Property of SWOSU
under the care of
Jeremy Evert
580-774-7050
jeremy.evert@swosu.edu

OBJECT-ORIENTED DATA STRUCTURES

USING

Java™

FOURTH EDITION

NELL DALE
UNIVERSITY OF TEXAS, AUSTIN

DANIEL T. JOYCE
VILLANOVA UNIVERSITY

CHIP WEEMS
UNIVERSITY OF MASSACHUSETTS,
AMHERST

JONES & BARTLETT
LEARNING

World Headquarters
Jones & Bartlett Learning
5 Wall Street
Burlington, MA 01803
978-443-5000
info@jblearning.com
www.jblearning.com

Jones & Bartlett Learning books and products are available through most bookstores and online booksellers. To contact Jones & Bartlett Learning directly, call 800-832-0034, fax 978-443-8000, or visit our website, www.jblearning.com.

09820-4

Production Credits
VP, Executive Publisher: David D. Cella
Acquisitions Editor: Laura Pagluica
Editorial Assistant: Taylor Ferracane
Director of Vendor Management: Amy Rose
Marketing Manager: Amy Langlais
VP, Manufacturing and Inventory Control: Therese Connell
Composition and Project Management: S4Carlisle Publishing Services

Cover Design: Kristin E. Parker
Text Design: Scott Moden
Rights & Media Specialist: Merideth Tumasz
Media Development Editor: Shannon Sheehan
Cover Image: © Ake13bk/Shutterstock
Printing and Binding: Edwards Brothers Malloy
Cover Printing: Edwards Brothers Malloy

Library of Congress Cataloging-in-Publication Data
Names: Dale, Nell (Nell B.), author. | Joyce, Daniel T., author. | Weems,
  Chip., author.
Title: Object-oriented data structures using Java / Nell Dale, Daniel T.
  Joyce, Chip Weems.
Description: Fourth edition. | Burlington, MA : Jones & Bartlett Learning,
  [2017]
Identifiers: LCCN 2016025145 | ISBN 9781284089097 (casebound)
Subjects: LCSH: Object-oriented programming (Computer science) | Data
  structures (Computer science) | Java (Computer program language)
Classification: LCC QA76.64 .D35 2017 | DDC 005.13/3--dc23 LC record available at
  https://lccn.loc.gov/2016025145

6048

Printed in the United States of America
20 19 18 17 16   10 9 8 7 6 5 4 3 2 1

Preface

Welcome to the fourth edition of *Object-Oriented Data Structures Using Java™*. This book presents the algorithmic, programming, and structuring techniques of a traditional data structures course in an object-oriented context. You'll find the familiar topics of linked lists, recursion, stacks, queues, collections, indexed lists, trees, maps, priority queues, graphs, sorting, searching, and complexity analysis, all covered from an object-oriented point of view using Java. We stress software engineering principles throughout, including modularization, information hiding, data abstraction, stepwise refinement, the use of visual aids, the analysis of algorithms, and software verification methods.

To the Student

You know that an algorithm is a sequence of unambiguous instructions for solving a problem. You can take a problem of moderate complexity, design a small set of classes/objects that work together to solve the problem, code the method algorithms needed to make the objects work, and demonstrate the correctness of your solution.

Algorithms describe actions. These actions manipulate data. For most interesting problems that are solved using computers, the structure of the data is just as important as the structure of the algorithms used to manipulate the data. Using this text you will discover that the way you structure data affects how efficiently you can use the data; you will see how the nature of the problem you are attempting to solve dictates your structuring decisions; and you will learn about the data structures that computer scientists have developed over the years to help solve problems.

Object-Oriented Programming with Java

Our primary goal is to present both the traditional and modern data structure topics with an emphasis on problem solving and software design. Using the Java programming language as a vehicle for problem solutions, however, presents an opportunity for students to expand their familiarity with a modern programming language and the object-oriented paradigm. As our data structure coverage unfolds, we introduce and use the appropriate Java constructs that support our primary goal. Starting early and continuing throughout the text, we introduce and expand on the use of many Java features such as classes, objects, generics, polymorphism, packages, interfaces, library classes, inheritance, exceptions, and threads. We also use Universal Modeling Language (UML) class diagrams throughout to help model and visualize our objects, classes, interfaces, applications, and their interrelationships.

Features

Data Abstraction   In this text we view our data structures from three different perspectives: their specification, their application, and their implementation. The specification describes the logical or abstract level—*what* the logical relationships among the data elements are and *what* operations can be performed on the structure. The application level, sometimes called the client level, is concerned with how the data structure is used to solve a problem—*why* the operations do what they do. The implementation level involves the coding details—*how* the structures and operations are implemented. In other words we treat our data structures as abstract data types (ADTs).

Efficiency Analysis   In Chapter 1 we introduce order of growth efficiency analysis using a unique approach involving the interaction of two students playing a game. Time and space analysis is consistently applied throughout the text, allowing us to compare and contrast data structure implementations and the applications that use them.

Recursion Treatment   Recursion is introduced early (Chapter 3) and used throughout the remainder of the text. We present a design and analysis approach to recursion based on answering three simple questions. Answering the questions, which are based on formal inductive reasoning, leads the programmer to a solid recursive design and program.

Interesting Applications   Eight primary data structures (stacks, queues, collections, indexed lists, trees, maps, priority queues, and graphs) are treated in separate chapters that include their definition, several implementations, and one or more interesting applications based on their use. Applications involve, for example, balanced expressions, postfix expressions, image generation (new!), fractals (new!), queue simulation, card decks and games (new!), text analysis (new!), tree and graph traversals, and big integers.

Robust Exercises   We average more than 40 exercises per chapter. The exercises are organized by chapter sections to make them easier for you to manage. They vary in level of difficulty, including short and long programming problems (marked with "programming-required" icons—one icon to indicate short exercises and two icons for projects), the analysis of algorithms, and problems to test students' understanding of abstract concepts. In this edition we have streamlined the previous exercises, allowing us to add even more options for you to choose from. In particular we have added several larger programming exercises to many of the chapters.

Input/Output Options   It is difficult to know what background the students using a data structures text will have in Java I/O. To allow all the students using our text to concentrate on the primary topic of data structures, we use the simplest I/O approach we can, namely a command line interface. However, to support those teachers and students who prefer to work with graphical user interfaces (GUIs), we provide GUIs for many of our applications. Our modular approach to program design supports this approach—our applications separate the user interface code, problem solution code, and ADT implementation code into separate classes.

Concurrency Coverage   We are pleased to be one of the only data structures texts to address the topics of concurrency and synchronization, which are growing in importance as computer systems move to using more cores and threads to obtain additional performance with each new generation. We introduce this topic in Section 4.9, "Concurrency, Interference, and Synchronization," where we start with the basics of Java threads, continue through examples of thread interference and synchronization, and culminate in a discussion of efficiency concerns.

New to the *Fourth Edition*

This edition represents a major revision of the text's material, although the philosophy and style that our loyal adopters have grown to appreciate remain unchanged. We removed material we felt was redundant or of lesser/outdated importance to the core topic of data structures, added new key material, and reworked much of the material that we kept. Although the length of the textbook was reduced by about 10%, the coverage of data structures has been expanded. We believe this new edition is a great improvement over previous editions and hope you do, too. Major changes include:

- Simplified Architecture: We continue to use the Java interface construct to define the abstract view of our ADTs, but we have reduced the number of levels of inheritance, simplifying the architecture and making it easier to understand and use.
- New Chapters: Chapter 5, "The Collection ADT," and Chapter 8, "The Map ADT," are brand new. The Collection ADT material introduces the idea of a data structure as a repository and concentrates on storage and retrieval of data based on key attributes. The Map ADT has become increasingly important with the rise in popularity of scripting languages with built-in associative arrays.
- New Section: Section 1.6, "Comparing Algorithms: Order of Growth Analysis," was completely rewritten and features an introduction to efficiency analysis driven by a game played between two students, plus analysis of sequential search, binary search, and sequential sort algorithms.
- New Sections: In response to reader's suggestions, Chapter 3, "Recursion," features two new sections: Section 3.3, "Recursive Processing of Arrays," is devoted to recursive processing of arrays and Section 3.4, "Recursive Processing of Linked Lists," is devoted to recursive processing of linked lists. These new sections provide practical examples of the use of recursion, before the reader moves on to the less practical but nevertheless popular Towers of Hanoi example covered in Section 3.5, "Towers."
- New Section: Fractals! A fun section related to recursively generating fractal-based images now wraps up the examples of Chapter 3, "Recursion."

- New Sections: We added "Variations" sections to the Stack, Queue, Collection, List, Tree, and Map chapters. In the primary exposition of each of these ADTs we record design decisions and specify the operations to be supported by the ADT. We also develop or at least discuss various implementation approaches, in most cases highlighting one array-based approach and one reference/linked-list-based approach. The "Variations" section discusses alternate approaches to defining/implementing the ADT and in most cases reviews the ADT counterparts available in the standard Java Library. Some of these sections also introduce related ADTs, for example, in the "Variations" section of the Collection chapter we define and discuss both the Set and Bag ADTs.
- Glossary: The text's glossary has always been available online. With this edition we make it available as Appendix E. Throughout the text we highlight important terms that might be unfamiliar to the student in **green**, the first time they are featured, to indicate that their definition can be found in the glossary.

Prerequisite Assumptions

In this book, we assume that readers are familiar with the following Java constructs:

- Built-in simple data types and the array type
- Control structures *while*, *do*, *for*, *if*, and *switch*
- Creating and instantiating objects
- Basic user-defined classes:
  - variables and methods
  - constructors, method parameters, and the *return* statement
  - visibility modifiers
- Commonly used Java Library Classes: *Integer, Math, Random, Scanner, String,* and *System*

Chapter Content

Chapter 1 is all about **Getting Organized**. An overview of object orientation stresses mechanisms for organizing objects and classes. The Java exception handling mechanisms, used to organize response to unusual situations, are introduced. Data structures are previewed and the two fundamental language constructs that are used to implement those structures, the array and the reference (link/pointer), are discussed. The chapter concludes with a look at efficiency analysis—how we evaluate and compare algorithms.

    Chapter 2 presents **The Stack ADT**. The concept of abstract data type (ADT) is introduced. The stack is viewed from three different levels: the abstract, application, and implementation levels. The Java interface mechanism is used to support this three-tiered view. We also investigate using generics to support generally usable ADTs. The Stack ADT is implemented using both arrays and references. To support the reference-based approach we introduce the linked list structure. Sample applications include determining if a set of grouping symbols is well formed and the evaluation of postfix expressions.

Chapter 3 discusses **Recursion**, showing how recursion can be used to solve programming problems. A simple three-question technique is introduced for verifying the correctness of recursive methods. Sample applications include array processing, linked list processing, the classic Towers of Hanoi, and fractal generation. A detailed discussion of how recursion works shows how recursion can be replaced with iteration and stacks.

Chapter 4 presents **The Queue ADT**. It is also first considered from its abstract perspective, followed by a formal specification, and then implemented using both array-based and reference-based approaches. Example applications include an interactive test driver, a palindrome checker, and simulating a system of real-world queues. Finally, we look at Java's concurrency and synchronization mechanisms, explaining issues of interference and efficiency.

Chapter 5 defines **The Collection ADT**. A fundamental ADT, the Collection, supports storing information and then retrieving it later based on its content. Approaches for comparing objects for equality and order are reviewed. Collection implementations using an array, a sorted array, and a linked list are developed. A text processing application permits comparison of the implementation approaches for efficiency. The "Variations" section introduces two more well-known ADTs: the Bag and the Set.

Chapter 6 follows up with a more specific Collection ADT, **The List ADT**. In fact, the following two chapters also develop Collection ADTs. Iteration is introduced here and the use of anonymous inner classes to provide iterators is presented. As with the Collection ADT we develop array, sorted array, and linked-list–based implementations. The "Variations" section includes an example of how to "implement" a linked list within an array. Applications include a card deck model plus some card games, and a Big Integer class. This latter application demonstrates how we sometimes design specialized ADTs for specific problems.

Chapter 7 develops **The Binary Search Tree ADT**. It requires most of the chapter just to design and create our reference-based implementation of this relatively complex structure. The chapter also discusses trees in general (including breadth-first and depth-first searching) and the problem of balancing a binary search tree. A wide variety of special-purpose and self-balancing trees are introduced in the "Variations" section.

Chapter 8 presents **The Map ADT**, also known as a symbol table, dictionary, or associative array. Two implementations are developed, one that uses an *ArrayList* and the other that uses a hash table. A large part of the chapter is devoted to this latter implementation and the important concept of hashing, which provides a very efficient implementation of a Map. The "Variations" section discusses a map-based hybrid data structure plus Java's support for hashing.

Chapter 9 introduces **The Priority Queue ADT**, which is closely related to the Queue but with a different accessing protocol. This short chapter does present a sorted array-based implementation, but most of the chapter focuses on a clever, interesting, and very efficient implementation called a Heap.

Chapter 10 covers **The Graph ADT**, including implementation approaches and several important graph-related algorithms (depth-first search, breadth-first search, path existence, shortest paths, and connected components). The graph algorithms make use of stacks, queues, and priority queues, thus both reinforcing earlier material and demonstrating the general usability of these structures.

Chapter 11 presents/reviews a number of **Sorting and Searching Algorithms**. The sorting algorithms that are illustrated, implemented, and compared include straight selection sort, two versions of bubble sort, insertion sort, quick sort, heap sort, and merge sort. The sorting algorithms are compared using efficiency analysis. The discussion of algorithm analysis continues in the context of searching. Previously presented searching algorithms are reviewed and new ones are described.

Organization

Chapter Goals   Sets of knowledge and skill goals are presented at the beginning of each chapter to help the students assess what they have learned.

Sample Programs   Numerous sample programs and program segments illustrate the abstract concepts throughout the text.

Feature Sections   Throughout the text these short sections highlight topics that are not directly part of the flow of material but nevertheless are related and important.

Boxed Notes   These small boxes of information scattered throughout the text highlight, supplement, and reinforce the text material, perhaps from a slightly different point of view.

Chapter Summaries   Each chapter concludes with a summary section that reviews the most important topics of the chapter and ties together related topics. Some chapter summaries include a UML diagram of the major interfaces and classes developed within the chapter.

Appendices   The appendices summarize the Java reserved word set, operator precedence, primitive data types, the ASCII subset of Unicode, and provide a glossary of important terms used in the text.

Website   http://go.jblearning.com/oods4e

This website provides access to the text's source code files for each chapter. Additionally, registered instructors are able to access selected answers to the text's exercises, a test item file, and presentation slides. Please contact the authors if you have material related to the text that you would like to share with others.

Acknowledgments

We would like to thank the following people who took the time to review this text: Mark Llewellyn at the University of Central Florida, Chenglie Hu at Carroll College, Val Tannen at the University of Pennsylvania, Chris Dovolis at the University of Minnesota, Mike Coe at Plano Senior High School, Mikel Petty at University of Alabama in Huntsville, Gene Sheppard at Georgia Perimeter College, Noni Bohonak at the University of South Carolina–Lancaster, Jose Cordova at the University of Louisiana–Monroe, Judy Gurka at the Metropolitan State College of Denver, Mikhail Brikman at Salem State University, Amitava Karmaker at University of Wisconsin–Stout, Guifeng Shao at Tennessee State University, Urska Cvek at Louisiana State University at Shreveport, Philip C. Doughty Jr. at Northern Virginia Community College, Jeff Kimball at Southwest Baptist University, Jeremy T. Lanman at Nova Southeastern University, Rao Li at University of South Carolina Aiken, Larry Thomas at University of Toledo, and Karen Works at Westfield State University. A special thanks to Christine Shannon at Centre College, to Phil LaMastra at Fairfield University, to Allan Gottlieb of New York University, and to J. William Cupp at Indiana Wesleyan University for specific comments leading to improvements in the text. A personal thanks to Kristen Obermyer, Tara Srihara, Sean Wilson, Christopher Lezny, and Naga Lakshmi, all of Villanova University, plus Kathy, Tom, and Julie Joyce for all of their help, support, and proofreading expertise.

A virtual bouquet of roses to the editorial and production teams who contributed so much, especially Laura Pagluica, Taylor Ferracane, Amy Rose, and Palaniappan Meyyappan.

ND

DJ

CW

Contents

7 The Binary Search Tree ADT   421

Getting Organized

Knowledge Goals

You should be able to

- describe some benefits of object-oriented programming
- describe the genesis of the Unified Method
- explain the relationships among classes, objects, and applications
- explain how method calls are bound to method implementations with respect to inheritance
- describe, at an abstract level, the following structures: array, linked list, stack, queue, list, tree, map, and graph
- identify which structures are implementation dependent and which are implementation independent
- describe the difference between direct addressing and indirect addressing
- explain the subtle ramifications of using references/pointers
- explain the use of O notation to describe the amount of work done by an algorithm
- describe the sequential search, binary search, and selection sort algorithms

Skill Goals

You should be able to

- interpret a basic UML class diagram
- design and implement a Java class
- create a Java application that uses the Java class
- use packages to organize Java compilation units
- create a Java exception class
- throw Java exceptions from within a class and catch them within an application that uses the class
- predict the output of short segments of Java code that exhibit aliasing
- declare, initialize, and use one- and two-dimensional arrays in Java, including both arrays of a primitive type and arrays of objects
- given an algorithm, identify an appropriate size representation and determine its order of growth
- given a section of code determine its order of growth

B efore embarking on any new project, it is a good idea to prepare carefully—to "get organized." In this first chapter that is exactly what we do. A careful study of the topics of this chapter will prepare us for the material on data structures and algorithms, using the object-oriented approach, covered in the remainder of the book.

1.1   Classes, Objects, and Applications

Software design is an interesting, challenging, and rewarding task. As a beginning student of computer science, you wrote programs that solved relatively simple problems. Much of your effort went into learning the syntax of a programming language such as Java: the language's reserved words, its data types, its constructs for selection and looping, and its input/output mechanisms.

As your programs and the problems they solve become more complex it is important to follow a software design approach that modularizes your solutions—breaks them into coherent manageable subunits. Software design was originally driven by an emphasis on actions. Programs were modularized by breaking them into subprograms or procedures/functions. A subprogram performs some calculations and returns information to the calling program, but it does not "remember" anything. In the late 1960s, researchers argued that this approach was too limiting and did not allow us to successfully represent the constructs needed to build complex systems.

Two Norwegians, Kristen Nygaard and Ole-Johan Dahl, created Simula 67 in 1967. It was the first language to support object-oriented programming. Object-oriented languages promote the object as the prime modularization mechanism. Objects represent both information and behavior and can "remember" internal information from one use to the next. This crucial difference allows them to be used in many versatile ways. In 2001, Nygaard and Dahl received the Turing Award, sometimes referred to as the "Nobel Prize of Computing," for their work.

The capability of objects to represent both information (the objects have *attributes*) and behavior (the objects have *responsibilities*) allows them to be used to represent "real-world" entities as varied as bank accounts, genomes, and hobbits. The self-contained nature of objects makes them easy to implement, modify, and test for correctness.

Object orientation is centered on classes and objects. Objects are the basic run-time entities used by applications. An object is an instantiation of a class; alternatively, a class defines the structure of its objects. In this section we review these object-oriented programming constructs that we use to organize our programs.

Classes

A class defines the structure of an object or a set of objects. A class definition includes variables (data) and methods (actions) that determine the behavior of an object. The following Java code defines a `Date` class that can be used to create and manipulate `Date` objects—for example, within a school course-scheduling application. The `Date` class can be used to create `Date` objects and to learn about the year, month, or day of any particular

Date object.[1] The class also provides methods that return the Lilian Day Number of the date (the code details have been omitted—see the feature section on Lilian Day Numbers for more information) and return a string representation of the date.

> **Authors' Convention**
>
> Java-reserved words (when used as such), user-defined identifiers, class and file names, and so on, appear in `this font` throughout the entire text.

```
//-------------------------------------------------------------------
// Date.java              by Dale/Joyce/Weems             Chapter 1
//
// Defines date objects with year, month, and day attributes.
//-------------------------------------------------------------------
package ch01.dates;
public class Date
{
    protected int year, month, day;
    public static final int MINYEAR = 1583;

    // Constructor
    public Date(int newMonth, int newDay, int newYear)
    {
        month = newMonth; day = newDay; year = newYear;
    }

    // Observers
    public int getYear() { return year; }
    public int getMonth() { return month; }
    public int getDay(){ return day; }

    public int lilian()
    {
        // Returns the Lilian Day Number of this date.
        // Algorithm goes here. Code is included with the program files.
        // See Lilian Day Numbers feature section for details.
    }

    @Override[2]
    public String toString()
```

Nice.
That
sucks

---

[1] The Java library includes a `Date` class, `java.util.Date`. However, the familiar properties of dates make them a natural example to use in explaining object-oriented concepts. Here we ignore the existence of the library class, as if we must design our own `Date` class.

[2] The purpose of `@Override` is discussed in Section 1.2 "Organizing Classes."

```
// Returns this date as a String.
{
    return(month + "/" + day + "/" + year);
}
}
```

The Date class demonstrates two kinds of variables: instance variables and class variables. The instance variables of this class are `year`, `month`, and `day` declared as

```
protected int year, month, day;
```

need to Simplify the first Example

Their values vary for each "instance" of an object of the class. Instance variables provide the internal representation of an object's attributes.

The variable `MINYEAR` is declared as

```
public static final int MINYEAR = 1583;
```

`MINYEAR` is defined as being `static`, and thus it is a class variable. It is associated directly with the `Date` class, instead of with objects of the class. A single copy of a class variable is maintained for all objects of the class.

Remember that the `final` modifier states that a variable is in its final form and cannot be modified; thus `MINYEAR` is a constant. By convention, we use only capital letters when naming constants. It is standard procedure to declare constants as class variables. Because the value of the variable cannot change, there is no need to force every object of a class to carry around its own version of the value. In addition to holding shared constants, class variables can be used to maintain information that is common to an entire class. For example, a `BankAccount` class may have a class variable that holds the number of current accounts.

Authors' Convention

We highlight important terms that might be unfamiliar to the student in green, the first time they are featured, to indicate that their definition can be found in the glossary in Appendix E.

In the `Date` class example, the `MINYEAR` constant represents the first full year that the widely used Gregorian calendar was in effect. The idea here is that programmers should not use the class to represent dates that predate that year. We look at ways to enforce this rule in Section 1.3 "Exceptional Situations," where we discuss handling exceptional situations.

The methods of the class are `Date`, `getYear`, `getMonth`, `getDay`, `lilian`, and `toString`. Note that the `Date` method has the same name as the class. Recall that this means it is a special type of method, called a class **constructor**. Constructors are used to create new instances of a class—that is, to instantiate objects of a class. The other methods are classified as **observer** methods, because they "observe" and return information based on the instance variable values. Other names for observer methods are "accessor" methods and "getters," as in accessing or getting information. Methods that simply return the value of an instance variable, such as `getYear()` in our `Date` class, are very common and always follow the same code pattern consisting of a single `return` statement. For this reason we will format such methods as a single line of code. In addition to constructors

System.out.println("Hello, " + 7));

Go to Eclipse and start a new project

Everywhere
X

ransformer. As you
mple, a method that
r.

tected and public
modifiers. This dis-
ackages. Inheritance
class, called the sub-
perclass. We say that
ited classes together
tensively in the next

ble 1.1. The public
available; any code
that these methods
n the Date class us-

access. At the other
bles and methods as
rited by subclasses.
lasses to hide their
atside the class. For
ared to be public,
's month to strange

wn in the Date ex-
be accessed directly
statement

e application. Thus,
even though it is publicly accessible, no other code can change its value. It is not necessary

to hide it. The application code above also shows how to access a public class variable from outside the class. Because MINYEAR is a class variable, it is accessed through the class name, Date, rather than through an object of the class.

Private access affords the strongest protection. Access is allowed only within the class. However, if you plan to extend your classes using inheritance, you may want to use protected access instead.

Coding Convention
We use protected access extensively for instance variables within our classes in this text.

The protected access modifier used in Date provides visibility similar to private access, only slightly less rigid. It "protects" its data from outside access, but allows the data to be accessed from within its own package *or* from any class derived from its class. Therefore, the methods within the Date class can access year, month, and day, and if, as we will show in Section 1.2 "Organizing Classes," the Date class is extended, the methods in the extended class can also access those variables.

The remaining type of access is called package access. A variable or method of a class defaults to package access if none of the other three modifiers are used. Package access means that the variable or method is accessible to any other class in the same package.

Lilian Day Numbers

Various approaches to numbering days have been proposed. Most choose a particular day in history as day 1, and then number the actual sequence of days from that day forward with the numbers 2, 3, and so on. The Lilian Day Number (LDN) system uses October 15, 1582, as day 1, or LDN 1.

Our current calendar is called the Gregorian calendar. It was established in 1582 by Pope Gregory XIII. At that time 10 days were dropped from the month of October, to make up for small errors that had accumulated throughout the years. Thus, the day following October 4, 1582, in the Gregorian calendar is October 15, 1582, also known as LDN 1 in the Lilian day numbering scheme. The scheme is named after Aloysius Lilius, an advisor to Pope Gregory and one of the principal instigators of the calendar reform.

Originally, Catholic European countries adopted the Gregorian calendar. Many Protestant nations, such as England and its colonies, did not adopt the Gregorian calendar until 1752, at which

1582		OCTOBER			1582	
SUN	MON	TUE	WED	THU	FRI	SAT
	1	2	3	4	15	16
17	18	19	20	21	22	23
24	25	26	27	28	29	30
31						

time they also "lost" 11 days. Today, most countries use the Gregorian calendar, at least for official international business. When comparing historical dates, one must be careful about which calendars are being used.

In our `Date` class implementation, `MINYEAR` is 1583, representing the first full year during which the Gregorian calendar was in operation. We assume that programmers will not use the `Date` class to represent dates before that time, although this rule is not enforced by the class. This assumption simplifies calculation of day numbers, as we do not have to worry about the phantom 10 days of October 1582.

To calculate LDNs, one must understand how the Gregorian calendar works. Years are usually 365 days long. However, every year evenly divisible by 4 is a leap year, 366 days long. This aligns the calendar closer to astronomical reality. To fine-tune the adjustment, if a year is evenly divisible by 100, it is not a leap year but, if it is also evenly divisible by 400, it is a leap year. Thus 2000 was a leap year, but 1900 was not.

Given a date, the `lilian` method of the `Date` class counts the number of days between that date and the hypothetical date 1/1/0—that is, January 1 of the year 0. This count is made under the assumption that the Gregorian reforms were in place during that entire time period. In other words, it uses the rules described in the previous paragraph. Let us call this number the Relative Day Number (RDN). To transform a given RDN to its corresponding LDN, we just need to subtract the RDN of October 14, 1582, from it. For example, to calculate the LDN of July 4, 1776, the method first calculates its RDN (648,856) and then subtracts from it the RDN of October 14, 1582 (578,100), giving the result of 70,756.

Code for the `lilian` method is included with the program code files.

The Unified Method

The object-oriented approach to programming is based on implementing models of reality. But how do you go about this? Where do you start? How do you proceed? The best plan is to follow an organized approach called a **methodology**.

In the late 1980s, many people proposed object-oriented methodologies. By the mid-1990s, three proposals stood out: the Object Modeling Technique, the Objectory Process, and the Booch Method. Between 1994 and 1997, the primary authors of these proposals got together and consolidated their ideas. The resulting methodology was dubbed the Unified Method. It is now, by far, the most popular organized approach to creating object-oriented systems.

The Unified Method features three key elements:

1. It is use-case driven. A use-case is a description of a sequence of actions performed by a user within the system to accomplish some task. The term "user" here should be interpreted in a broad sense and could represent another system.

2. It is architecture-centric. The word "architecture" refers to the overall structure of the target system, the way in which its components interact.

```
                          Date
     #year:int
     #month:int
     #day:int
     +MINYEAR:int = 1583

     +Date(newMonth:int,newDay:int,newYear:int)
     +getYear():int
     +getMonth():int
     +getDay():int
     +lilian():int
     +toString():String
```

Figure 1.1   UML class diagram for the Date class

3. It is iterative and incremental. The Unified Method involves a series of development cycles, with each one building upon the foundation established by its predecessors.

One of the main benefits of the Unified Method is improved communication among the people involved in the project. The Unified Method includes a set of diagrams for this purpose, called the **Unified Modeling Language (UML).**[3] UML diagrams have become a de facto industry standard for modeling software. They are used to specify, visualize, construct, and document the components of a software system. We use UML class diagrams throughout this text to model our classes and their interrelationships.

A diagram representing the Date class is shown in **Figure 1.1**. The diagram follows the standard UML class notation approach. The name of the class appears in the top section of the diagram, the variables (attributes) appear in the next section, and the methods (operations) appear in the final section. The diagram includes information about the nature of the variables and method parameters; for example, we can see at a glance that year, month, and day are all of type int. Note that the variable MINYEAR is underlined; this indicates that it is a class variable rather than an instance variable. The diagram also indicates the visibility or protection associated with each part of the class (+ = public, # = protected).

Objects

Objects are created from classes at run time. They can contain and manipulate data. Multiple objects can be created from the same class definition. Once a class such as Date has been defined, a program can create and use objects of that class. The effect is similar to expanding the language's set of standard types to include a Date type. To create an object in Java we use the new operator, along with the class constructor, as follows:

```
Date myDate = new Date(6, 24, 1951);
Date yourDate = new Date(10, 11, 1953);
Date ourDate = new Date(6, 15, 1985);
```

---

[3] The official definition of the UML is maintained by the Object Management Group. Detailed information can be found at http://www.uml.org/.

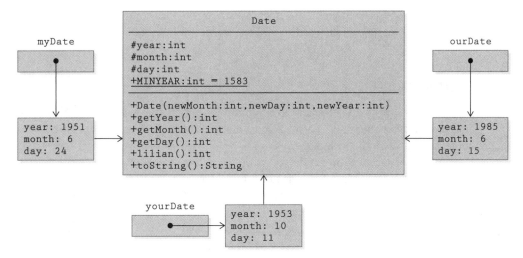

Figure 1.2   Class diagram showing `Date` objects

We say that the variables `myDate`, `yourDate`, and `ourDate` reference "objects of the class `Date`" or simply "objects of type `Date`." We could also refer to them as "`Date` objects."

Figure 1.2 extends our previous diagram (shown in Figure 1.1) to show the relationship between the instantiated `Date` objects and the `Date` class. As you can see, the objects are associated with the class, as represented by arrows from the objects to the class in the diagram. Notice that the `myDate`, `yourDate`, and `ourDate` variables are not objects, but actually hold references to the objects. The references are shown by the arrows from the variable boxes to the objects. In reality, references are memory addresses. The memory address of the instantiated object is stored in the memory location assigned to the variable. If no object has been instantiated for a particular variable, then its memory location holds a `null` reference.

Methods are invoked through the object upon which they are to act. For example, to assign the return value of the `getYear` method of the `ourDate` object to the integer variable `theYear`, a programmer would code

```
theYear = ourDate.getYear();
```

Recall that the `toString` method is invoked in a special way. Just as Java automatically changes an integer value, such as that returned by `getDay`, to a string in the statement

```
System.out.println("The big day is " + ourDate.getDay());
```

it automatically changes an object, such as `ourDate`, to a string in the statement

```
System.out.println("The party will be on " + ourDate);
```

The output from these statements would be

    The big day is 15
    The party will be on 6/15/1985

To determine how to change the object to a string, the Java compiler looks for a `toString` method for that object, such as the `toString` method we defined for `Date` objects in our `Date` class.

Applications

You should view an object-oriented program as a set of objects working together, by sending one another messages, to solve a problem. But where does it all begin? How are the objects created in the first place?

A Java program typically begins running when the user executes the **Java Virtual Machine** and passes it the program. How you begin executing the Java Virtual Machine depends on your environment. You may simply use the command "java" if you are working in a command line environment. Or, you may click a "run" icon if you are working within an integrated development environment. In any case, you indicate the name of a class that contains a `main` method. The Java Virtual Machine loads that class and starts executing that method. The class that contains the `main` method is called a **Java application**.

Suppose we want to write a program named `DaysBetween` that provides information about the number of days between two dates. The idea is for the program to prompt the user for two dates, calculate the number of days between them, and report this information back to the user.

In object-oriented programming a key step is identifying classes that can be used to help solve a problem. Our `Date` class is a perfect fit for the days-between problem. It allows us to create and access `Date` objects. Plus, its `lilian` method returns a value that can help us determine the number of days between two dates. We simply subtract the two Lilian Day Numbers. The design of our application code is straightforward—prompt for and read in the two dates, check that valid years are provided, and then display the difference between the Lilian Day Numbers.

Design Convention

Our application code usually consists of a class with a single method—`main`. Modularization is provided by using externally defined classes and objects.

The application code is shown below. Some items to note:

- The application imports the `util` package from the Java Class Library. The `util` package contains Java's `Scanner` class, which the application uses for input.

- The `DaysBetween` class contains just a single method, the `main` method. It is possible to define other methods within the class and to invoke them from the `main` method. Such functional modularization can be used if the `main` method becomes long and complicated. However, because we are emphasizing an object-oriented approach, our application code rarely subdivides a solution in that manner. Classes and objects are our primary modularization mechanisms, not application methods.

- Although the program checks to ensure the entered years of the dates are "modern," it does not do any other input correctness checking. In general, throughout the text, we assume the users of our applications are "friendly," that is, they enter input correctly.

```java
//------------------------------------------------------------------
// DaysBetween.java            by Dale/Joyce/Weems          Chapter 1
//
// Asks the user to enter two "modern" dates and then reports
// the number of days between the two dates.
//------------------------------------------------------------------
package ch01.apps;

import java.util.Scanner; import ch01.dates.*;

public class DaysBetween
{
  public static void main(String[] args)
  {
    Scanner scan = new Scanner(System.in);
    int day, month, year;

    System.out.println("Enter two 'modern' dates: month day year");
    System.out.println("For example, January 21, 1939, would be: 1 21 1939");
    System.out.println();
    System.out.println("Modern dates are not before " + Date.MINYEAR + ".");
    System.out.println();

    System.out.println("Enter the first date:");
    month = scan.nextInt(); day = scan.nextInt(); year = scan.nextInt();
    Date d1 = new Date(month, day, year);

    System.out.println("Enter the second date:");
    month = scan.nextInt(); day = scan.nextInt(); year = scan.nextInt();
    Date d2 = new Date(month, day, year);

    if ((d1.getYear() <= Date.MINYEAR) || (d2.getYear() <= Date.MINYEAR))
      System.out.println("You entered a 'pre-modern' date.");
    else
    {
      System.out.println("The number of days between");
      System.out.print(d1 + " and " + d2 + " is ");
      System.out.println(Math.abs(d1.lilian() - d2.lilian()));
    }
  }
}
```

Here is the result of a sample run of the application. User input is shown in `this color`.

```
Enter two 'modern' dates: month day year
For example, January 21, 1939, would be: 1 21 1939
Modern dates are not before 1583.
Enter the first date:
1 1 1900
Enter the second date:
1 1 2000
The number of days between
1/1/1900 and 1/1/2000 is 36524
```

1.2   Organizing Classes

During object-oriented development, dozens—even hundreds—of classes can be generated or reused to help build a system. The task of keeping track of all of these classes would be impossible without some type of organizational structure. In this section we review two of the most important ways of organizing Java classes: inheritance and packages. As you will see, both of these approaches are used "simultaneously" for most projects.

Inheritance

Inheritance is much more than just an organizational mechanism. It is, in fact, a powerful reuse mechanism. Inheritance allows programmers to create a new class that is a specialization of an existing class. The new class is a **subclass** of the existing class that in turn is the **superclass** of the new class.

A subclass "inherits" features from its superclass. It adds new features, as needed, related to its specialization. It can also redefine inherited features as necessary by overriding them. "Super" and "sub" refer to the relative positions of the classes in a hierarchy. A subclass is below its superclass and a superclass is above its subclasses.

Suppose we already have a `Date` class as defined previously, and we are creating a new application to manipulate `Date` objects. Suppose also that the new application is often required to "increment" a `Date` object—that is, to change a `Date` object so that it represents the next day. For example, if the `Date` object represents 7/31/2001, it would represent 8/1/2001 after being incremented. The algorithm for incrementing the date is not trivial, especially when you consider leap year rules. But in addition to developing the algorithm, another question that must be addressed is where to put the code that implements the algorithm. There are several options:

- Implement the algorithm within the application. The application code would need to obtain the month, day, and year from the `Date` object using the observer methods; calculate the new month, day, and year; instantiate a new Date object to hold the updated month, day, and year; and if required, assign all the variables that previously referenced the original Date to the new object. This might be a complex task so this is probably not the best approach. Besides, if future applications also need this functionality, their programmers would have to reimplement the solution for themselves. This approach does not promote reusability and possibly requires complex tracking of object aliases.

- Add a new method, called increment, to the Date class. This method would update the value of the current object. Such an approach allows future programs to use the new functionality. However, in some cases, a programmer may want a Date class with protection against any changes to its objects. Such objects are said to be **immutable**. Adding increment to the Date class undermines this protection.

- Add a new method, called nextDay, to the Date class. Rather than updating the value of the "current" object, nextDay would return a new Date object that represents the day after the Date object upon which it is invoked. An application could then reassign a Date variable to its next day, perhaps like this:

```
d1 = d1.nextDay();
```

This approach resolves the drawbacks of the previous approach in that the Date objects remain immutable, although if one wants all variables that referenced the original object to also reflect the updated information it is lacking. Aliases of the d1 object will not be updated.

- Use inheritance. Create a new class, called IncDate, that inherits all the features of the current Date class, but that also provides the increment method. This approach allows Date objects to remain immutable but at the same time provides a mutable Date-like class that can be used by the new application.

We now look at how to implement the final option, that is, to use inheritance to solve our problem. The inheritance relationship is often called an *is-a* relationship. An object of the class IncDate is also a Date object, because it can do anything that a Date object can do—and more. This idea

> **Important**
>
> Inheritance is a powerful reuse mechanism that allows us to define a new class as an extension of a current class. The new class is a specialization of the current class. New features can be added and inherited features can be redefined.

can be clarified by remembering that inheritance typically means specialization. IncDate *is-a* special case of Date, but not the other way around. Here is the code for IncDate:

```
package ch01.dates;
public class IncDate extends Date
{
    public IncDate(int newMonth, int newDay, int newYear)
```

```
    {
        super(newMonth, newDay, newYear);
    }


    public void increment()
    // Increments this IncDate to represent the next day.
    // For example, if this = 6/30/2005, then this becomes 7/1/2005.
    {
        // Increment algorithm goes here.
    }
}
```

Inheritance is indicated by the keyword ex-tends, that shows that IncDate inherits from Date. It is not possible in Java to inherit constructors, so IncDate must supply its own. In this case, the IncDate constructor simply takes the month, day, and year arguments and passes them to the constructor of its superclass (that is, to the Date class constructor) using the super reserved word.

The other part of the IncDate class is the new increment method, which is classified as a transformer because it changes the internal state of the object. The increment method changes the object's day and possibly the month and year values. The method is invoked through the object that it is to transform. For example, if aDate is an object of type IncDate then the statement

```
aDate.increment();
```

transforms the aDate object.

Although we have left out the details of the increment method because they are not crucial to our current discussion, note that it would require access to the year, month, and day instance variables of its superclass. Therefore, using protected rather than private access for those variables within the Date class, as we did, is crucial for our approach to be viable.

A program with access to each of the date classes can now declare and use both Date and IncDate objects. Consider the following program segment:

```
Date myDate = new Date(6, 24, 1951);
IncDate aDate = new IncDate(1, 11, 2001);

System.out.println("myDate day is:   " + myDate.getDay());
System.out.println("aDate day is:    " + aDate.getDay());

aDate.increment();
System.out.println("the day after is: " + aDate.getDay());
```

This program segment **instantiates** and initializes `myDate` and `aDate`, outputs the values of their days, increments `aDate`, and finally outputs the new day value of `aDate`. You might ask, "How does the system resolve the use of the `getDay` method by an `IncDate` object when `getDay` is defined in the `Date` class?" Understanding how inheritance is supported by Java provides the answer to this question. The extended class diagram in **Figure 1.3**, that shows the inheritance relationships and captures the state of the system after the `aDate` object has been incremented, helps us investigate the situation. As is standard with UML class diagrams, inheritance is indicated by a solid arrow with an open arrow head (a triangle). Note that the arrow points from the subclass to the superclass.

The compiler has available to it all the declaration information captured in the extended class diagram. Consider the `getDay` method call in the statement

```
System.out.println("the day after is: " + aDate.getDay());
```

To resolve this method call, the compiler follows the reference from the `aDate` variable to the `IncDate` class. It does not find a definition for a `getDay` method in the `IncDate`

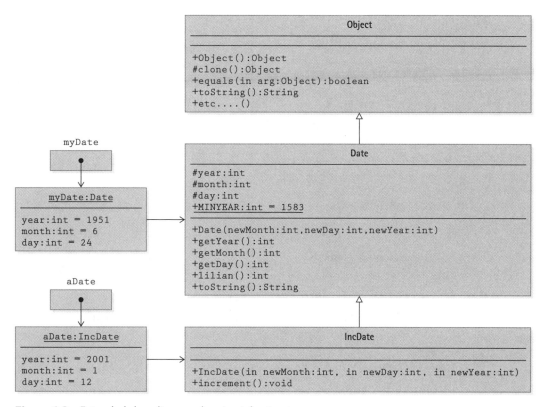

Figure 1.3 Extended class diagram showing inheritance

class, so it follows the inheritance link to the superclass `Date`. There it finds, and uses, the `getDay` method. In this case, the `getDay` method returns an `int` value that represents the `day` value of the `aDate` object. During execution, the system changes the `int` value to a `String`, concatenates it to the string "the day after is: ", and prints it to `System.out`.

The Inheritance Tree

Java supports single inheritance only. This means that a class can extend only one other class. Therefore, in Java, the inheritance relationships define an **inheritance tree**.

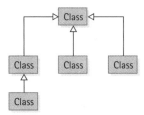

Figure 1.3 shows one branch of the overall system inheritance tree. Note that because of the way method calls are resolved, by searching *up* the inheritance tree, only objects of the class `IncDate` can use the `increment` method—if you try to use the `increment` method on an object of the class `Date`, such as the `myDate` object, no definition is available in either the `Date` class or any of the classes above `Date` in the inheritance tree. The compiler would report a syntax error in this situation.

Notice the `Object` class in Figure 1.3. Where did it come from? In Java, any class that does not explicitly extend another class implicitly extends the predefined `Object` class. Because `Date` does not explicitly extend any other class, it inherits directly from `Object`. The `Date` class is a direct subclass of `Object`.

All Java classes can be traced up to the `Object` class. We say that the `Object` class is the root of the inheritance tree. The `Object` class defines several basic methods: comparison for equality (`equals`), conversion to a string (`toString`), and so on. Therefore, for example, any object in any Java program supports the method `toString` because it is inherited from the `Object` class. Let us consider the `toString` example more carefully.

As discussed previously, just as Java automatically changes an integer value to a string in the statement

```
System.out.println("aDate day is:    " + aDate.getDay());
```

> **Important**
>
> Association of method names with method code is accomplished by moving up the inheritance tree. If a matching method is not found in the named class, then its superclass is searched. And if not found there, then the superclass above that and so on.

> **Java Note**
>
> In Java, the `Object` class is the root of the inheritance tree—all classes inherit from `Object`. Therefore, for example, all objects support `equals` and `toString`, although unless their class overrides the `Object` class definitions of those methods, they may not support those operations well.

so it automatically changes an object to a string in the statement

```
System.out.println("tomorrow: " + aDate);
```

To accomplish this, the Java compiler looks for a `toString` method for that object. In this case, the `toString` method is not found in the `IncDate` class, but it is found in its super-class, the `Date` class. However, if it was not defined in the `Date` class, the compiler would continue looking up the inheritance hierarchy and would find the `toString` method in the `Object` class. Given that all classes trace their roots back to `Object`, the compiler is always guaranteed to find a `toString` method eventually.

But wait a minute. What does it mean to "change an object to a string"? Well, that depends on the definition of the `toString` method that is associated with the object. The `toString` method of the `Object` class returns a string representing some of the internal system implementation details about the object. This information is somewhat cryptic and generally not useful to us. This situation is an example of where it is useful to redefine an inherited method by overriding it. We generally **override** the default `toString` method when creating our own classes so as to return a more relevant string, as we did with the `Date` class. This is why we use the `@Override` notation with the `toString` method as shown on page 3. By annotating our `toString` method as overriding an ancestor's `toString` method, we allow the compiler to double-check our syntax. If it cannot find an associated ancestor method with the same **signature**, it will generate an error. Additionally, some development environments will use the information to inform how they display the code.

Table 1.2 shows the output from the following program segment:

```
Date myDate = new Date(6, 24, 1951);
IncDate currDate = new IncDate(1, 11, 2001);
System.out.println("mydate:  " + myDate);
System.out.println("today:   " + currDate);

currDate.increment();
System.out.println("tomorrow: " + currDate);
```

The results on the left show an example of the output generated if the `toString` method of the `Object` class is used by default; the results on the right show the outcome if the `toString` method of our `Date` class is used.

Table 1.2 Output from Program Segment

Object Class toString Used		Date Class toString Used	
mydate:	Date@256a7c	mydate:	6/24/1951
today:	IncDate@720eeb	today:	1/11/2001
tomorrow:	IncDate@720eeb	tomorrow:	1/12/2001

Inheritance-Based Polymorphism

This is a good place to introduce an important object-oriented concept. The word **polymorphism** has Greek roots and literally means "many forms." Object-oriented languages that support polymorphism allow an object variable to reference objects of different classes at different times during the execution of a program—the variable can have "many types" and is called a polymorphic variable or polymorphic reference.

There are two ways to create polymorphic references with Java. Here we look at inheritance-based polymorphism. In Section 2.1, "Abstraction," we will look at interface-based polymorphism.

Typically in our programs we can tell exactly what method will be executed when a method is invoked through an object variable. For example, in the following code section the third and fourth lines respectively invoke the toString method of the String class and the toString method of the Date class.

```
String s = new String("Hello");
Date d = new Date(1,1,2015);
System.out.println(s.toString());
System.out.println(d.toString());
```

It is easy to see that this code will print "Hello" followed by "1/1/2015".

Remember that both String and Date inherit from the Object class. In terms of inheritance we say that a String "is-an" Object and that a Date also "is-an" Object. Due to the polymorphism built into the Java language this means that we can declare a variable to be of type Object, and then instantiate it as a String or as a Date. In fact, since the Object class is at the root of the Java inheritance tree, an Object reference can refer to an object of any class.

In the following code section assume that cutoff was assigned a random value between 1 and 100, perhaps through the Random class's nextInt method. Can you predict what method is invoked by the obj.toString() method invocation? Can you predict what will be printed? Do not forget that both the String class and the Date class override the toString method of the Object class.

```
Object obj;
if (cutoff <= 50)
    obj = new String("Hello");
else
    obj = new Date(1,1,2015);
System.out.println(obj.toString());
```

We cannot infer from the code whether the obj variable references a String or a Date. We can only infer that it references one or the other. The binding of the obj variable to a class occurs dynamically, at run time. As is implied by the arrows connecting objects to classes in Figure 1.3, each object carries information indicating the class to which it belongs. This can also be noticed in the output of the Object class's toString method, displayed on the left side of Table 1.2. Run-time (also called **dynamic**) **binding** and polymorphism go hand in hand. We can only predict that half of the time the toString method of the String class is invoked and the other half of the time the toString method of the Date class is invoked.

> **Important Concept**
>
> Inheritance, overriding of methods, and dynamic binding all interact to support polymorphic references. Because objects carry with them information about their class, that information can vary dynamically, as long as it satisfies the is-a relationship established by the inheritance tree.

You might ask how the compiler can parse a method invocation to ensure syntactical correctness when run-time binding is used. The key is that the Object class itself defines a toString method. The compiler is able to verify that the obj.toString() invocation correctly matches a defined method in the Object class, and after all, obj was declared to be of type Object. The Java Virtual Machine, however, when executing the method invocation, follows the dynamically created reference from obj to either the String class definition or the Date class definition and uses the toString method defined there.

Although the preceding example does demonstrate polymorphism, it does not really do justice to the power of inheritance-based polymorphism or demonstrate how it should be used. The example was selected due to its simplicity and conciseness. We will see another example of how polymorphism can be used in the next chapter, and although we will not make extensive use of it throughout the text, it is an important object-oriented concept, useful for creating easily maintained, versatile, adaptable systems of classes. Its true power becomes apparent when constructing large enterprise-level systems and their interfaces. If you continue to study object orientation, you will find it a powerful and crucial tool.

Packages

Java lets us group related classes together into a unit called a package. Packages provide several advantages:

- They let us organize our files.
- They can be compiled separately and imported into our programs.
- They make it easier for programs to use common class files.
- They help us avoid naming conflicts (two classes can have the same name if they are in different packages).

Package Syntax

The syntax for a package is extremely simple. All one has to do is to specify the package name at the start of the file containing the class. The first noncomment, nonblank line of the file must contain the keyword package followed by an identifier and a semicolon. By convention, Java programmers start a package identifier with a lowercase letter to distinguish package names from class names:

```
package someName;
```

Following the package name specification in the file, the programmer can write import declarations, so as to make the contents of other packages available to the classes inside the package being defined, and then one or more declarations of classes. Java calls this file a *compilation unit*. The classes defined in the file are members of the package. The imported classes are not members of the package.

The name of the file containing the compilation unit must match the name of the public class within the unit. Therefore, although a programmer can declare multiple classes in a compilation unit, only one of them can be declared public. All nonpublic classes in the file are hidden from the world outside the package. If a compilation unit can hold at most one public class, how do we create packages with multiple public classes? We have to use multiple compilation units, as described next.

Packages with Multiple Compilation Units

Each Java compilation unit is stored in its own file. The Java system identifies the file using a combination of the package name and the name of the public class in the compilation unit. Java restricts us to having a single public class per file so that it can use file names to locate public classes. Thus a package with multiple public classes is implemented as multiple compilation units, each in a separate file.

Using multiple compilation units has the further advantage of providing us with greater flexibility in developing the classes of a package. Team programming projects would be more cumbersome if Java made multiple programmers share a single package file.

We split a package among multiple files simply by placing its members into separate compilation units with the same package name. For example, we can create one file containing the following code (the . . . between the braces represents the code for each class):

```
package gamma;
public class One{ ... }
class Two{ ... }
```

A second file could contain this code:

```
package gamma;
class Three{ ... }
public class Four{ ... }
```

The result: The package gamma contains four classes. Two of the classes, One and Four, are public, so they are available to be imported by application code. The two file names must match the two public class names; that is, the files must be named One.java and Four.java, respectively.

How does the Java compiler manage to find these pieces and put them together? The answer is that it requires that all compilation unit files for a package be kept in a single directory or folder that matches the name of the package. For our preceding example, a programmer would store the source code in files called One.java and Four.java, both in a directory called gamma.

The Import Statement

To access the contents of a package from within a program, you must import it into your program. You can use either of the following forms of import statements:

```
import packagename.*;
import packagename.Classname;
```

An import declaration begins with the keyword import, the name of a package, and a dot (period). Following the dot you can write either the name of a class in the package or an asterisk (*). The declaration ends with a semicolon. If you want to access exactly one class in a particular package, then you can simply use its name in the import declaration. If you want to use more than one of the classes in a package, the asterisk is a shorthand notation to the compiler that says, "Import whatever classes from this package that this program uses."

Packages and Subdirectories

Many computer platforms use a hierarchical file system. The Java package rules are defined to work seamlessly with such systems. Java package names may also be hierarchical; they may contain "periods"

Java Note

The Java package construct is designed to work seamlessly with the commonly used hierarchical file system.

separating different parts of the name—for example, ch01.dates. In such a case, the package files must be placed underneath a set of subdirectories that match the separate parts of the package name. Continuing the same example, the package files should be placed in a directory named dates that is a subdirectory of a directory named ch01. You can then import the entire package into your program with the following statement:

```
import ch01.dates.*;
```

As long as the directory that contains the ch01 directory is on the ClassPath of your system, the compiler will be able to find the package you requested. The compiler automatically looks in all directories listed in ClassPath. Most programming environments provide a command to specify the directories to be included in the ClassPath. You will need to consult the documentation for your particular system to see how to do this. In our example, the compiler will search all ClassPath directories for a subdirectory named ch01 that contains a subdirectory named dates; upon finding such a subdirectory, it will import all of the members of the ch01.dates package that it finds there.

The Program Files

The files created to support this text are organized into packages. They are organized exactly as we have described and are available at the book's website, go.jblearning.com/oods4ecatalog/9781449613549/. All of the files are found in a directory named book-Files. It contains a separate subdirectory for each chapter of the book: ch01, ch02, etc. You will find the corresponding subdirectories underneath the chapter subdirectories.

For example, the ch01 subdirectory does, indeed, contain a subdirectory named dates, that in turn contains files that define Java classes related to dates. Each of the class files begins with the statement

```
package ch01.dates;
```

Thus they are all in the ch01.dates package. If you write a program that needs to use these files, you can simply import the package into your program and make sure the parent directory of the ch01 directory (that is, the bookFiles directory), is included in your computer's ClassPath.

We suggest that you copy the entire bookFiles directory to your computer's hard drive, ensuring easy access to all of the book's files and maintaining the crucial subdirectory structure required by the packages. Also, make sure you extend your computer's ClassPath to include your new bookFiles directory.

1.3 Exceptional Situations

In this section we take a look at various methods of handling exceptional situations that might arise when running a program.

Handling Exceptional Situations

Many different types of exceptional situations can occur when a program is running. Exceptional situations alter the flow of control of the program, sometimes resulting in a crash. Some examples follow:

- A user enters an input value of the wrong type.
- While reading information from a file, the end of the file is reached.
- A user presses a control key combination.
- A program attempts to invoke a method on a null object.
- An out-of-bounds value is passed to a method, for example, passing 25 as the month value to the Date constructor.

Java (along with some other languages) provides built-in mechanisms to manage exceptional situations. In Java an exceptional situation is referred to simply as an **exception**. The Java exception mechanism has three major parts:

- *Defining the exception.*   Usually as a subclass of Java's Exception class
- *Generating (raising) the exception.*   By recognizing the exceptional situation and then using Java's throw statement to "announce" that the exception has occurred.
- *Handling the exception.*   Using Java's try-catch statement to discover that an exception has been thrown and then take the appropriate action.

Java also includes numerous predefined built-in exceptions that are raised automatically under certain situations.

From this point on we use the Java term "exception" instead of the more general phrase "exceptional situation." Here are some general guidelines for using exceptions:

> **Java Note**
>
> In Java, exceptions are objects. They can be defined, instantiated, raised, thrown, caught, and handled. They allow us to control the flow of execution of a program to handle exceptional situations.

- An exception may be handled anywhere in the software hierarchy—from the place in the program module where it is first detected through the top level of the program.
- Unhandled built-in exceptions carry the penalty of program termination.
- Where in an application an exception is handled is a design decision; however, exceptions should be handled at a level that knows what the exception means.
- An exception need not be fatal.
- For nonfatal exceptions, the thread of execution should continue from the lowest level that can recover from the exception.

Exceptions and Classes: An Example

When creating our own classes we identify exceptions that require special processing. If the special processing is application dependent, we use the Java exception mechanism to throw the problem out of the class and force the application programmers to handle it. Conversely, if the exception handling can be hidden within the class, then there is no need to burden the application programmers with the task.

For an example of an exception created to support a programmer-defined class, we return to our `Date` class example. As currently defined, an application could invoke the `Date` constructor with an invalid month—for example, 25/15/2000. We can avoid the creation of such dates by checking the legality of the month argument passed to the constructor. But what should our constructor do if it discovers an illegal argument? Here are some options:

- Write a warning message to the output stream. This is not a good option because within the `Date` class we do not really know which output stream, if any, is used by the application.
- Instantiate the new `Date` object to some default date, perhaps 0/0/0. The problem with this approach is that the application program may just continue processing as if nothing is wrong and produce erroneous results. In general, it is better for a program to "bomb" than to produce erroneous results that may be used to make bad decisions.
- Throw an exception. This way, normal processing is interrupted and the constructor does not have to return a new object; instead, the application program is forced to acknowledge the problem (catch the exception) and either handle it or throw it to the next level.

Once we have decided to handle the situation with an exception, we must decide whether to use one of the Java library's predefined exceptions or to create one of our own. A study of the library in this case reveals a candidate exception called DataFormat-Exception, to be used to signal data format errors. We could use that exception but decide it does not really fit; it is not the format of the data that is the problem in this case, it is the value of the data.

We decide to create our own exception, DateOutOfBounds. It could be called MonthOutOfBounds, but we decide that we want to use the exception to indicate other potential problems with dates, not just problems with the month value. Our exception class is placed in a file named DateOutOfBounds.java.

Our DateOutOfBounds exception extends the library's Exception class. It is customary when creating your own exceptions to define two constructors, mirroring the two constructors of the Exception class. In fact, the easiest thing to do is define the constructors so that they just call the corresponding constructors of the superclass:

```java
package ch01.dates;
public class DateOutOfBoundsException extends Exception
{
    public DateOutOfBoundsException()
    {
        super();
    }
    public DateOutOfBoundsException(String message)
    {
        super(message);
    }
}
```

The first constructor creates an exception without an associated message. The second constructor creates an exception with a message equal to the string argument passed to the constructor.

Let us create a new class SafeDate. We could simply upgrade our previous Date class but do not want to invalidate our previous examples. So we will use the new class, SafeDate, to demonstrate the use of exceptions. Where, within our SafeDate class, should we throw the exception? All places within our class where a date value is created or changed should be examined to see if the resultant value could be an illegal date. If so, we should create an object of our exception class with an appropriate message and throw the exception.

Here is a SafeDate constructor that checks for legal months and years:

```java
public SafeDate(int newMonth, int newDay, int newYear)
            throws DateOutOfBoundsException
{
    if ((newMonth <= 0) || (newMonth > 12))
        throw new DateOutOfBoundsException("Month " + newMonth + " illegal.");
```

```
    else
        month = newMonth;

    day = newDay;

    if (newYear < MINYEAR)
        throw new DateOutOfBoundsException("Year " + newYear + " too early.");
    else
        year = newYear;
}
```

Notice that the message defined for each throw statement pertains to the problem discovered at that point in the code. This should help the application program that is handling the exception, or at least provide pertinent information to the user of the program if
the exception is propagated all the way to the user level.

   Finally, we see how an application program might use the SafeDate class. Consider
a program called UseSafeDate that prompts the user for a month, day, and year and creates a SafeDate object based on the user's responses. In the following code we hide the
details of how the prompt and response are handled by replacing those statements with
comments. This way we can *emphasize* the code related to our current discussion:

```
//------------------------------------------------------------------
// UseSafeDate.java          by Dale/Joyce/Weems          Chapter 1
//
// Example of re-throwing exceptions thrown by SafeDate class
//------------------------------------------------------------------

package ch01.apps;
public class UseSafeDate
{
    public static void main(String[] args) throws DateOutOfBoundsException
    {
        SafeDate theDate;

        // Program prompts user for a date.
        // M is set equal to user's month.
        // D is set equal to user's day.
        // Y is set equal to user's year.

        theDate = new SafeDate(M, D, Y);

        // Program continues ...
    }
}
```

When this program runs, if the user responds with an illegal value—for example, a year of 1051—the `DateOutOfBoundsException` is thrown by the `SafeDate` constructor; because it is not caught and handled within the program, it is thrown to the interpreter as indicated by the emphasized `throws` clause. The interpreter stops the program and displays a message like this:

```
Exception in thread "main" DateOutOfBoundsException: Year 1051 too early.
at SafeDate.<init>(SafeDate.java:18)
at UseSafeDate.main(UseSafeDate.java:57)
```

The interpreter's message includes the name and message string of the exception as well as a trace of calls leading up to the exception.

Alternatively, the `UseSafeDate` class could catch and handle the exception itself, rather than throw it to the interpreter. The application could ask for a new date when the exception occurs. Here is how `UseSafeDate` can be written to do this:

```
//-------------------------------------------------------------------------
// UseSafeDate.java          by Dale/Joyce/Weems          Chapter 1
//
// Example of catching exceptions thrown by SafeDate class
//-------------------------------------------------------------------------
package ch01.apps;

import java.util.Scanner; import ch01.dates.*;

public class UseSafeDate
{
  public static void main(String[] args)
  {
    int month, day, year;
    SafeDate theDate;
    boolean DateOK = false;
    Scanner scan = new Scanner(System.in);

    while (!DateOK)
    {
      System.out.println("Enter a date (month day and year):");
      month = scan.nextInt(); day = scan.nextInt(); year = scan.nextInt();
      try
      {
        theDate = new SafeDate(month, day, year);
        DateOK = true;
        System.out.println(theDate + " is a safe date.");
      }
```

```
      catch(DateOutOfBoundsException DateOBExcept)
      {
        System.out.println(DateOBExcept.getMessage() + "\n");
      }
    }
  // Program continues . . .
  }
}
```

If the new statement executes without any trouble, meaning the SafeDate constructor did not throw an exception, then the DateOK variable is set to true, the date is output, and the *while* loop terminates. However, if the DateOutOfBounds exception is thrown by the Date constructor, the latter two statements in the *try* clause are skipped and the exception is caught by the catch statement. This, in turn, prints the message from the exception and the *while* loop is executed, again prompting the user for a date. The program repeatedly prompts for date information until it is given a legal date. Notice that the main method no longer throws DateOutOfBoundsException, as it handles the exception itself.

One last important note about exceptions. The java.lang.Run-TimeException class is treated uniquely by the Java environment. Exceptions of this class are thrown when a standard run-time program error occurs. Examples of run-time errors include null-pointer-exception and array-index-out-of-bounds. Because run-time exceptions can happen in virtually any method or segment of code, we are not required to explicitly handle these exceptions. Otherwise, our programs would become unreadable because of so many try, catch, and throw statements. These errors are classified as **unchecked exceptions**.

> **Java Note**
>
> Java "Run-Time Exceptions" do not need to be handled explicitly. If we elect not to handle them and they are raised, they will eventually be thrown out to the Java Interpreter and our program will "bomb."

1.4 Data Structures

You are already familiar with various ways of organizing data. When you look up a course description in a catalog or a word in a dictionary, you are using an ordered list of words. When you take a number at a delicatessen or barbershop, you become part of a line/queue of people awaiting service. When you study the pairings in a sports tournament and try to predict which team or player will advance through all the rounds and become champion, you create a treelike list of predicted results.

Just as we use many approaches to organize data to deal with everyday problems, programmers use a wide variety of approaches to organize data when solving problems using computers. When programming, the way you view and structure the data that your programs manipulate greatly influences your success. A language's set of primitive types (Java's are byte, char, short, int, long, float, double, and boolean) can be very useful if we need a counter, a sum, or an index in a program. Generally, however, we must also deal with large amounts of data that have complex interrelationships.

Computer scientists have devised many organizational structures to represent data relationships. These structures act as a unifying theme for this text. In this section we introduce the topic in an informal way, by briefly describing some of the classic approaches.

Implementation-Dependent Structures

The internal representation of the first two structures is an inherent part of their definition. These structures act as building blocks for many of the other structures.

Array

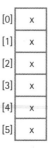

You have studied and used arrays in your previous work. An array's components are accessed by using their positions in the structure. Arrays are one of the most important organizational structures. They are available as a basic language construct in most high-level programming languages. Additionally, they are one of the basic building blocks for implementing other structures. We look at arrays more closely in Section 1.5, "Basic Structuring Mechanisms."

Linked List

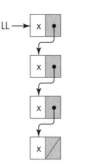

A linked list is a collection of separate elements, with each element linked to the one that follows it in the list. We can think of a linked list as a chain of elements. The linked list is a versatile, powerful, basic implementation structure and, like the array, it is one of the primary building blocks for the more complicated structures. Teaching you how to work with links and linked lists is one of the important goals of this text. We look at Java's link mechanism, the reference, in Section 1.5, "Basic Structuring Mechanisms." Additionally, throughout the rest of the text we study how to use links and linked lists to implement other structures.

Implementation-Independent Structures

Unlike the array and the linked list, the organizational structures presented in this subsection are not tied to a particular implementation approach. They are more abstract.

The structures presented here display different kinds of relationships among their constituent elements. For stacks and queues, the organization is based on when the elements were placed into the structure; for sorted lists, maps, and priority queues it is related to the values of the elements; and for trees and graphs, it reflects some feature of the problem domain that is captured in the relative positions of the elements.

These structures (and others) are treated separately later in the text, when we describe them in more detail, investigate ways of using them, and look at several possible implementations.

Stack

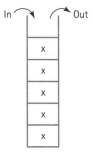

The defining feature of a stack is that whenever you access or remove an element, you work with the element that was most recently inserted. Stacks are "last in, first out" (LIFO) structures. To see how they work, think about a stack of dishes or trays. Note that the concept of a stack is completely defined by the relationship between its accessing operations, the operations for inserting something into it or removing something from it. No matter what the internal representation is, as long as the LIFO relationship holds, it is a stack.

Queue

Queues are, in one sense, the opposite of stacks. They are "first in, first out" (FIFO) structures. The defining feature of a queue is that whenever you access or remove an element from a queue, you work with the element that was in the queue for the longest time. Think about an orderly line of people waiting to board a bus or a group of people, holding onto their service numbers, at a delicatessen. In both cases, the people will be served in the order in which they arrived. In fact, this is a good example of how the abstract organizational construct, the queue, can have more than one implementation approach—an orderly line or service numbers.

Sorted List

George, John, Paul, Ringo

The elements of a sorted list display a linear relationship. Each element (except the first) has a predecessor, and each element (except the last) has a successor. In a sorted list, the relationship also reflects an ordering of the elements, from "smallest" to "largest," or vice versa.

You might be thinking that an array whose elements are sorted is a sorted list—and you would be correct! As we said earlier, arrays are one of the basic building blocks for constructing other structures. But that is not the only way to implement a sorted list. We will cover several other approaches.

Map

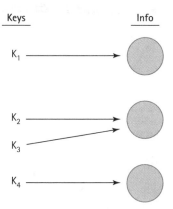

Maps, also known as dictionaries, tables, or associative arrays, are used to store "key"-"info" ordered pairs. Maps provide quick access to desired information when you provide an appropriate key. Consider, for example, when you enter a bank and provide a teller with your account number—within a few seconds (hopefully) the teller has access to your account information. Your account number is the "key"—it "maps" onto your account information. Although there are many ways to implement a map structure, they all must follow the same simple rules: keys are unique and a key maps onto a single information node.

Tree

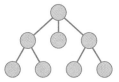

Trees and graphs are nonlinear. Each element of a tree is capable of having many successor elements, called its *children*. A child element can have only one *parent*. Thus, a tree is
a branching structure. Every tree has a special beginning element called the *root*. The root
is the only element that does not have a parent.

Trees are useful for representing hierarchical relationships among data elements. For
example, they can be used to classify the members of the animal kingdom or to organize
a set of tasks into subtasks. Trees can even be used to reflect the *is-a* relationship among
Java classes, as defined by the Java inheritance mechanism.

Graph

A graph is made up of a set of elements, usually called *nodes* or *vertices*, and a set of *edges*
that connect the vertices. Unlike with trees, there are no restrictions on the connections
between the elements. Typically, the connections, or edges, describe relationships among
the vertices. In some cases, values, also called *weights*, are associated with the edges to
represent some feature of the relationship. For example, the vertices may represent cities
and the edges may represent pairs of cities that are connected by airplane routes. Values
of the edges could represent the distances or travel times between cities.

What Is a Data Structure?

We divided our examples of structures into implementation-dependent and implementation-independent categories. Originally, in the infancy of computing, such a distinction
was not made. Most of the emphasis on the study of structures at that time dealt with
their implementation. The term "data structure" was associated with the details of coding
lists, stacks, trees, and so on. As our approaches to problem solving have evolved, we have
recognized the importance of separating our study of such structures into both abstract
and implementation levels.

As is true for many terms in the discipline of computing, you can find varied uses of the
term "data structure" throughout the literature. One approach is to say that a data structure
is the implementation of organized data. With this approach, of the structures described

in this section, only the implementation-dependent structures, the array and the linked list, are considered data structures. Another approach is to consider any view of organizing data as a data structure. With this second approach, the implementation-independent structures, such as the stack and the graph, are also considered data structures.

No matter how you label them, all of the structures described here are important tools for solving problems with programs. In this text we will explore all of these data structures, plus many additional structures, from several perspectives. When you are presented with a problem and are devising a computational solution, it is important to decide how you will store, access, and manipulate the information associated with the problem at an early stage of the solution design process. Knowledge of data structures allows you to successfully make and carry out this decision.

1.5   Basic Structuring Mechanisms

All of the structures described in Section 1.4 "Data Structures" can be implemented using some combination of two basic mechanisms, the reference and the array. Most general-purpose high-level languages provide these two mechanisms. In this section we review Java's versions of them. In Chapter 2 we will begin to use references and arrays to build structures.

Memory

All programs and data are held in memory. Although memory is buried under layers of system software that hides it from us and manages it for us, at its most basic level memory consists of a contiguous sequence of addressable words:

A variable in our program corresponds to a memory location. The compiler handles the translation so that every time the code references the same variable, the system uses the same memory location.

When doing low-level programming, assembly level or lower, there are typically many different addressing "modes" that can be used. However, the two most basic approaches are direct addressing and indirect addressing.

With *direct addressing* the memory location associated with the variable holds the value of the variable. This corresponds to how **primitive variables** are used in Java. For example, if the `char` variable `ch` holds the value 'A' and is associated with memory location **572**, it can be pictured as:

On the left, we show how things are implemented in memory—to clarify the figure we include the variable name `ch` beside its associated memory location. On the right, we show the Java code that declares and instantiates the variable, as well as how we model the variable and its contents in our abstract view of memory.

With *indirect addressing* the memory location associated with the variable holds the *address* of the location that holds the value of the variable. This corresponds to how **reference variables** are used in Java. For example, if the `String` object `str` holds the value "cat" and is associated with memory location **823**, with the actual object stored beginning at memory location **320**, it can be pictured as:

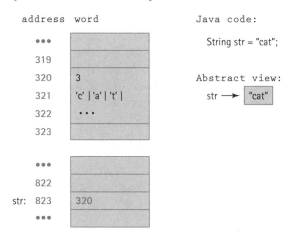

The variable `str` corresponds to location **823**, which holds the address of the location where the information about the `String` object begins—that location, location **320**, is where the system stores information about the string including the string length, the characters, and more—for example, a link to the `String` class. Note that the `String` variable, like all reference variables, is held in a single word (at address **823**) whereas the string itself requires several words. In our abstract view we represent the former location with the variable name "str" and the latter location with the arrow. Throughout the text we will use arrows to represent references—in actuality they represent memory locations.

References

To help present the concepts of this section, we assume access to a `Circle` class. The `Circle` class defines circular objects of different diameters. It provides a constructor that accepts an integer value that represents the diameter of the circle. The `Circle` class provides a convenient example, allowing us to graphically represent objects in our figures—we simply use actual circles of various diameters to represent the `Circle` objects.

Variables of an object class hold references to objects—they use indirect addressing. Consider the effects of the following Java statements:

```
Circle circleA;
Circle circleB = new Circle(8);
```

The first statement reserves memory space for a variable of class `Circle`. The second statement does the same thing, but also creates an object of class `Circle` and places a reference to that object in the `circleB` variable.

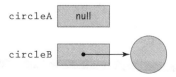

The reference is indicated by an arrow, but the reference is actually a memory address, as discussed in the previous subsection. References are sometimes referred to as *links*, *addresses*, or *pointers*. The memory address of the `Circle` object is stored in the memory location assigned to the `circleB` variable. Note how we are representing the `Circle` object with an actual circle. In reality, it would consist of a section of memory allocated to the object.

Because no object has been instantiated or assigned to the `circleA` variable, its memory location holds a `null` reference. Java uses the reserved word `null` to indicate an "absence of reference." If a reference variable is declared without being assigned an instantiated object, it is automatically initialized to whatever the system uses to represent the value `null`. You can also explicitly assign `null` to a variable:

```
circleB = null;
```

In addition, you can use `null` in a comparison:

```
if (circleA == null)
    System.out.println("The Circle does not exist");
```

Reference Types Versus Primitive Types

It is important to understand the differences in how primitive and nonprimitive types are handled in Java. Primitive types, such as the `int` type, are handled "by value."

Nonprimitive types, such as arrays and classes, are handled "by reference." Whereas the variable of a primitive type holds the value of the variable, the variable of a nonprimitive type holds a *reference* to the value of the variable. That is, the variable holds the address where the system can find the value associated with the variable.

> **Java Note**
>
> In Java, variables of a primitive type such as int or char are stored using direct addressing. We say they are stored "by value." Variables of a reference type, such as type Circle, are stored using indirect addressing. We say they are stored "by reference."

The difference in how "by value" and "by reference" variables are handled is seen dramatically in the result of a simple assignment statement. **Figure 1.4** shows the result of the assignment of one int variable to another int variable, and the result of the assignment of one Circle variable to another Circle variable.

Aliases

When we assign a variable of a primitive type to another variable of the same type, the latter becomes a copy of the former. After the integer assignment statement in Figure 1.4 both intA and intB contain the value 10.

Although the same occurs for reference variables, that is, a value is copied, when we assign a variable of a reference type to another variable of the same type, the effect is quite different. Because the value being copied is a reference in this case, the result is that both variables now point to the same object. Thus we have two "names" for the same object. In this case, we have an **alias** of the object. Good programmers avoid aliases when possible because they make programs difficult to understand. An object's state can change, even though it appears that the program did not access the object, when the object is accessed through the alias. For example, consider the IncDate class that was defined in Section 1.3 "Exceptional Situations." If date1 and date2 are aliases for the same IncDate object, then the code

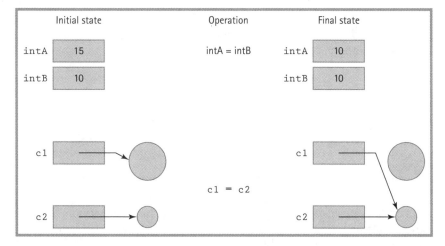

Figure 1.4   Results of assignment statements

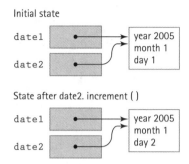

Figure 1.5   Aliases can be confusing

```
System.out.println(date1);
date2.increment();
System.out.println(date1);
```

would print out two different dates, even though at first glance it would appear that it should print out the same date twice (see **Figure 1.5**). This behavior can be very confusing for a maintenance programmer and lead to hours of frustrating testing and debugging.

Garbage

It would be fair to ask in the situation depicted in the lower half of Figure 1.4, "What happens to the space being used by the larger circle?" After the assignment statement the program has lost its reference to the large circle, so it can no longer be accessed. This kind of memory space, that has been allocated to a program but can no longer be accessed by a program, is called **garbage**. Garbage can be created in several other ways in a Java program. For example, the following code would create 100 objects of class `Circle`, but only one of them can be accessed through the `c1` variable after the loop finishes executing:

```
Circle c1;
for (n = 1; n <= 100; n++)
{
    Circle c1 = new Circle(n);
    // Code to initialize and use c1 goes here.
}
```

The other 99 objects cannot be reached by the program. They are garbage.

When an object is unreachable, the Java run-time system marks it as garbage. The system regularly performs an operation known as **garbage collection**, in which it identifies unreachable objects and **deallocates** their storage space, returning the space to the free pool for the creation of new objects.

This approach—creating and destroying objects at different points in the application by allocating and deallocating space in the free pool—is called **dynamic memory management**. Without it, the computer would be much more likely to run out of storage space for data.

Comparing Objects

The fact that nonprimitive types are handled by reference affects the results returned by the == comparison operator. Two variables of a nonprimitive type are considered identical, in terms of the == operator, only if they are aliases for each other. This makes sense when you consider that the system compares the contents of the two variables; that is, it compares the two references that those variables contain. So even if two variables of type Circle reference circles with the same diameter, they are not considered equal in terms of the comparison operator. **Figure 1.6** shows the results of using the comparison operator in various situations.

Parameters

When methods are invoked, they are often passed information (arguments) through parameters. Some programming languages allow the programmer to control whether arguments are passed by value (a copy of the argument's value is used) or by reference (a copy of the argument's address is used). Java does not allow such control. Whenever a variable is passed as an argument, the value stored in that variable is copied into the method's corresponding parameter variable. In other words, all Java arguments are passed by value.

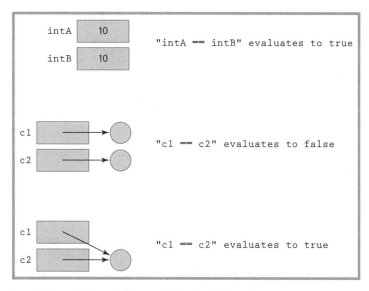

Figure 1.6 Comparing primitive and nonprimitive variables

Therefore, if the argument is of a primitive type, the actual value (int, double, etc.) is passed to the method. However, if the argument is a reference type, an object, or an array, then the value passed to the method is the value of the reference—it is the address of the object or the array.

As a consequence, passing an object variable as an argument causes the receiving method to create an alias of the object. If the method uses the alias to make changes to the object, then when the method finishes, an access via the original variable finds the object in its modified state.

Java Note

All java arguments are "passed by value." If the argument is of a primitive type, it represents the value of the primitive. If the argument is of a reference type, then it represents the address of the object.

Arrays

The second basic structuring construct is the array. An array allows the programmer to access a sequence of locations using an indexed approach. We assume you are already familiar with the basic use of arrays from your previous work. In this subsection we review some of the subtle aspects of using arrays in Java.

Arrays in Java are a nonprimitive type and, therefore, are handled by reference, just like objects. Thus they need to be treated carefully, just like objects, in terms of aliases, comparison, and their use as arguments. And like objects, in addition to being declared, arrays must be instantiated. At instantiation you specify how large the array will be:

```
numbers = new int[10];
```

As with objects, you can both declare and instantiate arrays with a single command:

```
int[] numbers = new int[10];
```

Let us discuss a few questions you may have about arrays in Java:

- What are the initial values in an array instantiated by using new? If the array components are primitive types, they are set to their default value. If the array components are reference types, such as arrays or classes, the components are set to null.

- Can you provide initial values for an array? Yes. An alternative way to create an array is with an initializer list. For example, the following line of code declares, instantiates, and initializes the array numbers:

```
int numbers[] = {5, 32, -23, 57, 1, 0, 27, 13, 32, 32};
```

- What happens if we try to execute the statement

```
numbers[n] = value;
```

  when n is less than 0 or when n is greater than 9? A memory location outside the array would be indicated, which causes an out-of-bounds exception. Some languages—C++, for instance—do not check for this error, but Java does. If your program attempts to use an index that is not within the bounds of the array, an ArrayIndexOutOfBoundsException is thrown.

In addition to component selection, one other "operation" is available for our arrays. In Java, each array that is instantiated has a public instance variable of type int, called length, associated with it that contains the number of components in the array. You access this variable using the same syntax you use to invoke object methods—you use the name of the object followed by a period, followed by the name of the instance variable. For the numbers example, the expression "numbers.length" would have the value 10.

Arrays of Objects

Although arrays with primitive-type components are very common, many applications require a collection of objects. In such a case we can simply define an array whose components are objects.

Here we define an array of Circle objects. Declaring and creating the array of objects is exactly like declaring and creating an array where the components are primitive types:

```
Circle[] allCircles = new Circle[10];
```

This means allCircles is an array that can hold 10 references to Circle objects. What are the diameters of the circles? We do not know yet. The array of circles has been instantiated, but the Circle objects themselves have not. Another way of saying this is that allCircles is an array of references to Circle objects, that are set to null when the array is instantiated. The objects must be instantiated separately. The following code segment initializes the first and second circles. We will assume that a Circle object myCircle has already been instantiated and initialized to have a diameter of 8.

```
Circle[] allCircles = new Circle[10];
allCircles[0] = myCircle;
allCircles[1] = new Circle(4);
```

Figure 1.7 provides a visual representation of the array.

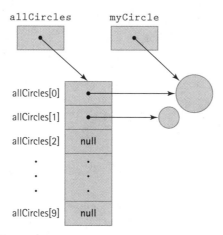

Figure 1.7 The allCircles array

Generating Images

The BufferedImage class in the Java Library allows us to create and manipulate images using a two-dimensional model. It supports most of the popular image types. In this feature we see how to generate JPEG images using this class. Consider the following program:

```java
//****************************************************************
//
//  ImageGen01.java          By Dale/Joyce/Weems          Chapter 1
//
//  Demonstrates image generation
//
//****************************************************************
package ch01.apps;

import java.awt.image.*;
import java.awt.Color;
import java.io.*;
import javax.imageio.*;

public class ImageGen01
{
    public static void main (String[] args) throws IOException
    {
        String fileOut = args[0];   // destination file

        // create BufferedImage of SIZE and TYPE
        final int SIDE = 1024;
        final int TYPE = BufferedImage.TYPE_INT_RGB;
        BufferedImage image = new BufferedImage(SIDE, SIDE, TYPE);

        final int LIMIT = 255; // limit of RGB values
        int c;                 // specific value for R G and B
        Color color;

        for (int i = 0; i < SIDE; i++)
          for (int j = 0; j < SIDE; j++)
          {
             c = (i + j) % LIMIT;
             color = new Color(c, c, c);  // creates 'gray' values
             image.setRGB(i, j, color.getRGB());  // saves pixel
          }

        File outputfile = new File(fileOut);
        ImageIO.write(image, "jpg", outputfile);
    }
}
```

The `ImageGen01` application is in the `ch01.apps` package. It uses a run-time argument as the name of its output file. It is best to use a standard JPEG file extension within this name, for example `test.jpg`. The program instantiates a `BufferedImage` object image of size 1024 × 1024 and of type RGB. Images of this type consist of pixels (picture elements) that use a red-green-blue model. The values for red, green, and blue can range from 0 to 255. Individual pixels can be set using the `setRGB` method, for example

```
color = new Color(200, 20, 125);
image.setRGB(10, 20, color.getRGB);
```

sets the pixel in the 10th row and 20th column to a pinkish purplish color. In the above snippet of code we first create a `Color` object with a red value of 200, a green value of 20, and a blue value of 125. The method `getRGB` invoked on that `Color` object returns a single `int` value that represents the corresponding color. It is that value that is used by the setRGB method to set the value of the pixel.

To create "black and white" images for our textbook we use the fact that within the RGB color model, colors with identical red, green, and blue values are "gray". For example (0, 0, 0) represents black, (255, 255, 255) represents white and (127, 127, 127) represents a medium gray. The double for-loop in the `ImageGen01` program walks through the entire image, from top left to bottom right. The loop body generates an int value c based on the expression `(i + j) % LIMIT`. The corresponding `Color` object, which is set to an RGB value of `(c, c, c)` will cycle through grey values from black to white. The resulting image is shown in **Figure 1.8(a)** below. By varying the expression used for the value of c, alternate images can be generated. It is not difficult to generate interesting images using this approach. For example Figure 1.8 (b) shows the image resulting from the expression `(i * j) % LIMIT`.

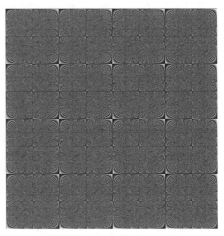

(a) Using `(i + j) % LIMIT`   (b) Using `(i * j) % LIMIT`

Figure 1.8   Generated images

Two-Dimensional Arrays

A one-dimensional array is used to represent elements in a list or a sequence of values. A two-dimensional array is used to represent elements in a table with rows and columns. Two dimensional arrays are useful when we need to store multiple pieces of information about multiple elements. They can also be used to represent images (see the Feature: Generating Images).

Figure 1.9 shows a two-dimensional array with 100 rows and 9 columns. The rows are accessed by an integer ranging from 0 through 99; the columns are accessed by an integer ranging from 0 through 8. Each component is accessed by a row—column pair—for example, [0][5].

A two-dimensional array variable is declared in exactly the same way as a one-dimensional array variable, except that there are two pairs of brackets. A two-dimensional array object is instantiated in exactly the same way, except that sizes must be specified for two dimensions.

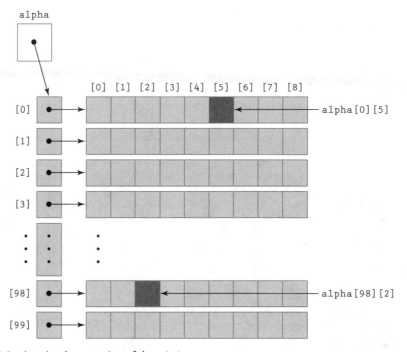

Figure 1.9 Java implementation of the alpha array

The following code fragment would create the array shown in Figure 1.8, where the data in the table are of type `double`.

```
double[][] alpha;
alpha = new double[100][9];
```

The first dimension specifies the number of rows, and the second dimension specifies the number of columns.

To access an individual component of the `alpha` array, two expressions (one for each dimension) are used to specify its position. We place each expression in its own pair of brackets next to the name of the array:

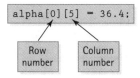

Note that `alpha.length` would give the number of rows in the array. To obtain the number of columns in a row of an array, we access the `length` field for the specific row. For example, the statement

```
rowLength = alpha[30].length;
```

stores the length of row 30 of the array `alpha`, which is 9, into the `int` variable `rowLength`.

It is not difficult to imagine many ways that a two-dimensional array can be used—rows could represent students and columns could be test grades, rows could represent employees and columns the hours they work each day, and so on.

Remember that in Java each row of a two-dimensional array is itself a one-dimensional array. Many programming languages directly support two-dimensional arrays; Java doesn't. In Java, a two-dimensional array is an array of references to array objects. If higher dimension arrays are required we simply extend the number of levels of arrays used, so for example, a three-dimensional array can be created as an two-dimensional array whose elements are arrays.

1.6   Comparing Algorithms: Order of Growth Analysis

Alice: "I'm thinking of a number between 1 and 1,000."

Bob: "Is it 1?"

Alice: "No ... it's higher."

Bob: "Is it 2?"

Alice: "No ... it's higher."

Bob: "Is it 3?"

Alice: rolls her eyes ...

Eventually, Bob will guess the secret number by incrementing his guess by 1 each time. Despite Alice's obvious frustration with him, he is following a valid **algorithm** known as **sequential search.**

The analysis of algorithms is an important area of theoretical computer science. In this section we introduce you to this topic to an extent that will allow you to determine which of two algorithms requires fewer resources to accomplish a particular task. The efficiency of algorithms and the code that implements them can be studied in terms of both time (how fast it runs) and space (the amount of memory required). When appropriate throughout this text we point out space considerations, but usually we concentrate on the time aspect—how fast the algorithm is, as opposed to how much space it uses.

Before continuing with a discussion of the time efficiency of algorithms we should point out that quite often time efficiency and space efficiency are interrelated, and trade-offs between time and space efficiency can be made. Consider, for example, the problem of sorting a deck of cards numbered 1–300. Suppose you are sitting on a bus with these cards and have to sort them while holding them in your hands. You will spend a lot of time shuffling through the cards, and you will most likely need to look at each card many times. Alternately, imagine trying to sort the same set of cards if you are standing in front of a table large enough to hold all 300 of them. In this situation you can look at each card just once and place it in its correct spot on the table. The extra space afforded by the table allows for a more time-efficient sorting algorithm.

Measuring an Algorithm's Time Efficiency

How do programmers compare the time efficiency of two algorithms? The first approach that comes to mind is simply to code the algorithms and then compare the execution times after running the two programs. The one with the shorter execution time is clearly the better algorithm. Or is it? Using this technique, we really can determine only that program A is more efficient than program B on a particular computer at a particular time using a particular set of input data. Execution times are specific to a particular computer, because different computers run at different speeds. Sometimes they are dependent on what else the computer is doing in the background. For example, if the Java run-time engine is performing garbage collection, it can affect the execution time of the program. Coding style and input conditions can also effect the time of a running program. We need a better approach.

A standard technique, and the one we use in this text, is to isolate a particular operation fundamental to the algorithm and count the number of times that this operation is performed. When selecting which operation to count, we want to be sure to select an operation that is executed at least as many times as any other operation during the course of the algorithm.

Consider, for example, Bob's use of the sequential search algorithm to guess Amy's secret number for the Hi-Lo game.

Hi-Lo Sequential Search
Set guess to 0
do
Increment guess by 1
Announce guess
while (guess is not correct)

It is clear that "Announce guess" is a fundamental operation for the Hi-Lo Sequential Search algorithm. It is found inside the loop so it executes over and over again, and it is directly related to the goal of discovering the hidden number.

So, how many times is "Announce guess" executed? How many guesses does Bob make?

Complexity Cases

If Bob is lucky, Alice is thinking of a low number and he will not need to make many guesses. On the other hand, if he is unlucky he will be guessing for a long time, for example, if Alice is thinking of the number 998.

Clearly, the number of "guesses" required by the Hi-Lo Sequential Search algorithm depends upon the input conditions. This is not unusual. To handle this situation, analysts define three complexity cases:

- **Best case complexity** tells us the complexity when we are very lucky. It represents the fewest number of steps that an algorithm can take. For Alice's guessing game, the best case occurs when she is thinking of the number 1 and Bob only needs to make one guess. In general, best case complexity is not very useful as a complexity measure. We would not want to choose an algorithm due to its best case complexity and then hope we get lucky in terms of the input conditions.

- **Average case complexity** represents the average number of steps required, considering all possible inputs. In the guessing game case this is not difficult to determine: if all of the numbers between 1 and 1,000 are equally likely to occur, then on average it will require $(1 + 1,000)/2 = 500.5$ guesses to guess a number. Average case complexity analysis can be useful but it is often difficult to define for a specific algorithm.

- **Worst case complexity** represents the highest number of steps that an algorithm would require. If Alice is thinking of the number 1,000 then Bob will need to make 1,000 guesses. With his approach he would never need to make more than 1,000 guesses. For our purposes we will usually use worst case analysis. It is typically easier to define and calculate than the average case and it gives us useful information. If we know that we can afford the amount of work required in the worst case then we can confidently use the algorithm under review.

We conclude that in the worst case the Hi-Lo Sequential Search algorithm requires 1,000 guesses. But wait—what if the game is changed slightly?

Size of Input

Bob: "Is it 366?"

Alice, patiently: "No . . . it's higher."

Bob: "Is it 367?"

Alice: "Yes!"

Bob: "Ha—that was easy."

Alice: "Want to play again?"

Bob: "Sure."

Alice: "OK. I'm thinking of a number between 1 and 1,000,000."

Bob: blinks

If we perform worst case analysis of the Hi-Lo Sequential Search algorithm for this new version of the game, we arrive at a different answer—1,000,000 steps. Clearly, the number of steps required by the algorithm depends on the range of possible numbers. Rather than saying the algorithm requires 1,000 steps under this condition and 1,000,000 steps under that condition we can describe the complexity of the algorithm as a function of the input size. If the game is to guess a number between 1 and N, the size of the input is N, and for the sequential search algorithm, the worst case number of guesses required is also N.

Most algorithms require more work to solve larger problems. For example, clearly it is more difficult to sort a list of 500 numbers than it is to sort a list of 10 numbers. Therefore, it makes sense to speak of an algorithm's efficiency in terms of the input size, and to use that size as a parameter when describing the efficiency of the algorithm. For the problems we address in this text it is usually obvious how to identify the required size parameter although for some interesting complex algorithms this is not the case. Most of the problems in this book involve data structures—stacks, queues, lists, maps, trees, and graphs. Each structure is composed of elements. We develop algorithms to add an element to the structure and to modify or delete an element from the structure. We can describe the work done by these operations in terms of N, where N is the number of elements in the structure.

Comparing Algorithms

Carlos: "What's up?"

Bob: "Alice wants me to guess a number between 1 and 1,000,000. No way."

Carlos: "Hmmm. I'll try. Is it 500,000?"

Alice: "No, it's lower."

Carlos: "Is it 250,000?"

Alice: "No, it's higher."

Carlos: "Is it 375,000?"

. . .

As you can see, Carlos is using a different algorithm than Bob. It is called **binary search** and leverages the fact that Carlos can eliminate half the remaining numbers each time by cleverly choosing a number in the middle of the range. Carlos will need, in the worst case, only 20 guesses to guess a number between 1 and 1,000,000!

Hi-Lo Binary Search(N)[4]

Set range to 1 . . . N
do
    Set guess to middle of range
    Announce guess
    if (guess was too high)
        Set range to first half of range
    if (guess was too low)
        Set range to second half of range
while (guess is not correct)

What is the worst case complexity of the Hi-Lo Binary Search algorithm? Let us again count how many times, in the worst case, the statement "Announce guess" is executed. Each time an incorrect guess is made, the remaining range of possible numbers is cut in half. So, another way of asking this is "How many times can you reduce N by half, before you get down to 1?" The answer is $\log_2 N$.[5] After $\log_2 N$ guesses all of the numbers except

---

[4] Code that implements this algorithm is found in the `SelSortAndBinSearch.java` file of the `ch01.apps` package.

[5] Recall that $\log_2 N$ is the power that you raise 2 to, in order to get N. For example, $\log_2 8 = 3$ because $2^3 = 8$. But another way of looking at this is to consider that $\log_2 N$ is the number of times you can cut N in half before reaching 1. We can cut 8 in half 3 times: $8 \rightarrow 4 \rightarrow 2 \rightarrow 1$.

Clever Algorithms

Devising clever algorithms that efficiently solve problems is an exciting part of computer science. Proving such algorithms are correct, analyzing space/time trade-offs, devising heuristics for special cases, and determining optimal bounds are all key steps in the evolution of our understanding of computation. Such work also has important practical benefits as evidenced by advancements in areas such as genome sequencing, modeling, signal processing, encryption, data compression, and network analysis.

one would have been eliminated so with one last guess you will be correct. Therefore, in the worst case Hi-Lo Binary Search requires $\log_2 N + 1$ guesses as compared to the N guesses of Hi-Lo Sequential Search. Of course, $\log_2 N$ is not always an integer—we can "round down" in the case of a nonintegral result. For an input size of 1,000,000, this equates to 20 guesses for binary search as opposed to 1,000,000 guesses for sequential search.

Obviously, the binary search approach is faster than the sequential search approach. Or is it? Each time a guess is made using the binary search approach, the algorithm must do more calculations than when using sequential search. Determining the middle of the remaining range is more time consuming than just adding 1 to the previous guess. Just by looking at the descriptions of the two algorithms we can see that the sequential search is simpler than the binary search. So which is better?

Let us try, in this one case, to count the operations more carefully. For sequential search the initial guess is set to 0, and then each time a guess is made the value must be both incremented and announced. In the worst case this will require two steps (increment, announce) for each guess plus the one initial step resulting in a total of $2N + 1$ steps. For binary search the algorithm must set the low value and high value of the range, and then each time a guess is made it must add together the low value and high value, divide, round, announce the guess, and adjust the range. It must also make the final guess. In the worst case, this will require five steps for each guess (add, divide, round, announce, and adjust) plus the two initial steps and one final step, resulting in a total of $5 \log_2 N + 3$ steps. The accompanying table compares the counts of our two algorithms for various values of N.

Size	Sequential Search	Binary Search
N	$2N + 1$ steps	$5 \log_2 N + 3$ steps
2	5	8
4	9	13
8	17	18
16	33	23
32	65	28
1,024	2,049	53
1,000,000	2,000,001	98
1,000,000,000	2,000,000,001	148

A study of the table shows that if the size of the problem is 8 or less, fewer steps are required by sequential search than by binary search. And for problem sizes like 16 and 32, the difference in number of steps needed by the two algorithms is not much. On the other hand, as the size of the problem grows, the difference in the number of steps required becomes dramatic, in favor of binary search.

Our example is typical. For many problems we can devise simple "brute force" algorithms that are easy to understand and that perform adequately when the size of the problem is small but as the problem size increases they become prohibitively expensive. If you play the Hi-Lo guessing game where the range of possible numbers is small, go ahead and use Bob's brute force approach—but as that range increases you will be much better off emulating the cleverer Carlos.

In general, we are interested in finding solutions to large problems. If you want to sort a list of three names into alphabetical order, you most likely would not need to consider an automated solution right? But what if it was a list of a million names? The study of algorithms focuses on large problem sizes.

Order of Growth

We must point out that the counting steps exercise of the previous subsection, although enlightening, is also somewhat futile. It is difficult to count accurately the number of steps required by an algorithm. At what level should you count? The pseudo-code description, the high-level language encoding, the machine language translation? And how to handle the issue that all steps are not created equal, for example, "increment a number" and "divide two numbers" will require different amounts of time.

Besides, the detailed counts do not really give us extra information in terms of comparing algorithms. Consider the following table, identical to the previous one, except it does not use any of the detailed step counting information. Here we simply use an estimate of how many times the fundamental operation occurs, N steps for sequential search and $\log_2 N$ (rounded to closest integer) steps for binary search.

Size	Sequential Search	Binary Search
N	N steps	$\log_2 N$ steps
2	2	1
4	4	2
8	8	3
16	16	4
32	32	5
1,024	1,024	10
1,000,000	1,000,000	20
1,000,000,000	1,000,000,000	30

From this table we can still conclude that as the size of the problem increases, the binary search vastly outperforms the sequential search. That is the focus of our analysis—determining which algorithm is better for large problems.

Computer scientists take advantage of the fact that what really matters when comparing algorithms is the highest order of the polynomial that represents the number of steps needed. We simply report that order to describe the efficiency. Perhaps the number of steps needed for the sequential search is $f(N) = 2N + 1$, but we say that it is "**Order of Growth** N" or even $O(N)$ read as "Oh of N" or "Order N."[6] Perhaps the number of steps needed for binary search is $f(N) = 5 \log_2 N + 3$, but we say it is $O(\log_2 N)$. Here are some more examples:

$$2N^5 + N^2 + 37 \text{ is } O(N^5) \quad 2N^2 \log_2 N + 3N^2 \text{ is } O(N^2 \log_2 N) \quad 1 + N^2 + N^3 + N^4 \text{ is } O(N^4)$$

By focusing only on the critical information provided by the order of growth, our analysis is simplified. We are able to simply look at an algorithm like Hi-Lo Sequential Search, recognize that in the worst case the loop will account for every number in the range, and state confidently that the efficiency of the algorithm is $O(N)$. Similarly, with the Hi-Lo Binary Search algorithm, we recognize that half the range is removed from consideration each time through the loop and that therefore the algorithm is $O(\log_2 N)$. There is no need to count operations in detail.

Selection Sort

Let us analyze one more example using the techniques we developed in this section. Putting an unsorted list of data elements into order—*sorting*—is a very common and useful operation. Entire books have been written about sorting algorithms. Here we look at a relatively simple brute-force algorithm that is somewhat similar to the approach many people use to sort a hand of randomly dealt cards in games such as bridge or poker.

Given an unsorted list of elements, the algorithm scans through the list and finds the smallest element. It then *selects* that element and swaps it with the first element. Next it scans the list again to find the second smallest element, again *selecting* it and swapping it with the second element. As the algorithm repeatedly *selects* the next smallest element and swaps it into its "correct" position, the sorted section of the list grows larger and the unsorted section of the list grows smaller, until eventually the entire list is sorted. For reasons which should be obvious, this algorithm is called the *Selection Sort*.

Before we can analyze the Selection Sort algorithm we need to identify the size of the input. It is easy to see that the larger the list, the more work is required to sort it. So the number of elements in the list is the natural choice for the size of the input for the sorting problem. We will use N to indicate this size. Here is a more formal description of the

---

[6] Many people read the notation as "Big Oh of N". There is a specific mathematical definition of the concept of "Big Oh" that is related to the order of growth and is used in the analysis of algorithms; however, the way we pursue analysis in this text is more properly called "order of growth" and we will use that term.

algorithm, where our goal is to sort an array `values` of size N (the indices of the array go from 0 to $N - 1$):

Selection Sort(values[0 ... N – 1])

for current going from 0 to $N - 2$
  Set minIndex to index of smallest unsorted element
  Swap the elements at indices current and minIndex

Figure 1.10 shows the steps taken by the algorithm to sort a five-element array. Each section of the figure represents one iteration of the *for* loop. The first part of a section represents the "find the smallest unsorted element" step. To do that it repeatedly examines the unsorted elements asking if each one is the smallest seen so far. The second part of a

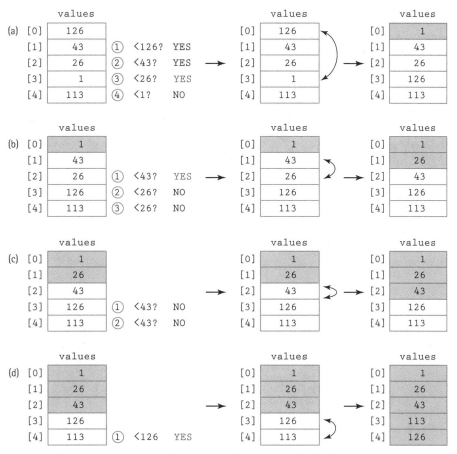

Figure 1.10   Example of a Selection Sort (sorted elements are shaded)

section shows the two-array elements to be swapped and the final part shows the result of the swap.

During the progression, we can view the array as being divided into a sorted part and an unsorted part. Each time it performs the body of the *for* loop, the sorted part grows by one element and the unsorted part shrinks by one element. Except at the very last step the sorted part grows by two elements—do you see why? When all the array elements except the last one are in their correct locations, the last one is in its correct location also, by default. This is why our *for* loop can stop at index $N - 2$, instead of at the end of the array, index $N - 1$.

We must be careful in identifying the "operation fundamental to the algorithm" to use in our analysis. Can we use "Swap the elements"? Although it appears to be a fundamental operation and is executed once for each iteration of the *for* loop, it is not the operation that is executed the most. Consider that in the act of finding the smallest element in the remaining part of the array each time through the loop we must "look at" all the remaining elements. If we add more detail to our algorithm, we see that we actually have a loop inside a loop:

Selection Sort(values[0 ... $N - 1$])[7]

for current going from 0 to $N - 2$
  Set minIndex to current
  for check going from (current + 1) to ($N - 1$)
    if (values[check] $<$ values[minIndex])
      Set minIndex to check
  Swap the elements at indices current and minIndex

Clearly, the innermost operation, the comparison of the two-array elements, is the fundamental operation that occurs most frequently. This is also evident from a study of Figure 1.10, where we can count 10 comparisons that occur in contrast to only four swaps. We describe the number of comparisons as a function of the number of elements in the array, that is, N.

The comparison operation is in the inner loop. We know that this loop is executed $N - 1$ times because the outer loop goes from 0 to $N - 2$. Within the inner loop, the number of comparisons varies, depending on the value of current. The first time the inner loop is executed, current is 0 so the algorithm checks locations 1 to $N - 1$, so there are $N - 1$ comparisons; the next time the current is 1 so there are $N - 2$ comparisons, and so on, until in the last call, there is only one comparison. The total number of comparisons is

$$(N - 1) + (N - 2) + (N - 3) + \ldots + 2 + 1$$

Applying a well-known summation formula tells us this sum is equal to $N(N - 1)/2$. To accomplish our goal of sorting an array of N elements, the selection sort requires

---

[7] Code that implements this algorithm is found in the `SelSortAndBinSearch`.java file of the `ch01.apps` package.

$N(N - 1)/2$ comparisons. The particular arrangement of values in the array does not affect the amount of work done at all. Even if the array is in sorted order before using Selection Sort, the algorithm still makes $N(N - 1)/2$ comparisons. Best case, average case, and worst case all require $N(N - 1)/2$ comparisons.

How do we describe this algorithm in terms of order of growth? If we expand $N(N - 1)/2$ as $\frac{1}{2}N^2 - \frac{1}{2}N$, it is easy to see. In order of growth notation we only consider the term "$\frac{1}{2}N^2$, " because it increases fastest relative to N. Further, we ignore the constant coefficient, $\frac{1}{2}$, making this algorithm $O(N^2)$. This means that, for large values of N, the computation time is approximately proportional to N^2.

Computer scientists who study and analyze many algorithms reach the point where they can often quickly determine the order of growth of an algorithm. For example, they could look at the Selection Sort algorithm described above and they would immediately know it is $O(N^2)$ because they have seen that pattern—a loop inside a loop with conditions interrelated in the same way—many times before. The exercises for this section hopefully will help you reach that level of expertise!

Common Orders of Growth

In this subsection we discuss some common orders of growth, listed from most efficient to least efficient.

$O(1)$ is called "bounded time." The amount of work is bounded by a constant and is not dependent on the size of the problem. Initializing a sum to 0 is $O(1)$. Although bounded time is often called constant time, the amount of work is not necessarily constant. It is, however, bounded by a constant.

$O(\log_2 N)$ is called "logarithmic time." The amount of work depends on the logarithm, in base 2, of the size of the problem. Algorithms that successively cut the amount of data to be processed in half at each step, like the binary search algorithm, typically fall into this category. Note that in the world of computing we often just say "log N" when we mean $\log_2 N$. The base 2 is assumed.

$O(N)$ is called "linear time." The amount of work is some constant times the size of the problem. Algorithms that work through all the data one time to arrive at a conclusion, like the sequential search algorithm, typically fall into this category.

$O(N \log_2 N)$ is called (for lack of a better term) "N log N time". Algorithms of this type typically involve applying a logarithmic algorithm N times. The better sorting algorithms, such as Quicksort presented in Chapter 11, have N log N complexity.

$O(N^2)$ is called "quadratic time." Algorithms of this type typically involve applying a linear algorithm N times. Most simple sorting algorithms, such as the Selection Sort algorithm, are $O(N^2)$ algorithms.

This pattern of increasingly time complex algorithms continues with $O(N^2 \log_2 N)$, $O(N^3)$, $O(N^3 \log_2 N)$, and so on.

$O(2^N)$ is called "exponential time." These algorithms are extremely costly and require more time for large problems than any of the polynomial time algorithms previously listed. An example of a problem for which the best known solution is exponential is the

Table 1.3 Comparison of Rates of Growth

N	$\log_2 N$	$N \log_2 N$	N^2	N^3	2^N
1	0	1	1	1	2
2	1	2	4	8	4
4	2	8	16	64	16
8	3	24	64	512	256
16	4	64	256	4,096	65,536
32	5	160	1,024	32,768	4,294,967,296
64	6	384	4,096	262,144	approximately 20 billion billion
128	7	896	16,384	2,097,152	It would take a fast computer a trillion billion years to execute this many instructions
256	8	2,048	65,536	16,777,216	Do not ask!

traveling salesman problem—given a set of cities and a set of roads that connect some of them, plus the lengths of the roads, find a route that visits every city exactly once and minimizes total travel distance.

Table 1.3 presents the values of various common orders of growth functions for several different values of N. As you can see in the table, the differences in the function values become quite dramatic as the size of N increases.

Summary

This chapter is all about organization.

Object orientation allows developers to organize their solutions around models of reality, accruing benefits of understandability, reusability, and maintainability. The primary construct for creating systems using this approach is the class. Classes are used to create objects that work together to provide solutions to problems. Java's inheritance mechanism and package construct help us organize our classes.

Java's exception handling mechanisms provide a powerful way to organize our system's responses to special situations. We can choose to handle exceptional situations where they are first encountered or to throw the responsibility out to another level. A good understanding of this mechanism is a crucial ingredient for creating safe, reliable systems.

Programs operate on data, so how the data are organized is of prime importance. Data structures deal with this organization. Several classic organizational structures have been identified through the years to help programmers create correct and efficient solutions to problems. The Java language provides basic structuring mechanisms for creating these structures—namely, the array and the reference mechanisms. Order of growth notation is an approach for classifying the efficiency of the algorithms that we will employ when implementing and using our data structures.

Programmers are problem solvers. Object orientation allows seamless integration of problem analysis and design, resulting in problem solutions that are maintainable and reusable. Data structures provide ways of organizing the data of the problem domain so that solutions are correct and efficient. Staying organized is the key to solving difficult problems!

Exercises

1.1 Classes, Objects, and Applications

1. *Research Question*: The Turing Award has been awarded annually since 1966 to a person or persons for making contributions of lasting and major technical importance to the computer field. Locate information about this award on the Web. Study the list of award winners and their contributions. Identify those winners whose contribution dealt directly with programming. Then identify those winners whose contributions dealt directly with object orientation.

2. *Research Question*: List and briefly describe the UML's 14 main diagramming types.

3. What is the difference between an object and a class? Give some examples.

4. Describe each of the four levels of visibility provided by Java's access modifiers.

5. According to the `DaysBetween` application, how many days are between 1/1/1900 and 1/1/2000? How many leap years are there between those dates? What about between 1/1/2000 and 1/1/2100? Explain the difference in these answers.

6. Use the `DaysBetween` application to answer the following:

   a. How old are you, in days?

   b. How many days has it been since the United States adopted the Declaration of Independence, on July 4, 1776?

   c. How many days between the day that Jean-François Pilâtre de Rozier and François Laurent became the first human pilots, traveling 10 kilometers in a hot air balloon on November 21, 1783, near Paris and the day Neil Armstrong took one small step onto the moon, at the Sea of Tranquility, on July 20, 1969?

7. Think about how you might test the `DaysBetween` application. What type of input should give a result of 0? Of 1? Of 7? Of 365? Of 366? Try out the test cases that you identified.

8. Modify the `Date` class so that it includes a `compareTo` method with signature

   ```
   int compareTo(Date anotherDate)
   ```

   This method should return the value 0 if this date (the date of the object upon which the method is invoked) is equal to the argument date; a value less than 0 if this date is a date earlier than the argument date; and a value greater than 0 if this date is a date later than the argument date. Create a **test driver** that shows that your method performs correctly.

9. A common use of an object is to "keep track" of something. The object is fed data through its transformer methods and returns information through its observer methods. Define a reasonable set of instance variables, class variables, and methods for each of the following classes. Indicate the access level for each construct. Note that each of these class descriptions are somewhat "fuzzy" and allow multiple varied "correct" answers.

   a. *A time counter*—this will keep track of total time; it will be fed discrete time amounts (in either minutes and seconds or just in seconds); it should provide information about the total time in several "formats," number of discrete time units, and average time per unit. Think of this class as a tool that could be used to keep track of the total time of a collection of music, given the time for each song.

   b. *Basketball statistics tracker*—this will keep track of the score and shooting statistics for a basketball team (not for each player but for the team as a unit); it should be fed data each time a shot is taken; it should provide information about shooting percentages and total score when requested.

   c. *Tic-Tac-Toe game tracker*—this will keep track of a tic-tac-toe game; it should be fed moves and return an indication of whether or not a move was legal; it should provide information about the status of the game (is it over? who won?) when requested.

10. For one or more of the classes described in the previous exercise

   a. Implement the class.

   b. Design and implement an application that uses the class.

   c. Use your application to help verify the correctness of your class implementation.

11. You will create a class that models a standard pair of dice.

   a. Create a class called `PairOfDice`. Objects of this class represent a single pair of six-sided dice. The only attributes of such an object are the face values of the dice. Provide a constructor. Provide a `roll` method that simulates rolling the dice. Provide a `value` method that returns the sum of the face values of the dice. Provide a `toString` method that returns a nicely formatted string representing the pair of dice, for example "5 : 3 = 8". Finally, create a "test driver" that demonstrates that your `PairOfDice` class performs correctly.

   b. The game of Craps is played in casinos all over the world. The basic bet made by the "shooter" in this game is the pass-line bet. To start a pass-line round, the shooter makes a "come-out" roll. A come-out roll of 2, 3, or 12 is called "craps" or "crapping out," and the shooter loses. A come-out roll of 7 or 11 is a "natural," and the shooter wins. The other possible numbers are the point numbers: 4, 5, 6, 8, 9, and 10. If the shooter rolls one of these numbers on the come-out roll, this establishes the "point"—to win, the point number must be rolled again be-fore a seven. So in the case where a "point" is established the shooter rolls over and over until either the point is rolled (a win) or a seven is rolled (a loss). Using your `PairOfDice` class simulate 100,000 pass-line bets and output how many result in a win, and how many result in a loss. *Hint*: Your result should tell you to be wary of casinos.

12. You will create a class that keeps track of the total cost, average cost, and number of items in a shopping bag.

   a.   Create a class called `ShoppingBag`. Objects of this class represent a single shopping bag. Attributes of such an object include the number of items in the bag and the total retail cost of those items. Provide a constructor that accepts a tax rate as a `double` argument. Provide a transformer method called `place` that models placing a number of identically priced items into the bag—it accepts an `int` argument indicating the number of items and a `double` argument that indicates the cost of each of the items. For example, `myBag.place(5, 10.5)` represents placing five items that cost $10.50 each into `myBag`. Provide getter methods for both the number of items in the bag and their total retail cost. Provide a `totalCost` method that returns the total cost with tax included. Provide a `toString` method that returns a nicely formatted string that summarizes the current status of the shopping bag. Finally, provide a program, a "test driver," that demonstrates that your `ShoppingBag` class performs correctly.

   b.   Create an application that repeatedly prompts the user for a number of items to put in the bag, followed by a prompt for the cost of those items. Use a 0 for the number of items to indicate that there are no more items. The program then displays a summary of the status of the shopping bag. Assume the tax rate is 6%. A short sample run might look something like this:

```
Enter count (use 0 to stop): 5
Enter cost: 10.50
Enter count (use 0 to stop): 2
Enter cost: 2.07
Enter count (use 0 to stop): 0
The bag contains seven items. The retail cost of the items is $56.64.
The total cost of the items, including tax, is $60.04.
```

13. You will create a class that represents a polynomial; for example, it could represent $5x^3 + 2x - 3$ or $x^2 - 1$.

   a.   Create a class called `Polynomial`. Objects of this class represent a single poly-nomial. Attributes of such an object include its `degree` and the `coefficients` of each of its terms. Provide a constructor that accepts the degree of the poly-nomial as an `int` argument. Provide a transformer method called `setCoeffi-cient` that accepts as `int` arguments the degree of the term it is setting and the coefficient to which it should be set. For example, the polynomial $5x^3 + 2x - 3$ could be created by the sequence of statements:

```
Polynomial myPoly = new Polynomial(3);
myPoly.setCoefficient(3,5);
myPoly.setCoefficient(1,2);
myPoly.setCoefficient(0,-3);
```

Provide an `evaluate` method that accepts a `double` argument and returns the value of the polynomial, as a `double`, as evaluated at the argument value. For example, given the previous code the following sequence of code would print −3.0, 4.0, and −1.375.

```
System.out.println(myPoly.evaluate(0.0));
System.out.println(myPoly.evaluate(1.0));
System.out.println(myPoly.evaluate(0.5));
```

Finally, provide a program, a "test driver," that demonstrates that your `Polynomial` class performs correctly.

b. Create an application that accepts the degree of a polynomial and the coefficients of the polynomial, from highest degree to lowest, as a command line argument and then creates the corresponding `Polynomial` object. For example, the polynomial $5x_3 + 2x - 3$ would be represented by the command line argument "3 5 0 2 − 3." The program should then repeatedly prompt the user for a double value at which to evaluate the polynomial and report the result of the evaluation. A sample run, assuming the previously stated command line argument, might look something like this:

```
Enter a value> 0.0
The result is -3.0
Continue?> Yes
Enter a value> 1.0
The result is 4.0
Continue?> Yes
Enter a value> 0.5
The result is -1.375
Continue?> No
```

c. Create an application that accepts the degree of a polynomial and the coefficients of the polynomial as a command line argument as in part b. The program should then prompt the user for two `double` values that will represent the end points of an interval on which the polynomial is defined. Your program should then calculate and output the approximation of the definite integral of the polynomial on the indicated interval, using 1,000 bounding rectangles.

1.2 Organizing Classes

14. Describe the concept of inheritance, and explain how the inheritance tree is traversed to bind method calls with method implementations in an object-oriented system.

15. *Research*: Find the Java library description of the `ArrayList` class and answer the following questions:

    a. What class does it directly inherit from?

    b. How many direct subclasses does it have?

    c. How many methods does it implement?

    d. How many methods does it inherit?

    e. If we invoke the `toString` method on an object of class `ArrayList`, which class's `toString` method will be used?

16. Given the definition of the `Date` and `IncDate` classes in this chapter, and the following declarations

    ```
    int temp;
    Date date1 = new Date(10,2,1989);
    IncDate date2 = new IncDate(12,25,2001);
    ```

    indicate which of the following statements are illegal, and which are legal. Explain your answers.

    a. `temp = date1.getDay();`

    b. `temp = date2.getYear();`

    c. `date1.increment();`

    d. `date2.increment();`

17. Design a set of at least three classes related by inheritance from the world of

    a. *Banking*—for example, account, checking account, savings account

    b. *Gaming*—for example, creature, hero, villain, pet

    c. *Travel*—for example, vehicle, plane, boat

    d. *Whatever*—use your imagination

18. Devise a program that demonstrates polymorphism, using the example provided on page 18.

19. Explain how packages are used to organize Java files.

20. *Research*: Copy the program files to your system and answer the following questions:

    a. How many classes are in the `support` package?

    b. How many classes are in the `ch01.apps` package?

    c. The `CSInfo` class is in the `ch05.apps` package:

        i.   What four packages does it import from?

        ii. How do the import statements differ?

    d.　The `Dates` class is in the `ch01.dates` class:

        i.　What happens if you change its package statement from `package ch01.dates` to `package ch01.date` and compile it? Explain.

        ii.　What happens if you remove its package statement and compile it? Explain.

        iii.　What happens if you remove its package statement and compile the `Days-Between` application that is in the `ch01.apps` package? Explain.

21. Suppose file 1 contains   and file 2 contains

```
package media.records;        package media.records;
public class Labels{ . . . }   public class Length{ . . . }
class Check { . . . }          class Review { . . . }
```

    a.　Are the `Check` class and the `Review` class in the same package?

    b.　What is the name of file 1?

    c.　What is the name of file 2?

    d.　What is the name of the directory that contains the two files?

    e.　What is that directory a subdirectory of?

1.3 Exceptional Situations

22. Explain the difference between a programmer-defined exception that extends the Java `Exception` class and one that extends the Java `RunTimeException` class.

23. Create a program that asks users to enter an integer and then thanks them. If they do not enter an integer your program should ask again, until they do. Running your program might result in this sort of console trace:

```
Please enter an integer.
OK
That is not an integer. Please enter an integer.
Twenty-seven
That is not an integer. Please enter an integer.
64
Thank you.
```

24. Create a `BankAccount` class that models a typical bank account where you deposit and withdraw money. To keep things simple, assume this bank account deals only with integral amounts.

    a.　You should provide a constructor, a `toString` method, a `getTotal` method that returns an `int`, and both `deposit` and `withdraw` methods that take `int` arguments and return `void`. Also create an application `UseBankAccount` that demonstrates that the `BankAccount` class works correctly.

    b.　Create a `BankAccountException` class. Change your `deposit` method so that it throws an appropriate exception if an attempt is made to deposit a negative amount. Do the same with the `withdraw` method, but also have it throw an exception if an attempt is made to withdraw more money than is available. In each case include appropriate exception messages. Create three short applications that demonstrate each of the three exceptional situations—it is OK if the applications bombs, as long as it demonstrates that the appropriate exception has been thrown.

c.   Create a new application, `Banker`, that creates a `BankAccount` object and then interacts with users, allowing them to deposit or withdraw funds, or to request an account total. This application should not bomb in any of the exceptional situations—it should catch the exception, pass the message to the user, and continue processing.

25. There are three parts to this exercise:

a.   Create a "standard" exception class called `ThirteenException`.

b.   Write a program that repeatedly prompts the user to enter a string. After each string is entered, the program outputs the length of the string, unless the length of the string is 13, in which case the `ThirteenException` is thrown with the message "Use thirteen letter words and stainless steel to protect yourself!" Your `main` method should simply throw the `ThirteenException` exception out to the run-time environment. A sample run of the program might be:

```
Input a string > Villanova University
That string has length 20.
Input a string > Triscadecaphobia
That string has length 16.
Input a string > misprogrammed
```

At this point the program bombs and the system provides some information, including the "Use thirteen letter words and stainless steel to protect yourself!" message.

c.   Create another program similar to the one you created for part b, except this time, within your code, include a *try-catch* clause so that you catch the exception when it is thrown. If it is thrown, then catch it, print its message, and end the program "normally."

1.4 Data Structures

26. *Research Question*: On the Web find two distinct definitions of the term "data structure." Compare and contrast them.

27. Identify things in the following story that remind you of the various data structures described in the section. Be imaginative. How many can you find? What are they? [*Note*: We can find nine!]

Kaede arrives at the train station with just a few minutes to spare. This weekend is shaping up to be a disaster. She studies the electronic map on the wall for a few seconds in confusion. She then realizes she just needs to select her destination from the alphabetized list of buttons on the right. When she presses Gloucester a path on the map lights up—so, she should take the Blue train to Birmingham where she can connect to the Red train that will take her to Gloucester. The wait in line to buy her ticket does not take long time. She hurries to the platform and approaches the fourth car of the train. Double-checking that her ticket says "car 4," she boards the train and finds a seat. Whew, just in time, as a few seconds later the train pulls out the station. About an hour into the journey Kaede decides it is time for lunch. She walks through cars 5, 6, and 7, to arrive at car 8, the dining car. She grabs the top tray (it is still warm from the tray dryer) and heads for the candy machine, thinking to herself, "May as well figure out what to have for dessert first, as usual. Hmmm, that's an interesting Pez dispenser in slot F4." She presses the button contentedly, and thinks "Looks like this is going to be a nice weekend after all. Thank goodness for data structures."

28. Describe three uses of a tree structure as a way of organizing information.

29. Some aspect of each of the following can be modeled with a graph structure. Describe, in each case, what the nodes would represent and what the edges would represent.

    a. Trips available using a specific airline
    b. Countries and their borders
    c. A collection of research articles about data structures
    d. Actors (research the "six degrees of Kevin Bacon")
    e. The computers at a university
    f. A labyrinth
    g. The Web

1.5 Basic Structuring Mechanisms

30. Draw images similar to those shown in the *Memory* subsection of Section 1.5 "Basic Structuring Mechanisms" that represent the contents of memory resulting from the following code segments. Assume that i is associated with memory location 123, j with 124, the str1 variable with 135 and its associated object with 100, and the str2 variable with 136.

    a.
    ```
    int i = 10;
    int j = 20;
    String str1 = "cat";
    ```

    b.
    ```
    int i = 10;
    int j = i;
    String str1 = "cat";
    String str2 = str1;
    ```

31. What is an alias? Show an example of how it is created by a Java program. Explain the dangers of aliases.

32. Assume that date1 and date2 are objects of class IncDate as defined in Section 1.2 "Organizing Classes." What would be the output of the following code?

```
date1 = new IncDate(5, 5, 2000);
date2 = date1;
System.out.println(date1);
System.out.println(date2);
date1.increment();
System.out.println(date1);
System.out.println(date2);
```

33. What is garbage? Show an example of how it is created by a Java program.

34. Assume that date1 and date2 are objects of class IncDate as defined in Section 1.2 "Organizing Classes." What would be the output of the following code?

```
date1 = new IncDate(5, 5, 2000);
date2 = new IncDate(5, 5, 2000);
if (date1 = = date2)
   System.out.println("equal");
else
   System.out.println("not equal");
date1 = date2;
if (date1 = = date2)
   System.out.println("equal");
else
   System.out.println("not equal");
date1.increment();
if (date1 = = date2)
   System.out.println("equal");
else
   System.out.println("not equal");
```

35. Write a program that declares a 10-element array of int, uses a loop to initialize each element to the value of its index squared, and then uses another loop to print the contents of the array, one integer per line.

36. Write a program that declares a 10-element array of Date, uses a loop to initialize the elements to December 1 through 10 of 2005, and then uses another loop to print the contents of the array, one date per line.

37. Create an application that instantiates a 20 × 20 two-dimensional array of integers, populates it with random integers drawn from the range of 1 to 100, and then outputs the index of the row with the highest sum among all the rows and the index of the column with the highest sum among all the columns.

38. Compile and run the `ImageGen01` application. Experiment with alternate formulas for the value of `c`. Add two more `int` variables so that you can separately set the RGB values of `color` and experiment some more. Share your most interesting results with your classmates.

1.6 Comparing Algorithms: Order of Growth Analysis

39. We examined two approaches to guessing the secret number for the Hi-Lo Guessing Game: Hi-Lo Sequential Search and Hi-Lo Binary Search. What is the best and worst case number of guesses required by each of these approaches if the highest possible number is (a) 10, (b) 1,000, (c) 1,000,000, and (d) 1,000,000,000.

40. For each of the following problems briefly describe an algorithm that solves the problem, identify a good "operation fundamental to the algorithm" that could be used to calculate the algorithm's efficiency, succinctly describe the size of the problem, and state the number of times the fundamental operation occurs as a function of the problem size in the best case and worst case. For example, if the problem was "guess the secret number in the Hi-Lo Guessing Game" your answer might be "start at 1 as my first guess and keep adding one to my guess until I guess the number; announce my guess; the highest possible number—call it N; best case 1 time, worst case N times".

    a. Finding *The Art of Computer Programming* on a shelf of unsorted books.

    b. Sorting an array of integers.

    c. Finding the cheapest pair of shoes in a shoe catalog.

    d. Figuring out how much money is in a piggy bank.

    e. Computing $N!$ for a given N.

    f. Computing the sum of the numbers 1 to N, for a given N.

    g. Multiplying two $N \times N$ matrices.

41. Compare each of the following pairs of functions $f(x)$ and $g(x)$ by graphing them on the set of nonnegative numbers (yes, just like in algebra class). Note that in each case the higher ordered function g eventually becomes larger than the lower ordered function f. Identify the x value where this occurs.

    a. $f(x) = 3 \log_2 x$ $g(x) = x$

    b. $f(x) = 5 \log_2 x + 3$ $g(x) = 2x + 1$

    c. $f(x) = 4 x^2$ $g(x) = x^3$

    d. $f(x) = 8 x^2$ $g(x) = 2^x$

42. Describe the order of growth of each of the following functions using O notation.

    a. $N^2 + 3N$

    b. $3N^2 + N$

    c. $N^5 + 100N^3 + 245$

   d. $3N\log_2 N + N^2$

   e. $1 + N + N^2 + N^3 + N^4$

   f. $(N * (N - 1)) / 2$

43. Describe the order of growth of each of the following code sections, using O notation:

   a.
```
count = 0;
for (i = 1; i <= N; i++)
   count++;
```

   b.
```
count = 0;
for (i = 1; i <= N; i++)
   for (j = 1; j <= N; j++)
      count++;
```

   c.
```
value = N;
count = 0;
while (value > 1)
{
   value = value / 2;
   count++;
}
```

   d.
```
count = 0;
value = N;
value = N * (N - 1);
count = count + value;
```

   e.
```
count = 0;
for (i = 1; i <= N; i++)
   count++;
for (i = N; i >= 0; i--)
   count++;
```

   f.
```
count = 0;
for (i = 1; i <=N; i++)
   for (j = 1; j <= 5; j++)
      count++;
```

44. The method Sum listed below returns the sum of the integers between 1 and n. What is its order of growth? Create a new method that performs the same function that is a lower order of growth.

```
public int Sum (int n)
// Precondition: n is > 0
{
   int total = 0;
   for (int i = 1; i <= n; i++)
      total = total + i;
   return total;
}
```

45. Assume that `numbers` is a large array of integers, currently holding N values in locations 0 through $N-1$. Describe the order of growth (worst case) of each of the following operations, using O notation:

    a. Set location N of `numbers` to 17.

    b. Shift all values in the `numbers` array to the "right" one location to make room at location 0 for a new number without disrupting the order of the current values; insert the number 17 into location 0.

    c. Randomly choose a location L from 0 to $N-1$; Shift all the values in the `numbers` array, from location L to location $N-1$, to the right one location to make room at location L for a new number; insert the number 17 into location L.

46. Show the sequence of changes the array `values` undergoes while it is sorted using selection sort.

    values

27	15	83	12	104	28	57	30

47. For this exercise you must implement the selection sort algorithm.

    a. Create a program named `SelectionSort` that instantiates an array of `int` of size 100 and initializes it with random numbers between 1 and 1000. The program should display the integers from the array in five columns. Next it sorts the array using selection sort. Finally, it prints the contents of the array again, in columns of 5.

    b. Augment your program from part a so that it also counts the number of comparisons and the number of swaps executed during the selection sort. It should report these numbers after printing the sorted array. Based on the analysis of selection sort in this section what are the expected values for the number of comparisons and the number of swaps? How do the values reported by your program compare to the "theoretical" values?

    c. Augment your program from part b so that it works first with an array of size 10, then 100, then 1000, then 10,000, and finally 100,000 (remove the code that prints out the array values of course). For each array size your program should display the number of comparisons and swaps. Have the program display these numbers in a nice tabular format.

The Stack ADT

Knowledge Goals

You should be able to

- explain the following terms and their relationships: abstraction, information hiding, data abstraction, data encapsulation, and abstract data type (ADT)
- describe the benefits of using an abstract data type
- define, for the Java programming language, the meanings of abstract method and interface
- describe the benefits of using a Java interface to specify an ADT
- list three options for making a collection ADT generally usable
- explain three ways to "handle" exceptional situations when defining an ADT
- describe the Stack ADT from three perspectives: abstract level, application level, and implementation level
- classify a given stack operation as a constructor, observer, or transformer
- describe an algorithm for determining whether grouping symbols (such as parentheses) within a string are balanced, using a stack
- describe an algorithm for evaluating postfix expressions, using a stack

Skill Goals

You should be able to

- use the Java interface construct to formally specify an ADT
- specify the preconditions and postconditions (effects) of a public method
- use the Java generics mechanism when designing and/or implementing and/or using an ADT
- define and use a self-referential class to build a linked list
- draw figures representing a sequence of operations on a linked list
- implement the Stack ADT using an array
- implement the Stack ADT using the Java library's `ArrayList` class
- implement the Stack ADT using a linked list
- draw diagrams showing the effect of stack operations for a particular implementation of a stack
- determine the order of growth efficiency of stack implementation operations
- throw Java exceptions from within an ADT and catch them within an application that uses the ADT
- evaluate a postfix expression "by hand"
- use the Stack ADT as a component of an application

This chapter introduces the stack, an important data structure. A stack is a "last in, first out" structure. We begin the chapter with a discussion of using abstraction in program design. We review the related concepts of abstraction and information hiding and show how these techniques encourage us to view our data at three different "levels": the application, abstract, and implementation levels. This approach is used with the stack structure. At the abstract level our stack is formally defined using a Java `interface`. We discuss many applications of stacks and look, in particular, at how stacks are used to determine whether a set of grouping symbols is well formed and to support the evaluation of mathematical expressions. Stacks are then implemented using two basic approaches: arrays and links (references). To support the link-based approach, we introduce the linked list structure. Finally, we also present an implementation using the Java library's `ArrayList` class.

2.1 Abstraction

The universe is filled with complex systems. We learn about such systems through models. A model may be mathematical, like equations describing the motion of satellites around the Earth. A physical object such as a model airplane used in wind-tunnel tests is another form of model. Typically, only the *relevant* characteristics of the system being studied are modeled; irrelevant details are ignored. For example, in-flight movies are not included in the model airplanes used to study aerodynamics. When irrelevant details are omitted we have an abstract view of the system.

An **abstraction** is a model of a system that includes only the details essential to the perspective of the viewer of the system. What does abstraction have to do with software development? Writing software is difficult because both the systems we model and the processes we use to develop the software are complex. Abstractions are the fundamental way that we manage complexity. In every chapter of this text we make use of abstractions to simplify our work.

> **Important**
>
> Abstraction is a key tool in the construction of large complex systems. We partition our systems into separate modules, each with their own responsibilities. The details of each module are hidden inside the module—a module presents only a controlled interface to its functionality to the outside.

Information Hiding

Many software design methods are based on decomposing a problem's solution into modules. A "module" is a cohesive system subunit that performs a share of the work. In Java, the primary module mechanism is the *class*. Decomposing a system using classes and objects generated from classes helps us handle complexity.

Classes/objects are abstraction tools. The complexity of their internal representation can be hidden from the rest of the system. As a consequence, the details involved in implementing a class are isolated from the details of the rest of the system. Why is hiding the details desirable? Shouldn't the programmer know everything? *No!* Hiding the implementation details of each module within the module helps manage the complexity of a system because a programmer can safely concentrate on different parts of a system at different times. **Information hiding** is the practice of hiding details within a module with the goal of simplifying the view of the module for the rest of the system.

Of course, a program's classes/objects are interrelated; that is, they work together to solve the problem. They provide services to one another through carefully defined interfaces. The interface in Java is usually provided by the public and/or protected methods of a class. Programmers of one class do not need to know the internal details of the classes with which it interacts, but they do need to know the interfaces. Consider a driving analogy: you can start a car without knowing how many cylinders are in the engine. You just have to understand the interface; that is, you only need to know how to turn the key.

Data Abstraction

Any data, such as a value of type `int`, processed by a computer is just a collection of bits that can be turned on or off. The computer manipulates data in this form. People, however, tend to think of data in terms of more abstract units such as numbers and lists, and thus we want our programs to refer to data in a way that makes sense to us. To hide the irrelevant details of the computer's view of data from our own, we create another view. **Data abstraction** is the separation of a data type's logical properties from its implementation.

Here we take a closer look at the very concrete—and very abstract—integer you have been using since you wrote your earliest programs. Just what is an integer? Integers are physically represented in different ways on different computers. However, knowing exactly how integers are represented on your computer is not a prerequisite for using integers in a high-level language. With a high-level language you use an abstraction of an integer. This is one of the reasons it is called a "high"-level language.

The Java language encapsulates integers for us. **Data encapsulation** is a programming language feature that enforces information hiding, allowing the internal

> **Did You Know?**
>
> You have been using data abstraction since you started programming. For example, if you ever used an `int` variable in a Java program then you made use of data abstraction. You take advantage of the logical properties of an `int` without worrying about the details of its internal representation.

representation of data and the details of the operations on the data to be encapsulated together within a single construct. The programmer using the data does not see the internal representation but deals with the data only in terms of its logical picture—its abstraction.

But if the data are encapsulated, how can the programmer get to them? Simple. The language provides operations that allow the programmer to create, access, and change the data. As an example, look at the operations Java provides for the encapsulated data type `int`. First, you can create variables of type `int` using declarations in your program.

```
int a, b, c;
```

Then you can assign values to these integer variables by using the assignment operator and perform arithmetic operations on them by using the +, -, *, /, and % operators.

```
a = 3;   b = 5;
c = a + b;
```

The point of this discussion is that you have *already* been dealing with a logical data abstraction of integers. The advantages of doing so are clear: You can think of the data and the operations in a logical sense and can consider their use without having to worry about implementation details. The lower levels are still there—they are just hidden from you. The only information you really need to know about the int type is its range [$-2{,}147{,}483{,}648$ to $2{,}147{,}483{,}647$] and the effects of the supported operations, for example, $+$, $-$, $\times$, $/$, and $\%$. You do not need to understand two's complement binary number representation nor how to arrange a circuit of logic gates in order to code the integer addition statement, even though such technologies are used to implement the operation.

We refer to the set of all possible values (the domain) of an encapsulated data "object," plus the specifications of the operations that are provided to create and manipulate the data, as an abstract data type. An **abstract data type (ADT)** is a data type whose properties (domain and operations) are specified independently of any particular implementation.

In effect, all of Java's built-in types, such as int, are ADTs. A Java programmer can declare variables of those types without understanding the actual representation. The programmer can initialize, modify, and access the information held by the variables via the provided operations.

In addition to the built-in ADTs, Java programmers can use the Java *class* mechanism to create their own ADTs. For example, the Date class defined in Chapter 1 can be viewed as an ADT. Yes, it is true that the programmers who created it needed to know about its actual representation; for example, they needed to know that a Date is composed of three int instance variables, and they needed to know the names of the instance variables. The application programmers who use the Date class, however, do *not* need this information. They simply need to know how to create a Date object and how to invoke its exported methods so as to use the object.

Data Levels

In this text we define, create, and use ADTs. We deal with ADTs from three different perspectives, or levels:

1. *Application (or user or client or external) level*   As the application programmer, we use the ADT to solve a problem. When working on the application we only need to know what program statements to use to create instances of the ADT and invoke its operations. That is, our application is a **client** of the ADT. There can be many different clients that use the same ADT. We should note that a client of an ADT does not have to be an application—any code that uses the ADT is considered to be its client—it could even be code used in the implementation of another ADT.

2. *Abstract (or logical) level*   This level provides an abstract view of the data values (the domain) and the set of operations to manipulate them. Here we deal with the

what questions: What is the ADT? What does it model? What are its responsibilities? What is its interface? At this level, the ADT designer, sometimes in consultation with intended client programmers, provides a specification of the properties of the ADT. This specification is used by the application/client programmer to decide when and how to use the ADT. And it is used by the implementation programmer who needs to create code that fulfills the specification.

3. *Implementation (or concrete or internal) level* The implementation programmer designs and develops a specific representation of the structure to hold the data as well as the implementation (coding) of the operations. Here we deal with the *how* questions: How do we represent and manipulate the data? How do we fulfill the responsibilities of the ADT? There can be many different answers to these questions, resulting in multiple implementation approaches.

When you write a program, you often deal with data at *each* of these three levels. In this section, which features abstraction, the focus is the abstract level. In one sense, the ADT approach centers on the abstract level. The abstract level provides a model of the implementation level for use at the application level. Its description acts as a contract created by the designer of the ADT, relied upon by the application programmers who use the ADT, and fulfilled by the programmers who implement the ADT.

> **Important**
>
> Understanding the differences between and relationships among the three ways of viewing data described here is crucially important. Sometimes you will work at the application level and use an ADT; at other times you will implement the ADT used by applications. In all cases the abstract view will act as your guide.

For the most part the abstract level provides independence between the application and implementation levels. Keep in mind, however, that there is one way that the implementation details can affect the applications that use the ADT—in terms of efficiency. The decisions we make about the way data are structured affect how efficiently we can implement the various operations on that data. The efficiency of operations can be important to the users of the data.

Preconditions and Postconditions

Suppose we want to design an ADT to provide a service. Access to the ADT is provided through its exported methods. To ensure that an ADT is usable at the application level, we must clarify how to use these methods. To be able to invoke a method, an application programmer must know its exact interface: its name, the types of its expected arguments, and its return type. But this information is not enough: The programmer also needs to know any assumptions that must be true for the method to work correctly and the effects of invoking the method.

Preconditions of a method are the conditions that must be true when invoking a method for the method to work correctly. For example, the `increment` method of the `IncDate` class, described in Chapter 1, could have preconditions related to legal date values and the start of the Gregorian calendar. Such preconditions should be listed at the beginning of the method declaration as a comment:

```
public void increment()
// Preconditions:    Values of day, month, and year represent a valid date.
//                   The value of year is not less than MINYEAR.
```

Establishing the preconditions for a method creates a contract between the programmer who implements the method and the programmers who use the method. The contract says that the method meets its specifications if the preconditions are satisfied. It is up to the programmers who use the method to ensure that the preconditions are true whenever the method is invoked. This approach is sometimes called "programming by contract."

We must also specify which conditions are true when the method is finished. **Postconditions (effects)** of a method are the results expected at the exit of the method, assuming that the preconditions were met. Postconditions do not tell us *how* these results are accomplished; they merely tell us *what* the results should be. We use the convention of stating the main effects—that is, the postconditions—within the opening comment of a method, immediately after any preconditions that are listed. For example,

```
public void increment()
// Preconditions:    Values of day, month, and year represent a valid date.
//                   The value of year is not less than MINYEAR.
//
// Increments this IncDate to represent the next day.
```

Java Interfaces

Java provides a construct, the `interface`, that can be used to formally specify the abstract level of our ADTs.

The word "interface" means a common boundary shared by two interacting systems. We use the term in many ways in computer science. For example, the user interface of a program is the part of the program that interacts with the user, and the interface of a method is its name, the set of parameters it requires, and the return value it provides.

In Java, the word "interface" has a very specific meaning. In fact, `interface` is a Java keyword. It represents a specific type of program unit. A Java interface looks very similar to a Java class. It can include variable declarations and methods. However, all variables declared in an interface must be constants and all the methods must be abstract.[1] An **abstract method** includes only a description of its parameters; no method bodies or implementations are allowed. In other words, only the *interface* of the method is included.

Unlike a class, a Java interface cannot be instantiated. What purpose can a Java interface serve if it can only hold abstract methods and cannot be instantiated? It provides

---

[1] As of March 2014 and the release of Java SE 8, Java interfaces may also include `default` and `static` methods. We do not use either of these within the interfaces defined in this text.

a template for classes to fit. To make an interface useful, a separate class must "implement" it. That is, a class must be created that supplies the bodies for the method headings specified by the interface. In essence, Java interfaces are used to describe requirements for classes.

Here is an example of an interface with one constant (PI) and two abstract methods (perimeter and area):

```
package ch02.figures;
public interface FigureInterface
{
   final double PI = 3.14;

   double perimeter();
   // Returns perimeter of this figure.

   double area();
   // Returns area of this figure.
}
```

Although Java provides the keyword abstract that we can use when declaring an abstract method, we should not use it when defining the methods in an interface. Its use is redundant, because all nonstatic methods of an interface must be abstract. Similarly, we can omit the keyword public from the method signatures. It is best not to use these unnecessary modifiers when defining an interface, as future versions of Java may not support their use.

Interfaces are compiled just like classes and applications. Each of our interfaces is kept in a separate file. The name of the file must match the name of the interface. For example, the interface shown above must reside in a file called FigureInterface.java. The compiler checks the interface code for errors; if there are none, it generates a Java byte code file for the interface. In our example, that file would be called Figure-Interface.class.

To use this interface a programmer could, for example, create a Circle class that implements the interface. When a class implements an interface, it receives access to all of the constants defined in the

> **Java Note**
>
> Java interfaces cannot be instantiated. They can only be implemented by classes or extended by other interfaces.

interface and it must provide an implementation—that is, a body—for all of the abstract methods declared in the interface. Thus, the Circle class, and any other class that implements the FigureInterface interface, would be required to repeat the declarations of the methods perimeter and area, and provide code for their bodies as shown here:

```
package ch02.figures;
public class Circle implements FigureInterface
{
  protected double radius;

  public Circle(double radius)
  {
    this.radius = radius;
  }

  public double perimeter()
  {
    return(2 * PI * radius);
  }

  public double area()
  {
    return(PI * radius * radius);
  }
}
```

Note that many different classes can all implement the same interface. For example, the following Rectangle class also implements FigureInterface.

```
package ch02.figures;
public class Rectangle implements FigureInterface
{
  protected double length, width;

  public Rectangle(double length, double width)
  {
    this.length = length;
    this.width = width;
  }

  public double perimeter()
  {
    return(2 * (length + width));
  }

  public double area()
  {
    return(length * width);
  }
}
```

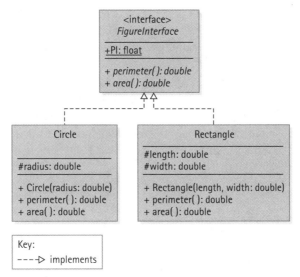

Figure 2.1   UML for Figure ADT

You can imagine many other classes such as `Square` and `Parallelogram`, all of which implement the `FigureInterface` interface. A programmer who knows that these classes implement the interface can be guaranteed that each provides implementations for the `perimeter` and `area` methods.

The Unified Modeling Language (UML) class diagram in **Figure 2.1** shows the relationship between the `FigureInterface` interface and the `Circle` and `Rectangle` classes. The dotted arrow with the open arrowhead indicates a class implementing an interface. Classes that implement an interface are not constrained only to implement the abstract methods of the interface as in this example; they can also add data fields and methods of their own.

Interfaces are a versatile and powerful programming construct. Among other things, they can be used to specify the abstract view of an ADT. Within the interface we define abstract methods that correspond to the exported methods of the ADT implementation. We use comments to describe the preconditions and postconditions of each abstract method. An implementation programmer, who intends to create a class that implements the ADT, knows that he or she must fulfill the contract spelled out by the interface. An application programmer, who wants to use the ADT, can use any class that implements the interface.

> **Authors' Convention**
>
> Throughout the text we will use interfaces to define the logical view of the data structures (ADTs) under consideration.

Using the Java interface construct in this way for our ADT specifications produces several benefits:

1. We can formally check the syntax of our specification. When the interface is compiled, the compiler uncovers any syntactical errors in the method interface definitions.

2. We can formally verify that the syntactical part of the interface "contract" is satisfied by the implementation. When the implementation is compiled, the compiler ensures that the method names, parameters, and return types match those defined in the interface.

3. We can provide a consistent interface to applications from among alternative implementations of the ADT. Some implementations may optimize the use of memory space; others may emphasize speed. An implementation may also provide extra functionality beyond that defined in the interface. Yet all of the implementations will have the specified interface in common.

Note that it is possible to declare a variable to be of an interface type. Given access to `FigureInterface`, `Circle`, and `Rectangle`, the following code is completely "legal."

```
FigureInterface myFigure;
myFigure = new Circle(5);
myFigure = new Rectangle(2,4);
```

As long as a class implements the `FigureInterface` interface, we can instantiate an object of the class and assign it to `myFigure`. This is an example of polymorphism.

Interface-Based Polymorphism

In Section 1.2, "Organizing Classes," we introduced the concept of polymorphism. You may want to review that material before continuing. In that section we discussed inheritance-based polymorphism. Here we discuss the other approach to polymorphism supported by Java, interface-based polymorphism.

Recall from the discussion in Chapter 1 that the word "polymorphism" has Greek roots and literally means "many forms" or "many shapes." It is therefore lucky that we have our `FigureInterface` interface to use in this discussion. We will actually be defining object references that can refer to "many shapes"!

Polymorphic object variables are able to reference objects of different classes at different times during the execution of a program. They cannot reference just any class, but they can reference a set of related classes. In inheritance-based polymorphism, the relationship among the classes is defined by the inheritance tree. The related classes are descendants of a common class. With interface-based polymorphism the relationship is even simpler. The related classes implement the same interface.

Consider the following application. Can you predict what it will output?

```
//-----------------------------------------------------------------
// RandomFigs.java          by Dale/Joyce/Weems          Chapter 2
//
// Demonstrates polymorphism.
//-----------------------------------------------------------------
package ch02.apps;
```

```
import ch02.figures.*;
import java.util.Random;
import java.text.DecimalFormat;

public class RandomFigs
{
    public static void main(String[] args)
    {
        DecimalFormat df = new DecimalFormat("#.###");
        Random rand = new Random();
        final int COUNT = 5;
        double totalArea = 0;

        FigureInterface[] figures = new FigureInterface[COUNT];

        // generate figures
        for (int i = 0; i < COUNT; i++)
        {
            switch (rand.nextInt(2))
            {
                case 0:    figures[i] = new Circle(1.0);
                           System.out.print("circle area     3.14\n");
                           break;

                case 1:    figures[i] = new Rectangle(1.0, 2.0);
                           System.out.print("rectangle area 2.00\n");
                           break;
            }
        }

        // sum areas
        for (int i = 0; i < COUNT; i++)
            totalArea = totalArea + figures[i].area();
        System.out.println("\nTotal: " + df.format(totalArea));
    }
}
```

As you can see, we declare an array figures of FigureInterface objects. An object of any class that implements FigureInterface can be stored in this array. The first *for* loop inserts five figure objects into the array; however, because of the random nature of this code, we cannot tell which types of figures are inserted simply by reading the code. The binding of the array slots to the objects is performed dynamically at run time. So we can see what happens when running the program, the first loop also prints out a string description of each object inserted into the array. The second *for* loop walks through the array and adds up the areas of the inserted objects. Within that loop the decision of which area method, that of the Circle class or that of the Rectangle class, to execute must be made at run time. Each of the array slots is a polymorphic reference. Here are three sample program runs:

```
circle area      3.14      rectangle area  2.00      rectangle area  2.00
rectangle area   2.00      rectangle area  2.00      rectangle area  2.00
rectangle area   2.00      circle area     3.14      circle area     3.14
rectangle area   2.00      circle area     3.14      circle area     3.14
rectangle area   2.00      rectangle area  2.00      circle area     3.14
Total: 11.14              Total: 12.28              Total: 13.42
```

It is not difficult to imagine many uses for interface-based polymorphism. For example, an array of FigureInterface objects could form the basis of a Geometry tutorial or an array of CreatureInterface objects could be used in an adventure game. It is not necessary to use arrays to benefit from this type of polymorphism. Later in this chapter we define a StackInterface; we will create multiple classes that implement this interface. We could create a program that declares a variable of type StackInterface and then dynamically chooses which of the implementations to use when instantiating the variable, perhaps based on some user responses to queries or the state of the system. With such an approach our program would be dynamically adaptable to the current situation.

2.2   The Stack

Consider the items pictured in **Figure 2.2**. Although the objects are all different, each illustrates a common concept—the stack. At the abstract level, a stack is an ordered group of homogeneous elements. The removal of existing elements and the addition of new ones can take place only at the top of the stack. For instance, if your favorite blue shirt is underneath a faded, old, red one in a stack of shirts, you first take the red shirt from the top of the stack. Then you remove the blue shirt, which is now at the top of the stack. The red shirt may then be put back on the top of the stack. Or it could be thrown away!

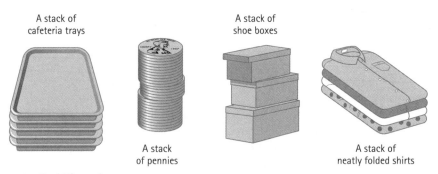

Figure 2.2   Real-life stacks

A stack may be considered "ordered" because elements occur in sequence according to how long they have been in the stack. The elements that have been in the stack the longest are at the bottom; the most recent are at the top. At any time, given any two elements in a stack, one is higher than the other. (For instance, the red shirt was higher in the stack than the blue shirt.)

Because elements are added and removed only from the top of the stack, the last element to be added is the first to be removed. There is a handy mnemonic to help you remember this rule of stack behavior: A stack is a LIFO (last in, first out) structure. To summarize, a **stack** is an access-controlled structure in which elements are added or removed from only one end, a LIFO structure.

Operations on Stacks

The logical picture of the structure is only half the definition of an abstract data type. The other half is a set of operations that allows the user to access and manipulate the elements stored in the structure. What operations do we need to use a stack?

When we begin using a stack, it should be empty. Thus we assume that our stack has at least one class constructor that sets it to the empty state.

The operation that adds an element to the top of a stack is usually called *push*, and the operation that removes the top element from the stack is referred to as *pop*. Classically, the *pop* operation has both removed the top element of the stack and returned the top element to the client that invoked *pop*. More recently, programmers have been defining two separate operations to perform these actions because operations that combine observations and transformation can result in confusing programs.

We follow modern convention and define a *pop* operation that removes the top element from a stack and a *top* operation that returns the top element of a stack.[2] Our *push* and *pop* operations are strictly transformers, and our *top* operation is strictly an observer. **Figure 2.3** shows how a stack, envisioned as a stack of building blocks, is modified by several *push* and *pop* operations.

Using Stacks

Suppose you are relaxing at the kitchen table reading the newspaper and the phone rings. You make a mental note of where you stop reading as you stand to answer the phone. While chatting on the phone with your friend, the doorbell chimes. You say "just a minute, hold that thought" and put the phone down as you answer the door. As you are about to sign for the package that is being delivered, your dog Molly runs out the open door. What do you do? Obviously you retrieve Molly, then sign for the package, then finish the phone call, and finally return to reading your paper. Whether you realize it or not, you have been storing your postponed obligations on a mental stack! Each time you are interrupted you

---

[2] Another common approach is to define a **pop** operation in the classical way—that is, it removes and returns the top element—and to define another operation, often called **peek**, that simply returns the top element.

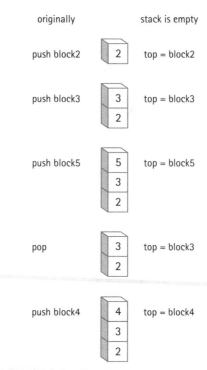

Figure 2.3 The effects of push and pop operations

push the current obligation onto this stack and then, when you are free, you pop it from the stack and resume handling it.

Stacks are very useful ADTs, especially in the field of computing system software. They are most often used in situations, like the example above, in which we must deal with postponed obligations. For example, programming language systems typically use a stack to keep track of operation calls. The main program calls operation A, that in turn calls operation B, that in turn calls operation C. When C finishes, control returns to B, the postponed obligation; when B finishes, control returns to A, the previous postponed obligation; and so on. The call and return sequence is essentially a LIFO sequence of postponed obligations.

You may have encountered a case where a Java exception has produced an error message that mentions "a system stack trace." This trace shows the nested sequence of method calls that ultimately led to the exception being thrown. These calls were saved on the "system stack."

Compilers use stacks to analyze language statements. A program often consists of nested components, for example, a *for* loop containing an *if-then* statement that contains a *while* loop. As a compiler is working through such nested constructs, it "saves" information about what it is currently working on in a stack; when it finishes its work on the innermost construct, it can "retrieve" its previous status (the postponed obligation) from the stack and pick up where it left off.

Similarly, an operating system will save information about the current executing process on a stack so that it can work on a higher-priority interrupting process. If that process is interrupted by an even higher-priority process, its information can also be pushed on the process stack. When the operating system finishes its

Use of Stacks

Stacks are often used to store postponed obligations. When possible or necessary the previously postponed obligation is removed from the stack in which it was stored and processing continues on it. Many variations on this theme occur within computing systems software, including call-return stacks and process stacks.

work on the highest-priority process, it retrieves the information about the most recently stacked process and continues working on it, much like the scenario described above where you were interrupted while reading the paper.

Stacks are also useful in situations where decisions are made on a tentative basis, for example, when traversing a maze. Given the choice between passages A or B you choose passage A, but store the option of trying passage B on a stack, so that you can return to it if A does not work out. While wandering down passage A you are given a choice between passages C or D and choose C, storing D on the stack. When C turns out to be a dead end, you pop the most recent alternate passage off the stack, in this case passage D, and continue from there. With a complex maze many such decisions could be stored on the stack, allowing us to simulate investigating various paths through the maze by retracing our steps. This stack-based algorithm for exploring a maze is called a *depth-first search* and is often used to explore tree and graph data structures.

2.3 Collection Elements

A stack is an example of an access-controlled collection ADT. A **collection** is an object that holds other objects. Typically we are interested in inserting, removing, and obtaining the elements of a collection.

A stack *collects* together elements for future use, while maintaining a LIFO access ordering among the elements. Before continuing our coverage of stacks, we will examine the question of which types of elements can be stored in a collection. We will look at several variations that are possible when structuring collections of elements and describe the approaches used throughout this text. It is important to understand the various options, along with their strengths and weaknesses, so that you can make informed decisions about which approach to use based on your particular situation.

Generally Usable Collections

A straightforward approach to implementing several stacks to hold different types of objects would be to create a unique stack class for each type of object. If we want to have a stack of something—say, strings or integers or programmer-defined bank account objects—we would have to design and code an ADT for each targeted type. (See **Figure 2.4a**)

Although this approach would provide us with the needed stacks, it requires a lot of redundant coding, and it would be difficult to track and maintain so many different stack classes.

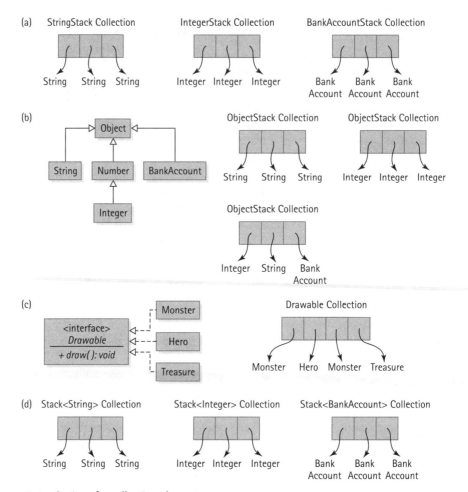

Figure 2.4 Options for collection elements

Collections of Class Object

One approach to creating generally usable collections is to have the collection ADT hold variables of class Object. Because all Java classes ultimately inherit from Object, such an ADT is able to hold a variable of any class. (See Figure 2.4b) This approach works well, especially when the elements of the collection do not have any special properties, for example, if the elements do not have to be sorted.

Although this approach is simple, it is not without problems. One drawback: whenever an element is removed from the collection, it can be referenced only as an Object. If you intend to use it as something else, you must cast it into the type that you intend to use. For example, suppose you place a string into a collection and then retrieve it. To use the retrieved object as a String object you must cast it, as <u>emphasized</u> here:

```
collection.push("E. E. Cummings");        // push string on a stack
String poet = (String) collection.top();  // cast top to String
System.out.println(poet.toLowerCase());   // use the string
```

Without the cast you will get a compile error because Java is a strongly typed language and will not allow you to assign a variable of type `Object` to a variable of type `String`. The `cast` operation tells the compiler that you, the programmer, are guaranteeing that the `Object` is, indeed, a `String`.

The `Object` approach works by converting every element into class `Object` as it is stored in the collection. Users of the collection must remember what kinds of objects have been stored in the collection, and then explicitly cast those objects back into their original classes when they are removed from the collection.

As shown by the third `ObjectStack` collection in Figure 2.4(b), this approach allows a program to mix the types of elements in a single collection. That collection holds an `Integer`, a `String`, and a `BankAccount`. In general, such mixing is *not* considered to be a good idea, and it should be used only in rare cases under careful control. Its use can easily lead to a program that retrieves one type of object—say, an `Integer`—and tries to cast it as another type of object—say, a `String`, which is an error.

Collections of a Class That Implements a Particular Interface

Sometimes we may want to ensure that all of the objects in a collection support a particular operation or set of operations. As an example, suppose the objects represent elements of a video game. Many different types of elements exist, such as monsters, heroes, and treasure. When an element is removed from the collection it is drawn on the screen, using a `draw` operation. In this case, we would like to ensure that only objects that support the `draw` operation can be placed in the collection.

Recall from Section 2.1, "Abstraction," that a Java interface can include only abstract methods, that is, methods without bodies. Once an interface is defined we can create classes that implement the interface by supplying the missing method bodies. For our video game example we could create an interface with an abstract `draw` method. A good name for the interface might be `Drawable`, as classes that implement this interface provide objects that can be drawn. The various types of video game elements that can be drawn on the screen should all be defined as implementing the `Drawable` interface.

Now we can ensure that the elements in our example collection are all "legal" by designing it as a collection of `Drawable` objects—in other words, objects that implement the `Drawable` interface. In this way we ensure that only objects that support a `draw` operation are allowed in the collection. (See Figure 2.4c) This approach was discussed in more detail in the "Interface-Based Polymorphism" subsection of Section 2.1, "Abstraction,".

Generic Collections

Beginning with version 5.0, the Java language supports generics. Generics allow us to define a set of operations that manipulate objects of a particular class, without specifying the class of the objects being manipulated until a later time. Generics represented one of the most significant changes to the language in version 5.0 of Java.

In a nutshell, **generics** are *parameterized types*. You are already familiar with the concept of a parameter. For example, in our `Circle` class the constructor has a `double` parameter named `radius`. When invoking that method we must pass it a `double` argument, such as "10.2":

```
Circle myCircle = new Circle(10.2);
```

Generics allow us to pass type names such as `Integer`, `String`, or `BankAccount` as arguments. Notice the subtle difference: with generics we actually pass a *type*, for example, `String`, instead of a *value* of a particular type, for example, "Elvis."

With this capability, we can define a collection class, such as `Stack`, as containing elements of a type T, where T is a placeholder for the name of a type. The name of the placeholder (convention tells us to use T) is indicated within braces; that is, <T>, in the header of the class.

```
public class Stack<T>
{
    protected  T[] elements ;     // array that holds objects of class T
    protected int topIndex = -1;  // index of the top element in the stack
    ...
```

In a subsequent application we can supply the actual type, such as `String`, `Integer`, or `BankAccount`, when the collection is instantiated (See Figure 2.4d).

```
Stack<String> answers;
Stack<Integer> numbers;
Stack<BankAccount> investments;
```

Pass `BankAccount` as the argument, get a `BankAccount` stack; pass `String`, get a `String` stack; and so on.

Generics provide the flexibility to design generally usable collections yet retain the benefit of Java's strong type checking. They are an excellent solution, and we will use this approach throughout most of the remainder of this text.

2.4 The Stack Interface

In this section we use the Java interface construct to create a formal specification of our Stack ADT; that is, we formally specify the abstract view of our stacks. To specify any collection ADT we must determine which types of elements it will hold, which operations it will export, and how exceptional situations will be handled. Some of these decisions have already been documented.

Recall from Section 2.2, "The Stack," that a stack is a LIFO structure, with three primary operations:

- push   Adds an element to the top of the stack.
- pop   Removes the top element from the stack.
- top   Returns the top element of a stack.

In addition to these operations a constructor is needed that creates an empty stack.

As noted in Section 2.3, "Collection Elements," our Stack ADT will be a generic stack. The type of information that a stack stores will be specified by the client code at the time the stack is instantiated. Following the common Java coding convention, we use <T> to represent the class of objects stored in our stack.

Now we look at exceptional situations. As you will see, this exploration can lead to the identification of additional operations.

Exceptional Situations

Are there any exceptional situations that require handling? The constructor simply initializes a new empty stack. This action, in itself, cannot cause an error—assuming that it is coded correctly.

The remaining operations all present potential problem situations. The descriptions of the pop and top operations both refer to manipulating the "top element of the stack." But what if the stack is empty? Then there is no top element to manipulate. Suppose an application instantiates a stack and immediately invoked the top or pop operation? What should happen? There are three potential ways to address this "error" situation:

- handle the error within the method itself
- throw an exception
- ignore it

How might the problem be handled within the methods themselves? Given that the pop method is strictly a transformer, it could simply do nothing when it is invoked on an empty stack. In effect, it could perform a vacuous transformation. For top, which must return an Object reference, the response might be to return null. For some applications this might be a reasonable approach, but in most cases it would merely complicate the application code. We will use a different approach.

What if we state a precondition that a stack must not be empty before calling top or pop? Then we do not have to worry about handling the situation within the ADT. Of course, we cannot expect every application that uses our stack to keep track of whether it is empty; that should be the responsibility of the Stack ADT itself. To address this requirement we define an observer called isEmpty that returns a boolean value of true if the stack is empty. Then the application can prevent misuse of the pop and top operations.

```
if (!myStack.isEmpty())
    myObject = myStack.top();
```

This approach appears promising but can place an unwanted burden on the application. If an application must perform a guarding test before every stack operation, its code might become inefficient and difficult to read. Therefore, it is also a good idea to provide an exception related to accessing an empty stack. Consider the situation where a large number of stack calls take place within a section of code. If we define an exception—for example, StackUnderflowException—to be thrown by both pop and top if they are called when the stack is empty, then such a section of code could be surrounded by a single *try-catch* statement, rather than use multiple calls to the isEmpty operation.

Our Approach

For our stacks we throw exceptions when inappropriate operations are invoked, such as a pop from an empty stack. But we also provide the tools for an application to avoid making such errors.

We decide to use this last approach. That is, we define a StackUnderflowException, to be thrown by both pop and top if they are called when the stack is empty. To provide flexibility to the application programmer, we also include the isEmpty operation in our ADT. Now the application programmer can decide either to prevent popping or accessing an empty stack by using the isEmpty operation as a guard or, as shown next, to "try" the operations on the stack and "catch and handle" the raised exception, if the stack is empty.

```
try
{
    myObject = myStack.top();
    myStack.pop();
    myOtherObject = myStack.top();
    myStack.pop();
}
catch (StackUnderflowException underflow)
{
    System.out.println("There was a problem in the ABC routine.");
    System.out.println("Please inform System Control.");
    System.out.println("Exception: " + underflow.getMessage());
    System.exit(1);
}
```

We define StackUnderflowException to extend the Java RuntimeException, as it represents a situation that a programmer can avoid by using the stack properly. The RuntimeException class is typically used in such situations. Recall that such exceptions are unchecked; in other words, they do not have to be *explicitly* caught by a program.

Here is the code for our StackUnderflowException class:

```
package ch02.stacks;
public class StackUnderflowException extends RuntimeException
{
```

```
public StackUnderflowException()
{
  super();
}

public StackUnderflowException(String message)
{
  super(message);
}
}
```

Because `StackUnderflowException` is an unchecked exception, if it is raised and not caught it is eventually thrown to the run-time environment, which displays an error message and halts. An example of such a message follows:

```
Exception in thread "main" ch02.stacks.StackUnderflowException: Top
attempted on an empty stack.
at ch02.stacks.ArrayStack.top(ArrayStack.java:78)
at MyTestStack.main(MyTestStack.java:25)
```

On the other hand, if the programmer explicitly catches the exception, as we showed in the `try-catch` example, the error message can be tailored more closely to the specific problem:

```
There was a problem in the ABC routine.
Please inform System Control.
Exception: top attempted on an empty stack.
```

A consideration of the `push` operation reveals another potential problem: What if we try to push something onto a stack and there is no room for it? In an abstract sense, a stack is never conceptually "full." Sometimes, however, it is useful to specify an upper bound on the size of a stack. We might know that memory is in short supply or problem-related constraints may dictate a limit on the number of `push` operations that can occur without corresponding `pop` operations.

We can address this problem in a way analogous to the stack underflow problem. First, we provide an additional `boolean` observer operation called `isFull`, that returns `true` if the stack is full. The application programmer can use this operation to prevent misuse of the `push` operation. Second, we define `StackOverflowException`, that is thrown by the `push` operation if it is called when the stack is full. Here is the code for the `StackOverflowException` class:

```
package ch02.stacks;
public class StackOverflowException extends RuntimeException
{
  public StackOverflowException()
  {
    super();
  }

  public StackOverflowException(String message)
```

```
      {
        super(message);
      }
    }
```

As with the underflow situation, the application programmer can decide either to prevent pushing information onto a full stack through use of the `isFull` operation or to "try" the operation on a stack and "catch and handle" any raised exception. The `StackOverflowException` is also an unchecked exception.

The Interface

We are now ready to formally specify our Stack ADT. As planned, we use the Java `interface` construct. Within the interface we include method signatures for the three basic stack operations `push`, `pop`, and `top`, plus the two observers `isEmpty` and `isFull`, as discussed above.

```
//-----------------------------------------------------------------------------
// StackInterface.java              by Dale/Joyce/Weems          Chapter 2
//
// Interface for a class that implements a stack of T.
// A stack is a last in, first out structure.
//-----------------------------------------------------------------------------
package ch02.stacks;

public interface StackInterface<T>
{
    void push(T element) throws StackOverflowException³;
    // Throws StackOverflowException if this stack is full,
    // otherwise places element at the top of this stack.

    void pop() throws StackUnderflowException;
    // Throws StackUnderflowException if this stack is empty,
    // otherwise removes top element from this stack.

    T top() throws StackUnderflowException;
    // Throws StackUnderflowException if this stack is empty,
    // otherwise returns top element of this stack.

    boolean isFull();
    // Returns true if this stack is full, otherwise returns false.
```

---

[3] Because our stack exceptions are unchecked exceptions, including them in the interface actually has no effect on anything from a syntactic or run-time error-checking point of view. They are not checked. However, we still list them as being thrown because we are also trying to communicate our requirements to the implementation programmer.

```
    boolean isEmpty();
    // Returns true if this stack is empty, otherwise returns false.
}
```

In Section 2.3, "Collection Elements," we presented our intention to create generic collection ADTs. This means that in addition to implementing our ADTs as generic classes—that is, classes that accept a parameter type upon instantiation—we also will define generic interfaces for those classes. Note the use of `<T>` in the header of `StackInterface`. As with generic classes, `<T>` used in this way indicates that `T` is a placeholder for a type provided by the client code. `T` represents the class of objects held by the specified stack. Since the `top` method returns one of those objects, in the interface it is listed as returning `T`. This same approach is used for ADT interfaces throughout the remainder of the text.

Note that we document the effects of the operations, the postconditions, as comments. For this ADT there are no preconditions because we have elected to throw exceptions for all error situations.

> **Java Note**
>
> Like classes, Java interfaces can be defined generically. When used within an application to declare a variable, a type argument is supplied and replaces the generic type for that particular variable. For example:
>
> `StackInterface<String> s;`
>
> declares s to be a stack of strings.

Example Use

The simple `ReverseStrings` example below shows how to use a stack to store strings provided by a user and then to output the strings in the opposite order from which they were entered. The code uses the array-based implementation of a stack developed in Section 2.5, "Array-Based Stack Implementations,". The parts of the code directly related to the creation and use of the stack are <u>emphasized</u>. We declare the stack to be of type `StackInterface<String>` and then instantiate it as an `ArrayBoundedStack<String>`. Within the *for* loop, three strings provided by the user are pushed onto the stack. The *while* loop repeatedly removes and prints the top string from the stack until the stack is empty. If we try to push any type of object other than a `String` onto the stack, we will receive a compile-time error message saying that the `push` method cannot be applied to that type of object.

```
//---------------------------------------------------------------------------
// ReverseStrings.java              by Dale/Joyce/Weems              Chapter 2
//
// Sample use of stack. Outputs strings in reverse order of entry.
//---------------------------------------------------------------------------
package ch02.apps;

import ch02.stacks.*;
import java.util.Scanner;

public class ReverseStrings
{
```

```java
public static void main(String[] args)
{
  Scanner scan = new Scanner(System.in);

  StackInterface<String> stringStack;
  stringStack = new ArrayBoundedStack<String>(3);

  String line;

  for (int i = 1; i <= 3; i++)
  {
    System.out.print("Enter a line of text > ");
    line = scan.nextLine();
    stringStack.push(line);
  }

  System.out.println("\nReverse is:\n");
  while (!stringStack.isEmpty())
  {
    line = stringStack.top();
    stringStack.pop();
    System.out.println(line);
  }
}
}
```

Here is the output from a sample run:

```
Enter a line of text > the beginning of a story
Enter a line of text > is often different than
Enter a line of text > the end of a story

Reverse is:

the end of a story
is often different than
the beginning of a story
```

2.5   Array-Based Stack Implementations

This section presents an array-based implementation of the Stack ADT. Additionally, we look at an alternative implementation that uses the Java library's `ArrayList` class. Note that Figure 2.16 in the Summary on page 146 shows the relationships among the primary classes and interfaces created to support our Stack ADT, including those developed in this section.

The ArrayBoundedStack Class

Here we develop a Java class that implements the `StackInterface`. We call this class `ArrayBoundedStack`, because it uses an array as the implementation structure and the resultant stack has a limited size. An array is a reasonable structure to hold the elements of a stack. We can put elements into sequential slots in the array, placing the first element pushed onto the stack into the first array position, the second element pushed into the second array position, and so on. The floating "high-water" mark is the top element in the stack. Given that stacks grow and shrink from only one end, we do not have to worry about inserting an element into the middle of the elements already stored in the array.

What instance variables does our implementation need? It needs the stack elements themselves and a variable indicating the top of the stack. We declare a protected array called `elements` to hold the stack elements and a protected integer variable called `topIndex` to indicate the index of the array that holds the top element. The `topIndex` is initialized to −1, as nothing is stored on the stack when it is first created (to depict how stacks grow and shrink from one end we draw our arrays vertically):

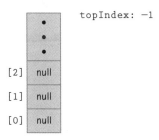

As elements are pushed and popped, we increment and decrement the value of `topIndex`. For example, starting with an empty stack and pushing "A," "B," and "C" results in:

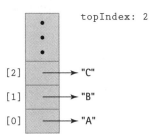

We provide two constructors for use by clients of the `ArrayBoundedStack` class: One allows the client to specify the maximum expected size of the stack, and the other assumes a default maximum size of 100 elements. To facilitate the latter constructor, we define a constant DEFCAP (default capacity) set to 100.

The beginning of the ArrayBoundedStack.java file is shown here:

```
//----------------------------------------------------------------------------
// ArrayBoundedStack.java          by Dale/Joyce/Weems          Chapter 2
//
// Implements StackInterface using an array to hold stack elements.
//
// Two constructors are provided: one that creates an array of a default size
// and one that allows the calling program to specify the size.
//----------------------------------------------------------------------------
package ch02.stacks;

public class ArrayBoundedStack<T> implements StackInterface<T>
{
  protected final int DEFCAP = 100;   // default capacity
  protected T[] elements;             // holds stack elements
  protected int topIndex = -1;        // index of top element in stack

  public ArrayBoundedStack()
  {
    elements = (T[]) new Object[DEFCAP];⁴
  }

  public ArrayBoundedStack(int maxSize)
  {
    elements = (T[]) new Object[maxSize];⁴
  }
```

Note that this class uses a generic parameter <T> as listed in the class header. The elements variable is declared to be of type T[], that is, an array of class T. This class implements a stack of T's—the class of T is not yet determined. It will be specified by the client class that uses the bounded stack. Because the Java translator will not generate references to a generic type, our code must specify Object along with the *new* statement within our constructors. Thus, although we declare our array to be an array of class T, we must instantiate it to be an array of class Object. Then, to ensure that the desired type checking takes place, we cast array elements into class T, as shown here:

```
elements = (T[]) new Object[DEFCAP];
```

Even though this approach is somewhat awkward and typically generates a compiler warning, it is how we must create generic collections using arrays in Java. We could

---

⁴An unchecked cast warning may be generated because the compiler cannot ensure that the array contains objects of class T—the warning can safely be ignored.

use the Java library's generic-compliant `ArrayList` to rectify the problem, but we prefer to use the more basic array structure for pedagogic reasons. The compiler warning can safely be ignored.

> **Java Note**
>
> To use generics with an array-based ADT we must declare our array to be of type `Object` and cast it as type T. Some compilers will generate a warning in this situation—the warning can be safely ignored.

Definitions of Stack Operations

For the array-based approach, the implementations of `isFull` and its counterpart, `isEmpty`, are both very simple. The stack is empty if the top index is equal to –1, and the stack is full if the top index is equal to one less than the size of the array.

```
public boolean isEmpty()
// Returns true if this stack is empty, otherwise returns false.
{
    return (topIndex == -1);
}


public boolean isFull()
// Returns true if this stack is full, otherwise returns false.
{
    return (topIndex == (elements.length - 1));
}
```

Now let us write the method to push an element of type T onto the top of the stack. If the stack is already full when `push` is invoked, there is nowhere to put the element. Recall that this condition is called stack overflow. Our formal specifications state that the `push` method should throw the `StackOverflowException` in this case. We include a pertinent error message when the exception is thrown. If the stack is not full, `push` must increment `topIndex` and store the new element into `elements[topIndex]`. The implementation of the method is straightforward:

```
public void push(T element)
// Throws StackOverflowException if this stack is full,
// otherwise places element at the top of this stack.
{
  if (isFull())
    throw new StackOverflowException("Push attempted on a full stack.");
  else
  {
    topIndex++;
    elements[topIndex] = element;
  }
}
```

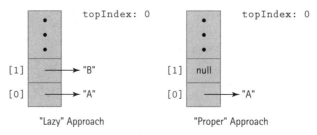

Figure 2.5   Lazy versus proper pop approaches for an array-based stack after push("A"), push("B"), and pop()

The pop method is essentially the reverse of push: Instead of putting an element onto the top of the stack, we remove the top element from the stack by decrementing top-Index. It is good practice to also "null out" the array location associated with the current top. Setting the array value to null removes the physical reference. **Figure 2.5** shows the difference between the "lazy" approach to coding pop and the "proper" approach.

If the stack is empty when pop is invoked, there is no top element to remove and we have stack underflow. As with the push method, the specifications say to throw an exception.

```
public void pop()
// Throws StackUnderflowException if this stack is empty,
// otherwise removes top element from this stack.
{
  if (isEmpty())
    throw new StackUnderflowException("Pop attempted on empty stack.");
  else
  {
    elements[topIndex] = null;
    topIndex--;
  }
}
```

Finally, the top operation simply returns the top element of the stack, the element indexed by topIndex. Consistent with our generic approach, the top method shows type T as its return type. As with the pop operation, if the top operation is invoked on an empty stack, a stack underflow results.

```
public T top()
// Throws StackUnderflowException if this stack is empty,
// otherwise returns top element of this stack.
{
  T topOfStack = null;
  if (isEmpty())
    throw new StackUnderflowException("Top attempted on empty stack.");
  else
```

```
        topOfStack = elements[topIndex];
    return topOfStack;
}
```

That does it. We have just completed the creation of our first data structure ADT. Of course, we still need to test it; in fact, as the authors developed the code shown above they ran several tests along the way. We discuss testing of ADTs more thoroughly in the nearby feature section "Testing ADTs."

Before continuing, we again want to emphasize the distinctions among the application, abstract, and implementation views of a stack. Suppose an application executes the following code (assume A and B represent strings):

```
StackInterface<String> myStack;
myStack = new ArrayBoundedStack<String>(3);
myStack.push(A);
myStack.push(B);
```

Figure 2.6 shows, left to right, the application, implementation, and abstract views that result from executing the above code. Note that the application has a reference

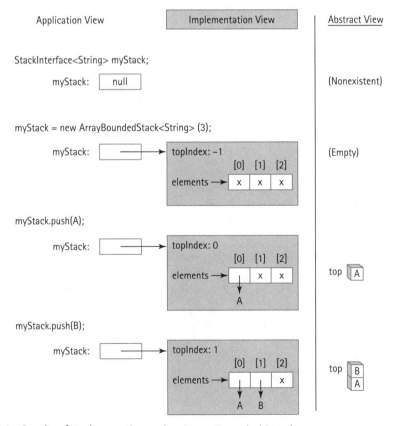

Figure 2.6 Results of stack operations using `ArrayBoundedStack`

variable `myStack` that points to an object of class `ArrayBoundedStack`. Within this `ArrayBoundedStack` object is hidden the reference variable `elements` that points to the array holding the strings and the `int` variable `topIndex` that indicates the array index where the top of the stack is stored.

Alternate Views

The programmer who creates the array-based stack implementation views a stack as an array and an index indicating the location of the top of the stack in the array. Programmers who write applications that use the array-based stack class view the stack abstractly, as a LIFO list, upon which they can invoke operations such as push and pop.

From the point of view of the application programmer the stack object is a black box—the details are hidden. In the figure we get a peek inside that black box. As the Stack ADT implementation programmers, we *create* the black box. It is important for you to see the difference between the variable `myStack`, which is an application variable and the variables `element` and `topIndex`, which are hidden *inside* the stack object.

One final note: the stack we implemented is bounded because it uses an array as its hidden data holder. We can also use arrays to implement unbounded stacks. One approach is to instantiate increasingly larger arrays, as needed during processing, copying the current array into the larger, newly instantiated array. We investigate this approach when implementing the Queue ADT in Chapter 4.

Testing ADTs

In this text we study, discuss, visualize, specify, design, code, and use data structures. We encapsulate our data structures as ADTs, which means we separate the code that specifies a data structure, for example, the `StackInterface` interface, and the code that implements it, for example, the `ArrayBoundedStack` class, and the code that uses it, for example, the `ReverseStrings` application. It is crucial for our code at all levels to work correctly. In addition to carefully specifying, designing, and creating our code it is *important* for us to test it—to demonstrate that it functions as expected.

Integrated Testing

Software testing is often conceived as a process that occurs after coding is completed. In reality, both for students and for professionals, it is important to test *during* the development stage. Within the main body of this text we usually present our ADTs as a collection of clearly conceived and completed classes. However, we do not describe the entire process that was followed in developing and testing this code. There is not enough space in this text to cover all of that! It is not unusual for people to use this approach when describing something: an automobile company advertises the sleek final product of its engineering without describing all the intermediate failed designs required to create the beautiful machine; an artist displays a sculpture without showing all the flawed models used during the creative process; a mathematician lays out a brilliant proof of a theorem without revealing all the false starts and backtracking needed to arrive at the polished logic.

   When creating an ADT such as our stack, we create *in parallel* a test driver or set of test drivers. We do this from the very beginning of the coding process. For example, our first pass at creating the `ArrayBoundedStack` was to create a "shell" of the class as shown here:

```
package ch02.stacks;
public class ArrayBoundedStack<T> implements StackInterface<T>
{
  public ArrayBoundedStack()
  {     }

  public void push(T element)
  {    }

  public void pop()
  {    }

  public T top()
  {    return null;    }

  public boolean isEmpty()
  {    return true;    }

  public boolean isFull()
  {    return false;    }
}
```

We next create an application, our test driver that "uses" the class:

```
package ch02.apps;
import ch02.stacks.*;

public class StackDriver
{
  public static void main(String[] args)
  {
    StackInterface<String> test;
    test = new ArrayBoundedStack<String>();
  }
}
```

You might protest, "But that application does not do anything!" Nevertheless, if these two files correctly compile it shows us that we have the files in the correct folders on our system, the packages are being used properly, and that the stack class includes the method names, parameter types, and return types as required by the interface. It might not do anything, but it *accomplishes* a lot!

Now we can add functionality a little at a time, expanding our implementation (`ArrayBoundedStack`) and test driver (`StackDriver`) concurrently as we go. Add the code for `isEmpty`. Add a test case for `isEmpty` and run it. Does it return `true`? Add the code for `push` and a test case that invokes `push` and then `isEmpty`. Does it return false? Repeatedly designing, coding, and testing a small increment to your code is possibly the best way to develop software.

Note that it might be helpful to export a special "helper" method within the implementation class to be used strictly during testing, that returns a string representing both the structure and contents of the hidden data. This method can be used during testing to ensure that the code is acting as expected. In many cases a typical `toString` method can suffice. For example, to test that your `push` code works as expected, it is useful to see the contents of the hidden `elements` array and the `topIndex` variable. In the exercises you are asked to create such a method for the various stack implementations.

As we add functionality to our implementation and test our methods, we should pay special attention to boundary conditions. It is common for programmers to handle general cases correctly, yet either not consider, or incorrectly design for, special cases. For example, when testing the push method for a stack, although we do need to test pushing an element onto a partially populated stack, many other situations should also be tested. For example,

| | Important: Evolve Your Code! |

Learn to evolve your code. You start with an overall design in mind, of course, but as you code move ahead in small increments. Design, code, and test—design, code, and test—design, code, and test. This approach allows you to focus on one feature at a time, and when you do make errors, and you will, it limits the scope of the error making it easier to identify and fix.

- Pushing onto a new stack
- Pushing onto a newly empty stack
- Pushing onto a stack containing a single element
- Pushing onto a full stack
- Pushing onto an almost full stack (`isFull` returns `false` beforehand and `true` afterwards)
- Pushing onto a stack that was full but now contains one free slot

Professional Testing

In a production environment where hundreds or even thousands of test cases need to be performed on a daily basis, automated test drivers are created to run in batch mode. For example, a software engineer constructing a test case that addresses pushing an element onto a partially populated stack might create the following program. (Assume this is test case number 34.)

```
import ch02.stacks.*;
public class Test034
{
  public static void main(String[] args)
  {
    StackInterface<String> test = new ArrayBoundedStack<String>( );
    test.push("trouble in the fields");
    test.push("love at the five and dime");
    test.push("once in a very blue moon");
    String s = test.top();
    if (s.equals("once in a very blue moon"))
      System.out.println("Test 34 passed");
    else
      System.out.println("Test 34 failed");
  }
}
```

This program can run without user intervention and will report whether the test case has been passed. By developing an entire suite of such programs, software engineers can automate the testing process. A prime benefit of such an approach is that the same set of test programs can be used over and over again throughout the development and maintenance stages of the software process. Frameworks exist that simplify the creation, management, and use of batch test suites. For example, you can find information about JUnit, a popular Java-based testing framework, at www.junit.org.

The ArrayListStack Class

There are often many ways to implement an ADT. This subsection presents an alternate implementation for the Stack ADT based on the `ArrayList` class. The `ArrayList` is a useful ADT provided by the Java Class Library.

The defining quality of objects of the `ArrayList` class are that they can grow and shrink in response to the program's needs. As a consequence, when using the `ArrayList` approach we do not have to worry about our stacks being bounded. Our constructor no longer needs to declare a stack size. The `isFull` operation can simply return `false`, because the stack is never full. We do not have to handle stack overflows.

One could argue that if a program runs completely out of memory, then the stack could be considered full and should throw `StackOverflowException`. However, in that case the run-time environment throws an "out of memory" exception anyway; we do not have to worry about the situation going unnoticed. Furthermore, running out of system memory is a serious problem (and ideally a rare event) and cannot be handled in the same way as a Stack ADT overflow.

The fact that an `ArrayList` automatically grows as needed makes it a good choice for implementing an unbounded Stack. Additionally, it provides a `size` method that can be used to keep track of the top of our stack. The index of the top of the stack is always the `size` minus one.

Study the following code. Compare this implementation to the previous implementation. They are similar, yet different. One is based directly on arrays, whereas the other uses arrays indirectly through the `ArrayList` class. Note that with the approach shown below the internal representation of our Stack ADT is another ADT—the `ArrayList` (that in turn is built on top of an array). Just as it is possible to have many levels of procedural abstraction in programs, it is possible to have many levels of data abstraction.

One nice benefit of using the `ArrayList` approach is we no longer receive the annoying unchecked cast warning from the compiler. This is because an `ArrayList` object, unlike the basic array, is a first-class object in Java and fully supports the use of generics. Despite the obvious benefits of using `ArrayList`, we will continue to use arrays as one of our basic ADT implementation structures throughout most of the rest of this text. Learning to use the standard array is important for future professional software developers.

```
//-----------------------------------------------------------------
// ArrayListStack.java          by Dale/Joyce/Weems          Chapter 2
//
// Implements an unbounded stack using an ArrayList.
//-----------------------------------------------------------------
package ch02.stacks;
import java.util.*;

public class ArrayListStack<T> implements StackInterface<T>
{
  protected ArrayList<T> elements;  // ArrayList that holds stack elements

  public ArrayListStack()
  {
    elements = new ArrayList<T>();
  }

  public void push(T element)
  // Places element at the top of this stack.
  {
    elements.add(element);
  }

  public void pop()
  // Throws StackUnderflowException if this stack is empty,
  // otherwise removes top element from this stack.
```

```java
{
  if (isEmpty())
    throw new StackUnderflowException("Pop attempted on empty stack.");
  else
    elements.remove(elements.size() - 1);
}

public T top()
// Throws StackUnderflowException if this stack is empty,
// otherwise returns top element of this stack.
{
  T topOfStack = null;
  if (isEmpty())
    throw new StackUnderflowException("Top attempted on empty stack.");
  else
    topOfStack = elements.get(elements.size() - 1);
  return topOfStack;
}

public boolean isEmpty()
// Returns true if this stack is empty, otherwise returns false.
{
  return (elements.size() == 0);
}

public boolean isFull()
// Returns false - an ArrayListStack is never full.
{
  return false;
}
}
```

2.6 Application: Balanced Expressions

Stacks are great for "remembering" things that have to be taken care of at a later time; in other words, handling postponed obligations. In this sample application we tackle a problem that perplexes many beginning programmers: matching parentheses, brackets, and braces in writing code. Matching *grouping symbols* is an important problem in the world of computing. For example, it is related to the legality of arithmetic equations, the syntactical correctness of computer programs, and the validity of XHTML tags used to define Web pages. This problem is a classic situation for using a stack, because we must "remember" an open symbol (e.g., (, [, or {) until it is "taken care of" later by matching a corresponding close symbol (e.g.,),], or }, respectively). When the grouping symbols in

Well-Formed Expressions	Ill-Formed Expressions
(xx (xx ( )) xx)	(xx (xx ( )) xxx) xxx)
[ ] ( ) { }	] [
([ ] { xxx } xxx ( ) xxx)	(xx [xxx) xx]
([{ [(([{ x }]) x)] } x])	([{ [(([{ x }]) x)] } x })
xxxxxxxxxxxxxxxxxxxxxxx	xxxxxxxxxxxxxxxxxxxxxx {

Figure 2.7 Well-formed and ill-formed expressions

an expression are properly matched, computer scientists say that the expression is *well formed* and that the grouping symbols are *balanced*.

Given a set of grouping symbols, our problem is to determine whether the open and close versions of each symbol are matched correctly. Let us focus on the normal pairs: (), [], and {}. In theory we could define any pair of symbols (e.g., <> or /\) as grouping symbols. Any number of other characters may appear in the input expression before, between, or after a grouping pair, and an expression may contain nested groupings. Each close symbol must match the last unmatched open symbol, and each open symbol must have a matching close symbol. Thus, expressions can be ill formed for two reasons: There is a mismatched close symbol (e.g., {]) or there is a missing close symbol (e.g., {{[]}). **Figure 2.7** shows examples of both well-formed and ill-formed expressions.

The Balanced Class

To help solve our problem we create a class called `Balanced`, with a single exported method `test` that takes an expression as a string argument and checks whether the grouping symbols in the expression are balanced. As there are two ways that an expression can fail the balance test, there are three possible results. We use an integer to indicate the result of the test:

0 means the symbols are balanced, such as (([xx])xx)

1 means the expression has a mismatched close symbol, such as (([xx}xx))

2 means the expression is missing a close symbol, such as (([xxx])xx

> **Reminder: Programming by Contract**
>
> A precondition is a contract. Within the `Balanced` class we do not need to check that the preconditions are met—we assume they are.

We include a single constructor for the Balanced class. To make the class more generally usable, we require the application to specify the open and close symbols. We thus define two string parameters for the constructor, `openSet` and `closeSet`, through which the application can pass the symbols. The symbols in the two sets match up by position. For our specific problem the two arguments could be "([{" and ")] }."

It is important that each symbol in the combined open and close sets is unique and that the sets be the same size. We use programming by contract and state these criteria in a precondition of the constructor.

```
public Balanced(String openSet, String closeSet)
// Preconditions: No character is contained more than once in the
//                 combined openSet and closeSet strings.
//                 The size of openSet == the size of closeSet.
{
   this.openSet = openSet;
   this.closeSet = closeSet;
}
```

Now we turn our attention to the `test` method. It is passed a `String` argument through its `expression` parameter and must determine, based on the characters in `openSet` and `closeSet`, whether the symbols in `expression` are balanced. The method processes the characters in `expression` one at a time. For each character, it performs one of three tasks:

- If the character is an open symbol, it is pushed on the stack.
- If the character is a close symbol, it is checked against the last open symbol, obtained from the top of the stack. If they match, processing continues with the next character. If the close symbol does not match the top of the stack or if the stack is empty, then the expression is ill formed.
- If the character is not a special symbol, it is skipped.

The stack is the appropriate data structure in which to save the open symbols because we always need to examine the most recent one. When all of the characters have been processed, the stack should be empty; otherwise, the expression is missing a close symbol.

Now we are ready to write the main algorithm for `test`. We assume an instance of our Stack ADT as defined by `StackInterface`. We also declare a `boolean` variable `still-Balanced`, initialized to `true`, to record whether the expression, as processed so far, is balanced.

Test for Well-Formed Expression Algorithm (String expression)

Create a new stack of size equal to the length of expression
Set stillBalanced to true
Get the first character from expression
while (the expression is still balanced AND there are still more characters to process)
  Process the current character
  Get the next character from expression
if (!stillBalanced)
  return 1
else if (stack is not empty)
  return 2
else
  return 0

The part of this algorithm that requires expansion before moving on to the coding stage is the "Process the current character" command. We previously described how to handle each type of character. Here are those steps in algorithmic form.

```
if (the character is an open symbol)
    Push the open symbol character onto the stack
else if (the character is a close symbol)
    if (the stack is empty)
        Set stillBalanced to false
    else
        Set open symbol character to the value at the top of the stack
        Pop the stack
        if the close symbol character does not "match" the open symbol character
            Set stillBalanced to false
else
    Skip the character
```

The code for the `Balanced` class is listed next. Because the focus of this chapter is stacks, we have <u>emphasized</u> the code related to the stack in the code listing. There are several interesting things to note about the `test` method of the class:

1. Within the `test` method we declare our stack to be of type `StackInterface`, but instantiate it as class `ArrayBoundedStack`. It is good practice for a client program to declare an ADT at as abstract a level as possible. This approach makes it easier to change the choice of implementation later.

2. The length of the expression limits the number of symbols that need to be pushed onto the stack. Therefore, we instantiate the stack with a size argument equal to the length of `expression`.

3. We use a shortcut for determining whether a close symbol matches an open symbol. According to our rules, the symbols match if they share the same relative position in their respective sets. This means that on encountering an open special symbol, rather than save the actual character on the stack, we can push its *position* in the `openSet` string onto the stack. Later in the processing, when encountering a close symbol, we can just compare its position with the position value on the stack. Thus, rather than push a character value onto the stack, we push an integer value.

4. We instantiate our stacks to hold elements of type `Integer`. But, as just mentioned, in the `test` method we push elements of the primitive type `int` onto our stack, thus taking advantage of Java's *Autoboxing* feature. If a programmer uses a value of a primitive type as an `Object`, it is automatically converted (boxed) into an object of its corresponding wrapper class. So when the test method says

```
stack.push(openIndex);
```

the integer value of `openIndex` is automatically converted to an `Integer` object before being stored on the stack. A corresponding feature called *Unboxing* reverses the effect of the *Autoboxing*. When the top of the stack is accessed with the statement

```
openIndex = stack.top();
```

the `Integer` object at the top of the stack is automatically converted to an integer value.

5. In processing a closing symbol, we access the stack to see if its top holds the corresponding opening symbol. If the stack is empty, it indicates an unbalanced expression. There are two ways to check whether the stack is empty: use the `isEmpty` method or try to access the stack and catch a `StackUnderflowException`. We choose the latter approach. It seems to fit the spirit of the algorithm because we expect to find the open symbol and finding the stack empty is the "exceptional" case.

6. In contrast, we use `isEmpty` to check for an empty stack at the end of processing the expression. Here, we do not want to extract an element from the stack—we just need to know whether it is empty.

Here is the code for the entire class:

```
//-------------------------------------------------------------------------------
// Balanced.java          by Dale/Joyce/Weems            Chapter 2
//
// Checks for balanced expressions using standard rules.
//
// Matching pairs of open and close symbols are provided to the
// constructor through two string arguments.
//-------------------------------------------------------------------------------
package ch02.balanced;

import ch02.stacks.*;

public class Balanced
{
  protected String openSet;
  protected String closeSet;

  public Balanced(String openSet, String closeSet)
  // Preconditions: No character is contained more than once in the
  //                combined openSet and closeSet strings.
  //                The size of openSet = the size of closeSet.
  {
    this.openSet = openSet;
    this.closeSet = closeSet;
  }
```

```java
public int test(String expression)
// Returns 0 if expression is balanced.
// Returns 1 if expression has unbalanced symbols.
// Returns 2 if expression came to end prematurely.
{
  char currChar;          // current character being studied
  int  currCharIndex;     // index of current character
  int  lastCharIndex;     // index of last character in expression

  int openIndex;          // index of current character in openSet
  int closeIndex;         // index of current character in closeSet

  boolean stillBalanced = true; // true while expression balanced

  StackInterface<Integer> stack;    // holds unmatched open symbols
  stack = new ArrayBoundedStack<Integer>(expression.length());

  currCharIndex = 0;
  lastCharIndex = expression.length() - 1;

  while (stillBalanced && (currCharIndex <= lastCharIndex))
  // while expression still balanced and not at end of expression
  {
    currChar = expression.charAt(currCharIndex);
    openIndex = openSet.indexOf(currChar);

    if(openIndex != -1)   // if current character in openSet
    {
      // Push the index onto the stack.
      stack.push(openIndex);
    }
      else
      {
          closeIndex = closeSet.indexOf(currChar);
          if(closeIndex != -1)  // if current character in closeSet
          {
              try    // try to pop an index off the stack
              {
                  openIndex = stack.top();
                  stack.pop();
                  if (openIndex != closeIndex)  // if not a match
                      stillBalanced = false;      // then not balanced
              }
```

```
            catch(StackUnderflowException e) // if stack was empty
            {
                stillBalanced = false;    // then not balanced
            }
        }
    }
    currCharIndex++;       // set up processing of next character
}

if (!stillBalanced)
    return 1;    // unbalanced symbols
else
if (!stack.isEmpty())
    return 2;    // premature end of expression
else
    return 0;    // expression is balanced
    }
}
```

The Application

Now that we have the Balanced class, it is not difficult to finish our application.

Our approach to program design in this text is to separate the user interface code from the rest of the program. We design classes, such as Balanced, that use our ADTs to solve some type of problem. We then design an application class that interacts with the user, taking advantage of the previously defined classes. Our extended examples present a command line interface (CLI) application program. However, behind the scenes, we sometimes also create graphical user interface (GUI) applications and provide the code for those programs with the program code files. The GUI-based application is often presented briefly, at the conclusion of the CLI application exposition, for those readers who are interested. Here we describe the CLI application in some detail. By separating the problem-solving aspect from the user interface aspect of our design we can easily reuse the problem-solving classes with different user interfaces.

> **Reminder: Class Evolution**
>
> As the authors designed and coded the Balanced class, we also tested it. As described before, we evolved the class, it did not just spring forth whole from our fingertips. Within the text we do not have the space to describe the evolution so we often just present our classes as finished products.

Because the Balanced class is responsible for determining whether grouping symbols are balanced, all that remains is to implement the user input and output. Rather than processing just one expression, the user can enter a series of expressions, indicating they are finished by entering the expression "X." We call our program BalancedCLI. Note that when the Balanced class is instantiated, the constructor is passed the strings "({ [" ")]}" so that it corresponds to our specific problem.

```java
//-------------------------------------------------------------------------
// BalancedCLI.java               by Dale/Joyce/Weems           Chapter 2
//
// Checks for balanced grouping symbols.
// Input consists of a sequence of expressions, one per line.
// Special symbol types are (), [], and {}.
//-------------------------------------------------------------------------
package ch02.apps;

import java.util.Scanner;
import ch02.balanced.*;

public class BalancedCLI
{
  public static void main(String[] args)
  {
    Scanner scan = new Scanner(System.in);

    // Instantiate new Balanced class with grouping symbols.
    Balanced bal = new Balanced("([{", ")]}");

    int result; // 0 = balanced, 1 = unbalanced, 2 = premature end

    String expression = null;    // expression to be evaluated
    final String STOP = "X";     // indicates end of input

    while (!STOP.equals(expression))
    {
      // Get next expression to be processed.
      System.out.print("Expression (" + STOP + " to stop): ");
      expression = scan.nextLine();
      if (!STOP.equals(expression))
      {
        // Obtain and output result of balanced testing.
        result = bal.test(expression);
        if (result == 1)
          System.out.println("Unbalanced \n");
        else
        if (result == 2)
          System.out.println("Premature end of expression \n");
        else
```

```
                  System.out.println("Balanced \n");
            }
       }
   }
}
```

Here is the output from a sample run:

```
Expression (X to stop): (xx[yy]{ttt})
Balanced

Expression (X to stop): ((())
Premature end of expression

Expression (X to stop): (tttttt]
Unbalanced

Expression (X to stop): (){}{}[({{[{({})}]}})]
Balanced

Expression (X to stop): X
```

The GUI Approach

As promised, we include here a GUI-based implementation of this application. We start with an example of the opening screen. The simple GUI consists of an input text field, a status label, and two action buttons.

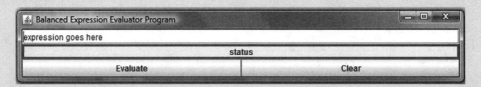

When the application is executed, the above window appears. The cursor is found in the text field containing the phrase "expression goes here." The user replaces that string with his or her own expression and then clicks on the Evaluate button. For example, if the user enters "((xx [ ] ([bb])))" and clicks the Evaluate button the window will now look like this:

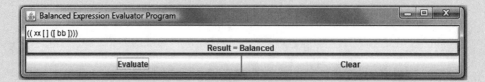

As you can see, the result of the evaluation is displayed in the middle "status" panel.

To evaluate another expression, the user simply clicks the Clear button and enters a new expression. Here is the result of entering "((hh)[}}":

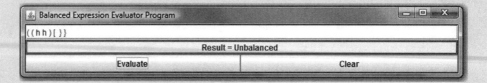

The GUI application is contained in the `BalancedGUI` class in the `ch02.apps` package. We do not list the code for that class here, but you can find it with the rest of the text code on the website. A look at that code reveals a straightforward implementation:

- It defines an internal static class containing the code that reacts to buttons being clicked. It also declares the input text field and the output status label statically at the global level so that they are accessible by both the main method and the button listener code.
- In the main method, one after another is declared and instantiated the surrounding frame, the text field, the status label, and the buttons. They are arranged in a simple layout, with the various objects added to it in the appropriate order. Finally, everything is "packed" together and displayed.
- The primary processing occurs in the button listener code. The code associated with the evaluate button instantiates a new `Balanced` object, uses it to determine the result of testing the current expression, and sets the result label to display the appropriate response. The code associated with the clear button sets the result label to "cleared" and the input text field to blank.
- We use a similar approach to provide GUI-based versions of our sample applications throughout the text.

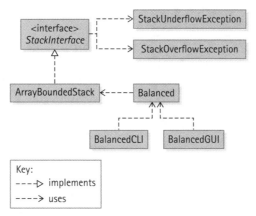

Figure 2.8 Program architecture

The Software Architecture

Figure 2.8 is a UML diagram showing the relationships among our interfaces and classes used in the balanced expression applications. The intent is to show the general architecture, so we do not include details about attributes and operations.

2.7 Introduction to Linked Lists

Recall from Section 1.4, "Data Structures," that the array and the linked list are the two primary building blocks for the more complex data structures. This section discusses linked lists in more detail, showing how to create linked lists using Java and introducing operations on linked lists. We use linked lists of strings in our examples.

This is a very important section. Understanding linked structures is crucial for computer scientists.

Arrays Versus Linked Lists

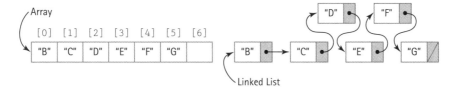

The figure depicts abstract views of an array of strings and a linked list of strings. An important difference between the two approaches is the internal representation of the data in memory and the way in the individual elements are accessed. With an array, we view all the elements as being grouped together, sitting in one block of memory. With a linked

Authors' Convention

Note that sometimes in our figures we indicate an object such as the `String` "B" as sitting inside an array slot or a list node, rather than showing an arrow inside the slot/node pointing to the object. We do this to simplify the figures—making it easier for the reader to concentrate on the concept being illustrated. Please remember that unless they hold primitive values, those slots and nodes do contain references to the objects and not the objects themselves.

list, each element sits separately in its own block of memory. We call this small separate block of memory a "node."

An array is a built-in structure in Java and most other programming languages. In contrast, although a few languages provide built-in linked lists (e.g., Lisp and Scheme), most do not. Java does support common types of linked lists through its class library. Even though the linked lists in the library are sufficient for many applications, software engineers need to understand how they work, both to appreciate their limitations and also to be able to build custom linked structures when the need arises.

As you know, an array allows us to access *any* element directly via its index. In comparison, the linked list structure seems very limited, as its nodes can only be accessed in a *sequential* manner, starting at the beginning of the list and following the links. So why should we bother to use a linked list in the first place? There are several potential reasons:

- The size of an array is fixed. It is provided as an argument to the `new` command when the array is instantiated. The size of a linked list varies. The nodes of a linked list can be allocated on an "as needed" basis. When no longer needed, the nodes can be returned to the memory manager.

- For some operations a linked list is a more efficient implementation approach than an array. For example, to place an element into the front of a collection of elements with an array you must shift all elements by one place toward the back of the array. This task requires many steps, especially if the array contains many elements. With a linked list you simply allocate a new node and link it to the front of the list. This task requires only three steps: create the new node and update two links. The following figure depicts the steps required to add an element to the front of an array and an equivalent linked list:

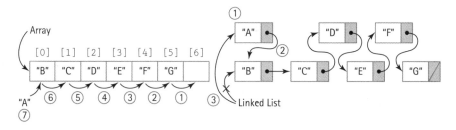

- For some applications you never have to directly access a node that is deep within the list without first accessing the nodes that precede it on the list. In those cases, the fact that nodes of a linked list must be accessed sequentially does not adversely affect performance.

The basic approaches that support linked list management also allow us to create and use more complex structures such as the trees and graphs developed in later chapters.

The LLNode Class

To create a linked list we need to know how to do two things: allocate space for a node dynamically and allow a node to link to, or reference, another node. Java supplies an operation for dynamically allocating space, an operation we have been using for all of our objects—the new operation. Clearly, that part is easy. But how can we allow a node to reference another node? Essentially a node in a linked list is an object that holds some important information, such as a string or other object, plus a link to another node. That other node is the exact same type of object—it is also a node in the linked list.

When defining the node class, we must allow the objects created from it to reference node class objects. This type of class is a **self-referential class**. The definition of our node class includes two instance variables: one that holds the important information that the linked list is maintaining and one that is a reference to an object of its same class. To allow our linked lists to be generally usable we use generics. The generic placeholder <T> is used to represent the information held by a node of the linked list. This approach allows us to create linked lists of strings, bank accounts, student records, and virtually anything.

We call our self-referential class LLNode. Objects of this class are the linked list nodes. Because we use this class to support link-based implementations of several of our ADTs later in the text, we place it in the support package. Its declarations include self-referential code, which is <u>emphasized</u> here:

```
package support;
public class LLNode<T>
{
    protected T info;              // information stored in list
    protected  LLNode<T> link;     // reference to a node
. . .
```

The LLNode class defines an instance variable info to hold a reference to the object of class T represented by the node and an instance variable link to reference another LLNode object. That next LLNode can hold a reference to an object of class T and a reference to another LLNode object, that in turn holds a reference to an object of class T and a reference to another LLNode object, and so on. The chain ends when the LLNode holds the value null in its link, indicating the end of the linked list. As an example, here is a linked list with three nodes, referenced by the LLNode<String> variable letters.[5] Given that we know how the nodes of our linked list are implemented, we now present a more detailed view in our figures.

---

[5] Throughout this section we use nodes with an info field that references a **String**. Do not forget, however, that we can create linked lists using any type of class for the info field.

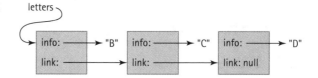

We define one constructor for the LLNode class:

```
public LLNode(T info)
{
  this.info = info;
  link = null;
}
```

The constructor accepts an object of class T as an argument and sets the info variable to that object. For example,

```
LLNode<String> sNode1 = new LLNode<String>("basketball");
```

results in the structure

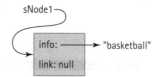

Other constructors are possible, such as one that accepts an LLNode<T> reference as an argument and sets the link variable. We do not think they would add much to the usability of the class.

Note that our constructor essentially creates a linked list with a single element. How, then, can you represent an empty linked list? You do so by declaring a variable of class LLNode but not instantiating it with the new operation:

```
LLNode<String> theList;
```

In that case, the value held in the node variable is null:

theList: null

Completing the class are the definitions of the setters and getters. Their code is standard and straightforward. The setLink method is used to link nodes together into a list. For example, the following code

```
LLNode<String> sNode1 = new LLNode<String>("basketball");
LLNode<String> sNode2 = new LLNode<String>("baseball")";
sNode1.setLink(sNode2);
```

results in the structure

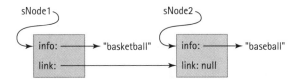

The complete `LLNode` class is shown next. It is used in Section 2.8, "A Link-Based Stack," to create a link-based implementation of the Stack ADT. Before we see how that is accomplished, we introduce the standard operations on linked lists.

```
//-------------------------------------------------------------------------
// LLNode.java                by Dale/Joyce/Weems              Chapter 2
//
// Implements<T> nodes for a Linked List.
//-------------------------------------------------------------------------
package support;

public class LLNode<T>
{
    protected T info;
    protected LLNode<T> link;

    public LLNode(T info)
    {
        this.info = info;
        link = null;
    }

    public void setInfo(T info){ this.info = info;}
    public T getInfo(){ return info; }
    public void setLink(LLNode<T> link){this.link = link;}
    public LLNode<T> getLink(){ return link;}
}
```

Operations on Linked Lists

Our node class `LLNode` provides a building block. It is up to us to use this building block to create and manipulate linked lists.

Three basic operations are performed on linked lists: A linked list can be traversed to obtain information from it, a node can be added to a linked list, and a node can be removed from a linked list. Look more carefully at each of these categories. To help simplify our presentation, we assume the existence of this linked list of `LLNode<String>` objects referenced by the variable `letters`:

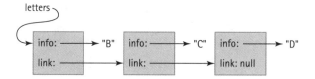

Traversal

Information held in a linked list is retrieved by traversing the list. There are many potential reasons for traversing a list; for the purposes of this discussion let us assume that we want to display the information contained in the `letters` linked list one line at a time, starting at the beginning of the list and finishing at the end of the list.

To traverse the linked list we need some way to keep track of our current position in the list. With an array we use an index variable. That approach will not work with a linked list because it is not indexed. Instead we need to use a variable that can reference the current node of interest on the list. Let us call it `currNode`. The traversal algorithm is

Set currNode to first node on the list
while (currNode is not pointing off the end of the list)
   Display the information at currNode
   Change currNode to point to the next node on the list

We refine this algorithm, transforming it into Java code as we go. Our `letters` list is a linked list of `LLNode<String>` objects. Therefore, `currNode` must be an `LLNode<String>` variable. We initialize `currNode` to point to the beginning of the list.

LLNode<String> currNode = letters;
while (currNode is not pointing off the end of the list)
   Display the information at currNode
   Change currNode to point to the next node on the list

Next we turn our attention to the body of the *while* loop. Displaying the information at `currNode` is achieved using the `getInfo` method. That part is easy:

```
System.out.println(currNode.getInfo());
```

But how do we "Change `currNode` to point to the next node on the list"? Consider the situation after `currNode` has been initialized to the beginning of the linked list:

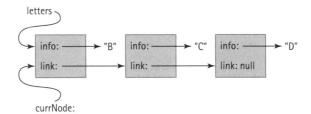

We want to change `currNode` to point to the next node, the node where the `info` variable points to the string "C." In the preceding figure notice what points to that node— the `link` variable of the node currently referenced by `currNode`. Therefore, we use the `getLink` method of the `LLNode` class to return that value and set the new value of `currNode`:

```
currNode = currNode.getLink();
```

Putting this all together we now have the following pseudocode.

```
LLNode<String> currNode = letters;
while (currNode is not pointing off the end of the list)
{

  System.out.println(currNode.getInfo());
  currNode = currNode.getLink();
}
```

The only thing left to do is determine when `currNode` is pointing off the end of the list. The value of `currNode` is repeatedly set to the value in the `link` variable of the next node. When we reach the end of the list, the value in this variable is `null`. So, as long as the value of `currNode` is not `null`, it is "not pointing off the end of the list." Our final code segment is

```
LLNode<String> currNode = letters;
while (currNode != null)
{
    System.out.println(currNode.getInfo());
    currNode = currNode.getLink();
}
```

Figure 2.9 traces through this code, graphically depicting what occurs at each step using our example linked list.

Before leaving this example we should see how our code handles the case of the

Important Algorithm

You can use the algorithmic pattern described here for traversing a linked list repeatedly in your programming. Create a reference to "walk down" the list. Set it to the start of the list. While you have not reached the end of the list, set it to the next node. Visit each node appropriately as you go.

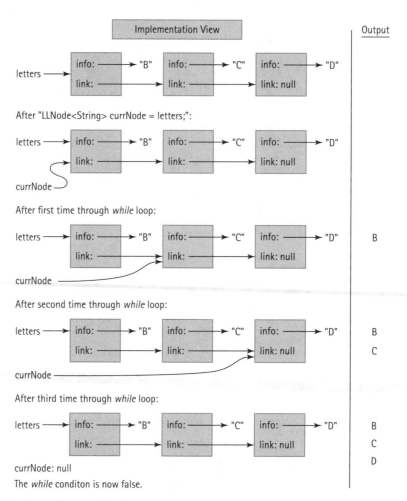

Figure 2.9 Trace of traversal code on `letters` linked list

empty linked list. The empty linked list is an important boundary condition. Whenever you are dealing with linked lists, you should always double-check that your approach works for this oft-encountered special case.

Recall that an empty linked list is one in which the value in the variable that represents the list is `null`:

letters: null

What does our traversal code do in this case? The `currNode` variable is initially set to the value held in the `letters` variable, which is `null`. Therefore, `currNode` starts out `null`, the *while* loop condition

```
(currNode != null)
```

is immediately false, and the *while* loop body is not entered. Essentially, nothing happens—exactly what we would like to happen when traversing an empty list! Our code passes this desk check. We should also remember to check this case with a test program.

Insertion

Three general cases of insertion into a linked list must be considered: insertion at the beginning of the list, insertion in the interior of the list, and insertion at the end of the list.

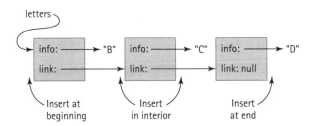

Let us consider the case in which we want to insert a node into the beginning of the list. Suppose we have the node newNode to insert into the beginning of the letters linked list:

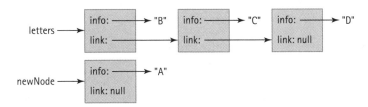

Our first step is to set the link variable of the newNode node to point to the beginning of the list:

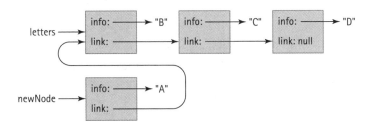

To finish the insertion, we set the `letters` variable to point to the `newNode`, making it the new beginning of the list:

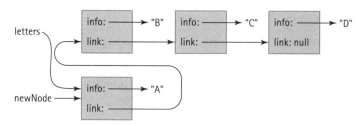

The insertion code corresponding to these two steps is

```
newNode.setLink(letters);
letters = newNode;
```

Note that the order of these statements is critical. If we reversed the order of the statements, we would end up with this:

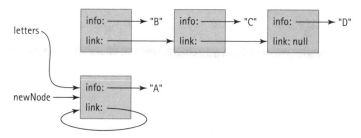

You must be very careful when manipulating references. Drawing figures to help you follow what is going on is usually a good idea.

Design Tip

When you work with link-based structures, draw lots of pictures like the ones shown here. Visualizing the links is the best possible way to make sure your design is correct, that you are listing statements in the correct order, and that you have not left anything out.

As we did for the traverse operation, we should ask what happens if our insertion code is called when the linked list is empty. **Figure 2.10** depicts this situation graphically. Does the method correctly link the new node to the beginning of the empty linked list? In other words, does it correctly create a list with a single node? First, the `link` of the new node is assigned the value of `letters`. What is this value when the list is empty? It is `null`, which is exactly what we want to put into the `link` of the only node of a linked list. Then `letters` is reset to point to the new node. The new node becomes the first, and only, node on the list. Thus this method works for an empty linked list as well as a linked list that contains elements. It is always gratifying (and an indication of good design) when our general case algorithm also handles the special cases correctly.

Implementation of the other two kinds of insertion operations requires similar careful manipulation of references.

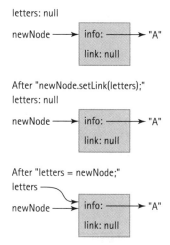

Figure 2.10   Results of insertion code on an empty linked list

Remaining Operations

So far this section has developed Java code that performs a traversal of a linked list and an insertion into the beginning of a linked list. We provided these examples to give you an idea of how you can work with linked lists at the code level.

Our purpose in introducing linked lists was to enable us to use them later for implementing ADTs. We defer development of the remaining linked list operations, including deletions, until they are needed to support the implementation of a specific ADT. For now, we will simply say that, as with insertion, there are three general cases of deletion of nodes from a linked list: deletion at the beginning of the list, deletion in the interior of the list, and deletion at the end of the list.

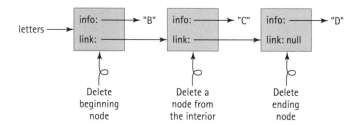

2.8   A Link-Based Stack

In the previous section we introduced linked lists and explained how they provide an alternative to arrays when implementing collections. It is important for you to learn both approaches. Recall that a "link" is the same thing as a "reference." The Stack ADT implementation presented in this section is therefore referred to as a reference- or link-based implementation.

Figure 2.16, in the Summary on page 146, shows the relationships among the primary classes and interfaces created to support our Stack ADT, including those developed in this section.

The LinkedStack Class

We call our new stack class `LinkedStack` to differentiate it from our array-based stack implementations. `LinkedStack` implements the `StackInterface`. Determining names for our classes is important and not always easy. See the nearby boxed feature "Naming Constructs" for more discussion of this topic.

Only one instance variable is required in the `LinkedStack` class, one that holds a reference to the linked list of objects that represents the stack. Needing quick access to the top of the stack, we maintain a reference to the node representing the top, that is, the most recent element pushed onto the stack. That node will, in turn, hold a reference to the node representing the next most recent element. This pattern continues until a particular node holds a `null` reference in its `link` attribute, signifying the bottom of the stack. We call the original reference variable `top`, as it will always reference the top of the stack. It is a reference to an `LLNode`. When instantiating an object of class `LinkedStack`, we create an empty stack by setting `top` to `null`. The beginning of the class definition is shown here. Note the `import` statement that allows us to use the `LLNode` class.

```
//-------------------------------------------------------------------------------
// LinkedStack.java    by Dale/Joyce/Weems       Chapter 2
//
// Implements StackInterface using a linked list to hold the stack elements.
//-------------------------------------------------------------------------------

package ch02.stacks;

import support.LLNode;
public class LinkedStack<T> implements StackInterface<T>
{
    protected LLNode<T> top; // reference to the top of this stack

    public LinkedStack()
    {
       top = null;
    }
. . .
```

Next, we see how we implement our link-based stack operations.

Naming Constructs

Choosing appropriate names for programmer-defined constructs is an important task. In this special feature, we discuss this task and explain some of the naming conventions used in this text.

Java is very lenient in terms of its rules for programmer-defined names. We have been following standard conventions when naming the constructs created for this text. Our class and interface names all begin with an uppercase letter, such as `ArrayBoundedStack` and `StackInterface`. Our method and variable names all begin with a lowercase letter, such as `insert` and `elements`. If a name contains more than one word, we capitalize the start of each additional word, such as `topIndex`. Finally, when naming constants such as `MIN-YEAR`, we use all capital letters.

The name assigned to a construct should provide useful information to someone who is working with that construct. For example, if you declare a variable within a method that should hold the maximum value of a set of numbers, you should name it based on its use: Name it `maximum` or `maxValue` instead of `X`. The same is true for class, interface, and method names.

Because classes tend to represent objects, we typically name them using nouns, for example, `Date` and `Rectangle`. Because methods tend to represent actions, we generally name them using verbs, for example, `insert` and `contains`.

When creating interfaces to specify ADTs, we use the name of the ADT plus the term "interface" within the name of our interface, for example, `StackInterface`. Although this nomenclature is a bit redundant, it is the approach favored by the Java library creators. Note that the name of the interface does not imply any implementation detail. Classes that implement the `StackInterface` interface can use arrays, vectors, array lists, or references—the interface itself does not restrict implementation options and its name does not imply anything about implementation details. The name does help us identify the purpose of the construct; thus `StackInterface` defines the interface required by the Stack ADT.

We must confess that we were hesitant to use names such as `ArrayBoundedStack` and `LinkedStack` for our classes. Can you guess why? Recall our goal of information hiding: We want to hide the implementation used to support our ADTs. Using terms such as "Array" and "Linked" in the names of our ADTs reveals clues about the very information we are trying to hide. However, we finally settled on using implementation-dependent terms within our class names. There are several reasons for this approach:

1. It is the same approach used by the Java library, for example, the `ArrayList` class.

2. Although information hiding is important, some information about the implementation is valuable to the client programmer because it affects the space used by objects of the class and the execution efficiency of the methods of the class. Using "array" and "linked" in the class names does help convey this information.

3. We already have a construct associated with our ADTs whose name is independent of implementation: the interface.

4. In this text we create multiple implementations of many different ADTs; this multiplicity is fundamental to the study of data structures. Using implementation-dependent names makes it easier to distinguish among these different implementations.

The push Operation

Pushing an element onto the stack means creating a new node and linking it to the current chain of nodes. **Figure 2.11** shows the result of the sequence of operations listed here. Like Figure 2.6 it shows the application, implementation, and abstract views of the stack. It graphically demonstrates the dynamic allocation of space for the references to the stack elements. Assume A, B, and C represent objects of class String.

```
StackInterface<String> myStack;
myStack = new LinkedStack<String>();
myStack.push(A);
myStack.push(B);
myStack.push(C);
```

When performing the push operation we must allocate space for each new node dynamically. Here is the general algorithm:

push(element)

Allocate space for the next stack node
  And set the node info to element
Set the node link to the previous top of stack
Set the top of stack to the new stack node

Figure 2.12 graphically displays the effect of each step of the algorithm, starting with a stack that already contains A and B and showing what happens when C is pushed onto it. This is the same algorithm studied in Section 2.7, "Introduction to Linked Lists," for insertion into the beginning of a linked list. We have arranged the node boxes visually to emphasize the LIFO nature of a stack.

Let us look at the algorithm line by line, creating our code as we go. Follow our progress through both the algorithm and Figure 2.12 during this discussion. We begin by allocating space for a new stack node and setting its info attribute to the element:

```
LLNode<T> newNode = new LLNode<T>(element);
```

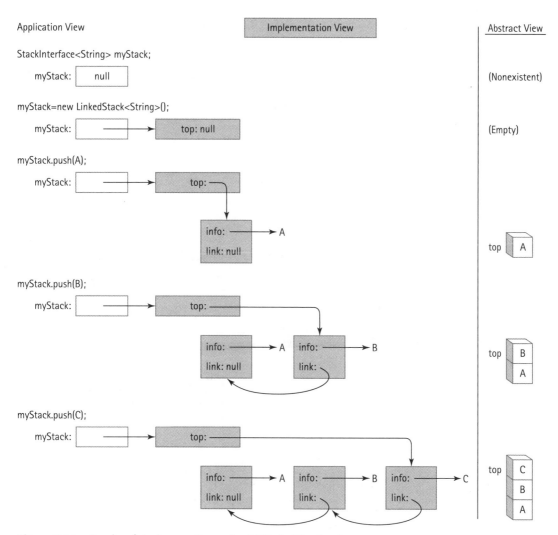

Figure 2.11   Results of stack operations using `LLNode<String>`

Thus, `newNode` is a reference to an object that contains two attributes: `info` of class `T` and `link` of the class `LLNode`. The constructor has set the `info` attribute to reference `element` (the argument C in our example), as required. Next we need to set the value of the `link` attribute:

```
newNode.setLink(top);
```

Now `info` references the `element` pushed onto the stack, and the `link` attribute of that element references the previous top of stack.

Finally, we need to reset the top of the stack to reference the new node:

```
top = newNode;
```

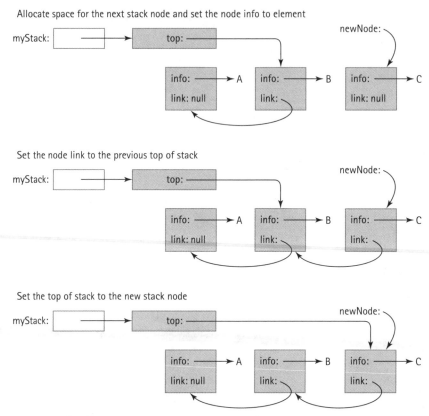

Figure 2.12   Results of push (C) operation

Putting it all together, the code for the push method is

```
public void push(T element)
// Places element at the top of this stack.
{
    LLNode<T> newNode = new LLNode<T>(element);
    newNode.setLink(top);
    top = newNode;
}
```

Note that the order of these tasks is critical. If we reset the top variable before setting the link of the new node, we would lose access to the stack nodes. This situation is generally true when dealing with a linked structure: You must be very careful to change the references in the correct order so that you do not lose access to any of the data. Do not hesitate to draw pictures such as those shown in our figures to help ensure you code the correct sequence of steps.

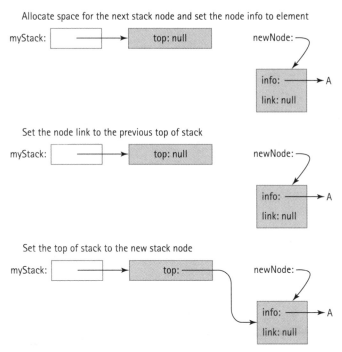

Figure 2.13   Results of push operation on an empty stack

You have seen how the algorithm works on a stack that contains elements. What happens if the stack is empty? Although we verified in Section 2.7, "Introduction to Linked Lists," that our approach works in this case, we should trace through it again. **Figure 2.13** shows graphically what occurs.

Coding Tip

It is always a good idea to check your code against borderline cases, such as an empty stack or a stack containing a single element. It is often in these situations where we make errors.

Space is allocated for the new node, and the node's info attribute is set to reference element. Now we need to correctly set the various links. The link of the new node is assigned the value of top. What is this value when the stack is empty? It is null, which is exactly what we want to put into the link of the last (bottom) node of a linked stack. Then top is reset to point to the new node, making the new node the top of the stack. The result is exactly what is desired—the new node is the only node on the linked list, and it is the current top of the stack.

The pop Operation

The pop operation is equivalent to deleting the first node of a linked list. It is essentially the reverse of the push operation.

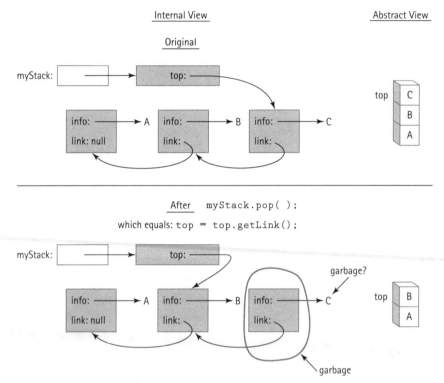

Figure 2.14 Results of pop operation

To accomplish it simply reset the stack's top variable to reference the node that represents the next element. Resetting top to the next stack node effectively removes the top element from the stack. See **Figure 2.14**. This requires only a single line of code:

```
top = top.getLink();
```

The assignment copies the reference from the link attribute of the top stack node into the variable top. After this code is executed, top refers to the LLNode object just below the prior top of the stack. We can no longer reference the previous top object because we overwrote our only reference to it. As indicated in Figure 2.14, the former top of the stack becomes garbage; the system garbage collector will eventually reclaim the space. If the info attribute of this object is the only reference to the data object labeled C in the figure, it, too, is garbage and its space will be reclaimed.

Are there any special cases to consider? Given that an element is being removed from the stack, we should be concerned with empty stack situations. What happens if we try to pop an empty stack? In this case the top variable contains null and the assignment statement "top = top.getLink;" results in a run-time error: NullPointerException.

Therefore, we protect the assignment statement using the Stack ADT's `isEmpty` operation. The code for our `pop` method is shown next.

```
public void pop()
// Throws StackUnderflowException if this stack is empty,
// otherwise removes top element from this stack.
{
    if (isEmpty())
      throw new StackUnderflowException("Pop attempted on an empty stack.");
    else
      top = top.getLink();
}
```

We use the same `StackUnderflowException` we used in our array-based approaches.

There is one more special case: popping from a stack with only one element. We need to make sure that this operation results in an empty stack. Let us see if it does. When our stack is instantiated, `top` is set to `null`. When an element is pushed onto the stack, the `link` of the node that represents the element is set to the current `top` variable; therefore, when the first element is pushed onto our stack, the `link` of its node is set to `null`. Of course, the first element pushed onto the stack is the last element popped off. This means that the last element popped off the stack has an associated `link` value of `null`. Because the `pop` method sets `top` to the value of this `link` attribute, after the last value is popped, `top` again has the value `null`, just as it did when the stack was first instantiated. We conclude that the `pop` method works for a stack of one element. **Figure 2.15** graphically depicts pushing a single element onto a stack and then popping it off.

The Other Stack Operations

Recall that the `top` operation simply returns a reference to the top element of the stack. At first glance this might seem very straightforward. Simply code

```
return top;
```

as `top` references the element on the top of the stack. However, remember that `top` references an LLNode object. Whatever program is using the Stack ADT is not concerned about LLNode objects. The client program is only interested in the object that is referenced by the `info` variable of the LLNode object.

Let us try again. To return the `info` of the top LLNode object we code

```
return top.getInfo();
```

That is better, but we still need to do a little more work. What about the special case when the stack is empty? In that situation we throw an exception instead of returning an object. The final code for the `top` method is shown next.

```
public T top()
// Throws StackUnderflowException if this stack is empty,
// otherwise returns top element of this stack.
```

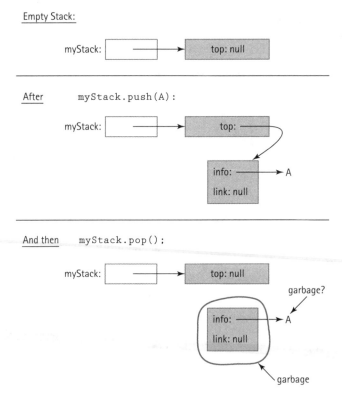

Figure 2.15   Results of push, then pop on an empty stack

```
{
   if (isEmpty())
      throw new StackUnderflowException("Top attempted on an empty stack.");
   else
      return top.getInfo();
}
```

That was not bad, but the isEmpty method is even easier. If we initialize an empty stack by setting the top variable to null, then we can detect an empty stack by checking for the value null.

```
public boolean isEmpty()
// Returns true if this stack is empty, otherwise returns false.
{
   return (top == null);
}
```

Because a linked stack is never full (we can always allocate another node) the `isFull` method simply returns `false`:

```
public boolean isFull()
// Returns false - a linked stack is never full.
{
    return false;
}
```

The linked implementation of the Stack ADT can be tested using a similar test plan as was presented for the array-based version.

Comparing Stack Implementations

Here we compare our two classic implementations of the Stack ADT, `ArrayBoundedStack` and `LinkedStack`, in terms of storage requirements and efficiency of the algorithms. First we consider the storage requirements. An array that is instantiated to match the maximum stack size takes the same amount of memory, no matter how many array slots are actually used. The linked implementation, using dynamically allocated storage, requires space only for the number of elements actually on the stack at run time. Note, however, that the elements are larger because we must store the reference to the next element as well as the reference to the user's data.

Efficiency of Stack Operations

For both our array-based and link-based implementations, the order of growth efficiency of the five basic stack operations (`isEmpty`, `isFull`, `push`, `pop`, and `top`) are all O(1).

We now compare the relative execution "efficiency" of the two implementations. The implementations of `isFull` and `isEmpty` are clearly O(1); they always take a constant amount of work. What about `push`, `pop`, and `top`? Does the number of elements in the stack affect the amount of work required by these operations? No, it does not. In all three implementations, we directly access the top of the stack, so these operations also take a constant amount of work. They, too, have O(1) complexity.

Only the class constructor differs from one implementation to the other in terms of the order of growth efficiency. In the array-based implementation, when the array is instantiated, the system creates and initializes each of the array locations. As it is an array of objects, each array slot is initialized to `null`. The number of array slots is equal to the maximum number of possible stack elements. We call this number N and say that the array-based constructor is O(N). For the linked approach, the constructor simply sets the `top` variable to `null`, so it is only O(1).

Overall, the two stack implementations are roughly equivalent in terms of the amount of work they do. So, which is better? The answer, as usual, is "it depends." The linked implementation does not have space limitations, and in applications where the number of stack elements can vary greatly, it wastes less space when the stack is small. Why would we ever want to use the array-based implementation? Because it is short, simple, and efficient. If pushing occurs frequently, the array-based implementation executes faster than the link-based implementation because it does not incur the run-time overhead of repeatedly invoking the new operation. When the maximum size is small and we know the maximum size with certainty, the array-based implementation is a good choice.

2.9   Application: Postfix Expression Evaluator

Postfix notation is a notation for writing arithmetic expressions in which the operators appear after their operands.[6] For example, instead of writing

$$(2 + 14) \times 23$$

we write

$$2\ 14\ +\ 23\ \times$$

With postfix notation, there are no precedence rules to learn, and parentheses are never needed. Because of this simplicity, some popular handheld calculators of the 1980s used postfix notation to avoid the complications of the multiple parentheses required in traditional algebraic notation. Postfix notation is also used by compilers for generating nonambiguous expressions.

Discussion

In elementary school you learned how to evaluate simple expressions that involve the basic binary operators: addition, subtraction, multiplication, and division. These are called *binary operators* because they each operate on two operands. It is easy to see how a child would solve the following problem:

$$2 + 5 = ?$$

As expressions become more complicated, the pencil-and-paper solutions require a little more work. Multiple tasks must be performed to solve the following problem:

$$(((13 - 1) / 2) \times (3 + 5)) = ?$$

These expressions are written using a format known as *infix* notation, which is the same notation used for expressions in Java. The operator in an infix expression is written *in between* its operands. When an expression contains multiple operators such as

$$3 + 5 \times 2$$

we need a set of rules to determine which operation to carry out first. You learned in your mathematics classes that multiplication is done before addition. You learned Java's operator-precedence rules[7] in your first Java programming course. We can use parentheses

---

[6]Postfix notation is also known as reverse Polish notation (RPN), so named after the Polish logician Jan Lukasiewicz (1875–1956) who developed it.

[7]See Appendix B, Java Operator Precedence.

to override the normal ordering rules. Still, it is easy to make a mistake when writing or interpreting an infix expression containing multiple operations.

Evaluating Postfix Expressions

Postfix notation is another format for writing arithmetic expressions. In this notation, the operator is written after (*post*) the two operands. For example, to indicate addition of 3 and 5:

$$5 \ 3 \ +$$

The rules for evaluating postfix expressions with multiple operators are much simpler than those for evaluating infix expressions; simply perform the operations from left to right. Consider the following postfix expression containing two operators.

$$6 \ 2 \ / \ 5 \ +$$

We evaluate the expression by scanning from left to right. The first item, 6, is an operand, so we go on. The second item, 2, is also an operand, so again we continue. The third item is the division operator. We now apply this operator to the two previous operands. Which of the two saved operands is the divisor? The one seen most recently. We divide 6 by 2 and substitute 3 back into the expression, replacing 6 2 /. Our expression now looks like this:

$$3 \ 5 \ +$$

We continue our scanning. The next item is an operand, 5, so we go on. The next (and last) item is the operator +. We apply this operator to the two previous operands, obtaining a result of 8.

Here are some more examples of postfix expressions containing multiple operators, equivalent expressions in infix notation, and the results of evaluating them. See if you get the same results when you evaluate the postfix expressions.

Postfix Expression	Infix Equivalent	Result
4 5 7 2 + – ×	$4 \times (5 - (7 + 2))$	–16
3 4 + 2 × 7 /	$((3 + 4) \times 2)/7$	2
5 7 + 6 2 – ×	$(5 + 7) \times (6 - 2)$	48
4 2 3 5 1 – + × + ×	$? \times (4 + (2 \times (3 + (5 - 1))))$	not enough operands
4 2 + 3 5 1 – × +	$(4 + 2) + (3 \times (5 - 1))$	18
5 3 7 9 + +	$(3 + (7 + 9)) \ ... \ 5???$	too many operands

Our task is to write a program that evaluates postfix expressions entered interactively by the user. In addition to computing and displaying the value of an expression, our program must display error messages when appropriate ("not enough operands," "too many operands," and "illegal symbol").

Postfix Expression Evaluation Algorithm

As so often happens, our by-hand algorithm can serve as a guideline for our computer algorithm. From the previous discussion it is clear that there are two basic items in a postfix expression: operands (numbers) and operators. We access items (an operand or an operator) from left to right, one at a time. When the item is an operator, we apply it to the preceding two operands.

We must save previously scanned operands in a collection object of some kind. A stack is the ideal place to store the previous operands, because the top item is always the most recent operand and the next item on the stack is always the second most recent operand— just the two operands required when we find an operator. The following algorithm uses a stack to evaluate a postfix expression.

Evaluate Expression

```
while more items exist
    Get an item
    if item is an operand
        stack.push(item)
    else
        operand2 = stack.top()
        stack.pop()
        operand1 = stack.top()
        stack.pop()
        Set result to (apply operation corresponding to item to operand1 and operand2)
        stack.push(result)
result = stack.top()
stack.pop()
return result
```

Each iteration of the *while* loop processes one operator or one operand from the expression. When an operand is found, there is nothing to do with it (we have not yet found the operator to apply to it), so it is saved on the stack until later. When an operator is found, we get the two topmost operands from the stack, perform the operation, and put the result back on the stack; the result may be an operand for a future operator.

Let us trace this algorithm. Before we enter the loop, the input remaining to be processed and the stack look like this:

5 7 + 6 2 − *

After one iteration of the loop, we have processed the first operand and pushed it onto the stack.

$$5\ 7\ +\ 6\ \ 2\ \ -\ \ast$$

```
|      |
|      |
|      |
|      |
|  5   |
```

After the second iteration of the loop, the stack contains two operands.

$$5\ 7\ +\ 6\ \ 2\ \ -\ \ast$$

```
|      |
|      |
|  7   |
|  5   |
```

We encounter the + operator in the third iteration. We remove the two operands from the stack, perform the operation, and push the result onto the stack.

$$5\ 7\ +\ 6\ \ 2\ \ -\ \ast$$

```
|      |
|      |
|      |
|  12  |
```

In the next two iterations of the loop, we push two operands onto the stack.

$$5\ 7\ +\ 6\ \ 2\ \ -\ \ast$$

```
|      |
|  2   |
|  6   |
|  12  |
```

When we find the − operator, we remove the top two operands, subtract, and push the result onto the stack.

$$5\ 7\ +\ 6\ \ 2\ \ -\ \ast$$

```
|      |
|      |
|  4   |
|  12  |
```

When we find the * operator, we remove the top two operands, multiply, and push the result onto the stack.

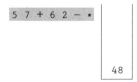

Now that we have processed all of the items on the input line, we exit the loop. We remove the result, 48, from the stack, and return it.

This discussion has glossed over a few "minor" details, such as how to recognize an operator, how to know when we are finished, and when to generate error messages. We discuss these issues as we continue to evolve the solution to our problem.

Error Processing

Our application will read a series of postfix expressions, some of which might be illegal. Instead of displaying an integer result when such an expression is entered, the application should display error messages as follows:

Type of Illegal Expression	Error Message
An expression contains a symbol that is not an integer or not one of "+," "-," " * ," and " / "	Illegal symbol
An expression requires more than 50 stack items	Too many operands—stack overflow
There is more than one operand left on the stack after the expression is processed; for example, the expression 5 6 7 + has too many operands	Too many operands—operands left over
There are not enough operands on the stack when it is time to perform an operation; for example, 6 7 + + +; and, for example, 5 + 5	Not enough operands—stack underflow

Assumptions

1. The operations in expressions are valid at run time. This means there is no division by zero. Also, no numbers are generated that are outside of the range of the Java `int` type.
2. A postfix expression has a maximum of 50 operands.

To facilitate error management we create an exception class called `PostFixException` similar to the exceptions created for the Stack ADT.

The PostFixEvaluator Class

The purpose of this class is to provide an `evaluate` method that accepts a postfix expression as a string and returns the value of the expression. We do not need any objects of the class, so we implement `evaluate` as a `public static` method. This means that it is invoked through the class itself, rather than through an object of the class.

The `evaluate` method must take a postfix expression as a string argument and return the value of the expression. The code for the class is listed below. It follows the basic postfix expression algorithm that was developed earlier, using an `ArrayBoundedStack` object to hold operands of class `Integer` until they are needed. Note that it instantiates a `Scanner` object to "read" the string argument and break it into tokens.

Let us consider error message generation. Because the `evaluate` method returns an `int` value, the result of evaluating the postfix expression, it cannot directly return an error message. Instead we turn to Java's exception mechanism. Look through the code for the lines that throw `PostFixException` exceptions. You should be able to see that we cover all of the error conditions identified previously. As would be expected, the error messages directly related to the stack processing are all protected by *if* statements that check whether the stack is empty (not enough operands) or full (too many operands). The only other error trapping occurs if the string stored in `operator` does not match any of the legal operators, in which case an exception with the message "Illegal symbol" is thrown. This is a very appropriate use of exceptions.

```
//-----------------------------------------------------------------------
// PostFixEvaluator.java        by Dale/Joyce/Weems          Chapter 2
//
// Provides a postfix expression evaluation.
//-----------------------------------------------------------------------
package ch02.postfix;

import ch02.stacks.*;
import java.util.Scanner;

public class PostFixEvaluator
{
  public static int evaluate(String expression)
  {
    Scanner tokenizer = new Scanner(expression);
    StackInterface<Integer> stack = new ArrayBoundedStack<Integer>(50);

    int value;
    String operator;
```

```
    int operand1, operand2;
    int result = 0;
    Scanner tokenizer = new Scanner(expression);

    while (tokenizer.hasNext())
    {
      if (tokenizer.hasNextInt())
      {
        // Process operand.
        value = tokenizer.nextInt();
        if (stack.isFull())
          throw new PostFixException("Too many operands-stack overflow");
        stack.push(value);
      }
      else
      {
        // Process operator.
        operator = tokenizer.next();

        // Check for illegal symbol
        if (!(operator.equals("/") || operator.equals("*") ||
              operator.equals("+") || operator.equals("-")))
          throw new PostFixException("Illegal symbol: " + operator);

        // Obtain second operand from stack.
        if (stack.isEmpty())
          throw new PostFixException("Not enough operands-stack underflow");
        operand2 = stack.top();
        stack.pop();

        // Obtain first operand from stack.
        if (stack.isEmpty())
          throw new PostFixException("Not enough operands-stack underflow");
        operand1 = stack.top();
        stack.pop();

        // Perform operation.
        if (operator.equals("/"))
          result = operand1 / operand2;
        else
        if(operator.equals("*"))
          result = operand1 * operand2;
        else
        if(operator.equals("+"))
          result = operand1 + operand2;
```

```
         else
         if(operator.equals("-"))
           result = operand1 - operand2;

         // Push result of operation onto stack.
         stack.push(result);
      }
   }

   // Obtain final result from stack.
   if (stack.isEmpty())
     throw new PostFixException("Not enough operands-stack underflow");
   result = stack.top();
   stack.pop();

   // Stack should now be empty.
   if (!stack.isEmpty())
     throw new PostFixException("Too many operands-operands left over");

   // Return the final.
   return result;
  }
}
```

The PFixCLI Class

This class is the main driver for our CLI-based application. Using the PostFixEvaluator and PostFixException classes, it is easy to design our program. We follow the same basic approach used for BalancedCLI earlier in the chapter—namely, repeatedly prompt the user for an expression, allowing him or her to enter "X" to indicate he or she is finished, and if the user is not finished, evaluate the expression and return the results. Note that the main program does not directly use a stack; it uses the PostFixEvaluator class, which in turn uses a stack.

```
//---------------------------------------------------------------------------
// PFixCLI.java              by Dale/Joyce/Weems              Chapter 2
//
// Evaluates postfix expressions entered by the user.
// Uses a command line interface.
//---------------------------------------------------------------------------
package ch02.apps;

import java.util.Scanner;
import ch02.postfix.*;
```

```java
public class PFixCLI
{
  public static void main(String[] args)
  {
    Scanner scan = new Scanner(System.in);
    String expression = null;    // expression to be evaluated
    final String STOP = "X";     // indicates end of input
    int result;                  // result of evaluation

    while (!STOP.equals(expression))
    {
      // Get next expression to be processed.
      System.out.print("\nPostfix Expression (" + STOP + " to stop): ");
      expression = scan.nextLine();

      if (!STOP.equals(expression))
      {
        // Obtain and output result of expression evaluation.
        try
        {
          result = PostFixEvaluator.evaluate(expression);

          // Output result.
          System.out.println("Result = " + result);
        }
        catch (PostFixException error)
        {
          // Output error message.
          System.out.println("Error in expression - " + error.getMessage());
        }
      }
    }
  }
}
```

Here is a sample run of our console-based application:

```
Postfix expression (X to stop): 5 7 + 6 2 - *
Result = 48
Postfix expression (X to stop): 4 2 3 5 1 - + * + *
Error in expression Not enough operands-stack underflow
Postfix expression (X to stop): X
```

The GUI Approach

The GUI-based implementation of the Postfix Evaluation application looks similar to the GUI approached used earlier in this chapter for the Balanced application. As was the case with Balanced, because we have separated the user interface code from the code that does the "work," it is easy to create a new application using a different interface approach. Here are a few screen shots from that application. The code is provided in a file named `PFixGUI.java` found in the `ch02.apps` package.

The start screen:

Here is the result of a successful evaluation:

Here is what happens if an illegal expression is evaluated:

2.10 Stack Variations

In the primary exposition of our ADTs in this text we record design decisions and specify the operations to be supported by the ADT. We also develop or at least discuss various implementation approaches, in most cases highlighting one array-based approach and one reference/linked list–based approach.

There are alternate approaches to defining/implementing any data structure. Therefore, for each of the major data structures presented in this text, we include a section that investigates variations of the structure. The stack, being a relatively simple data structure, does not permit a great amount of variation as compared, for example, to the tree structure for which dozens of variations exist. Nevertheless, a look at stack variations is still instructive.

Revisiting Our Stack ADT

Let us briefly review the design decisions made when we defined our Stack ADT and consider alternate approaches:

- Our stacks are generic, that is, the type of element held in our stack is specified by the application when the stack is instantiated. Alternately, we could define stacks to hold elements of class `Object` or of a class that implements a specified interface. These approaches were discussed in detail in Section 2.3, "Collection Elements,".

- Classically, stacks provide two operations:
  - `void push (T element)`—pushes `element` onto the stack
  - `T pop ( )`—removes and returns the top element of the stack

  For our stacks we redefined `pop` and added a third operation `top`, giving us:
  - `void push (T element)`—pushes `element` onto the stack
  - `void pop ( )`—removes the top element of the stack
  - `T top( )`—returns the top element of the stack

  Obviously, we could have chosen to use the classic approach. In one sense the `top` method we define is superfluous, as we can create the same result by using the classic `pop` immediately followed by a `push`. We chose our approach to emphasize the design benefits of defining methods that only do one thing. Thus we avoid the dual action of the classic `pop` that both removes and returns an element. However, the classic approach is also valid, and you will find it in many texts and code libraries.

- Our stacks throw exceptions in the case of underflow or overflow. An alternative approach is to state as a precondition for the stack methods that they will not be invoked in a situation where an underflow or overflow will be generated. In that case the implementation of the operations can just ignore the possibility. Yet another approach is to catch the issue within the method and prevent the overflow or underflow from occurring by nullifying the operation. With this latter approach we might redefine our three operations to return information about whether or not the operation completed successfully:
  - `boolean push (T element)`—pushes the element onto the stack; returns `true` if element successfully pushed, `false` otherwise

- boolean pop ( )—removes the top element of the stack; returns true if element successfully popped, false otherwise
- T top( )—if the stack is not empty, returns the top element of the stack; otherwise returns null

Rather than redefining our operations we could also just add new operations with unique names such as safePush or offer.

The Java Stack Class and the Collections Framework

The Java library provides classes that implement ADTs that are based on common data structures: stacks, queues, lists, maps, sets, and more. The library's Stack[8] is similar to the Stack ADT we develop in this chapter in that it provides a LIFO structure. However, in addition to our push, top, and isEmpty[9] operations, it includes two other operations:

- T pop( )—The classic "pop" operation removes and returns the top element from the stack.
- int search(Object o)—Returns the position of object o on the stack.

Because the library Stack class extends the library Vector class, it also inherits many operations defined for Vector (such as capacity, clear, clone, contains, isEmpty, toArray, and toString) and its ancestor Object.

Here is how you might implement the reverse strings application (see Section 2.4, "The Stack Interface,") using the Stack class from the Java library. The minimal differences between this application and the one using our Stack ADT are <u>emphasized</u>.

```
//-----------------------------------------------------------------------
// ReverseStrings2.java          by Dale/Joyce/Weems          Chapter 2
//
// Sample use of the library Stack.
// Outputs strings in reverse order of entry.
//-----------------------------------------------------------------------
package ch02.apps;

import java.util.Stack;
import java.util.Scanner;
```

---

[8]Since Java 1.6 was released in 2006 the library **Stack** class has been supplanted by the **Deque** class. Nevertheless, it is instructive for us to briefly consider the **Stack** class in this section.

[9]In the library isEmpty is called empty, and top is called peek.

```
public class ReverseStrings2
{
    public static void main(String[] args)
    {
        Scanner scan = new Scanner(System.in);

        Stack<String> stringStack = new Stack<String>();

        String line;

        for (int i = 1; i <= 3; i++)
        {
            System.out.print("Enter a line of text > ");
            line = scan.nextLine();
            stringStack.push(line);
        }

        System.out.println("\nReverse is:\n");
        while (!stringStack.empty())
        {
            line = stringStack.peek();
            stringStack.pop();
            System.out.println(line);
        }
    }
}
```

The library pop method both removes and returns the top element of the stack. Therefore, the body of the *while* loop in ReverseStrings2 could be coded as

```
line = stringStack.pop();
System.out.println(line);
```

or even as

```
System.out.println(stringStack.pop());
```

Which approach is best? It is really a matter of personal preference. We believe the approach used in ReverseStrings2 is the easiest to read and understand. However, one could also argue that the one-line approach shown immediately above is clear enough and properly uses the pop method.

The Collections Framework

As discussed in Section 2.2, "The Stack," another term for a data structure is "collection." The Java developers refer to the set of library classes, such as Stack, that support data structures as the **Collections Framework**. This framework includes both interfaces and classes. It also includes documentation that explains how the developers intend for us to use them. As of Java 5.0 all the structures in the Collections Framework support generics.

The Java library's Collections Framework comprises an extensive set of tools. It does more than just provide implementations of data structures; it provides a unified architecture for working with collections. The `Stack` class has been part of the Java Library from the beginning. More recently the library includes a set of `Deque` classes that can and should be used in place of the legacy `Stack` class. We will discuss the `Deque` classes in the *Variations* section of Chapter 4.

In this text we do not cover the Java Collections Framework in great detail. This text is meant to teach you about the fundamental nature of data structures and to demonstrate how to define, implement, and use them. It is not an exploration of how to use Java's specific library architecture of similar structures. Nevertheless, when we discuss a data structure that has a counterpart in the Java library, we will briefly describe the similarities and differences between our approach and the library's approach, as we did here for stacks.

Before you become a professional Java programmer you should carefully study the Collections Framework and learn how to use it productively. This text prepares you to do this not just for Java, but for other languages and libraries as well. If you are interested in learning more about the Java Collections Framework, you can study the extensive documentation available at Oracle's website.

Summary

Data can be viewed from multiple perspectives. Java encapsulates the implementations of its predefined types and allows us to encapsulate our own class implementations. In this chapter we specified a Stack ADT using the Java interface construct and created several implementations: one based on arrays, one based on the library's `ArrayList` class, and one based on linked lists. The concept of a linked list, new to many readers, was introduced in its own section. The Stack ADT allowed us to create applications that checked whether the grouping symbols in a string are balanced and evaluated postfix arithmetic expressions.

When using data abstraction to work with data structures such as a stack, there are three levels or views from which to consider our structures. The abstract level describes *what* the ADT provides to us. This view includes the domain of what the ADT represents and what it can do, as specified by its interface. At the application level, we *use* the ADT to solve problems. Finally, the implementation level provides the specific details of *how* to represent our structure and the code that supports the operations. The abstract level acts as a contract between the application level "above" it and the implementation level "below" it.

What do we gain by separating these views of the data? First, we reduce complexity at the higher levels of the design, making the client program easier to understand. Second, we make the program more readily modifiable: The implementation can be changed

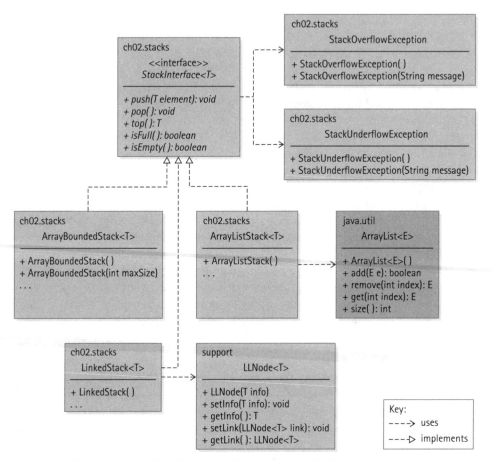

Figure 2.16   The stack-related interfaces and classes developed in Chapter 2

without affecting the program that uses the data structure. Third, we develop software that is *reusable*: The implementation operations can be used by other programs, for completely different applications, as long as the correct interfaces are maintained.

Figure 2.16 is a UML-like diagram showing the stack-related interfaces and classes developed in this chapter, along with a few other supporting classes, and their relationships. Our diagrams vary somewhat from traditional UML class diagrams:

- We show the name of the package in the upper-left corner of the class/interface rectangle.

- We omit private and protected information.

- If a class implements an interface we do *not* relist the methods defined within the interface within the class rectangle. We indicate that some methods have not been listed but placing "..." at the bottom of the method list.

- In an effort to present clear, uncluttered diagrams we sometimes omit arrows indicating "uses," if the information can be inferred. For example, the `Array-BoundedStack` class uses the `StackUnderflowException`. Since the `Array-BoundedStack` class implements `StackInterface`, and we already show that `StackInterface` uses `StackUnderflowException`, we can safely omit the arrow connecting `ArrayBoundedStack` to `StackUnderflowException`.
- Library classes included in our diagrams are shaded. We only include such classes if they are directly related to the implementation of the ADT.

Exercises

2.1 Abstraction

1. Describe four ways you use abstraction in your everyday life.
2. Name three different perspectives from which we can view data. Using the example "a list of student academic records," describe how we might view the data from each perspective.
3. Describe one way that the implementation details can affect the applications that use an ADT, despite the use of data abstraction.
4. What is an abstract method?
5. What happens if a Java interface specifies a particular method signature, and a class that implements the interface provides a different signature for that method? For example, suppose interface `SampleInterface` is defined as:

```
public interface SampleInterface
{
   public int sampleMethod();
}
```

and the class `SampleClass` is

```
public class SampleClass implements SampleInterface
{
   public boolean sampleMethod()
   {
      return true;
   }
}
```

6. True or False? Explain your answers.
   a. You can define constructors for a Java interface.
   b. Classes implement interfaces.
   c. Classes extend interfaces.

d. A class that implements an interface can include methods that are not required by the interface.

e. A class that implements an interface can leave out methods that are required by an interface.

f. You can instantiate objects of an interface.

7. What is wrong with the following method, based on our conventions for handling error situations?

```
public void method10(int number)
// Precondition:    number is > 0.
// Throws NotPositiveException if number is not > 0,
// otherwise ...
```

8. A friend of yours is having trouble instantiating an object of type `FigureInterface`. His code includes the statement

```
FigureInterface myFig = new FigureInterface(27.5);
```

What do you tell your friend?

9. Create Java classes that implement the `FigureInterface` interface:

a. `Square`—constructor accepts a single argument of type `double` which indicates the length of a side of the square

b. `RightTriangle`—constructor accepts two arguments of type `double` that indicate the lengths of the two legs

c. `IsoscelesTriangle`—constructor accepts two arguments of type `double` that indicate the height and the base

d. `Parallelogram`—constructor accepts three arguments of type `double` that indicate the height, the base, and the angle between the nonbase side and the base

10. Update the `RandomFigs` application so that it also uses the new `FigureInterface` classes you implemented for the previous question.

11. For this problem you must define a simple interface `NumTrackerInterface` and two implementations of the interface, `Tracker1` and `Tracker2`.

a. Define a Java interface named `NumTrackerInterface`. A class that implements this interface must keep track of both the sum and the count of numbers that are submitted to it through its `add` method, and provide getters for the sum, the count, and the average of those numbers. The `add` method should accept an argument of type `int`, the `getSum` and `getCount` methods should both return values of type `int`, and the `getAverage` method should return a value of type `double`. Suppose a class named `Tracker1` implements the `NumTrackerInterface`. A simple sample application that uses `Tracker1` is shown here. Its output would be "3 29 9.67."

```
public class Sample
{
    public static void main (String[] args)
    {
        NumTrackerInterface nt = new Tracker1();
        nt.add(5); nt.add(15); nt.add(9);
        System.out.print(nt.getCount() + " ");
        System.out.print(nt.getSum() + " ");
        System.out.println(nt.getAverage());
    }
}
```

b. Create a class called `Tracker1` that implements the `NumTrackerInterface`. This class should use three instance variables, `count`, `sum`, and `average`, to hold information. The getters should simply return the information when requested. Create a test driver application that demonstrates that the `Tracker1` class works correctly.

c. Create a class called `Tracker2` that implements the `NumTrackerInterface`. This class should use two instance variables, `count` and `sum`, to hold information. The average should be calculated only when needed with this approach. Create a test driver application that demonstrates that the `Tracker2` class works correctly.

d. Discuss the difference in the design philosophies exhibited by `Tracker1` and `Tracker2`.

2.2 The Stack

12. True or False?
    a. A stack is a first in, first out structure.
    b. The item that has been in a stack the longest is at the "bottom" of the stack.
    c. If you push five items onto an empty stack and then pop the stack five times, the stack will be empty again.
    d. If you push five items onto an empty stack and then perform the top operation five times, the stack will be empty again.
    e. The push operation should be classified as a "transformer."
    f. The top operation should be classified as a "transformer."
    g. The pop operation should be classified as an "observer."
    h. The top operation always returns the most recently pushed item.
    i. If we first push `itemA` onto a stack and then push `itemB`, then the top of the stack is `itemB`.
    j. On a stack a push operation followed by a pop operation has no effect on the status of the stack.
    k. On a stack a pop operation followed by a push operation has no effect on the status of the stack.

13. Describe the differences between the classic stack pop operation and the pop operation as defined in this text.

14. In the following command sequences numbered blocks are pushed and popped from a stack. Suppose that every time a block is popped, its numerical value is printed. Show the sequence of values that are printed in each of the following sequences. Assume you begin with an empty stack:

    a.   push block5; push block7 ; pop;   pop; push block2; push block1; pop; push block8;

    b.   push block5; push block4; push block3; push block2; pop; push block1; pop; pop; pop;

    c.   push block1; pop; push block1; pop; push block1; pop; push block1; pop;

15. Describe how you might use a stack in each of the following scenarios:

    a.   Help a forgetful friend discover where he left his umbrella during a night out "on the town."

    b.   Track an auction where the current highest bidder is allowed to retract her bid.

2.3 Collection Elements

16. In Section 2.3, "Collection Elements," we looked at four approaches to defining the types of elements we can hold in a collection ADT. Briefly describe each of the four approaches.

17. For this problem you must define a simple generic interface `PairInterface`, and two implementations of the interface, `BasicPair` and `ArrayPair`.

    a.   Define a Java interface named `PairInterface`. A class that implements this interface allows creation of an object that holds a "pair" of objects of a specified type—these are referred to as the "first" object and the "second" object of the pair. We assume that classes implementing `PairInterface` provide constructors that accept as arguments the values of the pair of objects. The `PairInterface` interface should require both setters and getters for the first and second objects. The actual type of the objects in the pair is specified when the `PairInterface` object is instantiated. Therefore, both the `PairInterface` interface and the classes that implement it should be generic. Suppose a class named `BasicPair` implements the `PairInterface` interface. A simple sample application that uses `BasicPair` is shown here. Its output would be "apple orange."

```
public class Sample
{
    public static void main (String[] args)
    {
        PairInterface myPair<String> =
                    new BasicPair<String>("apple", "peach");
        System.out.print(myPair.getFirst() + " ");
```

```
            myPair.setSecond("orange");
            System.out.println(myPair.getSecond());
        }
    }
```

b. Create a class called `BasicPair` that implements the `PairInterface` interface. This class should use two instance variables, `first` and `second`, to represent the two objects of the pair. Create a test driver application that demonstrates that the `BasicPair` class works correctly.

c. Create a class called `ArrayPair` that implements the `PairInterface` interface. This class should use an array[10] of size 2 to represent the two objects of the pair. Create a test driver application that demonstrates that the `ArrayPair` class works correctly.

2.4 Formal Specification

18. The `StackInterface` interface represents a contract between the implementer of a Stack ADT and the programmer who uses the ADT. List the main points of the contract.

19. Based on our Stack ADT specification, an application programmer has two ways to check for an empty stack. Describe them and discuss when one approach might be preferable to the other approach.

20. Show what is written by the following segments of code, given that `item1`, `item2`, and `item3` are `int` variables, and `s` is an object that fits the abstract description of a stack as given in the section. Assume that you can store and retrieve variables of type `int` on `s`.

a.
```
item1 = 1; item2 = 0; item3 = 4;
s.push(item2); s.push(item1); s.push(item1 + item3);
item2 = s.top();
s.push (item3*item3); s.push(item2); s.push(3);
item1 = s.top();
s.pop();
System.out.println(item1 + " " + item2 + " " + item3);
while (!s.isEmpty())
{
   item1 = s.top(); s.pop();
   System.out.println(item1);
}
```

b.
```
item1 = 4; item3 = 0; item2 = item1 + 1;
s.push(item2); s.push(item2 + 1); s.push(item1);
item2 = s.top(); s.pop();
```

---

[10]Section 2.5, "Array-Based Stack Implementations," shows how to use an array with generics.

```
item1 = item2 + 1;
s.push(item1); s.push(item3);
while (!s.isEmpty())
{
   item3 = s.top(); s.pop();
   System.out.println(item3);
}
System.out.println(item1 + " " + item2 + " " + item3);
```

21. Your friend Bill says, "The push and pop stack operations are inverses of each other. Therefore, performing a push followed by a pop is always equivalent to performing a pop followed by a push. You get the same result!" How would you respond to that? Do you agree?

22. In each plastic container of Pez candy, the colors are stored in random order. Your little brother Phil likes only the yellow ones, so he painstakingly takes out all the candies one by one, eats the yellow ones, and keeps the others in order, so that he can return them to the container in exactly the same order as before—minus the yellow candies, of course. Write the algorithm to simulate this process. (You may use any of the stack operations defined in the Stack ADT, but may not assume any knowledge of how the stack is implemented.)

23. Using the Stack ADT:

    a. Download the text code files and set them up properly on your laptop/desktop. Run the `ReverseStrings` application.

    b. Create a similar program that uses a stack. Your new program should ask the user to input a line of text and then it should print out the line of text in reverse. To do this your application should use a stack of `Character`.

24. A Century Stack is a stack with a fixed size of 100. If a Century Stack is full, then the element that has been on the stack, the longest, is removed to make room for the new element. Create a `CenturyStackInterface` file that captures this specification of a Century Stack.

2.5 Array-Based Stack Implementations

25. Show the implementation representation (the values of the instance variables `elements` and `topIndex`) at each step of the following code sequence:

```
StackInterface<String> s = new ArrayBoundedStack<String> (5);
s.push("Elizabeth");
s.push("Anna Jane");
s.pop();
s.push("Joseph");
s.pop();
```

26. Show the implementation representation (the values of the instance variables `elements` and `topIndex`) at each step of the following code sequence:

    ```
    StackInterface<String> s = new ArrayBoundedStack<String> (5);
    s.push("Adele");
    s.push("Heidi");
    s.push("Sylvia");
    s.pop();s.pop();s.pop();
    ```

27. Describe the effects each of the changes would have on the `ArrayBoundedStack` class.

    a. Remove the `final` attribute from the `DEFCAP` instance variable.

    b. Change the value assigned to `DEFCAP` to 10.

    c. Change the value assigned to `DEFCAP` to –10.

    d. In the first constructor change the statement to

        ```
        elements = (T[]) new Object[100];
        ```

    e. In `isEmpty`, change "`topIndex == -1`" to "`topIndex < 0`".

    f. Reverse the order of the two statements in the *else* clause of the `push` method.

    g. Reverse the order of the two statements in the *else* clause of the `pop` method.

    h. In the `throw` statement of the `top` method change the argument string from "Top attempted on an empty stack" to "Pop attempted on an empty stack."

28. Add the following methods to the `ArrayBoundedStack` class, and create a test driver for each to show that they work correctly. In order to practice your array related coding skills, code each of these methods by accessing the internal variables of the `ArrayBoundedStack`, not by calling the previously defined public methods of the class.

    a. `String toString()`—creates and returns a string that correctly represents the current stack. Such a method could prove useful for testing and debugging the class and for testing and debugging applications that use the class. Assume each stacked element already provided its own reasonable `toString` method.

    b. `int size()`—returns a count of how many items are currently on the stack. Do not add any instance variables to the `ArrayBoundedStack` class in order to implement this method.

    c. `void popSome(int count)`—removes the top `count` elements from the stack; throws `StackUnderflowException` if there are less than `count` elements on the stack.

    d. `boolean swapStart()`—if there are less than two elements on the stack returns `false`; otherwise it reverses the order of the top two elements on the stack and returns `true`.

    e. `T poptop( )`—the "classic" pop operation, if the stack is empty it throws `StackUnderflowException`; otherwise it both removes and returns the top element of the stack.

29. Perform the tasks listed in Exercise 28, but update the `ArrayListStack`.

30. Using the `ArrayBoundedStack` class, create an application `EditString` that prompts the user for a string and then repeatedly prompts the user for changes to the string, until the user enters an X, indicating the end of changes. Legal change operations are:

    U—make all letters uppercase
    L—make all letters lowercase
    R—reverse the string
    C ch1 ch2—change all occurrences of ch1 to ch2
    Z—undo the most recent change

    You may assume a "friendly user," that is, the user will not enter anything illegal. When the user is finished the resultant string is printed. For example, if the user enters:

    ```
    All dogs go to heaven
    U
    R
    Z
    C O A
    C A t
    Z
    ```

    the output from the program will be "ALL DAGS GA TA HEAVEN"

31. During software development when is the appropriate time to begin testing?

32. Create a noninteractive test driver, similar to `Test034`, that performs robust testing of the listed method of the `ArrayBoundedStack` class:

    a. `isEmpty`

    b. `top`

    c. `push`

    d. `pop`

33. Perform the tasks listed in Exercise 32, but test the `ArrayListStack`. *Note:* If you completed Exercise 32 then this should be a trivial exercise.

34. Implement a Century Stack (see Exercise 24).

    a. Using an array (can you devise a solution that maintains O(1) efficiency for the *push* operation?).

    b. Using an `ArrayList`.

2.6 Application: Balanced Expressions

35. Suppose each of the following well-formed expressions (using the standard paren-thesis, brackets, and braces) is passed to the `test` method of our `Balanced` class. Show the contents of the stack, from bottom to top, at the point in time when the stack holds the most elements, for each expression. Include ties.

   a. (x x (xx ( )) xx) [ ]

   b. ( ) [ ] { } ( ) [ ] { }

   c. (( )) [[[ ]]] {{{{ }}}}

   d. ({ [[{ ( ) } [{ ( ) }]]] } ( ))

36. Suppose each of the following ill-formed expressions (using the standard paren-thesis, brackets, and braces) is passed to the `test` method of our `Balanced` class. Show the contents of the stack, from bottom to top, at the point in time when it is discovered the expression is ill-formed.

   a. (x x (xx ( ) xx) [ ]

   b. ( ) [ ] { ( ) [}] { }

   c. (( )) [[[ ]]] {{{{ }}}})

   d. ({ [[{ ( ) } [{ ({) }]]] } ( ))

37. Answer the following questions about the `Balanced` class:

   a. Is there any functional difference between the class being instantiated in the fol-lowing two ways?

   ```
   Balanced bal = new Balanced ("abc", "xyz");
   Balanced bal = new Balanced ("cab", "zxy");
   ```

   b. Is there any functional difference between the class being instantiated in the fol-lowing two ways?

   ```
   Balanced bal = new Balanced ("abc", "xyz");
   Balanced bal = new Balanced ("abc", "zxy");
   ```

   c. Is there any functional difference between the class being instantiated in the fol-lowing two ways?

   ```
   Balanced bal = new Balanced ("abc", "xyz");
   Balanced bal = new Balanced ("xyz", "abc");
   ```

   d. Which type is pushed onto the stack? A `char`? An `int`? An `Integer`? Explain.

   e. Under which circumstances is the first operation performed on the stack (not counting the `new` operation) the `top` operation?

   f. What happens if the string `expression`, that is passed to the `test` method, is an empty string?

2.7 Introduction to Linked Lists

38. What is a self-referential class?

39. Draw figures representing our abstract view of the structures created by each of the following code sequences. Assume that each case is preceded by these three lines of code:

```
LLNode<String> node1 = new LLNode<String>("alpha");
LLNode<String> node2 = new LLNode<String>("beta");
LLNode<String> node3 = new LLNode<String>("gamma");
```

 a. `node1.setLink(node3);` `node2.setLink(node3);`

 b. `node1.setLink(node2);` `node2.setLink(node3);`
  `node3.setLink(node1);`

 c. `node1.setLink(node3); node2.setLink(node1.getLink());`

40. We developed Java code for traversing a linked list. Here are several alternate, possibly flawed, approaches for using a traversal to print the contents of the linked list of strings accessed through `letters`. Critique each of them:

 a.
```
LLNode<String> currNode = letters;
while (currNode != null)
{
   System.out.println(currNode.getInfo());
   currNode = currNode.getLink();
}
```

 b.
```
LLNode<String> currNode = letters;
while (currNode != null)
{
   currNode = currNode.getLink();
   System.out.println(currNode.getInfo());
}
```

 c.
```
LLNode<String> currNode = letters;
while (currNode != null)
{
   System.out.println(currNode.getInfo());
   if (currNode.getLink() != null)
     currNode = currNode.getLink();
   else
     currNode = null;
}
```

41. Assume `numbers` points to a linked list of `LLNode<Integer>`. Write code that prints the following. Do not forget to consider the case where the list is empty. Recall that `LLNode` exports setters and getters for both `info` and `link`.

a. The sum of the numbers on the list

b. The count of how many elements are on the list

c. The count of how many positive numbers are on the list

d. The enumerated contents of the list; for example, if the list contains 5, 7, and −9 the code will print

```
1.   5
2.   7
3.  -9
```

e. The reverse enumerated contents of the list (*hint*: use a stack); for example, if the list contains 5, 7, and −9 the code will print

```
1.  -9
2.   7
3.   5
```

42. Using the same style of algorithm presentation as found in this section, describe an algorithm for

a. Removing the first element from a linked list

b. Removing the second item from a linked list

c. Swapping the first two elements of a linked list (you can assume the list has at least two elements)

d. Adding an element with info attribute I as the second element of a linked list (you can assume the list has at least one element)

2.8 A Link-Based Stack

43. What are the main differences, in terms of memory allocation, between using an array-based stack and using a link-based stack?

44. Consider the code for the `push` method of the `LinkedStack` class. What would be the effect of the following changes to that code?

a. Switch the first and second lines.

b. Switch the second and third lines.

45. Show the implementation representation (draw the linked list starting with `topIndex`) at each step of the following code sequence:

```
StackInterface<String> s = new LinkedStack<String>();
s.push("Elizabeth");
s.push("Anna Jane");
s.pop();
s.push("Joseph");
s.pop();
```

46. Show the implementation representation (draw the linked list starting with `topIndex`) at each step of the following code sequence:

```
StackInterface<String> s = new LinkedStack<String>();
s.push("Adele");
s.push("Heidi");
s.push("Sylvia");
s.pop();s.pop();s.pop();
```

47. Repeat Exercise 28, but add the methods to the `LinkedStack` class.

48. Use the `LinkedStack` class to support an application that tracks the status of an online auction. Bidding begins at 1 (dollars, pounds, euros, or whatever) and proceeds in increments of at least 1. If a bid arrives that is less than the current bid, it is discarded. If a bid arrives that is more than the current bid, but less than the maximum bid by the current high bidder, then the current bid for the current high bidder is increased to match it and the new bid is discarded. If a bid arrives that is more than the maximum bid for the current high bidder, then the new bidder becomes the current high bidder, at a bid of one more than the previous high bidder's maximum. When the auction is over (the end of the input is reached), a history of the actual bids (the ones not discarded), from high bid to low bid, should be displayed. For example:

New Bid	Result	High Bidder	High Bid	Maximum Bid
7 John	New high bidder	John	1	7
5 Hank	High bid increased	John	5	7
10 Jill	New high bidder	Jill	8	10
8 Thad	No change	Jill	8	10
15 Joey	New high bidder	Joey	11	15

The bid history for this auction would be

Joey	11
Jill	8
John	5
John	1

Input/output details can be determined by you or your instructor. In any case, as input proceeds the current status of the auction should be displayed. The final output should include the bid history as described above.

49. Implement a Century Stack (see Exercise 24) using a linked list.

2.9 Application: Postfix Expression Evaluator

50. Evaluate the following postfix expressions.

    a. 5 7 8 * +

    b. 5 7 8 + *

    c. 5 7 + 8 *

    d. 1 2 + 3 4 + 5 6 * 2 * * +

51. Evaluate the following postfix expressions. Some of them may be ill-formed expressions—in that case, identify the appropriate error message (e.g., too many operands, too few operands).

    a. 1 2 3 4 5 + + +

    b. 1 2 + + 5

    c. 1 2 * 5 6 *

    d. / 23 * 87

    e. 4567 234 / 45372 231 * + 34526 342 / + 0 *

52. Revise and test the postfix expression evaluator program as specified here.

    a. Use the `ArrayListStack` class instead of the `ArrayBoundedStack` class— do not worry about stack overflow.

    b. Catch and handle the divide-by-zero situation that was assumed not to happen. For example, if the input expression is 5 3 3 - /, the result would be the message "illegal divide by zero."

    c. Support a new operation indicated by "^" that returns the larger of its operands. For example, 5 7 ^ = 7.

    d. Keep track of statistics about the numbers pushed onto the stack during the evaluation of an expression. The program should output the largest and smallest numbers pushed, the total numbers pushed, and the average value of pushed numbers.

2.10 Stack Variations

53. In the discussion of our Stack ADT, as compared to the classic definition of a stack, we stated that our `top` method is superfluous. Assume `myStack` is a stack of strings that uses the classic definition of the `pop` method. Create a code section that is functionally equivalent to the following line of code, but that does not use the `top` method:

```
System.out.println(myStack.top());
```

54. As discussed in this section, instead of having our stack methods throw exceptions in the case of "erroneous" invocations, we could have the stack methods handle the situation themselves. We define the following three "safe" methods:

    • `boolean safePush (T element)` —pushes `element` onto the stack; returns `true` if element successfully pushed, `false` otherwise

- `boolean safePop ( )` —removes the top element of the stack; returns `true` if element successfully popped, `false` otherwise
- `T safeTop( )` —if the stack is not empty returns the top element of the stack, otherwise returns `null`

a. Add these operations to the `ArrayBoundedStack` class. Create a test driver application to demonstrate that the added code works correctly.

b. Add these operations to the `ArrayListStack` class. Create a test driver application to demonstrate that the added code works correctly.

c. Add these operations to the `LinkedStack` class. Create a test driver application to demonstrate that the added code works correctly.

Exercises 55 to 58 require "outside" research.

55. Describe the major differences between the Java library's `Vector` and `ArrayList` classes.

56. Explain how the iterators in the Java Collections Framework are used.

57. What is the defining feature of the Java library's `Set` class?

58. Which classes of the Java library implement the `Collection` interface?

Recursion

Knowledge Goals

You should be able to

- define recursion
- discuss recursion as a problem-solving technique
- describe the three questions used to analyze a recursive approach
- do the following, given a recursive-problem description:
  - determine the base cases
  - determine the general cases
  - design the solution using recursion
- compare and contrast dynamic and static storage allocation
- explain how recursion works internally by showing the contents of the run-time stack
- explain why recursion may or may not be a good choice to implement the solution of a problem

Skill Goals

You should be able to

- do the following, given a recursive method:
  - determine under what conditions the method halts
  - determine the base cases
  - determine the general cases
  - determine what the method does
  - determine whether the method is correct and, if it is not, correct it
- verify a recursive method, using the Three-Question Approach
- decide whether a recursive solution is appropriate for a problem
- implement a recursive solution to a problem, if appropriate
- use a recursive approach to process an array
- use a recursive approach to process a linked list
- solve the Towers of Hanoi problem recursively
- generate a fractal image using recursion
- create an iterative version of a program that uses tail recursion
- replace a recursive solution with a solution based on a stack

This chapter introduces the topic of recursion—a distinct algorithmic problem-solving approach supported by many computer languages (Java included). What is recursion? Let us look first at a visual analogy.

You may have seen a set of brightly painted Russian dolls that fit inside one another. Inside the first doll is a smaller doll, inside of which is an even smaller doll, inside of which is yet a smaller doll, and so on. Solving a problem recursively is like taking apart such a set of Russian dolls. You first create smaller and smaller versions of the same problem until a version is reached that can no longer be subdivided (and that is easily solved)—that is, until the smallest doll is reached. Determining the overall solution often requires combining the smaller solutions, analogous to putting the dolls back together again.

Recursion, when applied properly, is an extremely *powerful* and *useful* problem solving tool. And it is fun! We will use it many times in upcoming chapters to support our work.

3.1 Recursive Definitions, Algorithms, and Programs

Recursive Definitions

You are already familiar with recursive definitions. Consider the following definition of the folder (or catalog, or directory) you use to organize files on a computer: A *folder* is an entity in a file system that contains a group of files and other *folders*. This definition is recursive because it expresses *folder* in terms of itself. A **recursive definition** is a definition in which something is defined in terms of smaller versions of itself.

Mathematicians regularly define concepts in terms of themselves. For instance, $n!$ (read "n factorial") is used to calculate the number of permutations of n elements. A nonrecursive definition of $n!$ is

$$n! = \begin{cases} 1 & \text{if } n = 0 \\ n \times (n-1) \times (n-2) \times \ldots \times 1 & \text{if } n > 0 \end{cases}$$

Consider the case of 4!. Because $n > 0$, we use the second part of the definition:

$$4! = 4 \times 3 \times 2 \times 1 = 24$$

This definition of $n!$ is not mathematically rigorous. It uses the three dots, rather informally, to stand for intermediate factors. For example, the definition of 8! is $8 \times 7 \times 6 \times \cdots \times 1$, with the . . . in this case standing for $5 \times 4 \times 3 \times 2$.

We can express $n!$ more elegantly, without using the three dots, by using recursion:

$$n! = \begin{cases} 1 & \text{if } n = 0 \\ n \times (n-1)! & \text{if } n > 0 \end{cases}$$

This is a recursive definition because it expresses the factorial function in terms of itself. The definition of 8! is now $8 \times 7!$.

Recursive Algorithms

Let us walk through the calculation of 4! using our recursive definition. We use a set of index cards to help track our work—not only does this demonstrate how to use a recursive definition, but it also models the actions of a computer system executing a recursive program.

We take out an index card and write on it:

Calculate 4!
4! =

Looking at our recursive definition we determine that 4 is greater than 0, so we use the second part of the definition and continue writing:

Calculate 4!
4! = 4 × (4 − 1)!
4! = 4 × 3!
4! = 4 × ☐

Of course, we cannot complete the third line because we do not know the value of 3!. Before continuing with our original problem (calculating 4!), we have to solve this new problem (calculating 3!). So we take out another index card, stack it on top of our original card, and write down our new problem:

Calculate 4!
4! Calculate 3!
4! 3! =
4!

Again we look at our recursive definition. We determine that 3 is greater than 0, so we use the second part of the definition and continue writing:

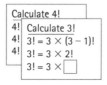

As before, we cannot complete the third line because we do not know the value of 2!. We take out another index card and write down our new problem. Continuing in this way we eventually have five cards stacked on our desk:

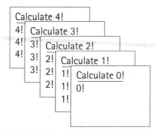

At this point, when we turn to our recursive definition to calculate 0! we find that we can use the first part of the definition: 0! equals 1. We can complete the top card as shown here:

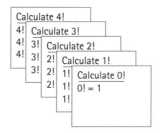

That finishes the problem at the top of our stack of cards. Its result is 1. Remembering that result, we throw away the top card, write the "1" into the empty slot on the card that is now on top (the *Calculate 1!* card), and continue working on that problem. Because we know how to calculate 1×1, we can quickly finish that problem and enter its result.

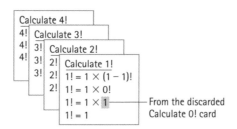

As before, we remember this result, discard the top card, enter the result onto the next card (the *Calculate 2!* card), and continue. In quick succession we determine that

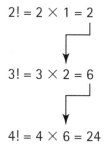

$$2! = 2 \times 1 = 2$$

$$3! = 3 \times 2 = 6$$

$$4! = 4 \times 6 = 24$$

ending with the solution to our original problem:

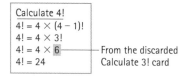

Calculate 4!
4! = 4 × (4 − 1)!
4! = 4 × 3!
4! = 4 × 6 ——————— From the discarded
4! = 24   Calculate 3! card

Note that we stopped creating new problem cards when we reached a case for which we know the answer without resorting to the recursive part of the definition. In this example, that point occurred when we reached *Calculate 0!*. We know that value is 1 directly from the definition without having to resort to recursion.

When the answer for a case is directly known, without requiring further recursion, it is called a **base case**. A recursive definition may have more than one base case. The case for which the solution is expressed in terms of a smaller version (or versions) of itself is called the **recursive or general case**. A recursive definition may also have more than one recursive case. A **recursive algorithm** is an algorithm that expresses a solution in terms of smaller versions of itself. A recursive algorithm must terminate; that is, it must have a base case, and the recursive cases must eventually lead to a base case.

Here is our recursive algorithm for calculating *n*! based directly on the recursive definition. It assumes that *n* is a nonnegative integer.

Factorial (int *n*)

```
// Precondition: n >= 0
if (n == 0)
      return (1)
else
      return (n * Factorial (n - 1))
```

Recursive Programs

In Java, a method can invoke other methods. A method can even invoke itself. When a method invokes itself, it is making a **recursive call**. It is only natural to use recursive method calls to implement recursive-problem solutions.

Here is a Java method that corresponds to our recursive factorial algorithm. It uses a recursive call (<u>emphasized</u>) to calculate the factorial of its integer argument.

```
public static int factorial(int n)
// Precondition: n is nonnegative
//
// Returns the value of "n!"
{
    if (n == 0)
        return 1;         // Base case
    else
        return (n * factorial(n - 1));      // General case

}
```

The argument in the recursive call, n - 1, is different from the argument in the original call, n. This is an important and necessary condition; otherwise, the method would continue calling itself indefinitely.

Suppose, for example, an application with access to the above method invokes the following statement:

```
System.out.println(factorial(4));
```

Much the same as with our index card example above, when the system is executing `factorial(4)` it invokes `factorial(3)`, that in turn invokes `factorial(2)`, that in turn invokes `factorial(1)`, that in turn invokes `factorial(0)` the base case. As you can see, the recursive calls lead to the base case where the chain of calls ends; otherwise it would recurse forever. At this point the chain of `return` statements begins, with `factorial(0)` returning 1, `factorial(1)` returning 1, `factorial(2)` returning 2, `factorial(3)` returning 6, and `factorial(4)` returning 24 which the application prints.

The `factorial` method is an example of direct recursion. **Direct recursion** is recursion in which a method directly calls itself. All of the examples in this chapter involve direct recursion. **Indirect recursion** is recursion in which a chain of two or more methods calls return to the method that originated the chain. For example, method A calls method B, and method B calls method A; the chain of method calls could be even longer, but if it eventually leads back to method A, then it is indirect recursion.

Iterative Solution for Factorial

Recursion is a powerful programming technique, but we must be careful when using it. Recursive solutions can be less efficient than iterative solutions to the same problem. In fact, some of the examples presented in this chapter, including `factorial`, are better suited to iterative approaches. This topic is discussed in depth in Section 3.8, "When to Use a Recursive Solution."

We used the factorial algorithm to demonstrate recursion because it is familiar and easy to visualize. In practice, we would never want to solve this problem using recursion, as a straightforward, more efficient iterative solution exists. Here we look at the iterative solution to the problem:

> **Important**
>
> We introduce recursion using the factorial problem because it is familiar to students and provides a clear example of a recursive definition, algorithm, and program. However, the iterative solution to factorial presented here is just as easy to understand as the recursive version and is more efficient because it does not require the overhead of so many method calls.

```
public static int factorial2(int n)
// Precondition: n is nonnegative
//
// Returns the value of retValue: n!
{
    int retValue = 1;
    while (n != 0)
    {
        retValue = retValue * n;
        n = n - 1;
    }
    return(retValue);
}
```

Iterative solutions tend to employ loops, whereas recursive solutions tend to have selection statements—either an *if* or a *switch* statement. A branching structure is usually the main control structure in a recursive method. A looping structure is the corresponding control structure in an iterative method. The iterative version of factorial has two local variables (`retValue` and n), whereas the recursive version has none. There are usually fewer local variables in a recursive method than in an iterative method. The iterative solution is more efficient because starting a new iteration of a loop is a faster operation than calling a method. Both the iterative and the recursive factorial methods are included within the `TestFactorial` application in the `ch03.apps` package.

3.2 The Three Questions

This section presents three questions to ask about any recursive algorithm or program. Using these questions helps us verify, design, and debug recursive solutions to problems.

Verifying Recursive Algorithms

The kind of walk-through presented in Section 3.1, "Recursive Definitions, Algorithms, and Programs" (using index cards), is useful for understanding the recursive process, but it is not sufficient for validating the correctness of a recursive algorithm. After all, simulating the execution of `factorial(4)` tells us the method works when the argument equals 4, but it does not tell us whether the method is valid for other arguments.

We use the Three-Question Approach for verifying recursive algorithms. To verify that a recursive solution works, we must be able to answer yes to all three of these questions:

1. *The Base-Case Question*   Is there a nonrecursive way out of the algorithm, and does the algorithm work correctly for this base case?
2. *The Smaller-Caller Question*   Does each recursive call to the algorithm involve a smaller case of the original problem, leading inescapably to the base case?
3. *The General-Case Question*   Assuming the recursive call(s) to the smaller case(s) works correctly, does the algorithm work correctly for the general case?

Let us apply these three questions to the `factorial` algorithm:

Factorial (int n)

```
// Precondition: n >= 0
if (n == 0)
     return (1)
else
     return (n * Factorial (n - 1))
```

1. *The Base-Case Question*   The base case occurs when *n* is 0. The `Factorial` algorithm then returns the value of 1, which is the correct value of 0! by definition. The answer is yes.
2. *The Smaller-Caller Question*   The parameter is *n* and the recursive call passes the argument *n* – 1. Therefore each subsequent recursive call sends a smaller value, until the value sent is finally 0, which is the base case. The answer is yes.
3. *The General-Case Question*   Assuming that the recursive call `Factorial(n - 1)` gives us the correct value of (*n* – 1)!, the *return* statement computes *n* * (*n* – 1)!. This is the definition of a factorial, so we know that the algorithm works in the general case—assuming it works in the smaller case. The answer is yes.

Because the answers to all three questions are yes, we can conclude that the algorithm works. If you are familiar with inductive proofs, you should recognize what we have done. Having made the assumption that the algorithm works for the smaller case, we have shown that the algorithm works for the general case. Because we have also shown that the algorithm works for the base case of 0, we have inductively shown that it works for any integer argument greater than or equal to 0.

Determining Input Constraints

For the factorial problem we assumed the original value for n is greater than or equal to 0. Note that without this assumption we cannot answer the smaller-caller question affirmatively. For example, starting with $n = -5$, the recursive call would pass an argument of -6, which is farther from the base case, not closer, as required.

These kinds of constraints often exist on the input arguments for a recursive algorithm. We can typically use our three-question analysis to determine these constraints. Simply check whether there are any starting argument values for which the smaller call does not produce a new argument that is closer to the base case. Such starting values are invalid. Constrain your legal input arguments so that these values are not permitted.

Writing Recursive Methods

The questions used for verifying recursive algorithms can also be used as a guide for writing recursive methods. Here is a good approach to designing a recursive method:

1. Get an exact definition of the problem to be solved.
2. Determine the size of the problem to be solved. On the initial call to the method, the size of the whole problem is expressed in the value(s) of the argument(s).
3. Identify and solve the base case(s) in which the problem can be expressed nonrecursively. This ensures a yes answer to the base-case question.
4. Identify and solve the general case(s) correctly in terms of a smaller case of the same problem—a recursive call. This ensures yes answers to the smaller-caller and general-case questions.

In the case of the factorial problem, the definition of the problem is summarized in the definition of the factorial function. The size of the problem is the number of values to be multiplied: n. The base case occurs when n is 0, in which case we take the nonrecursive path. The general case occurs when $n > 0$, resulting in a recursive call to `factorial` for a smaller case: `factorial(n - 1)`. Summarizing this information in table form:

Recursive factorial(int *n*) method: returns int

Definition:	Calculates and returns *n*!
Precondition:	*n* is nonnegative
Size:	Value of *n*
Base Case:	If *n* equals 0, return 1
General Case:	If $n > 0$, return $n *$ factorial($n - 1$)

Debugging Recursive Methods

Because of their nested calls to themselves, recursive methods can be confusing to debug. The most serious problem is the possibility that the method recurses forever. A typical symptom of this problem is an error message telling us that the system has run out of space in the run-time stack, due to the level of recursive calls. (Section 3.7, "Removing Recursion," looks at how recursion uses the run-time stack.) Using the Three-Question Approach to verify recursive methods and determine argument constraints should help us avoid this problem.

Success with the three questions does not guarantee, however, that the program will not fail due to lack of space. Section 3.8, "When to Use a Recursive Solution," discusses the amount of space overhead required to support recursive method calls. Because a call to a recursive method may generate many levels of method calls to itself, the space consumed might be more than the system can handle.

One error that programmers often make when they first start writing recursive methods is to use a looping structure instead of a branching one. Because they tend to think of the problem in terms of a repetitive action, they inadvertently use a *while* statement rather than an *if* statement. The body of a recursive method should always break down into base and recursive cases. Hence, we use a branching statement. It is a good idea to double-check our recursive methods to make sure that we used an *if* or *switch* statement to select the recursive or base case.

3.3   Recursive Processing of Arrays

Many problems related to arrays lend themselves to a recursive solution. After all, a subsection of an array (a "subarray") can also be viewed as an array. If we can solve an array-related problem by combining solutions to a related problem on subarrays, we may be able to use a recursive approach.

Binary Search

The general problem addressed in this section is finding a target element in a sorted array. Our approach is to examine the midpoint of the array and compare the element found there to our target element—if we are lucky they are "equal," but even if not lucky we are able to eliminate half the array from further consideration depending on whether our target element is greater than or less than the examined element. We repeatedly examine the middle element in the remaining part of the array, eliminating half the remaining elements until we either find our target or determine that it is not in the array.

This approach is an example of the "decrease and conquer" algorithm design technique—we conquer the problem by decreasing the size of the array subsection to search at each stage of

---

Recognize the Algorithm?

You may recognize the algorithm used in this section—it is the Binary Search algorithm, one of the approaches used in Section 1.6, "Comparing Algorithms: Order of Growth Analysis," to play the Hi-Lo guessing game. Our analysis in Section 1.6 revealed that this is an efficient search approach, $O(\log_2 N)$ where N represents the size of the original search area.

the solution process. The specific decrease and conquer algorithm used here is called the Binary Search algorithm.

Binary Search is a good fit for a recursive implementation. At the end of any stage in which the target is not located we continue by searching a portion of the original array—and we can use Binary Search to search that subarray.

Assume we have a sorted array of int named `values` that is accessible from within the recursive method `binarySearch`. Our specific problem is to determine if a given int named `target` is in the array. We pass our recursive method the target element and both the starting and ending indices of the portion of the array we are still searching. The signature for the method therefore is

```
boolean binarySearch(int target, int first, int last)
```

Here we use a specific example to help us add detail to our algorithm and create our code. Let us search for the value 20 in an array containing 4, 6, 7, 15, 20, 22, 25, and 27. At the beginning of our search `first` is 0 and `last` is 7; therefore we invoke `binarySearch(20, 0, 7)` resulting in

target: 20

	first=0						last=7
	[0]	[1]	[2]	[3]	[4]	[5]	[6]	[7]
values:	4	6	7	15	20	22	25	27

The midpoint is the average of `first` and `last`

```
midpoint = (first + last) / 2;
```

giving us the following:

target: 20

	first=0			midpoint=3			last=7
	[0]	[1]	[2]	[3]	[4]	[5]	[6]	[7]
values:	4	6	7	15	20	22	25	27

If `values[midpoint]` (which is 15) equals `target` (which is 20) then we are finished and can return `true`. Unfortunately it does not. However, since `values[midpoint]` is less than `target` we know we can eliminate the lower half of the array from consideration. We set `first` to `midpoint + 1` and recursively call `binarySearch(20, 4, 7)`. A new `midpoint` is calculated resulting in

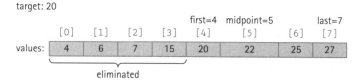

This time `values[midpoint]` is greater than `target` so we can eliminate the upper half of the remaining portion of the array from consideration. We set `last` to

`midpoint - 1` and recursively call `binarySearch(20, 4, 4)`, again calculating a new `midpoint`, resulting in

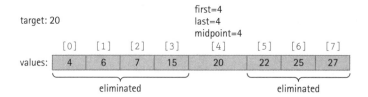

Finally, `values[midpoint]` equals `target` so we are finished and can return `true`.

Through this example we have identified how to handle the cases where the element at array location `midpoint` is less than, greater than, and equal to `target`. But we still need to determine how to terminate the algorithm if the targeted element is not in the array.

Consider the above example again, but this time with 18 replacing 20 as the fifth element of `values`. The same sequence of steps would occur until at the very last step we have the following:

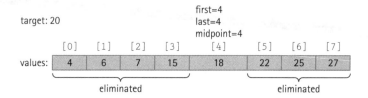

Continuing from this point we see that `values[midpoint]` is less than `target` so we set `first` to `midpoint + 1` and recursively call `binarySearch(20, 5, 4)`:

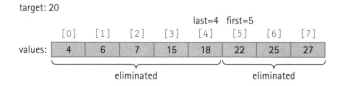

Note that we have eliminated the entire array from consideration and are invoking `binarySearch` with a `first` argument that is larger than the `last` argument. This is obviously a degenerate situation—attempting to search a space in the array that does not exist. It is in this situation where the method returns `false`, indicating that `target` is not in the array.

Here is a summary table for the algorithm:

Binary Search(target, first, last): returns boolean

Definition:	returns true if target is in sorted array values between index first and index last inclusive, otherwise returns false
Precondition:	first and last are valid array indices
Size:	last − first + 1
Note:	midpoint is calculated as (first + last)/2
Base Cases:	if first > last return false
	if values[midpoint] == target return true
General Cases:	if values[midpoint] < target return BinarySearch(target, midpoint+1, last)
	if values[midpoint] > target return BinarySearch(target, first, midpoint−1)

Let us verify Binary Search using the Three-Question approach:

1. *The Base-Case Question* There are two base cases.
   a. If `first` > `last` the algorithm returns `false`. This is correct because in this case there are no array elements to search.
   b. If `values[midpoint]` == `target` the algorithm returns `true`. This is correct because `target` has been found.

   The answer is yes.

2. *The Smaller-Caller Question* In the general case `binarySearch` is called with parameters `first` and `last` indicating the start and end of a subarray to search, with `first <= last`. Because the `midpoint` is calculated as `(first + last)/2` it must be `>= first` and `<= last`. Therefore, the size of the ranges (`midpoint+1`, `last`) and (`first`, `midpoint-1`) must be less than the range (`first`, `last`). The answer is yes.

3. *The General-Case Question*
   Assuming that the recursive calls `binarySearch(target, midpoint+1, last)` and `binarySearch(target, first, midpoint-1)` give the correct result, then the `return` statement

> **Preventing Overflow**
>
> If a large array is being searched and the search has been narrowed down to the higher end of the array, it is possible that both `first` and `last` are large numbers. Adding together two large numbers can cause arithmetic overflow. Therefore, it is safer in such cases to use "`first + (last - first) / 2`" to calculate the midpoint. Nevertheless, for the sake of clarity, we will use "`(first + last) / 2`" within the text code. In most practical situations it is safe and it is easier to read and understand.

gives the correct result because it has already been determined that `target` could not be in the other part of the array—whether or not it is in the array completely depends on whether or not it is in the indicated subarray. The answer is yes.

Because the answers to all three questions are yes, we can conclude that the algorithm works. Here is the code:

```
boolean binarySearch(int target, int first, int last)
// Precondition: first and last are legal indices of values
//
// If target is contained in values[first,last] return true
// otherwise return false.
{
    int midpoint = (first + last) / 2;
    if (first > last)
        return false;
    else
        if (target == values[midpoint])
            return true;
        else
        if (target > values[midpoint])    // target too high
            return binarySearch(target, midpoint + 1, last);
        else                              // target too low
            return binarySearch(target, first, midpoint - 1);
}
```

This code can be found in a file `BinarySearch.java` in the package `ch03.apps`. The code also includes an iterative version of the algorithm that is not much different than the recursive version. Note that this algorithm has already been analyzed for efficiency. It is $O(\log_2 N)$—see the latter part of Section 1.6, "Comparing Algorithms: Order of Growth Analysis."

3.4   Recursive Processing of Linked Lists

Arrays and linked lists (references) are our two basic building blocks for creating data structures. The previous section discussed some examples of recursive processing with arrays. This section does the same for linked lists. To simplify our linked list figures in this section, we sometimes use a capital letter to stand for a node's information, an arrow to represent the link to the next node (as always), and a slash to represent the `null` reference.

Recursive Nature of Linked Lists

Recursive approaches often work well for processing linked lists. This is because a linked list is itself a recursive structure, even more so than the array. Section 2.7, "Introduction to Linked Lists" introduced the LLNode class, our building block for linked lists. It noted that LLNode is a self-referential class, indicating that an LLNode object contains a reference to an LLNode object as emphasized in the following code segment:

```
public class LLNode<T>
{
    protected T info;             // information stored in list
    protected LLNode<T> link;     // reference to a node
    . . .
```

Self-referential classes are closely related to recursion. In a certain sense, they are recursive.

A linked list is either empty or consists of a node containing two parts: information and a linked list. For example, list1 is empty whereas list2 (the list containing A, B, and C) contains a reference to an LLNode object that contains information (A) and a linked list (the list containing B and C):

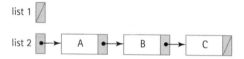

Note that the link value in the "last" node on the list is always null. When we process linked lists recursively, processing this null value is typically a base case.

Traversing a Linked List

Traversing a linked list in order to visit each element and perform some type of processing is a common operation. Suppose we wish to print the contents of the list. The recursive algorithm is straightforward—if the list is empty do nothing; otherwise, print the information in the current node, followed by printing the information in the remainder of the list (see **Figure 3.1**).

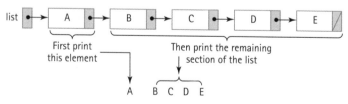

Figure 3.1   Printing a list recursively

Transforming this algorithm into code is also straightforward:

```
void recPrintList(LLNode<String> listRef)
// Prints the contents of the listRef linked list to standard output
{
    if (listRef != null)
    {
        System.out.println(listRef.getInfo());
        recPrintList(listRef.getLink());
    }
}
```

Within the *if* statement the content of the first node on the list pointed to by listRef is printed, followed by the recursive call to recPrintList that prints the remainder of the list. Our base case occurs when we reach the end of the list and listRef is null, in which case the *if* statement is skipped and processing stops. Here we verify recPrintList using the Three-Question Approach.

1. *The Base-Case Question* When listRef is equal to null, we skip the *if* body and return. Nothing is printed, which is appropriate for an empty list. The answer is yes.

2. *The Smaller-Caller Question* The recursive call passes the list referenced by lis-tRef.getLink(), which is one node smaller than the list referenced by listRef. Eventually it will pass the empty list; that is, it will pass the null reference found in the last node on the original list. That is the base case. The answer is yes.

3. *The General-Case Question* We assume that the statement

   ```
   recPrintList (listRef.getLink());
   ```

   correctly prints out the rest of the list; printing the first element followed by correctly printing the rest of the list gives us the whole list. The answer is yes.

Note that it is also easy to traverse a linked list using an iterative (nonrecursive) approach. When we first looked at linked lists in Section 2.7, "Introduction to Linked Lists," we developed an iterative approach to printing the contents of a linked list. It is instructive to compare the two approaches side-by-side:

Iterative

```
while (listRef != null)
{
  System.out.println(listRef.getInfo());
  listRef = listRef.getLink();
}
```

Recursive

```
if (listRef != null)
{
  System.out.println(listRef.getInfo());
  recPrintList(listRef.getLink());
}
```

The iterative version moves through the list using a *while* loop, looping until it encounters the end of the list. Similarly, the recursive version moves through the list until it reaches the end but in this case the repetition is achieved through the repetitive recursive calls.

The same coding patterns we see above can be used to solve many other problems related to traversing a linked list. For example, consider the following two methods that return the number of elements in the linked list passed as an argument and that use the same patterns established above. The first method uses the iterative approach and the second a recursive approach.

```
int iterListSize(LLNode<String> listRef)
// Returns the size of the listRef linked list
{
    int size = 0;
    while (listRef != null)
    {
        size = size + 1;
        listRef = listRef.getLink();
    }
    return size;
}
```

```
int recListSize(LLNode<String> listRef)
// Returns the size of the listRef linked list
{
    if (listRef == null)
        return 0;
    else
        return 1 + recListSize(listRef.getLink());
}
```

Note that the iterative version declares a variable (`size`) to hold the intermediate values of the computation. This is not necessary for the recursive version because the intermediate values are generated by the recursive *return* statements.

An interesting variation of the print list problem more clearly demonstrates the usefulness of recursion, because it is more easily solved recursively than iteratively. Suppose we want to print the list in reverse order—print the information in the last node first, then the information in the next-to-last node second, and so on. As when printing in the forward direction, the recursive algorithm is straightforward (at least it is if you are comfortable with recursion)—if the list is empty do nothing; otherwise, reverse print the information in the second-through-last nodes, followed by printing the information in the first node (see **Figure 3.2**).

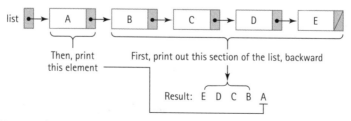

Figure 3.2   Printing a list in reverse recursively

The corresponding code is almost identical to `recPrintList`—we just need to switch the order of the two statements within the *if statement* and, of course, we also change the name of the method:

```
void recRevPrintList(LLNode<String> listRef)
// Prints the contents of the listRef linked list to standard output
// in reverse order
{
   if (listRef != null)
   {
      recRevPrintList(listRef.getLink());
      System.out.println(listRef.getInfo());
   }
}
```

Attempting to solve this version of the list printing problem is not as easy if you use an iterative method. One approach is to traverse the list and count the elements, then repeatedly retraverse the list to the next element to be printed, carefully counting one less element each time. That is an $O(N^2)$ approach. A more efficient approach is to traverse the list only once, pushing each element onto a stack. When you reach the end of the list you repeatedly pop the elements off the stack and print them. Using a stack to "replace" recursion is not uncommon—we will return to that idea in Section 3.7, "Removing Recursion."

Transforming a Linked List

This subsection considers operations that transform a linked list, for example, adding or removing elements. Using recursive methods to make these types of changes to a linked list is more complicated than just traversing the list. We will use lists of strings in our examples in this subsection.

Suppose we wish to create a recursive method `recInsertEnd` that accepts a `String` argument and a list argument (a variable of type `LLNode<String>`), and inserts the string at the end of the list. We reason that if the link of the list argument is not `null` then we need to insert the string into the sublist pointed to by that link—this is our recursive call. Our base case is when the link is `null`, which indicates the end of the list where the insertion occurs. Based on this reasoning we devise the following code:

```
void recInsertEnd(String newInfo, LLNode<String> listRef)
// Adds newInfo to the end of the listRef linked list
{
   if (listRef.getLink() != null)
      recInsertEnd(newInfo, listRef.getLink());
   else
      listRef.setLink(new LLNode<String>(newInfo));
}
```

There is a problem, though, with this approach. Do you see it?

The code does work in the general case. Suppose we have a linked list of strings named `myList` consisting of "Ant" and "Bat."

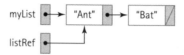

We wish to insert "Cat" at the end of this list so we invoke

`recInsertEnd("Cat", myList);`

As processing within the method begins we have the following arrangement:

It is not difficult to trace the code and see that because the link in the "Ant" node, the node referenced by `listRef`, is *not* `null`, the *if* clause will be executed. Therefore, `recInsertEnd` is invoked again, this time with a reference to the "Bat" node:

In this case the *else* clause of `recInsertEnd` is executed, because the link of the "Bat" node *is* `null`, and a new node containing "Cat" is created and appended to the list. So, where is the problem?

As always when designing solutions we need to ask if our approach works for all situations, in particular for special situations, what some call "borderline" conditions. What special situation can occur when inserting into a linked list? What if the list is empty to start with?

If we invoke

`recInsertEnd("Cat", myList);`

under this condition there is trouble—we pass a `null` reference to the method, so `listRef` is `null` and the method immediately attempts to use `listRef` to invoke `getLink`:

`if (listRef.getLink() != null). . .`

It is not possible to invoke a method on a `null` reference—a null pointer exception is thrown by the run-time system—to prevent this we need to handle the special case of insertion into an empty list.

In the case of an empty list we want to set the list reference itself to point to a new node containing the argument string. In our example we wish to be left with the following:

Due to Java's pass-by-value only policy, we cannot directly change myList within the re-cInsertEnd method. As is shown in the figures above, the parameter listRef is an alias of the argument myList and as an alias it lets us access whatever myList is referencing (the list), but it does not give us access to myList itself. We cannot change the reference contained in myList using this approach. We need to find another way.

The solution to this dilemma is to have the recInsertEnd method return a reference to the new list. The returned reference can be assigned to the myList variable. Therefore, instead of invoking

```
recInsertEnd("Cat", myList);
```

we invoke

```
myList = recInsertEnd("Cat", myList);
```

This is the only way to change the value held in myList. We use this same approach later in the text to create transformer algorithms for trees.

Other than the fact that we return a list reference, our processing is similar to that used in the previous (erroneous) solution. Here is the corresponding code:

```
LLNode<String> recInsertEnd(String newInfo, LLNode<String> listRef)
// Adds newInfo to the end of the listRef linked list
{
    if (listRef != null)
        listRef.setLink(recInsertEnd(newInfo, listRef.getLink()));
    else
        listRef = new LLNode<String>(newInfo);
    return listRef;
}
```

Tracing this code on the case of inserting "Cat" at the end of an empty myList we see that the *else* clause creates a new node containing "Cat" and returns a reference to it, and therefore myList correctly references the singleton "Cat" node.

Now we must return to the general case and verify that our new approach works correctly. Again, we have a linked list of strings named myList consisting of "Ant" and "Bat."

We wish to insert "Cat" at the end of this list so we invoke

```
myList = recInsertEnd("Cat", myList);
```

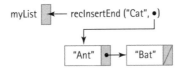

The call to `recInsertEnd` would return a link to the list obtained by inserting "Cat" at the end of the list "Ant"-"Bat." It operates on the node containing "Ant." Because that list is not empty, this first instance of `recInsertEnd` would recursively invoke `recInsertEnd`, setting the link of the node containing "Ant" to the list obtained by inserting "Cat" at the end of the list "Bat."

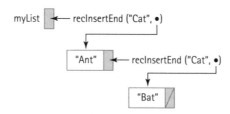

Within this second instance of the method it is still the case the list is not empty, so it would invoke a third instance, setting the link of the node containing "Bat" to the list obtained by inserting "Cat" at the end of the empty list.

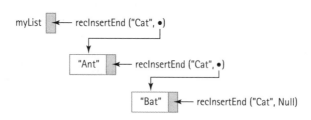

The third instance of `recInsertEnd` is invoked on an empty list, so the *if* clause is finally triggered and a node containing "Cat" is created. A reference to this new node is returned to the second instance, which sets the link of the node containing "Bat" to the new node.

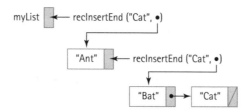

The second instance returns a reference to the node containing "Bat" to the first instance, which sets the link of the first node on the list to refer to the "Bat" node (*note:* it already did refer to that node so no change is really made here).

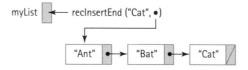

And finally, the first instance returns a reference to the node containing "Ant," and `myL-ist` is set equal to that value (again, it already did refer to that node so no change is really made here).

All of the code developed in this section is included in the file `LinkedListRecursive.java` in the `ch03.apps` package. The application includes the methods plus test code that exercises each of the methods on lists of size 0, 1, and 5.

3.5 Towers

The Towers of Hanoi is a popular example of the expressiveness of recursion. We are able to solve a seemingly complex problem with just a few lines of recursive code.

One of your first toys may have been a plastic contraption with pegs holding colored rings of different diameters. If so, you probably spent countless hours moving the rings from one peg to another. If we put some constraints on how they can be moved, we have an adult puzzle game called the Towers of Hanoi. When the game begins, all the rings are on the first peg in order by size, with the smallest on the top. The object of the game is to move the rings, one at a time, to the third peg. The catch is that a ring cannot be placed on top of one that is smaller in diameter. The middle peg can be used as an auxiliary peg, but it must be empty at the beginning and at the end of the game. The rings can only be moved one at a time. Our task is to create a method that prints out the series of moves required to solve this puzzle.

The Algorithm

To gain insight into how we might solve the Towers of Hanoi problem, consider a puzzle that starts with four rings, as shown in **Figure 3.3a**. Our task is to move the four rings from the start peg, peg 1, to the end peg, peg 3, with the aid of the auxiliary peg, peg 2.

It turns out that due to the constraints of the problem and the fact that we should not recreate a previous configuration (that might leave us in an infinite loop), each move is fairly obvious. For the first move we must move the smallest ring, so we move it to peg 2 resulting in the configuration shown in Figure 3.3b. Next, because there is no reason to move the smallest ring again, we move the second smallest ring from peg 1 to peg 3, resulting in the configuration shown in Figure 3.3c. You can follow all 15 required moves in Figure 3.3. The small arrows in the figure point to the most recent target peg.

Note the intermediate configuration of the puzzle in Figure 3.3h, after seven moves have been made, the moves represented by

The Towers Legend

The Towers of Hanoi puzzle was invented by Édouard Lucas in 1883. The legend behind the puzzle is instructive. A temple exists in Hanoi where monks work day and night to solve a version of the problem. The monks make one move every second. When they complete their task the world will disappear! No worries, however, their tower consists of 64 rings and requires many moves to solve. How many moves and how much time? Well for that answer, solve Exercise 22.

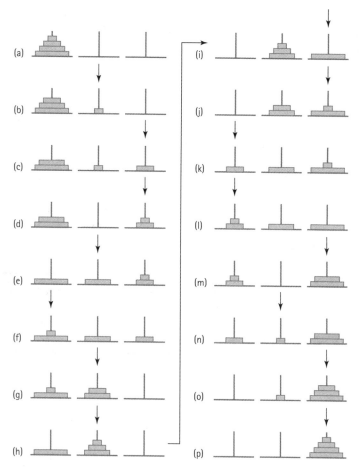

Figure 3.3 Towers of Hanoi solution for four rings

Figures 3.3a through 3.3h. At this point we have successfully moved the three smallest rings from peg 1 to peg 2, using peg 3 as an auxiliary peg as summarized here.

This allows us to move the largest ring from peg 1 to peg 3.

Can you see why at this point we are halfway to our completed solution? What remains is to move the three smallest rings from peg 2 to peg 3, using peg 1 as an auxiliary peg. This task is achieved by the seven moves represented by Figures 3.3i through 3.3p.

These seven moves are essentially the same moves made in the first seven steps, albeit with different starting, ending, and auxiliary pegs (compare the patterns of the small arrows to verify this statement). Those last seven moves are summarized here.

We solve the puzzle for four rings by first moving three rings from peg 1 to peg 2, then moving the largest ring from peg 1 to peg 3, and finally by moving three rings (again) from peg 2 to peg 3. Aha! We solve the puzzle for four rings by solving the puzzle for three rings—in fact by solving the puzzle for three rings twice.

It is this insight, the recognition of a solution to the problem that uses solutions to smaller versions of the problem, that leads us to our recursive solution. We can solve the general problem for *n* rings the same way. The general recursive algorithm for moving *n* rings from the starting peg to the destination peg is as follows.

Move n Rings from Starting Peg to Destination Peg

Move n – 1 rings from starting peg to auxiliary peg
Move the *n*th ring from starting peg to destination peg
Move n – 1 rings from auxiliary peg to destination peg

The Method

Let us write a recursive method that implements this algorithm. We can see that recursion works well because the first and third steps of the algorithm essentially repeat the overall algorithm, albeit with a smaller number of rings. Notice, however, that the starting peg, the destination peg, and the auxiliary peg are different for the subproblems; they keep changing during the recursive execution of the algorithm. To make the method easier to follow, the pegs are called `startPeg`, `endPeg`, and `auxPeg`. These three pegs, along with the number of rings on the starting peg, are the parameters of the method. The program will not actually move any rings but it will print out a message describing the moves.

Our algorithm explicitly defines the recursive or general case, but what about a base case? How do we know when to stop the recursive process? The key is to note that if there is only one ring to move we can just move it; there are no smaller disks to worry about. Therefore, when the number of rings equals 1, we simply print the move. That is the base case. The method assumes the arguments passed are valid.

```
public static void doTowers(
        int n,           // Number of rings to move
        int startPeg,    // Peg containing rings to move
        int auxPeg,      // Peg holding rings temporarily
        int endPeg)      // Peg receiving rings being moved
```

```
{
    if (n == 1) // Base case - Move one ring
        System.out.println("Move ring " + n + " from peg " + startPeg
                                + " to peg " + endPeg);
    else
    {
        // Move n - 1 rings from starting peg to auxiliary peg
        doTowers(n - 1, startPeg, endPeg, auxPeg);
        // Move nth ring from starting peg to ending peg
        System.out.println("Move ring " + n + " from peg " + startPeg
                                + " to peg " + endPeg);
        // Move n - 1 rings from auxiliary peg to ending peg
        doTowers(n - 1, auxPeg, startPeg, endPeg);
    }
}
```

It is hard to believe that such a simple method actually works, but it does. Let us investigate using the Three-Question Approach:

1. *The Base-Case Question*   Is there a nonrecursive way out of the method, and does the method work correctly for this base case? If the doTowers method is passed an argument equal to 1 for the number of rings (parameter n), it prints the move, correctly recording the movement of a single ring from startPeg to endPeg, and skips the body of the *else* statement. No recursive calls are made. This response is appropriate because there is only one ring to move and no smaller rings to worry about. The answer to the base-case question is yes.

2. *The Smaller-Caller Question*   Does each recursive call to the method involve a smaller case of the original problem, leading inescapably to the base case? The answer is yes, because the method receives a ring count argument n and in its recursive calls passes the ring count argument n - 1. The subsequent recursive calls also pass a decremented value of the argument, until finally the value sent is 1.

3. *The General-Case Question*   Assuming the recursive calls work correctly, does the method work in the general case? The answer is yes. Our goal is to move *n* rings from the starting peg to the ending peg. The first recursive call within the method moves *n* – 1 rings from the starting peg to the auxiliary peg. Assuming that operation works correctly, we now have one ring left on the starting peg and the ending peg is empty. That ring must be the largest, because all of the other rings were on top of it. We can move that ring directly from the starting peg to the ending peg, as described in the output statement. The second recursive call now moves the *n* – 1 rings that are on the auxiliary peg to the ending peg, placing them on top of the largest ring that was just moved. As we assume this transfer works correctly, we now have all *n* rings on the ending peg.

We have answered all three questions affirmatively.

The Program

We enclose the doTowers method within a driver class called Towers. It prompts the user for the number of rings and then uses doTowers to report the solution. Our program ensures that doTowers is called with a positive integral argument. The Towers application can be found in the ch03.apps package. Here is the output from a run with four rings:

```
Input the number of rings: 4
Towers of Hanoi with 4 rings
Move ring 1 from peg 1 to peg 2
Move ring 2 from peg 1 to peg 3
Move ring 1 from peg 2 to peg 3
Move ring 3 from peg 1 to peg 2
Move ring 1 from peg 3 to peg 1
Move ring 2 from peg 3 to peg 2
Move ring 1 from peg 1 to peg 2
Move ring 4 from peg 1 to peg 3
Move ring 1 from peg 2 to peg 3
Move ring 2 from peg 2 to peg 1
Move ring 1 from peg 3 to peg 1
Move ring 3 from peg 2 to peg 3
Move ring 1 from peg 1 to peg 2
Move ring 2 from peg 1 to peg 3
Move ring 1 from peg 2 to peg 3
```

Try the program for yourself. But be careful—with two recursive calls within the doTowers method, the amount of output generated by the program grows quickly. In fact, every time you add one more ring to the starting peg, you more than double the amount of output from the program. A run of Towers on the author's system, with an input argument indicating 16 rings, generated a 10-megabyte output file.

3.6   Fractals

As discussed in the "Generating Images" boxed feature in Chapter 1, digitized images can be viewed as two dimensional arrays of picture elements called pixels. In this section we investigate an approach to generating interesting, beautiful images with a simple recursive program.

There are many different ways that people define the term "fractal." Mathematicians study continuous but not differentiable functions, scientists notice patterns in nature that repeat certain statistical measurements within themselves,

Practical Fractals

In addition to being interesting and eye-pleasing, there are practical uses for fractals. Computer graphics experts use them to help generate realistic-looking scenery, engineers use them to build strong antenna, and scientists use them to model the weather, fluid dynamics, and coastline formations, among other things.

and engineers create hierarchical self-similar structures. For our purposes we define a fractal as an image that is composed of smaller versions of itself. Using recursion it is easy to generate interesting and eye-pleasing fractal images.

A T-Square Fractal

In the center of a square black canvas we draw a white square, one-quarter the size of the canvas (see **Figure 3.4a**). We then draw four more squares, each centered at a corner of the original white square, each one-quarter the size of the original white square, that is, one-eighth the size of the canvas (see Figure 3.4b). For each of these new squares we do the same, drawing four squares of smaller size at each of their corners (see Figure 3.4c). And again (see Figure 3.4d). We continue this recursive drawing scheme, drawing smaller and smaller squares, until we can no longer draw any more squares, that is until our integer division gives a result of zero (see Figure 3.4e and a larger version in **Figure 3.5a**). Theoretically, using real number division, we could continue dividing the size of the squares by four forever. This is why people sometimes view fractals as infinitely recursive.

Our resulting image is a fractal called a T-square because within it we can see shapes that remind us of the technical drawing instrument of the same name. The approach used to create the T-square is similar to approaches used to create some better-known fractals, specifically the Koch snowflake and Sierpinski triangle, both based on recursively drawing equilateral triangles and the Sierpinski carpet, which is also based on recursively drawing squares but features eight squares drawn along the border of the original square.

The following program creates a 1,000 × 1,000 pixel jpg file containing a T-square fractal image. The name of the file to hold the generated image is provided as a command line argument. The program first "paints" the entire image black and then calls the recursive `drawSquare` method, passing it the coordinates of the "first" square and the length of a side. The `drawSquare` method computes the corners of the square, "paints" the square white, and then recursively calls itself, passing as arguments the coordinates of its four corners and the required smaller side dimension. This calling pattern repeats over and over until the base case is reached. The base case occurs when the size of the side of the square to be drawn is 0. The visual result of running the program can be seen in Figure 3.5a.

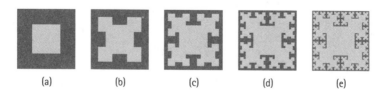

(a)   (b)   (c)   (d)   (e)

Figure 3.4   Stages of drawing a T-square

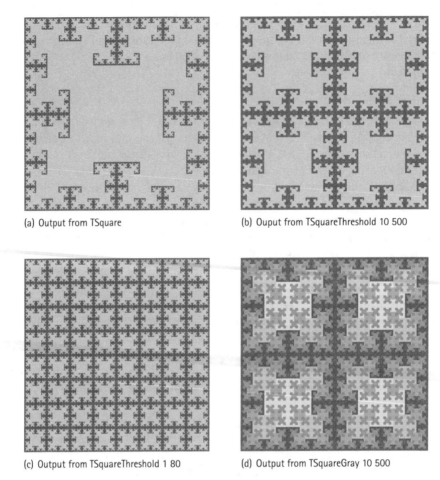

(a) Output from TSquare

(b) Ouput from TSquareThreshold 10 500

(c) Output from TSquareThreshold 1 80

(d) Output from TSquareGray 10 500

Figure 3.5 Samples of variations on the T-square application

```
//***********************************************************************
// TSquare.java            By Dale/Joyce/Weems            Chapter 3
//
// Creates a jpg file containing a recursive TSquare.
// Run argument 1: full name of target jpg file
//
//***********************************************************************
package ch03.fractals;

import java.awt.image.*;        import java.awt.Color;
import java.io.*;               import javax.imageio.*;
```

```java
public class TSquare
{
    static final int SIDE = 1000;      // image is SIDE X SIDE
    static BufferedImage image =
            new BufferedImage(SIDE, SIDE, BufferedImage.TYPE_INT_RGB);
    static final int WHITE = Color.WHITE.getRGB();
    static final int BLACK = Color.BLACK.getRGB();

    private static void drawSquare(int x, int y, int s)
    // center of square is x,y length of side is s
    {
        if (s <= 0) // base case
            return;
        else
        {
            // determine corners
            int left = x - s/2;      int right = x + s/2;
            int top = y - s/2;       int bottom = y + s/2;

            // paint the white square
            for (int i = left; i < right; i++)
                for (int j = top; j < bottom; j++)
                {
                    image.setRGB(i, j, WHITE);
                }

            // recursively paint squares at the corners
            drawSquare(left, top, s/2);
            drawSquare(left, bottom, s/2);
            drawSquare(right, top, s/2);
            drawSquare(right, bottom, s/2);
        }
    }
    public static void main (String[] args) throws IOException
    {
        String fileOut = args[0];

        // make image black
        for (int i = 0; i < SIDE; i++)
            for (int j = 0; j < SIDE; j++)
            {
                image.setRGB(i, j, BLACK);
            }
```

```
        // first square
        drawSquare(SIDE/2, SIDE/2, SIDE/2);

        // save image
        File outputfile = new File(fileOut);
        ImageIO.write(image, "jpg", outputfile);
    }
}
```

Variations

By slightly modifying our TSquare.java program we can generate additional interesting images. Figure 3.5 shows some examples generated by the program variations described below. Part (a) of the figure shows the output from the original TSquare program.
Note that all of the applications in this section are found in the ch03.fractals package.

The TSquareThreshold.java application allows the user to supply two additional arguments, both of type int, that indicate when to start and when to stop drawing squares. The first int argument indicates an inner threshold—if drawSqaure
is invoked with a side value less than or equal to this threshold then it does nothing.
For this program the base case occurs when we reach a square with a side less than or
equal to this inner threshold value, rather than a base case of 0. The second int argument provides an outer threshold. Squares whose sides are greater than or equal to this
threshold are also not drawn—although the recursive calls to drawSquare at their four
corners are still executed. Suppressing the drawing of the larger squares allows more of
the finer low-level details of the fractal image to appear. Simple *if statements* within the
drawSquare method provide this additional functionality. Figure 3.5(b) shows the output from TSquareThreshold with arguments 10, 500 while part (c) shows the output
with arguments 1, 80.

Considerations of printing costs preclude us from experimenting here with different
colors (although some of the exercises point you in that direction). We can, however, play
with gray levels as we did in the "Generating Images" boxed feature in Chapter 1. As explained in that feature, within the RGB color model, colors with identical red, green, and
blue values are "gray." For example, (0, 0, 0) represents black, (255, 255, 255) represents
white, and (127, 127, 127) represents a medium gray. The TSquareGray.java program
takes advantage of this balanced approach to "grayness" to use different gray scale levels
when drawing each set of differently sized squares. A *while* loop in the main method calculates the number of levels needed and sets the variable grayDecrement appropriately—
so that the widest range of gray possible is used within the fractal. A gray scale parameter
is included for the recursive drawSquare method. It is originally passed an argument
indicating white, and each time a new level of squares to be drawn is reached, the value
is decremented before the recursive calls to draw the four smaller squares are executed.
Figure 3.5(d) shows the output from TSquareGray with command line arguments 10,
500. The same arguments were used to generate the completely black and white image in
part (b) of the figure directly above it. Can you see how the two figures are related?

3.7   Removing Recursion

Some languages do not support recursion. Sometimes, even when a language does support recursion, a recursive solution is not desired because it is too costly in terms of space or time. This section considers two general techniques that are often used to replace recursion: eliminating tail recursion and direct use of a stack. First it looks at how recursion is implemented. Understanding how recursion works helps us see how to develop nonrecursive solutions.

The Java Programming Model

Java is generally used as an interpreted language. When you compile a Java program, it is translated into a language called Java bytecode. When you run a Java program, the bytecode version of your program is interpreted. The interpreter dynamically generates machine code based on the bytecode and then executes the machine code on your computer. You can also use a Java bytecode compiler to translate your bytecode files directly into machine code. In that case, you can run your programs directly on your computer without having to use an interpreter. In either case, your Java programs must be transformed into the machine language of your computer at some point in time.

In this section, we discuss the machine language representation of programs. Programmers working with most other high-level languages typically use compilers that translate programs directly into machine language.

How Recursion Works

The translation of high-level programs into machine language is a complex process. To facilitate our study of recursion, we make several simplifying assumptions about this process. Furthermore, we use a simple program, called `Kids`, that is not object-oriented; nor is it a good example of program design. It does provide a useful example for the current discussion, however.

Static Storage Allocation

A compiler that translates a high-level language program into machine code for execution on a computer must perform two functions:

1. Reserve space for the program variables.
2. Translate the high-level executable statements into equivalent machine language statements.

Typically, a compiler performs these tasks modularly for separate program subunits. Consider the following program.

```
package ch03.apps;
public class Kids
{
    private static int countKids(int girlCount, int boyCount)
    {
        int totalKids;
        totalKids = girlCount + boyCount;
        return(totalKids);
    }

    public static void main(String[] args)
    {
        int numGirls;
        int numBoys;
        int numChildren;

        numGirls = 12;
        numBoys = 13;
        numChildren = countKids(numGirls, numBoys);

        System.out.println("Number of children is " + numChildren);
    }
}
```

A compiler could create two separate machine code units for this program: one for the countKids method and one for the main method. Each unit would include space for its variables plus the sequence of machine language statements that implement its high-level code.

In our simple Kids program, the only invocation of the countKids method is from the main program. The flow of control of the program is

The compiler might arrange the machine code that corresponds to the Kids program in memory something like this:

```
-
    space for the main method variables
-
main method code that initializes variables
jump to the countKids method
main method code that prints information
exit
```

```
-
space for the countKids method parameters and local variables
-
the countKids method code
return to the main program
```

Static allocation like this is the simplest approach possible. But it does not support recursion. Do you see why?

The space for the `countKids` method is assigned to it at compile time. This strategy works well when the method will be called once and then always return, before it is called again. But a recursive method may be called again and again before it returns. Where do the second and subsequent calls find space for their parameters and local variables? Each call requires space to hold its own values. This space cannot be allocated statistically because the number of calls is unknown at compile time. A language that uses only static storage allocation cannot support recursion.

Dynamic Storage Allocation

Dynamic storage allocation provides memory space for a method when it is called. Local variables are thus not associated with actual memory addresses until run time.

Let us look at a simplified version of how this approach might work in Java. (The actual implementation depends on the particular system.) When a method is invoked, it needs space to keep its parameters, its local variables, and the return address (the address in the calling code to which the computer returns when the method completes its execution). This space is called an **activation record** or **stack frame**. Consider our recursive `factorial` method:

```java
public static int factorial(int n)
{
    if (n == 0)
        return 1;      // Base case
    else
        return (n * factorial(n - 1));      // General case
}
```

A simplified version of an activation record for method `factorial` might have the following "declaration":

```java
class ActivationRecordType
{
    AddressType returnAddr;          // Return address
    int result;                      // Returned value
    int n;                           // Parameter
}
```

Each call to a method, including recursive calls, causes the Java run-time system to allocate additional memory space for a new activation record. Within the method, references to the parameters and local variables use the values in the activation record. When the method ends, the activation record space is released.

What happens to the activation record of one method when a second method is invoked? Consider a program whose `main` method calls `proc1`, which then calls `proc2`. When the program begins executing, the "main" activation record is generated (the `main` method's activation record exists for the entire execution of the program).

At the first method call, an activation record is generated for `proc1`.

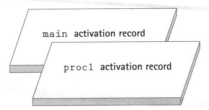

When `proc2` is called from within `proc1`, its activation record is generated. Because `proc1` has not finished executing, its activation record is still around. Just like the index cards we used in Section 3.1, "Recursive Definitions, Algorithms, and Programs," the activation record is stored until needed:

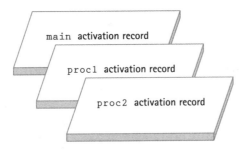

When `proc2` finishes executing, its activation record is released. But which of the other two activation records becomes the active one: `proc1`'s or `main`'s? You can see that `proc1`'s activation record should now be active. The order of activation follows the last in, first out (LIFO) rule. We know of a structure that supports LIFO access—the stack—so it should come as no surprise that the structure that keeps track of activation records at run time is called the **run-time** or **system stack**.

When a method is invoked, its activation record is pushed onto the run-time stack. Each nested level of method invocation adds another activation record to the stack. As each method completes its execution, its activation record is popped from the stack. Re-cursive method calls, like calls to any other method, cause a new activation record to be generated.

The number of recursive calls that a method goes through before returning deter-mines how many of its activation records appear on the run-time stack. The number of these calls is the **depth of the recursion**.

Now that we have an understanding of how recursion works, we turn to the primary topic of this section: how to develop nonrecursive solutions to problems based on recur-sive solutions.

Tail Call Elimination

When the recursive call is the last action executed in a recursive method, an interesting situation occurs. The recursive call causes an activation record to be put on the run-time stack; this record will contain the invoked method's arguments and local variables. When the recursive call finishes executing, the run-time stack is popped and the previous values of the variables are restored. Execution continues where it left off before the recursive call was made. Because the recursive call is the last statement in the method, however, there is nothing more to execute, and the method terminates without using the restored local variable values. The local variables did not need to be saved. Only the arguments in the call and its return value are actually significant.

In such a case we do not really need recursion. The sequence of recursive calls can be replaced by a loop structure. For instance, for the `factorial` method presented in Section 3.1, "Recursive Definitions, Algorithms, and Programs," the recursive call is the last statement in the method:

```
public static int factorial(int n)
{
    if (n == 0)
        return 1;        // Base case
    else
        return (n * factorial(n - 1));      // General case
}
```

Now we investigate how we could move from the recursive version to an iterative version using a *while* loop.

For the iterative solution we need to declare a variable to hold the intermediate values of our computation. We call it `retValue`, because eventually it holds the final value to be returned.

A look at the base case of the recursive solution shows us the initial value to assign to `retValue`. We must initialize it to 1, the value that is returned in the base case. This way the iterative method works correctly in the case when the loop body is not entered.

Now we turn our attention to the body of the *while* loop. Each time through the loop should correspond to the computation performed by one recursive call. Therefore, we multiply our intermediate value, retValue, by the current value of the n variable. Also, we decrement the value of n by 1 each time through the loop—this action corresponds to the smaller-caller aspect of each invocation.

Finally, we need to determine the loop termination conditions. Because the recursive solution has one base case—if the n argument is 0—we have a single termination condition. We continue processing the loop as long as the base case is not met:

```
while (n != 0)
```

Putting everything together we arrive at an iterative version of the method:

```
private static int factorial(int n)
{
    int retValue = 1;       // return value
    while (n != 0)
    {
        retValue = retValue * n;
        n = n - 1;
    }
    return(retValue);
}
```

Cases in which the recursive call is the last statement executed are called tail **recursion**. Tail recursion always can be replaced by iteration following the approach just outlined. In fact, some optimizing compilers will remove tail recursion automatically when generating low-level code.

Direct Use of a Stack

When the recursive call is not the last action executed in a recursive method, we cannot simply substitute a loop for the recursion. For instance, consider the method recRev-PrintList, which we developed in Section 3.4, "Recursive Processing of Linked Lists," for printing a linked list in reverse order:

```
void recRevPrintList(LLNode<String> listRef)
// Prints the contents of the listRef linked list to standard output
// in reverse order
{
    if (listRef != null)
    {
        recRevPrintList(listRef.getLink());
        System.out.println(listRef.getInfo());
    }
}
```

Here we make the recursive call and then print the value in the current node. In cases like this one, to remove recursion we can replace the stacking of activation records

that is done by the system with stacking of intermediate values that is done by the program.

For our reverse printing example, we must traverse the list in a forward direction, saving the information from each node onto a stack, until reaching the end of the list (when our current reference equals null). Upon reaching the end of the list, we print the information from the last node. Then, using the information we saved on the stack, we back up (pop) and print again, back up and print, and so on, until we have printed the information from the first list element.

Here is the code:

```
static void iterRevPrintList(LLNode<String> listRef)
// Prints the contents of the listRef linked list to standard output
// in reverse order
{
    StackInterface<String> stack = new LinkedStack<String>();
    while (listRef != null) // put info onto the stack
    {
        stack.push(listRef.getInfo());
        listRef = listRef.getLink();
    }
    // Retrieve references in reverse order and print elements
    while (!stack.isEmpty())
    {
        System.out.println(stack.top());
        stack.pop();
    }
}
```

Notice that the programmer stack version of the reverse print operation is quite a bit longer than its recursive counterpart, especially if we add in the code for the stack methods push, pop, top, and isEmpty. This extra length is caused by our need to stack and unstack the information explicitly. Knowing that recursion uses the system stack, we can see that the recursive algorithm for reverse printing is also using a stack—an invisible stack that is automatically supplied by the system. That is the secret to the elegance of recursive-problem solutions.

The reverse print methods presented in this section are included in the cho3.apps package in the file LinkedListReverse.java. The application includes both the recursive and iterative reverse print methods plus test code that exercises each of the methods on lists of size 0, 1, and 5.

3.8   When to Use a Recursive Solution

We might consider several factors when deciding whether to use a recursive solution to a problem. The main issues are the efficiency and the clarity of the solution.

Recursion Overhead

A recursive solution is often more costly in terms of both computer time and space than a nonrecursive solution. (This is not always the case; it really depends on the problem, the computer, and the compiler.) A recursive solution usually requires more "overhead" because of the nested recursive method calls, in terms of both time (each call involves processing to create and dispose of the activation record and to manage the run-time stack) and space (activation records must be stored). Calling a recursive method may generate many layers of recursive calls. For instance, the call to an iterative solution to the factorial problem involves a single method invocation, causing one activation record to be put on the run-time stack. Invoking the recursive version of factorial requires $n + 1$ method calls and pushes $n + 1$ activation records onto the run-time stack. That is, the depth of recursion is $O(n)$. Besides the obvious run-time overhead of creating and removing activation records, for some problems the system just may not have enough space in the run-time stack to run a recursive solution.

Inefficient Algorithms

Another potential problem is that a particular recursive solution might just be inherently inefficient. Such inefficiency is not a reflection of how we choose to implement the algorithm; rather, it is an indictment of the algorithm itself.

Combinations

Consider the problem of determining how many combinations of a certain size can be made out of a group of items. For instance, if we have a group of 20 students and want to form a panel (subgroup) consisting of five student members, how many different panels are possible?

A recursive mathematical formula can be used for solving this problem. Given that C is the total number of combinations, *group* is the total size of the group to pick from, *members* is the size of each subgroup, and *group > members*,

$$C(group, members) = \begin{cases} group, & \text{if members} = 1 \\ 1, & \text{if members} = group \\ C(group - 1, members - 1) + C(group - 1, members) & \text{if group} > members > 1 \end{cases}$$

The reasoning behind this formula is as follows:

- The number of ways you can select a single member of a group (a subgroup of size 1) is equal to the size of the group (you choose the members of the group one at a time).
- The number of ways you can create a subgroup the same size as the original group is 1 (you choose everybody in the group).

- If neither of the aforementioned situations apply then you have a situation where each member of the original group will be in some subgroups but not in other subgroups; the combination of the subgroups that a member belongs to and the subgroups that member does not belong to represents all of the subgroups; therefore, identify a member of the original group randomly and add together the number of subgroups to which that member belongs [$C(group - 1, members - 1)$] (our identified member belongs to the subgroup but we still need to choose members - 1 members from the remaining group - 1 possibilities) and the number of subgroups that member does not belong too [$C(group - 1, members)$] (we remove the identified member from consideration).

Because this definition of C is recursive, it is easy to see how a recursive method can be used to solve the problem.

```
public static int combinations(int group, int members)
{
    if (members == 1)
        return group;                  // Base case 1
    else if (members == group)
        return 1;                      // Base case 2
    else
        return (combinations(group - 1, members - 1) +
            combinations(group - 1, members));
}
```

The recursive calls for this method, given initial arguments (4, 3), are shown in **Figure 3.6**.

Returning to our original problem, we can now find out how many panels of five student members can be made from the original group of 20 students with the statement

```
System.out.println("Combinations = " + combinations(20, 5));
```

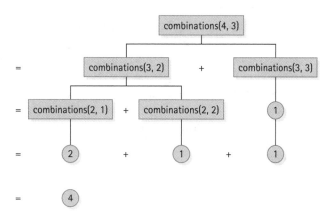

Figure 3.6   Calculating `combinations(4,3)`

that outputs "Combinations = 15504." Did you guess that it would be that large of a number? Recursive definitions can be used to define functions that grow quickly!

Although it may appear elegant, this approach to calculating the number of combinations is extremely inefficient. The example of this method illustrated in Figure 3.6, combinations(4,3), seems straightforward enough. But consider the execution of combinations(6,4), as illustrated in **Figure 3.7**. The inherent problem with this method is that the same values are calculated over and over. For example, combinations(4,3) is calculated in two different places, and combinations(3,2) is calculated in three places, as are combinations(2,1) and combinations(2,2).

It is unlikely that we could solve a combinatorial problem of any large size using this method. For large problems the program runs "forever"—or until it exhausts the capacity of the computer; it is an exponential-time, $O(2^N)$, solution to the problem.

Although our recursive method is very easy to understand, it is not a practical solution. In such cases, you should seek an alternative solution. A programming approach called *dynamic programming*, where solutions to subproblems that are needed repeatedly are saved in a data structure instead of being recalculated, can often prove useful. Or, even better, you might discover an efficient iterative solution. For the combinations problem an easy (and efficient) iterative solution does exist, as mathematicians can provide us with another definition of the function C:

$$C \text{ (group, members)} = \text{group!}/((\text{members!}) \times (\text{group} - \text{members})!)$$

A carefully constructed iterative program based on this formula is much more efficient than our recursive solution.

Clarity

The issue of the clarity of a problem solution is also an important factor in determining whether to use a recursive approach. For many problems, a recursive solution is simpler and more natural for the programmer to write. The total amount of work required to solve a problem can be envisioned as an iceberg. By using recursive programming, the application programmer may limit his or her view to the tip of the iceberg. The system takes care of the great bulk of the work below the surface.

Compare, for example, the recursive and nonrecursive approaches to printing a linked list in reverse order that were developed earlier in this chapter. In the recursive version, the system took care of the stacking that we had to do explicitly in the nonrecursive method. Thus, recursion is a tool that can help reduce the complexity of a program by hiding some of the implementation details. With the cost of computer time and memory decreasing and the cost of a programmer's time rising, it is worthwhile to use recursive solutions to such problems.

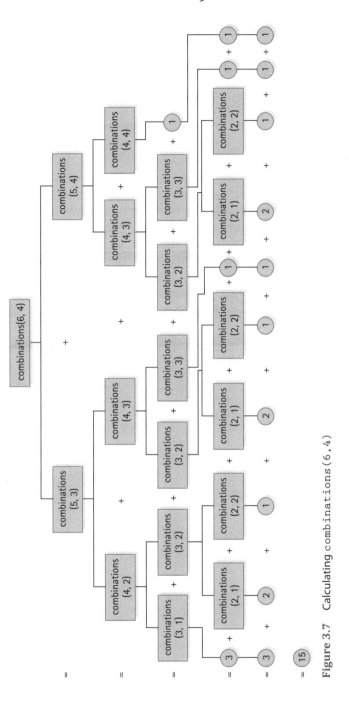

Figure 3.7 Calculating combinations(6,4)

Summary

Recursion is a very powerful problem-solving technique. Used appropriately, it can simplify the solution of a problem, often resulting in shorter, more easily understood source code. As usual in computing, trade-offs become necessary: Recursive methods are often less efficient in terms of both time and space, due to the overhead of many levels of method calls. The magnitude of this cost depends on the problem, the computer system, and the compiler.

A recursive solution to a problem must have at least one base case—that is, a case in which the solution is derived nonrecursively. Without a base case, the method recurses forever (or at least until the computer runs out of memory). The recursive solution also has one or more general cases that include recursive calls to the method. These recursive calls must involve a "smaller caller." One (or more) of the argument values must change in each recursive call to redefine the problem to be smaller than it was on the previous call. Thus, each recursive call leads the solution of the problem toward the base case.

Many data structures, notably trees but even simpler structures such as arrays and linked lists, can be treated recursively. Recursive definitions, algorithms, and programs are a key part of the study of data structures.

Exercises

Basics (Sections 3.1 and 3.2)

Exercises 1 to 3 use the following three mathematical functions (assume $N \geq 0$):

- $Sum(N) = 1 + 2 + 3 + \ldots + N$
- $BiPower(N) = 2^N$
- $TimesFive(N) = 5N$

1. Define recursively
   a. $Sum(N)$
   b. $BiPower(N)$
   c. $TimesFive(N)$

2. Create a recursive program that prompts the user for a nonnegative integer N and outputs.
   a. $Sum(N)$
   b. $BiPower(N)$
   c. $TimesFive(N)$
   Describe any input constraints in the opening comment of your recursive methods.

3. Use the Three-Question Approach to verify the program(s) you created for Exercise 2. Exercises 4 to 5 use the following method:

```
int puzzle(int base, int limit)
{
    if (base > limit)
        return -1;
    else
        if (base == limit)
            return 1;
        else
            return base * puzzle(base + 1, limit);
}
```

4. Identify
   a. The base case(s) of the `puzzle` method
   b. The general case(s) of the `puzzle` method
   c. Constraints on the arguments passed to the `puzzle` method

5. Show what would be written by the following calls to the recursive method `puzzle`.
   a. `System.out.println(puzzle(14, 10));`
   b. `System.out.println(puzzle(4, 7));`
   c. `System.out.println(puzzle(0, 0));`

6. Given the following method:

```
int exer(int num)
{
    if (num == 0)
        return 0;
    else
        return num + exer(num + 1);
}
```

   a. Is there a constraint on the value that can be passed as an argument for this method to pass the smaller-caller test?
   b. Is `exer(7)` a valid call? If so, what is returned from the method?
   c. Is `exer(0)` a valid call? If so, what is returned from the method?
   d. Is `exer(-5)` a valid call? If so, what is returned from the method?

7. For each of the following recursive methods, identify the base case, the general case, and the constraints on the argument values, and explain what the method does.
   a.
```
int power(int base, int exponent)
{
    if (exponent == 0)
        return 1;
```

```
        else
            return (base * power(base, exponent-1));
        }
    b.  int factorial (int n)
        {
            if (n > 0)
                return (n * factorial (n - 1));
            else
                if (n == 0)
                    return 1;
        }
    c.  int recur(int n)
        {
            if (n < 0)
                return -1;
            else if (n < 10)
                return 1;
            else
                return (1 + recur(n / 10));
        }
    d.  int recur2(int n)
        {
            if (n < 0)
                return -1;
            else if (n < 10)
                return n;
            else
                return ((n % 10) + recur2(n / 10));
        }
```

8. Code the methods described in parts a and b. *Hint*: Use recursion to iterate across the lines of asterisks, but use a *for loop* to generate the asterisks within a line.

    a. Code a recursive method `printTriangleUp(int n)` that prints asterisks to `System.out` consisting of n lines, with one asterisk on the first line, two on the second line, and so on. For example, if n is 4 the final result would be:

```
   *
  * *
 * * *
* * * *
```

b. Code a recursive method `printTriangleDn(int n)` that prints asterisks to `System.out` consisting of n lines, with n asterisk on the first line, n-1 on the second line, and so on. For example, if n is 4 the final result would be:

```
* * * *

* * *

* *

*
```

9. The greatest common divisor of two positive integers *m* and *n*, referred to as gcd(*m*, *n*), is the largest divisor common to *m* and *n*. For example, gcd(24, 36) = 12, as the divisors common to 24 and 36 are 1, 2, 3, 4, 6, and 12. An efficient approach to calculating the gcd, attributed to the famous ancient Greek mathematician Euclid, is based on the following recursive algorithm:

gcd(m, n)

```
if m < n, then swap the values of m, n
if n is a divisor of m, return n
else return gcd(n, m % n)
```

Design, implement, and test a program `Euclid` that repeatedly prompts the user for a pair of positive integers and reports the gcd of the entered pair. Your program should use a recursive method `gcd` based on the above algorithm.

3.3 Recursive Processing of Arrays

10. The sorted values array contains 16 integers 5, 7, 10, 13, 13, 20, 21, 25, 30, 32, 40, 45, 50, 52, 57, 60.

a. Indicate the sequence of recursive calls that are made to `binarySearch`, given an initial invocation of `binarySearch(32,0,15)`.

b. Indicate the sequence of recursive calls that are made to `binarySearch`, given an initial invocation of `binarySearch(21,0,15)`.

c. Indicate the sequence of recursive calls that are made to `binarySearch`, given an initial invocation of `binarySearch(42,0,15)`.

d. Indicate the sequence of recursive calls that are made to `binarySearch`, given an initial invocation of `binarySearch(70,0,15)`.

11. You must assign the grades for a programming class. Right now the class is studying recursion, and students have been given this assignment: Write a recursive method `sumValues` that is passed an index into an array values of `int` (this array is accessible from within the `sumValues` method) and returns the sum of the values in the array between the location indicated by `index` and the end of the array. The

argument will be between 0 and `values.length` inclusive. For example, given this configuration:

	[0]	[1]	[2]	[3]	[4]	[5]
values:	7	2	5	8	3	9

then `sumValues(4)` returns 12 and `sumValues(0)` returns 34 (the sum of all the values in the array). You have received quite a variety of solutions. Grade the methods below. If the solution is incorrect, explain what the code actually does in lieu of returning the correct result. You can assume the array is "full." You can assume a "friendly" user—the method is invoked with an argument between 0 and `values.length`.

a.
```
int sumValues(int index)
{
    if (index == values.length)
        return 0;
    else
        return index + sumValues(index + 1);
}
```

b.
```
int sumValues(int index)
{
    int sum = 0;
    for (int i = index; i < values.length; i++)
        sum = sum + values[i];
    return sum;
}
```

c.
```
int sumValues(int index)
{
    if (index == values.length)
        return 0;
    else
        return (1 + sumValues(index + 1);
}
```

d.
```
int sumValues(int index)
{
    return values[index] + sumValues(index + 1);
}
```

e.
```
int sumValues(int index)
{
    if (index > values.length)
        return 0;
```

```
        else
            return values[index] + sumValues(index + 1);
    }
```

f.
```
    int sumValues(int index)
    {
        if (index >= values.length)
            return 0;
        else
            return values[index] + sumValues(index + 1);
    }
```

g.
```
    int sumValues(int index)
    {
        if (index < 0)
            return 0;
        else
            return   values[index] + sumValues(index - 1);
    }
```

12. Assume we have an unsorted array of int named values that is accessible from within the recursive method smallestValue. Our specific problem is to determine the smallest element of the array. Our approach is to use the fact that the smallest element in a subarray is equal to the smaller of the first element in the subarray and the smallest element in the remainder of the subarray. The subarrays we examine will always conclude at the end of the overall array; therefore we only need to pass our recursive method a single parameter, indicating the start of the subarray currently being examined. The signature for the method is

```
int smallestValue(int first)
```

For example, given the values array from Exercise 11, smallestValue(4) returns 3 and smallestValue(0) returns 2 (the smallest value in the array). Design and code the recursive method smallestValue plus a test driver.

13. Consider that we can define the reverse of a string s recursively as:

$$
reverse(s) = \begin{cases} s \text{ if } s.equals("") \text{ (an empty string is its own reverse)} \\ \\ s.charAt(s.length() - 1) \\ \quad\quad + reverse(s.substring(0, s.length() - 1)) \end{cases}
$$

a. Create an application that prompts the user for a string, then outputs the string in reverse. For example, if the user inputs "abcd efg," then your application should output "gfe dcba." Within your application include a static recursive method reverse based on the above definition, that takes a String argument and returns a String that is the reverse of the argument.

b. Show the sequence of method calls to reverse that your application makes if the user inputs "RECURSE."

3.4 Recursive Processing of Linked Lists

14. This exercise uses the methods `recPrintList`, `recListSize`, and `recRev-PrintList` defined in Section 3.4. Assume `list` is of type `LLNode<String>` and points to the start of a linked list containing the following strings, in the order shown: `alpha beta comma delta emma`. For each of the following, indicate the sequence of recursive calls that results from the initial call shown. Include in your answer an indication of the information in the LLNode that is the argument of the call, for example, "`recPrintList(pointer to node containing delta)`."

   a. Initial call is `recPrintList(list)` (in other words `recPrintList(pointer to node containing alpha)`).

   b. Initial call is `recListSize(list)` (in other words `recListSize(pointer to node containing alpha)`).

   c. Initial call is `recRevPrintList(list)` (in other words `recRevPrintList(pointer to node containing alpha)`).

15. You must assign the grades for a programming class. Right now the class is studying recursion, and students have been given this assignment: Write a recursive method `sumSquares` that is passed a reference to a linked list of `Integer` elements and returns the sum of the squares of the elements. The list nodes are of class `LLNode<Integer>`. The objects in the list are all of class `Integer`. Example:

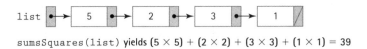

`sumsSquares(list)` yields $(5 \times 5) + (2 \times 2) + (3 \times 3) + (1 \times 1) = 39$

Assume that the list is not empty. You have received quite a variety of solutions. Grade the methods below, marking errors where you see them.

   a.
```
int sumSquares(LLNode<Integer> list)
{
    return 0;
    if (list != null)
      return (list.getInfo()* list.getInfo()+
    sumSquares(list.getLink())));
}
```

   b.
```
int sumSquares(LLNode<Integer> list)
{
    int sum = 0;
    while (list != null)
    {
        sum = list.getInfo() + sum;
        list = list.getLink();
```

```
        }
        return sum;
    }
```

c.
```
    int sumSquares(LLNode<Integer> list)
    {
        if (list == null)
            return 0;
        else
            return list.getInfo() * list.getInfo() +
                sumSquares(list.getLink());
    }
```

d.
```
    int sumSquares(LLNode<Integer> list)
    {
        if (list.getLink() == null)
            return list.getInfo() * list.getInfo();
        else
            return list.getInfo() * list.getInfo() +
                sumSquares(list.getLink());
    }
```

e.
```
    int sumSquares(LLNode<Integer> list)
    {
        if (list == null)
            return 0;
        else
            return (sumSquares(list.getLink()) *
                sumSquares(list.getLink()));
    }
```

For exercises 16 to 19 assume we have a sorted linked list of `Integer`. The start of the linked list is referenced by `values` which, of course, is of type `LLNode<Integer>`. For example purposes, assume `values` points to a list containing 3, 6, 6, 9, 12, 15, 18, 19, 19, and 20. You can and should assume the list in question is sorted in nondecreasing order. For each of these exercises you should also create a driver application that demonstrates that your new method operates correctly.

16. Write a recursive method `numEvens(LLNode<Integer> list)` that returns how many even numbers are contained in `list`. For our example list `numEvens(values)` would return 5 (the even numbers are 6, 6, 12, 18, and 20).

17. Write a recursive method `contains(int target, LLNode<Integer> list)` that returns `true` if `list` contains `target` and `false` otherwise. For our example list `contains(15, values)` would return true while `contains(10, values)` would return `false`.

18. Write a recursive method `remove(int target, LLNode<Integer> list)` that removes all occurrences of `target` from `list` and returns a reference to the new list. For our example list the statement

```
values = remove(6, values);
```

would result in `values` referencing the list containing 3 9 12 15 18 19 19 and 20. If `target` is not contained in `list` then the list remains unchanged.

19. Write a recursive method `insertOrdered(int target, LLNode<Integer> list)` that adds `target` to the ordered linked list referenced by `list`, such that the linked list remains sorted, and returns a reference to the new list. For our example list the statement

```
values = insertOrdered(16, values);
```

would result in `values` referencing the list containing 3   6   6   9   12   16   18   19   19 and 20.

3.5 Towers

20. What are the constraints on the arguments for parameter n of the `doTowers` method? What happens if the constraints are not met?

21. Change the Towers of Hanoi program so that it does the following:

   a. Counts the number of ring moves and prints that out instead of the sequence of moves. Use a static variable `count` of type `int` to hold the number of moves.

   b. Repeatedly prompts the user for the number of rings and reports the results, until the user enters a number less than 0.

22. Using your version of the Towers of Hanoi program from Exercise 21, answer the following:

   a. Fill in the table with the number of moves required to solve the problem, starting with the given number of rings.

Rings	Moves
1	
2	
3	
4	
5	
6	
7	

   b. Describe the pattern you see in the number of moves listed in your table.

   c. Assuming $n > 0$, define the number of moves required to move n rings using a recursive mathematical formula.

d. Suppose you have a physical Towers of Hanoi puzzle with 11 rings. If it takes one second to move a ring from one peg to another, how long would it take you to "solve" the puzzle?

e. In Java the data type `int` uses 32 bits and can represent integers in the range −2,147,483,648 to 2,147,483,647. By experimenting with your program from Exercise 12, figure out the largest number of rings that the program can handle before "blowing up"—that is, before the value in `count` overflows.

f. What is the number of moves reported for that number of rings? How close is that to the maximum `int` value? Explain.

g. In the legend described on page xxx the monks are solving a tower that has 64 rings. How many moves are required? At the rate of one move per second, how long will it take for the monks to complete the puzzle (and end the world!)?

 23. *Towers of Hanoi Variation*: In this new version of the Towers of Hanoi puzzle we add the additional constraint that every move *must* use the middle peg. For example, if the pegs are labeled 1, 2, and 3 left to right and we start with two rings, 1 and 2 (with 1 being the smaller ring) on peg 1, then to move the rings to peg 3 we would make the following moves: move ring 1 from peg 1 to peg 2, move ring 1 from peg 2 to peg 3, move ring 2 from peg 1 to peg 2, move ring 1 from peg 3 to peg 2, move ring 1 from peg 2 to peg 1, move ring 2 from peg 2 to peg 3, move ring 1 from peg 1 to peg 2, move ring 1 from peg 2 to peg 3. Done! Note that every move used peg 2, the middle peg.

a. Write a program named `TowersVariation`, similar to the `Towers` program, which prompts the user for the number of rings and then prints out the sequence of moves needed to solve the Towers of Hanoi Variation problem.

b. Revise your program so that it counts the number of ring moves and prints that out instead of the sequence of moves. Use a static variable `count` of type `int` to hold the number of moves. Your program should now repeatedly prompt the user for the number of rings and reports the results, until the user enters a number less than 0.

c. Create a table that compares the number of ring moves needed when solving the standard Towers problem as compared to the number required for the variation, for 1 to 10 rings.

3.6 Fractals

 24. Create an application `DiminishingSquares` that accepts a command line integer argument n and then outputs a "square" of asterisks of size n × n, followed by another of size (n - 1) × (n - 1), and so on, stopping after it draws a 1 × 1 square. Your application should include a recursive `drawSquares(int side)`

method that is called once by the main method and that handles all of the output. For example, if the argument to the application is 3, the output would be:

```
* * *

* * *

* * *

* *

* *

*
```

25. Three fractal drawing applications were presented in this section. Here we ask you to make some modifications to these programs. Some of the modifications require knowledge about the Java `Color` class, which you can find on the Oracle website.

   a. Create `TSquare01` by modifying `TSquare` so that it only draws squares at every other level. Therefore, it draws the largest square at level one, skips drawing the four smaller squares at level two, and draws the eight even smaller squares at level three, and so on.

   b. Create `TSquare02` by modifying `TSquare` so that it uses two interesting colors (instead of black and white) for the background and the squares.

   c. Create `TSquare03` by modifying `TSquare` so that it uses a black background, red for the odd numbered levels of squares, and yellow for the even numbered levels. Feel free to experiment with different color combinations until you find one that you like.

   d. Create `TSquareGray01` by modifying `TSquareGray` so that it uses a random color at each level.

   e. Create `TSquareGray02` by modifying `TSquareGray` so that it uses a random color for each square.

   f. Create `TSquareGray03` by modifying `TSquareGray` so that it uses a consistent color pattern. Figure out a way to vary the colors used at each level using a mathematical pattern.

26. The Sierpinski carpet is a well-known plane fractal based on recursive squares.

   a. Using `TSquare.java` as a guide, create an application called `Sierpinski-Carpet.java`. For this fractal imagine dividing the original square canvas into nine congruent squares, essentially creating a 3 × 3 grid of smaller squares. Fill in the central square. Recursively repeat the dividing and filling in on each of the outer eight squares.

   b. Experiment with shades of gray and colors as described in the previous problem.

27. Design your own image generation program that uses some type of recursion. Perhaps your class can have an Art Exhibit.

3.7 Removing Recursion

28. Explain what is meant by the following terms:

    a. Run-time stack

    b. Static storage allocation

    c. Dynamic storage allocation

    d. Activation record

    e. Tail recursion

29. Explain the relationship between dynamic storage allocation and recursion.

30. Create an iterative version of the `Euclid` program from Exercise 9. Call your program `Euclid2`. Use what you learned in this section about removing tail recursion to design your iterative approach.

31. Implement a program that repeatedly asks the user to input a positive integer and outputs the factorial of that input integer. Your program should be based on our recursive solution to the factorial problem, but instead of using recursion you should use a stack.

3.8 When to Use a Recursive Solution

32. Using the `combinations` method from Section 3.8:

    a. Create a program that repeatedly prompts the user for two integers, N and M, and outputs the number of combinations of M items that can be made out of N items.

    b. Enhance your program so that it also outputs the number of times the `combinations` method is invoked when determining each result.

    c. Experiment with your enhanced program, using different variations of input values. Write a short report about the results of your experiment.

33. The Fibonacci sequence is the series of integers

    0, 1, 1, 2, 3, 5, 8, 13, 21, 34, 55, 89 . . .

    See the pattern? Each element in the series is the sum of the preceding two elements. Here is a recursive formula for calculating the nth number of the sequence:

$$\text{Fib}(N) = \begin{cases} N, & \text{if } N = 0 \text{ or } 1 \\ \text{Fib}(N-2) + \text{Fib}(N-1), & \text{if } N > 1 \end{cases}$$

    a. Write a recursive method `fibonacci` that returns the nth Fibonacci number when passed the argument n.

    b. Write a nonrecursive version of the method `fibonacci`.

    c. Write a driver to test your two versions of the method `fibonacci`.

    d. Compare the recursive and iterative versions for efficiency. (Use words, not O( ) notation.)

Additional Problems

34. The following defines a function that calculates an approximation of the square root of a `number`, starting with an approximate answer (`approx`), within the specified tolerance (`tol`).

$$\text{sqrRoot(number, approx, tol)} = \begin{cases} \text{approx} & \text{if } \left|\text{approx}^2 - \text{number}\right| \leq \text{tol} \\ \text{sqrRoot}\left(\text{number}, \dfrac{(\text{approx}^2 + \text{number})}{(2 * \text{approx})}, \text{tol}\right) & \text{if } \left|\text{approx}^2 - \text{number}\right| > \text{tol} \end{cases}$$

    a. What limitations must be placed on the values of the arguments if this function is to work correctly?

    b. Write a recursive method `sqrRoot` that implements the function.

    c. Write a nonrecursive version of the method `sqrRoot`.

    d. Write a driver to test the recursive and iterative versions of the method `sqrRoot`.

35. A palindrome is a string that reads the same forward as well as backward. For example, "otto" and "never odd or even" are palindromes. When determining if a string is a palindrome, we ignore characters that are not letters.

    a. Give a recursive definition of a palindrome. (*Hint:* Consider what you get if you remove the first and last letters of a palindrome.)

    b. What is the base case of your definition?

    c. Write a recursive program based on your definition that repeatedly prompts the user for a string and then reports whether the string is a palindrome.

    d. Write an iterative program that does the same thing.

    e. Compare your two programs in terms of time and space efficiency.

36. Create a program that uses methods provided by the Java class library for exploring files and folders. (*Hint:* The `File` class is a good place to start.) The path to a specific file folder is provided to your program as a command line argument. Your program should do each of the following tasks:

    a. "Print" to standard output a list of all of the files in the argument folder plus their size, along with a list of any folders in the argument folder. Include for each listed folder a list of its files (including sizes) and folders. Do this "recursively" as long as there are subfolders to be listed. Your output should display the hierarchy of folders and files in a visually appealing manner.

    b. "Print" to standard output the name, path name, and size of the largest file in the list generated in part a.

    c. Create a report about your program that includes a program listing, sample output, and a description of your experience creating the program.

37. A Context Free Grammar (CFG) is a quadruple <V, T, P, S> where

V is a finite set of variables (nonterminals)

T is a finite set of terminal symbols

P is a finite set of productions:

A production is a rewriting rule of the form:

$$V \rightarrow \alpha$$

where V is a nonterminal, α is any string of terminals/nonterminals or the empty string,

S is a special symbol called the start symbol and is a variable

We will assume that variables are surrounded by < >, and that the empty string is represented by [ ].

A CFG can be used to generate random sentences.

We will use weighted productions where the probability that a production is used is equal to its weight divided by 100. In our list of productions we assume the sum of the weights of all productions with the same variable on the left side is 100. For example, a set of productions could be:

```
100 <S> = My homework is <rl> late because\n<reason>.
30 <reason> = it is <rl> always late
30 <reason> = my <rl> <hungry thing> ate it
20 <hungry thing> = younger <sibling>
20 <hungry thing> = older <sibling>
50 <sibling> = brother
50 <sibling> = sister
30 <hungry thing> = dog
30 <hungry thing> = printer
10 <reason> = <reason>\nand besides <rl> <reason>
20 <rl> = like
80 <rl> = []
30 <reason> = I forgot my flash drive
```

Sentences that could be generated based on the above set of productions include, for example:

```
My homework is late because          My homework is like late because
it is like always late               I forgot my flash drive
and besides my older sister ate it
```

a. List five other sentences that could be generated from the given grammar.

b. Design your own interesting CFG following the format shown above.

c. Create a program `SentenceGen` that will read a set of productions such as that shown above, and that will, at the user's request, generate and display a random "sentence" from the grammar, until the user indicates he or she wants to quit.

CHAPTER

4

The Queue ADT

Knowledge Goals

You should be able to

- describe a queue and its operations at an abstract level
- define a queue interface
- describe algorithms for implementing queue operations using an array
- compare fixed and floating-front approaches to an array-based implementation of a queue
- explain how to implement an unbounded queue using arrays
- describe algorithms for implementing queue operations using a linked list
- use order of growth analysis to describe and compare the efficiency of queue algorithms
- define interarrival time, service time, turnaround time, and waiting time for elements on a queue
- explain how concurrent threads can interfere with each other resulting in errors, and how such interference can be prevented

Skill Goals

You should be able to

- implement the bounded Queue ADT using an array
- implement the unbounded Queue ADT using an array
- implement the unbounded Queue ADT using a linked list
- draw diagrams showing the effects of queue operations for a particular implementation of a queue
- use the Queue ADT as a component of an application
- calculate turnaround and waiting times for queue elements, given arrival times and service requirements
- use our queue simulation system to investigate properties of real-world queues
- implement a program that properly uses threads to take advantage of the parallelism inherent within a problem solution

In this chapter we consider the queue, the logical counterpart of the stack. Whereas the stack is a "last in, first out" (LIFO) structure, a queue is a "first in, first out" (FIFO) structure. Whichever element is in the queue the longest time is the next element to be removed. Like the stack, the queue has many important uses related to systems programming and also is an appropriate structure for many other applications.

We study the queue as an ADT, looking at it from the abstract, application, and implementation levels. At the abstract level, queues are defined using a Java `interface`. Several applications of queues are discussed, and in particular we look at how queues are used to determine whether a string is a palindrome and to investigate properties of real-world queues. Two basic approaches are used to implement queues: arrays and linked lists. In addition to using an array to implement a bounded queue, we see how to implement an unbounded queue using an array. In a bit of a departure from our normal sequential processing view of things, the final section of the chapter discusses how queues are used to hold tasks targeted for parallel execution, and how to use Java to safely exploit such parallelism if it can be used to improve performance.

4.1   The Queue

The stacks studied in Chapter 2 are structures in which elements are always added to and removed from the same end. But what if we need to represent a collection that operates in a different manner? Suppose we want to simulate cars passing through the stages of a car wash. The cars go in one end and come out the other end. A data structure in which elements enter at one end and are removed from the opposite end is called a queue. The queue data structure, like the car wash, has the property that the first element (car) to go in is the first element (car) to come out.

Several variations on this basic form of queue exist, so to distinguish it we sometimes refer to this version as a FIFO queue. Other versions of queues are presented in Section 4.7, "Queue Variations" and in Chapter 9, "The Priority Queue ADT." For now we concentrate on the classic version of a queue—so when we say "queue" we mean a FIFO queue. As with the stack, we consider the queue as an ADT from three levels: abstract, implementation, and application.

A **queue** is an access-controlled group of elements in which new elements are added at one end (the "rear") and elements are removed from the other end (the "front"). As another example of a queue, consider a line of students waiting to pay for their books at a university bookstore (see **Figure 4.1**). In theory, if not in practice, each new student gets in line at the rear. When the cashier is ready for a new customer, the student at the front of the line is served.

To add elements to a queue, we access the rear of the queue; to remove elements, we access the front. The middle elements are logically

Queue Uses

In addition to the uses described here, queues often play a key role in parallel processing systems. Processes called producers, working in parallel, create tasks and place them in a queue. Processes called consumers, working in parallel, remove the tasks from the queue and perform them. The queue acts as a synchronization mechanism. We introduce some of Java's parallel processing features in Section 4.9 "Concurrency, Interference, and Synchronization."

Front of Queue

Rear of Queue

next...

PAY HERE

Figure 4.1   A FIFO queue

inaccessible. It is convenient to picture the queue as a linear structure with the front at the left end and the rear at the right end. However, we must stress that the "ends" of the queue are abstractions; their "leftness" and "rightness" may or may not correspond to any characteristics of the queue's implementation. The essential property of the queue is its FIFO access.

Operations on Queues

The bookstore example suggests two operations that can be applied to a queue. First, new elements can be added to the rear of the queue, an operation called *enqueue*. Second, elements can be removed from the front of the queue, an operation called *dequeue*. **Figure 4.2** shows how a series of these operations would affect a queue, envisioned as a series of blocks.

Unlike the stack operations `push` and `pop`, the addition and removal operations for a queue do not have standard names. The *enqueue* operation is sometimes called enq, enque, add, or insert; *dequeue* is also called deq, deque, remove, or serve.

Using Queues

Chapter 2 discussed how operating systems and compilers use stacks. Similarly, queues are often used for system programming purposes. For example, an operating system often maintains a queue of processes that are ready to execute or that are waiting for a particular event to occur.

As another example, computer systems must often provide a "holding area" for messages that are being transmitted between two processes, two programs, or even two

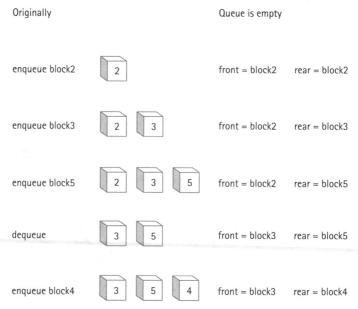

Originally		Queue is empty	
enqueue block2	2	front = block2	rear = block2
enqueue block3	2 3	front = block2	rear = block3
enqueue block5	2 3 5	front = block2	rear = block5
dequeue	3 5	front = block3	rear = block5
enqueue block4	3 5 4	front = block3	rear = block4

Figure 4.2 The effects of enqueue and dequeue operations

systems. This holding area is usually called a "buffer" and is often implemented as a queue. For example, if a large number of mail messages arrive at a mail server at about the same time, the messages are held in a buffer until the mail server can get around to processing them. If it processes the messages in the order they arrived—in FIFO order—then the buffer is a queue.

Many other applications need to store requests before processing. Consider applications that provide services to customers—for example, selling airline or theater tickets. Such applications typically use a queue to manage the requests.

As shown by the bookstore example, our software queues have counterparts in real-world queues. We wait in queues to buy pizza, to enter movie theaters, to drive on a turnpike, and to ride on a roller coaster. Another important application of the queue data structure is to help us simulate and analyze such real-world queues, as we will see in the sample application in Section 4.8, "Application: Average Waiting Time."

4.2   The Queue Interface

This section formally specifies our Queue ADT. Other than the fact that we support the operations enqueue and dequeue rather than push, pop, and top, we use the same basic approach as we did for our Stack ADT:

- Our queues are generic—the type of object held by a particular queue is indicated by the client at the time the queue is instantiated.
- The classes defined to support our queues are grouped together in the ch04. queues package.

- We provide an observer operation `size` so that an application can determine the size of a queue. The size of a queue might be important to an application because it can give an indication of how long an element will remain in the queue.

- We provide observer operations `isEmpty` and `isFull` so that a client, when appropriate, can prevent itself from trying to remove an element from an empty queue or add an element to a full queue.

- We create `QueueUnderflowException` and `QueueOverflowException` classes.

- We create a `QueueInterface` that defines the signatures of the queue methods. An implementation of a queue should `implement` this interface.

The code for the two exception classes is essentially the same as that used for the two stack exception classes in Chapter 2, so we do not show it here. As with stacks, the application programmer can decide to prevent problems by using the `isFull` and `isEmpty` observers before accessing a queue, or the application can "try" the access operations and "catch and handle" any raised exception.

Here is the `QueueInterface`. As you can see, it defines the signatures of the five queue methods—enqueue, dequeue, isEmpty, isFull, and size.

```
//---------------------------------------------------------------------------
// QueueInterface.java          by Dale/Joyce/Weems          Chapter 4
//
// Interface for a class that implements a queue of T.
// A queue is a "first in, first out" structure.
//---------------------------------------------------------------------------
package ch04.queues;

public interface QueueInterface<T>
{
    void enqueue(T element) throws QueueOverflowException¹;
    // Throws QueueOverflowException if this queue is full;
    // otherwise, adds element to the rear of this queue.

    T dequeue() throws QueueUnderflowException;
    // Throws QueueUnderflowException if this queue is empty;
    // otherwise, removes front element from this queue and returns it.

    boolean isFull();
    // Returns true if this queue is full;
    // otherwise, returns false.
```

---

[1] The queue exceptions are unchecked exceptions; therefore, including them in the interface has no effect from a syntactic or run-time error-checking standpoint. We show them in the interfaces to describe our expectations for the implementation.

```
boolean isEmpty();
// Returns true if this queue is empty;
// otherwise, returns false.

int size();
// Returns the number of elements in this queue.
}
```

Example Use

As we did for stacks we provide a simple example use of a queue to end this section about the formal specification of the Queue ADT. The `RepeatStrings` example shows how to use a queue to store strings provided by a user and then to output the strings in the same order in which they were entered. The code uses the array-based implementation of a queue developed in the next section. The parts of the code directly related to the creation and use of the queue are <u>emphasized.</u> We declare the queue to be of type `QueueInterface<String>` and then instantiate it as an `ArrayBoundedQueue<String>`. Within the *for* loop, three strings provided by the user are enqueued. The *while* loop repeatedly dequeues and prints the front string from the queue until the queue is empty.

Authors' Note

This example closely resembles the example provided for the Stack ADT on page 89. It might be helpful for you to compare and contrast the two programs and their outputs.

```
//----------------------------------------------------------------
// RepeatStrings.java        by Dale/Joyce/Weems         Chapter 4
//
// Sample use of a queue. Outputs strings in same order of entry.
//----------------------------------------------------------------
package ch04.apps;

import ch04.queues.*;
import java.util.Scanner;

public class RepeatStrings
{
  public static void main(String[] args)
  {
    Scanner scan = new Scanner(System.in);

    QueueInterface<String> stringQueue;
    stringQueue = new ArrayBoundedQueue<String>(3);

    String line;

    for (int i = 1; i <= 3; i++)
```

```
    {
      System.out.print("Enter a line of text > ");
      line = scan.nextLine();
      stringQueue.enqueue(line);
    }

    System.out.println("\nOrder is:\n");
    while (!stringQueue.isEmpty())
    {
      line = stringQueue.dequeue();
      System.out.println(line);
    }
  }
}
```

Here is the output from a sample run:

```
Enter a line of text > the beginning of a story
Enter a line of text > is often different than
Enter a line of text > the end of a story

Order is:

the beginning of a story
is often different than
the end of a story
```

4.3   Array-Based Queue Implementations

This section presents two array-based implementations of the Queue ADT: one that implements a bounded queue and one that implements an unbounded queue. We continue to simplify some of our figures by using a capital letter to represent an element's information.

Note that Figure 4.16, in the chapter's summary, shows the relationships among all the classes and interfaces created to support our Queue ADT.

The ArrayBoundedQueue Class

First we develop a Java class that implements a fixed-size queue. Such a queue is often called a "bounded buffer" because it has a limited size (it is bounded), and it can be used to temporarily hold information until it is needed (it is a buffer). We call our class ArrayBoundedQueue, in recognition of the fact that it uses an array as the internal implementation. The term Bounded is part of the class name to distinguish this class from the array-based unbounded queue that is developed later in this section.

Our first task is to decide how to store the queue in the array: We need some way of determining the front and rear elements of the queue. Several possible alternatives are available.

Fixed-Front Design Approach

In our array-based implementation of the Stack ADT we began by inserting an element into the first array position, setting `topIndex` to 0, and then adjusting the location of `topIndex` with subsequent `push` and `pop` operations. The bottom of the stack, however, was always the first slot in the array. Can we use a similar solution for a queue, keeping the front of the queue fixed in the first array slot and letting the rear move as new elements are added?

Let us see what happens after a few `enqueue` and `dequeue` operations if we add the first element into the first array position, the second element into the second position, and so on. To simplify our figures in this chapter, we show the element sitting inside its corresponding array slot—keep in mind that, in actuality, the array slot holds a reference to the element. After four calls to `enqueue` with arguments A, B, C, and D, the queue would look like this:

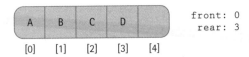

Remember that the front of the queue is fixed at the first slot in the array, whereas the rear of the queue moves back with each enqueue. Now we dequeue the front element from the queue:

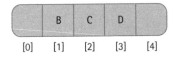

This operation removes the element in the first array slot and leaves a hole. To keep the front of the queue fixed at the top of the array, we need to move every element in the queue forward one slot:

With this design the `enqueue` operation is the same as the array-based stack's `push`, simply add the element into the next available array slot. The `dequeue` operation is more complicated than the stack's `pop`, because the remaining elements of the queue have to shift up toward the front of the array.

Let us evaluate this design. Its strengths are its simplicity and ease of coding; it is almost as simple as the stack implementation. Although the queue is accessed from both ends rather than one (as in the stack), we just have to keep track of the rear, because the front is fixed. Only the `dequeue` operation is more complicated. What is the weakness of the design? It is the complexity and inefficiency of the `dequeue` operation. *All* of the elements must move forward one array slot every time we dequeue, which increases the amount of work done.

> **Implementation Efficiency**
>
> In general we try to design the most efficient implementation of an ADT in terms of order of growth analysis that is possible, but it is not always clear how to measure efficiency. Sometimes efficiency depends upon how the implementation will be used by the applications.

How serious is this weakness? To make this judgment, we have to know something about how the queue will be used. If it will hold large numbers of elements, the processing required to move the elements with each dequeue makes this solution a poor one. Conversely, if the queue generally contains only a few elements, the data movement may not be too costly. Although this design can be made to work and has acceptable performance in some situations, in general it is not the most efficient choice. Let us develop a design that avoids the need to move all the queue elements for each `dequeue` operation.

Floating-Front Design Approach

The need to move the elements in the array was created by our decision to keep the front of the queue fixed in the first array slot and to let only the rear move. What if we allow both the front and the rear to move? As before, an `enqueue` operation adds an element at the rear of the queue and adjusts the location of the rear. But now a `dequeue` operation removes the element at the front and simply adjusts the location of the front. No movement of elements is required. However, we now have to keep track of the array indices of both the front and the rear of the queue.

Figure 4.3 shows how several `enqueue` and `dequeue` operations would affect a queue that uses this approach.

Letting the queue elements float in the array creates a new problem when the rear indicator gets to the end of the array. In our first design, this situation told us that the queue was full. Now, however, the rear of the queue could potentially reach the end of the array when the queue is not yet full (**Figure 4.4a**).

Because there may still be space available at the beginning of the array, the obvious solution is to let the queue elements "wrap around" the end of the array. In other words, the array can be treated as a circular structure in which the last slot is followed by the first slot (Figure 4.4b). To get the next position for the rear indicator, for instance, we can use an *if* statement. Assume `capacity` represents the size of the array:

```
if (rear == (capacity - 1))
    rear = 0;
else
    rear = rear + 1;
```

Another way to reset `rear` is to use the modulo (%) operator:

```
rear = (rear + 1) % capacity;
```

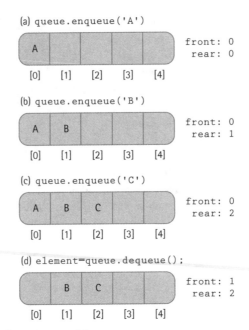

(a) queue.enqueue('A')

front: 0
rear: 0

(b) queue.enqueue('B')

front: 0
rear: 1

(c) queue.enqueue('C')

front: 0
rear: 2

(d) element=queue.dequeue();

front: 1
rear: 2

Figure 4.3 The effect of enqueue and dequeue

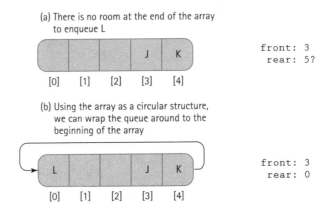

(a) There is no room at the end of the array to enqueue L

front: 3
rear: 5?

(b) Using the array as a circular structure, we can wrap the queue around to the beginning of the array

front: 3
rear: 0

Figure 4.4 Wrapping the queue elements around the array

Comparing Design Approaches

The circular array (floating-front) solution is not as simple as the fixed-front design. What do we gain by adding this complexity to our design? By using a more efficient dequeue operation, we achieve better performance. The fixed-front version of dequeue is an $O(N)$ operation. The floating-front design requires dequeue to perform just a few simple operations. The amount of work never exceeds some fixed constant, no matter how many elements are in the queue, so the algorithm's complexity is O(1).

We will use the more efficient floating-front approach.

The Instance Variables and Constructors

Simplicity Versus Efficiency

Usually when we design a more efficient ADT implementation approach it is also a more complex approach—in terms of the complexity of the code. In some cases the less complex, less efficient approach may be preferred. Simpler designs are easier to imagine, code, test, and maintain, saving human time and cost. Sometimes this savings outweighs the benefits of more efficient code.

What instance variables does our implementation need? We need the queue elements themselves; they are held in an array named `elements`. From our earlier analysis, we know that we must add two instance variables to the class: `front` and `rear`. And we know that to help wrap around the array it is useful to know its capacity—that is, the maximum number of elements the queue can hold. The capacity is supplied by the array's *length* attribute.

We are now confident that we can handle the `enqueue` and `dequeue` operations, but what about the remaining operations? To facilitate the observer operations `isEmpty`, `isFull`, and `size`, we decide to use one more instance variable, `numElements`. The `numElements` variable holds the current number of elements in the queue. Here is the beginning of `ArrayBoundedQueue`:

```
//-----------------------------------------------------------------
// ArrayBoundedQueue.java          by Dale/Joyce/Weems          Chapter 4
//
// Implements QueueInterface with an array to hold the queue elements.
// Two constructors are provided: one that creates a queue of a default
// capacity and one that allows the calling program to specify the capacity.
//-----------------------------------------------------------------
package ch04.queues;
public class ArrayBoundedQueue<T> implements QueueInterface<T>
{
  protected final int DEFCAP = 100;  // default capacity
  protected T[] elements;            // array that holds queue elements
  protected int numElements = 0;     // number of elements in the queue
  protected int front = 0;           // index of front of queue
  protected int rear;                // index of rear of queue

  public ArrayBoundedQueue()
  {
    elements = (T[]) new Object[DEFCAP]²;
    rear = DEFCAP - 1;
  }
}
```

---

[2] An unchecked cast warning is generated because the compiler cannot ensure that the array contains objects of class T—the warning can safely be ignored.

```
public ArrayBoundedQueue(int maxSize)
{
   elements = (T[]) new Object[maxSize]³;
   rear = maxSize - 1;
}
```

As you can see, our class includes the two standard constructors for a bounded structure: one for which the client program specifies a maximum size and one that defaults to a maximum size of DEFCAP elements (the default capacity is 100). Recall that because the Java translator will not generate references to a generic type, our code must specify Object along with the *new* statement within our constructors. Thus, we declare our arrays to be arrays of class T but instantiate them to be arrays of class Object. Then, to ensure that the desired type checking takes place, we cast array elements into class T. Even though this approach is somewhat awkward and typically generates a compiler warning, it is how we must create generic collections using arrays in Java.

The rear variable is initialized to the last array index. Due to the wraparound approach used, the first time something is enqueued this value is set to 0, indicating the array slot that should hold that first element. The front variable is initialized to 0, as that is the array index of the first element that is dequeued. Note that when the queue holds just one element, front and rear will have the same value.

Definitions of Queue Operations

Given the preceding discussion, the implementations of our queue operations are straightforward. Recall that for the bounded queue the enqueue method should throw an exception if the queue is full. If the queue is not full, the method should simply increment the rear variable, "wrapping it around" if necessary, place the element into the rear location, and increment the numElements variable.

```
public void enqueue(T element)
// Throws QueueOverflowException if this queue is full;
// otherwise, adds element to the rear of this queue.
{
  if (isFull())
    throw new QueueOverflowException("Enqueue attempted on a full queue.");
  else
  {
    rear = (rear + 1) % elements.length;
    elements[rear] = element;
    numElements = numElements + 1;
  }
}
```

³ An unchecked cast warning is generated because the compiler cannot ensure that the array contains objects of class T—the warning can safely be ignored.

The dequeue method is essentially the reverse of enqueue. It throws an exception if the queue is empty. Otherwise, it increments front, also wrapping if necessary, decrements numElements, and returns the element previously indicated by the front variable. This methods starts by copying the reference to the object it eventually returns. It does so because during its next step, it removes the reference to the object from the array.

```
public T dequeue()
// Throws QueueUnderflowException if this queue is empty;
// otherwise, removes front element from this queue and returns it.
{
  if (isEmpty())
    throw new QueueUnderflowException("Dequeue attempted on empty queue.");
  else
  {
    T toReturn = elements[front];
    elements[front] = null;
    front = (front + 1) % elements.length;
    numElements = numElements - 1;
    return toReturn;
  }
}
```

Note that dequeue, like the stack pop operation, sets the value of the array location associated with the removed element to null. This allows the Java garbage collection process to work with up-to-date information.

The observer methods are very simple, thanks to the fact that we keep track of the size of the queue in the numElements variable:

```
public boolean isEmpty()
// Returns true if this queue is empty; otherwise, returns false
{
    return (numElements == 0);
}
```

```
public boolean isFull()
// Returns true if this queue is full; otherwise, returns false.
{
    return (numElements == elements.length);
}
```

```
public int size()
// Returns the number of elements in this queue.
{
        return numElements;
}
```

That completes the development of our array-based bounded queue implementation.

The ArrayUnboundedQueue Class

Next we develop a Java class that uses an array and implements an unbounded queue. It may seem surprising to implement an unbounded structure using an array, given that once an array is created its capacity cannot be changed. The trick is to create a new, larger array, when needed, and copy the structure into the new array.

To create the ArrayUnboundedQueue class we can reuse some of the design and code from our previous work. There are several options:

- We could extend the ArrayBoundedQueue class, overwriting any methods affected by the change—both the enqueue and the isFull methods. This is a valid approach. As a general rule, however, we hesitate to extend concrete classes. Doing so creates a tight coupling between the two classes that can create issues later on, if the base class is modified.

- We could "wrap" a bounded queue inside of our unbounded queue implementation. In other words, instead of directly using an array to hold our unbounded queue, use a bounded queue to hold it. When needed, instantiate a new larger bounded queue, copying over the contents of the previous bounded queue using a sequence of dequeue/enqueue operations. This approach also works although it adds an extra level of abstraction.

- We could reuse the basic parts of our bounded queue design, redesigning it as necessary to make the queue unbounded. In other words, literally make a copy of the ArrayBoundedQueue.java file, rename the file to ArrayUnboundedQueue, and then make the required changes to this file. We opt for this third approach.

Starting with ArrayBoundedQueue, what changes are needed so that the queue never becomes full? Of course, we change the name of the class to ArrayUnboundedQueue. We also change the isFull() method so that it always returns false, since an unbounded queue is never full.

Those are the "easy" changes. Now we address the issue of making the structure unbounded. We must change the enqueue method to increase the capacity of the array if it has run out of space. Because enlarging the array is conceptually a separate operation from enqueuing, we implement it as a separate method named enlarge. So the enqueue method begins with the following statement:

```
if (numElements == elements.length)
enlarge();
```

Next we need to implement the enlarge method. By how much should we increase the size of the array? Again, several options are possible:

- Set a constant increment value or multiplying factor within the class.
- Allow the application to specify an increment value or multiplying factor when the queue is instantiated.
- Use the original capacity as the increment value.

Because `enlarge` must copy the contents of the entire array, it is a O(*N*) operation—therefore we do not want to invoke it too often. This fact implies that we should increment the capacity by a large amount. But if we increment by too large an amount, we waste both time and space.

> **Solution Reuse I**
>
> The approach we describe here for creating an array-based unbounded queue can be used for other array-based unbounded structures. In fact, it is used to implement some of the similar structures found in the Java library such as the `ArrayList`.

Let us use the original capacity as the increment value. Our `enlarge` method instantiates an array with a size equal to the current capacity plus the original capacity. Our constructor code stores the value of the original capacity using an instance variable `origCap`.

Within `enlarge`, when copying the contents from the old array into the new array, we must be careful to step through the elements of the queue, beginning at `front`, and properly wrapping around the end of the array on our way to `rear`. In the new array the elements are placed at the beginning of the array. After the copy operation, we update instance variables appropriately. Here are the declarations and affected methods of the `ArrayUnboundedQueue` class, with the code changes from the bounded version <u>emphasized</u>.

```
//-------------------------------------------------------------------------
// ArrayUnboundedQueue.java      by Dale/Joyce/Weems          Chapter 4
//
// Implements QueueInterface with an array to hold queue elements.
//
// Two constructors are provided; one that creates a queue of a default
// original capacity and one that allows the calling program to specify the
// original capacity.
//
// If an enqueue is attempted when there is no room available in the array, a
// new array is created, with capacity incremented by the original capacity.
//-------------------------------------------------------------------------
package ch04.queues;

public class ArrayUnboundedQueue<T> implements QueueInterface<T>
{
  protected final int DEFCAP = 100;  // default capacity
  protected T[] elements;            // array that holds queue elements
  protected int origCap;             // original capacity
  protected int numElements = 0;     // number of elements in the queue
  protected int front = 0;           // index of front of queue
  protected int rear;                // index of rear of queue
```

```
public ArrayUnboundedQueue()
{
  elements = (T[]) new Object[DEFCAP]⁴;
  rear = DEFCAP - 1;
  origCap = DEFCAP;
}

public ArrayUnboundedQueue(int origCap)
{
  elements = (T[]) new Object[origCap]⁵;
  rear = origCap - 1;
  this.origCap = origCap;
}

private void enlarge()
// Increments the capacity of the queue by an amount
// equal to the original capacity.
{
  // create the larger array
  T[] larger = (T[]) new Object[elements.length + origCap];

  // copy the contents from the smaller array into the larger array
  int currSmaller = front;
  for (int currLarger = 0; currLarger < numElements; currLarger++)
  {
    larger[currLarger] = elements[currSmaller];
    currSmaller = (currSmaller + 1) % elements.length;
  }

  // update instance variables
  elements = larger;
  front = 0;
  rear = numElements - 1;
}
public void enqueue(T element)
// Adds element to the rear of this queue.
{
  if (numElements == elements.length)
    enlarge();
```

[4, 5] An unchecked cast warning is generated because the compiler cannot ensure that the array contains objects of class T—the warning can safely be ignored.

```
    rear = (rear + 1) % elements.length;
    elements[rear] = element;
    numElements = numElements + 1;
  }


// dequeue, isEmpty and size code not printed - they are unchanged


  public boolean isFull()
  // Returns false - an unbounded queue is never full.
  {
    return false;
  }
}
```

In our bounded queue implementation the enqueue method exhibits O(1) complexity. That is not the case for our unbounded queue, at least not in the worst case. Do you see why? If the number of enqueue invocations exceeds the number of dequeue invocations, eventually the elements array becomes full and the enqueue method will invoke the enlarge method. Because the enlarge method is $O(N)$ we must say that the corresponding call to enqueue also required $O(N)$ steps. Thus in the worst case, enqueue is $O(N)$.

Note that there can be a long sequence of enqueue and dequeue operations executed before the enlarge method is invoked; in fact, there can be applications that use our unbounded queue that never cause the array to become full. At the very least there must be $N + 1$ calls to the enqueue method before the enlarge method is invoked on an array of size N. If we distribute the cost of the enlarge method across these $N + 1$ calls, then the average cost of the enqueue method is still O(1). Using this average cost approach we can consider the execution efficiency of the enqueue method to be O(1). The analysis employed in this paragraph is called **amortized analysis**—amortization is a financial term related to spreading a payment of a debt across several payments as opposed to paying in one lump sum.

> **Amortized Cost**
>
> If occasionally a method requires extra processing, we might consider the cost of the extra processing to be spread across all the invocations of the method, softening the perceived drawback of the extra processing. Using average case analysis in place of worst case analysis like this, to spread the cost of unusual extra processing, is sometimes called amortized analysis.

Note that if you are working within an environment where consistent efficiency is important, for example, with some real-time systems, then average case efficiency might not be the appropriate measure to consider. In such environments you must be cautious in your choice of ADT implementation.

Section 2.5, "Array-Based Stack Implementations," includes a description about implementing an unbounded stack using the Java library ArrayList class. ArrayList can also be used to implement an unbounded queue—in fact, it is a good choice for the implementation because it provides a structure that grows in size as needed *and* it supports the use of generic types without the generation of any compiler warnings. Exercise 14 asks you to explore this implementation approach.

4.4 An Interactive Test Driver

Section 2.5, "Array-Based Stack Implementations," addressed testing our ADTs. It discussed the importance of developing a test driver application in parallel with the development of the ADT implementation class. It also discussed the importance of batch testing tools in a professional environment. Here we take a slightly different approach. We create an interactive test driver for our `ArrayBoundedQueue` class. Not only does this application act as an example use of the `ArrayBoundedQueue` class, it can also be used by students to experiment and learn about the Queue ADT and the relationships among its exported methods. The approach outlined in this section can be used to create similar test drivers for any of the ADT implementation classes presented in the text (or elsewhere in fact). Our interactive test driver will use elements of type `String` to be stored and retrieved from the ADT.

The General Approach

Every ADT that we implement supports a set of operations. For each ADT we therefore can create an interactive test driver program that allows us to test the operations in a variety of sequences. How can we write a single test driver that allows us to test numerous operation sequences? The solution is to create a test driver that repeatedly presents the user—that is, the tester—with a choice of operations representing the exported methods of the ADT. In this way the tester can test any sequence of operations he or she chooses. When the tester chooses an operation that requires one or more arguments, then the test driver prompts the tester to supply that information also.

Interactive test drivers can all follow the same basic algorithm. Here is a pseudo-code description:

Interactive Test Driver for ADT Implementation

Prompt for, read, and display test name
Determine which constructor to use, obtain needed parameters, instantiate a new instance of the ADT
while (testing continues)
{
  Display a menu of operation choices, one choice for each
    method exported by the ADT implementation, plus a "stop testing" choice
  Get the user's choice and obtain any needed parameters
  Perform the chosen operation
    if an exception is thrown, catch it and report its message
    if a value is returned, report it
}

The interactive test driver obtains the operation requests from the user one at a time, performs the operation by invoking the methods of the class being tested, and reports the results to an output stream. This approach provides us with maximum flexibility when we are testing our ADTs.

Notice that the first step prompts for, reads, and displays the test name. This step might seem unnecessary for an interactive program given that the name of the test is reported directly back to the user who enters it. However, the programmer performing the test may want to save a record of the interactive dialogue for later study or as archival test documentation, so establishing a name for the interactive dialogue can prove useful.

> **Solution Reuse II**
>
> The approach we describe here for creating an interactive test driver for our array-based bounded queue implementation can also be used to test many other classes. Exercise 18 asks you to do just that, create similar test programs. It is even conceivable to imagine creating a program that would generate such test programs automatically, given a particular ADT implementation class as input. It is observations such as this that lead to the creation of software development tools.

A Test Driver for the ArrayBoundedQueue Class

The application `ITDArrayBoundedQueue` is included in the `ch04.queues` package with the program files. The leading "ITD" stands for Interactive Test Driver.

Study the test driver program. You should be able to follow the control logic and recognize that it is a refinement of the pseudo-code presented above. You should also understand the purpose of each statement. Although the program is straightforward, a few points require further explanation. The program starts by using `new` to instantiate `test`, an `ArrayBoundedQueue` variable. It then proceeds to ask the user to select one of the two available constructors and, under the control of the first *switch* statement, instantiates `test` again. It does not appear that the first use of the `new` command, in the opening statement of the `main` method, is necessary. It seems to be redundant. However, some Java compilers require that statement. Without it they report an error such as "variable `test` might not have been initialized" because the later `new` commands are embedded within a decision structure (the *switch* statement) that includes a branch without a `new` command (the default branch). These compilers conclude that `new` may not be executed. Including the `new` command in the opening statement resolves the problem.

The test driver does some error checking to ensure that user inputs are valid, but it does not represent a completely robust program. For instance, it does not verify that the size provided for the second constructor is a positive number, and it does not prevent the user from inserting too many elements into an `ArrayBoundedQueue`. Although both of these situations are disallowed by the contract of `ArrayBoundedQueue`, based on the stated preconditions, they should not be prevented by our test driver program. The user of the test driver, who is testing the `ArrayBoundedQueue`, might wish to determine what happens when preconditions are not met and, therefore, needs the ability to violate the preconditions during a test run.

Using the Test Driver

Figure 4.5 shows the result of a sample run of the test driver. User input is shown in **blue**. The repeated display of the operation menu has been replaced with `"..."` in most places. As you can see, in this test the user chooses to use the first constructor to

```
What is the name of this test?     1
Sample Test                        Enter string to enqueue:
                                   Test Line 2
This is test Sample Test           enqueue("Test Line 2")
                                   Choose an operation:
Choose a constructor:              . . .
1: ArrayBoundedQueue( )            3
2: ArrayBoundedQueue(int maxSize)  isFull()
1                                  Result: false

Choose an operation:               Choose an operation:
1: enqueue(element)                . . .
2: String dequeue()                2
3: boolean isFull()                dequeue()
4: boolean isEmpty()               Result: Test Line 1 was
5: int size()                      returned.
6: stop Testing
4                                  Choose an operation:
isEmpty()                          . . .
Result: true                       2
                                   dequeue()
Choose an operation:               Result: Test Line 2 was
. . .                              returned.
1                                  Choose an operation:
Enter string to enqueue:           . . .
Test Line 1                        2
enqueue("Test Line 1")             dequeue()
                                   Underflow Exception: Dequeue
                                   attempted on empty queue.
Choose an operation:
. . .                              Choose an operation:
4                                  . . .
isEmpty()                          6
Result: false                      End of Interactive Test Driver

Choose an operation:
. . .
```

Figure 4.5 Output from interactive test driver

create the queue and then requests the following sequence of operations: `isEmpty()`, `enqueue("Test Line 1")`, `isEmpty()`, `enqueue("Test Line 2")`, `isFull()`, `dequeue()`, `dequeue()`, and `dequeue()`. Our `ArrayBoundedQueue` class passed the test! The reader is encouraged to try this test driver yourself.

4.5 Link-Based Queue Implementations

In this section we implement an unbounded queue using a linked list. We call our class `LinkedQueue`. As we did for the linked implementation of stacks presented in Chapter 2, we use the `LLNode` class from our `support` package to provide the nodes for the internal representation.

In the array-based implementation of a queue, we kept track of two indices that indicated the front and rear boundaries of the data in the queue. In a linked representation, we can use two references, `front` and `rear`, to mark the front and the rear of the queue, respectively. When the queue is empty, both of these references should equal `null`. Therefore, the constructor for the queue initializes them both accordingly. The beginning of our class definition is as follows:

```
//--------------------------------------------------------------------
// LinkedQueue.java              by Dale/Joyce/Weems          Chapter 4
//
// Implements QueueInterface using a linked list.
//--------------------------------------------------------------------
package ch04.queues;
import support.LLNode;

public class LinkedQueue<T> implements QueueInterface<T>
{
  protected LLNode<T> front;     // reference to the front of this queue
  protected LLNode<T> rear;      // reference to the rear of this queue
  protected int numElements = 0; // number of elements in this queue

  public LinkedQueue()
  {
    front = null;  rear = null;
  }
}
```

Figure 4.6 graphically depicts our queue representation. We often depict queues by showing their instance variables (`front` and `rear`) in different areas of the figure. Recall that these variables are actually collected together in a single queue object. Also, recall that dynamically allocated nodes in linked structures exist "somewhere in the system memory" although we show the nodes arranged linearly for clarity. We will not include the `numElements` variable in our figures in this section.

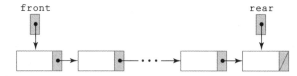

Figure 4.6 A linked queue representation

The Enqueue Operation

In our linked implementation of the Stack ADT, we saw how to add and delete a node at the beginning of a linked list. We add new elements to a queue by inserting them at the rear of the structure—we have not yet seen that operation. We need an algorithm to implement the enqueue operation. The steps in the algorithm are numbered and steps 1, 2, and 3 correspond to the labeled parts of **Figure 4.7**.

Enqueue(element)

1. Create a node for the new element
2. Add the new node at the rear of the queue
3. Update the reference to the rear of the queue
4. Increment the number of elements

Here we look at these four steps, one at a time:

1. The first step is familiar. We create a new node for the element by instantiating a new LLNode object and passing it the element as an argument:

   ```
   LLNode<T> newNode = new LLNode<T>(element);
   ```

2. Next we add our new node at the rear of the queue. We set the link of the current last node to reference the new node, using the LLNode setLink method:

   ```
   rear.setLink(newNode);
   ```

   But what happens if the queue is empty when we enqueue the element? When using references, you must always be sure to handle the special case of null; you cannot use it to access an object. If the queue is empty when we add the element, the value of rear would be null and the use of rear.setLink would raise a run-time exception. In other words, we cannot "set the link of the current last node to reference the new node" because there is no "current last node." In this case we must set front to point to the new node since it is the first node in the queue:

   ```
   if (rear == null)
     front = newNode;
   else
     rear.setLink(newNode);
   ```

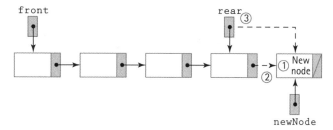

Figure 4.7 The enqueue operation

3. The next task in the `enqueue` algorithm, updating the `rear` reference, simply involves the assignment:

```
rear = newNode;
```

Does this work if it is the first node in the queue—that is, if we are inserting into an empty queue? Yes, because we always have `rear` pointing to the new node following a call to `enqueue`, regardless of how many elements are in the queue.

4. Incrementing the number of elements is straightforward:

```
numElements++;
```

Putting this all together, we get the following code for the `enqueue` method:

```
public void enqueue(T element)
// Adds element to the rear of this queue.
{
    LLNode<T> newNode = new LLNode<T>(element);
    if (rear == null)
        front = newNode;
    else
        rear.setLink(newNode);
    rear = newNode;
    numElements++;
}
```

The Dequeue Operation

The `dequeue` operation is similar to the stack's `pop` operation because it removes an element from the beginning of the linked list. However, recall that `pop` only removed the top element from the stack, whereas `dequeue` both removes and returns the element. Also, as with the stack's `top` operation, we do not want to return the entire `LLNode`, just the information the node contains.

In writing the `enqueue` algorithm, we noticed that inserting into an empty queue is a special case because we need to make `front` point to the new node. Similarly, in our `dequeue` algorithm we need to allow for the special case of deleting the only node in the

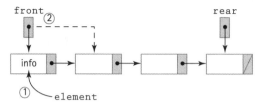

Figure 4.8   The `dequeue` operation

queue, leaving it empty. If `front` is `null` after being reset, the queue is empty and we need to set `rear` to `null`. The first few steps of the algorithm for removing and returning the front element from a linked queue are illustrated in **Figure 4.8**.

Dequeue: returns Object

1. Set element to reference the information in the front node
2. Remove the front node from the queue
3. if the queue is empty
     Set rear to null
4. Decrement the number of elements
5. return element

Let us look at the implementation line by line.

1. We "remember" the information in the first node so that we can return it later. We declare a local T variable `element` and then assign the information (i.e., the reference to the information) from the front queue element to it:

    ```
    T element;
    element = front.getInfo();
    ```

2. We remove the front node from the queue. This step is easy: just set `front` to the link to the next element. This approach works even if the resultant queue is empty, because the link would be `null`:

    ```
    front = front.getLink();
    ```

3. If the queue becomes empty, also set the `rear` of the queue to `null`, as discussed earlier:

    ```
    if (front == null)
        rear = null;
    ```

4. Decrementing the number of elements is straightforward:

    ```
    numElements--;
    ```

5. Now just return the information saved earlier:

    ```
    return element;
    ```

Finally, we must remember to throw a `QueueUnderflowException` if the dequeue operation is attempted on an empty queue. Putting it all together, the code is as shown here;

```
public T dequeue()
// Throws QueueUnderflowException if this queue is empty;
// otherwise, removes front element from this queue and returns it.
{
  if (isEmpty())
    throw new QueueUnderflowException("Dequeue attempted on empty queue.");
  else
  {
    T element;
    element = front.getInfo();
    front = front.getLink();
    if (front == null)
      rear = null;
    numElements--;
    return element;
  }
}
```

The remaining operations `isEmpty`, `isFull`, and `size` are all very straightforward. The code for the entire class can be found within the `ch04.queues` package.

A Circular Linked Queue Design

Our `LinkedQueue` class contains two instance variables, one to reference each end of the queue. This design is based on the linear structure of the linked queue. Can we implement the class using only one instance variable? Given only a reference to the front of the queue, we could follow the links to get to the rear of the queue, but this approach makes accessing the rear (to enqueue an element) an O(N) operation. If instead we set the only reference to the rear of the queue, it is impossible to access the front because the links only go from front to rear, so this approach also will not work well.

However, we can efficiently access both ends of the queue from a single reference if the queue is **circularly linked**. That is, the link of the rear node would reference the front node of the queue (see **Figure 4.9**). A `LinkedQueue` could then have only one instance

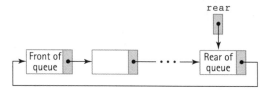

Figure 4.9 A circular linked queue

variable, referencing the rear of the queue, rather than two. This queue implementation differs from the abstract picture of a queue as a linear structure with two ends. Instead, it is a circular structure with no ends. What makes it a queue is its support of FIFO access.

To enqueue an element, we access the "rear" node directly through the reference `rear`. To dequeue an element, we must access the "front" node of the queue. We do not have a reference to this node, but we do have a reference to the node preceding it—`rear`. The reference to the "front" node of the queue is in `rear.getLink()`. For an empty queue, `rear` would be `null`. Designing and coding the Queue ADT operations using a circular linked implementation is left for you as an exercise.

Comparing Queue Implementations

We have now looked at several different implementations of the Queue ADT. How do they compare? We consider two different factors: the amount of memory required to store the structure and the amount of "work" the solution requires, as expressed in order of growth notation. Let us first compare the `ArrayBoundedQueue` and `LinkedQueue` implementations.

The internal array in an `ArrayBoundedQueue` consumes the same amount of memory, no matter how many slots are actually used; we need to reserve space for the maximum number of elements. The linked implementation using dynamically allocated storage space requires space only for the number of elements actually in the queue. Note, however, that the node elements are twice as large, because we must store the link (the reference to the next node) as well as the reference to the element.

Figure 4.10 illustrates each queue implementation approach, assuming a current queue size of 5 and a maximum queue size (for the array-based implementation) of 100. To simplify, we ignore the instance variables related to capacity and number of elements. Note that the array-based implementation requires space for two integers and 101 references (one for the array reference variable `elements` and one for each array slot) regardless of the size of the queue. The linked implementation requires space for only 12 references (one for `front`, one for `rear`, and two for each of the current queue elements). However, for the linked implementation the required space increases as the size of the queue increases, based on the following formula:

```
Number of required references = 2 + ( 2 * size of queue)
```

A simple analysis reveals that the breakeven point between the two approaches in terms of space used is when the actual queue size is approximately half the maximum queue size. For smaller queues the linked representation requires less space than the array-based representation, and beyond that size, the linked representation requires more space. In any case, unless the maximum queue size is significantly larger than the average queue size, the difference between the two implementations in terms of space is probably not important.

We can also compare the relative execution "efficiency" of the two implementations in terms of order of growth notation. In both implementations, the complexity of the

Queues with
    Maximum size 100 (Array-Based)
    Current size 5
    x = null

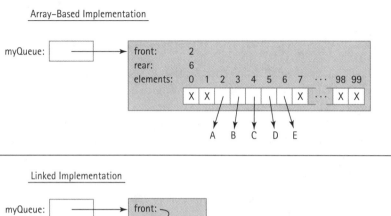

Array–Based Implementation

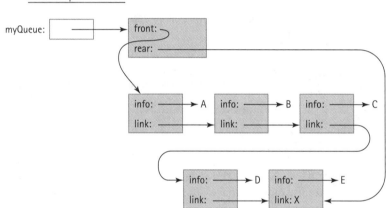

Linked Implementation

Figure 4.10   Comparing queue implementations

observer methods (isFull, isEmpty, and size) is clearly O(1). These methods always take the same amount of work regardless of how many elements are on the queue. As was the case for stacks, the queue constructor requires O(N) steps for the array representation, but is O(1) for the linked representation.

What about enqueue and dequeue? Does the number of elements in the queue affect the amount of work done by these operations? No, it does not; in both implementations, we can directly access the front and the rear of the queue. The amount of work done by these operations is independent of the queue size, so these operations also have O(1) complexity. As with the array-based and linked implementations of stacks, both queue implementations are roughly equivalent in terms of the amount of work they do.

Now we briefly consider our ArrayUnboundedQueue approach. The analysis for the bounded approach applies to the unbounded approach. However, with the unbounded approach we could start with an array size that handles an average-size queue; only if the queue becomes larger is the array expanded. Thus we do not pay as big a penalty in terms of extra space. The drawback is the extra time, $O(N)$, required to resize the array. For most applications this operation is not required very often, and as discussed earlier, we can consider the $O(N)$ cost of this operation to be spread across many enqueue invocations.

4.6 Application: Palindromes

In this section we develop a short application that uses both a queue and a stack related to palindromes. This is a simple, fun application that serves to remind us that we can often use more than one ADT when solving problems.

A *palindrome* is a string that reads the same forward and backward. While we are not sure of their general usefulness, identifying them provides us with a good example for the use of both queues and stacks. Besides, palindromes can be entertaining. Consider these famous palindromes:

- A tribute to Teddy Roosevelt, who orchestrated the creation of the Panama Canal: "A man, a plan, a canal—Panama!"
- Allegedly muttered by Napoléon Bonaparte upon his exile to the island of Elba (although this is difficult to believe given that Napoléon mostly spoke French!): "Able was I ere, I saw Elba."
- Overheard in a busy Chinese restaurant: "Won ton? Not now!"
- Possibly the world's first palindrome: "Madam, I'm Adam."
- Followed immediately by one of the world's shortest palindromes: "Eve."

As you can see, the rules for what is a palindrome are somewhat lenient. Typically, we do not worry about punctuation, spaces, or matching the case of letters.

The Palindrome Class

As with previous applications, we separate the user interface from the part of the program that does the main processing. First we concentrate on that main processing—identifying a palindrome.

The class Palindrome exports a single static method test that takes a candidate string argument and returns a boolean value indicating whether the string is a palindrome. Because the method is static, we do not define a constructor for the class. Instead, we invoke the test method using the name of the class.

The test method, when invoked, creates a new stack of characters and a new queue of characters. It then repeatedly pushes each letter from the input line onto the stack, and also enqueues the same letter into the queue. It discards any nonletter characters because they are not considered part of a palindrome. To simplify the comparison later, we push and enqueue lowercase versions of the characters.

When all of the characters of the candidate string have been processed, the program repeatedly pops a letter from the stack and dequeues a letter from the queue. As long as these letters match each other the entire way through this process (until the structures are empty), we have a palindrome. Can you see why? Because the queue is a FIFO structure, the letters are returned from the queue in the same order they appear in the string. But the letters taken from the stack, a LIFO structure, are returned in the opposite order. Thus we are comparing the forward view of the string to the backward view of the string.

Here is the code for the `Palindrome` class.

```java
//-------------------------------------------------------------------------
// Palindrome.java          by Dale/Joyce/Weems          Chapter 4
//
// Provides a method to test whether a string is a palindrome.
// Non letters are skipped.
//-------------------------------------------------------------------------
package ch04.palindromes;

import ch02.stacks.*;
import ch04.queues.*;


public class Palindrome
{
  public static boolean test(String candidate)
  // Returns true if candidate is a palindrome, false otherwise.
  {
    char ch;                    // current candidate character being processed
    int length;                 // length of candidate string
    char fromStack;             // current character popped from stack
    char fromQueue;             // current character dequeued from queue
    boolean stillPalindrome;    // true if string might still be a palindrome

    StackInterface<Character> stack; // holds non blank string characters
    QueueInterface<Character> queue; // also holds non blank string characters

    // initialize variables and structures
    length = candidate.length();
    stack = new ArrayBoundedStack<Character>(length);
    queue = new ArrayBoundedQueue<Character>(length);
```

```
      // obtain and handle characters
      for (int i = 0; i < length; i++)
      {
        ch = candidate.charAt(i);
        if (Character.isLetter(ch))
        {
          ch = Character.toLowerCase(ch);
          stack.push(ch);
          queue.enqueue(ch);
        }
      }

      // determine if palindrome
      stillPalindrome = true;
      while (stillPalindrome && !stack.isEmpty())
      {
        fromStack = stack.top();
        stack.pop();
        fromQueue = queue.dequeue();
        if (fromStack != fromQueue)
          stillPalindrome = false;
      }

      // return result
      return stillPalindrome;
  }
}
```

Note that we use both the bounded stack and the bounded queue implementations. It is appropriate to use bounded structures because the structures need not be larger than the length of the candidate string. Also note that we make use of Java's autoboxing and unboxing features, when adding and removing variables of the primitive type char to and from the structures. The system automatically wraps the char values in a Character object before addition, then unwraps the returned Character object back into a char value after it is removed.

The Applications

The Palindrome class does most of the work for us. All that is left to do now is to implement the user I/O. The PalindromeCLI program found in the ch04.apps package is similar to the command line interface programs presented in previous chapters. Its basic flow is to prompt the user for a string, use the Palindrome class's test method to determine whether the string is a palindrome, output the result, and then ask the user to enter another string, until the user enters a special "stop" string, in this case the string "X". Here is a sample run of the program:

```
String (X to stop): racecar
is a palindrome.

String (X to stop): aaaaaaaaabaaaaaaaa
is NOT a palindrome.

String (X to stop): fred
is NOT a palindrome.

String (X to stop): Are we not drawn onward, we few? Drawn onward
to new era!
is a palindrome.

String (X to stop): X
```

The program `PalindromeGUI`, also found in `ch04.apps`, implements a graphical user interface (GUI)-based interface providing the same functionality as `PalindromeCLI`.

There are other—probably better—ways of determining whether a string is a palindrome. In fact, in Exercise 35 of Chapter 3 we asked you to consider some other approaches. We included this example application for several reasons: it is interesting but not too complicated, it is fun, it clearly demonstrates the association between a stack and a queue, and it reminds us that we can use more than one ADT when solving a problem. **Figure 4.11** is an abbreviated Unified Modeling Language (UML) diagram showing the relationships among the stack and queue interfaces and classes used in the palindrome applications.

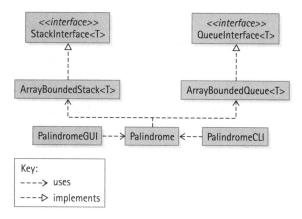

Figure 4.11   Palindrome program architecture

4.7 Queue Variations

As we did with stacks, we look at some variations of the queue. It is important to understand that there are many approaches to defining and implementing data structures. We first consider some alternate ways to define the classic queue operations. Next we look at additional operations that could be included in a Queue ADT, some that allow us to "peek" into the queue and others that expand the access rules, essentially creating a more versatile structure that can be used as both a queue or a stack. Finally, we review the Java Standard Library queue support.

Before continuing we should mention an important ADT closely related to the queue. The Priority Queue ADT is often considered along with queues. A priority queue enqueues elements in any order but when an element is dequeued, it returns the highest priority element. So unlike with the traditional queue, the order in which elements enter the queue has no relationship to the order in which they are removed. The Priority Queue is an important ADT; we return to it in Chapter 9.

Exceptional Situations

Our queues throw exceptions in the case of underflow or overflow. Another approach is to test for the exceptional situation within the method implementation, prevent the over/underflow from occurring by nullifying the operation, and return a value that indicates failure. With this latter approach we might redefine `enqueue` and `dequeue` as follows:

> `boolean enqueue(T element)` adds `element` to the rear of this queue; returns `true` if element is successfully added, `false` otherwise
>
> `T dequeue()` returns `null` if this queue is empty, otherwise removes front element from this queue and returns it

In the case of `enqueue`, the most common reason for failure to complete the operation would be an attempt to add an element to a full, bounded queue. We also could define alternate versions of queues that have rules about what will or will not be accepted for entry—for example a queue that disallows duplicate elements or a queue that only accepts elements with certain features (only students who ate their vegetables may queue up for ice cream). In the case of `dequeue` the primary reason for failure is that the queue is empty.

Rather than redefining our operations we could just add new operations exhibiting the functionality described above, with unique names such as `safeEnqueue` and `safe-Dequeue` to differentiate them from the regular queue operations.

The GlassQueue

An application that uses our Stack ADT, as defined in Chapter 2, has the option of either obtaining the top element of the stack (the `top` method) or removing the top element from the stack (the `pop` method). This means that an application can "look at" the top element of the stack without removing it from the stack. An application might use this feature to determine whether or not to pop a stack under some circumstances, or perhaps to choose which of several stacks to pop at a particular time.

The ability to look into a data structure without removing an element is often called "peeking." As discussed in Chapter 2, including this operation with stacks makes looking at the top element of the stack easy, but it is a superfluous operation. The same result can be obtained by using the classic pop operation, followed by examining the returned element, followed by a push operation that returns the element to the top of the stack. For queues, however, this is not the case. One cannot just simply dequeue an element, examine it, and then enqueue it back to its original position in the queue. Trying to do so would result in moving the element from the front of the queue to the rear of the queue. For this reason, adding the ability to peek into a queue can be very useful.

We define a new type of queue that includes the ability to peek into both the front and the rear of the queue. We call this queue a Glass Queue, because the queue's contents are somewhat transparent, as if the queue was made from glass. Our Glass Queue must support all of the operations of a "regular" queue plus the new operations peekFront and peekRear. First we define a GlassQueueInterface class.

Java supports **inheritance of interfaces**—one interface can extend another interface. In fact, the language supports **multiple inheritance of interfaces**—a single interface can extend any number of other interfaces. The fact that a Glass Queue requires all of the operations of our current Queue ADT makes this a perfect place to use inheritance. We define our GlassQueueInterface as a new interface that extends QueueInterface but also requires peekFront and peekRear methods. Here is the code for the new interface (note the <u>emphasized</u> extends clause):

```java
//-------------------------------------------------------------------------
// GlassQueueInterface.java         by Dale/Joyce/Weems         Chapter 4
//
// Interface for a class that implements a queue of T and includes operations
// for peeking at the front and rear elements of the queue.
//-------------------------------------------------------------------------
package ch04.queues;

public interface GlassQueueInterface<T> extends QueueInterface<T>
{
  public T peekFront();
  // If the queue is empty, returns null.
  // Otherwise, returns the element at the front of this queue.

  public T peekRear();
  // If the queue is empty, returns null.
  // Otherwise, returns the element at the rear of this queue.
}
```

As you can see, the interface is a simple extension of the `QueueInterface`. Similarly, an implementation of a `LinkedGlassQueue` class, that implements our new `GlassQueue-Interface`, is a straightforward extension of the `LinkedQueue` class:

```
//--------------------------------------------------------------------------
// LinkedGlassQueue.java          by Dale/Joyce/Weems          Chapter 4
//
// Extends LinkedQueue with operations to access the front and rear queue
// elements without removing them.
//--------------------------------------------------------------------------
package ch04.queues;
public class LinkedGlassQueue<T> extends LinkedQueue<T>
                                 implements GlassQueueInterface<T>
{
  public LinkedGlassQueue()
  {
    super();
  }

  public T peekFront()
  // If the queue is empty, returns null.
  // Otherwise returns the element at the front of this queue.
  {
    if (isEmpty())
      return null;
    else
      return front.getInfo();
  }

  public T peekRear()
  // If the queue is empty, returns null.
  // Otherwise returns the element at the rear of this queue.
  {
    if (isEmpty())
      return null;
    else
      return rear.getInfo();
  }
}
```

We will use the `LinkedGlassQueue` class to help us solve the problem presented in Section 4.8, "Application: Average Waiting Time."

The Double-Ended Queue

Stacks are a linear structure permitting addition and removal of elements from one end, called the top. Queues are a linear structure permitting addition to one end, called the rear, and removal from the other end, called the front. Why can we not define a structure that allows both addition and removal from both ends? Well—there is no reason why not. In fact, we can and many people have! Such a structure is classically called a **Double-Ended Queue**. "Double-Ended Queue" is sometimes shortened to "Dequeue" but because that term is identical to one of the standard queue operations, the more common term used for this ADT is **Deque**, pronounced "Deck."

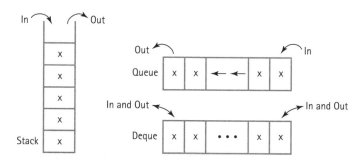

When defining a Deque ADT we must differentiate between two addition methods (front and rear) and two removal methods (front and rear). A few changes and additions to our `QueueInterface` class results in the following `DequeInterface` class:

```java
//-----------------------------------------------------------------------------
// DequeInterface.java          by Dale/Joyce/Weems              Chapter 4
//
// Interface for a class that implements a deque of T.
// A deque is a linear structure allowing addition/removal at both ends.
//-----------------------------------------------------------------------------
package ch04.queues;

public interface DequeInterface<T>
{
  void enqueueFront(T element) throws QueueOverflowException;
  // Throws QueueOverflowException if this queue is full;
  // otherwise, adds element to the front of this queue.

  void enqueueRear(T element) throws QueueOverflowException;
  // Throws QueueOverflowException if this queue is full;
  // otherwise, adds element to the rear of this queue.
```

```
T dequeueFront() throws QueueUnderflowException;
// Throws QueueUnderflowException if this queue is empty;
// otherwise, removes front element from this queue and returns it.

T dequeueRear() throws QueueUnderflowException;
// Throws QueueUnderflowException if this queue is empty;
// otherwise, removes rear element from this queue and returns it.

boolean isFull();
// Returns true if this queue is full; otherwise, returns false.

boolean isEmpty();
// Returns true if this queue is empty; otherwise, returns false.

int size();
// Returns the number of elements in this queue.
}
```

Instead of defining an entirely new interface for the Deque ADT we could define the DequeInterface class as an extension of the QueueInterface class, as we did for our Glass Queue. With that approach we only need to include the two methods enqueue-Front and dequeueRear in the interface, as all the other method declarations would be inherited. In fact, lots of structural variations of interfaces and implementation classes involving generalizations and/or specializations are possible, considering the relationships among the Stack, Queue, and Deque ADTs. Here we decided to take the simplest approach—we defined an entirely new interface.

Implementations of array-based and link-based deques are left as exercises.

Doubly Linked Lists

If you attempt to create a Deque using a linked list you will discover that it is difficult to implement the dequeueRear operation. In order to remove the last node in a linked list you need access to the previous node, and the only way to gain that access in a standard linked list is to walk through the entire list. In cases like this, where we need to access the node that precedes a given node, a doubly linked list is useful. In a doubly linked list, the nodes are linked in both directions. Each node of a doubly linked list contains three parts:

    info: the element stored in the node

    link: the reference to the following node

    back: the reference to the preceding node

A deque that uses a linear doubly linked list might look like this:

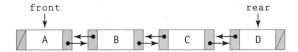

The back reference of the first node and the link reference of the last node contain null. Nodes for such a list could be provided by the following DLLNode class, which is similar to our previously defined LLNode class.

```java
//----------------------------------------------------------------------
// DLLNode.java              by Dale/Joyce/Weems              Chapter 4
//
// Implements nodes holding info of class <T> for a doubly linked list.
//----------------------------------------------------------------------
package support;

public class DLLNode<T>
{
  private T info;
  private DLLNode<T> forward, back;

  public DLLNode(T info)
  {
    this.info = info; forward = null; back = null;
  }

  public void setInfo(T info){this.info = info;}
  public T getInfo(){return info;}

  public void setForward(DLLNode<T> forward){this.forward = forward;}
  public void setBack(DLLNode<T> back){this.back = back;}

  public DLLNode getForward(){return forward;}
  public DLLNode getBack(){return back;}
}
```

Note that yet another alternate approach, called a Circular Doubly Linked List, exists where the back reference of the first node points to the last node and the link reference of the last node points to the first node—see Exercise 33.

The dequeueRear Operation

When we make changes (additions/deletions) to a doubly linked list we must be careful to properly manage all of the references and to handle the special cases. Let us look at an example. Imagine implementing a Deque ADT with a doubly linked list that uses the DLLNode class. Let us discuss the `dequeueRear` method. Consider our sample deque:

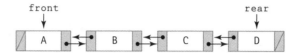

As with the dequeue operation of our "regular" Queue ADT we throw an exception if the queue is empty, and otherwise remove and return an element from the queue and decrement the count of the number of elements. If removing the only element from the queue we also need to update the front reference. Here we concentrate on the pointer manipulation. In our example, we want to make the node containing C become the rear node. Therefore we need to set the forward link of the node containing C to null, and set the `rear` reference of the queue to point to the node containing C. How do we access the node containing C? Due to the doubly linked nature of our implementation this is easy—it is `rear.getBack()`. After setting the forward link of the C node to null (using the `setLink` method) we have the following:

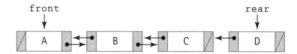

Now we set the value of the rear reference to indicate the next-to-last node, the node containing C. Assuming no other references are pointing at the node containing D, it becomes garbage, and that space will eventually be reclaimed by the system.

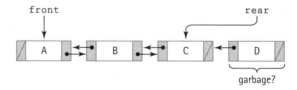

Putting this all together along with the code for handling the special cases (empty and one element queues) and returning the element we arrive at the following implementation of a dequeueRear method:

```
public T dequeueRear()
// Throws QueueUnderflowException if this deque is empty;
// otherwise, removes rear element from this queue and returns it.
```

```
{
  if (isEmpty())
    throw new QueueUnderflowException("dequeue rear attempted on empty
queue.");
  else
  {
    T element;
    element = rear.getInfo();
    if (rear.getBack() == null)
    {
      front = null; rear = null;
    }
    else
    {
      rear.getBack().setLink(null);
      rear = rear.getBack();
    }
    numElements--;
    return element;
  }
}
```

This `dequeueRear` implementation is O(1). The same operation for our "standard" linked queue would require O(N) steps since the next to last node is not readily available. The increased efficiency is not without some cost. The nodes of a doubly linked list require more space than those of a singly linked list.

> **Space/Time Trade-offs**
>
> Quite often (but not always) in the design of data structures and related algorithms we must trade space efficiency for time efficiency, or vice versa. Using a doubly linked list to allow an O(1) implementation of the `dequeueRear` operation is an example where a little extra space, per node, allows for a much faster operation.

The Java Library Collection Framework Queue/Deque

A `Queue` interface was added to the Java Library Collection Framework with Java 5.0 in 2004. As expected, the library's approach to queues is similar to our approach in that elements are always removed from the "front" of the queue. However, their approach also exhibits several important differences:

- It does not require elements to be added only at the "rear" of the queue. For example, added elements might be ordered based on a priority value. In other words, it allows Priority Queue ADT (Chapter 9) implementations.

- It provides two operations for enqueuing: `add`, that throws an exception if invoked on a full queue, and `offer`, that returns a boolean value of `false` if invoked on a full queue.

- It provides two operations for dequeuing: `remove`, that throws an exception, and `poll`, that returns `false`, when invoked on an empty queue.
- Inspection operations, for obtaining the front element without removing it, are included.

As with the library Stack, the library Queue was supplanted by the Deque with the release of Java 6.0 in 2006. The library `Deque` interface is similar to the `DequeInterface` previously discussed—it requires operations allowing for additions, deletions, and inspections at both ends of the queue. By carefully restricting method use, a class that implements the interface could be used by an application as a stack (only allow enqueuing and dequeuing at the front) or as a queue (only allow enqueuing to the rear and dequeuing from the front) or even as some sort of stack-queue combination. There are four library classes that implement the `Deque` interface: `ArrayDeque`, `ConcurrentLinkedDeque`, `Linked-BlockingDeque`, and `LinkedList`.

Here is how you might implement the repeat strings application (see Section 4.2, "The Queue Interface") using the `ArrayDeque` class from the Java library. The minimal differences between this application and the one using our Queue ADT are <u>emphasized</u>.

```
//-------------------------------------------------------------------
// RepeatStrings2.java         by Dale/Joyce/Weems        Chapter 4
//
// Sample use of the library ArrayDeque.
// Outputs strings in same order of entry.
//-------------------------------------------------------------------
package ch04.apps;

import java.util.ArrayDeque;
import java.util.Scanner;

public class RepeatStrings2
{
  public static void main(String[] args)
  {
    Scanner scan = new Scanner(System.in);

    ArrayDeque<String> stringQueue;
    stringQueue = new ArrayDeque<String>(3);

    String line;

    for (int i = 1; i <= 3; i++)
    {
      System.out.print("Enter a line of text > ");
```

```
      line = scan.nextLine();
      stringQueue.addLast(line);
    }

    System.out.println("\nOrder is:\n");
    while (!stringQueue.isEmpty())
    {
      line = stringQueue.removeFirst();
      System.out.println(line);
    }
  }
}
```

If you are interested in learning more about the Java Collections Framework, you can study the extensive documentation available on Oracle's website.

4.8   Application: Average Waiting Time

Queues are useful data structures within computer systems: for example, there are process queues, print job queues, and service queues. Queues are also commonly seen in the real world: tollbooth queues, ticket-counter queues, and fast-food queues.

The primary function of such queues is to provide a place for a "customer" to wait before receiving a "service." Processes are waiting for a processor, print jobs are waiting for a printer, and hungry people are waiting for their hamburgers. Sometimes management is interested in how much time customers spend waiting in queues. For example, a computer system manager wants quick system response time, and a fast-food restaurant manager wants to keep his or her customers happy. These goals are achieved by minimizing the time spent in the queues.

One way to minimize queue waiting time is to add more servers, and therefore more queues, to the system.[6] Print jobs spend less time in the print queue if there are 10 printers to churn out jobs than they do if there is only one printer. Likewise, a fast-food restaurant with six teller lines can handle more customers, more quickly, than a restaurant with only two lines. However, additional servers are not free—there is usually some cost associated with them. Management must balance the benefits of adding extra servers against the costs when deciding how many servers to provide.

In this section we create a program that simulates a system of queues. The goal is to help management analyze queuing systems. Computer simulations are a powerful and widely used technique for analysis of complicated real-world problems. Our program simulates a series of customers arriving for service, entering a queue, waiting, being served, and finally leaving the queue. It tracks the time the customers spend waiting in queues and outputs the average waiting time.

---

[6] Some systems have several queues feeding into one server. In this section we assume that each queue has its own dedicated server.

Problem Discussion and Example

How do we calculate the waiting time of a customer? To simplify things, we assume that time is measured in integer units, and that our simulation starts at time 0. Suppose a customer arrives at time X and leaves at time Y. Is the waiting time for that customer equal to $Y - X$? No, part of that time the customer was being served. The time $Y - X$ is called the *turnaround time*; it is the total time the customer spends in the system, including the service time. Waiting time is turnaround time minus service time.

To calculate waiting time we need to know the arrival time, finish time, and service time. The arrival time and service time depend on the individual customers—when they show up and how much service they need. The finish time depends on the number of queues, the number of other customers in the queues, and the service needs of those other customers.

Each simulation should take customers in the order they arrive and place them into queues. We assume that a customer always chooses the smallest queue available. In case of a tie, the customer chooses the smaller-numbered queue. The program has to model only two situations: a customer arriving for service and a customer leaving after being served. When a customer leaves, the program must remember the customer's waiting time so that it can calculate the overall average waiting time.

As an example, consider a case with the following four customers:

Customer	Arrival Time	Service Time
1	3	10
2	4	3
3	5	10
4	25	7

Suppose we have two queues. The first customer arrives at time 3 and enters queue 0. We can see that the expected finish time is 13, because the service time is 10. The second customer arrives before the first is finished and enters queue 1. The finish time is 7. This scenario is represented by the following chart:

Time	1 2 3 4 5 6 7 8 9 10 11 12 13 14 15 16 17 18 19 20 21 22 23 24 25
Q0	cust1
Q1	cust2

The third customer arrives at time 5, before either of the preceding customers is finished. Because both queues have the same number of customers, customer 3 enters the smaller numbered queue, queue 0, and has an expected finish time of 23. Do you see why? Customer 1 finishes at time 13 so it is not until then that the service for customer 3 begins— because their service time is 10, their finish time will be 13 + 10 = 23. Note that for this simulation customers may not "jump" queues—once they enter a queue they stay in it.

Time	1 2 3 4 5 6 7 8 9 10 11 12 13 14 15 16 17 18 19 20 21 22 23 24 25
Q0	cust1 ⟶ cust3
Q1	cust2

If you continue this simulation by hand, you should get the following results, for an average waiting time of 8 ÷ 4 = 2.0 time units.

Customer	Arrival Time	Service Time	Finish Time	Wait Time
1	3	10	13	0
2	4	3	7	0
3	5	10	23	8
4	25	7	32	0

The Customer Class

As we just saw, customers have four associated values: arrival time, service time, finish time, and wait time. We create a Customer class to model these values. Objects of this class will be enqueued to and dequeued from our queue objects, simulating customers entering and leaving real-world queues.

What are the responsibilities of objects of the Customer class? The arrival and service times of the customer can be provided as arguments to the constructor when a Customer object is instantiated. A Customer must provide observer methods for those attributes, and it should also provide methods to both set and observe the finish time. Given that the object eventually knows its arrival, service, and finish times, it can be responsible for calculating and returning its own waiting time.

Because we may want to use customers in other applications later in the text, we place the Customer class in the support package. The class is very straightforward:

```
//-----------------------------------------------------------------------
// Customer.java          by Dale/Joyce/Weems              Chapter 4
//
// Supports customer objects having arrival, service, and finish time
// attributes. Responsible for computing and returning wait time.
//
// Clients should not request wait time unless finish time has been set.
//-----------------------------------------------------------------------

package support;

public class Customer
{
  protected int arrivalTime;
  protected int serviceTime;
  protected int finishTime;

  public Customer(int arrivalTime, int serviceTime)
  {
    this.arrivalTime = arrivalTime;
    this.serviceTime = serviceTime;
  }

  public int getArrivalTime(){return arrivalTime;}
  public int getServiceTime(){return serviceTime;}
  public void setFinishTime(int time){finishTime = time;}
  public int getFinishTime(){return finishTime;}

  public int getWaitTime()
  {
    return (finishTime - arrivalTime - serviceTime);
  }
}
```

For our simulation where do the customers come from? To create a sequence of customer objects we need to know their arrival times and service requirements. These values can be obtained in several ways. One approach is to read the values from a file. This strategy is great for testing because it allows the programmer to completely control the input values. However, it is awkward if you want to simulate a large number of customers.

Another approach is to generate the values randomly. We take this approach. It is easy to generate the random service times: The user simply enters the minimum and maximum expected service times, and using Java's Random class our program generates service times between those two values.

We follow a slightly different algorithm with arrival times. Service time measures an amount of time, but arrival time specifies when the customer arrives. For example, customer 1 arrives at 10:00 a.m., customer 2 at 10:05, customer 3 at 10:07, and so on. In our simulation, we simply start the clock at 0 and keep the arrival time as an integer. We cannot directly create a sequence of increasing times by using the random number generator. Instead, we randomly generate the times between customer arrivals (the interarrival times), and keep a running total of those values.

For example, we might generate a sequence of interarrival times of 5, 7, 4, 10, and 7. Given that our simulation starts at time 0, the arrival times are then 5, 12, 16, 26, and 33. To constrain the range of interarrival times, we can let the user specify a minimum value and a maximum value. Note that we are assuming that both the interarrival and service time values are distributed uniformly between their minimums and maximums. Simulations can, of course, also be based on other distributions.

For each customer our program generates an arrival time and a service time. Through the simulation it then determines the finish time and, based on those values, calculates the waiting time. We create a `CustomerGenerator` class. An object of this class is passed the minimum and maximum interarrival and service times of the customers upon instantiation. Its primary responsibility is to generate and return the "next" customer when requested.

The customer generator class uses the Java library's `Random` class. Recall that a call to `rand.nextInt(N)` returns a random integer between 0 and *N* – 1. Note that a `Customer Generator` object keeps track of the current time, so it can calculate the next arrival time. We also place this class in the `support` package.

```java
//-----------------------------------------------------------------------
// CustomerGenerator.java        by Dale/Joyce/Weems          Chapter 4
//
// Generates a sequence of random Customer objects based on the
// constructor arguments for min and max interarrival and service times.
// Assumes a flat distribution of both interarrival and service times.
// Assumes time starts at 0.
//-----------------------------------------------------------------------
package support;

import java.util.Random;

public class CustomerGenerator
{
  protected int minIAT;    // minimum interarrival time
  protected int maxIAT;    // maximum interarrival time
  protected int minST;     // minimum service time
  protected int maxST;     // maximum service time

  protected int currTime = 0;    // current time

  Random rand = new Random();    // to generate random numbers
```

```
public CustomerGenerator (int minIAT, int maxIAT, int minST, int maxST)
// Preconditions: all arguments >= 0
//                 minIAT <= maxIAT
//                 minST  <= maxST
{
  this.minIAT = minIAT;    this.maxIAT = maxIAT;
  this.minST  = minST;     this.maxST  = maxST;
}


public void reset()
{
  currTime = 0;
}


public Customer nextCustomer()
// Creates and returns the next random customer.
{
  int IAT;  // next interarrival time
  int ST;   // next service time

  IAT = minIAT + rand.nextInt(maxIAT - minIAT + 1);
  ST  = minST  + rand.nextInt(maxST - minST + 1);

  currTime = currTime + IAT;  // updates current time to the arrival
                              // time of next customer

  Customer next = new Customer(currTime, ST);
  return next;
}
}
```

The Simulation

Our application will generate a sequence of customers and simulate them entering queues, waiting, and being serviced. It will output the average waiting time of a customer. What should be the input to our application? What does the user want to vary under their control?

We allow the user of the application to indicate customer information in the form of the minimum and maximum interarrival and service times, and the total number of customers. The application also obtains the number of simulated queues from the user. We index the queues starting at 0; if there are N queues, they are indexed 0 to $N - 1$. To ease the input burden, our program will allow the user to enter the sets of minimum and maximum time parameters once, and then run repeated simulations where he or she indicates the number of queues and customers.

As with our previous applications, we separate the user interaction from the classes that perform the "work" of the program. Therefore, we next create a `Simulation` class. We place it in a package called `ch04.simulation`. A `Simulation` object can be created based on the parameters obtained from the user, perform the simulation, and return the average waiting time. Because the user must be able to run multiple simulations using the same customer parameters (the time-related parameters), we decide to pass these parameters to the `Simulation` object once, at instantiation—that is, through the constructor of the `Simulation` object. The constructor, in turn, creates a `CustomerGenerator` object to use during the subsequent simulation runs. Next, the application can "ask" the `Simulation` object to run simulations, always using the same `CustomerGenerator` but with differing numbers of queues and customers.

Let us now consider the actual simulation process. As already determined, our program uses an array of queues to hold the customers. It must be able to take the next-generated `Customer` from the `CustomerGenerator` and add it into the correct queue. But how can it determine the correct queue? It must pick the smallest queue; therefore, it will use the queue's `size` method to determine which queue to use.

Do we need any special operations for our queues? After the program determines which queue to use, it must `enqueue` the customer into that queue. Recall that we can determine the finish time of a customer as soon as we know which queue the customer is entering. If the queue is empty, then that customer's finish time is equal to the arrival time plus the service time. If the queue is not empty, then the new customer's finish time is equal to the finish time of the customer at the rear of the queue plus the new customer's own service time. Thus the program can set the finish time of a customer before enqueuing the customer. Note that if the queue is nonempty, the program must be able to peek at the customer at the rear of the queue before it can set the finish time for the current customer. For this reason, we add peeking at the rear of a queue to our list of desired operations.

To perform the simulation the program must also be able to determine when the "next" customer is ready to leave a queue, and then remove and return that customer. How does it determine when a customer is ready to leave a queue? Because customers in a queue know their finish times, the program just needs to compare the finish times of the customers at the front of each queue and determine which is the earliest. Therefore, the program must be able to peek at the customer at the front of a queue. That is one more operation to add to our list.

So, in addition to the standard queue operations we need to be able to peek at both the front and the rear elements in our queues. The `GlassQueue` class developed in Section 4.7, "Queue Variations," provides these capabilities.

The `simulate` method of the `Simulation` class works through the simulation until finished. Each time through the *while*

Discrete Event Simulation

The application developed in this section is an example of discrete-event simulation. Within a discrete-event simulation a system is modeled as a sequence of separate events (customers arriving or leaving in our case). The application repeatedly determines what event occurs next, and models the effect of that event, updating the state of the system and possibly generating more events.

loop one of two things is simulated: a new customer is added into the queues or a customer is removed from a queue. To decide which of these two actions to simulate, the method determines and compares the next arrival time and the next departure time. The constant

MAXTIME is used to simplify the code; an arrival/departure time value of MAXTIME indicates that there are no arrivals/departures.

```java
//---------------------------------------------------------------------
// Simulation.java              by Dale/Joyce/Weems           Chapter 4
//
// Models a sequence of customers being serviced
// by a number of queues.
//---------------------------------------------------------------------
package ch04.simultion;

import support.*;        // Customer, CustomerGenerator
import ch04.queues.*;    // LinkedGlassQueue

public class Simulation
{
  final int MAXTIME = Integer.MAX_VALUE;

  CustomerGenerator custGen;    // a customer generator
  float avgWaitTime = 0.0f;     // average wait time for most recent
                                // simulation

  public Simulation(int minIAT, int maxIAT, int minST, int maxST)
  {
    custGen = new CustomerGenerator(minIAT, maxIAT, minST, maxST);
  }

  public float getAvgWaitTime()
  {
    return avgWaitTime;
  }

  public void simulate(int numQueues, int numCustomers)
  // Preconditions: numQueues > 0
  //                numCustomers > 0
  //                No time generated during simulation is > MAXTIME
  //
  // Simulates numCustomers customers entering and leaving
  // a queuing system with numQueues queues
  {
    // the queues
```

```
LinkedGlassQueue<Customer>[] queues = new LinkedGlassQueue[numQueues]⁷;

Customer nextCust;       // next customer from generator
Customer cust;           // holds customer for temporary use

int totWaitTime = 0;     // total wait time
int custInCount = 0;     // count of customers started so far
int custOutCount = 0;    // count of customers finished so far

int nextArrTime;         // next arrival time
int nextDepTime;         // next departure time
int nextQueue;           // index of queue for next departure

int shortest;            // index of shortest queue
int shortestSize;        // size of shortest queue
Customer rearCust;       // customer at rear of shortest queue
int finishTime;          // calculated finish time for customer being
                         //    enqueued

// instantiate the queues
for (int i = 0; i < numQueues; i++)
  queues[i] = new LinkedGlassQueue<Customer>();

// set customer generator and get first customer
custGen.reset();
nextCust = custGen.nextCustomer();

while (custOutCount < numCustomers)  // while still more customers
{
  // get next arrival time
  if (custInCount != numCustomers)
    nextArrTime = nextCust.getArrivalTime();
  else
    nextArrTime = MAXTIME;

  // get next departure time and set nextQueue
  nextDepTime = MAXTIME;
  nextQueue = -1;
  for (int i = 0; i < numQueues; i++)
    if (queues[i].size() != 0)
    {
      cust = queues[i].peekFront();
```

---

⁷ An unchecked cast warning is generated because the compiler cannot ensure that the array actually contains objects of class `GlassQueue<Customer>`.

```
      if (cust.getFinishTime() < nextDepTime)
      {
        nextDepTime = cust.getFinishTime();
        nextQueue = i;
      }
  }

  if (nextArrTime < nextDepTime)
  // handle customer arriving
  {
    // determine shortest queue
    shortest = 0;
    shortestSize = queues[0].size();
    for (int i = 1; i < numQueues; i++)
    {
      if (queues[i].size() < shortestSize)
      {
        shortest = i;
        shortestSize = queues[i].size();
      }
    }

    // determine the finish time
    if (shortestSize == 0)
      finishTime = nextCust.getArrivalTime() + nextCust.getServiceTime();
    else
    {
      rearCust = queues[shortest].peekRear();
      finishTime = rearCust.getFinishTime() + nextCust.getServiceTime();
    }

    // set finish time and enqueue customer
    nextCust.setFinishTime(finishTime);
    queues[shortest].enqueue(nextCust);

    custInCount = custInCount + 1;

    // if needed, get next customer to enqueue
    if (custInCount < numCustomers)
      nextCust = custGen.nextCustomer();
  }
  else
  // handle customer leaving
```

```
    {
        cust = queues[nextQueue].dequeue();
        totWaitTime = totWaitTime + cust.getWaitTime();
        custOutCount = custOutCount + 1;
    }
} // end while

avgWaitTime = totWaitTime/(float)numCustomers;
}
}
```

The Application

This application is similar in structure to those presented previously in the text. The primary responsibility of the application is interacting with the user. We make the simplifying assumption that the user is well behaved—in other words, the user provides valid input data. For example, the minimum service time the user enters is not larger than the maximum service time.

We provide two versions of the application in the ch04.apps package. SimulationCLI uses the command line interface. Here is an output from a sample run:

```
Enter minimum interarrival time: 0
Enter maximum interarrival time: 10
Enter minimum service time: 5
Enter maximum service time: 20

Enter number of queues: 2
Enter number of customers: 2000
Average waiting time is 1185.632

Evaluate another simulation instance? (Y=Yes): y
Enter number of queues: 3
Enter number of customers: 2000
Average waiting time is 5.7245

Evaluate another simulation instance? (Y=Yes): n
Program completed.
```

As you can see, our program provides us with a powerful analysis tool. Under the conditions of interarrival times between 0 and 10 and service times between 5 and 20, with only two queues the waiting time "blows up." But by simply adding one more queue, the expected waiting time becomes very reasonable.

A screenshot of a run of our second version of the application, SimulationGUI, is shown in **Figure 4.12**. A benefit of the GUI approach is that the user can easily change just

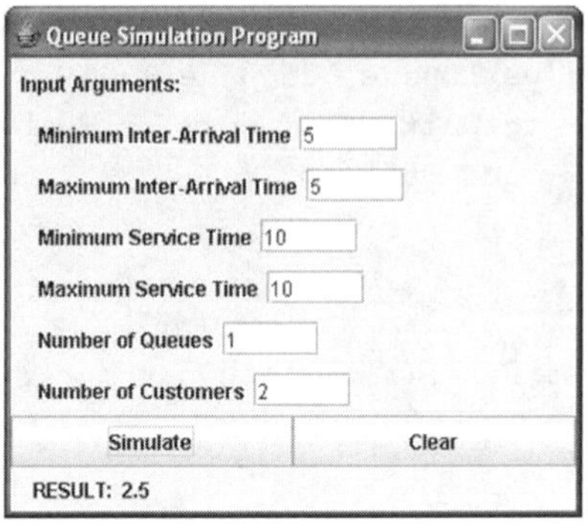

Figure 4.12 Screenshot of the `SimulationGUI` program in action

one input value and rerun the simulation to see the effect of that change. A drawback of the approach is that the previous result is no longer readily visible, as it is with the command line approach.

Testing Considerations

How do we know our program works? Besides being careful with the design and coding, we must test it. We should test each of the classes separately as we create them. To do so, we need to create test driver programs that allow us to evaluate the classes under different conditions.

We can test the overall system by carefully selecting the values we enter for input. For example, if we enter the minimum and maximum interarrival times both as 5, then we know that a customer should arrive every 5 time units. By controlling the arrival times and service requirements, along with the number of available queues, we can see whether our system provides reasonable answers. Finally, we could tweak the `CustomerGenerator` code slightly, so that it outputs the arrival and service times of each of the customers it generates. Using this information, we can hand-check the results of a simulation to confirm that it is correct.

An abbreviated UML diagram showing our classes and interfaces related to the Simulation applications is shown in **Figure 4.13**.

4.9 Concurrency, Interference, and Synchronization

The complexities of today require many people to engage in **multitasking**—performing more than one task at a time. For example, right now you may be texting on your phone while watching TV and eating lunch, all at the same time you are doing your data structures homework! Computers also multitask. A computer system can be printing a document, running a virus checker, and interacting with a user all at the same time.

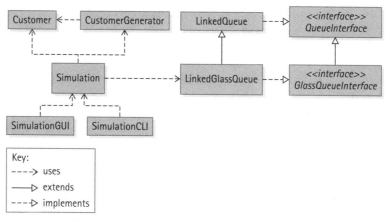

Figure 4.13 Queue waiting time simulation program architecture

Many computer programs require multitasking capabilities. For example, a game program might have separate code sequences to react to changes in user input, to detect collisions between the objects in the game, and to update a scoreboard reflecting the game status. For such a game to be playable each of the code sequences must be active simultaneously and they must interact with each other. Programs that perform this way are called concurrent programs. **Concurrent programs** consist of several interacting code sequences executing simultaneously, possibly through an interleaving of their statements by a single processor, possibly through execution on distinct processors.

On a single processor system concurrency is achieved through the interleaving of the instructions of the various code sequences. The computer jumps back and forth among code sequences, executing a "few" instructions from one sequence, and then a "few" from another sequence, and so on. On systems with dual processors, quad processors, or higher levels of physical support for parallelism, the concurrency can be "real." The computer's operating system hides the presence or absence of physical concurrency support from the program designer so that as programmers we need not be concerned with the details of that support.

In many ways queues are the data structure most directly associated with concurrency. Imagine a system where some processes, called producers, create tasks that need attention, while other processes, called consumers, are able to handle the tasks. How do we coordinate between the producers and consumers? The Queue ADT is an obvious choice to act as a buffer between the producers and the consumers. Producers repeatedly generate tasks and place them in the queue—consumers repeatedly remove a task from the queue

> **Concurrent Programs**
>
> Concurrent programs are very common—programs that control systems, provide games, support work productivity, or allow communication are usually concurrent. Concurrency can be provided "automatically" by an operating system or indicated directly by an application programmer. Additionally, tools exist that analyze a sequential program and transform it into one that takes advantage of concurrency.

and handle it. The queue itself is a shared data structure and as such access to it must be carefully coordinated. We must be careful that producers do not improperly interleave access to the shared queue while scheduling tasks. We must coordinate removal of tasks from the queue by consumers, to ensure that a specific task is not consumed multiple times. Coordinating a shared resource like this is at the heart of the study of concurrent programming.

A formal study of program concurrency is typically provided in operating system, database, or algorithm courses within a computing curriculum and is beyond the scope of this book. However, in this section we introduce the topic by:

- Defining terminology related to concurrency.
- Showing how to indicate that parts of a Java program should be executed concurrently.
- Explaining how concurrent code sequences might interfere with each other.
- Demonstrating how to synchronize the execution of the code sequences so that such interference does not occur.

The Counter Class

To support our investigation of the topics of this section we use the following simple Counter class. It provides an integral attribute that is originally zero and that can be incremented through calls to an increment method. All auxiliary classes created for this section of the text are placed into the ch04.threads package.

```java
//-----------------------------------------------------------------
// Counter.java              by Dale/Joyce/Weems           Chapter 4
//
// Tracks the current value of a counter.
//-----------------------------------------------------------------
package ch04.threads;
public class Counter
{
    private int count;

    public Counter()
    {
        count = 0;
    }

    public void increment()
    {
```

```
        count++;
    }


    public int getCount(){return count;}
}
```

The sample program `Demo01` instantiates a `Counter` object c, increments it three times, and then prints its value. The sample output is as expected, showing a count of 3. All of the application programs created for this section of the text are placed into the `ch04.concurrency` folder.

```
package ch04.concurrency;
import ch04.threads.*;

public class Demo01
{
    public static void main(String[] args)
    {
        Counter c = new Counter();
        c.increment();
        c.increment();
        c.increment();
        System.out.println("Count is: " + c.getCount());
    }
}
```

The output of the program is: `Count is:  3`

Java Threads

The Java concurrency mechanism we present is the thread. Every Java program that executes has a thread, the "main" thread of the program. The main thread has the ability to generate additional threads. The various threads of the program run concurrently. The program terminates when all of its threads terminate.

The `java.lang` package, which is automatically imported into all programs, provides a `Thread` class. We create thread objects by first defining a class that implements the Java library's `Runnable` interface. Such classes must provide a public `run` method. As an example, see the following `Increase` class that accepts a `Counter` object and an integer amount through its constructor, and provides a `run` method that increments the `Counter` object the number of times indicated by the value of `amount`.

```
package ch04.threads;
public class Increase implements Runnable
{
        private Counter c;  private int amount;
```

```
    public Increase (Counter c, int amount)
    {
       this.c = c;        this.amount = amount;
    }

    public void run()
    {
       for (int i = 1; i <= amount; i++)
          c.increment();
    }
}
```

We can now instantiate a `Thread` object by passing its constructor an `Increase` object (or any `Runnable` object). The instantiated `Thread` object can be used to execute the `Increase` object's run method in a separate thread from the main program thread. To do this we call the thread object's `start` method. Consider the `Demo02` example:

```
package ch04.concurrency;
import ch04.threads.*;
public class Demo02
{
  public static void main(String[] args) throws InterruptedException[8]
  {
     Counter   c = new Counter();
     Runnable r = new Increase(c, 10000);
     Thread    t = new Thread(r);
     t.start();
     System.out.println("Expected: 10000");
     System.out.println("Count is: " + c.getCount());
  }
}
```

The `Demo02` program instantiates a `Counter` object c, uses c plus the integer literal 10,000 to instantiate a `Runnable` object r, and uses r to instantiate a `Thread` object t. The thread object runs, in a separate thread, after the call to its `start` method. The program displays the value of the counter object before terminating. What value will it display? Considering that the `Increase` object will increment the counter 10,000 times we expect the output of the program to be the following:

```
Expected: 10000
Count is: 10000
```

---

[8] The **Thread** object can throw the checked run-time **InterruptedException** exception. Therefore, we must either catch and handle that exception or throw it out to the execution environment.

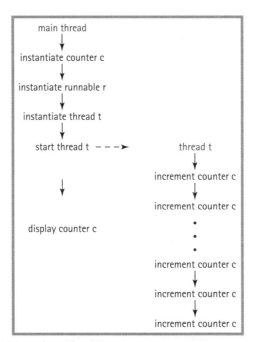

Figure 4.14   Execution of the `Demo02` program

But the increment of the counter and the display of its value occur in different threads, as shown in **Figure 4.14**. There is no guarantee that the incrementing of the counter by the second thread will finish before its value is displayed by the main thread. In fact, it is very likely that a value other than 10,000 will be output. When run on the author's computer, the `Demo02` program displays output such as:

```
Expected: 10000
Count is: 3074
```

We can indicate that we want one thread to wait for the completion of another thread by using the `join` command. The following program produces the "correct" output, reporting a count of 10,000, since it indicates that the main thread should wait for completion of the `t` thread before displaying the value of the counter object. The line of code that accomplishes this is <u>emphasized</u>.

```
package ch04.concurrency;
import ch04.threads.*;

public class Demo03
{
    public static void main(String[] args) throws InterruptedException
```

```
    {
        Counter   c = new Counter();
        Runnable  r = new Increase(c, 10000);
        Thread    t = new Thread(r);

        t.start();
        t.join();

        System.out.println("Expected: 10000");
        System.out.println("Count is: " + c.getCount());
    }
}
```

The `join` command indicates that the main thread should wait until completion of the thread t before continuing. Therefore, the counter is incremented completely before its value is output.

Interference

When two or more threads of a program make changes to the same data at the same time they can interfere with each other and create unintended, undesired results. Consider the Demo04 program that has a total of three threads: the main thread and two others, t1 and t2.

```
package ch04.concurrency;
import ch04.threads.*;

public class Demo04
{
    public static void main(String[] args) throws InterruptedException
    {
        Counter   c = new Counter();
        Runnable r1 = new Increase(c, 5000);
        Runnable r2 = new Increase(c, 5000);
        Thread   t1 = new Thread(r1);
        Thread   t2 = new Thread(r2);

        t1.start();
        t2.start();
        t1.join();
        t2.join();

        System.out.println("Count is: " + c.getCount());
    }
}
```

As you can see, the Demo04 program runs two separate threads, each of which increments the shared counter object 5,000 times. The program uses the `join` method to ensure that all auxiliary threads are finished before it accesses and displays the final values of the counter. Again we ask—what values will this program display? Clearly we would expect the result to be

```
Count is: 10000
```

However, we would be wrong. This example demonstrates the dangers of working with concurrency. Programmers who use concurrency must be very careful how they wield its power. Three separate runs of the Demo04 program on the author's computer produce the following three outputs:

```
Count is: 9861
Count is: 9478
Count is: 9203
```

The reason for these unexpected results is that the two incrementing threads interfere with each other. Consider that to increment a counter requires three steps in Java byte code: obtain the current value of the counter, add one to that value, and store the result. If two threads executing simultaneously interleave the execution of these steps, then the resultant value of the counter will be one less than the expected value. For example, consider the following sequence of steps, where the counter begins with the value 12 and both threads increment the counter. Although we would expect the resultant value to be 14, due to the "interference" the final value is only 13:

```
Thread t1                           Thread t2
Step 1: obtains value 12
              ↓
                                    Step 2: obtains value 12
Step 3: increments value to 13                 ↓
Step 4: stores the value 13                    ↓
                                    Step 5: increments value to 13
                                    Step 6: stores the value 13
```

Examining the output from the Demo04 program we conclude that such interference occurs multiple times during the execution of the code. When concurrent threads make changes to shared variables, such as in the Demo04 program, they must synchronize their access of the shared information.

Synchronization

In Java we can force synchronization at either the statement level or the method level. We use method-level synchronization. In the Demo04 example, the method that requires synchronization is the `increment` method of the `Counter` class. To demonstrate the use of a synchronized method we create a separate counter class `SyncCounter`. Indicating that a method is synchronized simply requires the use of the `synchronized` keyword as a modifier in the method declaration line, as <u>emphasized</u> in the following code.

```
//-------------------------------------------------------------------------
// SyncCounter.java                   by Dale/Joyce/Weems              Chapter 4
//
// Tracks the current value of a counter.
// Provides synchronized access to the increment method.
//-------------------------------------------------------------------------
package ch04.threads;

public class SyncCounter
{
  private int count;
  public SyncCounter()
  {
    count = 0;
  }

  public synchronized void increment()
  {
    count++;
  }

  public int getCount(){return count;}
}
```

Thread access to the `increment` method of the `SyncCounter` class will be executed in a safe fashion. If one thread is in the middle of executing code within the method, no other thread will be given access to the method. No interleaving of Java byte code statements for this method will occur. This prevents the interference that led to the unexpected results in the `Demo04` program.

Whenever the `Demo05` program below is executed it correctly reports the expected value for the counter of 10,000. The `IncreaseSync` class used in the program is identical to the `Increase` class except that it accepts a `SyncCounter` instead of `Counter` as its first parameter.

```
package ch04.concurrency;
import ch04.threads.*;

public class Demo05
{
  public static void main(String[] args) throws InterruptedException
```

```
{
   SyncCounter sc = new SyncCounter();
   Runnable r1 = new IncreaseSync(sc, 5000);
   Runnable r2 = new IncreaseSync(sc, 5000);
   Thread t1 = new Thread(r1);
   Thread t2  =  new Thread(r2);

   t1.start(); t2.start();
   t1.join(); t2.join();

   System.out.println("Count is: " + sc.getCount());
 }

}
```

A Synchronized Queue

Data collections are sometimes at the heart of concurrent programs. The Queue ADT in particular is often used concurrently, for example, to store tasks generated by "producer" threads of a system that need to be handled later by separate "consumer" threads of the system, in essence acting as a repository for unfinished work. When a collection is used by multiple threads, access to it must be synchronized. Otherwise some elements may be mistakenly skipped and others may be erroneously accessed more than once, as threads interfere with each other while manipulating the data structure that underlies the collection.

In this subsection we investigate using a queue as described in the previous paragraph. We use a simple example so that we can concentrate on the synchronization issues. First we look at an unsynchronized version of the program and discuss its potential problems, then we see how to resolve the raised issues. Here is the first version of the program:

```
package ch04.concurrency;
import ch04.threads.*;
import ch04.queues.*;

public class Demo06
{
  public static void main(String[] args) throws InterruptedException
  {
    int LIMIT = 100;
    SyncCounter c = new SyncCounter();
    QueueInterface<Integer> q;
    q = new ArrayBoundedQueue<Integer>(LIMIT);
```

```
    for (int i = 1; i <= LIMIT; i++)
      q.enqueue(i);

    Runnable r1 = new IncreaseUseArray(c, q);
    Runnable r2 = new IncreaseUseArray (c, q);
    Thread   t1 = new Thread(r1);
    Thread   t2 = new Thread(r2);

    t1.start(); t2.start();
    t1.join(); t2.join();

    System.out.println("Count is: " + c);
  }
}
```

The Demo06 program above creates a queue of integers and inserts the integers from 1 to 100 into the queue. It then generates and runs two threads: t1 and t2. These threads each contain a copy of an IncreaseUseArray object (see the code that follows). Therefore, each of the threads checks the queue to see whether it is empty, and if not, the thread removes the next number from the queue and increments the shared counter object that number of times. So perhaps the t1 thread increments the counter once while the t2 counter is incrementing the counter twice; and then the t2 thread may increment the counter three times while the t1 counter is incrementing the counter four times, and so on. Remember that access to the counter is synchronized. After both threads complete, the value of the counter is output.

```
package ch04.threads;
import ch04.queues.*;

public class IncreaseUseArray implements Runnable
{
   private SyncCounter c;
   private QueueInterface<Integer> q;

   public IncreaseUseArray (SyncCounter c, QueueInterface<Integer> q)
   {
      this.c = c; this.q = q;
   }
   public void run()
   {
      int hold;
      while (!q.isEmpty())
      {
         hold = q.dequeue();
```

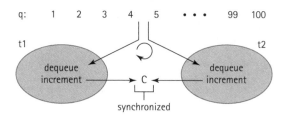

Figure 4.15   Threads t1 and t2 increment c—expected result is 5050

```
        for (int i = 1; i <= hold; i++)
            c.increment();
    }
  }
}
```

Let us review. The Demo06 program inserts the numbers from 1 to 100 into the queue q. As shown in **Figure 4.15**, the t1 and t2 threads repeatedly remove numbers from that queue and increment the counter c accordingly. The value of the counter is then output. What is that value? It should be 5050, which is equal to the sum of the integers between 1 and 100, correct? When executed on the author's computer the result is 5050. Good. So the program works as expected. Not so fast—when dealing with concurrent programs it is possible for interference errors to occur intermittently. Such errors depend on the timing of thread interleaving, and so although the program may work as expected on one run, on another run we may get unexpected results.

We ran this program 10 times, and 10 times the result was 5050. But the 11th test run produced a result of 4980. And the 16th test run produced a null pointer exception. Although access to the counter is synchronized, access to the queue itself is not. That is the source of these unexpected results. Interference during access to the dequeue method, perhaps multiple times, would explain both of these unexpected results. Readers are encouraged to try this experiment for themselves to see what happens on their systems.

To create a reliable version of this program we need to create a synchronized queue class. Fortunately, this is not difficult. We simply add the synchronized keyword to the qualifiers of each of the exported methods of our queue implementation as <u>emphasized</u> in the SyncArrayBoundedQueue class below. Adding the synchronized keyword to multiple methods guarantees that if one thread is active in any of those methods, then no other thread will be allowed into the same method or any of the other methods. Using this class in place of the ArrayBoundedQueue class in the Demo06 program creates a reliable example (see Demo7). We ran this new program 100 times and received the expected result of 5050 every time.

```java
//------------------------------------------------------------------------
// SyncArrayBoundedQueue.java          by Dale/Joyce/Weems          Chapter 4
//
// Implements QueueInterface with an array to hold the queue elements.
// Operations are synchronized to allow concurrent access.
//------------------------------------------------------------------------
package ch04.queues;

public class SyncArrayBoundedQueue<T> implements QueueInterface<T>
{
protected final int DEFCAP = 100; // default capacity
protected T[] elements;           // array that holds queue elements
protected int numElements = 0;    // number of elements in the queue
protected int front = 0;          // index of front of queue
protected int rear;               // index of rear of queue

public SyncArrayBoundedQueue()
{
    elements = (T[]) new Object[DEFCAP];
    rear = DEFCAP - 1;
  }

  public SyncArrayBoundedQueue(int maxSize)
  {
    elements = (T[]) new Object[maxSize];
    rear = maxSize - 1;
  }

  public synchronized void enqueue(T element)
  // Throws QueueOverflowException if this queue is full;
  // otherwise, adds element to the rear of this queue.
  {
  if (isFull())
      throw new QueueOverflowException("Enqueue attempted on full queue.");
  else
  {
      rear = (rear + 1) % elements.length;
      elements[rear] = element;
      numElements = numElements + 1;
  }
  }
```

```
public synchronized T dequeue()
// Throws QueueUnderflowException if this queue is empty;
// otherwise, removes front element from this queue and returns it.
{
if (isEmpty())
  throw new QueueUnderflowException("Dequeue attempted on empty queue");
else
{
  T toReturn = elements[front];
  elements[front] = null;
  front = (front + 1) % elements.length;
  numElements = numElements - 1;
  return toReturn;
  }
}


public synchronized boolean isEmpty()
// Returns true if this queue is empty; otherwise, returns false.
  {
    return (numElements == 0);
  }


public synchronized boolean isFull()
// Returns true if this queue is full; otherwise, returns false.
  {
    return (numElements == elements.length);
  }


public synchronized int size()
// Returns the number of elements in this queue.
  {
    return numElements;
  }
}
```

We have avoided the interference problems by making all of the queue access and increment methods synchronized. As a result, every attempt to access the queue waits if the other thread is currently accessing it. Once a thread has the increment value from the queue, it attempts to access the shared counter, but because it too is synchronized, the thread will wait until the other thread is done incrementing the counter. As a result, there are very few concurrent operations taking place. While one thread is incrementing, the other thread can access the queue, and vice versa. If our goal is to make use of two physical processors in the computer to finish the task twice as quickly, the actual speed improvement will be disappointing.

Programmers of concurrent systems often encounter situations such as this. To ensure correctness, they must include so much synchronization that most of the work done by the threads takes place sequentially rather than concurrently. To get greater concurrency, it may be necessary to rethink the solution to the problem.

For example, if each of our threads had its own private counter, they could each get values from the synchronized queue and perform their increments concurrently on their own counters. On completion, each thread would return its counter value, and the main thread would add the two values to get the final result. The threads would only wait on occasions where they interfere in accessing the queue and would no longer need to wait when accessing a counter. Executing this solution on two processors could yield nearly a doubling of performance.

We say "could" because there are other factors involved in achieving good performance with concurrent processing. For example, creating each new thread requires the run-time system to do some work. If the work to be done by each thread is less than the work required to create the thread, then it actually takes longer to create the threads and do the work concurrently than to do the work in the usual sequential way. As you can see, concurrency brings many additional considerations to programming.

In every new generation of computer chip, manufacturers add more cores (processors), with each core capable of running multiple threads simultaneously. Taking advantage of these capabilities requires programs to divide their work among multiple threads. Concurrent programming is thus an important future trend in computing.

Concurrency and the Java Library Collection Classes

In Section 4.7, "Queue Variations," a subsection discussed the Java Library Collection Framework Queue and explained that the library includes a Queue interface and a Deque interface. Nine classes in the library implement the Queue interface, and four implement the Deque interface. As we emphasized in the current section, queues are often used in concurrent programs. Lending credence to this statement is the fact that most of the queue interface implementations in the Java library support concurrent use in one way or another:

- The ArrayBlockingQueue, LinkedBlockingQueue, DelayQueue, Synchronous-Queue, and PriorityBlockingQueue all share the feature that a thread attempting to put an element into a full queue object will block until such time that the queue object has space available, and that a thread attempting to retrieve an element from an empty queue object will block until an element is available.

- The ConcurrentLinkedQueue is thread safe. This means that like the SyncArray-BoundedQueue we developed in this section, operations on objects of the ConcurrentLinked-Queue are synchronized to allow concurrent access.

Originally most of the collection classes in the Collections Framework were thread safe, just like the ConcurrentLinkedQueue class. These include the Vector, Stack,

`Dictionary`, and `HashTable` classes. However, due to the protection processing required there is an execution time cost associated with maintaining thread safeness. Furthermore, many users of the collection classes do not need nor want to use concurrent threads, so the built-in cost of thread safeness was considered unnecessary overhead. Therefore, with the release of Java 2, similar nonthread-safe classes were included in the library for all of the original collection classes. For example, the `ArrayList` class is a nonthread-safe alternative for the `Vector` class and `HashSet` or `HashMap` are alternatives to `HashTable`.

The original set of collection classes, the thread-safe collection classes, are now known as the "historical" collection classes. Most programmers prefer not to use them; instead, programmers use the collection classes introduced with Java 2 or later. There are facilities in the library for transforming these newer classes into thread-safe classes. For example, you could create a synchronized `Set` collection using the unsynchronized `HashSet` class with the statement

```
Set s = Collection.synchronizedSet(new HashSet());
```

Summary

A queue is a "first in, first out" (FIFO) structure. We defined a queue at the abstract level as an ADT, creating a queue interface that requires both enqueue and dequeue operations plus several observer operations. Two array-based implementations were developed—one bounded and one unbounded. We also created a link-based implementation and discussed several other implementations that would use links. **Figure 4.16** displays a diagram of the *major* queue-related interfaces and classes developed in this chapter. The diagram follows the same conventions we listed on page 146 for the Stack ADT diagram.

Queues are often used to hold information until it needs to be used or jobs until they can be served. The palindrome identifier application highlighted this nature of queues, using a queue to hold a sequence of characters until they could be compared to the characters from a stack.

We developed a second application, a tool to analyze queue behavior. Our program allowed us to control the arrival rate and service needs of queue elements, and discover the average amount of time an element spent waiting on a queue. By varying the number of queues, we could determine the suitability of adding new servers to a queuing system. This application used a variation of our standard queue, a "glass" queue that allowed an application to look inside the queue abstraction. In addition to the glass queue variation we discussed several other variations and took a quick look at the support for queues in the Java library.

Finally, we also discussed the use of queues for managing tasks that can be executed concurrently and looked at some of Java's mechanisms for indicating concurrency and for synchronizing concurrent threads.

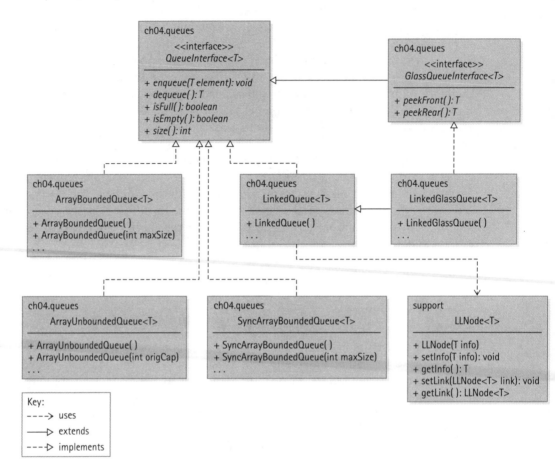

Figure 4.16   The queue-related interfaces and classes developed in Chapter 4

Exercises

4.1 The Queue

1. True or False? Explain your answers.

   a. A queue is a "first in, first out" structure.

   b. The element that has been in a queue the longest is at the "rear" of the queue.

   c. If you `enqueue` five elements into an empty queue and then `dequeue` five elements, the queue will be empty again.

   d. If you `enqueue` five elements into an empty queue and then perform the `isEmpty` operation five times, the queue will be empty again.

e.   The `enqueue` operation should be classified as a "transformer."

f.   The `isEmpty` operation should be classified as a "transformer."

g.   The `dequeue` operation should be classified as an "observer."

h.   If we first `enqueue elementA` into an empty queue and then `enqueue`
     `elementB`, the `front` of the queue is `elementA`.

2. Indicate whether a queue would be a suitable data structure to use in each of the
    following applications.

a.   An ailing company wants to evaluate employee records so that it can lay off
     some workers on the basis of service time (the most recently hired employees
     are laid off first).

b.   A program is to keep track of patients as they check into a clinic, assigning them
     to doctors on a "first come, first serve" basis.

c.   A program to solve a maze is to backtrack to an earlier position (the last place
     where a choice was made) when a dead-end position is reached.

d.   An operating system is to process requests for computer resources by allocating
     the resources in the order in which they are requested.

e.   A grocery chain wants to run a simulation to see how average customer wait
     time would be affected by changing the number of checkout lines in its stores.

f.   Customers are to take numbers at a bakery and be served in order when their
     number comes up.

g.   Gamblers take numbers in the lottery and win if their numbers are picked.

4.2 The Queue Interface

3. Based on our Queue ADT specification, a programmer has two ways to check for an
    empty queue. Describe them and discuss when one approach might be preferable to
    the other approach.

4. Show what is written by the following segments of code, given that `element1`,
    `element2`, and `element3` are `int` variables, and `q` is an object that fits the abstract
    description of a queue as given in Section 4.2, "The Queue Interface." Assume you
    can store and retrieve values of type `int` in `q`.

a.
```
element1 = 1;    element2 = 0;    element3 = 4;
q.enqueue(element2);
q.enqueue(element1);
q.enqueue(element1 + element3);
element2 = q.dequeue();
q.enqueue(element3*element3);
q.enqueue(element2);
q.enqueue(3);
```

```
        element1 = q.dequeue();
        System.out.println(element1 + " " + element2 + " " + element3);
        while (!q.isEmpty())
        {
            element1 = q.dequeue(); System.out.println(element1);
        }
```

b.
```
    element1 = 4;   element3 = 0;   element2 = element1 + 1;
    q.enqueue(element2);
    q.enqueue(element2 + 1);
    q.enqueue(element1);
    element2 = q.dequeue();
    element1 = element2 + 1;
    q.enqueue(element1);
    q.enqueue(element3);
    while (!q.isEmpty())
    {
        element1 = q.dequeue();
        System.out.println(element1);
    }
    System.out.println(element1 + " " + element2 + " " + element3);
```

5. Your friend Bill says, "The enqueue and dequeue queue operations are inverses of each other. Therefore, performing an enqueue followed by a dequeue is always equivalent to performing a dequeue followed by an enqueue. You get the same result!" How would you respond to that? Do you agree?

6. Using the Queue ADT: For this exercise you should use the methods listed in the QueueInterface interface and standard Java control operations. Assume all of the queues are able to hold elements of type int and have sufficient capacity to fulfill the problem specifications.

    a. Assume startQ contains elements of type int and both evenQ and oddQ are empty. Devise a section of code that moves all of the integers from startQ to the other two queues such that when finished, startQ is empty, evenQ contains the even integers, and oddQ contains the odd integers.

    b. Assume queueA and queueB contain integers and queueC is empty. Devise a section of code that will alternately move an integer from queueA to queueC and then from queueB to queueC until either or both of the source queues are empty—if anything is left in a source queue then those integers are also copied to queueC. For example, if you start with queueA containing 1 2 3 4 and queueB containing 5 6 then when the code finishes executing the two source queues are empty and queueC contains 1 5 2 6 3 4.

4.3 Array-Based Queue Implementations

7. Discuss the relative efficiency of the `enqueue` and `dequeue` operations for an array-based queue implemented with a fixed-front approach as opposed to a floating-front approach.

8. Draw the internal representation of the queue q for each step of the following code sequence:

```
ArrayBoundedQueue<String> q = new ArrayBoundedQueue<String>(5);
q.enqueue("X");
q.enqueue("M");
q.dequeue();
q.enqueue("T");
```

Your drawings should be similar to the array-based implementation part of Figure 4.10.

9. Using the Queue ADT: Write a segment of code (application level) to perform each of the following operations. Assume `myQueue` is an object of the class `ArrayBounded Queue` and is a queue of strings, containing at least three elements. You may call any of the public methods. You may also use additional `ArrayBoundedQueue` objects.

   a. Set the string variable `secondElement` to the second element from the beginning of `myQueue`, leaving `myQueue` without its original two front elements.

   b. Set the string variable `last` equal to the rear element in `myQueue`, leaving `myQueue` empty.

   c. Set the string variable `last` equal to the rear element in `myQueue`, leaving `myQueue` unchanged.

   d. Print out the contents of `myQueue`, leaving `myQueue` unchanged.

10. Using the Queue ADT: Write a program that repeatedly prompts the user to enter strings, using the string "x done" to indicate when finished. The user is assumed to only enter strings of the form "f name" or "m name." Output the names that had "m" indicated in the same order they were entered, preceded by the string "males:" and then do the same for the names that had "f" indicated, preceded by the string "females: ". Use two `ArrayBoundedQueue` objects in your program.

Sample Run

```
Input a gender and name (x done to quit) > m Fred
Input a gender and name (x done to quit) > f Wilma
Input a gender and name (x done to quit) > m Barney
Input a gender and name (x done to quit) > m BamBam
Input a gender and name (x done to quit) > f Betty
Input a gender and name (x done to quit) > x done
males: Fred Barney BamBam  females: Wilma Betty
```

11. Describe the effects each of the following changes would have on the `ArrayBounded`
    `Queue` class:

    a. Remove the `final` attribute from the `DEFCAP` instance variable.

    b. Change the value assigned to `DEFCAP` to 10.

    c. Change the value assigned to `DEFCAP` to −10.

    d. In the first constructor, change the first statement to

        ```
        elements = (T[]) newObject[100];
        ```

    e. In the first constructor, change the last statement to

        ```
        rear = DEFCAP;
        ```

    f. In the first constructor, change the last statement to

        ```
        rear = -1;
        ```

    g. Reverse the order of the first two statements in the *else* clause of the `enqueue`
        method.

    h. Reverse the order of the last two statements in the *else* clause of the `enqueue`
        method.

    i. Reverse the order of the first two statements in the *else* clause of the `dequeue`
        method.

    j. In `isEmpty`, change "`==`" to "`=`".

12. Add the following methods to the `ArrayBoundedQueue` class, and create a test
    driver for each to show that they work correctly. In order to practice your array
    coding skills, code each of these methods by accessing the internal variables of the
    `ArrayBoundedQueue`, not by calling the previously defined public methods of the
    class.

    a. `String toString()` creates and returns a string that correctly represents the
        current queue. Such a method could prove useful for testing and debugging the
        class and for testing and debugging applications that use the class. Assume each
        queued element already provides its own reasonable `toString` method.

    b. `int space()` returns an integer indicating how many empty spaces remain in
        the queue.

    c. `void remove(int count)` removes the front `count` elements from the
        queue, and throws `QueueUnderflowException` if there are less than `count`
        elements in the queue.

    d. `boolean swapStart()` returns `false` if there are less than two elements
        in the queue; otherwise it reverses the order of the front two elements in the
        queue and returns `true`.

    e. `boolean swapEnds()` returns `false` if there are less than two elements
        in the queue; otherwise it swaps the first and last elements of the queue and
        returns `true`.

13. Consider our array-based unbounded queue implementation.

    a. What would be the effect of starting with a capacity of 1?

    b. What would be the effect of starting with a capacity of 0?

14. Create an `ArrayListUnboundedQueue` class that implements the `QueueInter-face`, using an `ArrayList` instead of an array as the internal representation. Also create a test driver application that demonstrates that the class works correctly.

15. A "deque" is like a queue, but it also allows you to add to the front of the queue and to remove from the rear of the queue. Create an array-based `DeQue` class and a test driver that demonstrates that it works correctly.

4.4 An Interactive Test Driver

16. Devise a test plan that uses the `ITDArrayBoundedQueue` application to demonstrate that each of the following `ArrayBoundedQueue` methods works correctly. Submit a description of your plan, an argument as to why it is a robust plan, and the output from using the interactive test driver to carry out the test.

    a. `boolean isEmpty()`

    b. `int size()`

    c. `void enqueue(T element)`

17. As in Exercise 12a, add a `toString` method to the `ArrayBoundedQueue` class. Next enhance the `ITDArrayBoundedQueue` class to include a menu option that invokes the new `toString` method and displays the returned string. Finally, demonstrate that everything works correctly by using the `ITDArrayBoundedQueue`.

18. Following the approach used to create the `ITDArrayBoundedQueue` class, devise similar test drivers for each of the following classes. Demonstrate that your program works correctly.

    a. The `ArrayUnboundedQueue` class

    b. The `ArrayBoundedStack` class (see package `ch02.stacks`)

    c. The `LinkedStack` class (see package `ch02.stacks`)

4.5 Link-Based Queue Implementations

19. Draw the internal representation of the queue q for each step of the following code sequence:

```
LinkedQueue<String> q;
q = new LinkedQueue<String>();
q.enqueue("X");
q.enqueue("M");
q.dequeue();
q.enqueue("T");
```

Your drawings should be similar to the linked implementation part of Figure 4.10.

20. Describe the effects each of the following changes would have on the `LinkedQueue` class:

    a. In the constructor, change "`rear = null`" to "`rear = front`."

    b. In the `enqueue` method, move the statement "`rear = newNode`" to just before the *if* statement.

    c. In the `enqueue` method, change the `boolean` expression "`rear == null`" to "`front == null`."

    d. In the `dequeue` method, switch the second and third statements in the *else* clause.

21. Consider Figure 4.6. Suppose we switched the relative positions of the front and rear references. How would that affect our queue implementation? How would you implement the `dequeue` method if this new approach was used?

22. Add the following methods to the `LinkedQueue` class, and create a test driver for each to show that they work correctly. In order to practice your linked list coding skills, code each of these methods by accessing the internal variables of the `LinkedQueue`, not by calling the previously defined public methods of the class.

    a. `String toString()` creates and returns a string that correctly represents the current queue. Such a method could prove useful for testing and debugging the class and for testing and debugging applications that use the class. Assume each queued element already provides its own reasonable `toString` method.

    b. `void remove(int count)` removes the front `count` elements from the queue; throws `QueueUnderflowException` if less than `count` elements are in the queue.

    c. `boolean swapStart()` returns `false` if less than two elements are in the queue, otherwise reverses the order of the front two elements in the queue and returns `true`.

    d. `boolean swapEnds()` returns `false` if there are less than two elements in the queue, otherwise swaps the first and last elements of the queue and returns `true`.

23. With the linked implementation of a queue, what are the ramifications of an application enqueuing the same object twice before dequeuing it?

24. A "deque" is like a queue, but it also allows you to add to the front of the queue and to remove from the rear of the queue. Create a link-based `DeQue` class and a test driver that demonstrates that it works correctly.

25. Implement the Queue ADT using a circular linked list as shown in Figure 4.9.

26. Assume the maximum queue size is 200.

    a. How many references are needed for:

        i. Our bounded array-based queue holding 20 elements?

        ii. Our bounded array-based queue holding 100 elements?

iii. Our bounded array-based queue holding 200 elements?

iv. Our reference-based queue holding 20 elements?

v. Our reference-based queue holding 100 elements?

vi. Our reference-based queue holding 200 elements?

b. For what size queue do the array-based and reference-based approaches use approximately the same number of references?

4.6 Application: Palindromes

27. Consider the `test` method of the `Palindrome` class. What is the effect of:

a. Switching the order of the `push` and `enqueue` statements in the *for* loop?

b. Removing the `stack.pop()` statement?

c. The `candidate` argument string being `null`?

d. The `candidate` argument string having no letters?

28. How would you change the `test` method of the `Palindrome` class so that it considers all characters, not just letters? Identify the statements you would change, and how you would change them.

29. This question deals with palindromic dates—that is, dates that read the same forward and backward.

a. The year 2002 was a palindromic year. When is the next palindromic year?

b. If dates are written MMDDYYYY, then May 2, 2050, is a palindromic date. What is the earliest palindromic date of the 21st century?

c. Create a program that identifies all palindromic dates in a given year. First a user enters a year. Then the program reports the palindromic dates. Finally, the program asks the user if he or she wishes to try again. Note that you need a class similar to the `Palindrome` class, but one that permits testing "digit" characters.

4.7 Queue Variations

30. As discussed in this section, instead of having our queue methods throw exceptions in the case of "erroneous" invocations, we could have the queue methods handle the situation themselves. We define the following two "safe" methods:

- `boolean safeEnqueue (T element)` adds `element` to the rear of the queue; returns `true` if element successfully added, `false` otherwise

- `T safeDequeue ( )` returns `null` if this queue is empty; otherwise removes front element from this queue and returns it

a. Add these operations to the `ArrayBoundedQueue` class. Create a test driver application to demonstrate that the added code works correctly.

b. Add these operations to the `LinkedQueue` class. Create a test driver application to demonstrate that the added code works correctly.

31. Show what is written by the following segment of code, given that `element1`, `element2`, and `element3` are `int` variables, and `glassQ` is an object that fits the abstract description of a glass queue as given in Section 4.7, "Queue Variations." Assume that you can store and retrieve values of type `int` in `glassQ`.

```
element1 = 1;   element2 = 0;   element3 = 4;
glassQ.enqueue(element2);   glassQ.enqueue(element1);
glassQ.enqueue(element3);
System.out.println(glassQ.peekFront());
System.out.println(glassQ.peekRear());
element2 = glassQ.dequeue();
glassQ.enqueue(element3*element3);
element1 = glassQ.peekRear();   glassQ.enqueue(element1);
System.out.println(element1 + " " + element2 + " " + element3);
while (!glassQ.isEmpty())
{
    element1 = glassQ.dequeue(); System.out.println(element1);
}
```

32. Following the approach used to create the `ITDArrayBoundedQueue` class, devise a similar test driver for the `LinkedGlassQueue` class. Demonstrate that your program works correctly.

33. Using the circular doubly linked list below, give the expression corresponding to each of the following descriptions.

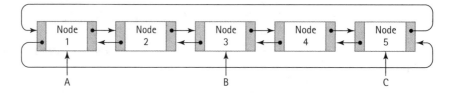

For example, the expression for the `info` value of node 1, referenced from reference A, would be `A.getInfo()`.

a. The `info` value of node 1, referenced from reference C
b. The `info` value of node 2, referenced from reference B
c. The `link` value of node 2, referenced from reference A
d. The `link` value of node 4, referenced from reference C
e. Node 1, referenced from reference B
f. The `back` value of node 4, referenced from reference C
g. The `back` value of node 1, referenced from reference A

34. This exercise shares some content with Exercises 15 and 24. Create a class that implements the `DequeInterface` and a test driver that demonstrates it works correctly:

    a. Create an array-based bounded implementation.

    b. Create a linked list–based implementation.

    c. Create a doubly linked list–based implementation. Use the `DLLNode` class for the nodes.

    Questions 35–38 require "outside" research.

35. List the Java library classes that implement the Java library `Queue` interface.

36. In the Java library, the `BlockingQueue` interface extends the `Queue` interface. Briefly describe the main differences between a "blocking" queue and a "normal" queue.

37. The informal description provided of the Java library `Queue` suggests that addition of a `null` object into a queue be disallowed. Why?

38. Describe the differences among the four Java library classes that implement the Library `Deque` interface.

4.8 Application: Average Waiting Time

39. Complete the following table:

Customer	Arrival Time	Service Time	Finish Time	Wait Time
1	0	10		
2	8	3		
3	8	10		
4	9	40		
5	20	15		
6	32	18		

    a. Assuming one queue, what is the average waiting time?

    b. Assuming two queues, what is the average waiting time?

    c. Assuming three queues, what is the average waiting time?

40. In the Average Waiting Time program, which class (`Customer`, `CustomerGenerator`, `GlassQueue`, `Simulation`, or `SimulationCLI`) is responsible for:

    a. Providing the size of a queue?

    b. Deciding which queue a customer enters?

    c. Obtaining the number of queues from the user?

    d. Calculating the arrival time of a customer?

e. Calculating the finish time of a customer?

f. Calculating the waiting time for a customer?

g. Calculating the average waiting time?

41. Use the Average Waiting Time program to determine a reasonable number of queues to use if there are 1,000 customers and:

a. The interarrival time is 5 and the service time is 5.

b. The interarrival time is 1 and the service time is 5.

c. The interarrival time ranges from 0 to 20, and the service time ranges from 20 to 100.

d. The interarrival time ranges from 0 to 2, and the service time ranges from 20 to 100.

42. Revise the Average Waiting Time program to do the following:

a. Also output the largest number of customers who were on a queue at the same time.

b. Also output the percentage of the time at least one server was "idle."

c. Choose the queue for a customer to enter based on shortest finish time, rather than shortest size. The user should have the ability to choose which approach to use for any simulation run.

4.9 Concurrency, Interference, and Synchronization

43. Seats to events such as concerts are often sold online, at ticket kiosks, and at walk-up ticket booths, simultaneously. Discuss potential interference problems in such situations and options for controlling the interference.

44. What is the output of each of the following code sequences? List all possible results and explain your answers.

a.
```
Counter c = new Counter();
c.increment(); c.increment();
System.out.println(c);
```

b.
```
Counter c = new Counter();
Runnable r = new Increase(c, 3);
Thread t = new Thread(r);
t.start();
System.out.println(c);
```

c.
```
Counter c = new Counter();
Runnable r = new Increase(c, 3);
Thread t = new Thread(r);
c.increment(); t.start();
System.out.println(c);
```

d.
```
Counter c = new Counter();
Runnable r = new Increase(c, 3);
Thread t = new Thread(r);
t.start(); c.increment();
System.out.println(c);
```

e.
```
Counter c = new Counter();
Runnable r = new Increase(c, 3);
Thread t = new Thread(r);
t.start(); t.join();
c.increment();
System.out.println(c);
```

f.
```
Counter c = new Counter();
Runnable r = new Increase(c, 3);
Thread t = new Thread(r);
t.start(); c.increment();
t.join();
System.out.println(c);
```

g.
```
SyncCounter sc = new SyncCounter();
Runnable r = new IncreaseSync(sc, 3);
Thread t = new Thread(r);
t.start(); sc.increment();
t.join();
System.out.println(sc);
```

45. Create a `PrintChar` class that implements `Runnable`. The constructor should accept a character and an integer as parameters. The `run` method should print the character the number of times indicated by the integer. Create an application that instantiates two `PrintChar` objects, one passed "A" and 200 and one passed "B" and 200. It then instantiates and starts two thread objects, one for each of the two `PrintChar` objects. Experiment with the resulting system, using different numerical parameters for the `PrintChar` objects. Create a report about the results of your experimentation.

46. Create an application that instantiates a 20 × 20 two-dimensional array of integers, populates it with random integers drawn from the range 1 to 100, and then outputs the index of the row with the highest sum among all the rows. To support your solution, create a class from which you can instantiate `Runnable` objects, each of which will sum one row of the two-dimensional array and then place the sum of that row into the appropriate slot of a one-dimensional, 20-element array. To summarize, your application will:

a. Generate the two-dimensional array of random integers.

b. Start 20 concurrent threads, each of which places the sum of one row of the two-dimensional array into the corresponding slot of a one-dimensional array.

c. Output the index of the row with the maximum value.

The Collection ADT

Knowledge Goals

You should be able to

- describe a collection and its operations at an abstract level
- explain the difference between comparing objects for equality using the == operator and the `equals` method
- explain the concept of a "key" of a class and how it is used with a Collection ADT class
- describe the purpose of the Java `Comparable` interface
- explain what it means for the `compareTo` and `equals` methods of a class to be compatible
- define vocabulary density
- describe an algorithm for determining the vocabulary density of a text
- describe the difference between implementing an ADT "by copy" or "by reference" and give an example
- perform order of growth efficiency analysis for a given implementation of a collection
- define the Bag ADT
- define the Set ADT

Skill Goals

You should be able to

- given a class, define a suitable `equals` method for it and explain why it is suitable
- create a class that implements the `Comparable` interface
- implement the Collection ADT using an array
- implement the Collection ADT using a sorted array
  - implement the `find` method using binary search
- implement the Collection ADT using a linked list
- show the internal view of a specific Collection ADT implementation for a given application
- predict the output of an application that uses the Collection ADT
- use the Collection ADT as a component of an application
- implement the basic Set ADT using inheritance from a Collection implementation class
- implement the basic Set ADT by wrapping a Collection implementation class

This chapter introduces one of the most fundamental ADTs, the Collection ADT. This ADT provides the ability to store information and then access the stored information. As you can imagine, storing and retrieving information is often at the heart of computer processing. There are other ADTs that provide these same operations, perhaps with certain restrictions on the information stored or the order in which it can be accessed. In fact, you might recall that we have referred to both of our previously defined ADTs, the Stack and the Queue, as "access-controlled" collections.

Typical Collection ADTs (unlike the Stack and the Queue) allow retrieval of information based on the contents of the information. Therefore, we return to the topic of object comparison in this chapter, considering what it means for two objects to be "equal" or for one object to be "less than" or "greater than" another object. Being able to compare objects allows us to store them in sorted order, which, in turn, permits relatively fast retrieval options. This allows us, for example, to analyze more information during processing—we demonstrate this ability using a text processing application developed with our Collection ADT.

5.1   The Collection Interface

Stacks and queues are useful ADTs allowing us to solve many different types of problems. Stacks are perfect for situations where we need to process the most recent data first, such as matching grouping symbols in arithmetic expressions and queues make good buffers for storing information that needs to be handled in a first in first out sequence. The restrictions on how to insert and remove information when using stacks and queues ensure that when we use them in these situations we properly access the data.

Terms with Multiple Meanings

The set of attributes that uniquely identify an object is called its key. The term "key" is used in similar fashion across computing, in particular in the fields of databases and information management. However, like so many other terms it does have alternate meanings such as the keys used with encryption algorithms or even the keys you press on your keyboard to enter data.

But what about problems where we need to retrieve information regardless of the order in which it is stored—for example obtaining bank account information based on an ID number or determining if a specific item is in stock at a warehouse? In these situations we need a structure that allows us to store information and retrieve it later based on some key part of the information. Many solutions to this problem exist—lists, maps, tables, search trees, and databases just to name a few. This chapter presents the most basic ADT that provides the required functionality—the Collection ADT.

Our Collection ADT allows us to collect together information for later access. The order in which we add information to a collection has no effect on when we can retrieve it. Once an object is added to a collection we can retrieve it and/or remove it based on its contents.

To provide content-based access the Collection ADT uses the `equals` method. All classes provide an `equals` method—if they do not implement the method directly then they inherit it. We know this because the `equals` method is implemented in the `Object` class that is the root of the inheritance tree (see Section 1.2, "Organizing Classes"). The `equals` method of the `Object` class only considers two objects to be equal if they are aliases of each other. Usually we want equality to be related to the contents of the objects, not their memory address. Therefore, objects stored in our collections should override the `equals` method of the `Object` class. We return to this topic in Section 5.4, "Comparing Objects Revisited." For now we will use the `String` class in our examples—the `String` class *does* provide a content-based `equals` method.

Assumptions for Our Collections

Many variations of collections are possible. Here we define a basic collection, a content-based repository that supports addition, removal, and retrieval of elements.

Our collections *allow* duplicate elements. Element `first` is considered to be a duplicate of element `second` if `first.equals(second)` returns `true`. When an operation involves "finding" such an element, it can "find" any one of the duplicates. There is no distinction among duplicate elements in these cases.

As with our stacks and queues, collections do *not* support `null` elements. As a general precondition for all of our collection methods, `null` elements cannot be used as arguments. Rather than stating this precondition for each method, we state it once in the lead comment of the interface. This is a standard precondition when defining ADTs. It simplifies coding, which removes the need for testing for `null` pointers every time we use an argument within a method.

Other than prohibiting `null` elements, our collection classes have *minimal* preconditions for operations. For example, it is possible to specify a `remove` operation that requires a matching object to be present in the collection. We do not do this. Instead, we define a `remove` operation that returns a `boolean` value indicating whether the operation succeeded. This approach provides greater flexibility to applications. Similarly we could require that the `add` operation not be invoked on a full collection, perhaps stating that in such a situation it throws a "Collection Overflow" exception. Instead we use the same approach as with `remove`—`add` returns a `boolean` indicating success or failure of the operation. An attempt to `add` to a full collection would return `false`.

The Interface

As we did with stacks and queues, we capture the formal specifications of our Collection ADT using the Java interface construct. Our collections are generic—the type of object held by any particular collection is indicated by the client at the time the list is instantiated. It is the client's responsibility to use a class whose `equals` method definition suits their needs. Here is the code for our `CollectionInterface`. Study the comments and method signatures to learn more about the details. As you can see, this interface is part of the `ch05.collections` package. The implementation classes are also stored in the same package.

```
//-------------------------------------------------------------------------
// CollectionInterface.java         by Dale/Joyce/Weems          Chapter 5
//
// Interface for a class that implements a collection of T.
// A collection allows addition, removal, and access of elements.
// Null elements are not allowed. Duplicate elements are allowed.
//-------------------------------------------------------------------------
package ch05.collections;

public interface CollectionInterface<T>
{
  boolean add(T element);
  // Attempts to add element to this collection.
  // Returns true if successful, false otherwise.

  T get(T target);
  // Returns an element e from this collection such that e.equals(target).
  // If no such element exists, returns null.

  boolean contains(T target);
  // Returns true if this collection contains an element e such that
  // e.equals(target); otherwise returns false.

  boolean remove (T target);
  // Removes an element e from this collection such that e.equals(target)
  // and returns true. If no such element exists, returns false.

  boolean isFull();
  // Returns true if this collection is full; otherwise, returns false.

  boolean isEmpty();
  // Returns true if this collection is empty; otherwise, returns false.


  int size();
  // Returns the number of elements in this collection.
}
```

Figure 5.4, in this chapter's summary, shows the relationships among the primary classes and interfaces created to support our Collection ADT.

5.2   Array-Based Collection Implementation

This section develops an array-based implementation of our Collection ADT. We look at another array-based solution in Section 5.5, "Sorted Array-Based Collection Implementation," and discuss a link-based solution in Section 5.6, "Link-Based Collection Implementation."

Our basic approach is simple: If a collection has *N* elements, we hold the elements in the first *N* locations of the array, locations 0 to *N*−1. We maintain an instance variable, numElements, to hold the current number of elements in the collection. This example shows how we would represent a collection of country abbreviations:

numElements: 4

	[0]	[1]	[2]	[3]	[4]	[5]
elements:	"BRA"	"MEX"	"PER"	"ARG"		

When an element is added to the collection, we simply place it in the next available slot, the slot indicated by numElements, and increment numElements by one. The result of adding Columbia ("COL") to the above collection is as follows:

numElements: 4̸ 5

	[0]	[1]	[2]	[3]	[4]	[5]
elements:	"BRA"	"MEX"	"PER"	"ARG"	"COL"	

When an element is removed we could shift all the elements at higher indices one position lower, to fill the gap left by the removal. Instead we take advantage of the unsorted nature of the array and simply move the element at the end of the collection into the position occupied by the element to be removed. Let us remove Mexico from the above collection:

numElements: 4̸5̸4

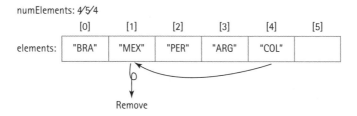

Remove

The ArrayCollection class implements the CollectionInterface using the basic approach described above. The implementation of the ArrayCollection class is straightforward, especially if you are familiar with the array-based implementations of the Stack ADT from Chapter 2 and of the Queue ADT from Chapter 4.

As was the case with our array-based generic stacks and queues, the instantiation of an array as an array of Object, and subsequent casting of it as an array of T, typically generates a compiler warning. Even though this approach is somewhat awkward and results in a compiler warning, it is how we must create generic collections using arrays in Java. Two constructors are provided: one that instantiates a collection based on a default capacity of 100, and another that allows the client to indicate the capacity.

For our ArrayCollection class we place the code for array search in a protected helper method, called find, which is invoked by each method that needs to search for an element. The find method sets the values of the protected instance variables found and location, thereby indicating the results of the search. The algorithm used here for searching the array for an element is the Sequential Search algorithm presented in Section 1.6, "Comparing Algorithms: Order of Growth Analysis." The find method is an example of procedural abstraction. Its existence removes the need to create similar code across the methods remove, contains, and get, and greatly simplifies the code for each of those methods.

Here is the code for the ArrayCollection class:

```
//-------------------------------------------------------------------------
// ArrayCollection.java          by Dale/Joyce/Weems          Chapter 5
//
// Implements the CollectionInterface using an array.
//
// Null elements are not allowed. Duplicate elements are allowed.
//
// Two constructors are provided: one that creates a collection of a default
// capacity, and one that allows the calling program to specify the capacity.
//-------------------------------------------------------------------------
package ch05.collections;

public class ArrayCollection<T> implements CollectionInterface<T>
{
  protected final int DEFCAP = 100; // default capacity
  protected T[] elements;           // array to hold collection's elements
  protected int numElements = 0;    // number of elements in this collection

  // set by find method
  protected boolean found;  // true if target found, otherwise false
  protected int location;   // indicates location of target if found

  public ArrayCollection()
  {
    elements = (T[]) new Object[DEFCAP];
  }
```

```
public ArrayCollection(int capacity)
{
  elements = (T[]) new Object[capacity];
}


protected void find(T target)
// Searches elements for an occurrence of an element e such that
// e.equals(target). If successful, sets instance variables found to true
// and location to the index of e. If not successful, sets found to false.
{
  location = 0; found = false;
  while (location < numElements)
  {
    if (elements[location].equals(target))
    {
      found = true;
      return;
    }
    else
      location++;
  }
}


public boolean add(T element)
// Attempts to add element to this collection.
// Returns true if successful, false otherwise.
{
  if (isFull())
    return false;
  else
  {
    elements[numElements] = element;
    numElements++;
    return true;
  }
}


public boolean remove (T target)
// Removes an element e from this collection such that e.equals(target)
// and returns true; if no such element exists, returns false.
{
  find(target);
  if (found)
```

```
      {
        elements[location] = elements[numElements - 1];
        elements[numElements - 1] = null;
        numElements--;
      }
      return found;
    }

    public boolean contains (T target)
    // Returns true if this collection contains an element e such that
    // e.equals(target); otherwise, returns false.
    {
      find(target);
      return found;
    }

    public T get(T target)
    // Returns an element e from this collection such that e.equals(target);
    // if no such element exists, returns null.
    {
      find(target);
      if (found)
        return elements[location];
      else
        return null;
    }

    public boolean isFull()
    // Returns true if this collection is full; otherwise, returns false.
    {
      return (numElements == elements.length);
    }

    public boolean isEmpty()
    // Returns true if this collection is empty; otherwise, returns false.
    {
      return (numElements == 0);
    }

    public int size()
    // Returns the number of elements in this collection.
    {
      return numElements;
    }
  }
```

5.3 Application: Vocabulary Density

The vocabulary density of a text is the total number of words in the text divided by the number of unique words in the text. In this section we develop an application that computes the vocabulary density of a given text.

The problem is clear—read the text and count how many words it contains and also the number of unique words it contains. We define a word to be a sequence of letter characters (A through Z) plus the apostrophe character ('). The apostrophe is included so as to treat words such as "it's" and "Molly's" as a single word. We ignore the case of letters when determining uniqueness—for example, "The" and "the" are considered to be the same word.

> **Vocabulary Density**
>
> Vocabulary density indicates the variation in the vocabulary and is used by computational linguists as a tool to help analyze texts. One way of looking at the vocabulary density is that it indicates the average number of words one reads within a text before encountering a "new" word. In general, if the vocabulary density ratio is small, the vocabulary is more complex; as the number increases, the text becomes easier. On the other hand, the longer a text is the lower its vocabulary density tends to be, so it should only be used to compare texts of similar length when looking at complexity.

To count the number of unique words we need to keep track of all the words encountered so far while reading through the text. Our Collection ADT is the perfect tool to accomplish this. The algorithm is simple—read through the text word by word, checking each word to see if it is already in the collection and if not, add it to the collection. When finished, the size of the collection provides us the number of unique words. As we proceed through the words we also keep track of the total number of words processed. We use the total number of words and the number of unique words to calculate the vocabulary density. More formally:

Vocabulary Density Calculation

Initialize variables and objects
while there are more words to process
  Get the next word
  if the collection does not contain the word
    Add the word to the collection
  Increment total number of words
Display (total number of words/size of the collection)

Input to our application will reside in a text file. The name/location of the file should be indicated as a command line argument to the program. Here is the application—the parts of the code directly related to the use of the Collection ADT are <u>emphasized</u>:

```
//--------------------------------------------------------------------------
// VocabularyDensity.java        by Dale/Joyce/Weems              Chapter 5
//
// Displays the number of total words, unique words in the input text file,
// and the resulting vocabulary density.
// Input file indicated by a command line argument.
//--------------------------------------------------------------------------
```

```java
package ch05.apps;

import java.io.*;
import java.util.*;
import ch05.collections.*;

public class VocabularyDensity
{
  public static void main(String[] args) throws IOException
  {
    final int CAPACITY = 1000;     // capacity of collection
    String fname = args[0];        // input file of text
    String word;                   // current word
    int numWords = 0;              // total number of words
    int uniqWords;                 // number of unique words
    double density;                // vocabulary density

    CollectionInterface<String> words =
                          new ArrayCollection<String>(CAPACITY);

    // Set up file reading
    FileReader fin = new FileReader(fname);
    Scanner wordsIn = new Scanner(fin);
    wordsIn.useDelimiter("[^a-zA-Z']+"); // delimiters are nonletters,'

    while (wordsIn.hasNext())        // while more words to process
    {
      word = wordsIn.next();
      word = word.toLowerCase();
      if (!words.contains(word))
        words.add(word);
      numWords++;
    }

    density = (double)numWords/words.size();
    System.out.println("Analyzed file " + fname);
    System.out.println("\n\tTotal words:  " + numWords);
    if (words.size() == CAPACITY)
      System.out.println("\tUnique words: at least " + words.size());
    else
```

```
  {
    System.out.println("\tUnique words: " + words.size());
    System.out.printf("\n\tVocabulary density: %.2f", density);
  }
 }
}
```

Some observations about the application:

- The code is short and simple—this is because so much of the complexity is handled by the `ArrayCollection` class. This is a good example of the power and utility of abstraction.

- This program demonstrates how to read input from a file. The `FileReader` constructor will throw `IOException` if there are issues finding/opening the indicated file. Because that is a checked exception, we must either catch it or rethrow it. We chose the latter approach as you can see on the line declaring the `main` method. The `FileReader` `fin` is passed as an argument to a `Scanner`, allowing us to use the scanner to read the file.

- We use Java's `Scanner` to break the input file into words. It allows us to know when "there are more words to process" and allows us to "get the next word." The `Scanner` class permits us to define the set of delimiters used to separate the tokens found in its input source by invoking its `useDelimiter` method. This method accepts a regular expression as an argument. In our program we indicate that the delimiters are "[^a-zA-Z']+"; this regular expression means any sequence of one or more characters that are not a letter ("a-zA-Z" indicates all the characters between 'a' and 'z' plus all the characters between 'A' and 'Z') or an apostrophe (note the ' that follows the 'Z' in the expression)—the '^' symbol acts to negate that set of characters, and the + sign indicates "one or more" of the characters in the bracketed set that proceeds it. Thus, "one or more characters that are not a letter or an apostrophe." See documentation about the Java `Pattern` class for more information.

- The `toLowerCase` method of the `String` class changes all letters of a word to lowercase before checking if the word is in the collection, fulfilling the specification to ignore the case of letters when determining uniqueness.

- The constant `CAPACITY` is used to instantiate the `ArrayCollection` variable `words`. Therefore, the `words` collection can hold at most `CAPACITY` words, in our case 1,000. If the capacity is reached we display the phrase "at least" because we cannot determine the exact number of unique words in the file. In that case we do not display the density as it would be meaningless.

- Once the capacity is reached the `add` method no longer adds words to the collection—instead it simply returns the value `false` over and over as the program continues to process the input file. Exercise 5.12a asks you to modify the program so that in the case of reaching a full capacity it stops processing and outputs an appropriate message.

The reader is encouraged to test this program and to use it to analyze some text files of their choice. Here are the results of running the program on three related, important, historical documents—the 1215 British Magna Carta (translated to English from the original Latin but minus the list of those in attendance), the 1776 U.S. Declaration of Independence (minus the list of signatures), and the 1930 Indian Purna Swaraj:

Analyzed file BritishMagnaCarta.txt	Analyzed file USAdeclaration.txt	Analyzed file IndiaPurnaSwaraj.txt
Total words: 3310	Total words: 1341	Total words: 594
Unique words: 698	Unique words: 540	Unique words: 288
Vocabulary density: 4.74	Vocabulary density: 2.48	Vocabulary density: 2.06

5.4   Comparing Objects Revisited

With stacks and queues, we access only the ends of our structures. We push or pop the top element of a stack, or we enqueue a value at the tail of a queue and dequeue it from the head. We do not access elements stored at other places within the structure. With a collection, however, access is permitted to elements anywhere within the structure. Therefore, to understand collections we need to understand how an element within a structure is identified—we need to understand equality of objects.

In the next section we consider an approach to storing the elements of a collection that improves the efficiency of finding any given element. If we can store the elements in "increasing order" then we can use the binary search algorithm to locate them. But what does it mean to store elements "in order"? To understand this we need to understand object comparison.

This section reviews both the `equals` method, used to determine equality, and the `compareTo` method (along with the `Comparable` interface), used to determine order.

The equals Method

Section 1.5, "Basic Structuring Mechanisms," discussed comparing objects using the comparison operator (`==`). Recall that when using `==`, the comparison is actually made between the contents of the two reference variables that point to the objects, and not between the contents of the objects themselves. This is demonstrated in **Figure 5.1** (which replicates Figure 1.6).

The comparison operator does not compare the contents of objects. What else can we do? How do we compare the actual objects? One option is to use the `equals` method. Because this method is exported from the `Object` class that is the root of the Java inheritance tree, it can be used with objects of any Java class. If `c1` and `c2` are objects of the class `Circle`, then we can compare them using:

```
c1.equals(c2)
```

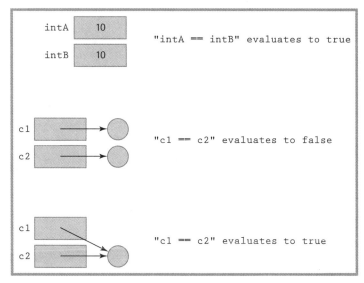

Figure 5.1   Comparing primitive and nonprimitive variables

The `equals` method, as defined in the `Object` class, acts in much the same way as the comparison operator. It returns true if and only if the two variables reference the same object. To circumvent this problem we can, within a class, redefine the `equals` method to fit the purpose of the class.

Suppose we have a `Circle` class that features a `radius` attribute of type `int`. A reasonable definition for equality of `Circle` objects is that they are equal if they have the same radii. To implement this approach, we include the following method in the `Circle` class:

```
@Override
public boolean equals(Object obj)
// Returns true if obj is a Circle with same radius as this Circle,
// otherwise returns false.
{
    if (obj == this)
        return true;
    else
    if (obj == null || obj.getClass() != this.getClass())
        return false;
    else
    {
        Circle c = (Circle) obj;
        return (this.radius == c.radius);
    }
}
```

This design of the `equals` method reflects standard good practice. A few notes about the design follow:

- The `@Override` notation indicates to the compiler that we are overriding an ancestor's method. The compiler double-checks our syntax and ensures that we are in fact overriding a method.
- The first *if* clause checks to see if we are comparing a circle to itself. In that case we return `true`.
- The second *if* clause checks to see if the argument is `null`. If so we return `false`. Due to the short-circuit nature of the Java || operator the second part of the *or* expression is only evaluated if the first part is false, protecting us from a null pointer exception. In the second part of the expression we check to make sure the two objects being compared are of the same type—if not we return `false`.
- If processing reaches the final *else* clause we can safely cast the `obj` argument as a `Circle` and compare the two radii.

Now when a statement such as

```
c1.equals(c2)
```

is encountered, the customized `equals` method of the `Circle` class is used, rather than the `equals` method of the `Object` class. Even though `c1` and `c2` may reference different `Circle` objects, if those objects have equal radii, the `equals` method returns `true`. As discussed previously in Section 5.1, "The Collection Interface," we sometimes refer to the attribute, or combination of attributes, of an object used by the `equals` method to determine equality as the key of the class. The **key** of a class, from the point of view of an application, is the set of attributes that are used to determine the identity of an object of the class, for that application. For example, if an application uses the `Circle` class `equals` method to determine identity, then the radius of a circle is the key.

The FamousPerson class

Let us look at another example, one that we will use in several applications. This example should help clarify what is meant by the *key* attributes of a class. Consider a class, `FamousPerson`, whose objects will represent famous people. The information we wish to capture about a famous person is their name (first name and last name), the year they were born, and some short interesting fact about the person.

The `FamousPerson` class can be found in the `support` package. It includes protected variables `firstName`, `lastName`, `yearOfBirth`, and `fact` to hold its attributes, all of which are initialized through its constructor. The class also includes getters plus `equals`, `compareTo`, and `toString` methods. Here we show the equals method that demonstrates that equality *can* sometimes depend on a subset of the attributes, in this case the first and last name attributes. We say that the combination of `firstName` and `lastName` is the key of the class.

```
@Override
public boolean equals(Object obj)
// Returns true if 'obj' is a FamousPerson with same first and last
// names as this FamousPerson, otherwise returns false.
{
    if (obj == this)
        return true;
    else
    if (obj == null || obj.getClass() != this.getClass())
        return false;
    else
    {
        FamousPerson fp = (FamousPerson) obj;
        return (this.firstName.equals(fp.firstName) &&
                this.lastName.equals(fp.lastName));
    }
}
```

Let us create an application that uses our Collection ADT and the FamousPerson class. A text file named FamousCS.txt is included in the input folder—it contains information about famous computer scientists, one scientist per line, in the format: first name, last name, year of birth, and fact. We make the simplifying assumptions that the only commas in the file are those used to separate the information, and that the scientists' names do not contain "white space."

Our application will read the information from the file and store it in a collection of FamousPerson. It will then interact with the user, displaying the information about the scientists based on the user's queries. The application is easy to write because the more complex parts are already implemented by the ArrayCollection and FamousPerson classes. We call the application CSInfo, representing Computer Scientist Information.

```
//-------------------------------------------------------------------------
// CSInfo.java               by Dale/Joyce/Weems              Chapter 5
//
// Reads information about famous computer scientists from the file
// FamousCS.txt. Allows user to enter names and provides them the information
// from the file that matches the name.
//-------------------------------------------------------------------------
package ch05.apps;

import java.io.*;
import java.util.*;
import ch05.collections.*;
import support.FamousPerson;
```

```java
public class CSInfo
{
  public static void main(String[] args) throws IOException
  {
    // instantiate collection
    final int CAPACITY = 300;
    ArrayCollection<FamousPerson> people
          = new ArrayCollection<FamousPerson>(CAPACITY);

    // set up file reading
    FileReader fin = new FileReader("input/FamousCS.txt");
    Scanner info = new Scanner(fin);
    info.useDelimiter("[,\\n]");  // delimiters are commas, line feeds

    Scanner scan = new Scanner(System.in);
    FamousPerson person;
    String fname, lname, fact;
    int year;

    // read the info from the file and put in collection
    while (info.hasNext())
    {
      fname = info.next();    lname = info.next();
      year = info.nextInt(); fact = info.next();
      person = new FamousPerson(fname, lname, year, fact);
      people.add(person);
    }

    // interact with user, getting names and displaying info
    final String STOP = "X";
    System.out.println("Enter names of computer scientists.");
    System.out.println("Enter: firstname lastname (" + STOP + " to exit)\n");
    fname = null; lname = null;
    while (!STOP.equals(fname))
    {
      System.out.print("Name> ");
      fname = scan.next();
      if (!STOP.equals(fname))
      {
        lname = scan.next();
        person = new FamousPerson(fname, lname, 0, "");
        if (people.contains(person))
```

```
        {
            person = people.get(person);
            System.out.println(person);
        }
        else
            System.out.println("No information available\n");
    }
  }
 }
}
```

Here is a sample run of the application:

```
Enter names of computer scientists.
Enter: firstname lastname (X to exit)

Name> Ada Lovelace
Ada Lovelace(Born 1815): Considered by many to be first computer programmer.

Name> Molly Joyce
No information available

Name> Edsger Dijkstra
Edsger Dijkstra(Born 1930): 1972 Turing Award winner.

Name> X
```

As you study the code of the application, take particular note of the following line:

```
person = people.get(person);
```

It might seem strange to be passing `person` to the collection to get back a `FamousPerson` object and assign it to `person`. This is an example of how the key attributes of an object let us retrieve information from a collection. Suppose the user enters "Ada Lovelace" in response to the name prompt. In that case the line

```
person = new FamousPerson(fname, lname, 0, "");
```

creates a new `Person` object with attributes

```
firstName: "Ada"  lastName: "Lovelace"  yearOfBirth: 0
fact: ""
```

When the `get` method is invoked with this object as an argument, the object is compared to each of the objects held in the collection—based on the way `equals` is defined for `FamousPerson` objects, a match is found for the `Person` object with attributes

```
firstName: "Ada"  lastName: "Lovelace"  yearOfBirth: 1815
fact: "Considered by many to be first computer programmer."
```

It is this matched object that is returned, that is a reference to it is returned, and assigned to the `person` variable. Now the `person` variable references the object that is in the collection, the object with the complete information, and it is this information that is used in the `println` statement on the following line. As long as we provide a partial object that contains the correct key information, we can retrieve the complete object from the collection.

The Comparable Interface

The `equals` method allows us to check whether a particular element is in a collection. But in addition to checking objects for equality, we need another type of comparison. We often need to be able to tell when one object is less than, equal to, or greater than another object. The Java library provides an interface, called `Comparable`, that can be used to ensure that a class provides this functionality.

The `Comparable` interface consists of exactly one abstract method:

```
public int compareTo(T o);
// Returns a negative integer, zero, or a positive integer as this object
// is less than, equal to, or greater than the specified object.
```

The `compareTo` method returns an integer value that indicates the relative "size" relationship between the object upon which the method is invoked and the object passed to the method as an argument. As we see in the next section, this information can be used to order the objects of a collection within the internal representation structure, facilitating faster search. By convention the `compareTo` method of a class should support the standard order of a class—lexicographic order for strings, numeric order for numbers, low score to high score for bowlers, high score to low score for golfers, and so on. We call the order established by a class `compareTo` method the **natural order** of the class.

Any class that implements the `Comparable` interface defines its own `compareTo` method, with a signature that matches the abstract method defined in the interface. After all, the implementer of the class is in the best position to define how objects of the class should be compared—to know the natural order.

The Java `Comparable` interface is able to work with generics. Use of generic types with the `compareTo` method helps ensure that comparison takes place only between compatible objects.

Let us return to our famous person example. Recalling that people are compared on their first and last names when determining equality, we use the same two fields when determining relative order. Following standard procedure we first compare last names using the `String` class `equals` method—only if the two last names under consideration are equal do we turn our attention to the first names. When a key consists of multiple attributes, starting with the most significant attribute, first is the best approach. Here is the `compareTo` method implemented within our `FamousPerson` class (our `FamousPerson` class *does* implement the `Comparable` interface):

```
public int compareTo(FamousPerson other)
// Precondition: 'other' is not null
//
// Compares this FamousPerson with 'other' for order. Returns a
// negative integer, zero, or a positive integer as this object
// is less than, equal to, or greater than 'other'.
{
  if (!this.lastName.equals(other.lastName))
    return this.lastName.compareTo(other.lastName);
  else
    return this.firstName.compareTo(other.firstName);
}
```

Our `compareTo` method uses the `compareTo` method of the `String` class. This makes sense because the attributes upon which we are basing the comparison are strings. Notice that the `equals` method described previously and the `compareTo` method described here are consistent with each other. In other words, the `equals` method returns `true` for two people if and only if the `compareTo` method returns 0 for the two people. It is good programming

> **Operation Consistency**
>
> The `equals` and `compareTo` methods defined on a class not only should behave consistently with respect to each other but also with respect to their arithmetic counterparts. For example, if A and B are objects of the same class then `A.equals(B)` should return the same value as `B.equals(A)` (see Exercise 16). Similarly, unless A and B are "equal", `A.compareTo(B)` should return the opposite result as `B.compareTo(A)`.

practice to ensure consistency between these two methods. Unlike with the `equals` method it is common to assume the argument passed to `compareTo` is not `null`.

5.5 Sorted Array-Based Collection Implementation

In Section 5.2, "Array-Based Collection Implementation," we implemented a collection class that used an array. The `ArrayCollection` implementation featured a constant time `add`, but all the other basic operations—get, `contains`, and `remove`—require $O(N)$ time. Consider an application that builds a large collection and then repeatedly accesses the collection to see if it contains various elements—perhaps a spell-checker application. Although such an application can make use of the fast `add` operation, it might benefit even more from a fast `contains` operation. Is there some way we can structure our stored data so as to facilitate a faster search?

In Section 1.6, "Comparing Algorithms: Order of Growth Analysis," and Section 3.3, "Recursive Processing of Arrays," we studied the binary search algorithm—an $O(\log_2 N)$ algorithm for finding an element in a sorted array. If we use an array as the internal representation for a collection implementation, and keep that array in sorted order, then the binary search algorithm can be used to find elements in the collection. Not only will this significantly speed up the `contains` operation but since `get` and `remove` both require that we first find the element in question, those operations can also benefit. In this section we take this approach. We call our implementation the `SortedArrayCollection`.

Our goal with this new Collection ADT implementation is to increase the efficiency of the operations. Efficiency is typically only a concern for a collection when the collection holds a large number of elements. It makes sense, therefore, to make this implementation of the Collection ADT unbounded. We do this using the same approach we did with our array-based unbounded queue implementation—we include a protected `enlarge` method that can be invoked internally by the public `add` method when needed.

Comparable Elements

As elements are added to our collection we intend to keep the protected array sorted according to the natural order of the elements—therefore we intend to use the `compareTo` method associated with the elements. In order to do this we must ensure that only classes that implement the `Comparable` interface are used with our collection.

Is it possible to force applications to use `Comparable` classes when providing an argument for a generic type? Yes it is. We can use what is called a "bounded type." For example, we could design a class `Duo` that holds a pair of elements and that provides a `largest` operation to return the larger of the two elements:

```
public class Duo<T extends Comparable<T>>
{
  protected T first;
  protected T second;

  public Duo(T f, T s)
  {
    first = f; second = s;
  }

  public T larger()
  {
    if (first.compareTo(second) > 0)
      return first;
    else
      return second;
  }
}
```

Note that in the class declaration instead of indicating the generic parameter as <T> we used <T extends Comparable <T>>. This indicates that the generic argument must be of a class that implements the Comparable interface. If we instantiate a Duo object using a class that does not implement Comparable, a syntax error is generated.

Although it appears we can use the above approach to solve our problem of assuring that only Comparable classes are used with our SortedArrayCollection classes, it turns out that is not the case. Because we wish to use an array as our internal representation structure, we cannot use this approach due to type safety issues and differences between the way arrays and generic types are treated by Java. Attempting to declare an array of <T extends Comparable<T>> results in a syntax error. So we need to find a different approach.

Rather than try to enforce the use of Comparable classes using syntactic means we will use our "programming by contract" approach. We specify as a precondition of the add method that its argument is comparable to the previous objects added to the collection. As the add method is the only way for an element to get into the collection, we are guaranteed that all elements held in our SortedArrayCollection can be compared to each other. If a client class ignores the contract then it is likely that an exception will be thrown when they use the class.

The Implementation

The SortedArrayCollection class implements the CollectionInterface using an array. For this class we *are* concerned about the order in which we keep elements stored—the array must be kept sorted. Nevertheless, the implementation of the SortedArrayCollection class has much in common with the implementation of the ArrayCollection class developed in Section 5.2 "Array-Based Collection Implementation," so we do not provide complete code listings here. The code for the new class can be found in the ch05.collections package. A few notes follow.

- As already mentioned, this implementation is unbounded, using a protected en-large method as needed to increase the size of the internal representation array by the original capacity.

- The class includes a protected find method that serves the same function as the find method of the ArrayCollection class—search the collection for an occurrence of an element that is equal to the target element, and if successful set the instance variable found to true and set the instance variable location to the index where the target was found. For this class, however, the find method makes use of the binary search algorithm to provide excellent efficiency. The recursive approach to the binary search algorithm described in Section 3.3, "Recursive Processing of Arrays," is used.

- During the search process the compareTo operation is used. Therefore, within the find method we must cast elements as Comparable, so that the Java compiler will accept our use of the `compareTo` method. Some compilers will generate a warning message regarding an unchecked call to `compareTo`, because there is no way for the compiler to verify that the generic type T will actually implement `Comparable`. Because we understand the reason for the warning message and because our precondition prohibits the use of elements that do not implement `Comparable`, we can safely ignore the compiler warning. An application that ignores the precondition and adds elements to the `SortedArrayCollection` that are not `Comparable` will cause a type mismatch exception to be thrown—which is exactly the result we desire because incomparable elements should not be added to a sorted collection.

- Unlike with the `ArrayCollection` class we cannot simply add a new element in the next available location of the array. So that the add method can also make use of the `find` method, to determine where the new element should be inserted, the `find` method of the `SortedArrayCollection` class has additional functionality. In the case of an "unsuccessful" search, the `find` method sets the instance variable `found` to `false` and sets the instance variable `location` to the index where the target should be inserted.

- Once the index where the addition of the new element is identified, the add method creates room for the new element by shifting all of the elements from that index through the end of the collection, one index higher, and then inserts the new element in the free slot that is created:

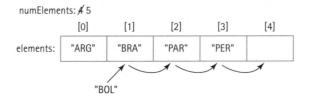

The code for the add method is as follows:

```
public boolean add(T element)
// Precondition:  element is Comparable to previously added objects
//
// Adds element to this collection.
{
  if (numElements == elements.length)
    enlarge();

  find(element); // sets location to index where element belongs

  for (int index = numElements; index > location; index--)
    elements [index] = elements[index - 1];
```

```
    elements [location] = element;
  numElements++;
  return true;
}
```

Note that since the `SortedArrayCollection` is unbounded the `add` method always returns `true`—it should always be able to add the given `element` successfully.

- Similarly, the remove method shifts elements one index lower in order to remove the targeted element without disrupting the already sorted array.

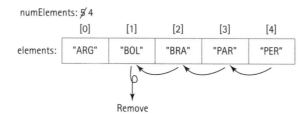

Implementing ADTs "by Copy" or "by Reference"

When designing an ADT, such as for a stack, queue, or collection, we have a choice about how to handle the elements—"by copy" or "by reference."

By Copy

With this approach, the ADT manipulates copies of the data used in the client program. When the ADT is presented with a data element to store, it makes a copy of the element and stores that copy. Making a valid copy of an object can be a complicated process, especially if the object is composed of other objects. Valid copies of an object are typically created using the object's `clone` method. Classes that provide a `clone` method must indicate this fact to the run-time system by implementing the `Cloneable` interface. In the examples that follow, we assume the object classes provide rigorous `clone` methods and implement the `Cloneable` interface. In that case, code for an unsorted collection `add` operation might be

```
public void add (T element)
// Adds a copy of the element to this collection
{
  elements[numElements] = element.clone();
  numElements++;
}
```

In Java, if the collection elements are objects, then it is really a reference to a copy of the element that is stored—because all Java objects are manipulated by reference. The key distinction here is that it is a reference to a copy of the element, and not a reference to the element itself, that is stored.

Similarly, when an ADT returns an element using the "by copy" approach, it actually returns a reference to a copy of the element. As an example, consider the code for a collection get operation:

```
public T get(T target)
// Returns a copy of element e from this collection such that e.equals(target);
// if no such element exists, returns null.
{
  find(target);
  if (found)
    return elements[location].clone();
  else
    return null;
}
```

This approach provides strong information hiding. In effect, the ADT is providing a separate repository for a copy of the client's data.

By Reference

For this approach, an ADT manipulates references to the actual elements passed to it by the client program. For example, code for an unsorted collection add operation might be

```
public void add (T element)
// Adds an element to this collection
{
    elements[numElements] = element;
    numElements++;
}
```

Because the client program retains a reference to the element, we have exposed the contents of the collection ADT to the client program. The ADT still hides the way the data is organized—for example, the use of an array of objects—but it allows direct access to the individual elements of the collection by the client program through the client program's own references. In effect, the ADT provides an organization for the original client data.

The "by reference" method is the most commonly used approach and the one we use throughout this text. It has the advantage that it takes less time and space than the "by copy" method. Copying objects takes time, especially if the objects are large and require complicated deep-copying methods. Storing extra copies of objects also requires extra memory. Thus, the "by reference" approach is an attractive strategy.

When we use the "by reference" approach, we create aliases of our elements, so we must deal with the potential problems associated with aliases. If our data elements are immutable, then no problems will occur. If the elements can be changed, however, problems can arise.

If an element is accessed and changed through one alias, it could disrupt the status of the element when it is accessed through the other alias. This situation is especially dangerous if the client program can change an attribute that the ADT uses to determine the internal organization of the elements. For example, if the client changes an attribute that determines an object's position within a sorted collection, then the object may no longer be in the proper place. Because the change did not go through a method of the sorted collection class, the class has no way of knowing that it should correct this situation. A subsequent `get` operation on this collection would likely fail.

An Example

The diagrams in **Figure 5.2** show the ramifications of both approaches. Suppose we have objects that hold a person's `name` and `weight`. Further suppose that we have a collection of these objects sorted by the variable `weight`. We add three objects into the collection, and then transform one of the objects with a `diet` method that changes the `weight` of the object. The left side of the figure models the approach of storing references to copies of the objects—the "by copy" approach. The right side models the approach of storing references to the original objects—the "by reference" approach.

The middle section of the figure, showing the state of things after the objects have been inserted into the collections, clearly demonstrates the differences in the internal implementations. The "by copy" approach creates copies and the collection elements reference them; these copies take up space that is not required in the "by reference" approach. It is also clear from the right side of the figure that the "by reference" approach creates aliases for the objects, as we can see more than one reference to an object. In both approaches, the collection elements are kept sorted by weight.

The situation becomes more interesting when we modify one of the objects. When the person represented by the `S1` object loses some weight, the `diet` method is invoked to decrease the weight of the object. In this scenario, both approaches display problems. In the "by copy" approach, we see that the `S1` object has been updated. The copy of the `S1` object maintained in the collection is clearly out of date. It holds the old weight value. A programmer must remember that such a collection stores only the values of objects as they existed at the time of the `add` operation and that changes to those objects are not reflected in the objects stored on the collection. The programmer must design the code to update the collection, if appropriate.

In the "by reference" approach, the object referred to by the collection contains the up-to-date weight information, because it is the same object referred to by the `S1` variable. The collection, however, is no longer sorted by the `weight` attribute. Because the update to `weight` took place without any collection activity, the collection objects remain in the same order as before. The collection structure is now corrupt, and calls to the collection

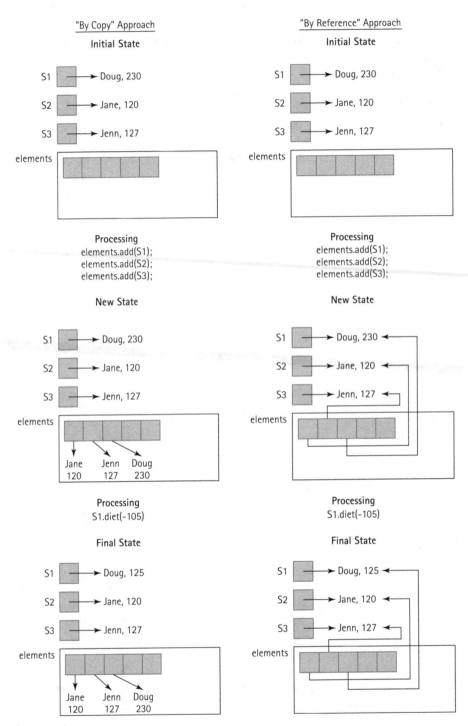

Figure 5.2 Store "by copy" versus store "by reference"

methods may behave unpredictably. Instead of directly updating the S1 object, the program should have removed the object from the collection, updated the object, and then reinserted it into the collection.

Summation

Which approach is better? That depends. If processing time and space are issues, and if we are comfortable counting on the application programs to behave properly, then the "by reference" approach is probably the best choice. If we are not overly concerned about time and space usage (maybe our collection objects are not too large), but we are concerned with maintaining careful control over the access to and integrity of our collections, then the "by copy" approach is probably the best choice. The suitability of either approach depends on how the collection is used.

Sample Application

To provide evidence that our new collection implementation works correctly we return to the vocabulary density problem introduced in Section 5.3, "Application: Vocabulary Density." The application developed in that section used the `ArrayCollection` class:

```
CollectionInterface<String> words =
                    new ArrayCollection<String>(CAPACITY);
```

The only thing we need to do, to use our new implementation, is to change the above line to use the `SortedArrayCollection` class:

```
CollectionInterface<String> words =
                    new SortedArrayCollection<String>(CAPACITY);
```

To compare the two approaches in terms of time efficiency we used a suite of text files, most obtained from the Project Gutenberg website, as input to both versions of the application. We timed the programs using the `currentTimeMillis` method of the Java Library `System` class. Although this approach to measuring execution time is not extremely precise, it is good enough for our purposes here.

See **Table 5.1** for the results of our experiment. The text files are presented in the table from smallest to largest. The "Linux Word File" is an alphabetical list of words used by the Linux Operating System's spell-checker program. It has the lowest density, essentially 1 (due to some words, for example "unix," being repeated in the file with different capitalization schemes, the number of words and number of unique words are not exactly the same). Other than that special case, the density tends to increase as the size of the file increases, as is expected. The "Mashup" file is a concatenation of 121 files from the Gutenberg site consisting of all the other files on the list (except the Linux Word File) plus other novels, "complete works," dictionaries, and technical manuals including Spanish, French, and German language texts in addition to the English.

Before running the program on a particular text file we made sure that the instantiated collection would be large enough to hold all of the unique words in the file—this way

Table 5.1 Results of Vocabulary Density Experiment[1]

Text	File Size	Results		Array-Collection	Sorted-Array-Collection
Shakespeare's 18th Sonnet	1 KB	words: unique: density:	114 83 1.37	20 msecs	23 msecs
Shakespeare's *Hamlet*	177 KB	words: unique: density:	32,247 4,790 6.73	236 msecs	128 msecs
Linux Word File	400 KB	words: unique: density:	45,404 45,371 1.00	9,100 msecs	182 msecs
Melville's *Moby-Dick*	1,227 KB	words: unique: density:	216,113 17,497 12.35	2,278 msecs or 2.3 seconds	382 msecs
The Complete Works of William Shakespeare	5,542 KB	words: unique: density:	900,271 26,961 33.39	9.7 seconds	1.2 seconds
Webster's Unabridged Dictionary	28,278 KB	words: unique: density:	4,669,130 206,981 22.56	4.7 minutes	9.5 seconds
11th Edition of the *Encyclopaedia Britannica*	291,644 KB	words: unique: density:	47,611,399 695,531 68.45	56.4 minutes	2.5 minutes
Mashup	608,274 KB	words: unique: density:	102,635,256 1,202,099 85.38	10 hours	7.2 minutes

we guaranteed that the bounded `ArrayCollection` was able to handle the problem and we did not "penalize" the unbounded `SortedArrayCollection` for time spent enlarging its internal storage.

The benefits of the sorted array approach are clear from the table. As the size of the input increases, the fast performance of the binary search used by the `SortedArrayCollection` as compared to the sequential search used by the `ArrayCollection` become obvious. This is most evident in the comparison of times for the large Mashup file, with the array-based approach requiring over 10 hours and the sorted array approach taking only 7 minutes, on the author's desktop computer.

---

[1]Project Gutenberg files contain technical instructions and legal disclaimers. We did not scrub these from the files before processing. For our purposes—exercising our algorithms—the extraneous data does not affect our results.

5.6   Link-Based Collection Implementation

In this section we design a link-based implementation of our Collection ADT. The internal representation structure will be an unsorted linked list. You will discover that most of the detailed work is already finished as we will be able to reuse code from previous ADT implementations. Throughout the discussion we compare and contrast the implementation of the operations within the previously defined `ArrayCollection` class and the `LinkedCollection` class currently under consideration. To study the code details not shown here please see the `LinkedCollection` class in the `ch05.collections` package.

The Internal Representation

As we did for our link-based stacks and queues, we again use the `LLNode` class from the `support` package to provide our nodes. The information attribute of a node contains the collection element; the link attribute contains a reference to the node holding the next collection element. We maintain a variable, `head` of type `LLNode<T>` that references the first node in the linked list. This linked list acts as the internal representation for the collection. It is an unsorted linked list. The start of the class is

```
package ch05.collections;
import support.LLNode;

public class LinkedCollection<T> implements CollectionInterface<T>
{
  protected LLNode<T> head;          // head of the linked list
  protected int numElements = 0;     // number of elements in this collection

  // set by find method
  protected boolean found;           // true if target found, else false
  protected LLNode<T> location;      // node containing target, if found
  protected LLNode<T> previous;      // node preceding location

  public LinkedCollection()
  {
    numElements = 0;
    head = null;
  }
}
```

There is only one constructor provided for `LinkedCollection`. There is no need to deal with capacity as there was with the array-based implementations. The constructor sets the instance variables `numElements` and `head`, essentially constructing an empty collection.

> **Naming Conventions**
>
> The first node in a linked list is called the head of the list. Therefore, for our link-based collection implementation, we choose to name the reference to the first node on the list head. For our link-based stack we used the identifier `top`, as the start of the linked list always represented the top of the stack. Likewise, for our link-based queue we called it `front`. Because a collection really does not have a "top" or a "front" we revert to linked-list terminology, and name it `head`.

The Operations

Why do we need a numElements instance variable? Recall that in the array-based approach, the numElements variable was used to indicate the first empty array location. Because we are now using a linked list, we do not have array locations. Nevertheless, to support the size operation we still maintain numElements, incrementing it whenever an element is added to the collection and decrementing it whenever an element is removed. The size method simply returns the value of numElements just as it does in ArrayCollection. The isEmpty method also remains unchanged from the array-based approach and the isFull method just trivially returns false because our linked structure is never full.

The add method is passed an argument of class T, and adds it to the collection. Because the internal linked list is unsorted, and order of the elements is not important, we can just add new elements to the front of the linked list. This is the easiest, most efficient approach, because head already provides a reference to this location. The code for the add method is very similar to that of the push method in the LinkedStack class developed in Section 2.8, "A Link-Based Stack." Note that since our LinkedCollection is unbounded, the add method always returns the value true—it should always be able to add the given element successfully.

```
public boolean add(T element)
// Adds element to this collection.
{
  LLNode<T> newNode = new LLNode<T>(element);
  newNode.setLink(head);
  head = newNode;
  numElements++;
  return true;
}
```

As we did for both the unsorted and sorted array-based implementation approaches, we create a protected helper method for our linked approach and call it find. Recall that this method sets the values of the instance variables found and location, which can then be used by the other methods. Given that the find method works correctly, coding both the contains and get methods become easy—in fact they are exactly the same as their counterparts in the array-based implementations:

```
public boolean contains (T target)        public T get(T target)
{                                          {
  find(target);                              find(target);
  return found;                              if (found)
}                                                return location.getInfo();
                                           else
                                                return null;
                                           }
```

The protected find method is also used by the remove method—we discuss remove below. For now, let us consider find in more detail. It follows the same algorithm as the find method of the array-based implementation: Walk through the internal representation of elements until the target element is found or the end of the representation is reached. The only difference is the use of linked list statements instead of array-related statements. Here is the code for both methods, for comparison. In the array-based approach, `location` is of type `int`, indicating the array index of the target element; in the link-based approach, `location` is an `LLNode`, indicating the node containing the target element.

Array-Based

```
protected void find(T target)
{
  location = 0;
  found = false;
  while (location < numElements)
  {
    if (elements[location].equals(target))
    {
      found = true;
      return;
    }
    else
      location++;
  }
}
```

Link-Based

```
protected void find(T target)
{
  location = head;
  found = false;
  while (location != null)
  {
    if (location.getInfo().equals(target))
    {
      found = true;
      return;
    }
    else
    {
      previous = location;
      location = location.getLink();
    }
  }
}
```

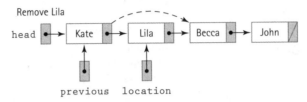

Figure 5.3   Removing element at location from a linked collection

Actually, we lied. There is another difference between the two find implementations. Do you see it? The link-based implementation assigns a value to a variable named previous that is not mentioned in the array-based implementation. This variable is used by the LinkedCollection remove method. We will take a closer look now at this method.

To remove the target, we must first find it. We do so using the find method, which sets the location variable to indicate the target element. As shown in **Figure 5.3**, however, to actually remove the node referenced by location, we must change the reference in the previous node. That is, we must change the link of the previous node to reference the node following the one being removed. We "jump over" the removed node. This is where we use the previous variable.

Not only does find set location, but it also sets previous so that the remove method has access to the previous node and can implement the "jump over" step. This is accomplished by remove with the statement:

```
previous.setLink(location.getLink());
```

Removing the first node must be treated as a special case because the main reference to the linked list (head) must be changed. We handle that special case with an *if* statement at the beginning of the code for remove. Is removing the last node a special case that requires additional code? No. The link within the last node is null. Therefore, in the case of removing the last node the above statement correctly sets the value of the link of the previous node to null, indicating that it is now the end of the list. Here is remove:

```
public boolean remove (T target)
// Removes an element e from this collection such that e.equals(target)
// and returns true; if no such element exists, returns false.
{
   find(target);
   if (found)
   {
      if (head == location)
         head = head.getLink();        // remove first node
      else
         previous.setLink(location.getLink());   // remove node at location
```

```
            numElements--;
        }
        return found;
    }
```

Comparing Collection Implementations

We have now looked at several different implementations of the Collection ADT. How do they compare? Let us briefly review each implementation—a summary of this discussion is found in **Table 5.2**.

All three implementation approaches, the `ArrayCollection`, `SortedArray-Collection`, and `LinkedCollection`, maintain an instance variable `numElements` that holds the current size of the collection. This allows simple O(1) implementations of the `size`, `isEmpty`, and `isFull` operations.

Our `ArrayCollection` implementation is a bounded implementation. It is the responsibility of the client to indicate the capacity of an `ArrayCollection` object at instantiation. If an `add` operation is invoked on a full collection the `add` operation returns `false` and there is no change to the collection. A client must therefore ensure the initial capacity is large enough to handle the problem they are addressing. Being an array-based implementation

> **Cost of Simplicity**
>
> Maintaining a `numElements` variable does simplify the implementation of the `isEmpty`, `isFull`, and `size` methods. However, we must realize that there is a hidden cost required for this simplicity. An extra statement must be executed every time an element is added to or removed from a collection, to maintain the correct value in `numElements`. So although it is true that the three aforementioned methods are all O(1), there is a hidden time cost.

the constructor is an O(N) operation, where N indicates the capacity—for any particular collection object we only execute the constructor once. The array in this implementation

Table 5.2 Comparison of Collection Implementations

Storage Structure	ArrayCollection Unsorted array	SortedArrayCollection Sorted array	LinkedCollection Unsorted linked list
Space	Bounded by original capacity	Unbounded—invokes `enlarge` method as needed	Unbounded—grows and shrinks
Class constructor	O(N)	O(N)	O(1)
size isEmpty isFull	O(1)	O(1)	O(1)
contains	O(N)	O($\log_2 N$)	O(N)
get	O(N)	O($\log_2 N$)	O(N)
add	O(1)	O(N)	O(1)
remove	O(N)	O(N)	O(N)

is unsorted—meaning the add operation is trivial and is O(1), whereas to locate a target element in the array for the contains, get, and remove operations requires a O(N) sequential search.

The SortedArrayCollection is also an array-based implementation; however, in this case we decided to make it an unbounded array-based implementation. If an add operation is invoked when the array is full then additional space is created using the enlarge method. This approach relieves the client of the responsibility of predetermining the needed capacity. Keeping the internal array sorted requires a more complex add method with a cost of O(N). However, it also means that the cost of locating a target element is now $O(\log_2 N)$ as we can use the binary search algorithm. This significantly lowers the time cost of both contains and get.

Capacity is not a concern for the LinkedCollection. In this unbounded implementation the amount of space used to hold the collection grows and shrinks along with the collection. As we pointed out when discussing linked implementations previously, we do require two reference variables for each element in the collection—one to hold the link and one to reference the collection element. The constructor for the LinkedCollection simply initializes the instance variables. Other than the constructor, the efficiency of the unsorted linked list approach is the same as that of the unsorted array approach. For both approaches it makes no difference where we add an element so the add method is fast. On the other hand, searching for a target element requires traversing the collection element by element.

5.7 Collection Variations

If you reflect on our Collection ADT you will realize it offers simple but crucial functionality– the ability to store and retrieve information. This functionality sits at the heart of information processing. Data structures, file systems, memory/storage, databases, the Cloud, the Internet all involve, at their core, storing and retrieving information.

Given the central importance of collections, this section about variations could go on and on! The lists, search trees, maps, hash tables, and priority queues we study in the upcoming chapters can all be considered forms of collections. Even the stacks and queues that we covered previously are collections, albeit collections with specific rules about addition and removal of elements. We will first briefly review the role of collections within the Java library. We then take a look at two commonly used collections not covered elsewhere in the text—bags and sets.

The Java Collections Framework

It is not surprising that the Java platform includes a "Collections Framework"—a unified architecture of classes and interfaces that provides powerful, flexible tools for storing and retrieving information. At the center of the framework is the Collection interface, found in the java.util package of the library. This interface supports 11 subinterfaces including `Deque`, `List`, and `Set` and has 33 implementing classes including the somewhat familiar `ArrayList`, `LinkedList`, `Stack`, and `PriorityQueue` and exotic-sounding classes such as `BeanContextServicesSupport` and `RoleUnresolvedList`.

There are 15 abstract methods defined within the Java `Collection` interface, including methods that mirror our `isEmpty`, `size`, `add`, `remove`, and `contains` methods. Note, however, that the interface does not define anything analogous to our `get` method. So how is one supposed to retrieve information from a collection? The answer is that the designers of the Collections Framework do not intend for anyone to directly implement the Collection interface. Instead it is used as the root of an inheritance tree of interfaces as previously mentioned, and it is those interfaces that are implemented. Various methods similar to our `get` method are defined within those interfaces.

It is instructive to look at some of the additional method definitions from the `Collection` interface:

`toArray`	Returns an array containing all of the elements of the collection
`clear`	Removes all elements
`equals`	Takes an `Object` argument, returning `true` if it is equal to the current collection and `false` otherwise
`addAll`	Takes a `Collection` argument and adds its contents to the current collection; returns a `boolean` indicating success or failure
`retainAll`	Takes a `Collection` argument and removes any elements from the current collection that are not in the argument collection; returns a `boolean` indicating success or failure
`removeAll`	Takes a `Collection` argument and removes any elements from the current collection that are also in the argument collection

Methods such as `equals`, `addAll`, `retainAll`, and `removeAll` allow clients to use collections as more than just separate repositories—collections can be combined and compared. The Set ADT we define below is a collection intended to be used in that fashion.

As mentioned in Chapter 2, in this text we do not cover the Collections Framework in great detail. This text is meant to teach you about the fundamental nature of data structures and to demonstrate how to define, implement, and use them. It is not an exploration of how to use Java's specific library architecture of similar structures. If you are interested in learning more about the Java Collections Framework, you can study the extensive documentation available at Oracle's website.

The Bag ADT

We want to define an ADT that fits our everyday notion of a bag—a bag of marbles, a bag of groceries, a bag of money! What assumptions should we make about our bag? What operations should we include?

Think about a bag of marbles. Suppose marbles are identified by their color. It certainly is possible to place more than one red marble into our bag—we decide that our Bag ADT should allow duplicate elements.

We can put marbles into the bag, look into the bag to see if it contains a particular marble ("is there a green marble in there?") and reach in and remove a specific marble. These activities correspond to our Collection ADT's add, contains, and remove operations. We can check to see if the bag is full or is empty and we could look inside and count how many marbles it contains—our isFull, isEmpty, and size operations. With a bit of a stretch of imagination we can think about reaching into the bag and pointing to a marble (which is essentially what our get operation does). In short, all of the operations we defined for our Collection ADT also make sense for our **Bag** ADT.

What other operations can we include? We could close our eyes and reach into the bag and draw out a random marble ("I hope I get the blue one"). We could peek into the bag and count all marbles of a specified color ("How many red ones are there?") or remove all marbles of a specified color ("I don't like the purple ones"). We could turn the bag upside down and empty it ("Watch out, here they come!"). We will add grab, count, removeAll, and clear to our Bag operations. Their formal definitions are included in our BagInterface listed below. As with our Collection ADT, our Bag ADT requires a valid equals method to be defined for the objects that it contains.

```
//----------------------------------------------------------------------------
// BagInterface.java          by Dale/Joyce/Weems          Chapter 5
//
// Interface for a class that implements a bag of T.
// A bag is a collection that supports a few extra operations.
//----------------------------------------------------------------------------
package ch05.collections;

public interface BagInterface<T> extends CollectionInterface
{
  T grab();
  // If this bag is not empty, removes and returns a random element of the
  // bag; otherwise returns null.
```

```
int count(T target);
// Returns a count of all elements e in this collection such that
// e.equals(target).

int removeAll(T target);
// Removes all elements e from this collection such that e.equals(target)
// and returns the number of elements removed.

void clear();
// Empties this bag so that it contains zero elements.
}
```

As you can see, the BagInterface is located in the ch05.collections package. The interface extends our CollectionInterface. Any class that implements BagInterface must provide concrete methods for the add, get, contains, remove, isFull, isEmpty, and size operations of the CollectionInterface in addition to the grab, count, removeAll, and clear operations that are explicitly listed in the interface.

The Bag ADT is suited for use by applications that need to be able to count specific elements in a collection or remove all of a specific element from a collection—perhaps applications that manage inventories or allow distribution of resources. Additionally, the unique grab operation allows the Bag ADT to be used for applications that require randomness, for example, games or tutorial programs. Implementation of the Bag ADT is left as an exercise.

The Set ADT

A feature of each of our collection ADTs so far is that they allow duplicate elements. If we change our approach, that is, if we disallow duplicate elements, we have a collection commonly known as a Set. The **Set** ADT models the mathematical set that is typically defined as a collection of distinct objects.

We can implement a Set class by copying and changing the code from one of our collection implementations—the only method we need to change is the add method. The new add method could be designed to check if the element argument is not already in the collection, and if not it would add the element and return true. Otherwise, of course, it returns false.

Instead of copying the code from one of our implementations is there another way we can reuse it? Yes, in fact, there are two common approaches. We can extend the implementation class or we can wrap an object of the class within the new implementation. Let us investigate each approach.

The BasicSet1 class below extends the LinkedCollection. Therefore, it inherits all of the methods of the LinkedCollection. To ensure that duplicate elements are not entered into the collection we redefine the add method as discussed above. Applications that instantiate a BasicSet1 object and use it to invoke the add method will use the safe add method, that prevents duplicate elements from being added, rather than the overridden method from the LinkedCollection class, which allows duplicates.

```
//------------------------------------------------------------------
// BasicSet1.java                  by Dale/Joyce/Weems            Chapter 5
//
// Implements the CollectionInterface by extending LinkedCollection.
// Overrides add method so that duplicate elements are not added.
//
// Null elements are not allowed.
// One constructor is provided, one that creates an empty collection.
//------------------------------------------------------------------
package ch05.collections;

public class BasicSet1<T> extends LinkedCollection<T>
                          implements CollectionInterface<T>
{
  public BasicSet1()
  {
    super();
  }

  @Override
  public boolean add(T element)
  // If element is not already contained in this collection adds element to
  // this collection and returns true; otherwise returns false.
  {
    if (!this.contains(element))
    {
      super.add(element);
      return true;
    }
    else
      return false;
  }
}
```

As you can see, the BasicSet1 class code is short and was easy to create owing to the effort already expended in the design and creation of the LinkedCollection class.

A drawback of the above approach is that future changes to the LinkedCollection implementation could invalidate the unique element provision of its BasicSet1 subclass. For example, suppose the LinkedCollection was enhanced with the following method:

```
public void addAll(LinkedCollection elements)
// Adds all the contents of the elements collection to this collection.
```

Because `BasicSet1` inherits from `LinkedCollection`, this new method would be available to `BasicSet1` objects. If the maintenance programmer does not update `BasicSet1` to override `addAll`, then the integrity of `BasicSet1` would be compromised as it is possible that `addAll` could be used to add duplicate elements.

Let us look at another reuse approach that does not suffer from this drawback. Rather than extending `LinkedCollection` we can use a `LinkedCollection` object inside our new basic set implementation. This approach is sometimes called "wrapping" because, similar to the Java wrapper classes such as `Integer`, we hold an object of one type within an object of another type and delegate calls to it. Here is the code:

```
//-----------------------------------------------------------------------
// BasicSet2.java              by Dale/Joyce/Weems              Chapter 5
//
// Implements the CollectionInterface by wrapping a LinkedCollection.
// Ensures that duplicate elements are not added.
//
// Null elements are not allowed.
// One constructor is provided, one that creates an empty collection.
//-----------------------------------------------------------------------
package ch05.collections;

public class BasicSet2<T> implements CollectionInterface<T>
{
  LinkedCollection<T> set;

  public BasicSet2()
  {
    set = new LinkedCollection<T>();
  }

  public boolean add(T element)
  // If element is not already contained in this collection adds element to
  // this collection and returns true; otherwise returns false.
  {
    if (!this.contains(element))
    {
      set.add(element);
      return true;
    }
    else
      return false;
  }
```

```
public int size(){return set.size();}
public boolean contains (T target){return set.contains(target);}
public boolean remove (T target){return set.remove(target);}
public T get(T target){return set.get(target);}
public boolean isEmpty(){return set.isEmpty();}
public boolean isFull(){return set.isFull();}
}
```

The only instance variable in the `BasicSet2` class is the variable `set` of type `LinkedCollection`. In the case of every method provided, except for the `add` method, the method just invokes the corresponding method of `LinkedCollection` through the `set` variable. In the case of `add` the corresponding `LinkedCollection` add is also invoked but only if it is safe to do so. Although `BasicSet2` is longer than `BasicSet1`, it does not require more work to create since the only method requiring extra code is the `add` method—as was also the case for `BasicSet1`. Furthermore, `BasicSet2` does not suffer from the maintenance issue discussed above for `BasicSet1`. Our `Basic-Set2` class is a good example of a hierarchical implementation. It is built on top of the `LinkedCollection` class that in turn uses the `LLNode` class.

It is possible to define a more complex Set ADT, one that supports the set operations we learned in mathematics classes such as *union* and *intersection*. Exercise 36 asks the reader to define and implement such an ADT.

Summary

We introduced the concept of a collection—an object that collects together other objects for later retrieval. The Collection ADT acts as the basis for many other structures. Following our standard approach, we defined the ADT using the Java `interface` construct.

Three separate implementations of the Collection ADT were developed—an unsorted array, a sorted array, and a linked list. **Figure 5.4** shows the relationships among the primary classes and interfaces we created to support this ADT. The diagram follows the same conventions we listed on page 146 for the Stack ADT diagram.

All collection implementations require checking elements for equality, and the sorted array implementation requires the ability to determine the relative order of elements. Therefore, we reviewed comparison of objects, considering both the `equals` and `compareTo` methods.

The primary application developed in this chapter to demonstrate the usefulness of the Collection ADT was a vocabulary density calculator. Using both the unsorted and sorted array-based implementations of the collection allowed us to demonstrate the difference in efficiency between the two approaches when analyzing large text files.

In Section 5.7, "Collection Variations," we reviewed the Java Library Collections Framework and defined two specific collection variants: the Bag and the Set. Implementations for a basic Set ADT using two approaches were developed, each dependent on reusing the `LinkedCollection` class. One approach demonstrated reuse through inheritance and the other demonstrated reuse by wrapping.

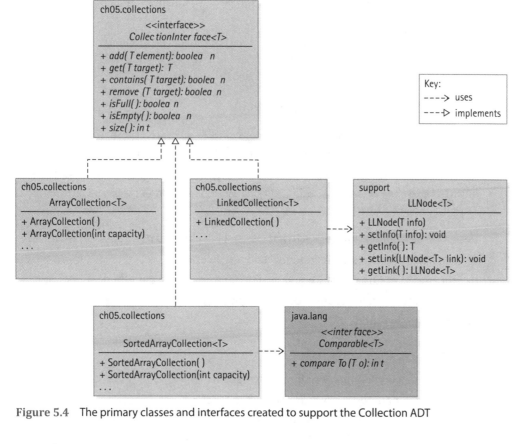

Figure 5.4   The primary classes and interfaces created to support the Collection ADT

Exercises

5.1 The Collection Interface

1. For each of the methods declared in `CollectionInterface`, identify what type of operation it is (observer, transformer, or both).

2. `CollectionInterface` defines seven abstract methods. Define at least three more operations that might be useful for a Collection ADT to provide.

3. Identify which attributes would make a good key for determining equality of objects for each of the following classes and explain your reasoning:

    a. A Golfer class that supports finding the latest score of your favorite golfer.

    b. A Student class for use by a university accounting office that includes name, ID number, and payment attributes.

    c. A Rectangle class with attributes length, width, area, and perimeter.

    d. A Book class for an online store that includes book name, author name, edition number, cost, and number of pages attributes.

4. Discuss the ramification of dropping the "null elements are not allowed" general precondition of `CollectionInterface`.

5. Discuss the difference between an operation that pushes an element onto a full (bounded) stack as defined by our `StackInterface` (Section 2.4, "The Stack Interface") and one that adds an element to a full collection.

5.2 Array-Based Collection Implementation

6. Show the values contained in the instance variables `elements` and `numElements` of the `sample` collection after the following sequence of operations:

   ```
   ArrayCollection<String> sample = new ArrayCollection<String>;
   sample.add("A"); sample.add("B"); sample.add("C"); sample.add("D");
   sample.remove("B");
   ```

7. Describe the ramifications of each of the following changes to `ArrayCollection`:

   a. the first three lines of the `add` method are deleted

   b. the `numElements++` statement is deleted from the `add` method

   c. in the `find` method "protected" is changed to "public"

   d. in the `find` method "<" is changed to "<="

   e. the `elements[numElements - 1] = null` statement is deleted from the `remove` method

   f. the "==" in the `isEmpty` method is changed to "="

   g. in the `get` method, "`found`" is changed to "`!found`"

8. Add the following methods to the `ArrayCollection` class, and create a test driver for each to show that they work correctly. In order to practice your array coding skills, code each of these methods by accessing the internal variables of the `ArrayCollection`, not by calling the previously defined public methods of the class.

   a. `String toString()` creates and returns a string that correctly represents the current collection. Such a method could prove useful for testing and debugging the class and for testing and debugging applications that use the class. Assume each stored element already provides its own reasonable `toString` method.

   b. `int count(T target)` returns a count of the number of elements e in the collection such that `e.equals(target)` is `true`.

   c. `void removeAll(T target)` removes all elements e from the collection such that `e.equals(target)` is `true`.

   d. `ArrayCollection<T> combine(ArrayCollection<T> other)` creates and returns a new `ArrayCollection` object that is a combination of `this` object and the argument object.

9. What would be the result of using the `ArrayCollection` class to hold objects of a class that has not overridden the `equals` method of the `Object` class?

5.3 Application: Vocabulary Density

10. The Vocabulary Density application allows you to analyze text, reporting on the total number of words, the number of unique words, and the vocabulary density. Use it to analyze one or more texts of your choice. Create a report on the results. This is a wide open exercise—we leave it up to you to figure out something interesting to analyze.

11. Study the Vocabulary Density application and answer the following questions:
    a. How is the name and location of the input file provided to the program?
    b. What happens if the input text contains more than `CAPACITY` unique words?
    c. What would be the effect of removing the ' (apostrophe) from the delimiters definition?
    d. What is the effect of removing the "`word = word.toLowerCase()`" statement?

12. Revise the Vocabulary Density application so that
    a. if the collection becomes full, then the application no longer continues processing—instead it displays a suitable message and then ends.
    b. it includes a constant `THRESHOLD` of type `int` and ignores words whose length is less than the threshold value—thus the word analysis would not include "short" words.
    c. it permits multiple filenames to be passed as command line arguments, and will proceed to separately analyze and report on each of the files.
    d. expand on the previous revision so that in addition to the separate analysis of the files it also performs a combined analysis, as if the combined files all represented a single text.

13. The file `Animals.txt` found in the `input` folder contains a long list of animal names, one per line. Create an application that reads that file and creates a collection of animal names. Use the `ArrayCollection` class. Your application should then generate a random character and challenge the user to repeatedly enter an animal name that begins with that character, reading the names entered by the user until they either enter a name that does not begin with the required character or is not in the collection, or they enter a name they used before. Finally, your application reports how many names they successfully entered.

14. The file `Keywords.txt` found in the `input` folder contains all the Java keywords. Create an application that accepts the name of a Java program file as a command line argument and displays a count of the total number of keywords the program contains. For example, if you use the `VocabularyDensity.java` program as your input, the application should display

`VocabularyDensity.java contains 24 Java keywords`

As part of your solution you should create a collection of keywords using the information in the `Keywords.txt` file. Do not worry about the fact that you might be counting keywords contained within comments or strings.

5.4 Comparing Objects Revisited

15. Based on the `equals` method for `Circle` objects defined in Section 5.4, "Comparing Objects Revisited," what is the output of the following code sequence?

```
Circle c1 = new Circle(5);
Circle c2 = new Circle(5);
Circle c3 = new Circle(15);
Circle c4 = null;
System.out.println(c1 == c1);
System.out.println(c1 == c2);
System.out.println(c1 == c3);
System.out.println(c1 == c4);
System.out.println(c1.equals(c1));
System.out.println(c1.equals(c2));
System.out.println(c1.equals(c3));
System.out.println(c1.equals(c4));
```

16. An `equals` method is supposed to provide an equivalence relation among the objects of a class. This means that if a, b, and c are non-null objects of the class, then

   i.   `a.equals(a)` is true.

   ii. `a.equals(b)` has the same value as `b.equals(a)`.

   iii. If `a.equals(b)` is true and `b.equals(c)` is true, then `a.equals(c)` is true.

   State whether the following definitions of `equals` are valid. If they are not, explain why not.

   a. Two circles are equal if they have the same area.

   b. Two circles are equal if their radii are within 10% of each other.

   c. Two integers are equal if they have the same remainder when divided by a specific integer, for example, when divided by 3.

   d. Two integers are equal if the second integer is a multiple of the first.

17. Suppose we have a `Rectangle` class that includes `length` and `width` attributes, of type `int`, both set by the constructor. Define an `equals` method for this class so that two rectangle objects are considered equal if

    a. They have the exact same `length` and `width`.

    b. They have the same dimensions—that is, they are congruent.

    c. They have the same shape—that is, they are similar.

    d. They have the same perimeter.

    e. They have the same area.

18. Which of the definitions of `equals` listed in Exercise 17 is valid, based on the criteria listed in Exercise 16?

19. Based on the `compareTo` method for `FamousPerson` objects defined in Section 5.4, "Comparing Objects Revisited," what is the output of the following code sequence? Answers may include phrases such as "a negative integer."

```
FamousPerson f1 = new FamousPerson("Peter","Parker",1962,"Spiderman");
FamousPerson f2 = new FamousPerson("Bonnie","Parker",1910,"Criminal");
FamousPerson f3 = new FamousPerson("Clark","Kent",1938,"Superman");
FamousPerson f4 = new FamousPerson("Clark","Kent",1938,"Reporter");
System.out.println(f1.compareTo(f1));
System.out.println(f1.compareTo(f2));
System.out.println(f2.compareTo(f1));
System.out.println(f1.compareTo(f3));
System.out.println(f3.compareTo(f4));
System.out.println(f4.compareTo(f3));
```

20. In Exercise 16 we stated some rules for the behavior of the `equals` method. What similar rule or rules should the `compareTo` method follow?

21. Suppose we have a `Rectangle` class that includes `length` and `width` attributes of type `int`, both set by the constructor. Create a `compareTo` method for this class so that rectangle objects are ordered based on their

    a. Perimeter.

    b. Area.

22. How many "known" classes in the Java library implement the `Comparable` interface? List five such classes that you have used before, or at least have studied.

5.5 Sorted Array-Based Collection Implementation

23. Show the values contained in the instance variables `elements` and `numElements` of the `sample` collection after the following sequence of operations:

```
SortedArrayCollection<String> sample
            = new SortedArrayCollection<String>;
sample.add("A"); sample.add("D"); sample.add("B"); sample.add("C");
sample.remove("B");
```

24. Fill in the following table with the order of growth of the indicated operations for the given implementation approach—assume the collection holds *N* elements:

operation	ArrayCollection	SortedArrayCollection
add		
get		
contains		
remove		
isEmpty		

25. Describe the ramifications of each of the following changes to `SortedArrayCollection`:

    a. in the `enlarge` method "`origCap`" is changed to "`DEFCAP`"

    b. the first two statements are deleted from the `find` method

    c. the `if (result > 0) location++` statement is deleted from the `recFind` method

26. Add the following methods to the `SortedArrayCollection` class, and create a test driver for each to show that they work correctly. Code each of these methods by accessing the internal variables of the `SortedArrayCollection`, not by calling the previously defined methods of the class.

    a. `String toString()` creates and returns a string that correctly represents the current collection. Such a method could prove useful for testing and debugging the class and for testing and debugging applications that use the class. Assume each stored element already provides its own reasonable `toString` method.

    b. `T smallest()` returns `null` if the collection is empty, otherwise returns the smallest element of the collection.

    c. `int greater(T element)` returns a count of the number of elements e in the collection that are greater than `element`, that is such that `e.compareTo(element)` is > 0.

    d. `SortedArrayCollection<T> combine(SortedArrayCollection<T> other)` creates and returns a new `SortedArrayCollection` object that is a combination of `this` object and the argument object.

27. Describe the functional difference between the following two sections of code:

```
CollectionInterface<String> c = new ArrayCollection<String>(10);
c.add("Tom"); c.add("Julie"); c.add("Molly");
System.out.println(c.contains("Kathy"));
```

```
CollectionInterface<String> c = new SortedArrayCollection<String>(10);
c.add("Tom"); c.add("Julie"); c.add("Molly");
System.out.println(c.contains("Kathy"));
```

5.6 Link-Based Collection Implementation

28. Show the values contained in the instance variables `head` and `numElements` of the `sample` collection after the following sequence of operations:

```
LinkedCollection<String> sample = new LinkedCollection<String>;
sample.add("A"); sample.add("B"); sample.add("C"); sample.add("D");
sample.remove("B");
```

29. Describe the ramifications of each of the following changes to `LinkedCollection`:
    a. the statement `newNode.setLink(head)` is deleted from the `add` method
    b. the statement `location = location.getLink()` is deleted from the `find` method
    c. the statement `head = head.getLink()` within the `remove` method is changed to `head = location.getLink()`

30. Add the following methods to the `LinkedCollection` class, and create a test driver for each to show that they work correctly. Code each of these methods by accessing the internal variables of the `LinkedCollection`, not by calling the previously defined methods of the class.
    a. `String toString()` creates and returns a string that correctly represents the current collection. Such a method could prove useful for testing and debugging the class and for testing and debugging applications that use the class. Assume each stored element already provides its own reasonable `toString` method.
    b. `int count(T target)` returns a count of the number of elements e in the collection such that `e.equals(target)` is true.
    c. `void removeAll(T target)` removes all elements e from the collection such that `e.equals(target)` is true.
    d. `LinkedCollection<T> combine(LinkedCollection<T> other)` creates and returns a new `SortedArrayCollection` object that is a combination of `this` object and the argument object.

31. Create a new collection class named `SortedLinkedCollection` that implements a collection using a sorted linked list. Include a `toString` method as described in Exercise 30a. Include a test driver application that demonstrates your class works correctly.

32. Recreate the contents of Table 5.2 (no peeking).

5.7 Collection Variations

33. Create a class that implements the `BagInterface`, plus a test driver that shows that your class operates correctly:
    a. Using an unsorted array (if you like, you can extend the `ArrayCollection` class)
    b. Using a sorted array (if you like, you can extend the `SortedArrayCollection` class)
    c. Using a linked list (if you like, you can extend the `LinkedCollection` class)

34. Create an application that creates a Bag of `FamousPerson` using one of your implementation classes from Exercise 33. Your application should use the information in the `input/FamousCS.txt` file (see Section 5.4, "Comparing Objects Revisited") to create the Bag. Next your application will repeat the following five times:

    - selects a random "famous person" from the bag
    - tells the user the year of birth and the fact about the person
    - asks the user to enter the last name of the famous person and reads their response
    - display all the information about the famous person

    Finally, your application tells the user how many they "got right" out of the five chances, that is, how many famous people they correctly identified.

35. Describe the three approaches discussed in the section to reuse the `LinkedCollection` class in the creation of a Basic Set ADT implementation.

36. An Advanced Set includes all the operations of a Basic Set plus operations for the union, intersection, and difference of sets.

    a. Define an Advanced Set interface.

    b. Implement the Advanced Set using an unsorted array; include a test driver that demonstrates your implementation works correctly.

    c. Implement the Advanced Set using a sorted array; include a test driver that demonstrates your implementation works correctly.

    d. Implement the Advanced Set using a linked list; include a test driver that demonstrates your implementation works correctly.

6

The List ADT

Knowledge Goals

You should be able to

- describe a list and its operations at an abstract level
- classify a given list operation as a constructor, observer, or transformer
- perform order of growth efficiency analysis for a given implementation of the list
- describe the purposes of the Java `Iterable` and `Iterator` interfaces
- explain how and why an anonymous inner class is created
- list and describe the potential exceptions that might be thrown by list implementation methods
- describe algorithms for list operations implemented using an array
- describe algorithms for list operations using a linked list
- if needed, define a new list approach to help solve a specified problem
- describe an approach for implementing large integers using linked lists

Skill Goals

You should be able to

- create a class that implements the `Iterable` interface
- use a *for-each* loop with an `Iterable` object
- define and analyze the Insertion Sort
- draw diagrams showing the effect of list operations for a particular implementation of a list
- predict the output of an application that uses the List abstract data type (ADT)
- use the List ADT as a component of an application
- use the `CardDeck` class as a component of an application
- implement the List ADT using
  - an array
  - a sorted array
  - a linked list
  - a linked list as an array of nodes

This chapter focuses on the List ADT: its definition, its implementation, and its use in problem solving. Lists are one of the most widely used ADTs in computer science, which is only natural given how often we use them in daily life. We make to-do lists, shopping lists, checklists, party invitation lists, and so on. We even make lists of lists!

Lists are extremely versatile ADTs. They are collections—they provide storage for information. They are similar to stacks and queues in that there is an order imposed on their elements, but unlike stacks and queues, they do not impose any limitations on how those elements are added, accessed, or removed. There are even languages in which the list is a built-in structure. In Lisp, for example, the list is the main data type provided by the language.

As you work through the chapter you may occasionally want to review Figure 6.9 in the chapter summary section—a diagram showing the relationships among the major interfaces and classes for our List ADT.

6.1 The List Interface

From a programming point of view a **list** is a collection of elements, with a **linear relationship** existing among its elements. A linear relationship means that, at the abstract level, each element on the list except the first one has a unique predecessor and each element except the last one has a unique successor. The linear relationship among list elements also means that each element has a position on the list. We can indicate this position using an index, just like we do with arrays. So in addition to our lists supporting the standard collection operations `add`, `get`, `contains`, `remove`, `isFull`, `isEmpty`, and `size`, they will support index-related operations.

The elements of a list are indexed sequentially, from zero to one less than the size of the list, just like an array. For example, if a list has five elements, they are indexed 0, 1, 2, 3, and 4. No "holes" are allowed in the indexing scheme, so if an element is removed from the "middle" of a list, other elements will have their indices lowered. We define methods for adding, retrieving, changing, and removing an element at an indicated index, as well as a method for determining the index of an element. Details can be seen in the `ListInterface` below.

Each method that accepts an index as an argument throws an exception if the index is invalid. Clients must use valid indices—they can determine the range of valid indices by using the `size` method. Indices go from 0 to (`size()` - 1). To allow addition of an element to the end of the list, the valid range for `add` includes `size()`.

We do not define our own exception class to use with the indexed list, because the Java library provides an appropriate exception called `IndexOutOfBoundsException`. This class extends `RuntimeException`, so it is unchecked.

Iteration

Because a list maintains a linear relationship among its elements, we can support iteration through the list. **Iteration** means that we provide a mechanism to process the entire list, element by element, from the first element to the last element. The Java library provides two related interfaces that deal with iteration: `Iterable` in the `java.lang` package, and `Iterator` in `java.util`.

Our lists will be required to implement the library's `Iterable` interface. This interface requires a single method, `iterator`, that creates and returns an `Iterator` object. Methods that create and return objects are sometimes called **Factory methods**.

What is an `Iterator` object? An `Iterator` object provides the means to iterate through the list. `Iterator` objects provide three operations: `hasNext`, `next`, and `remove`. When an `Iterator` object is created it is set to the beginning of the list. Repeated calls on the `next` method of the object will return elements of the list, one by one. The `hasNext` method returns `true` if the iterator object has not yet reached the end of the list. Clients are expected to use `hasNext` to prevent going past the end of the list during an iteration. The `remove` method removes the element that was most recently visited. The `Iterator` implementation keeps track of whatever information is needed to allow efficient removal of that element when requested.

Because our lists implement `Iterable`, clients can use the `iterator` method to obtain an `Iterator` object and then use the `Iterator` object to iterate through the list. An example should help clarify. Suppose `strings` is a List ADT object that contains the four strings "alpha," "gamma," "beta," and "delta." The following code would delete "gamma" from the list and display the other three strings:

```
Iterator<String> iter = strings.iterator();
String hold;
while (iter.hasNext())
{
  hold = iter.next();
  if (hold.equals("gamma"))
    iter.remove();
  else
    System.out.println(hold);
}
```

Note that a client can have several iterations through a list active at the same time, using different `Iterator` objects.

What happens if the program inserts or removes an element (by a means other than using the current iterator's `remove`) in the middle of iterating through the structure? Nothing good, you can be sure! Adding and deleting elements change the size and structure of the list. The results of using an iterator are unspecified if the underlying collection is modified in this fashion while the iteration is in progress.

Java provides an enhanced *for* loop to use with array or `Iterable` objects. Referred to as a *for-each* loop, this version of the *for* loop allows programmers to indicate that a block of instructions should be executed "for each" of the objects in the array or `Iterable` object. The following code would display all of the elements of the `strings` list:

```
for (String hold: strings)
  System.out.println(hold);
```

The *for-each* loop acts as an abstraction—it hides the use of the `Iterator` and its `hasNext` and `next` methods, making it even easier for us to iterate through a list.

Assumptions for Our Lists

So far we have determined that our lists will be collections and will support both index and iteration-related operations. Before formally specifying our List ADT we complete our informal specification with the following list of assumptions:

- Our lists are *unbounded*. When implementing a list with an array, we use the same approach as with our array-based unbounded queue and collection implementations. That is, if an element is added to a "full" list, then the capacity of the underlying array is increased.

- We *allow* duplicate elements on our lists. When an operation involves "finding" such an element, it can "find" any one of the duplicates. We do not specify any distinction among duplicate elements in these cases, with the exception of one indexed list method (indexOf).

- As with our other ADTs, we do *not* support null elements. As a general precondition for all of our list methods, null elements cannot be used as arguments. Rather than stating this precondition for each method, we state it once in the general list interface.

- The indices in use for a list are *contiguous*, starting at 0. If an indexed list method is passed an index that is outside the current valid range, it will throw an exception.

- Two of the index-related operations, add and set, are **optional**. Both of these operations allow the client to insert an element into a list at a specified index. For some list implementations, notably a sorted list implementation, this could invalidate the internal representation of the list. By indicating that these operations are optional we permit a sorted list implementation to throw an exception if one of these operations is invoked. Our implementations will throw the Java library supplied UnsupportedOperationException in such cases.

Unsupported Operations

Some operations fit well with one implementation of an ADT but do not make sense for another implementation. For example, we cannot allow an application to set the value of a specific list element if the elements are being kept in increasing order—the application could invalidate the ordering. In these cases we indicate in our interface that an operation is optional.

The Interface

Here is the code for our ListInterface. It is part of the ch06.lists package. Note that it extends both our CollectionInterface and the Java library's Iterable interface—classes that implement ListInterface must also implement those interfaces and therefore must provide operations add, get, contains, remove, isFull, isEmpty, size, and iterate, in addition to the index-related operations specified explicitly in ListInterface. Study the comments and method signatures of the interface, listed below, to learn more about the details of our List ADT.

```
//--------------------------------------------------------------------------
// ListInterface.java          by Dale/Joyce/Weems          Chapter 6
//
// Lists are unbounded and allow duplicate elements, but do not allow
// null elements. As a general precondition, null elements are not passed as
// arguments to any of the methods.
//
// During an iteration through the list the only change that can safely be
// made to the list is through the remove method of the iterator.
//--------------------------------------------------------------------------
package ch06.lists;

import java.util.*;
import ch05.collections.CollectionInterface;
public interface ListInterface<T> extends CollectionInterface<T>, Iterable<T>
{
  void add(int index, T element);
  // Throws IndexOutOfBoundsException if passed an index argument
  // such that index < 0 or index > size().
  // Otherwise, adds element to this list at position index; all current
  // elements at that position or higher have 1 added to their index.
  // Optional. Throws UnsupportedOperationException if not supported.

  T set(int index, T newElement);
  // Throws IndexOutOfBoundsException if passed an index argument
  // such that index < 0 or index >= size().
  // Otherwise, replaces element on this list at position index with
  // newElement and returns the replaced element.
  // Optional. Throws UnsupportedOperationException if not supported.

  T get(int index);
  // Throws IndexOutOfBoundsException if passed an index argument
  // such that index < 0 or index >= size().
  // Otherwise, returns the element on this list at position index.

  int indexOf(T target);
  // If this list contains an element e such that e.equals(target),
  // then returns the index of the first such element.
  // Otherwise, returns -1.

  T remove(int index);
  // Throws IndexOutOfBoundsException if passed an index argument
  // such that index < 0 or index >= size().
```

```
      // Otherwise, removes element on this list at position index and
      // returns the removed element; all current elements at positions
      // higher than index have 1 subtracted from their position.
}
```

6.2   List Implementations

In this section we develop an array-based and a link-based implementation of the List ADT. Because a list is a collection the implementations share some design and code with their Collection ADT counterparts. Here we emphasize the new functionality—the indexing and the iteration. The reader may want to review the design and code of the Collection ADT implementations from Chapter 5 before continuing.

Array-Based Implementation

We use the same approach for our array-based list as we did for our array-based collection. Elements are stored in an internal array and an instance variable `numElements` holds the size of the list. A list of five strings would be represented as:

numElements: 5

	[0]	[1]	[2]	[3]	[4]	[5]
elements:	"Bat"	"Ant"	"Cat"	"Ear"	"Dog"	

If a new string is added to the above list it is placed in array slot `numElements` and then `numElements` is incremented.

    You may recall that when removing an element from an array-based collection we replaced it with the "last" element in the array and decremented `numElements`:

numElements: 5̶/4

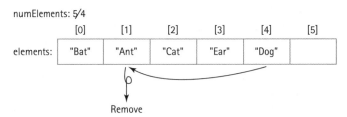

Remove

For a list we cannot use this approach because we must maintain the index order of the remaining elements. Therefore, we use the same approach we did for the sorted array collection:

numElements: 5̶ 4

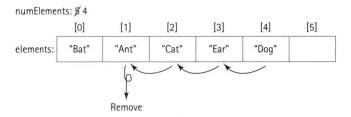

Remove

Here is the beginning of the ABList (Array-Based List) class:

```
//----------------------------------------------------------------------
// ABList.java                    by Dale/Joyce/Weems              Chapter 6
// Array-Based List
//
// Null elements are not permitted on a list. The list is unbounded.
//
// Two constructors are provided: one that creates a list of a default
// original capacity, and one that allows the calling program to specify the
// original capacity.
//----------------------------------------------------------------------
package ch06.lists;

import java.util.Iterator;

public class ABList<T> implements ListInterface<T>
{
  protected final int DEFCAP = 100;  // default capacity
  protected int origCap;             // original capacity
  protected T[] elements;            // array to hold this list's elements
  protected int numElements = 0;     // number of elements in this list

  // set by find method
  protected boolean found;  // true if target found, otherwise false
  protected int location;   // indicates location of target if found

  public ABList()
  {
    elements = (T[]) new Object[DEFCAP];
    origCap = DEFCAP;
  }
  public ABList(int origCap)
  {
    elements = (T[]) new Object[origCap];
    this.origCap = origCap;
  }
```

As you can see this is very similar to the declarations and constructors of previous array-based implementations of our ADTs. We leave it to the reader to examine the code for the protected helper methods enlarge and find, and the public methods add, remove, contains, get, size, isFull and isEmpty all of which are similar/identical to code we have developed previously.

Index-Related Operations

Now we turn our attention to the five required indexed methods. The four methods that accept an index parameter each follow the same pattern—check the index argument, and if it is outside the allowable range for that operation throw an exception—otherwise carry out the operation. Because of the close logical relationship between the internal representation, an array, and the ADT, an indexed list, the implementation of these operations is very straightforward. Here we examine the code for `set`:

```
public T set(int index, T newElement)
// Throws IndexOutOfBoundsException if passed an index argument
// such that index < 0 or index >= size().
// Otherwise, replaces element on this list at position index with
// newElement and returns the replaced element.
{
    if ((index < 0) || (index >= size()))
        throw new IndexOutOfBoundsException("Illegal index of " + index +
                            " passed to ABList set method.\n");

    T hold = elements[index];
    elements[index] = newElement;
    return hold;
}
```

Our list indexing starts at 0, just as does our array indexing. So the `index` argument can simply be used to access the array. The other indexed methods are similar, although of course the `add` and `remove` methods require shifting of array elements.

Iteration

Our lists support iteration. They implement the `ListInterface` that extends the `Iterable` interface, therefore our list classes must also implement `Iterable`. The `Iterable` interface requires a single public method:

```
Iterator<T> iterator( );
```

We must design an `iterator` method that creates and returns an `Iterator` object. `Iterator` objects provide three public methods—`hasNext`, `next`, and `remove`. In order for our `iterator` method to create an `Iterator` object we must define a new `Iterator` class that provides these three methods. Where do we put this new class? There are three approaches:

- *External class.* We could create a class that implements `Iterator` as a class in a separate file, for example, the `ABListIterator` class. The constructor of this class would accept an `ABList` object as a parameter. The class should be in the `ch06.lists` package so that it has access to the `protected` instance variables of `ABList`, which it needs to implement the required operations. For example, if the instance variable used to reference the `ABList` object within the iterator class is named `theList`, the `remove` method might include a line of code like

```
theList.elements[theList.numElements - 1] = null;
```

to properly reduce the size of the list after the removal is completed. Note the direct use of the `ABList` instance variables `elements` and `numElements`. Although we have decided to use a different approach, it is instructive for the reader to study the external class approach—we have included the code for `ABListIterator` with the text files. If we did use this approach then the code for the `iterator` method within the `ABList` class becomes simply:

```
public Iterator<T> iterator()
// Returns an Iterator over this list.
{
   return new ABListIterator<T>(this);
}
```

Why not use this approach? The greatest drawback is the unusual use of the instance variables of the `ABList` class within the separate `ABListIterator` class. Even though the two classes are in the same package this approach goes against the information hiding principles we practice throughout the rest of the text. This strong coupling between two classes that reside in separate files could create issues during later maintenance of the `ABList` class. We think it is better if the two classes reside in the same file, as is the case with the next two approaches we discuss.

- *Inner class.* Rather than creating an `Iterator` class in an external file we could place all of the code for it inside the `ABList.java` file. With this approach it is obvious to future maintenance programmers that the two classes are directly related. Furthermore, the inner class can directly access the instance variables of the surrounding class, as it *is* a member of the surrounding class. With this approach the fragment of code that corresponds to the `remove` method fragment shown before is simply

```
elements[numElements - 1] = null;
```
and the `iterator` method becomes
```
public Iterator<T> iterator()
// Returns an Iterator over this list.
{
   return new ABListIterator();
}
```

- *Anonymous inner class.* Java permits programmers to write anonymous classes, classes without names. Instead of defining a class in one place and then instantiating it somewhere else, as is the usual approach, we can define a class exactly at the place in the code where it is being instantiated. Because it is created at the same place it is defined there is no need for a class name. After all, the name is really just used as a connection between the definition and instantiation.

We use this last approach for our required `Iterator` class, that is, we define it as an anonymous inner class within the `iterator` method. The only reason we need an `Iterator` class is so that the `iterator` method can return it, thus using an anonymous inner class just at the point of need makes sense. The code is shown below. Note that the `iterator` method essentially consists of the following:

```java
public Iterator<T> iterator()
// Returns an Iterator over this list.
{
    return new Iterator<T>()
    {
        // code that implements an Iterator
    };
}
```

The entire method is listed below—the skeleton view of the method displayed above hopefully helps you to see that an object of type `Iterator` is being created dynamically and returned by the `iterator` method.

```java
public Iterator<T> iterator()
// Returns an Iterator over this list.
{
    return new Iterator<T>()
    {
        private int previousPos = -1;
        public boolean hasNext()
        // Returns true if the iteration has more elements; otherwise false
        {
            return (previousPos < (size() - 1)) ;
        }

        public T next()
        // Returns the next element in the iteration.
        // Throws NoSuchElementException - if the iteration has no more elements
        {
            if (!hasNext())
                throw new IndexOutOfBoundsException("Illegal invocation of next " +
                              " in LBList iterator.\n");
            previousPos++;
            return elements[previousPos];
        }
        public void remove()
        // Removes from the underlying representation the last element returned
        // by this iterator. This method should be called only once per call to
        // next(). The behavior of an iterator is unspecified if the underlying
```

```
  // representation is modified while the iteration is in progress in any
  // way other than by calling this method.
  {
    for (int i = previousPos; i <= numElements - 2; i++)
      elements [i] = elements[i+1];
    elements [numElements - 1] = null;
    numElements--;
    previousPos--;
  }
};
}
```

The entire implementation of ABList is found in the ch06.lists package.

Link-Based Implementation

As was the case for the array-based approaches, some of the link-based collection imple-mentation design and code can be reused for the link-based list. Here is the beginning of the class, showing the instance variables and constructor:

```
//-------------------------------------------------------------------
// LBList.java              by Dale/Joyce/Weems              Chapter 6
// Link-Based List
//
// Null elements are not permitted on a list. The list is unbounded.
//-------------------------------------------------------------------
package ch06.lists;
import java.util.Iterator;
import support.LLNode;

public class LBList<T> implements ListInterface<T>
{
  protected LLNode<T> front;      // reference to the front of this list
  protected LLNode<T> rear;       // reference to the rear of this list
  protected int numElements = 0;  // number of elements in this list
  // set by find method
  protected boolean found;            // true if target found, else false
  protected int targetIndex;          // list index of target, if found
  protected LLNode<T> location;    // node containing target, if found
  protected LLNode<T> previous;    // node preceding location
  public LBList()
  {
    numElements = 0;
    front = null;
    rear = null;
  }
```

All of the instance variables except two have counterparts in the link-based collection implementation of Chapter 5. To support the add method, which adds elements to the end of the list, we maintain a reference rear to the end of the list. Any transformer method must be careful to correctly update both the front and rear references, if appropriate. To support the indexOf method we include a targetIndex variable, which the find method sets, in addition to setting found, location, and previous.

The code for size, get, isEmpty, and isFull is straightforward and is exactly the same as that discussed in Chapter 5 for LinkedCollection. The code for find and remove is also very similar to their linked collection counterparts, although the list find must set the targetIndex variable and the list remove, being a transformer, must update the rear variable under certain conditions. The add method adds the argument element to the end of the list—exactly the same as the enqueue method developed in Chapter 4. The code for all of these methods can be studied by looking at the LBList class in the ch06.lists package.

Index-Related Operations

Here we consider the five required indexed methods. Designing these methods was very easy for the array-based implementation because of the close association between list indices and the underlying array indices. This is not the case for the link-based implementation. When an index is provided as an argument to a method there is only one way to access the associated element—we must walk through the list from the start, the front reference, until we reach the indicated element. For example, here is the code for set:

```
public T set(int index, T newElement)
// Throws IndexOutOfBoundsException if passed an index argument
// such that index < 0 or index >= size().
// Otherwise, replaces element on this list at position index with
// newElement and returns the replaced element.
{
    if ((index < 0) || (index >= size()))
        throw new IndexOutOfBoundsException("Illegal index of " + index +
                            " passed to LBList set method.\n");
    LLNode<T> node = front;
    for (int i = 0; i < index; i++)
        node = node.getLink();
    T hold = node.getInfo();
    node.setInfo(newElement);
    return hold;
}
```

The necessity of walking through the list from the front means that the indexed operation implementations are all going to have O(N) efficiency. If a client is going to use indexing heavily with its lists it might be best for it to use the array-based lists.

The transformer methods that deal with indices, add and remove, are complicated by special cases. For example, the add method follows the same pattern as set; however, the method must take care when adding to the front of list, to the rear of list, or to an empty list:

```
public void add(int index, T element)
// Throws IndexOutOfBoundsException if passed an index argument
// such that index < 0 or index > size().
// Otherwise, adds element to this list at position index; all current
// elements at that index or higher have 1 added to their index.
{
  if ((index < 0) || (index > size()))
    throw new IndexOutOfBoundsException("Illegal index of " + index +
                          " passed to LBList add method.\n");
  LLNode<T> newNode = new LLNode<T>(element);
  if (index == 0) // add to front
  {
    if (front == null) // adding to empty list
    {
      front = newNode; rear = newNode;
    }
    else
    {
      newNode.setLink(front);
      front = newNode;
    }
  }
  else
  if (index == size()) // add to rear
  {
    rear.setLink(newNode);
    rear = newNode;
  }
  else  // add in interior part of list
  {
    LLNode<T> node = front;
    for (int i = 0; i < (index - 1); i++)
      node = node.getLink();
    newNode.setLink(node.getLink());
    node.setLink(newNode);
  }
  numElements++;
}
```

We leave it to the reader to examine the code for the get, indexOf, and remove methods.

Iteration

As we did with the array-based list implementation, we use an anonymous inner class within the `iterator` method. The instantiated `Iterator` object keeps track of three instance variables to provide the iteration and to support the required `remove` operation: `currPos` references the node that was "just" returned, `prevPos` references the node before `currPos`, and `nextPos` references the node following `currPos`. For example, if the list contains the strings "Bat," "Ant," "Cat," "Ear," and "Dog" and an iteration has just returned "Cat," then the values of the references would be as shown here:

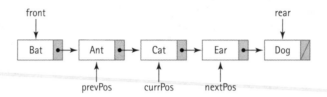

When the `Iterator` object is instantiated, `nextPos` is initialized to `front` and `currPos` and `prevPos` are both initialized to `null`, which properly sets up for the start of the iteration:

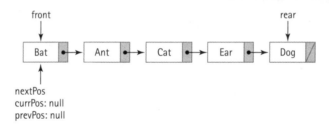

The `next` method, when invoked, first checks to see if there is a next element to return (if not it throws an exception), then "saves" the information to return, updates all three of the references, and returns the information. See the code below. For example, the first time `next` is invoked on our sample list it would return the string "Bat" and update the references resulting in this new state:

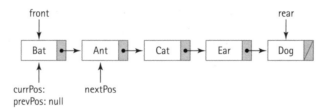

Recall that if we invoke `remove` in the middle of an iteration it is supposed to remove the element that was just returned, the element referenced by `currPos`. It does this by changing the link value of the element before `currPos`, the element referenced by `prev-Pos`. Here is how things would look in our example if the iteration most recently returned "Cat" and `remove` was then invoked:

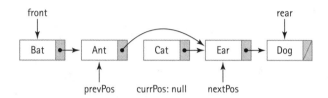

Note that `remove` sets the value of `currPos` to `null`, since after removal, the most recent element returned is no longer in the list. This is necessary so the `next` method does not inappropriately use an "out of date" `currPos` reference. In the above scenario the node containing "Cat" is potentially garbage and, if so, that memory space will be reclaimed by the Java garbage collector. Here is the iterator code in full. We encourage the readers to trace this code themselves, drawing pictures like those shown here, to validate both the code and their understanding.

```
public Iterator<T> iterator()
// Returns an Iterator over this list.
{
  return new Iterator<T>()
  {
    protected LLNode<T> prevPos = null;  // node before node just returned
    protected LLNode<T> currPos = null;  // node just returned
    protected LLNode<T> nextPos = front; // next node to return

    public boolean hasNext()
    // Returns true if the iteration has more elements; otherwise false
    {
      return (nextPos != null);
    }

    public T next()
    // Returns the next element in the iteration.
    // Throws NoSuchElementException - if the iteration has no more elements
    {
      if (!hasNext())
        throw new IndexOutOfBoundsException("Illegal invocation of next " +
                                    " in LBList iterator.\n");
```

```
      T hold = nextPos.getInfo();              // holds info for return
      if (currPos != null) prevPos = currPos;  // in case element was removed
      currPos = nextPos;
      nextPos = nextPos.getLink();
      return hold;
    }

    public void remove()
    // Removes from the underlying representation the last element returned
    // by this iterator. This method should be called only once per call to
    // next(). The behavior of an iterator is unspecified if the underlying
    // representation is modified while the iteration is in progress in any
    // way other than by calling this method.
    {
      if (currPos == null) // there is no last element returned by iterator
        return;
      else
      {
        if (prevPos == null)  // removing front element
        {
          front = nextPos;
          currPos = null;
          if (front == null) // removed only element
            rear = null;
        }
        else
        {
          prevPos.setLink(nextPos);
          currPos = null;
        }
        numElements--;
      }
    }
  };
}
```

The entire implementation of LBList is found in the ch06.lists package.

6.3 Applications: Card Deck and Games

Everyone is familiar with card games: poker, blackjack, hearts, bridge, solitaire, and others. In this section we use our List ADT to support a class that represents a deck of cards, and then use that class in a few sample applications. We create a class that provides a standard deck of 52 playing cards, with ranks of two through ace and the suits clubs, diamonds, hearts, and spades.

© Bardocz Peter/Shutterstock

The Card Class

Before creating the card deck class, which will use our List ADT, we need cards to put into the list—we need a `Card` class. We place both the `Card` class and the `CardDeck` class in the `support.cards` package. A `Card` object has two obvious attributes—a `rank` and a `suit`. The `Card` class provides two public enum classes, `Rank` and `Suit`, which are in turn used for the card attributes. As the enum classes are public they are available for use by other classes and applications. The `Card` class also provides an `image` attribute that lets us associate an image file with each card. The image files are also found in the `support.cards` package. The card images can be used in graphical programs to provide

Java Note—enum

The Java enum type is a special data type that allows a variable to represent one of a set of predefined constants. The variable must be equal to one of the values that have been predefined for it. For example, the suit variable within our card class can only take on the values Club, Diamond, Heart, and Spade. It is good to use enum types when you need to represent a fixed set of constants, especially when you know all possible values of the set at compile time.

a realistic look to an application. The rest of the Card class is very straightforward. The card attributes, rank, suit, and image are all set through the constructor—once instantiated a card cannot change—cards are immutable. Three getter methods are provided, along with the standard equals, compareTo, and toString. In many games cards are compared on rank only—we follow that approach.

```java
//-------------------------------------------------------------------
// Card.java              by Dale/Joyce/Weems           Chapter 6
//
// Supports playing card objects having a suit, a rank, and an image.
// Only rank is used when comparing cards. Ace is "high".
//-------------------------------------------------------------------
package support.cards;

import javax.swing.ImageIcon;

public class Card implements Comparable<Card>
{
   public enum Rank {Two, Three, Four, Five, Six, Seven, Eight, Nine,
                     Ten, Jack, Queen, King, Ace}

   public enum Suit {Club, Diamond, Heart, Spade}

   protected final Rank rank;
   protected final Suit suit;
   protected ImageIcon image;

   Card(Rank rank, Suit suit, ImageIcon image)
   {
      this.rank = rank; this.suit = suit; this.image = image;
   }

   public Rank getRank() { return rank; }
   public Suit getSuit() { return suit; }
   public ImageIcon getImage() {return image;}

   @Override
   public boolean equals(Object obj)
```

```
// Returns true if 'obj' is a Card with same rank
// as this Card, otherwise returns false.
{
   if (obj == this)
      return true;
   else
   if (obj == null || obj.getClass() != this.getClass())
      return false;
   else
   {
      Card c = (Card) obj;
      return (this.rank == c.rank);
   }
}


public int compareTo(Card other)
// Compares this Card with 'other' for order. Returns a
// negative integer, zero, or a positive integer as this object
// is less than, equal to, or greater than 'other'.
{
   return this.rank.compareTo(other.rank);
}


@Override
public String toString() { return suit + " " + rank; }

}
```

The CardDeck Class

Because we know the exact number of cards in a card deck we use our ABList as the internal representation for the Card-Deck class. We can instantiate a list of size 52. Note the use of levels of abstraction here—CardDeck is built on top of ABList and ABList is built on top of an array.

The constructor of the CardDeck class instantiates deck of class ABList<Card> and then uses a double *for* loop, iterating through all combinations of Suit and Rank, to add the desired cards to the deck. The card image files can be identified by manipulating the string representation of

> **Important Concept: Abstraction Hierarchy**
>
> Our CardDeck class provides an abstraction of a deck of cards. It hides the implementation details from an application, allowing an application to access the deck through its public methods shuffle, more, and next-Card. Meanwhile, the implementation of CardDeck uses ABList—an abstraction of a list. The card deck abstraction is built upon the list abstraction (which uses an array, yet another abstraction level albeit one provided as a core part of the Java language). Abstraction hierarchies are an important way to manage complexity. They help limit the scope of concern when we are working at any particular level in the hierarchy.

suit and rank; as the cards are thereby added to the deck, they are also associated with the appropriate image.

A second instance variable, deal, provides a Card iterator—one that simulates dealing the deck of cards. Creating deal is easy—we just call the iterator method of the deck object. Do not forget, deck is an ABList object and therefore provides an iterator method. Managing the deck and dealing cards is accessed through the public CardDeck methods hasNextCard and nextCard, both of which call the appropriate method of the deal iterator. In addition to creating the deck of cards the constructor initializes deal.

As you can see, the CardDeck class allows an application to "shuffle" the deck of cards. The shuffle algorithm is the same one used by the Java library Collections class. It works through the deck backward, selecting a random position from the preceding portion of the deck, and swaps the card at that position with the card at the current position. To select a random position it uses the Java library's Random class. The call to rand.nextInt(i) returns a random integer between 0 and i—1. Because the Random class does such a good job with randomization there is no need to "shuffle" the deck multiple times—once is enough. After the cards are shuffled a new deal object is created—one that is all set to deal from the reshuffled deck.

```java
//-------------------------------------------------------------------
// CardDeck.java          by Dale/Joyce/Weems          Chapter 6
//
// Models a deck of cards. Includes shuffling and dealing.
//-------------------------------------------------------------------

package support.cards;

import java.util.Random;
import ch06.lists.ABList;
import javax.swing.ImageIcon;

public class CardDeck
{
  public static final int NUMCARDS = 52;

  protected ABList<Card> deck;
  protected Iterator<Card> deal;

  public CardDeck()
  {
    deck = new ABList<Card>(NUMCARDS);
    ImageIcon image;
    for (Card.Suit suit : Card.Suit.values())
```

```
      for (Card.Rank rank : Card.Rank.values())
      {
        image = new ImageIcon("support/cards/" + suit + "_" + rank
                                + "_RA.gif");
        deck.add(new Card(rank, suit, image));
      }
   deal = deck.iterator();
}

public void shuffle()
// Randomizes the order of the cards in the deck.
// Resets the current deal.
{
  Random rand = new Random(); // to generate random numbers
  int randLoc;                // random location in card deck
  Card temp;                  // for swap of cards

  for (int i = (NUMCARDS - 1); i > 0; i--)
  {
    randLoc = rand.nextInt(i);  // random integer between 0 and i - 1
    temp = deck.get(randLoc);
    deck.set(randLoc, deck.get(i));
    deck.set(i, temp);
  }

  deal = deck.iterator();
}

public boolean hasNextCard()
// Returns true if there are still cards left to be dealt;
// otherwise, returns false.
{
  return (deal.hasNext());
}

public Card nextCard()
// Precondition:  this.hasNextCard() == true
//
// Returns the next card for the current 'deal'.
{
  return deal.next();
}
}
```

Application: Arranging a Card Hand

Our first example use of the CardDeck class, CardHandCLI, is a command line interface program that uses the class to generate one five-card hand of playing cards, and allows the user to arrange the cards in the order they prefer. In addition to using the CardDeck class we use an ABList of Card to hold and manage the hand. As cards are dealt one by one the hand, as arranged so far, is displayed using a *for each* loop (which is only possible because ABList implements Iterable), and the user can indicate where they want the next card placed. The indexed-based add method is then used to place the card in the correct slot.

```
//-----------------------------------------------------------------------
// CardHandCLI.java          by Dale/Joyce/Weems              Chapter 6
//
// Allows user to organize a hand of playing cards.
// Uses a command line interface.
//-----------------------------------------------------------------------

package ch06.apps;

import java.util.Scanner;
import java.util.Iterator;
import ch06.lists.*;
import support.cards.*;

public class CardHandCLI
{
  public static void main(String[] args)
  {
    Scanner scan = new Scanner(System.in);
    final int HANDSIZE = 5;
    int slot;

    Card card;                         // playing card
    CardDeck deck = new CardDeck();    // deck of playing cards

    ListInterface<Card> hand = new ABList<Card>(HANDSIZE); // user's hand

    deck.shuffle();
    hand.add(deck.nextCard());    // deals 1st card and places into hand

    for (int i = 1; i < HANDSIZE; i++)
    {
      System.out.println("\nYour hand so far:");
      slot = 0;
```

```
      for (Card c: hand)
      {
        System.out.println(slot + "\n  " + c);
        slot++;
      }
      System.out.println(slot);

      card = deck.nextCard();
      System.out.print("Slot between 0 and " + i + " to put "
                          + card + " > ");
      slot = scan.nextInt();
      hand.add(slot, card);
    }

    System.out.println("\nYour final hand is:");
    for (Card c: hand)
        System.out.println("  " + c);
  }
}
```

sample run of the program is:

```
Your hand so far:
0
  Six of Clubs
1
Slot between 0 and 1 to put Nine of Diamonds > 1
Your hand so far:
0
  Six of Clubs
1
  Nine of Diamonds
2
Slot between 0 and 2 to put Five of Diamonds > 0
Your hand so far:
0
  Five of Diamonds
1
  Six of Clubs
2
  Nine of Diamonds
3
Slot between 0 and 3 to put Ace of Clubs > 3
```

```
Your hand so far:
0
   Five of Diamonds
1
   Six of Clubs
2
   Nine of Diamonds
3
   Ace of Clubs
4
Slot between 0 and 4 to put Nine of Clubs > 2
Your final hand is:
   Five of Diamonds
   Six of Clubs
   Nine of Clubs
   Nine of Diamonds
   Ace of Clubs
```

Readers who are familiar with the game of poker will recognize this hand as a "Pair of Nines." Is that good? We will investigate that question in a subsection below.

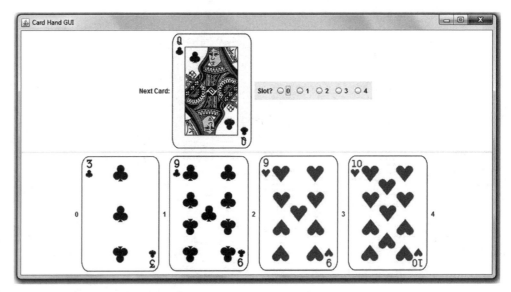

Figure 6.1 Sample screenshot of `CardHandGUI` in action
© Bardocz Peter/Shutterstock

In addition to the `CardHandCLI` program we also created `CardHandGUI`. It provides identical functionality, featuring a graphical user interface. A screenshot of the program is displayed in **Figure 6.1**. Another "Pair of Nines"! Interested readers are encouraged to examine the code, found in the `ch06.apps` package.

Application: Higher or Lower?

To further demonstrate the use of the `CardDeck` and `Card` classes, in particular card comparison, we develop a very simple interactive card game.

The game "Higher or Lower?" can be defined in one sentence. You are dealt a card from a deck of cards and you must predict whether or not the next card dealt will have a higher or lower rank. That is it—here is the application:

```
//----------------------------------------------------------------------
// HigherLower.java          by Dale/Joyce/Weems          Chapter 6
//
// Plays Higher or Lower? with user through command line interface.
//----------------------------------------------------------------------
package ch06.apps;

import support.cards.*;          // Card, CardDeck
import java.util.Scanner;

public class HigherLower
{
  public static void main(String[] args)
  {
    Scanner scan = new Scanner(System.in);
    char reply;

    Card card1, card2;
    CardDeck deck = new CardDeck();
    deck.shuffle();

    System.out.println("Welcome to \"Higher or Lower\". Good luck!");

    // First card
    card1 = deck.nextCard();
    System.out.println("\nFirst Card: " + card1);

    // Get prediction
    System.out.print("Higher (H) or Lower (L)? > ");
    reply = scan.nextLine().charAt(0);
```

```
    // Second card
    card2 = deck.nextCard();
    System.out.println("\nSecond Card: " + card2);

    // Determine and display results
    if ((card2.compareTo(card1) > 0) && (reply == 'H'))
      System.out.println("Correct");
    else
    if ((card2.compareTo(card1) < 0) && (reply == 'L'))
      System.out.println("Correct");
    else
      System.out.println("Incorrect");
  }
}
```

And a sample run:

```
Welcome to "Higher or Lower". Good luck!

First Card: Nine of Diamonds
Higher (H) or Lower (L)? > L

Second Card: Seven of Spades
Correct
```

Application: How Rare Is a Pair?

This example shows how to use program simulation to help verify formal analysis, and vice versa. Five-card stud is a popular poker game. Each player is dealt five cards from a standard 52-card playing deck. The player with the best hand wins. As you know playing cards have two qualities: suit (Club, Diamond, Heart, and Spade) and rank (Two through Ace). Hands are rated, from best to worst, as follows:

- *Royal Flush* All cards of the same suit. Ranks from 10 through Ace.
- *Straight Flush* All cards of the same suit. Rank in sequence.
- *Four of a Kind* Four cards with the same rank.
- *Full House* Three cards of one rank, and two cards of a second rank.
- *Flush* All cards of the same suit.
- *Straight* All cards with ranks in sequence (e.g., 4-5-6-7-8). Note that Ace can be used low or high.
- *Three of a Kind* Three cards with the same rank.
- *Two Pair* Two sets of cards of the same rank (e.g., 8-8-3-3-9).
- *One Pair* Two cards of the same rank.
- *High Card* If we have none of the above, the highest-ranking card in our hand is the "high card."

To help us understand the game of poker, we want to know the probability, when dealt a random five-card hand, that we get at least two cards of the same rank. We are not concerned with straights and flushes; we are only concerned with getting cards of the same rank.

There are two approaches to investigate this question: We can analyze the situation mathematically or we can write a program that simulates the situation. Let us do both. We can then compare and verify our results.

First we use the mathematical approach. The analysis is simplified by turning the question around. We figure out the probability (a real number in the range from 0 to 1) that we do *not* get two cards of the same rank, and then subtract that probability from 1 (which represents absolute certainty).

We proceed one card at a time. When we are dealt the first card, what is the probability we do not have two cards of the same rank? With only one card, it is certain that we do not have a matching pair! We calculate this fact mathematically by using the classic probability formula of *number of favorable events ÷ total number of possible events*:

$$\frac{52}{52} = 1$$

There are 52 total possible cards from which to choose, and picking any of the 52 has the desired "favorable" result (no matches). The probability we have a pair of matching cards is thus $1 - 1 = 0$ (impossible). It is impossible to have a pair of matching cards when we have only one card. Why do we need this mathematical complexity to say something that is so obvious? Because it acts as a foundation for our continuing analysis.

Now we are dealt the second card. The first card has some rank between two and ace. Of the 51 cards that are still in the deck, 48 of them do not have the same rank as the first card. Thus there are 48 chances out of 51 that this second card will not match the first card. To calculate the overall probability of two sequential events occurring, we multiply their individual probabilities. Therefore, after two cards the probability that we do not have a pair is

$$\frac{52}{52} \times \frac{48}{51} \approx 0.941$$

At this point, the probability that we do have a pair is approximately $1 - 0.941 = 0.059$.

For the third card dealt, there are 50 cards left in the deck. Six of those cards match one or the other of the two cards previously dealt, because we are assuming we do not have a pair already. Thus there are 44 chances out of 50 that we do not get a pair with the third card, giving us the probability

$$\frac{52}{52} \times \frac{48}{51} \times \frac{44}{50} \approx 0.828$$

Continuing in this way we get the following probability that we do not have a pair of matching cards after five cards are dealt:

$$\frac{52}{52} \times \frac{48}{51} \times \frac{44}{50} \times \frac{40}{49} \times \frac{36}{48} \approx 0.507$$

Therefore, the probability that we get at least two matching cards is approximately $1 - 0.507 = 0.493$. We should expect to get at least one pair a little less than half the time.

Now we address the same problem using simulation. Not only does this endeavor help us double-check our theoretical results, but it also helps validate our programming and the random number generator used to simulate shuffling the cards.

We create a program that deals 1 million five-card poker hands and tracks how many of them have at least one pair of identical cards. We use our `CardDeck` class to provide the deck of cards and, as we did in the previous example application, we represent the poker "hand" with a list of `Card` objects.

Our approach is to reshuffle the cards for every new hand. As cards are dealt, they are placed in a hand list. For each new card, we check the list to see whether an equivalent card is already in hand. Recall that card equality is based on the rank of the cards. Here is the `Pairs` application:

```
//-------------------------------------------------------------------
// Pairs.java              by Dale/Joyce/Weems              Chapter 6
//
// Simulates dealing poker hands to calculate the probability of
// getting at least one pair of matching cards.
//-------------------------------------------------------------------

import ch06.lists.*;
import support.cards.*;       // Card and CardDeck

public class Pairs
{
  public static void main(String[] args)
  {
    final int HANDSIZE = 5;           // number of cards per hand
    final int NUMHANDS = 1000000;     // total number of hands
    int numPairs = 0;                 // number of hands with pairs
    boolean isPair;                   // status of current hand
    float probability;                // calculated probability

    Card card;                            // playing card
    CardDeck deck = new CardDeck();   // deck of playing cards

    ListInterface<Card> hand = new ABList<Card>(HANDSIZE); // the poker hand
    for (int i = 0; i < NUMHANDS; i++)
    {
      deck.shuffle();
      hand = new ABList<Card>(HANDSIZE);
      isPair = false;
      for (int j = 0; j < HANDSIZE; j++)
```

```
  {
    card = deck.nextCard();
    if (hand.contains(card))
      isPair = true;
    hand.add(card);
  }
  if (isPair)
    numPairs = numPairs + 1;
}

probability = numPairs/(float)NUMHANDS;
System.out.println();
System.out.print("There were " + numPairs + " hands out of " + NUMHANDS);
System.out.println(" that had at least one pair of matched cards.");
System.out.print("The probability of getting at least one pair,");
System.out.print(" based on this simulation, is ");
System.out.println(probability);
}
}
```

As we have seen several times before, the use of predefined classes, such as our `ABList` class and our `CardDeck` class, makes programming much easier. Here is the result of one run of this program:

```
There were 492709 hands out of 1000000 that had at least one
  pair of matched cards.
The probability of getting at least one pair, based on this
  simulation, is 0.492709
```

This result is very close to our theoretical result. Additional program runs also produced acceptably close results.

6.4   Sorted Array-Based List Implementation

Many of the lists we use every day are sorted lists. A "To-Do" list is sorted from most important to least important, a list of students is likely to be in alphabetical order, and a well-organized grocery list is sorted by store aisle. Considering how common it is for us to work with sorted lists, it is a good idea to create a version of our List ADT where the elements are kept in sorted order. We will call our new array-based class `SortedABList`. Like `ABList` and `LBList`, `SortedABList` implements `ListInterface`.

In Section 5.5, "Sorted Array-Based Collection Implementation," we designed and coded a collection class whose internal representation was a sorted array. Our goal then was to increase the efficiency of the *find* operation, which gave us a much more efficient `contains` method ($O(\log_2 N)$ versus $O(N)$) and also improved the efficiency of several other operations. Here our goal is to be able to present a sorted list to the client—when they iterate through the list they know it will be presented to them in sorted order. We use the same basic approach to maintaining sorted order as we did for the sorted collection, and we do achieve most of the same efficiency benefits. Much of the design and code of the `SortedArrayCollection` from the `ch05.collections` package can be reused.

The Insertion Sort

Let us say the following four elements have previously been added to our list: "Cat," "Ant," "Ear," and "Dog." Because the list is being kept sorted its internal representation would be

numElements: 4

	[0]	[1]	[2]	[3]	[4]	[5]
list:	"Ant"	"Cat"	"Dog"	"Ear"		

Suppose now a new string "Bat" is added to the list. The add method invokes the `find` method that efficiently determines where the new element should be inserted. In this case the element belongs at index 1 so the `find` method sets the value of the instance variable `location` to 1 and then the `add` method proceeds to shift the necessary elements and insert "Bat" into the newly opened slot at index `location`:

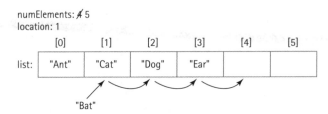

Because this same approach is used every time an element is added to the list, the list is maintained in sorted order.

The approach described above is actually a well-known sorting algorithm called *Insertion Sort*. Suppose we have a set of *N* elements that we wish to sort. We can instantiate a `SortedABList` object and repeatedly add the elements to it. As each successive element is added to the list, it is *inserted* into its proper place with respect to the other, already sorted elements. After all of the elements have been added we can iterate through the list to retrieve the elements in sorted order.

What is the order of growth efficiency for *Insertion Sort*? When we add an element to the list we may have to shift previously added elements one slot in order to make room for the new element. In the worst case when the new element is the "smallest" of the elements added so far—for example, consider adding "Aardvark" to the list shown above—we have to shift *all* of the current elements. If we are very unlucky and our original set of elements is presented to us in reverse order, then each time we add an element all of the previous elements need to be shifted.

Efficiency of Sorting Algorithms

The Selection Sort algorithm presented in Section 1.6, "Comparing Algorithms: Order of Growth Analysis," and the Insertion Sort algorithm described here are both $O(N^2)$ algorithms. For small- to medium-sized sets of elements these sorts are sufficient, but as the number of elements increases, faster algorithms become necessary. In Section 11.3 we develop several $O(N \log_2 N)$ sorting algorithms.

Shifting an element in the array and copying in the newly added element both are carried out with an assignment statement. So we can consider the assignment statement a fundamental operation for the *Insertion Sort* algorithm. We will count how many assignment statements are needed in the worst case scenario, and we will call the use of the assignment statement a "step."

When the first element is added nothing needs to be shifted, but the new element must be copied into the array. So that requires one step. When the second element is added we would need one shift and one copy; therefore two steps. By the time we add the Nth element we need $N - 1$ shifts and one copy, therefore N steps. The total number of steps required is

$$1 + 2 + 3 + \ldots + (N - 1) + N$$

Applying a well-known summation formula tells us this sum is equal to $N(N + 1)/2$. If we expand $N(N + 1)/2$ as $\frac{1}{2}N^2 + \frac{1}{2}N$, it is easy to see that the order of growth is N^2. This analysis and result is similar to what we did in Section 1.6, "Comparing Algorithms: Order of Growth Analysis," for the *Selection Sort* algorithm. Although an O(N^2) sorting algorithm is not considered to be "fast," the *Insertion Sort* is a good sorting approach to use in situations such as our List ADT where the elements to be sorted are passed to the storage container one at a time.

Unsupported Operations

As we just discussed, a `SortedABList` object keeps the elements added to it in sorted order. It does this by carefully inserting added elements into the appropriate location of the internal array. Note that besides the standard `add` method, the List ADT includes two other ways for elements to be placed into a list, the index-based `add` and `set` methods.

If we allow clients to `add` or `set` elements at a specified index of the list, then it is possible a client would invalidate the carefully created ordering of the array. This in turn would cause the `find` method to malfunction. There is a simple solution to this issue. We state as a general precondition of the class that the index-based `add` and `set` operations are not supported. If invoked we have those methods throw an `UnsupportedOperationException`, which is an unchecked exception provided by the Java library. Here is the code for the two unsupported methods:

```
public void add(int index, T element)
// Throws UnsupportedOperationException.
{
  throw new UnsupportedOperationException("Unsupported index-based add . . .
}

public T set(int index, T newElement)
// Throws UnsupportedOperationException.
{
  throw new UnsupportedOperationException("Unsupported index-based set . . .
}
```

Comparator Interface

For the `SortedArrayCollection` of Chapter 5 the elements in the array were maintained in natural order, that is, in the order defined by the element class's `compareTo` method. In that case we were only interested in increasing the efficiency of the `find` operation, so the natural order worked as well as any other ordering. We simply had to require that elements added to the collection implemented the `Comparable` interface, thus ensuring that they implemented the `compareTo` method.

For our List ADT, however, our goal is to present a sorted list to the client. It might be that a client does not want to use the natural order of the elements. After all, there often are many ways we can sort lists—a list of students could be sorted by name, by test average, by age, by height, and so on. We want to allow clients of our `SortedABList` to be able to specify for themselves how the elements should be sorted.

The Java library provides another interface related to comparing objects, a generic interface called `Comparator`. This interface defines two abstract methods:

```
public abstract int compare(T o1, T o2);
// Returns a negative integer, zero, or a positive integer to
// indicate that o1 is less than, equal to, or greater than o2

public abstract boolean equals(Object obj);
// Returns true if this Comparator equals obj; otherwise, false
```

The first method, `compare`, is very similar to the familiar `compareTo` method. It takes two arguments, however, rather than one. The second method, `equals`, is specified in the same way as the `equals` method of the `Object` class and can be inherited from `Object`. Recall that it usually is important for the `equals` and `compareTo` methods of a class to be consistent—likewise it is also important for the `equals` and `compare` methods of a `Comparator` class to be consistent. We do not address the `equals` method again in this discussion as we do not use it within our implementation of the sorted list.

Comparing two objects using `compareTo` requires invoking the method on one of the objects. For example, if `fp1` and `fp2` are both `FamousPerson` objects they could be compared as follows:

```
if (fp1.compareTo(fp2)) . . .
```

Java Note

With the release of Java 8, in 2014, another option is available for defining comparisons. Lambda expressions provide a functional programming aspect to Java—allowing programmers easily to define and manipulate functions, such as comparison, much like in languages such as Lisp and Scheme. Functional programming involves a problem-solving approach that is quite different from object-oriented programming, and it would take considerable space to explain and demonstrate properly. To maintain our focus on data structures and object orientation, we have elected not to use lambda expressions in this text.

There can be only one `compareTo` method defined on the `FamousPerson` class, and therefore only one way to sort such objects if we rely on the `compareTo` method. This is the so-called natural order, and in the case of the `FamousPerson` class the elements would be ordered alphabetically by last name, first name.

Using an approach based on the `Comparator` class allows for multiple sorting orders. We can define as many methods related to an element class that return a `Comparator` object as we want. Here is a method, `yearOfBirthComparator`, which returns a `Comparator` object allowing us to sort `FamousPerson` elements by year of birth. It is exported from the `FamousPerson` class and uses the anonymous inner-class technique introduced in the *Iteration* subsection of Section 6.2, "List Implementations":

```
public static Comparator<FamousPerson> yearOfBirthComparator()
{
  return new Comparator<FamousPerson>()
  {
    public int compare(FamousPerson element1, FamousPerson element2)
    {
      return (element1.yearOfBirth - element2.yearOfBirth);
    }
  };
}
```

Exercise 6.30 asks you to provide several more comparison options for the `Famous-Person` class.

Constructors

How does a client class of `SortedABList` specify which `Comparator` to use for ordering the elements? Simple, it passes the `Comparator` as an argument to the constructor of the class when it instantiates the sorted list. The `SortedABList` class includes a protected variable `comp` of type `Comparator<T>`:

```
protected Comparator<T> comp;
```

Here is the constructor of the class:

```
public SortedABList(Comparator<T> comp)
{
  list = (T[]) new Object[DEFCAP];
  this.comp = comp;
}
```

As you can see the value of the instance variable `comp` is set through the constructor. Within the `find` method of the class, comparison is accomplished using `comp`:

```
    result = comp.compare(target, elements[location]);
```

So, for example, if a client wants a list of `FamousPerson` sorted by their year of birth they would instantiate a `SortedABList` object with the appropriate comparator:

```
SortedABList<FamousPerson> people =
  new SortedABList<FamousPerson>(FamousPerson.yearOfBirthComparator());
```

But, what if the client *does* want to use the natural order of the element class, the order as defined by the `compareTo` method. To allow easy use of the natural order we define a second constructor, one that takes no parameters. This constructor generates a `Compar-ator` object based on the `compareTo` method of the element class, using the anonymous inner-class approach, and assigns that comparator to `comp`. So if the parameter-less constructor of `SortedABList` is invoked, then the natural ordering of the elements is used for sorting purposes by default. The second constructor is:

```
public SortedABList()
// Precondition: T implements Comparable
{
  list = (T[]) new Object[DEFCAP];
  comp = new Comparator<T>()
  {
    public int compare(T element1, T element2)
    {
      return ((Comparable)element1).compareTo(element2);
    }
  };
}
```

An Example

The following program reads information about famous computer scientists from a file named `FamousCS.txt` and uses it to create and then display a sorted list of the information. It allows the user of the program to indicate how to sort the information, either by name (the natural order) or by birth year. In the former case the program instantiates the list using the parameter-less constructor, and in the latter case it passes the constructor the "sort by year of birth" comparator. The code and sample output follows.

```
//---------------------------------------------------------------------------
// CSPeople.java              by Dale/Joyce/Weems              Chapter 6
//
// Reads information about famous computer scientists from the file
// input/FamousCS.txt. Allows user to indicate if they wish to see the list
// sorted by name or by year of birth.
//---------------------------------------------------------------------------
package ch06.apps;

import java.io.*;
import java.util.*;
import ch06.lists.*;
import support.*;
```

```java
public class CSPeople
{
  public static void main(String[] args) throws IOException
  {
    // Get user's display preference
    Scanner scan = new Scanner(System.in);
    int choice;
    System.out.println("1: Sorted by name? \n2: Sorted by year of birth?");
    System.out.print("\nHow would you like to see the information > ");
    choice = scan.nextInt();

    // Instantiate sorted list
    SortedABList<FamousPerson> people;
    if (choice == 1)
      people = new SortedABList<FamousPerson>(); // defaults to natural order
    else
      people = new
            SortedABList<FamousPerson>(FamousPerson.yearOfBirthComparator());

    // Set up file reading
    FileReader fin = new FileReader("input/FamousCS.txt");
    Scanner info = new Scanner(fin);
    info.useDelimiter("[,\\n]");  // delimiters are commas, line feeds
    FamousPerson person;
    String fname, lname, fact;
    int year;

    // Read the info from the file and add it to the list
    while (info.hasNext())
    {
      fname = info.next();    lname = info.next();
      year = info.nextInt(); fact = info.next();
      person = new FamousPerson(fname, lname, year, fact);
      people.add(person);
    }

    // Display the list, using the advanced for loop
    System.out.println();
    for (FamousPerson fp: people)
      System.out.println(fp);
  }
}
```

To save space we only show the first few lines of output. First we show the result if the user chooses option 1:

```
1: Sorted by name?
2: Sorted by year of birth?

How would you like to see the information > 1

John Atanasoff(Born 1903): Invented digital computer in 1930.
Charles Babbage(Born 1791): Concept of machine that could be programmed.
Tim Berners-Lee(Born 1955): "Inventor" of the World Wide Web.
Anita Borg(Born 1949): Founding director of IWT.
. . .
```

And if they choose option 2:

```
1: Sorted by name?
2: Sorted by year of birth?

How would you like to see the information > 2
Blaise Pascal(Born 1623): One of inventors of mechanical calculator.
Joseph Jacquard(Born 1752): Developed programmable loom.
Charles Babbage(Born 1791): Concept of machine that could be programmed.
Ada Lovelace(Born 1815): Considered by many to be first computer programmer.
. . .
```

This concludes our section. The code of the `SortedABList` class that we "skipped over" is essentially identical to code developed for previous ADTs. You can find `SortedABList` in the `ch06.lists` package.

6.5   List Variations

Just as there are many variations of types of, and uses for, lists in everyday life there are multiple approaches to implementing and using lists as a data structure.

Java Library Lists

In the *Variations* sections of Chapters 2, 4, and 5 we reviewed the Java Standard Library support for stacks, queues, and collections. We do not attempt to cover the Java Collections Application Programming Interface (API) in detail as a subject within this text. Our goal in these *Variations* sections related to the API is to point the interested reader to the information and encourage independent study of the topics. Moving forward, we will just briefly mention the library constructs related to the ADT under consideration when appropriate.

The library provides a `List` interface that inherits from both the `Collection` and `Iterable` interfaces of the library. The library's list interface is significantly more complex than ours, defining 28 abstract methods. It is implemented by the following classes: `AbstractList`, `AbstractSequentialList`, `ArrayList`, `AttributeList`, `CopyOnWriteArrayList`, `LinkedList`, `RoleList`, `RoleUnresolvedList`, `Stack`, and `Vector`. Of special note are the `ArrayList`—we used an `ArrayList` in Section 2.5, "Array-Based Stack Implementations," to implement a stack—and the `LinkedList`, that "implements a doubly linked list."

Linked List Variations

Linked lists are sometimes used as an ADT, for example, the `LinkedList` class of the Java library, and sometimes used as a means of implementing another structure, for example, the way we used linked lists so far to implement stacks, queues, collections, and lists.

We have already seen several kinds of linked list structures. We used a singly linked list with a single access link (**Figure 6.2a**) to implement a stack in Section 2.8, "A Link-Based Stack," and a collection in Section 5.6, "Link-Based Collection Implementation." We used a single linked list with access links to both the front and rear (Figure 6.2b) to implement a queue in Section 4.5, "Link-Based Queue Implementations," and a list in Section 6.2, "List Implementations." We discussed how to use a circular linked list with a single access reference (Figure 6.2c) to implement a queue in Section 4.5, "Link-Based Queue Implementations," and how to implement a deque using a doubly linked list (Figure 6.2d) in Section 4.7, "Queue Variations."

When implementing methods for a linked list, we see that special cases often arise for the first and last nodes on the list. One way to simplify these methods is to make sure that we never add or remove elements at the ends of the list. How can we do this? It is often a simple matter to set up dummy nodes to mark the ends of a list. This is especially true for sorted lists because we can indicate the dummy nodes by using values outside of the permitted range of the contents of the list. A **header node**, containing a value smaller than any possible list element key, can be placed at the beginning of the list. A **trailer node**, containing a value larger than any legitimate element key, can be placed at the end of the list (Figure 6.2e).

Sometimes linked lists are themselves linked together in multiple levels to form a more complex structure. We discuss using multiple levels of linked lists in Chapter 10 to implement a Graph ADT. Interconnected lists are sometimes used to support complex yet efficient algorithms, for example a Skip List is a multilevel list (Figure 6.2f) that supports both efficient addition of nodes and efficient search for nodes.

The material in this text provides you the foundations needed to study, understand, use, and create all of the above variations of linked lists and more.

A Linked List as an Array of Nodes

We tend to think of linked structures as consisting of self-referential nodes that are dynamically allocated as needed, as illustrated in **Figure 6.3a**. But this is not a requirement. A linked list could be implemented in an array; the elements might be stored in the array in any order and "linked" by their indices (see Figure 6.3b). In this subsection, we discuss an array-based linked list implementation.

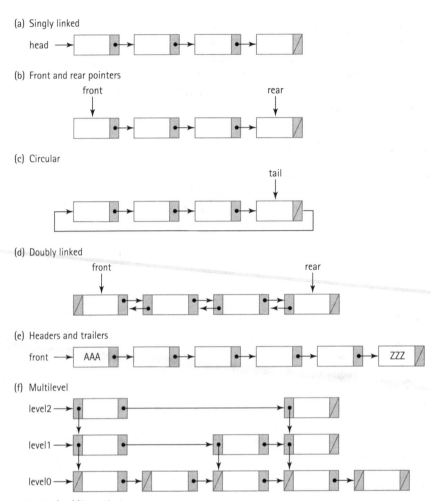

Figure 6.2 Linked list variations

In our previous reference-based implementations of lists, we used Java's built-in memory management services when we needed a new node for addition or when we were finished with a node and wanted to remove it. Obtaining a new node is easy in Java; we just use the familiar new operation. Releasing a node from use is also easy; just remove our references to it and depend on the Java run-time system's garbage collector to reclaim the space used by the node.

For the array-based linked representation, we must predetermine the maximum list size and instantiate an array of nodes of that size. We then directly manage the nodes in the array. We keep a separate list of the available nodes, and we write routines to allocate nodes to and deallocate nodes from this free list.

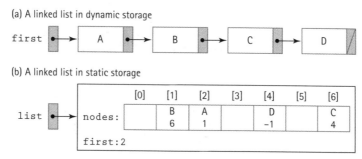

Figure 6.3   Linked lists in dynamic and static storage

Why Use an Array?

We have seen that dynamic allocation of list nodes has many advantages, so why would we even consider using an array-of-nodes implementation? Recall that dynamic allocation is just one advantage of choosing a linked implementation; another advantage is the greater efficiency of the add and remove algorithms. Most of the algorithms for operations on a linked structure can be used for either an array-based or a reference-based implementation. The main difference arises from the requirement that we manage our own free space in an array-based implementation. Sometimes managing the free space ourselves gives us greater flexibility.

Another reason to use an array of nodes is that some programming languages do not support dynamic allocation or reference types. You can still use linked structures if you are programming in one of these languages, using the techniques presented in this subsection.

Finally, sometimes dynamic allocation of each node, one at a time, is too costly in terms of time—especially in real-time system software such as operating systems, air traffic controllers, and automotive systems. In such situations, an array-based linked approach provides the benefits of linked structures without the same run-time costs.

A desire for static allocation is one of the primary motivations driving the array-based linked approach, so we drop our assumption that our lists are of unlimited size. Here, our lists will not grow as needed. Clients should not add elements to a full list.

How Is an Array Used?

Here we return to our discussion of how a linked list can be implemented in an array. We outline an approach and leave the actual implementation as an exercise. We can associate a next variable with each array node to indicate the array index of the succeeding node. The beginning of the list is accessed through a "reference" that contains the array index of the first element in the list. **Figure 6.4** shows how a sorted list containing the elements "David," "Joshua," "Leah," "Miriam," and "Robert" might be stored in an array of nodes.

nodes	.info	.next
[0]	David	4
[1]		
[2]	Miriam	6
[3]		
[4]	Joshua	7
[5]		
[6]	Robert	−1
[7]	Leah	2
[8]		
[9]		

first | 0

Figure 6.4 A sorted list stored in an array of nodes

Do you see how the order of the elements in the list is explicitly indicated by the chain of `next` indices?

What goes in the `next` index of the last list element? Its "null" value must be an invalid address for a real list element. Because the `nodes` array indices begin at 0, the value −1 is not a valid index into the array; that is, there is no `nodes[-1]`. Therefore, −1 makes an ideal value to use as a "null" address. We could use the literal value −1 in our programs:

```
while (location != -1)
```

It is better programming style to declare a named constant, however. We suggest using the identifier NUL and defining it to be −1:

```
protected static final int NUL = -1;
```

When an array-of-nodes implementation is used to represent a linked list, the programmer must write routines to manage the free space available for new list elements. Where is this free space? Look again at Figure 6.4. All of the array elements that do not contain values in the list constitute free space. Instead of the built-in allocator `new`, which allocates memory dynamically, we must write our own method to allocate nodes from the free space. Let us call this method `getNode`. We use `getNode` when we add new elements to the list.

When we remove an element from the list, we need to reclaim its space—that is, we need to return the removed node to the free space so it can be used again later. We cannot depend on a garbage collector; the node we remove remains in the allocated array so it is not reclaimed by the run-time engine. We need to write our own method, `freeNode`, to put a node back into the pool of free space.

We need a way to track the collection of nodes that are not being used to hold list elements. We can link this collection of unused array elements together into a second list, a linked list of free nodes. **Figure 6.5** shows the array nodes with both the list of elements and the list of free space linked through their `next` values. The `first` variable is a reference to a list that begins at index 0 (containing the value "David"). Following the links in `next`, we see that the list continues with the array slots at index 4 ("Joshua"), 7 ("Leah"), 2 ("Miriam"), and 6 ("Robert"), in that order. The free list begins at `free`, at index 1. Following the `next` links, we see that the free list also includes the array slots at indices 5, 3, 8, and 9. We see two NUL values in the next column because there are two linked lists contained in the nodes array; thus the array includes two end-of-list values.

That concludes our outline for an approach to implementing a linked list with an array. Of course, a lot of work remains to be done to actually accomplish the implementation. See Exercise 37.

nodes	.info	.next
[0]	David	4
[1]		5
[2]	Miriam	6
[3]		8
[4]	Joshua	7
[5]		3
[6]	Robert	NUL
[7]	Leah	2
[8]		9
[9]		NUL

first	0
free	1

Figure 6.5 An array with a linked list of values and free space

6.6 Application: Large Integers

In the previous section we reviewed several common variations of linked lists: singly linked, doubly linked, circular, lists with headers and trailers, lists with front only or front and rear pointers, and multilevel lists. More variations are possible, of course, especially considering you can "mix and match" approaches, for example, creating a circular linked list with a front-only pointer that uses headers and trailers, and so on.

In this section we will create a variant of the linked list that is designed to help us solve a specific problem. In addition to using classic data structures and creating reusable ADTs it is also important to be able to design, create, and use structures on an as-needed basis.

Large Integers

The range of integer values that can be supported in Java varies from one primitive integer type to another. Appendix C contains a table showing the default value, the possible range of values, and the number of bits used to implement each integer type. The largest type, `long`, can represent values between $-9,223,372,036,854,775,808$ and $9,223,372,036,854,775,807$. Wow! That would seem to suffice for most applications. Some programmer, however, is certain to want to represent integers with even larger values. We create a class `LargeInt` that allows the programmer to manipulate integers in which the number of digits is limited only by the amount of memory available.[1]

Because we are providing an alternative implementation for a mathematical object, an integer number, the operations are already familiar: addition, subtraction, multiplication, division, assignment, and the relational operators. In this section, we limit our attention to addition and subtraction. We ask you to enhance this ADT with some of the other operations in the exercises.

In addition to the standard mathematical operations, we need to consider how to create our `LargeInt` objects prior to attempting to add or subtract them. We cannot use a constructor with an integer parameter, because the desired integer might be too large to represent in Java—after all, that is the idea of this ADT. Therefore, we decide to include a constructor that accepts a string argument that represents an integer and instantiates the corresponding `LargeInt` object.

We assume the sign of a large integer is positive and provide a way to make it negative. We call the corresponding method `setNegative`. Additionally, we must have an observer operation that returns a string representation of the large integer. We follow the Java convention and call this operation `toString`.

---

[1]Note that the Java library already provides a similar class, `java.math.BigInteger`. We are implementing our own version here because it is a good demonstration of the use of lists and because it is informative to see how to implement such a class.

The Internal Representation

Before we look at the algorithms for these operations, we need to decide on our internal representation. The fact that a large integer can be any size leads us to a dynamic memory-based representation. Also, given that an integer is a list of digits, it is natural to investigate the possibility of representing it as a linked list of digits. **Figure 6.6** shows two ways of storing numbers in a singly linked list and an example of addition. Parts (a) and (c) show one digit per node; part (b) shows several digits per node. We develop our Large Integer ADT using a single digit per node. (You are asked in the exercises to explore the changes necessary to include more than one digit in each node.) Thus we have decided to represent our large integers as linked lists of digits. Because a single digit can be represented by Java's smallest integer type, the `byte`, we decide to use linked lists of `byte` values.

What operations must be supported by this linked list? The first thing to consider is how large integer objects are to be constructed. We have already decided to build our representation, one digit at a time, from left to right across a particular large integer. That is how we initialize large integers directly. But large integers can also be created as a result of arithmetic operations. Think about how you perform arithmetic operations such as addition—you work from the least significant digit to the most significant digit, obtaining the result as you proceed. Therefore, we also need to create large integers by inserting digits in order from least significant to most significant. Thus our linked list should support insertion of digits at both the beginning and the end of the list.

Given the unique requirements for our Large Integer representation we create a list class specifically for this project. We call it `LargeIntList`.

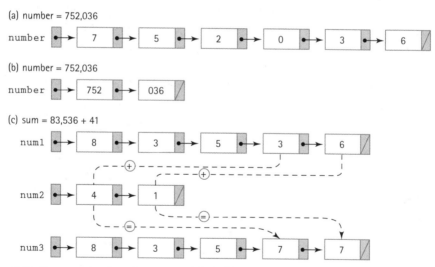

Figure 6.6   Representing large integers with linked lists

Figure 6.7   A doubly linked list with two references

The LargeIntList class

At this point we review our requirements. Our lists must hold elements of the primitive-type `byte`; we will use the wrapper class `Byte`. The lists need not support `isFull`, `isEmpty`, `add`, `contains`, `get`, `remove`, nor any of the indexed operations. In fact, the only list operations that we have been using that are required by this new list construct are the `size` operation and the iterator operations. We also need to process elements from left to right and from right to left, so we need to support two iterators: `forward` and `reverse`. In addition, we need to add elements at the front of our lists, `addFront`, and at the back of our lists, `addEnd`.

To support the requirement of traversing the list by going either forward or backward we decide to use a reference-based doubly linked structure for our implementation. To begin our backward traversals, and to support the new `addEnd` operation, it is clear that we need easy access to the end of the list. We decide to maintain two list references, one for the front of the list and one for the back of the list. **Figure 6.7** shows the general structure of the internal representation of our `LargeIntList` class.

Here is the beginning of the `LargeIntList` class. We use nodes of the `DLLNode` class (introduced in Section 4.7, "Queue Variations"). We use instance variables to track the first list element, the last list element, and the number of elements on the list. The `info` attribute of the `DLLNode` class holds a value of type `Byte`, as discussed earlier.

```
//-------------------------------------------------------------------------
// LargeIntList.java            by Dale/Joyce/Weems              Chapter 6
//
// A specialized list to support Large Integer ADT
//-------------------------------------------------------------------------
package ch06.largeInts;

import support.DLLNode;
import java.util.Iterator;

public class LargeIntList
{
  protected DLLNode<Byte> listFirst;    // Ref to the first node on list
  protected DLLNode<Byte> listLast;     // Ref to the last node on the list
  protected int numElements;            // Number of elements in the list
```

```
public LargeIntList()
// Creates an empty list object
{
  numElements = 0;
  listFirst = null;
  listLast = null;
}
```

The `size` method is essentially unchanged from previous implementations—it simply returns the value of the `numElements` instance variable.

```
public int size()
// Returns the number of elements on this list.
{
  return numElements;
}
```

The iterator methods are straightforward. There is no requirement for removing nodes during an iteration so the returned iterators need not support that operation. This simplifies their design considerably.

```
public Iterator<Byte> forward()
// Returns an Iterator that iterates from front to rear.
{
  return new Iterator<Byte>()
  {
    private DLLNode<Byte> next = listFirst; // next node to return
    public boolean hasNext()
    // Returns true if the iteration has more elements; otherwise false.
    {
      return (next != null);
    }

    public Byte next()
    // Returns the next element in the iteration.
    // Throws NoSuchElementException - if no more elements
    {
      if (!hasNext())
        throw new IndexOutOfBoundsException("Illegal invocation of " +
                      " next in LargeIntList forward iterator.\n");

      Byte hold = next.getInfo();        // holds info for return
      next = next.getForward();
      return hold;
    }
```

```
      public void remove()
      // Throws UnsupportedOperationException.
      {
        throw new UnsupportedOperationException("Unsupported remove " +
                    "attempted on LargeIntList forward iterator.");
      }
  };
}


public Iterator<Byte> reverse()
// Returns an Iterator that iterates from front to rear.
{
  return new Iterator<Byte>()
  {
    private DLLNode<Byte> next = listLast; // next node to return
    public boolean hasNext()
    // Returns true if the iteration has more elements; otherwise false.
    {
      return (next != null);
    }

    public Byte next()
    // Returns the next element in the iteration.
    // Throws NoSuchElementException - if no more elements
    {
      if (!hasNext())
        throw new IndexOutOfBoundsException("Illegal invocation of " +
                      "next in LargeIntList reverse iterator.\n");

      Byte hold = next.getInfo();          // holds info for return
      next = next.getBack();
      return hold;
    }

    public void remove()
    // Throws UnsupportedOperationException.
    {
      throw new UnsupportedOperationException("Unsupported remove " +
                  "attempted on LargeIntList forward iterator.");
    }
  };
}
```

The addition methods are simplified because we do not have to handle the general case of addition in the middle of the list. The addFront method always adds at the beginning of the list and the addEnd method always adds at the end of the list. Here we look at addFront (see **Figure 6.8a**).

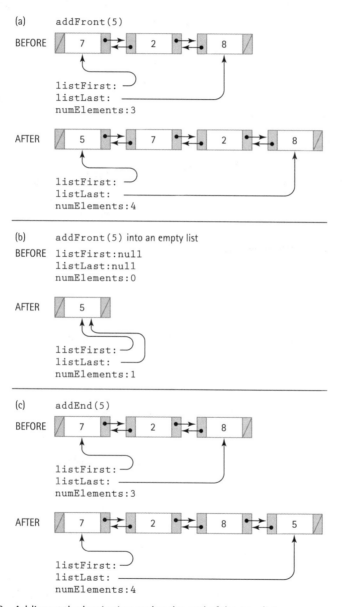

Figure 6.8 Adding at the beginning and at the end of the new list

The method begins by creating the new node and initializing its attributes. The new node is the new front of the list, so we know that its `forward` link should reference the current front of the list, and its `back` link should be `null`. An *if* statement guards the case when the addition occurs into an empty list (see Figure 6.8b). In that case, both the `list-First` and `listLast` instance variables must reference the new node, as it is both the first and last element of the list. Otherwise, the `back` link of the previous first element is set to reference the new element, along with the `listFirst` instance variable.

```
public void addFront (byte element)
// Adds the value of element to the beginning of this list
{
  DLLNode<Byte> newNode = new DLLNode<Byte>(element); // node being added
  newNode.setForward(listFirst);
  newNode.setBack(null);
  if (listFirst == null)    // Adding into an empty list
  {
    listFirst = newNode;  listLast = newNode;
  }
  else                    // Adding into a non-empty list
  {
    listFirst.setBack(newNode);
    listFirst = newNode;
  }
  numElements++;
}
```

The code for the `addEnd` method is similar (see Figure 6.8c):

```
public void addEnd (byte element)
// Adds the value of element to the end of this list
{
  DLLNode<Byte> newNode = new DLLNode<Byte>(element); // node being added
  newNode.setForward(null);
  newNode.setBack(listLast);
  if (listFirst == null)    // Adding into an empty list
  {
    listFirst = newNode;  listLast = newNode;
  }
  else                    // Adding into a non-empty list
  {
    listLast.setForward(newNode);
    listLast = newNode;
  }
  numElements++;
}
```

The LargeInt Class

We will use `LargeIntList` objects to hold the linked list of digits that form part of the internal representation of our Large Integers. Now we can concentrate on the rest of the definition of the class. In addition to digits, integers have a sign, which indicates whether they are positive or negative. We represent the sign of a large integer with a `boolean` instance variable `sign`. Furthermore, we define two `boolean` constants, PLUS = `true` and MINUS = `false`, to use with `sign`.

Here is the beginning of the class `LargeInt`. It includes the instance variables, two constructors, and the three methods `setNegative` (to make a large integer negative), `addDigit` (to build a large integer digit by digit), and `toString` (to provide a string representation of a large integer, complete with commas separating every three digits). We place it in the package `ch06.largeInts` along with `LargeIntList`.

```
//------------------------------------------------------------------------
// LargeInt.java            by Dale/Joyce/Weems            Chapter 6
//
// Provides a Large Integer ADT. Large integers can consist of any number
// of digits, plus a sign. Supports an add and a subtract operation.
//------------------------------------------------------------------------
package ch06.largeInts;

import java.util.Iterator;

public class LargeInt
{
  protected LargeIntList numbers;     // Holds digits

  // Constants for sign variable
  protected static final boolean PLUS = true;
  protected static final boolean MINUS = false;

  protected boolean sign;

  public LargeInt()
  // Instantiates an "empty" large integer.
  {
    numbers = new LargeIntList();
    sign = PLUS;
  }
```

```java
public LargeInt(String intString)
// Precondition: intString contains a well-formatted integer
//
// Instantiates a large integer as indicated by intString
{
  numbers = new LargeIntList();
  sign = PLUS;

  int firstDigitPosition;        // Position of first digit in intString
  int lastDigitPosition;         // Position of last digit in intString

  // Used to translate character to byte
  char digitChar;
  int digitInt;
  byte digitByte;

  firstDigitPosition = 0;
  if (intString.charAt(0) == '+')    //  Skip leading plus sign
    firstDigitPosition = 1;
  else
  if (intString.charAt(0) == '-')    // Handle leading minus sign
  {
    firstDigitPosition = 1;
    sign = MINUS;
  }

  lastDigitPosition = intString.length() - 1;

  for (int count = firstDigitPosition; count <= lastDigitPosition; count++)
  {
    digitChar = intString.charAt(count);
    digitInt = Character.digit(digitChar, 10);
    digitByte = (byte)digitInt;
    numbers.addEnd(digitByte);
  }
}

public void setNegative()
{
  sign = MINUS;
}
```

```
public String toString()
{
  Byte element;

  String largeIntString;
  if (sign == PLUS)
    largeIntString = "+";
  else
    largeIntString = "-";

  int count = numbers.size();
  Iterator<Byte> forward = numbers.forward();
  while (forward.hasNext())
  {
    element = forward.next();
    largeIntString = largeIntString + element;
    if ((((count - 1) % 3) == 0) && (count != 1))
      largeIntString = largeIntString + ",";
    count--;
  }
  return(largeIntString);
}
```

Note the many levels of abstraction used here with respect to our data. In a previous chapter we defined the doubly linked list node class DLLNode. That class was used above as part of the internal representation of the LargeIntList class, which in turn is being used here as part of the internal representation of the LargeInt class. Once we finish the creation of the LargeInt class we can use it within applications to manipulate large integers. The application uses LargeInt which uses LargeIntList which uses DLLNode which uses two references variables.

> **Important Concept Revisited: Abstraction Hierarchy**
>
> Here we see another example of an abstraction hierarchy. Applications use the LargeInt class, which uses the LargeIntList class, which uses the DLLNode class. When working at any level in this hierarchy as a programmer we need to know only how to use the next lower level – we do not need to know how it is implemented nor need we worry about the details of lower levels. Abstraction is indeed the key to conquering complexity.

Addition and Subtraction

Do you recall when you learned about addition of integers? Remember how special rules applied depending on what the signs of the operands were and which operand had the larger absolute value? For example, to perform the addition $(-312) + (+200)$, what steps would you take? Let us see: The numbers have unlike signs, so we subtract the smaller absolute value (200) from the larger absolute value (312), giving us 112, and use the sign of the larger absolute value (−), giving the final result of (−112). Try a few more additions:

$$(+200) + (+100) = ?$$
$$(-300) + (-134) = ?$$
$$(+34) + (-62) = ?$$
$$(-34) + (+62) = ?$$

Did you get the respective correct answers (+300, −434, −28, +28)?

Did you notice anything about the actual arithmetic operations that you had to perform to calculate the results of the summations listed above? You performed only two kinds of operations: adding two positive numbers and subtracting a smaller positive number from a larger positive number. That is it. In combination with rules about how to handle signs, these operations allow you to do all of your sums.

Helper Methods

In programming, as in mathematics, we also like to reuse common operations. Therefore, to support the addition operation, we first define a few helper operations. These base operations should apply to the absolute values of our numbers, which means we can ignore the `sign` for now. Which common operations do we need? Based on the preceding discussion, we need to be able to add together two lists of digits, and to subtract a smaller list from a larger list. That means we also have to be able to identify which of two lists of digits is larger. Thus we need three operations, which we call `addLists`, `subtractLists`, and `greaterList`.

Here we begin with `greaterList`. We pass `greaterList` two `LargeIntList` arguments; it returns `true` if the first argument represents a larger number than the second argument, and `false` otherwise. When comparing strings, we compare pairs of characters in corresponding positions from left to right. The first characters that do not match determine which number is greater. When comparing positive numbers, we have to compare the numbers digit by digit only if they are the same length. We first compare the lengths; if they are not the same, we return the appropriate result. If the number of digits is the same, we compare the digits from left to right. In the code, we originally set a `boolean` variable `greater` to `false`, and we change this setting if we discover that the first number is larger than the second number. In the end, we return the `boolean` value of `greater`.

```
protected static boolean greaterList(LargeIntList first,
                                      LargeIntList second)
// Precondition: first and second have no leading zeros
//
// Returns true if first represents a larger number than second;
// otherwise, returns false
```

```
{
  boolean greater = false;
  if (first.size() > second.size())
    greater = true;
  else
  if (first.size() < second.size())
    greater = false;
  else
  {
    byte digitFirst;
    byte digitSecond;
    Iterator<Byte> firstForward = first.forward();
    Iterator<Byte> secondForward = second.forward();

    // Set up loop
    int length = first.size();
    boolean keepChecking = true;
    int count = 1;

    while ((count <= length) && (keepChecking))
    {
      digitFirst = firstForward.next();
      digitSecond = secondForward.next();
      if (digitFirst > digitSecond)
      {
        greater = true;
        keepChecking = false;
      }
      else
      if (digitFirst < digitSecond)
      {
        greater = false;
        keepChecking = false;
      }
      count++;
    }
  }
  return greater;
}
```

If we exit the *while* loop without finding a difference, the numbers are equal and we return the original value of `greater`, which is `false` (because `first` is not greater than `second`). Because we blindly look at the lengths of the lists, we must assume that the numbers do not include leading zeros (e.g., the method would report that $005 > 14$). We make the `greaterList` method protected: Helper methods are not intended for use by the client programmer; they are intended for use only within the `LargeInt` class itself.

We look at `addLists` next. We pass `addLists` its two operands as `LargeIntList` parameters, and the method returns a new `LargeIntList` as the result. The processing for `addLists` can be simplified if we assume that the first argument is larger than the second argument. We already have access to a `greaterList` method, so we make this assumption.

We begin by adding the two least significant digits (the unit's position). Next, we add the digits in the 10s position (if present) plus the carry from the sum of the least significant digits (if any). This process continues until we finish with the digits of the smaller operand. For the remaining digits of the larger operand, we may need to propagate a carry, but we do not have to add digits from the smaller operand. Finally, if a carry value is left over, we create a new most significant location and place it there. We use integer division and modulus operators to determine the carry value and the value to insert into the result. The algorithm follows:

---

addLists (LargeIntList larger, LargeIntList smaller) returns LargeIntList

Set result to new LargeIntList();
Set carry to 0;
larger.resetBackward();
smaller.resetBackward();

for the length of the smaller list
    Set digit1 to larger.getPriorElement();
    Set digit2 to smaller.getPriorElement();
    Set temp to digit1 + digit2 + carry
    Set carry to temp/10
    result.addFront(temp % 10)
Finish up digits in larger, adding carries if necessary
if (carry != 0))
    result.addFront(carry)
return result

Apply the algorithm to the following examples to convince yourself that it works. The code follows.

322	388	399	999	3	1	988	0
44	108	1	11	44	99	100	0
- - -	- - -	- - -	- - -	- - -	- - -	- - -	- - -
366	496	400	1010	47	100	1088	0

```
protected static LargeIntList addLists(LargeIntList larger,
                                       LargeIntList smaller)
// Precondition: larger > smaller
//
// Returns a specialized list that is a byte-by-byte sum of the two
// argument lists
{
  byte digit1;
  byte digit2;
  byte temp;
  byte carry = 0;

  int largerLength = larger.size();
  int smallerLength = smaller.size();
  int lengthDiff;

  LargeIntList result = new LargeIntList();

  Iterator<Byte> largerReverse = larger.reverse();
  Iterator<Byte> smallerReverse = smaller.reverse();

  // Process both lists while both have digits
  for (int count = 1; count <= smallerLength; count++)
  {
    digit1 = largerReverse.next();
    digit2 = smallerReverse.next();
    temp = (byte)(digit1 + digit2 + carry);
    carry = (byte)(temp / 10);
    result.addFront((byte)(temp % 10));
  }

  // Finish processing of leftover digits
  lengthDiff = (largerLength - smallerLength);
  for (int count = 1; count <= lengthDiff; count++)
  {
    digit1 = largerReverse.next();
    temp = (byte)(digit1 + carry);
    carry = (byte)(temp / 10);
    result.addFront((byte)(temp % 10));
  }
  if (carry != 0)
    result.addFront((byte)carry);

  return result;
}
```

Now we examine the helper method subtractLists. Remember that we only need to handle the simplest case: Both integers are positive, and the smaller one is subtracted from the larger one. As with addLists, we accept two LargeIntList parameters, the first being larger than the second, and we return a new LargeIntList.

We begin with the pair of digits in the unit's position. Let us call the digit in the larger argument digit1 and the digit in the smaller argument digit2. If digit2 is less than digit1, we subtract and insert the resulting digit at the front of the result. If digit2 is greater than digit1, we borrow 10 and subtract. Then we access the digits in the 10s position. If we have borrowed, we subtract 1 from the new larger and proceed as before. Because we have limited our problem to the case where larger is larger than smaller, both either run out of digits together or larger still contains digits when smaller has been processed. This constraint guarantees that borrowing does not extend beyond the most significant digit of larger. See if you can follow the algorithm we just described in the code.

```
protected static LargeIntList subtractLists(LargeIntList larger,
                                             LargeIntList smaller)
// Precondition: larger >= smaller
//
// Returns a specialized list, the difference of the two argument lists
{
  byte digit1;
  byte digit2;
  byte temp;
  boolean borrow = false;

  int largerLength = larger.size();
  int smallerLength = smaller.size();
  int lengthDiff;

  LargeIntList result = new LargeIntList();

  Iterator<Byte> largerReverse = larger.reverse();
  Iterator<Byte> smallerReverse = smaller.reverse();

  // Process both lists while both have digits.
  for (int count = 1; count <= smallerLength; count++)
  {
    digit1 = largerReverse.next();
    if (borrow)
    {
      if (digit1 != 0)
      {
        digit1 = (byte)(digit1 - 1);
        borrow = false;
```

```
      }
      else
      {
        digit1 = 9;
        borrow = true;
      }
    }

    digit2 = smallerReverse.next();

    if (digit2 <= digit1)
      result.addFront((byte)(digit1 - digit2));
    else
    {
      borrow = true;
      result.addFront((byte)(digit1 + 10 - digit2));
    }
  }

  // Finish processing of leftover digits
  lengthDiff = (largerLength - smallerLength);
  for (int count = 1; count <= lengthDiff; count++)
  {
    digit1 = largerReverse.next();
    if (borrow)
    {
      if (digit1 != 0)
      {
        digit1 = (byte)(digit1 - 1);
        borrow = false;
      }
      else
      {
        digit1 = 9;
        borrow = true;
      }
    }
    result.addFront(digit1);
  }

  return result;
}
```

Addition

Now that we have finished the helper methods, we can turn our attention to the public methods provided to clients of the `LargeInt` class. First, we look at addition. Here are the rules for addition you learned when studying arithmetic:

Addition Rules

1. If both operands are positive, add the absolute values and make the result positive.
2. If both operands are negative, add the absolute values and make the result negative.
3. If one operand is negative and one operand is positive, subtract the smaller absolute value from the larger absolute value and give the result the sign of the larger absolute value.

We use these rules to help us design our `add` method. We can combine the first two rules as follows: "If the operands have the same sign, add the absolute values and make the sign of the result the same as the sign of the operands." Our code uses the appropriate helper method to generate the new list of digits and then sets the sign based on the rules. Remember that to use our helper methods we pass them the required arguments in the correct order (larger first). Here is the code for add:

```
public static LargeInt add(LargeInt first, LargeInt second)
// Returns a LargeInt that is the sum of the two argument LargeInts
{
  LargeInt sum = new LargeInt();

  if (first.sign == second.sign)
  {
    if (greaterList(first.numbers, second.numbers))
      sum.numbers = addLists(first.numbers, second.numbers);
    else
      sum.numbers = addLists(second.numbers, first.numbers);
    sum.sign = first.sign;
  }
  else    // Signs are different
  {
    if (greaterList(first.numbers, second.numbers))
    {
      sum.numbers = subtractLists(first.numbers, second.numbers);
      sum.sign = first.sign;
    }
    else
```

```
    {
      sum.numbers = subtractLists(second.numbers, first.numbers);
      sum.sign = second.sign;
    }
  }

  return sum;
}
```

The add method accepts two `LargeInt` objects and returns a new `LargeInt` object equal to their sum. Because it is passed both operands as parameters and returns the result explicitly, it is defined as a `static` method that is invoked through the class, rather than through an object. For example, the code

```
LargeInt LI1 = new LargeInt();
LargeInt LI2 = new LargeInt();
LargeInt LI3;
LI1.addDigit((byte)9);
LI1.addDigit((byte)9);
LI1.addDigit((byte)9);

LI2.addDigit((byte)9);
LI2.addDigit((byte)8);
LI2.addDigit((byte)7);

LI3 = LargeInt.add(LI1, LI2);
System.out.println("LI3 is " + LI3);
```

would result in the output of the string "LI3 is +1986."

Subtraction

Remember how subtraction seemed harder than addition when you were learning arithmetic? Not anymore! We need to use only one subtraction rule: "Change the sign of the subtrahend, and add." We do have to be careful about how we "change the sign of the subtrahend," because we do not want to change the sign of the actual argument passed to subtract—that would produce an unwanted side effect of our method. Therefore, we create a new `LargeInt` object, make it a copy of the second parameter, invert its sign, and then invoke add:

```
public static LargeInt subtract(LargeInt first, LargeInt second)
// Returns a LargeInt that is the difference of the two argument LargeInts
{
  LargeInt diff = new LargeInt();
```

```
  // Create an inverse of second
  LargeInt negSecond = new LargeInt();
  negSecond.sign = !second.sign;
  Iterator<Byte> secondForward = second.numbers.forward();
  int length = second.numbers.size();
  for (int count = 1; count <= length; count++)
    negSecond.numbers.addEnd(secondForward.next());

  // Add first to inverse of second
  diff = add(first, negSecond);

  return diff;
}
```

The LargeIntCLI Program

The `LargeIntCLI` program, in the `ch06.apps` package, allows the user to enter two large integers, performs the addition and subtraction of the two integers, and reports the results. Study the code below. You should be able to identify the statements that declare, instantiate and initialize, transform, and observe large integers.

```
//---------------------------------------------------------------------
// LargeIntCLI.java          by Dale/Joyce/Weems              Chapter 6
//
// Allows user to add or subtract large integers.
//---------------------------------------------------------------------
import java.util.Scanner;
import ch06.largeInts.LargeInt;

public class LargeIntCLI
{
  public static void main(String[] args)
  {
    Scanner scan = new Scanner(System.in);

    LargeInt first;
    LargeInt second;

    String intString;
    String more = null;     // used to stop or continue processing

    do
    {
      // Get large integers.
      System.out.println("Enter the first large integer: ");
      intString = scan.nextLine();
```

```
      first = new LargeInt(intString);

      System.out.println("Enter the second large integer: ");
      intString = scan.nextLine();
      second = new LargeInt(intString);
      System.out.println();

      // Perform and report the addition and subtraction.
      System.out.print("First number:   ");
      System.out.println(first);
      System.out.print("Second number: ");
      System.out.println(second);
      System.out.print("Sum:           ");
      System.out.println(LargeInt.add(first,second));
      System.out.print("Difference:    ");
      System.out.println(LargeInt.subtract(first,second));

      // Determine if there is more to process.
      System.out.println();
      System.out.print("Process another pair of numbers? (Y=Yes): ");
      more = scan.nextLine();
      System.out.println();
    }
  while (more.equalsIgnoreCase("y"));
  }
}
```

Here is the result of a sample run of the program:

```
Enter the first large integer:
15463663748473748374988477777777777777777
Enter the second large integer:
4536748465999347474948722222222222222223

First number:    +15,463,663,748,473,748,374,988,477,777,777,777,777,777
Second number:  +4,536,748,465,999,347,474,948,722,222,222,222,222,223
Sum:             +20,000,412,214,473,095,849,937,200,000,000,000,000,000
Difference:      +10,926,915,282,474,400,900,039,755,555,555,555,555,554
Process another pair of numbers? (Y=Yes): N
```

You are encouraged to try the program out for yourself. If you do, you may discover a few problem situations. These situations form the basis for some end-of-chapter exercises.

The GUI Approach: A Large Integer Calculator

The `LargeInt` class can also be used as the basis for an interactive large integer calculator. The interested reader can find the code for this calculator with the text files in the `ch06.apps` package. Here are some screenshots, to give you a feeling for the application. The user first sees this screen:

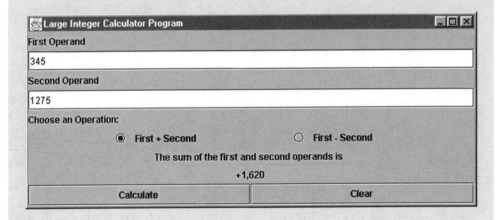

Here is the result of entering two operands, choosing addition, and clicking Calculate:

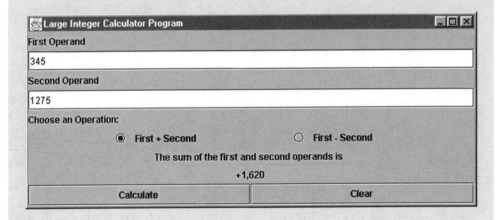

How about subtraction?

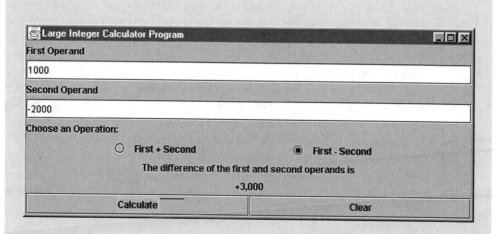

Wait a second; is that answer correct? Of course . . . remember that $1,000 - (-2,000) = 1,000 + 2,000$. We can look at an example using really big integers, which is the whole point of the Large Integer ADT:

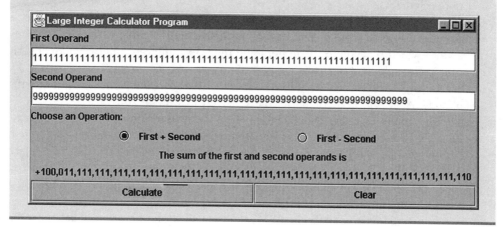

Summary

The List ADT is versatile and important. A list is a collection (providing add, remove, contains, and get operations) and supports indexed operations. A list is also iterable—to understand, design, and create list-related classes we studied iteration, and in particular the Java `Iterable` and `Iterator` interfaces. We learned how to use an anonymous inner class to create and return an `Iterator` object.

As has been our practice in previous chapters, we defined our List ADT as a Java interface and implemented it using both arrays and linked lists. Of special interest was the relatively complex task of supporting the iteration-related `remove` method for the linked list implementation—we tracked and used two extra reference variables, pointing into the linked list, during the iteration just to support this operation.

To demonstrate the utility of the List ADT we used it to create a `CardDeck` class. We also provided several examples of the use of `CardDeck`, some of which used additional list objects besides the deck itself.

Our sorted array-based list implementation provides the extra benefits to clients of keeping their data organized in "increasing" order. During the development of this implementation we learned how to indicate that an operation is not supported (throw the `UnsupportedOperationException`) since a sorted list cannot allow indexed-based add or set operations. We also learned how to use the `Comparator` interface so that clients of the class can indicate alternate ordering conditions in addition to the "natural ordering" of the elements.

In the variations section we briefly discussed the Java library list support and reviewed various kinds of linked lists. We even saw how to implement a linked list using an array—which really helps us understand there is a difference between an abstract concept such as "Linked List" and its internal representation, in this case an array. With this technique, the links are not references into the free store but rather indices into the array of nodes. This type of linking is used extensively in systems software.

The application presented at the end of the chapter designed a Large Integer ADT, for which the number of digits is bounded only by the size of memory. The Large Integer ADT required a specialized list for its implementation. Thus we created a new class `LargeIntegerList`. This case study provided a good example of how one ADT can be implemented with the aid of another ADT, emphasizing the importance of viewing systems as a hierarchy of abstractions.

Figure 6.9 is an abbreviated UML diagram showing the primary list-related classes and interfaces discussed or developed in this chapter. Note that the `Iterable`, `Comparable, and Comparator` interfaces shown in the diagram reside in the Java library. Everything else is found within the text's `bookfiles` folder.

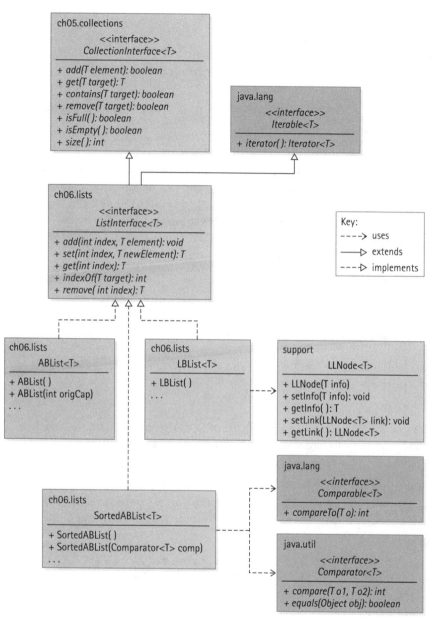

Figure 6.9   List-related classes and interfaces

Exercises

6.1 The List Interface

1. For each of the methods declared in `ListInterface` identify what type of operation it is (observer, transformer, or both).

2. How would you change `ListInterface` if we dropped our assumption that
    a. Lists are unbounded?
    b. Duplicate elements are not allowed on a list?

3. Suppose `indList` is a list that contains seven elements. Suppose `value` holds an element that is not already on the list. For each of the following method invocations, indicate whether they would result in the `IndexOutOfBoundsException` being thrown. Each part of this question is independent.
    a. `indList.add(6, value)`
    b. `indList.add(7, value)`
    c. `indList.add(8, value)`
    d. `indList.set(6, value)`
    e. `indList.set(7, value)`
    f. `indList.remove(value)`
    g. `indList.get(value)`
    h. `indList.remove(-1)`
    i. `indList.remove(0)`

4. Assume `strings` is an `Iterable` list of `String` objects. Using a *while* loop, list and iterator operations, create code with functionality equivalent to

    ```
    for (String hold: strings)
        System.out.println(hold);
    ```

5. Based on the definition of `ListInterface` and assuming `strings` is a `list` of `String` objects which has just been instantiated, show the output of:
    a.

    ```
    System.out.println(strings.isEmpty());
    System.out.println(strings.add("alpha"));
    strings.add("gamma");
    strings.add("delta");
    System.out.println(strings.add("alpha"));
    System.out.println(strings.remove("alpha"));
    System.out.println(strings.isEmpty());
    System.out.println(strings.get("delta"));
    System.out.println(strings.contains("delta"));
    System.out.println(strings.contains("beta"));
    System.out.println(strings.contains("alpha"));
    System.out.println(strings.size());
    ```

b.

```
strings.add(0,"alpha"));  strings.add(0,"gamma");
strings.add(1,"delta");   strings.add(1,"beta");
strings.add(1,"alpha");   strings.add(3,"omega");
strings.add(2,"pi");      strings.set(1,"comma");
strings.remove(3);
for (String hold: strings)
System.out.println(hold);
```

c.

```
strings.add(0,"alpha"));  strings.add(0,"gamma");
strings.add(1,"delta");   strings.add(1,"beta");
strings.add(1,"alpha");   strings.add(3,"omega");
strings.add(2,"pi");      strings.set(1,"comma");
Iterator<String> iter;    String temp;
while (iter.hasNext())
{
  temp = iter.next();
  if (temp.equals("alpha")) iter.remove();
}
for (String hold: strings)
              System.out.println(hold);
```

6.2 List Implementations

6. Describe/define/explain

   a. The relationship between Java's `Iterable` and `Iterator` interfaces

   b. An inner class

   c. An anonymous inner class

   d. The functionality of an `Iterator` `remove` method

7. Show the values contained in the instance variables of the `sample` list after each of the following sequences of operations.

   a.
   ```
   ABList<String> sample = new ABList<String>(5);
   sample.add("A"); sample.add("C"); sample.add("D");
   sample.add("A"); sample.contains("D"); sample.remove("C");
   ```

   b.
   ```
   ABList<String> sample = new ABList<String>(5);
   sample.add("A"); sample.add(0,"C"); sample.add(0,"D");
   sample.contains("E"); sample.remove(2); sample.set(1,"Z");
   sample.get("A"); sample.add(1,"Q");
   ```

   c.
   ```
   LBList<String> sample = new LBList<String>();
   sample.add("A"); sample.add("C"); sample.add("D");
   ```

```
sample.add("A"); sample.contains("D");
sample.remove("C");
```

d.

```
LBList<String> sample = new LBList<String>();
sample.add("A"); sample.add(0,"C"); sample.add(0,"D");
sample.contains("E"); sample.remove(2); sample.set(1,"Z");
sample.get("A"); sample.add(1,"Q");
```

8. Programming tasks:

a. Add a toString method to the ABList class that returns the contents of the list as a nicely formatted string. You should then use the toString method, as appropriate, in the rest of this exercise.

b. Create an application TestBasic that demonstrates that the "basic" list operations (add, remove, contains, get, and size) supported by ABList work as expected.

c. Create an application TestIndexed that demonstrates that the index-related list operations supported by ABList work as expected.

d. Create an application TestIterator that demonstrates that the iterator-related list operations supported by ABList work as expected.

9. Repeat the previous exercise except for the LBList class.

10. Describe the ramifications of each of the following changes to ABList:

a. The final statement in the enlarge method is deleted.

b. In the first statement in the indexed add method change ">" to ">=".

c. In the first statement in the set method, change ">=" to ">".

d. The statements T hold = elements[index]; and elements[index] = newElement; are reversed in the set method.

e. In the indexed remove method the −1 is deleted from the *for* loop termination condition.

f. In the iterator code the previousPos variable is initialized to 0 instead of −1.

g. In the iterator code, the final statement is deleted from the remove method.

11. Consider the indexed operation: removeAll(T target, int start, int end)—removes all elements from the list that are equal to target that are held in between index start and index end.

a. The removeAll method is not well specified. Carefully define your detailed vision for removeAll including preconditions and exceptions that will be thrown.

b. Implement removeAll for the ABList class and create a driver application that demonstrates it works correctly.

c. Implement removeAll for the LBList class and create a driver application that demonstrates it works correctly.

12. Describe the "special cases" specifically addressed by each of the following methods and how they are handled—for example, adding an element to an empty list is a "special case."

    a. The `ABList` add method

    b. The `ABList` set method

    c. The `LBList` indexed add method

    d. The `LBList` indexed remove method

    e. The `LBList` iterator remove method

13. Fill in the following table with the order of growth of the indicated operations for the given implementation approach—assume the list holds N elements:

operation	ABList	LBList
add		
get		
contains		
remove		
isEmpty		
indexed add		
indexed set		
indexOf		
indexed get		
iterator next		
iterator remove		

6.3 Applications: Card Deck and Games

14. Application: This chapter specifies and implements a List ADT.

    a. Design an algorithm for an application-level method `last` that accepts a `String` list as an argument and returns a `String`. If the list is empty, the method returns `null`. Otherwise, it returns the last element of the list. The signature for the method should be

    `String last(ListInterface<String> list)`

    b. Devise a test plan for your algorithm.

    c. Implement and test your algorithm.

15. Application: This chapter specifies and implements a List ADT.

    a. Design an algorithm for an application-level method `compare` that accepts two `String` lists as arguments and returns an `int` representing a count of the number of elements from the first list that are also on the second list. The signature for the method should be

    ```
    int compare(ListInterface<String> list1,
                ListInterface<String> list2)
    ```

    b. Devise a test plan for your algorithm.

    c. Implement and test your algorithm.

16. The `Card` Class developed in this section uses the Java enum type to help model a standard playing card. Describe two other useful models that could be created with the help of enum.

17. When you play cards you normally shuffle the deck several times before dealing. Yet the shuffling algorithm used in our `CardDeck` class "walks" through the deck of cards only once. Explain the difference between these two situations.

18. Describe the effects each of the following changes would have on the `CardDeck` class:

    a. In place of using the `ABList` class it uses the `LBList` class.

    b. The `NUMCARDS` constant is initialized to 100.

    c. Within the constructor the order of the double *for loop* is reversed—that is the ranks are the outer loop and the suits are the inner loop.

    d. Within the `shuffle` method the loop termination condition is changed to `i >= 0`.

19. Add the following methods to the `CardDeck` class, and create a test driver for each to show that they work correctly.

    a. `int cardsRemaining()` returns a count of the number of undealt cards remaining in the deck.

    b. `Card peek()` returns the next card from the deck without removing it—precondition is that `hasNext` returns `true`.

    c. `void reset()` resets the deck back to its original order, that is, to the order exhibited by a new deck.

20. The `CardHandCLI` application allows the user to "arrange" a hand of five cards. However, some poker games use seven cards per hand and in a game such as bridge there are 13 cards per hand. Change the `CardHandCLI` application so that the number of cards in the hand is passed to the application as a command line argument.

21. The following enhancements to the `HigherLower` application are intended to be completed in the sequence listed:

    a. It accepts upper- or lowercase H and L replies from the user.

    b. It repeatedly deals a hand until there are no more cards left in the deck.

    c. The user starts with a "stake" of 100 chips. After seeing the first card the user can risk from one to their total number of chips. If the user predicts correctly their number of chips is increased by the number of chips they risked; if they are incorrect it is decreased by that amount. The game ends when all the cards are dealt or when they run out of chips.

    d. If the second card is equal to the first card the user "loses" double their risk.

22. Implement a graphical user interface-based version of the Higher-Lower application.

23. In-Between is a well-known card game. Many variations exist—we define it as follows. One deck of cards is used. A game consists of one or more "hands." A player starts with a certain number of chips called the "stake" (say 100) and must risk one or more chips on each hand, before seeing any cards. As long as the player still has chips and there are three or more cards left in the deck (enough to play a hand), the game continues. For each hand the player must risk between one and their total number of chips. Two cards are dealt "face up." Then a third card is dealt. If the third card is "in-between" the first two cards, based on the ranks of the cards, the player's chips are increased by the amount risked. Otherwise they are decreased by that amount.

    a. Implement the game. The application user is the "player."

    b. If the first two cards dealt are the same rank, that hand is over and the player is awarded two chips.

    c. Allow the player at his or her discretion to double the risk after seeing the first two cards.

24. Implement a graphical user interface–based version of the In-Between game (see previous exercise).

25. Similar to Exercise 20, change the `Pairs` application so that the number of cards in a hand is passed to the application as a command line argument. Use the new program to investigate the probability of getting at least a pair in a seven-card poker hand. Calculate the theoretical probability of the same (or have your program do it for you!), using the approach described in this section, and compare it to the output of your program. Is it close?

26. In a "hand" of bridge a deck of cards is dealt to four players, each receiving 13 cards. The players then proceed to bid on who will get to play the hand—player's bid partially based on how highly he or she evaluates their hand and partially based on what their opponents and their partner bid. There are many different ways to evaluate a bridge hand, including various point counting systems. A simple point counting system is as follows: count each ace as 4 points, each king as 3 points, each queen as 2 points, and each jack as 1 point. Then add 1 additional point for each suit in which you have five cards, 2 points for a six-card suit, 3 points for a seven-card suit, and so on. For example, if your hand consists of the ace, queen, five, four, and three of clubs, the jack of diamonds, and the ace, king, queen, jack, ten, nine, and two of spades, your hand's point value would be 21 points.

a. Create an application `BridgeHand` that allows a user to arrange a hand of 13 cards, much like the `CardHand` application. The program then prompts the user to enter the point value of the hand, using the counting approach described. Finally, the program reads in the user's response and provides appropriate feedback ("Correct" or "Incorrect, the actual point value is . . .").

b. Create an application `HandsCounts` that generates 1,000,000 bridge hands and outputs the smallest, largest, and average point value, using the counting approach described above.

c. Expand `HandsCounts` so that when finished it also prints out one hand with the smallest point value and one hand with the highest point value.

6.4 Sorted Array-Based List Implementation

27. For each of the following lists describe several useful ways they might be sorted:

a. Books

b. University course descriptions

c. Professional golfer information

d. Summer camper registration information

28. Create an application (that uses the `SortedABList`) that reads a list of strings from a file and outputs them in alphabetical order.

29. Create an application (that uses the `SortedABList`) that allows a user to enter a list of countries that he or she has visited and then displays the list in alphabetical order, plus a count of how many countries are on the list. If the user mistakenly enters the same country more than once, the program should inform the user of their error and refrain from inserting the country into the list a second time.

30. Currently the `FamousPerson` class defines the natural order of its elements to be based on the alphabetical order of people names (last name, then first name). It also provides a `Comparator` that defines order based on increasing year of birth. Augment the class to include more `public static` methods that return Comparators as described below. Augment the `CSPeople` application to demonstrate that the new Comparators work properly.

a. Order alphabetically by name (first name, then last name)

b. Order by year of birth—decreasing

c. Order by length of "fact"—increasing

31. Fill in the following table with the order of growth of the indicated operations for the given implementation approach. Assume the list holds *N* elements (partial repeat of Exercise 13):

operation	ABList	LBList	SortedABList
add			
get			
contains			
remove			
isEmpty			
indexed add			
indexed set			
indexOf			
indexed get			
iterator next			
iterator remove			

32. A bridge hand consists of 13 playing cards. Many bridge players arrange their hands left to right first by decreasing suit (spades, hearts, diamonds, clubs) and within each suit by decreasing rank (ace through 2). Add a method `bridgeComparator` to the `Card` class of the `support` package that returns a `Comparator<Card>` object that can be used to sort cards in this fashion. Demonstrate by creating an application that instantiates a deck of cards, deals four bridge hands, and then displays the hands side by side, for example the output might start with something such as:

```
Ace of Spades      Ace of Hearts     Jack of Hearts     Ace of Diamonds
Queen of Hearts    Ace of Clubs      Ten of Clubs       King of Clubs
Queen of Clubs     King of Spades    Nine of Diamonds   Ten of Hearts
  . . .              . . .             . . .              . . .
```

33. These applications should create random five card poker hands using the `CardDeck` class. You may find that sorting the hand in various ways aids in the determination of the hand rank.

  a. `PokerValue` should generate a single five-card poker hand and output the best rank associated with the hand—is it a "three of a kind" or a "straight flush," and so forth? Hand ranks are listed from best to worst on page 370.

  b. `PokerOdds` should generate 10 million five-card poker hands and output the relative percentage of times each of the card ranks listed on page 370 occurs. Each hand contributes only to the count of its highest possible rank. Do some research and compare your result to the known probabilities for poker hands.

6.5 List Variations

34. John and Mary are programmers for the local school district. One morning John commented to Mary about the interesting last name the new family in the district had: "Have you ever heard of a family named ZZuan?" Mary replied "Uh, oh; we have some work to do. Let's get going." Can you explain Mary's response?

35. Assume you implemented our Sorted List ADT using the Linked List as an Array of Nodes approach described in this section. Assume the size of the array is N. What is the order of growth for the efficiency of initializing the free list? For the methods `getNode` and `freeNode`?

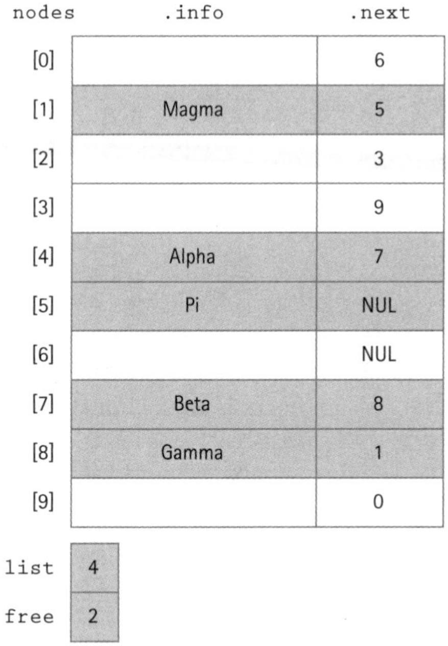

nodes	.info	.next
[0]		6
[1]	Magma	5
[2]		3
[3]		9
[4]	Alpha	7
[5]	Pi	NUL
[6]		NUL
[7]	Beta	8
[8]	Gamma	1
[9]		0

list	4
free	2

Figure 6.10 Linked list as an array of nodes

36. Use the linked lists contained in the array pictured in **Figure 6.10** to answer these questions. Each question is to be considered independently of the other questions.

  a. What is the order in which array positions (indices) appear on the free space list?

  b. Draw a figure that represents the array after the addition of "delta" to the list.

  c. Draw a figure that represents the array after the removal of "gamma" from the list.

37. Implement our List ADT using the Linked List as an Array of Nodes approach described in this section. Also implement a test driver application that demonstrates that your implementation works correctly.

6.6 Application: Large Integers

38. True or False? Explain your answers. The `LargeIntList` class

   a. Uses the "by copy" approach with its elements.

   b. Implements the `ListInterface` interface.

   c. Keeps its data elements sorted.

   d. Allows duplicate elements.

   e. Uses the `LLNode` class of the `support` package.

   f. Throws an exception if an iteration "walks off" the end of the list.

   g. Throws an exception if an element is added when it is "full."

   h. Supports addition of elements at the front of the list, the end of the list, and anywhere in between.

   i. Can hold objects of any Java class.

   j. Has only O(1) operations, including its constructor.

   k. Provides more than one `Iterator`.

39. Discuss the changes that would be necessary within the `LargeInt` class if more than one digit is stored per node.

40. The Large Integer Application does not "catch" ill-formatted input. For example, consider the following program run:

```
Enter the first large integer:
twenty

Enter the second large integer:
two

First number:    +-1-1-1,-1-1-1
Second number:  +-1-1-1
Sum:        +-1-1-1,-2-2-2
Difference:      +-1-1-1,000

Process another pair of numbers? (Y=Yes): n
```

Fix the program so that it is more robust, and so that in situations such as that shown above it writes an appropriate error message to the display.

41. Consider the multiplication of large integers.

   a. Describe an algorithm.

   b. Implement a multiply method for the `LargeInt` class.

   c. Add multiplication to the Large Integer Application.

42. The protected method `greaterList` of the `LargeInt` class assumes that its arguments have no leading zeros. When this assumption is violated, strange results can occur. Consider the following run of the Large Integer Application that claims $35 - 3$ is -968:

```
Enter the first large integer:
35

Enter the second large integer:
003
First number:    +35
Second number: +003
Sum:       +038
Difference:     -968

Process another pair of numbers? (Y=Yes): n
```

a. Why do leading zeros cause a problem?

b. Identify at least two approaches to correcting this problem.

c. Describe the benefits and drawbacks of each of your identified approaches.

d. Choose one of your approaches and implement the solution.

The Binary Search Tree ADT

Knowledge Goals

You should be able to

- define and use the following tree terminology:

  - tree
  - binary tree
  - binary search tree
  - root
  - parent

  - child
  - sibling
  - leaf
  - interior node
  - subtree

  - ancestor
  - descendant
  - level
  - height

- given a tree, identify the order the nodes would be visited for breadth-first and depth-first traversals
- given a binary tree, identify the order the nodes would be visited for preorder, inorder, and postorder traversals
- discuss the order of growth efficiency of a given binary search tree operation implementation
- describe an algorithm for balancing a binary search tree
- describe these tree variations: decision trees, expression trees, R-trees, tries, B-trees, AVL trees
- given a problem description, determine whether a binary search tree is an appropriate structure to help solve the problem

Skill Goals

You should be able to

- answer questions related to a given tree, such as which nodes are descendants of a given node
- show how a binary search tree would be structured after a series of insertions and removals
- implement the following binary search tree algorithms in Java:

  - find an element
  - count the number of nodes
  - add an element

  - remove an element
  - retrieve an element
  - traverse a tree in preorder, inorder, and postorder

- use a binary search tree as a component of a problem solution

Chapter 5 introduced the Collection ADT with core operations *add, remove, get,* and *contains.* Chapter 6 presented the List ADT—a list is a collection that also supports *iteration* and *indexing.* In this chapter we present another variation of a collection. The distinguishing features of a binary search tree are that it maintains its elements in *increasing* order and it provides, in the general case, *efficient* implementations of *all* the core operations. How can it do this?

The binary search tree can be understood by comparing a sorted linked list to a sorted array:

Consider the steps needed to add the value 985 to each of these structures. For the linked list we must perform a linear search of the structure in order to find the point of insertion. That is an O(N) operation. However, once the insertion point is discovered, we can add the new value by creating a new node and rearranging a few references, an O(1) operation. On the other hand, the sorted array supports the binary search algorithm (see Sections 1.6 and 3.3, "Comparing Algorithms: Order of Growth Analysis" and "Recursive Processing of Arrays") allowing us to quickly find the point of insertion, an O($\log_2 N$) operation. Even though we quickly find the insertion point we still need to shift all the elements "to the right" of the location one index higher in the array, an O(N) operation. In summation, the linked list exhibits a slow find but a fast insertion, whereas the array is the opposite, a fast find but a slow insertion.

Can we combine the fast search of the array with the fast insertion of the linked list? The answer is yes!—with a binary search tree. A binary search tree is a linked structure that allows for quick insertion (or removal) of elements. But instead of one link per node it uses two links per node as shown below on the right where we display the sorted list 5, 8, 12, 20, and 27 as a binary search tree, along with equivalent array and linked list representations.

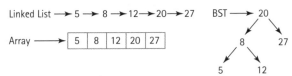

As you will see in this chapter, the availability of two links allows us to embed a binary search within the linked structure, thus combining fast binary search with fast node insertion—the best of both worlds. The binary search tree provides us with a data structure that retains the flexibility of a linked list while allowing quicker [O($\log_2 N$) in the general case] access to any node in the list.

A binary search tree is a special case of a more general data structure, the tree. Many variations of the tree structure exist. We begin this chapter with an overview of tree terminology and briefly discuss general tree implementation strategies and applications. We then concentrate on the design and use of a binary search tree.

7.1 Trees

Each node in a singly linked list may point to one other node: the one that follows it. Thus, a singly linked list is a *linear* structure; each node in the list (except the last) has a unique successor. A **tree** is a *nonlinear* structure in which each node is capable of having multiple successor nodes, called **children**. Each of the children, being nodes in a tree, can also have multiple child nodes, and these children can in turn have many children, and so on, giving the tree its branching structure. The "beginning" of the tree is a unique starting node called the **root**.

Trees are useful for representing lots of varied relationships. **Figure 7.1** shows four example trees. The first represents the hierarchical inheritance relationship among a set of Java classes, the second shows a naturally occurring tree—a tree of

> **Tree Definitions**
>
> The many definitions related to trees presented in this subsection are collected in Figure 7.3 at the end of the subsection and can also be found in the glossary.

cellular organisms, the third is a game tree used to analyze choices in a turn-taking game, and the fourth shows how a simply connected maze (no loops) can be represented as a tree.

Trees are recursive structures. We can view any tree node as being the root of its own tree; such a tree is called a **subtree** of the original tree. For example, in Figure 7.1a the node labeled "Abstract List" is the root of a subtree containing all of the Java list-related classes.

There is one more defining quality of a tree—a tree's subtrees are disjoint; that is, they do not share any nodes. Another way of expressing this property is to say that there is a unique path from the root of a tree to any other node of the tree. In the structure below these rules are violated. The subtrees of A are not disjoint as they both contain the node D; there are two paths from the root to the node containing D. Therefore, this structure is not a tree.

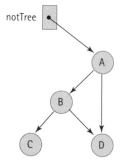

As you can already see, our tree terminology borrows from both genealogy; for example, we speak of "child" nodes, and from botany, for example, we have the "root" node. Computer scientists tend to switch back and forth between these two terminological models seamlessly. Let us expand our tree vocabulary using the tree of characters in **Figure 7.2** as an example.

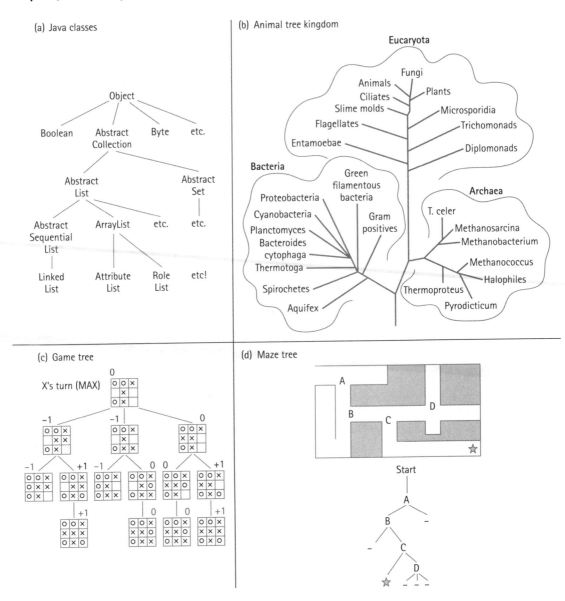

Figure 7.1   Example trees

The root of the tree is A (from the botany point of view we usually draw our trees up-side down!). The children of A are B, F, and X. Since they are A's children it is only natural to say that A is their **parent**. We also say that B, F, and X are **siblings**. Continuing with the genealogical trend, we can speak of a node's **descendants** (the children of a node, and their children, and so on recursively) and the **ancestors** of a node (the parent of the node, and their parent, and so on recursively). In our example, the descendants of X are H, Q, Z,

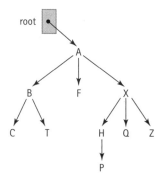

Figure 7.2   Sample tree

Ancestor   A parent of a node, or a parent of an ancestor

Children   The successors of a node are its children

Descendant   A child of a node, or a child of a descendant

Height   The maximum level of the tree

Interior node   A node that is not a leaf

Leaf   A node that has no children

Level   The level of a node is its distance from the root (the number of connections between itself and the root)

Parent   A node's unique predecessor is its parent

Root   The top node of the tree structure; a node with no parent

Siblings   Nodes with the same parent

Subtree   A node and all of its descendants form a subtree rooted at the node

Tree   A structure with a unique starting node (the root), in which each node is capable of having multiple child nodes, and in which a unique path exists from the root to every other node

---

Figure 7.3   Tree terminology

and P, and the ancestors of P are H, X, and A. Obviously, the root of the tree is the ancestor of every other node in the tree, but the root node has no ancestors itself.

A node can have many children but only a single parent. In fact, every node (except the root) must have a single parent. This is a consequence of the "all subtrees of a node are disjoint" rule—you can see that in the "not a tree" example on page 423 that D has two parents.

If a node in the tree has no children, it is called a **leaf**. In our example tree in Figure 7.2 the nodes C, T, F, P, Q, and Z are leaf nodes. Sometimes we refer to the nonleaf nodes as **interior nodes**. The interior nodes in our example are A, B, X, and H.

The **level** of a node refers to its distance from the root. In Figure 7.2, the level of the node containing A (the root node) is 0 (zero), the level of the nodes containing B, F, and X is 1, the level of the nodes containing C, T, H, Q, and Z is 2, and the level of the node containing P is 3. The maximum level in a tree determines its **height** so our example tree has a height of 3. The height is equal to the highest number of links between the root and a leaf.

Tree Traversals

To traverse a linear linked list, we set a temporary reference to the beginning of the list and then follow the list references from one node to the other, until reaching a node whose reference value is `null`. Similarly, to traverse a tree, we initialize our temporaryreference to the root of the tree. But where do we go from there? There are as many choices as there are children of the node being visited.

Breadth-First Traversal

Let us look at two important related approaches to traversing a general tree structure: breadth-first and depth-first. We think of the breadth of a tree as being from side-to-side and the depth of a tree as being from top-to-bottom. Accordingly, in a **breadth-first traversal** we first visit the root of the tree.[1] Next we visit, in turn, the children of the root (typically from leftmost to rightmost), followed by visiting the children of the children of the root and so on until all of the nodes have been visited. Because we sweep across the breadth of the tree, level by level, this is also sometimes called a **level-order traversal.**

Figure 7.4a shows that in a breadth-first traversal of our sample tree the order the nodes are visited is A B F X C T H Q Z P. But, how can we implement this traversal? As part of visiting a node of the tree we must store references to its children so that we can visit them later in the traversal. In our example, when visiting node A, we need to store references to nodes B, F, and X. When we next visit node B we need to store references to

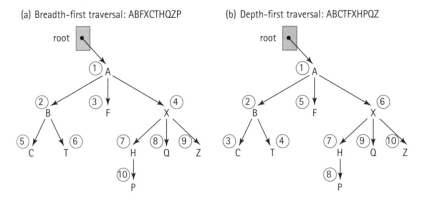

(a) Breadth-first traversal: ABFXCTHQZP   (b) Depth-first traversal: ABCTFXHPQZ

Figure 7.4   Tree Traversals

---

[1] When we say "visit" we mean that the algorithm does whatever it needs to do with the values in the node: print them, sum certain values, or change them for example.

nodes C and T—but they must be stored "behind" the previously stored F and X nodes so that nodes are visited in the desired order. What ADT supports this first in, first out (FIFO) approach? The Queue ADT. Here is a breadth-first traversal algorithm:

Breadth-First Traversal(root)

```
Instantiate a queue of nodes
if (root is not null)
{
    queue.enqueue(root)
    while (!queue.isEmpty())
    {
        node = queue.dequeue()
        Visit node;
        Enqueue the children of node (from left to right) into queue
    }
}
```

The Breadth-First Traversal algorithm begins by making sure the tree is not empty—if it is, no processing occurs. It is almost always a good idea to check for the degenerate case of an empty tree like this at the start of tree processing. Once it is determined that the tree is not empty, the algorithm enqueues the root node of the tree. We could just visit the root node at this point, but by enqueuing it, we set up the queue for the processing loop that follows. That loop repeatedly pulls a node off the queue, visits it, and then enqueues its children, until it runs out of nodes to process—that is, until the queue is empty.

Table 7.1 shows a trace of the algorithm on the sample tree of Figure 7.2. Trace the algorithm yourself and verify the contents of the table.

Traversal of our collection structures are needed in case we must visit every node in the structure to perform some processing. Suppose, for example, we had a tree of bank account information and wanted to sum all the amounts of all the accounts. A breadth-first traversal of the tree in order to retrieve all the account information is as good as any other traversal approach in this situation.

Besides allowing us to visit every node, for certain applications the breadth-first approach can provide additional benefits. For example, if our tree represents choices in a game (see Figure 7.1c) a breadth-first approach could provide a fast way to determine our next move. It amounts to looking at all possible next moves, and if desired all possible responses, and so on one level at a time. The point is we can avoid getting stuck traveling deeply down a tree path that represents a never-ending sequence of moves if we use breadth-first search. Using trees to represent sequences of alternatives and their ramifications, such as those found in a game, and traversing such trees using the breadth-first search to make a good choice among the alternatives, is a common artificial intelligence technique.

Table 7.1 Breadth-First Search Algorithm Trace

After Loop Iteration	Node	Visited So Far	Queue
0			A
1	A	A	B F X
2	B	A B	F X C T
3	F	A B F	X C T
4	X	A B F X	C T H Q Z
5	C	A B F X C	T H Q Z
6	T	A B F X C T	H Q Z
7	H	A B F X C T H	Q Z P
8	Q	A B F X C T H Q	Z P
9	Z	A B F X C T H Q Z	P
10	P	A B F X C T H Q Z P	null

Depth-First Traversal

A **depth-first traversal**, as might be expected, is the counterpart of the breadth-first traversal. Rather than visiting the tree level by level, expanding gradually away from the root, with a depth-first traversal we move quickly away from the root, traversing as far as possible along the leftmost path, until reaching a leaf, and then "backing up" as little as needed before traversing again down to a leaf. A depth-first traversal of a maze tree (see Figure 7.1d) represents going as far as possible down one corridor of the maze before backing up a little and trying another path—this might be a good approach if we need to escape the maze as soon as possible and are willing to gamble on being lucky, as opposed to a breadth-first approach that is almost guaranteed to take a long time unless we are already very close to an exit.

Figure 7.4b shows the order in which we visit nodes with a depth-first traversal of our sample tree: A B C T F X H P Q Z.

The algorithm is similar to that of the breadth-first traversal. Again, as part of visiting a node of the tree, we must store references to its children so that they can be visited later in the traversal. In our example, when visiting node A, we again need to store references to nodes B, F, and X. Upon visiting node B we need to store references to nodes C and T— but they must be stored "ahead of" the previously stored F and X nodes so that nodes are visited in the desired order. What ADT supports this last in, first out (LIFO) approach? The Stack ADT. When pushing the children of a node onto the stack we will do so from "right to left" so that they are removed from the stack in the desired "left to right" order. Here is a depth-first traversal algorithm:

Depth-First Traversal(root)

```
Instantiate a stack of nodes
if (root is not null)
{
    stack.push(root)
    while (!stack.isEmpty())
    {
        node = stack.top()
        stack.pop()
        Visit node;
        Push the children of node (from right to left) onto stack
    }
}
```

Tracing the algorithm on our sample tree is left as an exercise.

When we study graphs in Chapter 10 we will again use a queue to support a breadth-first traversal and a stack to support a depth-first traversal.

7.2 Binary Search Trees

As demonstrated in Figure 7.1, trees are very expressive structures, used to represent lots of different kinds of relationships. In this chapter, we concentrate on a particular form of tree: the binary tree. In fact, we concentrate on a particular type of binary tree: the binary search tree. The binary search tree provides an efficient implementation of a sorted collection.

Binary Trees

A **binary tree** is a tree where each node is capable of having at most two children. **Figure 7.5** depicts a binary tree. The root node of this binary tree contains the value A. Each node in the tree may have zero, one, or two children. The node to the left of a node, if it exists, is called its left child. For instance, the left child of the root node of our example tree contains the value B. The node to the right of a node, if it exists, is its right child. The right child of the root node contains the value C.

In Figure 7.5, each of the root node's children is itself the root of a smaller binary tree, or subtree. The root node's left child, containing B, is the root of its left subtree, whereas the right child, containing C, is the root of its right subtree. In fact, any node in the tree can be considered the root node of a binary subtree. The subtree whose root node has the value B also includes the nodes with values D, G, H, and E.

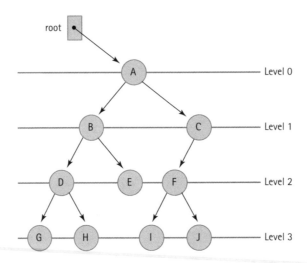

Figure 7.5 A binary tree

Our general tree terminology also applies to binary trees. The level of a node refers to its distance from the root. In Figure 7.5, the level of the node containing A (the root node) is 0 (zero), the level of the nodes containing B and C is 1, the level of the nodes containing D, E, and F is 2, and the level of the nodes containing G, H, I, and J is 3. The maximum level in a tree determines its height.

For a binary tree the maximum number of nodes at any level N is 2^N. Often, however, levels do not contain the maximum number of nodes. For instance, in Figure 7.5, level 2 could contain four nodes, but because the node containing C in level 1 has only one child, level 2 contains only three nodes. Level 3, which could contain eight nodes, has only four. We could make many differently shaped binary trees out of the 10 nodes in this tree. A few variations are illustrated in **Figure 7.6**. It is easy to see that the maximum number of levels in a binary tree with N nodes is N (counting level 0 as one of the levels). But what is the minimum number of levels? If we fill the tree by giving every node in each level two children until running out of nodes, the tree has $\lfloor \log_2 N \rfloor + 1$ levels (Figure 7.6a).[2] Demonstrate this fact to yourself by drawing "full" trees with 8 and 16 nodes. What if there are 7, 12, or 18 nodes?

The height of a tree is the critical factor in determining the efficiency of searching for elements. Consider the maximum-height tree shown in Figure 7.6c. If we begin searching at the root node and follow the references from one node to the next, accessing the node with the value J (the farthest from the root) is an $O(N)$ operation—no better than searching a linear list! Conversely, given the minimum-height tree depicted in Figure 7.6a, to access the node containing J, we have to look at only three other nodes—the ones containing E, A, and G—before finding J. Thus, if the tree is of minimum height, its structure supports $O(\log_2 N)$ access to any element.

---

[2] $\lfloor \log_2 N \rfloor$ says to apply the mathematical floor function ("rounding down") to the value of $\log_2 N$.

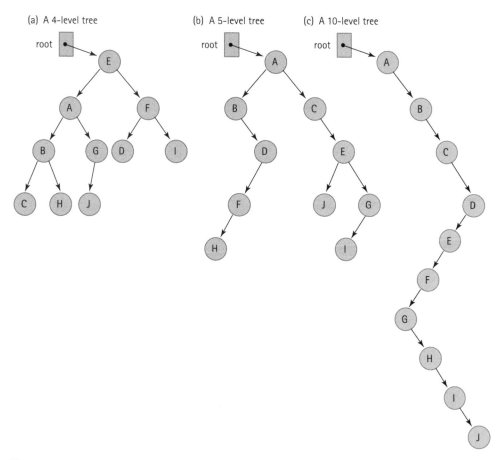

(a) A 4-level tree   (b) A 5-level tree   (c) A 10-level tree

Figure 7.6   Binary trees

The arrangement of the values in the tree pictured in **Figure 7.6a**, however, does not lend itself to quick searching. Suppose we want to find the value G. We begin searching at the root of the tree. This node contains E, not G, so the search continues. But which of its children should be inspected next, the right or the left? There is no special order to the nodes, so both subtrees must be checked. We could use a breadth-first search, searching the tree level by level, until coming across the value we are searching for. But that is an $O(N)$ search operation, which is no more efficient than searching a linear linked list.

Binary Search Trees

To support $O(\log_2 N)$ searching, we add a special property to our binary tree, the binary search property, based on the relationship among the values of its elements. We put all of the nodes with values smaller than or equal to the value in the root into its left subtree, and all of the nodes with values larger than the value in the root into its right subtree.

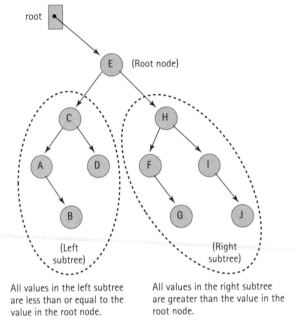

Figure 7.7 A binary search tree

Figure 7.7 shows the nodes from Figure 7.6a rearranged to satisfy this property. The root node, which contains E, references two subtrees. The left subtree contains all values smaller than or equal to E, and the right subtree contains all values larger than E.

When searching for the value G, we look first in the root node. G is larger than E, so G must be in the root node's right subtree. The right child of the root node contains H. Now what? Do we go to the right or to the left? This subtree is also arranged according to the binary search property: The nodes with smaller or equal values are to the left and the nodes with larger values are to the right. The value of this node, H, is greater than G, so we search to its left. The left child of this node contains the value F, which is smaller than G, so we reapply the rule and move to the right. The node to the right contains G—success.

A binary tree with the binary search property is called a **binary search tree**. As with any binary tree, it gets its branching structure by allowing each node to have a maximum of two child nodes. It gets its easy-to-search structure by maintaining the binary search property: The left child of any node (if one exists) is the root of a subtree that contains only values smaller than or equal to the node. The right child of any node (if one exists) is the root of a subtree that contains only values that are larger than the node.

> **External/Internal Views**
>
> We simplify most of our figures in this chapter by restricting them to our internal viewpoint, showing the reference to the root of the tree and the contents of the tree nodes. Do not forget that from the point of view of the client, the tree is wrapped in an object. Figure 7.9 shows both the external view (the client variable `example`) and the internal view.

Four comparisons instead of a maximum of ten does not sound like such a big deal, but as the number of elements in the structure increases, the difference becomes impressive. In the worst case—searching for the last node in a linear linked list—we must look at every node in the list; on average, we must search half of the list. If the list contains 1,000 nodes, it takes 1,000 comparisons to find the last node. If the 1,000 nodes were arranged in a binary search tree of minimum height, it takes no more than 10 comparisons— $\lfloor \log_2 1000 \rfloor + 1 = 10$—no matter which node we were seeking.

Binary Tree Traversals

We discussed two well-known traversal approaches for the general tree structure, the breadth-first and depth-first traversals. Due to the special structure of binary trees, where each node has a left subtree and a right subtree, there are additional traversal orders available for binary trees. Three common ones are defined in this subsection.

Our traversal definitions depend on the relative order in which we visit a root and its subtrees. Here are three possibilities:

1. **Preorder traversal.** Visit the root, visit the left subtree, visit the right subtree
2. **Inorder traversal.** Visit the left subtree, visit the root, visit the right subtree
3. **Postorder traversal.** Visit the left subtree, visit the right subtree, visit the root

The name given to each traversal specifies where the root itself is processed in relation to its subtrees. You might note that these definitions are recursive—we define traversing a tree in terms of traversing subtrees.

We can visualize each of these traversal orders by drawing a "loop" around a binary tree as shown in **Figure 7.8**. Before drawing the loop, extend the nodes of the tree that have fewer than two children with short lines so that every node has two "edges." Then draw the loop from the root of the tree, down the left subtree, and back up again, hugging the shape of the tree as you go. Each node of the tree is "touched" three times by the loop (the touches are numbered in Figure 7.8): once on the way down before the left subtree is reached; once after finishing the left subtree but before starting the right subtree; and once on the way up, after finishing the right subtree. To generate a preorder traversal, follow the loop and visit each node the first time it is touched (before visiting the left subtree). To generate an inorder traversal, follow the loop and visit each node the second time it is touched (in between visiting the two subtrees). To generate a postorder traversal, follow the loop and visit each node the third time it is touched (after visiting the right subtree). Use this method on the example tree in **Figure 7.9** and see whether you agree with the listed traversal orders.

You may have noticed that an inorder traversal of a binary search tree visits the nodes in order from the smallest to the largest. Obviously, this type of traversal would be useful when we need to access the elements in ascending key order—for example, to print a sorted list of the elements. There are also useful applications of the other traversal orders. For example, the preorder traversal (which is identical to depth-first

A binary tree

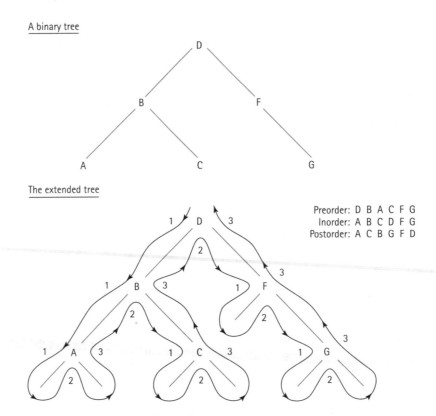

The extended tree

Preorder: D B A C F G
Inorder: A B C D F G
Postorder: A C B G F D

Figure 7.8   Visualizing binary tree traversals

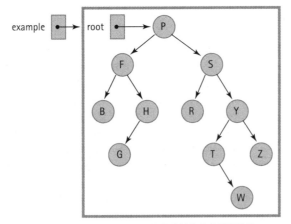

Inorder: B F G H P R S T W Y Z
Preorder: P F B H G S R Y T W Z
Postorder: B G H F R W T Z Y S P

Figure 7.9   Three binary tree traversals

order) can be used to duplicate the search tree—traversing a binary search tree in preorder and adding the visited elements to a new binary search tree as you go, will recreate the tree in the same exact shape. Since postorder traversal starts at the leaves and works backwards toward the root, it can be used to delete the tree, node by node, without losing access to the rest of the tree while doing so—this is analogous to the way a tree surgeon brings down a tree branch by branch, starting way out at the leaves and working backwards toward the ground, and is especially important when using a language without automatic garbage collection. As another example, preorder and postorder traversals can be used to translate infix arithmetic expressions into their prefix and postfix counterparts.

We mentioned that the preorder traversal results in visiting the nodes of the binary tree in a depth-first order. What about breadth-first (also known as level) order? We do not implement a breadth-first search for our binary search trees. However, an exercise asks you to explore and implement that option.

7.3   The Binary Search Tree Interface

In this section, we specify our Binary Search Tree ADT. As for stacks, queues, collections, and lists, we use the Java interface construct to formalize the specification.

Our binary search trees are defined to be similar to the lists of Chapter 6. Like the lists, our binary search trees will implement this text's `CollectionInterface` and the Java Library's `Iterable` interface. We make the same basic assumptions

> **Implied Requirements**
>
> Using the phrase "binary search tree" in regards to an ADT implies an implementation scheme that provides at least $O(\log_2 N)$ average case addition, removal, and search for elements. As discussed in the introduction to this chapter, a binary search tree provides the benefits of a sorted array when it comes to locating an element and the benefits of a linked list when it comes to adding or removing an element.

for our binary search trees as we did for our lists—they are unbounded, allow duplicate elements, and disallow null elements. In fact, our binary search trees act very much like sorted lists because the default iteration returns elements in increasing natural order. They can be used by some applications that require a sorted list.

So, what are the differences between the sorted list and the binary search tree? First, our binary search tree does not support the indexed operations defined for our lists. Second, we add two required operations (`min` and `max`) to the binary search tree interface that return respectively the smallest element in the tree and the largest element in the tree. Finally, as we have seen, binary search trees allow for multiple traversal orders so a `getIterator` method, that is passed an argument indicating which kind of iterator is desired—preorder, inorder, or postorder—and returns a corresponding `Iterator` object, is also required.

The Interface

Here is the interface. Some discussion follows.

```
//-----------------------------------------------------------------------
// BSTInterface.java           by Dale/Joyce/Weems           Chapter 7
//
// Interface for a class that implements a binary search tree (BST).
//
// The trees are unbounded and allow duplicate elements, but do not allow
// null elements. As a general precondition, null elements are not passed as
// arguments to any of the methods.
//-----------------------------------------------------------------------
package ch07.trees;

import ch05.collections.CollectionInterface;
import java.util.Iterator;

public interface BSTInterface<T> extends CollectionInterface<T>, Iterable<T>
{
   // Used to specify traversal order.
   public enum Traversal {Inorder, Preorder, Postorder};

   T min();
   // If this BST is empty, returns null;
   // otherwise returns the smallest element of the tree.

   T max();
   // If this BST is empty, returns null;
   // otherwise returns the largest element of the tree.


   public Iterator<T> getIterator(Traversal orderType);
   // Creates and returns an Iterator providing a traversal of a "snapshot"
   // of the current tree in the order indicated by the argument.
}
```

The BSTInterface extends both the CollectionInterface from the ch05.collections package and the Iterable interface from the Java library. Due to the former, classes that implement BSTInterface must provide add, get, contains, remove, isFull, isEmpty, and size methods. Due to the latter, they must provide an iterator method that returns an Iterator object that allows a client to iterate through the binary search tree.

The min and max methods are self-explanatory. We include them in the interface because they are useful operations and should be reasonably easy to implement in an efficient manner for a binary search tree.

The `BSTInterface` makes public an `enum` class `Traversal` that enumerates the three kinds of supported binary search tree traversals. The `getIterator` method accepts an argument from the client of type `Traversal` that indicates which tree traversal is desired. The method should return an appropriate `Iterator` object. For example, if a client wants to print the contents of a binary search tree named `mySearchTree`, which contains strings, using an inorder traversal the code could be:

```
Iterator<String> iter;
iter = mySearchTree.getIterator(BSTInterface.Traversal.Inorder);
while (iter.hasNext())
  System.out.println(iter.next());
```

In addition to the `getIterator` method, a class that implements the `BSTInterface` must provide a separate `iterator` method, because `BSTInterface` extends `Iterable`. This method should return an `Iterator` that provides iteration in the "natural" order of the tree elements. For most applications this would be an inorder traversal, and we make that assumption in our implementation. Therefore, for the above example, an alternate way to print the contents of the tree using an inorder traversal is to use the *for-each* loop, available to `Iterable` classes:

```
for (String s: mySearchTree)
  System.out.println(s);
```

We intend the iterators created and returned by `getIterator` and `iterator` to provide a **snapshot** of the tree as it exists at the time the iterator is requested. They represent the state of the tree at that time and subsequent changes to the tree should not affect the results returned by the iterator's `hasNext` and `next` methods. Because the iterators are using a snapshot of the tree it does not make sense for them to support the standard iterator `remove` method. Our iterators will throw an `UnsupportedOperationException` if `remove` is invoked.

To demonstrate the use of iterators with our binary search tree we provide an example application that first generates the tree shown in Figure 7.9 and then outputs the contents of the tree using each of the traversal orders. Next, the application demonstrates how to use the *for-each* loop, resulting in a repeat of the inorder traversal. Finally, it shows that adding elements to a tree *after* obtaining an iterator does *not* affect the results of the iteration. This example uses the binary search tree implementation developed in the upcoming chapter sections. Here is the code, and the example output follows:

```
//-----------------------------------------------------------------------------
// BSTExample.java          by Dale/Joyce/Weems              Chapter 7
//
// Creates a BST to match Figure 7.9 and demonstrates use of iteration.
//-----------------------------------------------------------------------------
package ch07.apps;

import ch07.trees.*;
import java.util.Iterator;
```

```java
public class BSTExample
{
  public static void main(String[] args)
  {
    BinarySearchTree<Character> example = new BinarySearchTree<Character>();
    Iterator<Character> iter;

    example.add('P'); example.add('F'); example.add('S'); example.add('B');
    example.add('H'); example.add('R'); example.add('Y'); example.add('G');
    example.add('T'); example.add('Z'); example.add('W');

    // Inorder
    System.out.print("Inorder:    ");
    iter = example.getIterator(BSTInterface.Traversal.Inorder);
    while (iter.hasNext())
      System.out.print(iter.next());

    // Preorder
    System.out.print("\nPreorder:   ");
    iter = example.getIterator(BSTInterface.Traversal.Preorder);
    while (iter.hasNext())
      System.out.print(iter.next());

    // Postorder
    System.out.print("\nPostorder: ");
    iter = example.getIterator(BSTInterface.Traversal.Postorder);
    while (iter.hasNext())
      System.out.print(iter.next());

    // Inorder again
    System.out.print("\nInorder:    ");
    for (Character ch: example)
      System.out.print(ch);

    // Inorder again
    System.out.print("\nInorder:    ");
    iter = example.getIterator(BSTInterface.Traversal.Inorder);
    example.add('A'); example.add('A'); example.add('A');
    while (iter.hasNext())
      System.out.print(iter.next());

    // Inorder again
    System.out.print("\nInorder:    ");
    iter = example.getIterator(BSTInterface.Traversal.Inorder);
```

```
    while (iter.hasNext())
      System.out.print(iter.next());
  }
}
```

Note that we recreate the tree in the figure within the application by adding the elements in "level order." The implementation details, presented in the next several sections, should clarify that this approach will indeed create a model of the tree shown in the figure. Here is the output from the BSTExample application:

```
Inorder:    BFGHPRSTWYZ
Preorder:   PFBHGSRYTWZ
Postorder: BGHFRWTZYSP
Inorder:    BFGHPRSTWYZ
Inorder:    BFGHPRSTWYZ
Inorder:    AAABFGHPRSTWYZ
```

7.4   The Implementation Level: Basics

We represent a tree as a linked structure whose nodes are allocated dynamically. Before continuing, we need to decide exactly what a node of the tree is. In our earlier discussion of binary trees, we talked about left and right children. These children are the structural references in the tree; they hold the tree together. We also need a place to store the client's data in the node and will continue to call it info. **Figure 7.10** shows how to visualize a node.

Here is the definition of a BSTNode class that corresponds to the picture in Figure 7.10.

```
//-------------------------------------------------------------------------
// BSTNode.java                by Dale/Joyce/Weems              Chapter 7
//
// Implements nodes holding info of class <T> for a binary search tree.
//-------------------------------------------------------------------------
package support;

public class BSTNode<T>
{
  private T info;                 // The node info
  private BSTNode<T> left;        // A link to the left child node
  private BSTNode<T> right;       // A link to the right child node

  public BSTNode(T info)
  {
    this.info = info; left = null; right = null;
  }
```

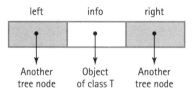

Figure 7.10 Binary tree nodes

```
public void setInfo(T info){this.info = info;}
public T getInfo(){return info;}

public void setLeft(BSTNode<T> link){left = link;}
public void setRight(BSTNode<T> link){right = link;}

public BSTNode<T> getLeft(){return left;}
public BSTNode<T> getRight(){return right;}
}
```

The careful reader may notice that the above class is similar to the DLLNode class introduced in the Variations section of Chapter 4. In fact, the two classes are essentially equivalent, with the left/right references of the BSTNode class corresponding to the back/forward references of the DLLNode class. Instead of creating a new node class for our Binary Search Tree ADT we could reuse the DLLNode class. Although reuse is good to take advantage of when possible, in this case we create an entirely new class. Our intent when creating the DLLNode class was to support doubly linked lists that are linear structures and *not* the same as binary search trees. Our intent when creating the BSTNode class is to support binary search trees. Furthermore, creating a new node class allows us to use appropriate method names for each structure, for example, getBack and setForward for a doubly linked list and getLeft and setRight for the binary search tree.

Now that the node class is defined, we turn our attention to the implementation. We will call our implementation class BinarySearchTree. It implements the BST-Interface and uses BSTNode. The relationships among our binary search tree classes and interfaces are depicted in Figure 7.24 in this chapter's "Summary" section.

The instance variable root references the root node of the tree. It is set to null by the constructor. The beginning of the class definition follows:

```
//-------------------------------------------------------------------------------
// BinarySearchTree.java            by Dale/Joyce/Weems            Chapter 7
//
// Defines all constructs for a reference-based BST.
// Supports three traversal orders Preorder, Postorder, & Inorder ("natural")
//-------------------------------------------------------------------------------
```

```java
package ch07.trees;

import java.util.*;    // Iterator, Comparator

import ch04.queues.*;
import ch02.stacks.*;
import support.BSTNode;

public class BinarySearchTree<T> implements BSTInterface<T>
{
  protected BSTNode<T> root;       // reference to the root of this BST
  protected Comparator<T> comp;    // used for all comparisons

  protected boolean found;    // used by remove

  public BinarySearchTree()
  // Precondition: T implements Comparable
  // Creates an empty BST object - uses the natural order of elements.
  {
    root = null;
    comp = new Comparator<T>()
    {
        public int compare(T element1, T element2)
        {
            return ((Comparable)element1).compareTo(element2);
        }
    };
  }


  public BinarySearchTree(Comparator<T> comp)
  // Creates an empty BST object - uses Comparator comp for order
  // of elements.
  {
   root = null;
   this.comp = comp;
  }
```

The class is part of the ch07.trees package. The reason for importing queues and stacks will become apparent as the rest of the class is developed. We call the variable that references the tree structure root, because it is a link to the root of the tree.

As we did with the sorted list implementation in Section 6.4, "Sorted Array-Based List Implementation," we allow the client to pass a Comparator to one of the two constructors. In that case the argument Comparator is used when determining relative order of the tree elements. This provides a versatile binary search tree class that can be used at different times with different keys for any given object class. For example, name, student number, age, or test score average could be used as the key when storing/retrieving objects that represent a student. The other constructor has no parameter. Instantiating a tree with this constructor indicates the client wishes to use the "natural" order of the elements, that is, the order defined by their compareTo method. A precondition on this constructor requires that type T implements Comparable, ensuring the existence of the compareTo method.

Next we look at the observer methods isFull, isEmpty, min, and max:

```java
public boolean isFull()
// Returns false; this link-based BST is never full.
{
  return false;
}


public boolean isEmpty()
// Returns true if this BST is empty; otherwise, returns false.
{
  return (root == null);
}


public T min()
// If this BST is empty, returns null;
// otherwise returns the smallest element of the tree.
{
  if (isEmpty())
     return null;
  else
  {
     BSTNode<T> node = root;
     while (node.getLeft() != null)
       node = node.getLeft();
     return node.getInfo();
  }
}


public T max()
// If this BST is empty, returns null;
// otherwise returns the largest element of the tree.
{
  if (isEmpty())
    return null;
  else
```

```
    {
        BSTNode<T> node = root;
        while (node.getRight() != null)
            node = node.getRight();
        return node.getInfo();
    }
}
```

The `isFull` method is trivial—as we have seen before, a link-based structure need never be full. The `isEmpty` method is almost as easy. One approach is to use the `size` method: If it returns 0, `isEmpty` returns `true`; otherwise, it returns `false`. But the `size` method will count the nodes on the tree each time it is called. This task takes at least $O(N)$ steps, where N is the number of nodes (as we see in Section 7.5, "Iterative Versus Recursive Method Implementations"). Is there a more efficient way to determine whether the list is empty? Yes, just see whether the root of the tree is currently `null`. This approach takes only $O(1)$ steps.

Now consider the `min` method. Examine any of the binary search trees seen so far and ask yourself, where is the minimum element? It is the leftmost element in the tree. In any binary search tree, if you start at the root and move downward left as far as possible you arrive at the minimum element. This is a result of the binary search property—elements to the left are less than or equal to their ancestors. To find the smallest element one must move left down the tree as far as possible. This is equivalent to traversing a linked list (the linked list that starts at `root` and continues through the `left` links) until reaching the end. The code shows the linked list traversal pattern we have seen many times before— while not at the end of the list, move to the next node. The code for the `max` method is equivalent, although movement is to the right through the tree levels instead of left.

7.5   Iterative Versus Recursive Method Implementations

Binary search trees provide us with a good opportunity to compare iterative and recursive approaches to a problem. You may have noticed that trees are inherently recursive: Trees are composed of subtrees, which are themselves trees. We even use recursive definitions when talking about properties of trees—for example, "A node is the *ancestor* of another node if it is the parent of the node, or the parent of some other *ancestor* of that node." Of course, the formal definition of a binary tree node, embodied in the class BSTNode, is itself recursive. Thus, recursive solutions will likely work well when dealing with trees. This section addresses that hypothesis.

First, we develop recursive and iterative implementations of the `size` method. The `size` method could be implemented by maintaining a running count of tree nodes (incrementing it for every `add` operation and decrementing it for every `remove` operation). In fact, that approach was used for our collections and lists. The alternative approach of traversing the tree and counting the nodes each time the number is needed is also viable, and we use it here.

After looking at the two implementations of the `size` method, we discuss the benefits of recursion versus iteration for this problem.

Recursive Approach to the size Method

Public/Private Pattern

When we use recursion to access our structures we usually need to pass a private/protected variable as an argument to the recursive method. As part of our information hiding approach, the client class does not have access to private/protected variables. We therefore create a public method that is invoked by the client, and this method in turn invokes the private recursive method passing it the needed argument.

As we have done in previous cases when implementing an ADT operation using recursion, we must use a public method to access the `size` operation and a private recursive method to do all the work.

The public method, `size`, calls the private recursive method, `recSize`, and passes it a reference to the root of the tree. We design the recursive method to return the number of nodes in the subtree referenced by the argument passed to it. Because `size` passes it the root of the tree, `recSize` returns the number of nodes in the entire tree to `size`, which in turn returns it to the client program. The code for `size` is very simple:

```
public int size()
// Returns the number of elements in this BST.
{
    return recSize(root);
}
```

In the introduction to recursion in Chapter 3 it states that the factorial of *N* can be computed if the factorial of *N* – 1 is known. The analogous statement here is that the number of nodes in a tree can be computed if the number of nodes in its left subtree and the number of nodes in its right subtree are known. That is, the number of nodes in a nonempty tree is

```
1 + number of nodes in left subtree + number of nodes in right subtree
```

This is easy. Given a method `recSize` and a reference to a tree node, we know how to calculate the number of nodes in the subtree indicated by the node: call `recSize` recursively with the reference to the subtree node as the argument. That takes care of the general case. What about the base case? A leaf node has no children, so the number of nodes in a subtree consisting of a leaf is 1. How do we determine that a node is a leaf? The references to its children are `null`. Let us summarize these observations into an algorithm, where `node` is a reference to a tree node.

recSize(node): returns int Version 1

```
if (node.getLeft() is null) AND (node.getRight() is null)
    return 1
else
    return 1 + recSize(node.getLeft()) + recSize(node.getRight())
```

Let us try this algorithm on a couple of examples to be sure that it works (see **Figure 7.11**).

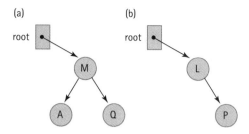

Figure 7.11   Two binary search trees

We call `recSize` with the tree in Figure 7.11a, using a reference to the node with element M as an argument. We evaluate the boolean expression and because the left and right children of the root node (M) are not `null` it evaluates to `false`. So we execute the *else* statement, returning

```
1 + recSize(reference to A) + recSize(reference to Q)
```

The result of the call to `recSize(reference to A)` is 1—when the boolean expression is evaluated using a reference to node A, both its left and right children are `null`, activating the `return 1` statement. By the same reasoning, `recSize(reference to Q)` returns 1 and therefore the original call to `recSize(reference to M)` returns 1 + 1 + 1 = 3. Perfect.

One test is not enough. Let us try again using the tree in Figure 7.11b. The left subtree of its root is empty; we need to see if this condition proves to be a problem. It is not true that both children of the root (L) are `null`, so the *else* statement is executed again, this time returning

```
1 + recSize(null reference) + recSize(reference to P)
```

The result of the call to `recSize(null reference)` is ... Oops! We do have a problem. If `recSize` is invoked with a `null` argument, a "null reference exception" is thrown when the method attempts to use the `null` reference to access an object. The method crashes when trying to access `node.getLeft()` with `node` equals `null`.

We need to check if the argument is `null` before doing anything else. As pointed out earlier, it is almost always a good idea to check for the degenerate case of an empty tree at the start of tree processing. If the argument is `null` then there are no elements so 0 is returned. Here is a new version of our algorithm:

recSize(node): returns int Version 2

```
if (node is null)
    return 0
else
if (node.getLeft() is null) AND (node.getRight() is null)
    return 1
else
    return 1 + recSize(node.getLeft()) + recSize(node.getRight())
```

Version 2 works correctly. It breaks the problem down into three cases:

- The argument represents an empty tree—return 0.
- The argument references a leaf—return 1.
- The argument references an interior node—return 1 + the number of nodes in its subtrees.

Version 2 of the algorithm is good. It is clear, efficient, and correct. It is also a little bit redundant. Do you see why? The section of the algorithm that handles the case of a leaf node is now superfluous. If we drop that case (the first *else* clause) and let the code fall through to the third case when processing a leaf node, it will return "1 + the number of nodes in its subtrees," which is $1 + 0 + 0 = 1$. This is correct! The first *else* clause is unnecessary. This leads to a third and final version of the algorithm:

---

recSize(node): returns int Version 3

```
if node is null
    return 0
else
    return recSize(node.getLeft()) + recSize(node.getRight()) + 1
```

We have taken the time to work through the versions containing errors and unnecessary complications because they illustrate two important points about recursion with trees: (1) Always check for the empty tree first, and (2) leaf nodes do not need to be treated as separate cases. Here is the code:

```
private int recSize(BSTNode<T> node)
// Returns the number of elements in subtree rooted at node.
{
    if (node == null)
        return 0;
    else
        return 1 + recSize(node.getLeft()) + recSize(node.getRight());
}
```

Iterative Approach to the size Method

An iterative method to count the nodes on a linked list is simple to write:

```
count = 0;
while (list != null)
{
    count++;
    list = list.getLink();
}
return count;
```

However, taking a similar approach to develop an iterative method to count the nodes in a binary tree quickly runs into trouble. We start at the root and increment the count. Now what? Should we count the nodes in the left subtree or the right subtree? Suppose we decide to count the nodes in the left subtree. We must remember to come back later and count the nodes in the right subtree. In fact, every time we make a decision on which subtree to count, we must remember to return to that node and count the nodes of its other subtree. How can we remember all of this?

In the recursive version, we did not have to record explicitly which subtrees still needed to process. The trail of unfinished business was maintained on the system stack for us automatically. For the iterative version, that information must be maintained explicitly, on our own stack. Whenever processing a subtree is postponed, we push a reference to the root node of that subtree on a stack of references. Then, when we are finished with our current processing, we remove the reference that is on the top of the stack and continue our processing with it. This is the depth-first traversal algorithm discussed in Section 7.1, "Trees," for general trees. Visiting a node during the traversal amounts to incrementing a count of the nodes.

Each node in the tree should be processed exactly once. To ensure this we follow these rules:

1. Process a node immediately after removing it from the stack.

2. Do not process nodes at any other time.

3. Once a node is removed from the stack, do not push it back onto the stack.

To initiate processing the tree root is pushed onto the stack (unless the tree is empty in which case we just return 0). We could just count the tree root node and push its children onto the stack, but pushing it primes the stack for processing. It is best to attempt to eliminate special cases if possible, and pushing the tree root node onto the stack allows us to treat it like any other node. Once the stack is initialized with the root, we repeatedly remove a node from the stack, add 1 to our count, and push the children of the node onto the stack. This guarantees that all descendants of the root are eventually pushed onto the stack—in other words, it guarantees that all nodes are processed.

Finally, we push only references to actual tree nodes; we do not push any `null` references. This way, when removing a reference from the stack, we can increment the count of nodes and access the left and right links of the referenced node without worrying about `null` reference errors. Here is the code:

```
public int size()
// Returns the number of elements in this BST.
{
  int count = 0;
  if (root != null)
  {
    LinkedStack<BSTNode<T>> nodeStack = new LinkedStack<BSTNode<T>>;
    BSTNode<T> currNode;
    nodeStack.push(root);
    while (!nodeStack.isEmpty())
```

```
    {
      currNode = nodeStack.top();
      nodeStack.pop();
      count++;
      if (currNode.getLeft() != null)
        nodeStack.push(currNode.getLeft());
      if (currNode.getRight() != null)
        nodeStack.push(currNode.getRight());
    }
  }
  return count;
}
```

Recursion or Iteration?

After examining both the recursive and the iterative versions of counting nodes, can we determine which is a better choice? Section 3.8, "When to Use a Recursive Solution," discussed some guidelines for determining when recursion is appropriate. Let us apply these guidelines to the use of recursion for counting nodes.

Is the depth of recursion relatively shallow?

Yes. The depth of recursion depends on the height of the tree. If the tree is well balanced (relatively short and bushy, not tall and stringy), the depth of recursion is closer to $O(\log_2 N)$ than to $O(N)$.

Is the recursive solution shorter or clearer than the nonrecursive version?

Yes. The recursive solution is shorter than the iterative method, especially if we count the code for implementing the stack against the iterative approach. Is the recursive solution clearer? In our opinion, yes. The recursive version is intuitively obvious. It is very easy to see that the number of nodes in a binary tree that has a root is 1 plus the number of nodes in its two subtrees. The iterative version is not as clear. Compare the code for the two approaches and see what you think.

Is the recursive version much less efficient than the nonrecursive version?

No. Both the recursive and the nonrecursive versions of size are $O(N)$ operations. Both have to count every node.

We give the recursive version of the method an "A"; it is a good use of recursion.

7.6 The Implementation Level: Remaining Observers

We still need to implement observer operations: contains, get, and the traversal-related iterator and getIterator, plus transformer operations add and remove. Note that nonrecursive approaches to most of these operations are also viable and, for some programmers, may even be easier to understand. These are left as exercises. We choose to use the recursive approach here because it does work well and many students need practice with recursion.

The `contains` and `get` Operations

At the beginning of this chapter, we discussed how to search for an element in a binary search tree. First check whether the target element searched for is in the root. If it is not, compare the target element with the root element and based on the results of the comparison search either the left or the right subtree.

This is a recursive algorithm since the left and right subtrees are also binary search trees. Our search terminates upon finding the desired element or attempting to search an empty subtree. Thus for the recursive `contains` algorithm there are two base cases, one returning `true` and one returning `false`. There are also two recursive cases, one with the search continuing in the left subtree and the other with it continuing in the right subtree.

We implement `contains` using a private recursive method called `recContains`. This method is passed the element being searched for and a reference to a subtree in which to search. It follows the algorithm described above in a straightforward manner.

```
public boolean contains (T target)
// Returns true if this BST contains a node with info i such that
// comp.compare(target, i) == 0; otherwise, returns false.
{
  return recContains(target, root);
}


private boolean recContains(T target, BSTNode<T> node)
// Returns true if the subtree rooted at node contains info i such that
// comp.compare(target, i) == 0; otherwise, returns false.
{
  if (node == null)
    return false;         // target is not found
  else if (comp.compare(target, node.getInfo()) < 0)
    return recContains(target, node.getLeft());    // Search left subtree
  else if (comp.compare(target, node.getInfo()) > 0)
    return recContains(target, node.getRight());   // Search right subtree
  else
    return true;          // target is found
}
```

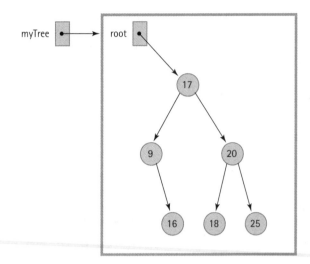

Figure 7.12 Tracing the contains operation

Here we trace this operation using the tree in **Figure 7.12**. In our trace we substitute actual arguments for the method parameters. It is assumed we can work with integers and are using their natural order. We want to search for the element with the key 18 in a tree myTree, so the call to the public method is

```
myTree.contains(18);
```

The contains method, in turn, immediately calls the recursive method:

```
return recContains(18, root);
```

Because root is not null and 18 > node.getInfo()—that is, 18 is greater than 17—the third *if* clause is executed and the method issues the recursive call:

```
return recContains(18, node.getRight());
```

Now node references the node whose key is 20, so because 18 < node.getInfo() the next recursive call is

```
return recContains(18, node.getLeft());
```

Now node references the node with the key 18, so processing falls through to the last *else* statement:

```
return true;
```

This halts the recursive descent, and the value true is passed back up the line of recursive calls until it is returned to the original contains method and then to the client program.

Next, we look at an example where the key is not found in the tree. We want to find the element with the key 7. The public method call is

```
myTree.contains(7);
```

followed immediately by

```
recContains(7, root)
```

Because node is not null and 7 < node.getInfo(), the first recursive call is

```
recContains(7, node.getLeft())
```

Now node is pointing to the node that contains 9. The second recursive call is issued

```
recContains(7, node.getLeft())
```

Now node is null, and the return value of false makes its way back to the original caller.

The get method is very similar to the contains operation. For both contains and get the tree is searched recursively to locate the tree element that matches the target element. However, there is one difference. Instead of returning a boolean value, a reference to the tree element that matches target is returned. Recall that the actual tree element is the info of the tree node; thus, a reference to the info object is returned. If the target is not in the tree null is returned.

```
public T get(T target)
// Returns info i from node of this BST where comp.compare(target, i) == 0;
// if no such node exists, returns null.
{
  return recGet(target, root);
}


private T recGet(T target, BSTNode<T> node)
// Returns info i from the subtree rooted at node such that
// comp.compare(target, i) == 0; if no such info exists, returns null.
{
  if (node == null)
    return null;                // target is not found
  else if (comp.compare(target, node.getInfo()) < 0)
    return recGet(target, node.getLeft());       // get from left subtree
  else
  if (comp.compare(target, node.getInfo()) > 0)
    return recGet(target, node.getRight());      // get from right subtree
  else
    return node.getInfo();  // target is found
}
```

The Traversals

The BSTExample.java application at the end of Section 7.3, "The Binary Search Tree Interface," demonstrated our Binary Search Tree ADTs support for tree traversal. You may want to review that code and its output before continuing here.

Let us review our traversal definitions:

- *Preorder traversal.* Visit the root, visit the left subtree, visit the right subtree.
- *Inorder traversal.* Visit the left subtree, visit the root, visit the right subtree.
- *Postorder traversal.* Visit the left subtree, visit the right subtree, visit the root.

Recall that the name given to each traversal specifies where the root itself is processed in relation to its subtrees.

Our Binary Search Tree ADT supports all three traversal orders through its getIterator method. As we saw in the BSTExample.java application, the client program passes getIterator an argument indicating which of the three traversal orders it wants. The getIterator method then creates the appropriate iterator and returns it. The returned iterator represents a snapshot of the tree at the time getIterator is invoked. The getIterator method accomplishes this by traversing the tree in the desired order, and as it visits each node it enqueues a reference to the node's information in a queue of T. It then creates an iterator using the anonymous inner class approach we used before for our list iterators. The instantiated iterator has access to the queue of T and uses that queue to provide its hasNext and next methods.

The generated queue is called infoQueue. It must be declared final in order to be used by the anonymous inner class—anonymous inner classes work with copies of the local variables of their surrounding methods and therefore must be assured that the original variables will not be changed. As a result, the returned iterator cannot support the remove method. Because we are creating a snapshot of the tree for iteration, the removal of nodes during a traversal is not appropriate anyway. Here is the code for getIterator:

```
public Iterator<T> getIterator(BSTInterface.Traversal orderType)
// Creates and returns an Iterator providing a traversal of a "snapshot"
// of the current tree in the order indicated by the argument.
// Supports Preorder, Postorder, and Inorder traversal.
{
  final LinkedQueue<T> infoQueue = new LinkedQueue<T>();
  if (orderType == BSTInterface.Traversal.Preorder)
    preOrder(root, infoQueue);
  else
  if (orderType == BSTInterface.Traversal.Inorder)
    inOrder(root, infoQueue);
```

```
else
if (orderType == BSTInterface.Traversal.Postorder)
  postOrder(root, infoQueue);

return new Iterator<T>()
{
  public boolean hasNext()
  // Returns true if iteration has more elements; otherwise returns false.
  {
    return !infoQueue.isEmpty();
  }


  public T next()
  // Returns the next element in the iteration.
  // Throws NoSuchElementException - if the iteration has no more elements
  {
    if (!hasNext())
      throw new IndexOutOfBoundsException("illegal invocation of next "
                              + " in BinarySearchTree iterator.\n");
    return infoQueue.dequeue();
  }


  public void remove()
  // Throws UnsupportedOperationException.
  // Not supported. Removal from snapshot iteration is meaningless.
  {
    throw new UnsupportedOperationException("Unsupported remove attempted "
                              + "on BinarySearchTree iterator.\n");
  }
};
}
```

As you can see, the queue holding the information for the iteration is initialized by passing it, along with a reference to the root of the tree, to a private method—a separate method for each traversal type. All that is left to do is to define the three traversal methods to store the required information from the tree into the queue in the correct order.

We start with the inorder traversal. We first need to visit the root's left subtree, which contains all the values in the tree that are smaller than or equal to the value in the root node. Then the root node is visited by enqueuing its information in our infoQueue.

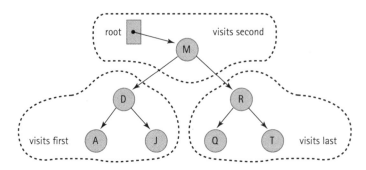

Figure 7.13 Visiting all the nodes in order

Finally, we visit the root's right subtree, which contains all the values in the tree that are larger than the value in the root node (see **Figure 7.13**).

Let us describe this problem again, developing our algorithm as we proceed. Our method is named `inOrder` and is passed arguments `root` and `infoQueue`. The goal is to visit the elements in the binary search tree rooted at `root` inorder; that is, first visit the left subtree inorder, then visit the root, and finally visit the right subtree inorder. As we visit a tree node we want to enqueue its information into `infoQueue`. Visiting the subtrees inorder is accomplished with a recursive call to `inOrder`, passing it the root of the appropriate subtree. This works because the subtrees are also binary search trees. When `inOrder` finishes visiting the left subtree, we enqueue the information of the root node and then call method `inOrder` to visit the right subtree. What happens if a subtree is empty? In this case the incoming argument is `null` and the method is exited—clearly there's no point to visiting an empty subtree. That is our base case.

Argument/Parameter Aliases

Our traversal methods illustrate a subtle point that might be missed on first glance. As discussed on page 37, when a reference variable is passed as an argument to a method, the parameter variable and the argument variable become aliases of each other. Thus, enqueuing elements into the local variable *q* in the private traversal methods *does* actually enqueue them into the queue associated with the argument variable `infoQueue`.

```
private void inOrder(BSTNode<T> node, LinkedQueue<T> q)
// Enqueues the elements from the subtree rooted at node into q in inOrder.
{
  if (node != null)
  {
    inOrder(node.getLeft(), q);
    q.enqueue(node.getInfo());
    inOrder(node.getRight(), q);
  }
}
```

The remaining two traversals are approached in exactly the same way, except that the relative order in which they visit the root and the subtrees is changed. Recursion certainly allows for an elegant solution to the binary tree traversal problem.

```
private void preOrder(BSTNode<T> node, LinkedQueue<T> q)
// Enqueues the elements from the subtree rooted at node into q in preOrder.
{
  if (node != null)
  {
    q.enqueue(node.getInfo());
    preOrder(node.getLeft(), q);
    preOrder(node.getRight(), q);
  }
}


private void postOrder(BSTNode<T> node, LinkedQueue<T> q)
// Enqueues the elements from the subtree rooted at node into q in postOrder.
{
  if (node != null)
  {
    postOrder(node.getLeft(), q);
    postOrder(node.getRight(), q);
    q.enqueue(node.getInfo());
  }
}
```

7.7   The Implementation Level: Transformers

To complete our implementation of the Binary Search Tree ADT we need to create the transformer methods *add* and *remove*. These are the most complex operations. The reader might benefit from a review of the subsection "Transforming a Linked List" in Section 3.4, "Recursive Processing of Linked Lists," because a similar approach is used here as was introduced in that subsection.

The add Operation

To create and maintain the information stored in a binary search tree, we must have an operation that inserts new nodes into the tree. A new node is always inserted into its appropriate position in the tree as a leaf. **Figure 7.14** shows a series of insertions into a binary tree.

For the implementation we use the same pattern that we used for contains and get. A public method, add, is passed the element for insertion. The add method invokes the recursive method, recAdd, and passes it the element plus a reference to the root of the tree. The CollectionInterface requires that our add method return a boolean

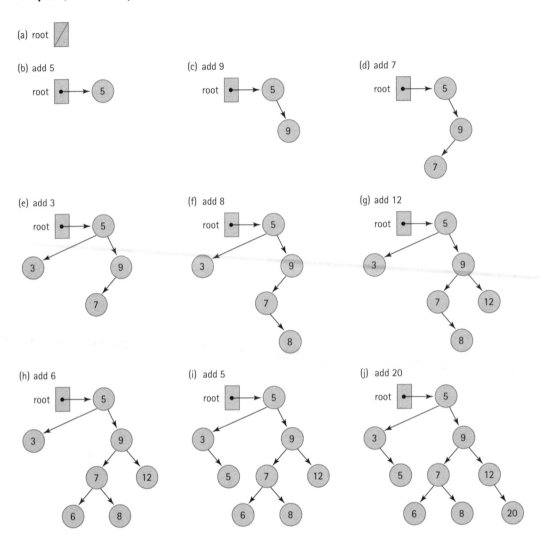

Figure 7.14 Insertions into a binary search tree

indicating success or failure. Given that our tree is unbounded the add method simply returns true—it is always successful.

```
public boolean add (T element)
// Adds element to this BST. The tree retains its BST property.
{
  root = recAdd(element, root);
  return true;
}
```

The call to `recAdd` returns a `BSTNode`. It returns a reference to the new tree—that is, to the tree that now includes `element`. The statement

```
root = recAdd(element, root);
```

can be interpreted as "Set the reference of the root of this tree to the root of the tree that is generated when the element is added to this tree." At first glance this might seem inefficient or redundant. We always perform insertions as leaves, so why do we have to change the root of the tree? Look again at the sequence of insertions in Figure 7.14. Do any of the insertions affect the value of the root of the tree? Yes, the original insertion into the empty tree changes the value held in the root. In the case of all the other insertions, the statement in the `add` method just copies the current value of the root onto itself; however, we still need the assignment statement to handle the special case of insertion into an empty tree. When does the assignment statement occur? After all the recursive calls to `recAdd` have been processed and have returned.

Before beginning the development of `recAdd`, we reiterate that every node in a binary search tree is the root node of a binary search tree. In **Figure 7.15a** we want to insert a node with the key value 13 into our tree whose root is the node containing 7. Because 13 is greater than 7, the new node belongs in the root node's right subtree. We have defined a smaller version of our original problem—insert a node with the key value 13 into the tree whose root is `root.right`. Note that to make this example easier to follow, in both the figure and the discussion here, we use the actual arguments rather than the formal parameters, so we use "13" rather than "element" and "`root.right`" rather than "`node.getRight()`"—"`root.right`" is a shorthand way of writing "the right attribute of the `BSTNode` object referenced by the `root` variable."

> **Nonrecursive Approach**
>
> It is also possible to design a nonrecursive approach to add an element to a binary search tree. The nonrecursive approach would maintain a trailing pointer as the search for the insertion location moves down the tree. When the insertion point is discovered the trailing pointer is used to access the parent node, which is the node that needs to be changed because it requires a new child pointer. Some people find the nonrecursive approach easier to understand. See Exercise 41b.

We have a method to insert elements into a binary search tree: `recAdd`. The `recAdd` method is called recursively:

```
root.right = recAdd(13, root.right);
```

Of course, `recAdd` still returns a reference to a `BSTNode`; it is the same `recAdd` method that was originally called from `add`, so it must behave in the same way. The above statement says "Set the reference of the right subtree of the tree to the root of the tree that is generated when 13 is inserted into the right subtree of the tree." See Figure 7.15b. Once again, the actual assignment statement does not occur until after the remaining recursive calls to `recAdd` have finished processing and have returned.

The latest invocation of the `recAdd` method begins its execution, looking for the place to insert 13 in the tree whose root is the node with the key value 15. The method compares 13 to the key of the root node; 13 is less than 15, so the new element belongs in the tree's left subtree. Again, we have obtained a smaller version of the problem—insert a

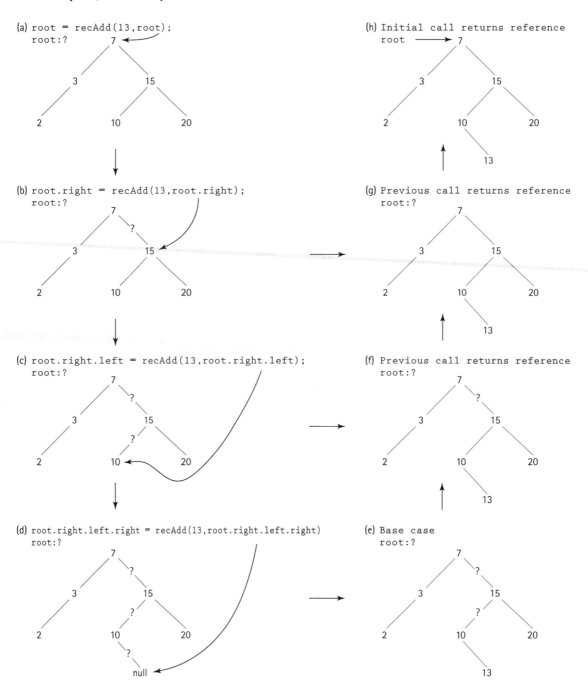

(a) `root = recAdd(13,root);`

(b) `root.right = recAdd(13,root.right);`

(c) `root.right.left = recAdd(13,root.right.left);`

(d) `root.right.left.right = recAdd(13,root.right.left.right)`

(e) Base case

(f) Previous call returns reference

(g) Previous call returns reference

(h) Initial call returns reference

Figure 7.15 The recursive add operation

node with the key value 13 into the tree whose root is `root.right.left`; that is, the subtree rooted at 10 (Figure 7.15c). Again `recAdd` is invoked to perform this task.

Where does it all end? There must be a base case, in which space for the new element is allocated and 13 copied into it. This case occurs when the subtree being searched is `null`—that is, when the subtree we wish to insert into is empty. (Remember, 13 will be added as a leaf node.) Figure 7.15d illustrates the base case. We create the new node and return a reference to it to the most recent invocation of `recAdd`, where the reference is assigned to the `right` link of the node containing 10 (see Figure 7.15e). That invocation of `recAdd` is then finished; it returns a reference to its subtree to the previous invocation (see Figure 7.15f), where the reference is assigned to the `left` link of the node containing 15. This process continues until a reference to the entire tree is returned to the original `add` method, which assigns it to `root`, as shown in Figure 7.15g and h.

While backing out of the recursive calls, the only assignment statement that actually changes a value is the one at the deepest nested level; it changes the right subtree of the node containing 10 from `null` to a reference to the new node containing 13. All of the other assignment statements simply assign a reference to the variable that held that reference previously. This is a typical recursive approach. We do not know ahead of time at which level the crucial assignment takes place, so we perform the assignment at every level.

The recursive method for insertion into a binary search tree is summarized as follows:

Method recAdd(element, node) returns node reference

Definition:	Inserts element into the binary search tree rooted at node
Size:	The number of elements in the path from node to insertion place
Base case:	If node is null, return a new node that contains element
General cases:	(1) If element <= node.getInfo(), return recAdd(element, node.getLeft())
	(2) If element > node.getInfo(), return recAdd(element, node.getRight())

Here is the code that implements this recursive algorithm:

```
private BSTNode<T> recAdd(T element, BSTNode<T> node)
// Adds element to tree rooted at node; tree retains its BST property.
{
  if (node == null)
    // Addition place found
    node = new BSTNode<T>(element);
  else if (comp.compare(element, node.getInfo()) <= 0)
    node.setLeft(recAdd(element, node.getLeft()));   // Add in left subtree
```

```
    else
        node.setRight(recAdd(element, node.getRight())); // Add in right subtree
    return node;
}
```

The remove Operation

The `remove` operation is the most complicated of the binary search tree operations and one of the most complex operations considered in this text. We must ensure that when we remove an element from the tree, the binary search tree property is maintained.

The setup of the `remove` operation is the same as that of the `add` operation. The private `recRemove` method is invoked by the public `remove` method with arguments equal to the target element to be removed and the subtree to remove it from. The recursive method returns a reference to the revised tree, just as it did for `add`. Here is the code for `remove`:

```
public boolean remove (T target)
// Removes a node with info i from tree such that comp.compare(target,i) == 0
// and returns true; if no such node exists, returns false.
{
    root = recRemove(target, root);
    return found;
}
```

As with our recursive *add* approach, in most cases the root of the tree is not affected by the `recRemove` call, in which case the assignment statement is somewhat superfluous, as it is reassigning the current value of `root` to itself. If the node being removed happens to be the root node, however, then this assignment statement is crucial. The `remove` method returns the `boolean` value stored in `found`, indicating the result of the removal. The `recRemove` method sets the value of `found` to indicate whether the element was found in the tree. Obviously, if the element is not originally in the tree, then it cannot be removed.

The `recRemove` method receives a target and a reference to a tree node (essentially a reference to a subtree), finds and removes a node matching the target's key from the subtree if possible, and returns a reference to the newly created subtree. We know how to determine whether the target is in the subtree; we did it for `get`. As with that operation, the recursive calls to `recRemove` progressively decrease the size of the subtree where the target node could be, until the node is located or it is determined that the node is not in the tree.

If located, we must remove the node and return a reference to the new subtree—this is somewhat complicated. This task varies according to the position of the target node in the tree. Obviously, it is simpler to remove a leaf node than to remove a nonleaf node. In fact, we can break down the removal operation into three cases, depending on the number of children linked to the node being removed:

1. *Removing a leaf (no children).* As shown in **Figure 7.16**, removing a leaf is simply a matter of setting the appropriate link of its parent to null.

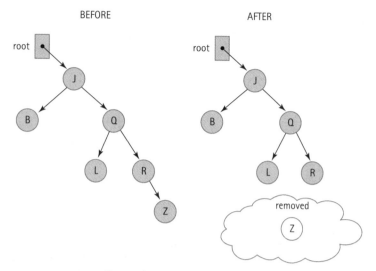

Remove the node containing Z

Figure 7.16   Removing a leaf node

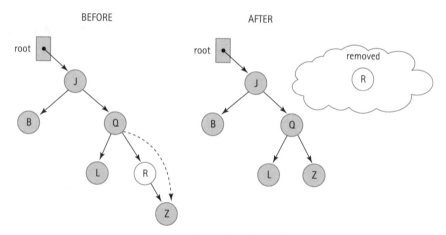

Remove the node containing R

Figure 7.17   Removing a node with one child

2. *Removing a node with only one child.* The simple solution for removing a leaf does not suffice for removing a node with a child, because we do not want to lose all of its descendants in the tree. We want to make the reference from the parent skip over the removed node and point instead to the child of the node being removed (see **Figure 7.17**).

3. *Removing a node with two children.* This case is the most complicated because we cannot make the parent of the removed node point to both of the removed node's

children. The tree must remain a binary tree and the search property must remain intact. There are several ways to accomplish this removal. The method we use does not remove the node but rather replaces its `info` with the `info` from another node in the tree so that the search property is retained. Then this other node is removed. Hmmm. That also sounds like a candidate for recursion. Let us see how this turns out.

Which tree element can be used to replace `target` so that the search property is retained? There are two choices: the elements whose keys immediately precede or follow the key of `target`—that is, the *logical* predecessor or successor of `target`. We elect to replace the `info` of the node being removed with the `info` of its logical predecessor—the node whose key is closest in value to, but less than or equal to, the key of the node to be removed.

Look back at Figure 7.14j and locate the logical predecessor of the interior nodes 5, 9, and 7. Do you see the pattern? The logical predecessor of the root node 5 is the leaf node 5, the largest value in the root's left subtree. The logical predecessor of 9 is 8, the largest value in 9's left subtree. The logical predecessor of 7 is 6, the largest value in 7's left subtree. The replacement value is always in a node with either zero or one child. After copying the replacement value, it is easy to remove the node that the replacement value was in by changing one of its parent's references (see **Figure 7.18**).

Examples of all three types of removals are shown in **Figure 7.19**.

It is clear that the removal task involves changing the reference from the parent node to the node to be removed. That explains why the `recRemove` method must

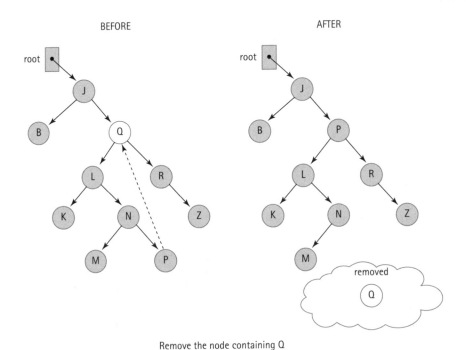

Remove the node containing Q

Figure 7.18 Removing a node with two children

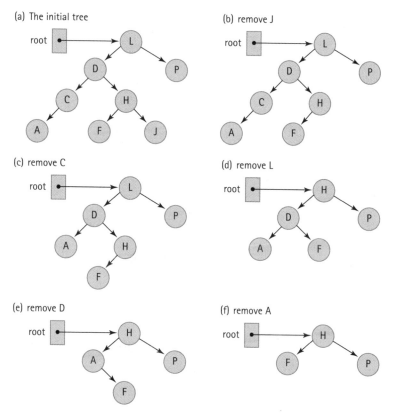

(a) The initial tree

(b) remove J

(c) remove C

(d) remove L

(e) remove D

(f) remove A

Figure 7.19 Removals from a binary search tree

return a reference to a BSTNode. Here we look at each of the three cases in terms of our implementation.

If both child references of the node to be removed are null, the node is a leaf and we just return null. The previous reference to this leaf node is replaced by null in the calling method, effectively removing the leaf node from the tree.

If one child reference is null, we return the other child reference. The previous reference to this node is replaced by a reference to the node's only child, effectively jumping over the node and removing it from the tree (similar to the way we removed a node from a singly linked list).

If neither child reference is null, we replace the info of the node with the info of the node's logical predecessor and remove the node containing the predecessor. The node containing the predecessor came from the left subtree of the current node, so we remove it from that subtree. We then return the original reference to the node (we have not created a new node with a new reference; we have just changed the node's info reference).

Let us summarize all of this in algorithmic form as removeNode. Within the algorithm and the code, the reference to the node to be removed is node.

removeNode (node): returns BSTNode

```
if (node.getLeft() is null) AND (node.getRight() is null)
   return null
else if node.getLeft() is null
   return node.getRight()
else if node.getRight() is null
   return node.getLeft()
else
   Find predecessor
   node.setInfo(predecessor.getInfo())
   node.setLeft(recRemove(predecessor.getInfo(), node.getLeft()))
   return node
```

Now we can write the recursive definition and code for `recRemove`.

Method recRemove (target, node) returns BSTNode

Definition:	Removes node with info target from tree rooted at node
Size:	The number of nodes in the path from node to the node to be removed
Base case 1:	If target is not in the tree (node is null), return false
Base case 2:	If target's info matches info in node, remove node and return true

General case:	If target < node.getInfo(),
	    return recRemove(target, node.getLeft());
	  else return recRemove(target, node.getRight())

```
private BSTNode<T> recRemove(T target, BSTNode<T> node)
// Removes element with info i from tree rooted at node such that
// comp.compare(target, i) == 0 and returns true;
// if no such node exists, returns false.
{
   if (node == null)
      found = false;
   else if (comp.compare(target, node.getInfo()) < 0)
      node.setLeft(recRemove(target, node.getLeft()));
   else if (comp.compare(target, node.getInfo()) > 0)
      node.setRight(recRemove(target, node.getRight()));
   else
```

```
{
  node = removeNode(node);
  found = true;
}
return node;
}
```

Before we code removeNode, we look at its algorithm again. We can eliminate one of the tests by noticing that the action taken when the left child reference is null also takes care of the case in which both child references are null. When the left child reference is null, the right child reference is returned. If the right child reference is also null, then null is returned, which is what we want if both nodes are null.

Here we write the code for removeNode using getPredecessor as the name of an operation that returns the info reference of the predecessor of the node with two children.

```
private BSTNode<T> removeNode(BSTNode<T> node)
// Removes the information at node from the tree.
{
  T data;
  if (node.getLeft() == null)
    return node.getRight();
  else if (node.getRight() == null)
    return node.getLeft();
  else
  {
    data = getPredecessor(node.getLeft());
    node.setInfo(data);
    node.setLeft(recRemove(data, node.getLeft()));
    return node;
  }
}
```

Now we must look at the operation for finding the logical predecessor. The logical predecessor is the maximum value in node's left subtree. Where is this value? The maximum value in a binary search tree is in its rightmost node. Therefore, starting from the root of node's left subtree, just keep moving right until the right child is null. When this occurs, return the info reference of that node. There is no reason to look for the predecessor recursively in this case. A simple iteration moving as far rightward down the tree as possible suffices.

```
private T getPredecessor(BSTNode<T> subtree)
// Returns the information held in the rightmost node of subtree
{
  BSTNode<T> temp = subtree;
```

```
      while (temp.getRight() != null)
        temp = temp.getRight();
      return temp.getInfo();
   }
```

That is it. We used four methods to implement the binary search tree's `remove` operation! Note that we use both types of recursion in our solution: direct recursion (`recRemove` invokes itself) and indirect recursion (`recRemove` invokes `removeNode`, which in turn may invoke `recRemove`). Due to the nature of our approach, we are guaranteed to never go deeper than one level of recursion in this latter case. Whenever `removeNode` invokes `recRemove`, it passes a target element and a reference to a subtree such that the target matches the largest element in the subtree. Therefore, the element matches the rightmost element of the subtree, which does not have a right child. This situation is one of the base cases for the `recRemove` method, so the recursion stops there.

If duplicate copies of the largest element in the subtree are present, the code will stop at the first one it finds—the one closest to the root of the tree. The remaining duplicates must be in that element's left subtree, based on the way we defined binary search trees and the way we implemented the `add` method. Thus, even in this case, the indirect recursion does not proceed deeper than one level of recursion.

7.8   Binary Search Tree Performance

A binary search tree is an appropriate structure for many of the same applications discussed previously in conjunction with other collection structures, especially those providing sorted lists. The special advantage of using a binary search tree is that it facilitates searching while conferring the benefits of linking the elements. It provides the best features of both the sorted array-based list and the linked list. Similar to a sorted array-based list, it can be searched quickly, using a binary search. Similar to a linked list, it allows insertions and removals without having to move large amounts of data. Thus, a binary search tree is particularly well suited for applications in which processing time must be minimized.

As usual, there is a trade-off. The binary search tree, with its extra reference in each node, takes up more memory space than a singly linked list. In addition, the algorithms for manipulating the tree are somewhat more complicated. If all of a list's uses involve sequential rather than random processing of the elements, a tree may not be the best choice.

Text Analysis Experiment Revisited

Let us return to the text analysis project introduced in Chapter 5, the Vocabulary Density project, and see how our binary search tree compares to the array-based and sorted array-based list approaches presented previously. Because the text analysis statistics remain unchanged we do not repeat them here—see Table 5.1 for that information. Here we

Table 7.2 Results of Vocabulary Density Experiment

Source	File Size	Array	Sorted Array	Binary Search Tree
Shakespeare's 18th Sonnet	1 KB	20 msecs	23 msecs	22 msecs
Shakespeare's *Hamlet*	177 KB	236 msecs	128 msecs	127 msecs
Linux Word File	400 KB	9,100 msecs	182 msecs	Stack overflow error, 33,760 msecs with revision
Melville's *Moby-Dick*	1,227 KB	2,278 msecs or 2.3 seconds	382 msecs	334 msecs
Complete Works of William Shakespeare	5,542 KB	9.7 seconds	1.2 seconds	0.9 seconds
Webster's Unabridged Dictionary	28,278 KB	4.7 minutes	9.5 seconds	4.2 seconds
11th Edition of the *Encyclopaedia Britannica*	291,644 KB	56.4 minutes	2.5 minutes	41.8 seconds
Mashup	608,274 KB	10 hours	7.2 minutes	1.7 minutes

concentrate solely on the execution time using three structures: an array. a sorted array, and a binary search tree. Results of the updated experiment are shown in **Table 7.2**.

As you can see, the binary search tree outperforms the other two approaches in most cases, especially as the size of the files increase. In the case of the largest file, the Mashup file, analysis using the binary search tree requires only 24% of the time needed by the sorted array approach and only 0.3% of the time needed by the unsorted array approach. This is a good result and shows that when dealing with large amounts of data that need to be stored and retrieved, the binary search tree approach is a good option.

A study of the table reveals that the performance gains from the binary search tree are only clearly evident as the size of the file increases. This is because the extra overhead associated with this approach, creating nodes, managing multiple references, and the like, counterbalance the benefits of the approach when applied to smaller data sets.

The table also reveals a serious issue when the binary search tree structure is used for the Linux Word file. The application bombs—it stops executing (about 70% of the way through the data on the author's computer) and reports a "Stack overflow error." The error is generated because the height of the underlying tree becomes so large that the system cannot support the recursive operations `add` and `size`. The author recoded these methods to be nonrecursive so that the experiment could be concluded. Now the application completes successfully, but the amount of time required, 34 seconds, is much longer than either of the other two approaches. The problem, as you may have surmised, is that the underlying tree is completely skewed.

Insertion Order and Tree Shape

Due to the way binary search trees are constructed, the order in which nodes are inserted determines the shape of the tree. **Figure 7.20** illustrates how the same data, inserted in different orders, produces very differently shaped trees.

If the values are inserted in order (or in reverse order), the tree is completely **skewed** (a long, "narrow" tree shape). This was the case with the Linux Word file—it is an alphabetically ordered list of words. The resulting tree has a depth of more than 45,000 nodes and is essentially a linked list of *right child* connections. No wonder the space allocated by

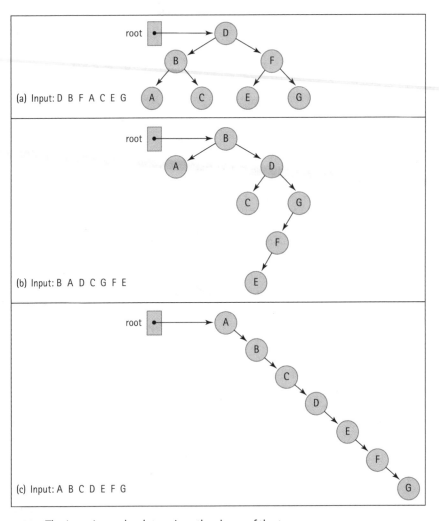

Figure 7.20 The insertion order determines the shape of the tree

the system for the method call-return stack is consumed when a recursive implementation is used.

Insertion of a random mix of the elements produces a shorter, **bushy** tree. Because the height of the tree determines the maximum number of comparisons during a search, the tree's shape is very important. Obviously, minimizing the height of the tree maximizes the efficiency of the search. Algorithms have been developed that adjust a tree to make its shape more desirable; some of these are discussed below; others in Section 7.10, "Tree Variations."

Balancing a Binary Search Tree

A beneficial enhancement to our Binary Search Tree ADT operations is a `balance` operation that balances the tree. When a binary search tree is balanced it provides $O(\log_2 N)$ search, addition, and removal. The specification of the operation is

```
public balance();
// Restructures this BST to be optimally balanced
```

There are several ways to restructure a binary search tree. Our approach is simple: traverse the tree, saving the information in an array,[3] and then traverse the array, saving the information back into the tree. The structure of the new tree depends on the order in which we save the information into the array and the order in which we access the array to insert the information back into the tree.

First traverse the tree *inorder* and insert the elements into the array. We end up with a sorted array. Next, to ensure a balanced tree we even out, as much as possible, the number of descendants in each node's left and right subtrees. Insert elements "root first," which means first insert the "middle" element. (If we list the elements from smallest to largest, the "middle" element is the one in the middle of the list—it has as many elements less than or equal to it as it has greater than it, or at least as close as possible.) The middle element becomes the root of the tree. It has about the same number of descendants in its left subtree as it has in its right subtree. Good. Which element do we insert next? We will work on the left subtree. Its root should be the "middle" element of all the elements that are less than or equal to the root. That element is inserted next. Now, when the remaining elements that are less than or equal to the root are inserted, about half of them will be in the left subtree of the element, and about half will be in its right subtree. Sounds recursive, does it not?

Here is an algorithm for balancing a tree based on the approach described above. The algorithm consists of two parts: one iterative and one recursive. The iterative part, Balance, creates the array and invokes the recursive part, InsertTree, which then rebuilds the tree.

---

[3] Because Java arrays do not support generics, we use an `ArrayList` to store the information.

Balance

```
Iterator iter = tree.getIterator(Inorder )
int index = 0
while (iter.hasnext())
    array[index] = iter.next( )
    index++
tree = new BinarySearchTree()
tree.InsertTree(0, index - 1)
```

InsertTree(low, high)

```
if (low == high)                // Base case 1
        tree.add(array[low])
else if ((low + 1) == high)     // Base case 2
        tree.add(array[low])
        tree.add(array[high])
else
        mid = (low + high) / 2
        tree.add(array[mid])
        tree.InsertTree(low, mid - 1)
        tree.InsertTree(mid + 1, high)
```

As planned we first store the nodes of the tree into our array using an inorder traversal (the default traversal), so they are stored, in order, from smallest to largest. The algorithm continues by invoking the recursive algorithm InsertTree, passing it the bounds of the array. The InsertTree algorithm checks the array bounds it is passed. If the low and high bounds are the same (base case 1), it inserts the corresponding array element into the tree. If the bounds differ by only one location (base case 2), the algorithm inserts both elements into the tree. Otherwise, it computes the "middle" element of the subarray, inserts it into the tree, and then makes two recursive calls to itself: one to process the elements less than the middle element and one to process the elements greater than the middle element.

Trace the InsertTree algorithm using sorted arrays of both even and odd length to convince yourself that it works. The code for balance and a helper method insertTree follows directly from the algorithm; writing it is left for you as an exercise. **Figure 7.21** shows the results of using this approach on a sample tree.

It is up to the client program to use the balance method appropriately. It should not be invoked too often, as it also has an execution cost associated with it. It is possible to provide a method that returns an indication of how balanced, or imbalanced, a tree is—which can then be used by a client to determine when to invoke balance. But testing for how balanced a tree is also has a cost. We ask you to investigate these ideas in Exercises 48 and 49.

(a) The original tree

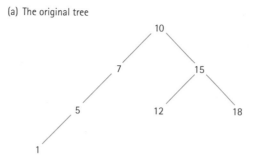

(b) The inorder traversal

(c) The resultant tree if InsertTree (0,6) is used

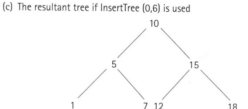

Figure 7.21 An optimal transformation

Another, and perhaps better, approach to the issue of imbalance is to implement a more complex add operation, one that maintains a balanced tree as elements are being included. Imbalance can also be created by repeated removal of nodes so a corresponding remove method, that also maintains balance, would also need to be created. Search trees using this approach are discussed in Section 7.10, "Tree Variations."

Application-Specific Knowledge

Some applications deal with random data and can safely use our binary search tree without worrying about the tree becoming skewed. Other applications deal with structured, maybe even sorted, data and if they use a binary search tree they may be best served by making periodic calls to the balance method despite its cost. Or, if they can withstand the added time required for each call to add and remove, they could use one of the self-balancing trees described in Section 7.10, "Tree Variations." Knowledge of your application area, possibly supplemented with experimentation, can help you choose the best approach.

7.9   Application: Word Frequency Counter

We have already established that our binary search tree is a good structure to use when analyzing text files, at least normal text files—that is, files representing novels, technical manuals, and news stories—we just do not want to use it without some sort of balancing strategy with files like the Linux Word file. In this section we develop a word frequency counter that uses our binary search tree. The application is to read a text file and generate an alphabetical listing of the unique words that the file contains, along with a count of how many times each word occurs.

To allow users to control the amount of useful output from the generator, based on the particular problem they are studying, the generator must allow users to specify a minimum word size and a minimum frequency count. The generator should skip over words smaller than the minimum word size; it should not include a word on its output list if the word occurs fewer times than the minimum frequency count. Finally, the generator should present a few summary statistics: the total number of words, the number of words whose length is at least the minimum word size, and the number of unique words of at least the specified size whose frequency is at least the minimum frequency count.

The WordFreq Class

To associate a count with each unique word from the file we create a class called WordFreq to hold a word frequency pair. A quick analysis tells us that we have to be able to initialize objects of the class, increment the frequency, and observe both the word and the frequency values.

The code for the WordFreq class is very straightforward. It is placed in the support package. A few observations are appropriate:

- The constructor initializes the freq variable to 0. As a consequence, the main program must increment a WordFreq object before placing it on the tree for the first time. We could have coded the constructor to set the original frequency to 1, but it is more natural to begin a frequency count at 0. There may be other applications that can use WordFreq where this feature would be important.

- In the toString method, we use Java's DecimalFormat class to force the string generated from the frequency count to be at least five characters wide. This helps line up output information for applications such as our word frequency generator.

```
//------------------------------------------------------------------------
// WordFreq.java              by Dale/Joyce/Weems            Chapter 7
//
// Defines word-frequency pairs
//------------------------------------------------------------------------
package support;

import java.text.DecimalFormat;

public class WordFreq implements Comparable<WordFreq>
{
  private String word;
  private int freq;

  DecimalFormat fmt = new DecimalFormat("00000");
```

```
public WordFreq(String newWord)
{
  word = newWord;
  freq = 0;
 }

public String getWordIs(){return word;}
public int getFreq(){return freq;}

public void inc()
{
  freq++;
}

public int compareTo(WordFreq other)
{
  return this.word.compareTo(other.word);
}

public String toString()
{
  return(fmt.format(freq) + " " + word);
}
}
```

The Application

Our approach for this application borrows quite a bit from the `VocabularyDensity` application developed in Chapter 5 and revisited in the previous section. The application scans the input file for words, and after reading a word, it checks to see if a match is already in the tree, and if not it insets the word. What is actually inserted is a `WordFreq` object that holds the word and a frequency count of 1.

Unlike the `VocabularyDensity` application, however, there is processing to attend to even if the word is already in the tree. In that case the application must increment the frequency associated with the word. It needs to get the corresponding `WordFreq` object from the tree, increment its count, and then add it back into the tree. But wait—if the application gets the object from the tree and then adds it back, there will be two copies of it in the tree. So it also needs to remove the object from the tree before processing it. If the word is not already in the tree it needs to insert it with a corresponding count of 1. The following algorithm summarizes this discussion. Assume that `wordFromTree` and `wordToTry` are `WordFreq` objects and that the latter contains the next word from the input file that is at least the minimum word size in length.

Handle the Next Word 1

```
boolean match = tree.contains(wordToTry)
if match
    wordFromTree = tree.get(wordToTry)
    tree.remove(wordFromTree)
    wordFromTree.inc()
    tree.add(wordfromTree)
else
    wordToTry.inc()   // to set its frequency to 1
    tree.add(wordToTry);
```

The first thing we notice is the repeated access to the tree required for each word. Potentially the application may have to check the tree to see whether the word is already there, get the word from the tree, remove the word from the tree, and save the word back into the tree. This is not good. Our input files could have tens of thousands of words, so even though the binary search tree provides an efficient structuring mechanism, it is not a good idea to access it so many times for each word. Can we do better?

Recall that our tree stores objects "by reference." When a WordFreq object is retrieved from the tree, it is actually a reference to the object that is retrieved. If that reference is used to access the object and increment its frequency count, the frequency count of the object in the tree is incremented. It is not necessary to remove the word from the tree and then add it back.

In our discussion of the perils of "store by reference" in the feature "Implementing ADTs 'by Copy' or 'by Reference'" found in Section 5.5, "Sorted Array-Based Collection Implementation," we stated that it is dangerous for the client to use a reference to reach into a data structure hidden by an ADT and change a data element. But as we also noted, this practice is dangerous only if the change affects the parts of the element used to determine the underlying organization of the structure. In this case, the structure is based on the *word* information of a WordFreq object; the application is changing the *frequency* information. It can reach into the tree and increment the frequency count of one of the tree's elements without affecting the tree's structure. We change the name of our variable to reflect the fact that the object is still in the tree. We can reduce our algorithm to:

Handle the Next Word 2

```
boolean match = tree.contains(wordToTry)
if match
    wordInTree = tree.get(wordToTry)
    wordInTree.inc()
else
    wordToTry.inc()   // to set its frequency to 1
    tree.add(wordToTry);
```

That is a significant improvement, but we can still do better. Do you see how? Instead of using `contains` to determine if the word is already in the tree we can use `get`. If `get` returns a `null`, then the word is not in the tree. If `get` returns a non-`null`, then the word is in the tree. Using this approach we reduce the number of accesses of the tree as we no longer need to execute both `contains` and `get`:

Handle the Next Word 3

```
wordInTree = tree.get(wordToTry)
if (wordInTree != null)
    wordInTree.inc()
else
    wordToTry.inc()  // to set its frequency to 1
    tree.add(wordToTry);
```

Overall, we have reduced the maximum number of times the tree is "searched" to handle a matched word from 4 to 1. Much better.

Figure 7.22 displays a trace of this algorithm, showing the changes that occur to the variables when "aardvark" is the next "word to try" and assuming that "aardvark" has already been processed five times, as well as "fox" (three times) and "zebra" (seven times). Part (a) of the figure shows the status before processing. Note that `wordInTree` is `null` at this point. Part (b) shows the status after the step

```
wordInTree = tree.get(wordToTry)
```

As you can see, `wordInTree` now holds a reference into the tree. Because the boolean expression (`wordInTree != null`) evaluates to `true`, the next statement executed is

```
wordInTree.inc()
```

that increments the frequency of the `WordFreq` object within the tree (as shown in part (c) of the figure).

The remainder of the application is straightforward. Based on the user input we do need to filter the words under consideration by word size and filter the output by word count. These requirements are both handled easily with simple *if* statements. The application is below.

```
//--------------------------------------------------------------------------
// WordFreqCounter.java          by Dale/Joyce/Weems          Chapter 7
//
// Displays a word frequency list of the words listed in the input file.
// Prompts user for minSize and minFreq.
// Does not process words less than minSize in length.
// Does not output words unless their frequency is at least minFreq.
//--------------------------------------------------------------------------
package ch07.apps;
```

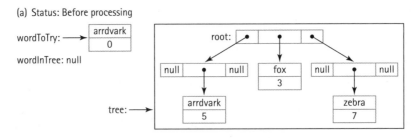

(a) Status: Before processing

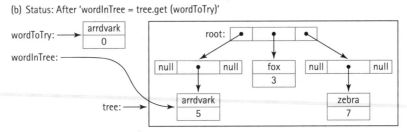

(b) Status: After 'wordInTree = tree.get (wordToTry)'

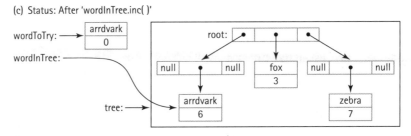

(c) Status: After 'wordInTree.inc( )'

Figure 7.22 Trace of "Handle the Next Word 3" algorithm

```java
import java.io.*;
import java.util.Scanner;
import ch07.trees.*;
import support.WordFreq;

public class WordFreqCounter
{
  public static void main(String[] args) throws IOException
  {
    String word;
    WordFreq wordToTry;
    WordFreq wordInTree;

    BinarySearchTree<WordFreq> tree = new BinarySearchTree<WordFreq>();

    int numWords = 0;
    int numValidWords = 0;
```

```
int numValidFreqs = 0;
int minSize;
int minFreq;
int treeSize;

// Set up command line reading
Scanner scan = new Scanner(System.in);

// Set up file reading
String fn;
System.out.print("File name > ");
fn = scan.next();
Scanner wordsIn = new Scanner(new FileReader(fn));
wordsIn.useDelimiter("[^a-zA-Z']");   // delimiters are nonletters,'

// Get word and frequency limits from user
System.out.print("Minimum word size> ");
minSize = scan.nextInt();
System.out.print("Minimum word frequency> ");
minFreq = scan.nextInt();

// Process file
while (wordsIn.hasNext())        // while more words to process
{
  word = wordsIn.next();
  numWords++;
  if (word.length() >= minSize)
  {
    numValidWords++;
    word = word.toLowerCase();
    wordToTry = new WordFreq(word);
    wordInTree = tree.get(wordToTry);
    if (wordInTree != null)
    {
      // word already in tree, just increment frequency
      wordInTree.inc();
    }
    else
    {
      // insert new word into tree
      wordToTry.inc();                 // set frequency to 1
      tree.add(wordToTry);
    }
  }
}
```

```
// Display results
System.out.println("The words of length " + minSize + " and above,");
System.out.println("with frequency counts " + minFreq + " and above:");
System.out.println();
System.out.println("Freq  Word");
System.out.println("----- ----------------");
for (WordFreq wordFromTree: tree)
{
  if (wordFromTree.getFreq() >= minFreq)
  {
    numValidFreqs++;
    System.out.println(wordFromTree);
  }
}
System.out.println();
System.out.println(numWords + " words in the input file.  ");
System.out.println(numValidWords + " of them are at least " + minSize
            + " characters.");
System.out.println(numValidFreqs + " of these occur at least "
            + minFreq + " times.");
System.out.println("Program completed.");
  }
}
```

Here we show the results of running the program on a text file containing the complete works of William Shakespeare. The minimum word size was set to 10 and the minimum frequency count was set to 100. Ten words meeting those criteria were found. This application is a useful text analysis tool—and it is fun, too. What is a "bolingbroke"?[4]

```
File name > input/literature/shakespeare.txt
Minimum word size> 10
Minimum word frequency> 100
The words of length 10 and above,
with frequency counts of 100 and above:

Freq  Word
----- ----------------
00219 antipholus
00141 attendants
```

---

[4] Henry Bolingbroke aka King Henry IV.

```
00175 bolingbroke
00254 buckingham
00120 conscience
00213 coriolanus
00572 gloucester
00102 honourable
00148 northumberland
00159 themselves

1726174 words in the input file.
15828 of them are at least 10 characters.
10 of these occur at least 100 times.
Program completed.
```

7.10   Tree Variations

Our goal in the Variations sections of this text is to instruct the reader about alternate definitions and implementation approaches for each of the ADTs studied. We also hope to arouse the reader's curiosity about the variety of data structures that exist and show that the possibilities are "unbounded" when it comes to defining new ways to structure our data. Nowhere is this more evident than with the Tree ADT, for which more variations may exist than for all the other ADTs considered together. Trees can be binary, trinary (up to three children per node), *n*-ary (up to *n* children per node), alternating-ary, balanced, not balanced, partially balanced, self-adjusting, and store information in their nodes or their edges or both. With trees, even the variations have variations!

Application-Specific Variations

Given the wide variety of trees it is difficult (but not impossible) to define a general tree ADT. The Java Library does not include a general tree structure and neither do most textbooks. Often with trees we let the specific target application dictate the definition, assumptions, rules, and operations associated with a specific implementation. Here we review some of the popular specific uses for trees.

Decision Trees

What to do today? The answer to this question might depend on the sequence of answers to a host of other questions: is my schoolwork up-to-date, how is the weather, what is my bank account balance? When we work through a series of questions and our answers lead to other questions, yet ultimately to a solution, we are traversing a decision tree.

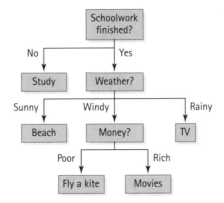

Support for creating and using such trees is often included in business management tools. These trees can consist of separate types of nodes such as boolean question nodes, multiple choice question nodes, chance nodes, and answer nodes. Static decision trees can be implemented using nested *if-else* and *switch* statements, whereas dynamic ones would require implementations similar to those we presented in this chapter.

Expression/Parse Trees

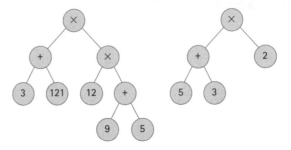

Arithmetic expressions can be ambiguous. For example, the expression $5 + 3 \times 2$ might evaluate to 16 or 11 depending on the order in which you perform the operations. We resolve this ambiguity by creating rules for order of evaluation or by using grouping symbols, such as parenthesis. Another way to solve the problem is to store the expression in a tree. A tree node that holds an operation indicates that the operation is to be performed on its children. There is no ambiguity. Specially designed tree traversals are used to evaluate the expression.

In addition to storing and helping us evaluate an expression in an unambiguous manner, expression trees can be used to translate expressions from one form to another. Looking at the tree on the right above we "see" the infix expression $(5 + 3) \times 2$. But consider the result of a postorder traversal: $5\ 3 + 2\ \times$. You might recognize that as the postfix expression that corresponds to the given infix expression. Similarly, we can generate "prefix" expressions using a preorder traversal.

Expressions trees can be binary or n-ary. Arithmetic expression trees are a specific form of a more general type of tree, a parse tree. Formal language definition relies on a sequence of expressions describing how strings may be combined into legal sentences. These expressions follow the same rules as arithmetic expressions and can, therefore, also be stored as trees. So expression trees, or parse trees as they are usually called, can be used to store a legal sentence of a formal grammar. Since programming languages are formal languages, a parse tree can be used to store an entire computer program!

R-Trees

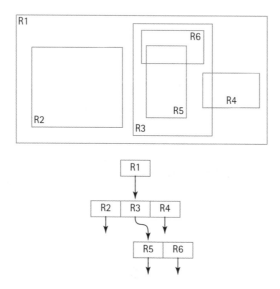

R-Trees (Rectangle Trees) and their variants deal with storing hierarchical spatial data and can be used in search and navigational systems. Desks sit within a classroom, classrooms line a hallway, hallways are on floors, floors are in wings, wings are in buildings, buildings are on campuses, and so on. R-trees can be used to store the relative locations of all of these things in a manner that supports efficient retrieval. Inner nodes represent bounding rectangles which contain, literally, all of their descendants. Leaf nodes represent specific objects.

R-Trees are a good example of a tree structure that was created to address a specific problem, in this case support for geo-data related applications (identify all the lakes within 40 miles of point X). Given the constraints of a particular problem, computer scientists design efficient structures to support problem solution.

Tries/Prefix Trees

A Trie is an interesting structure because the information it stores is associated with its edges. Tries are used as collections, with a goal toward making the `contains` operation as quick as possible. Trie is pronounced as "tree" as the name derives from the "trie" in "retrieval".

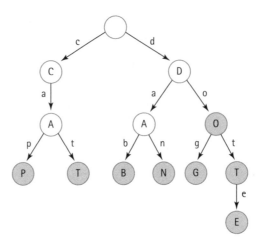

In particular, tries are useful for storing strings, or any other information that can be broken into a sequence of atomized parts, such as binary numbers. Let us look at how a trie stores strings of characters. In the example trie shown here the root represents the empty string. As we traverse from the root to a leaf we build a string, adding the character associated with each link as we go. When we arrive at a leaf we have built one of the strings that is contained in the trie. Contained strings can also be associated with inner nodes. The shaded nodes in our sample tree all indicate strings contained in the trie.

To determine if a given string is stored in our tree we simply access the string character by character, traversing the trie as we go. If we reach a point where no traversal path is possible before we reach the end of the string then the answer is "no, the string is not stored in the trie". If we reach the end of the string and are left in a "shaded" node within the trie then the answer is "Yes!".

Tries are useful for word game applications, spell checkers, and hyphenators. They are especially appropriate for autocompletion of text, such as the apps that suggest what word you are typing when you are texting. Do you see why?

Balanced Search Trees

The Binary Search Tree ADT presented in this chapter is an excellent collection structure for holding "random" data, but suffers from one major weakness—it can become unbalanced. In the extreme case (see Figure 7.20c) an unbalanced binary search tree acts no differently than a linked list—essentially it is a linked list. Many search tree variations have been invented to address this weakness, each in turn with their own strengths and weaknesses. Different variations have different definitions of what it means to be balanced.

B-Trees

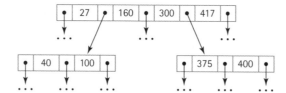

A B-Tree (B for "Balanced") is a search tree that allows internal nodes to hold multiple values and have multiple children. Within a node the values and child links are stored in order, and a form of the binary search tree property is maintained in terms of the relationship between the information in child nodes and their parents.

Since a B-Tree node can contain a great deal of information, processing that

> **Specialized Structures**
>
> B-Trees are another good example of how computer scientists analyzed a situation and created an appropriate data structure to fit the circumstances. If disk reads are the most expensive operation, create a structure that minimizes disk reads. To improve performance concentrate your efforts on the most expensive part of the processing.

information during a search or change to the tree requires more effort than processing a node of a binary search tree. B-trees were originally designed to support retrieval of information from disk storage systems and they are often used with large scale database systems. In these systems the time required to read information is the most costly part of processing. Since B-Trees store a lot of information in a "flat" tree they are perfect for such systems. A minimal number of time consuming "read from disk" operations are required to find information in the B-Tree and the extra time required for processing a node, once it has been read, is not important in the overall scheme of things.

B-Tree Variants

As we pointed out in the introduction to this section, with trees even our variants have variants. A popular variant of the B-Tree is the 2-3-4 tree, where nodes are constrained to hold 1, 2, or 3 values and therefore have 2, 3, or 4 subtrees (thus the name of the tree). Insertion of new nodes results in a 2-node becoming a 3-node, or a 3-node becoming a 4-node, or a 4-node becoming two 2-nodes (with one value propagating up the tree and possibly causing further changes). In any case, searching, insertion, and removal of information is always $O(\log_2 N)$ and the amount of work required to process the information within any node is constant.

A 2-3-4 tree can be implemented using a binary tree structure called a red-black tree. In this structure nodes are "colored" either red or black (each node must hold an extra `boolean` value that indicates this information). The color of a node indicates how its value fits into the corresponding 2-3-4 tree. For example, a 4-node holding the information [B, D, F] is modeled by a "black" node containing [D], with a left child "red" node containing [B] and a right child "red" node containing [F]. The rules for what constitutes a red-black tree are somewhat complicated but suffice it to say it provides all the benefits of a 2-3-4 tree plus the added benefit of only requiring a single node type, a binary tree node, to support its implementation. Although the defining rules are more complex, implementation is simpler.

Note that the Java Library does not provide a Tree ADT—but it does include two important classes that use tree implementations. The Java `TreeMap` class supports maps (see Chapter 8) and the Java `TreeSet` class supports sets (see Section 5.7, "Collection Variations"). In both cases the internal representation is a red-black tree.

AVL Trees

AVL trees were defined in a paper in 1962 written by **A**deleson-**V**elsky and **L**andis. They define balance from the local perspective of a single node—in an AVL tree the difference in height between a node's two subtrees can be at most 1. Let us call the difference in height between two subtrees of a node its "balance factor". Returning again to Figure 7.20, the tree in part (a) of the figure is an AVL tree since the balance factor of each of its nodes is 0. The tree in part (b) of the figure is *not* an AVL tree because, for example, the balance factor of its root node is 3. Obviously the tree in part (c) of the figure is also *not* an AVL tree.

Having each node in a tree exhibit a balance factor ≤ 1 results in a relatively well-balanced tree. Searching for information in an AVL tree is an $O(\log_2 N)$ operation, even in the worst case. But what about addition and removal of information? During addition and removal of nodes extra work is required to ensure the tree remains balanced. Let us consider addition of a node. **Figure 7.23a** shows an AVL tree containing five nodes. The balance factor of its nodes, top to bottom, left to right are 1, 0, 0, 0, 0. Figure 7.23b shows the result of adding 5 to the tree. The new tree is no longer an AVL tree, since the balance factor of its nodes, top to bottom, left to right are 2, 1, 0, 1, 0, 0. Any imbalance created in an AVL tree by an addition will be along the path of nodes that were visited to determine the addition location, and in this case the imbalance is exhibited at the root node.

Temporary imbalance in an AVL tree is handled by performing one of four potential rotations. In our example the rotation known as a "right rotation" or more simply the "R rotation" is performed on the root. The tree is "rotated" with the root moving down to the right and its left child moving up to become the new root. The result of the rotation, which is accomplished with three reference assignment statements, is shown in Figure 7.23c. Depending on the nature of the imbalance other rotations might be required (L, LR, and RL rotations). All needed rotations are accomplished with a few reference assignment statements. Although in some cases multiple rotations are required to rebalance a tree, the overall cost of additions and removals is never more than $O(\log_2 N)$.

Research shows that AVL trees perform especially well in situations where an original tree construction includes insertions of sequences of elements "in order", and is followed by long sequences of search operations.

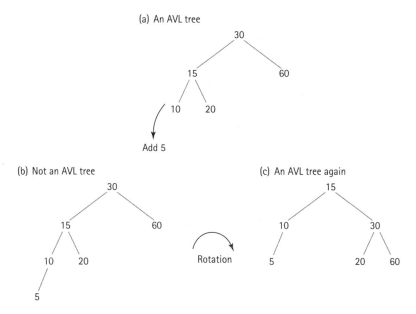

Figure 7.23   Adding a node to an AVL tree

Summary

In this chapter we learned about trees and their many uses. The binary search tree may be used to structure sorted information to reduce the search time for any particular element while at the same time allowing relatively fast addition and removal of information. For applications in which direct access to the elements in a sorted structure is needed, the binary search tree is a very useful data structure. If the tree is balanced, access to any node in the tree is an O($\log_2 N$) operation. The binary search tree combines the advantages of quick random access (like a binary search on a sorted linear list) with the flexibility of a linked structure.

We also saw that the binary search tree operations could be implemented very elegantly and concisely using recursion. This makes sense, because a binary tree is itself a "recursive" structure: Any node in the tree is the root of another binary tree. Each time we moved down a level in the tree, taking either the right or left path from a node, the size of the (current) tree is reduced, a clear case of the smaller-caller. For comparison we implemented the `size` operation both recursively and iteratively—the iterative version made use of our Stack ADT.

The benefits of a binary search tree diminish if the tree is skewed. We discussed a tree-balancing approach that can be used to keep a binary search tree balanced, and in the Variations section we introduced the concept of self-balancing trees.

Figure 7.24 is a UML diagram showing the relationships among the classes and interfaces involved in our Binary Search Tree ADT. It shows that the `BSTInterface` extends both this text's `CollectionInterface` and the library's `Iterable` interface.

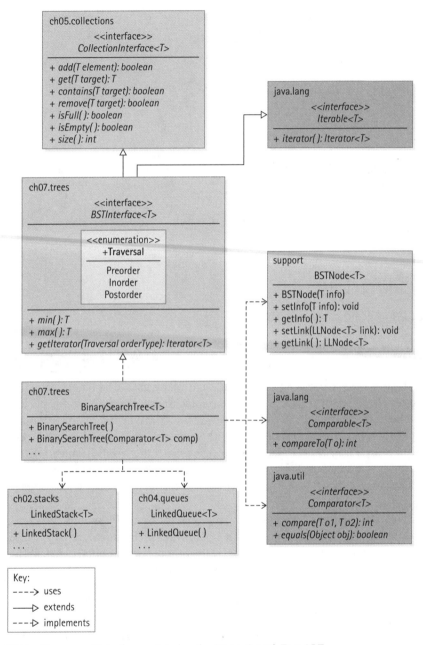

Figure 7.24   Classes and interfaces related to the Binary Search Tree ADT

Thus in addition to the `min`, `max`, and `getIterator` operations our binary search trees must implement all of the abstract methods found in those interfaces. Our `BinarySearchTree` class is the most complex class we have developed so far.

Exercises

7.1 Trees

1. For each of the following application areas state whether or not the tree data structure appears to be a good fit for use as a storage structure, and explain your answer:

    a. chess game moves

    b. public transportation paths

    c. relationship among computer files and folders

    d. genealogical information

    e. parts of a book (chapters, sections, etc.)

    f. programming language history

    g. mathematical expression

2. Java classes are related in a hierarchical manner defined by inheritance; in fact we sometimes speak of the "Java Inheritance Tree." The hierarchy within the `Java.lang` package is described here:

    `https://docs.oracle.com/javase/8/docs/api/java/lang/package-tree.html`.

    Answer the following questions about that hierarchy viewed as a tree.

    a. What is the root?

    b. What is the height of the tree?

    c. Which node has the most children?

    d. How many leaves are there?

3. Following the example in Figure 7.1d, draw a tree that represents this maze:

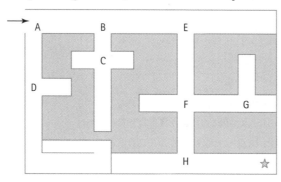

4. Answer the questions below about the following tree, using the letters that label the nodes:

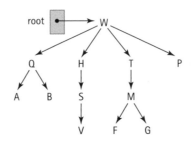

a. Which node is the root?

b. Which node is the parent of F?

c. Which node(s) are the children of H?

d. Which node(s) are the ancestors of M?

e. Which node(s) are the descendants of T?

f. Which node(s) are the siblings of S? of H?

g. What is the height of the tree?

h. In what order are the nodes visited by a breadth-first traversal?

i. In what order are the nodes visited by a depth-first traversal?

5. Create a table similar to Table 7.1 that shows a trace of a

a. Depth-First Traversal for the sample tree in Figure 7.2.

b. Breadth-First Traversal for the sample tree in Exercise 4.

c. Depth-First Traversal for the sample tree in Exercise 4.

6. Draw a tree (multiple answers might be possible) that

a. Has four nodes and is height 1.

b. Has four nodes and is height 3.

c. Has more nodes at level 2 than at level 1.

d. Has five nodes and three are leaves.

e. Has six nodes and two are leaves.

f. Has four interior nodes.

g. Has a breadth-first traversal of A B C D E F.

h. Has a depth-first traversal of A B C D E F.

i. Has a breadth-first traversal of A B C D E F and a depth-first traversal of A B C E F D.

7. Brainstorm: Describe two different approaches to implementing a general tree data structure.

7.2 Binary Search Trees

8. True/False. Explain your answer.

    a. Every binary tree is a binary search tree.

    b. Every binary search tree is a tree.

    c. Every binary search tree is a binary tree.

    d. A node in a binary tree must have two children.

    e. A node in a binary tree can have more than one parent.

    f. Each node of a binary search tree has a parent.

    g. In a binary search tree the info in all of the nodes in the left subtree of a node are less than the info in all of the nodes in the right subtree of the node.

    h. In a binary search tree the info in all of the nodes in the left subtree of a node are less than the info in the node.

    i. A preorder traversal of a binary search tree processes the nodes in the tree in the exact reverse order that a postorder traversal processes them.

9. Draw a single binary tree that has both inorder traversal E B A F D G and preorder traversal A B E D F G.

10. Draw a single binary tree which has inorder traversal T M Z Q A W V and postorder traversal Z M T A W V Q.

11. Draw three binary search trees of height 2 containing the nodes A, B, C, D, and E.

12. What is the

    a. maximum number of levels that a binary search tree with 100 nodes can have?

    b. minimum number of levels that a binary search tree with 100 nodes can have?

    c. maximum total number of nodes in a binary tree that has N levels? (Remember that the root is level 0.)

    d. maximum number of nodes in the Nth level of a binary tree?

    e. number of ancestors of a node in the Nth level of a binary search tree?

    f. number of different binary trees that can be made from three nodes that contain the key values 1, 2, and 3?

    g. number of different binary search trees that can be made from three nodes that contain the key values 1, 2, and 3?

13. Answer the following questions about the binary search tree with root referenced by `rootA` (see below).

    a. What is the height of the tree?

    b. Which nodes are on level 3?

    c. Which levels have the maximum number of nodes that they could contain?

    d. What is the maximum height of a binary search tree containing these nodes?

e.   What is the minimum height of a binary search tree containing these nodes?

f.   What is the order in which nodes are visited by a preorder traversal?

g.   What is the order in which nodes are visited by an inorder traversal?

h.   What is the order in which nodes are visited by a postorder traversal?

i.   What is the order in which nodes are visited by a depth-first traversal?

j.   What is the order in which nodes are visited by a breadth-first traversal?

14. Repeat the previous question but use binary search tree with root referenced by `rootB`.

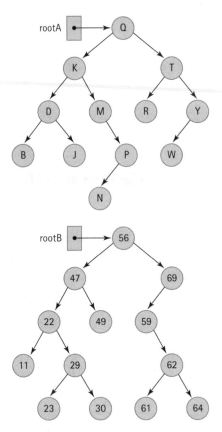

7.3 The Binary Search Tree Interface

15. List all the methods required by the `BSTInterface` and classify each as observer, transformer, or both.

16. In addition to the operations required by the `BSTInterface`, define at least three more operations that might be useful for a Binary Search Tree ADT to provide.

17. Explain the concept of a "snapshot" of a structure. Explain why it does not make sense for our binary search tree iterators to support a `remove` operation.

18. For this question assume that binary search tree `treeA` (with root referenced by `rootA` as shown above) has been declared and instantiated as an object of a class that correctly implements `BSTInterface`. What is the output of each of the following code sections (these sections are independent; that is, you start over again with the tree as shown in the figure above for each section):

a.
```
System.out.println(treeA.isFull());
System.out.println(treeA.isEmpty());
System.out.println(treeA.size());
System.out.println(treeA.min());
System.out.println(treeA.max());
System.out.println(treeA.contains('R'));
System.out.println(treeA.remove('R'));
System.out.println(treeA.remove('R'));
System.out.println(treeA.get('S'));
```

b.
```
Iterator<Character> iter;
iter = treeA.getIterator(BSTInterface.Traversal.Preorder);
while (iter.hasNext())
    System.out.print(iter.next());
System.out.println();
for (Character ch: treeA)
    System.out.print(ch);
System.out.println();
iter = treeA.iterator();
while (iter.hasNext())
    System.out.print(iter.next());
```

c.
```
Iterator<Character> iter;
iter = treeA.getIterator(BSTInterface.Traversal.Preorder);
treeA.remove('N'); treeA.remove('R');
while (iter.hasNext())
    System.out.print(iter.next());
iter = treeA.getIterator(BSTInterface.Traversal.Inorder);
while (iter.hasNext())
    System.out.print(iter.next());
```

19. Using the Binary Search Tree ADT: For this question you should use the methods listed in the `BSTInterface` and standard Java control operations.

a. Assume that binary search tree `words` has been declared and it holds `String` objects. Write a section of code that prompts the user for a sentence, and then displays the words from the sentence in alphabetical order.

b. Assume that binary search tree `numbers` has been declared and it holds `Integer` objects. Write a section of code that generates 1,000 random numbers between 1 and 10,000 and stores them in `numbers`. It then generates 20 more numbers and reports for each whether or not it is contained in `numbers`.

c.   Assume that binary search tree `numbers` has been declared and it holds `Integer` objects. Write a section of code that generates 1,000 random numbers between 1 and 10,000 and stores them in `numbers`. It then outputs the average value of the numbers and how many of the numbers are less than that average.

7.4 The Implementation Level: Basics

20. Compare and contrast the `DLLNode` and `BSTNode` classes found in this text's `support` package.

21. Explain the difference between the two constructors of the `BinarySearchTree` class.

22. Suppose `tree` is a variable of type `BinarySearchTree<String>` and represents a tree containing the strings "alpha," "beta," "gamma," and "zebra," with "gamma" as the root and "beta" as one of the leaves. Draw a detailed figure that demonstrates the contents of the external variable `tree`, the internal variable `root`, plus the contents of the four `BSTNode` objects.

23. The `FamousPerson` class is part of this text's `support` package and was introduced in Section 5.4, "Comparing Objects Revisited," and revisited in Section 6.4, "Sorted Array-Based List Implementation." Show how you would instantiate a binary search tree `people` to hold `FamousPerson` objects ordered by

a.   Last name, First name

b.   Year of birth

24. Which method of the `BinarySearchTree` class is more efficient, `max` or `min`? Explain your answer.

25. For each of the following trees, state how many times the body of the *while* loops of the `min` and `max` methods of the `BinarySearchTree` class would be executed, if the methods are invoked on:

a.   an empty tree

b.   a tree consisting of a single node

c.   the tree in Figure 7.20a

d.   the tree in Figure 7.20b

e.   the tree in Figure 7.20c

26. Suppose `numbers` is a variable of class `BinarySearchTree<Integer>` and `value` is a variable of type `int`. Write a Java statement that prints `true` if `value` is in-between the largest and smallest values stored in `numbers`, and `false` otherwise.

7.5 Iterative Versus Recursive Method Implementations

27. Compare and contrast the approach we used for the `size` method when implementing our List ADT for the `LBList` class in Chapter 6 (maintain an instance variable

© Photodic

representing size) to the approach used for the `BinarySearchTree` class (calculate the size when asked).

28. Use the Three-Question Method to verify the recursive version of the `size` method.

29. Design and implement a method `min2` for `BinarySearchTree`, functionally equivalent to the `min` method, which uses recursion.

30. Design and implement a method `leafCount` for `BinarySearchTree` that returns the number of leaves in the tree and

   a. uses recursion.

   b. does not use recursion.

31. Design and implement a method `oneChild` for `BinarySearchTree` that returns the number of nodes in the tree that have exactly one child and

   a. uses recursion.

   b. does not use recursion.

32. Design and implement a method `height` for `BinarySearchTree`, that returns the height of the tree and

   a. uses recursion.

   b. does not use recursion.

7.6 The Implementation Level: Remaining Observers

33. For each of the following trees state how many times the `getLeft`, `getRight`, and `getInfo` methods are invoked if the `contains` method of the `BinarySearchTree` class is called with an argument of D on:

   a. an empty tree

   b. a tree consisting of a single node that contains D

   c. a tree consisting of a single node that contains A

   d. a tree consisting of a single node that contains E

   e. the tree in Figure 7.20a

   f. the tree in Figure 7.20b

   g. the tree in Figure 7.20c

34. What would be the effect of changing the first < comparison to <= in the `recContains` method of the BinarySearchTree class?

35. Design and implement a method `contains2` for `BinarySearchTree`, functionally equivalent to the `contains` method, that does not use recursion.

36. Suppose `getIterator` is invoked on the tree in Figure 7.12 and passed an argument indicating that an inorder traversal is desired. Show the sequence of ensuing method calls (you can indicate arguments using an integer that represents the info in the node) that are made to build the queue. Repeat for a postorder traversal.

37. Suppose that in place of using a queue within our traversal generation code we used a stack. Instead of enqueuing and dequeuing we push and top/pop the elements, but we make no other changes to the code. What would such a change mean for

    a. the preorder traversal

    b. the inorder traversal

    c. the postorder traversal

38. Enhance the Binary Search Tree ADT so that it supports a "level-order" traversal of the nodes, in addition to preorder, inorder, and postorder traversals.

7.7 The Implementation Level: Transformers

39. Show how we visualize the binary search tree with root referenced by `rootA` (page 490) after each of the following changes. Also list the sequence of `Binary-SearchTree` method calls, both public and private, that would be made when executing the change. Use the original tree to answer each part of this question.

    a. Add node C.

    b. Add node Z.

    c. Add node Q.

    d. Remove node M.

    e. Remove node Q.

    f. Remove node R.

40. Draw the binary search tree that results from starting with an empty tree and

    a. adding 50 72 96 94 26 12 11 9 2 10 25 51 16 17 95

    b. adding 95 17 16 51 25 10 2 9 11 12 26 94 96 72 50

    c. adding 10 72 96 94 85 78 80 9 5 3 1 15 18 37 47

    d. adding 50 72 96 94 26 12 11 9 2 10, then removing 2 and 94

    e. adding 50 72 96 94 26 12 11 9 2 10, then removing 50 and 26

    f. adding 50 72 96 94 26 12 11 9 2 10, then removing 12 and 72

41. Alternate implementations of the `add` method:

    a. We implemented the `add` method by invoking a `recAdd` method as follows:

    ```
    root = recAdd(element, root);
    ```

    As explained in the text, we used this approach so that in the case of adding to an empty tree we correctly reset the value in `root`. An alternate approach is to first handle that special case within the `add` method itself, before invoking `recAdd`. With this new approach `recAdd` need not return anything; it just handles the addition of the element. Design and implement a method `add2` for `BinarySearchTree`, functionally equivalent to the `add` method, that uses this alternate approach.

    b. Design and implement a method `add3` for `BinarySearchTree`, functionally equivalent to the `add` method, that does not use recursion.

7.8 Binary Search Tree Performance

42. Suppose 1,000 integer elements are generated at random and are inserted into a sorted linked list and a binary search tree (BST). Compare the efficiency of searching for an element in the two structures.

43. Suppose 1,000 integer elements are inserted in order, from smallest to largest, into a sorted linked list and a binary search tree. Compare the efficiency of searching for an element in the two structures.

44. Fill in the following table with the worst case efficiency order for each of the listed operations, given the listed internal representation. Assume the collection contains *N* elements at the time the operation is invoked. Assume an efficient algorithm is used (as efficient as allowed by the representation). Assume the linked lists have a pointer to the "front" of the list only.

	Unsorted Array	Unsorted Linked List	Sorted Array	Sorted Linked List	Skewed BST	Bushy BST
isEmpty						
min						
max						
contains						
add						
remove						

45. Draw the new tree that would be created by traversing the binary search tree with root referenced by `rootA` (page 490) in the following order, and as the nodes are visited, adding them to the new tree:

   a. Preorder

   b. Inorder

   c. Postorder

   d. Levelorder

46. Using the *Balance* algorithm, show the tree that would be created if the following values represented the inorder traversal of the original tree.

   a. 3   6   9   15   17   19   29

   b. 3   6   9   15   17   19   29   37

   c. 1   2   3   3   3   3   3   3   3   24
       37

47. Revise our `BSTInterface` interface and `BinarySearchTree` class to include the `balance` method. How can you test your revision?

48. Fullness Experiment:

    a.   Design and implement a method `height` for `BinarySearchTree` that returns the height of the tree (you have already done this if you completed Exercise 32).

    b.   Define the fullness ratio of a binary tree to be the ratio between its minimum height and its height (given the number of nodes in the tree). For example, the tree in Figure 7.5a has a fullness ratio of 1.00 (its minimum height is 3 and its height is 3) and the tree in Figure 7.6c has a fullness ratio of 0.33 (its minimum height is 3 and its height is 9). Implement a method `fRatio` to be added to the `BinarySearchTree` class that returns the fullness ratio of the tree.

    c.   Create an application that generates 10 "random" trees, each with 1,000 nodes (random integers between 1 and 3,000). For each tree output its height, optimal height, and fullness ratio.

    d.   Submit a report that includes your code for the `height` method, the `fRatio` method, the application code, sample output, and a short discussion. The discussion should include consideration of how the `fRatio` method might be used by an application to keep its search trees reasonably well balanced.

49. Fullness Experiment Part 2 (assumes you did the previous exercise):

    a.   Create an application that is capable of creating a "random" tree of 1,000 nodes (integers between 1 and 3,000). Each time one of the integers is generated it has a k% chance of being 42 and a (1–k)% chance of being a random integer between 1 and 3,000. For example, if k is 20 then approximately 20% of the integers in the tree will be 42 and the other 80% will be spread between 1 and 3,000. The application should output the tree's height, optimal height, and fullness ratio. Test the application on various values of k.

    b.   Expand your application so that it generates 10 trees for each value of k varying between 10 and 90, in increments by 10. That is a total of 90 trees. For each value of k output the average tree height and fullness ratio.

    c.   Submit a report that includes your code, sample output, and a discussion. Include descriptions of situations where we might store information that is "uneven"—where certain values occur more frequently than others.

7.9 Application: Word Frequency Counter

50. List all of the classes used directly by the `WordFreqCounter` application.

51. Describe the effect that each of the following changes would have on the `WordFreqCounter` application.

    a.   Remove the call to the `useDelimiter` method of the `Scanner` class.

    b.   Remove the call to the `toLowerCase` method of the `String` class.

    c.   Change the call to the `toLowerCase` method to a call to the `toUpperCase` method.

    d.   In the inner *if* clause of the *while* loop, change the statement `wordInTree.inc()` to `wordToTry.inc()`.

52. Create an application that will read a text file (file name/location provided through a command line argument) and display the longest word (or words if there is a tie) in the file and how many times they occur.

53. Create an application that will read a text file (file name/location provided through a command line argument) and display the most frequently used word (or words if there is a tie) in the file and how many times they occur.

54. Create an application that will read a text file (file name/location provided through a command line argument) and display the word or words in the file that occur exactly once.

55. An *n*-gram is a sequence of *n* items (numbers, characters, words) from some source. For example, the phrase "scoo be do be do be" contains the word-based 2-grams "scoo be" (once), "be do" (twice), and "do be" (twice). *N*-grams are used by computational linguists, biologists, and data compression experts in a multitude of ways. They can be especially useful in prediction models, where you have the start of a sequence of items and want to predict what is next—for example, when you text on your phone it might predict what word you want next as a shortcut. Write and test code that

    a. Acts like the `WordFreqCounter` application but instead of asking the user for the minimum word and frequency size it asks the user for a value of *n* and an associated minimum *n*-gram frequency, then tracks the frequency of *n*-grams from the input text, for that *n*.

    b. Enhance your application from part (a) so that after reporting the results for the *n*-grams it allows the user repeatedly to enter a group of *n* words and it reports back the top three most likely words that follow that group, along with the percentage of time within the text that group of words is followed by the reported word. For example, the interaction from running the application might look like this:

```
File name > somefile.txt
n-gram length> 3
Minimum n-gram frequency> 40
The 3-grams with frequency counts of 40 and above:

Freq  3-gram
-----  ------------------
00218 one of the
00105 is in the
00048 at the end


Enter 3 words (X to stop): one of the

12.7% one of the most
 8.3%   one of the first
 3.4%   one of the last


 . . .
```

7.10 Tree Variations

56. Draw a decision tree for deciding where to eat.

57. For the following mathematical expression

$$(56 + 24) \times 2 - (15 / 3)$$

    a.   draw the expression tree.

    b.   what is a preorder traversal of the tree?

    c.   postorder?

58. Draw the trie containing the following words:

    dan   date   danger   dang   dog   data   daniel   dave

59. Bob decides that the efficiency of searching a B-tree is dependent on how many levels there are in the tree. He decides he will store his 1,000 elements in a B-tree which contains only one node, a root node with all 1,000 elements. Because the height of his tree is 0, he believes he will be rewarded with constant search time. What do you tell Bob?

60. In the subsection AVL Trees, we defined the "balance factor" of a node. What is the balance factor of

    a.   Node A in the tree in Figure 7.6a.

    b.   Node A in the tree in Figure 7.6b.

    c.   Node A in the tree in Figure 7.6c.

    d.   Node C in the tree in Figure 7.6a.

    e.   Node C in the tree in Figure 7.6b.

The Map ADT

Knowledge Goals

You should be able to

- describe the genesis of the term *symbol table*
- discuss the ramifications of allowing null values within a map
- describe a map and its operations at an abstract level
- perform order of growth efficiency analysis for a given implementation of a map
- given a problem description, determine whether a map is an appropriate structure for solving the problem
- describe the `MapEntry` class
- define the following terms related to hashing
  - hash function
  - compression function
  - collisions
  - linear probing
  - clustering
  - quadratic probing
  - buckets
- discuss the ramifications of allowing null keys for a hash table–based implementation of a map
- given a description of a hashing approach, discuss potential approaches to the remove operation
- describe the role of rehashing in a hashing system
- critique a given hash function for a given application domain
- give examples of hybrid data structures and their uses

Skill Goals

You should be able to

- determine if it represents a legal map, given a pairwise relationship between two sets of values
- create a class that implements our Map ADT using:
  - an array
  - a hash table
  - a linked list
  - a sorted array
  - a binary search tree
  - an `ArrayList`
- predict the output of an application that uses the Map ADT
- use the Map ADT as a component of a problem solution
- design and implement an appropriate hash function for an application or a class
- show the contents of the underlying array, given a description of an array-based hashing approach and a sequence of inserted keys
- implement a hash-based map, given a description of the collision resolution policy

In the early days of computing it became apparent that high-level languages such as Java were crucial for programmers to be productive. The compilers and interpreters that translated high-level languages into lower-level languages for machine execution were possibly the most complex programs that had ever been created at that time. To support these programs a data structure called a symbol table was devised. A symbol table did just as its name suggests—it provided a table that could hold symbols. The symbols we speak of actually were the identifiers used in the high-level programs being translated, and the tables held more than just the identifier names, of course; they also held important information related to the identifier such as its type, scope, and memory location:

Symbol	Type	Scope	Location
value	integer	global	47B43390
cost	float	local	537DA372
i	integer	loop	38DD2545

When the translation program first encountered an identifier it would add its information to the table. On subsequent encounters it would get the information related to the symbol from the table. Thus, a symbol table provided a mapping from symbols to the information related to the symbol:

$$cost \rightarrow float, local, 537DA372$$

In the years since the creation of symbol tables, we have come to realize that such a data structure, one that provides a map from a given value to information related to that value, can be used for more than just symbol tables. That is why in this chapter we use the more generic term **map** to describe this structure. Nevertheless, our Map ADT is essentially a symbol table. It is similar to our Collection ADT and, like all of our collections, it supports the addition, removal, and discovery of information. The primary difference between our Collection ADT and our Map ADT is that our Map ADT explicitly separates the key information from the element—the key and the value mapped to, from the key, are separate entities.

Following our typical pattern, we first define an interface for our Map ADT, and then look at implementations and applications. One implementation approach in particular is *very important*. Hashing traces its origins back to those early symbol tables, where it was crucial to be able to quickly locate a symbol in the table. As you will see, with a well-designed hashing approach the cost to find a key can be O(1). Yes, O(1)—you cannot do better than that! Today, hashing is still used to implement compiler symbol tables, in addition to such important uses as memory management, database indexing, and Internet routing.

8.1   The Map Interface

Our maps will associate a key with a value. When a map structure is presented with a key—for example, through a `get(key)` operation—it returns the associated value, if there is one. A map acts much like a mathematical function. In fact, within the functional programming paradigm the term "map" means applying a function to all elements of a list, and returning the new list. Functions in mathematics relate each input value to exactly one output value. Present the function $f(x) = x^2$ with the value 5, and it returns 5^2 or 25. The function f maps 5 onto 25, and nothing else. So it is with our maps. Another way of putting this is to say that a map structure does not permit duplicate keys (see **Figure 8.1a** which is *not* a map). The values on the other hand, may be duplicate—it is possible to have two distinct keys map onto the same value (see Figure 8.1(b) which is a map).

When we think of maps, keys, and associated values we typically think of using a key to retrieve the additional information associated with the key. For example, in **Figure 8.2a** the atomic number is used as a key to find the associated element name. However, it could be that the key itself is embedded in the information associated with it—much like the key fields of the elements in our collections. The key could be a string and the value associated with it could be a `WordFreq` object holding the same string plus the additional information of a count, as shown in Figure 8.2b. There can even be a situation where we want to use a map simply to hold keys, for example, to calculate the vocabulary density of a text we only need to store strings with no associated value. In such a case we can still use a map, by simply associating a key with itself as shown in Figure 8.2c.

We now define our `MapInterface`. Our maps will provide all of the basic operations associated with collections—the ability to add, remove, get, and determine membership

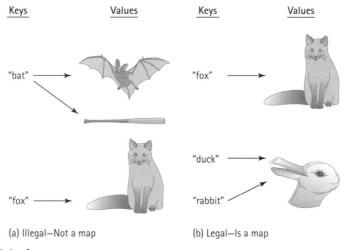

(a) Illegal—Not a map   (b) Legal—Is a map

Figure 8.1   Rules for maps

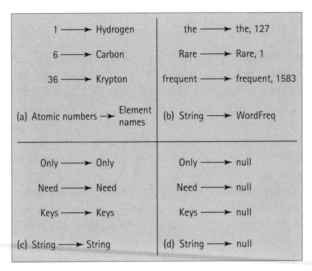

Figure 8.2 Legal mapping variations

of elements. However, given that maps separate keys from values, we cannot reuse the `CollectionInterface` abstract method definitions. With maps, all of these basic operations will refer separately to keys and values.

We have already stated that keys will be unique. Additionally, we disallow null keys. If a map operation is passed a null key as an argument, it will throw an `IllegalArgument Exception`. This unchecked exception is provided by the `java.lang` package.

Values, on the other hand, need not be unique (see Figure 8.1b) and can be null. Allowing null values permits us to store the fact that a key exists even though it is not yet associated with any value; for example, a new employee was hired but has not yet been assigned an office. Null values can also be used in the case where we are only interested in holding keys (see Figure 8.2d).

The Map interface takes two generic parameters, one indicating the key type and one indicating the value type. In addition to the basic collection-like operations mentioned above, it also requires our standard `isEmpty`, `isFull`, and `size` methods, plus an iterator. The code follows.

```
//------------------------------------------------------------------------
// MapInterface.java              by Dale/Joyce/Weems          Chapter 8
//
// A map provides (K = key, V = value) pairs, mapping the key onto the value.
// Keys are unique. Keys cannot be null.
//
// Methods throw IllegalArgumentException if passed a null key argument.
//
// Values can be null, so a null value returned by put, get, or remove does
// not necessarily mean that an entry did not exist.
//------------------------------------------------------------------------
```

```
package ch08.maps;

import java.util.Iterator;

public interface MapInterface<K, V> extends Iterable<MapEntry<K,V>>
{
    V put(K k, V v);
    // If an entry in this map with key k already exists then the value
    // associated with that entry is replaced by value v and the original
    // value is returned; otherwise, adds the (k, v) pair to the map and
    // returns null.

    V get(K k);
    // If an entry in this map with a key k exists then the value associated
    // with that entry is returned; otherwise null is returned.

    V remove(K k);
    // If an entry in this map with key k exists then the entry is removed
    // from the map and the value associated with that entry is returned;
    // otherwise null is returned.
    //
    // Optional. Throws UnsupportedOperationException if not supported.

    boolean contains(K k);
    // Returns true if an entry in this map with key k exists;
    // Returns false otherwise.

    boolean isEmpty();
    // Returns true if this map is empty; otherwise, returns false.

    boolean isFull();
    // Returns true if this map is full; otherwise, returns false.

    int size();
    // Returns the number of entries in this map.
}
```

Depending on the circumstances, the put, get, and remove methods might return null to indicate that there was no value associated with the provided key argument. The client must be careful how it interprets a returned null value, since it is possible to have keys associated with null. If the distinction between a null indicating "no entry" and a null indicating an entry with a null value is important to a client, then it should use the contains method first to determine whether the entry exists.

Because a map holds pairs of objects it is possible to consider three iteration approaches—we could provide an iteration that returns the keys, or that returns the values, or that returns the key-value pairs. We have decided to require the last of these, an iteration that returns key-value pairs, as part of our map requirements. We create a new class `MapEntry` to represent the key-value pairs. This class requires the `key` and `value` to be passed as constructor arguments, and provides getter operations for both, plus a setter operation for the value, plus a `toString`. It is a relatively simple class and is also part of the `ch08.maps` package:

```
//------------------------------------------------------------------------------
// MapEntry.java                by Dale/Joyce/Weems              Chapter 8
//
// Provides key, value pairs for use with a Map.
// Keys are immutable.
//------------------------------------------------------------------------------
package ch08.maps;

public class MapEntry<K, V>
{
  protected K key;
  protected V value;

  MapEntry(K k, V v)
  {
    key = k; value = v;
  }

  public K getKey()   {return key;}
  public V getValue(){return value;}
  public void setValue(V v){value = v;}

  @Override
  public String toString()
  // Returns a string representing this MapEntry.
  {
    return "Key  : " + key + "\nValue: " + value;
  }
}
```

Looking back at `MapInterface` you will see that it extends `Iterable<MapEntry<K,V>>`. This means that any class that implements the `MapInterface` must provide an `iterator` method that returns an `Iterator` over `MapEntry<K,V>` objects.

Let us look at a short sample application, just to clarify the use of a map. This example uses the implementation developed in the next section. Each output statement includes a description of the predicted output. This makes it easier to check if our expectations are met. You should trace through the code to see if you agree with the predictions.

```java
package ch08.apps;
import ch08.maps.*;

public class MapExample
{
  public static void main(String[] args)
  {
    boolean result;
    MapInterface<Character, String> example;
    example = new ArrayListMap<Character, String>();
    System.out.println("Expect 'true':\t" + example.isEmpty());
    System.out.println("Expect '0':\t" + example.size());

    System.out.println("Expect 'null':\t" + example.put('C', "cat"));
    example.put('D', "dog");    example.put('P', "pig");
    example.put('A', "ant");    example.put('F', "fox");
    System.out.println("Expect 'false':\t" + example.isEmpty());
    System.out.println("Expect '5:\t" + example.size());
    System.out.println("Expect 'true':\t" + example.contains('D'));
    System.out.println("Expect 'false':\t" + example.contains('E'));
    System.out.println("Expect 'dog':\t" + example.get('D'));
    System.out.println("Expect 'null':\t" + example.get('E'));

    System.out.println("Expect 'cat':\t" + example.put('C', "cow"));
    System.out.println("Expect 'cow':\t" + example.get('C'));
    System.out.print("Expect 5 animals: ");
    for (MapEntry<Character,String> m: example)
      System.out.print(m.getValue() + "\t");

    System.out.println("\nExpect 'pig':\t" + example.put('P', null));
    System.out.println("Expect 'dog':\t" + example.remove('D'));
    System.out.print("Expect 3 animals plus a 'null': ");
    for (MapEntry<Character,String> m: example)
      System.out.print(m.getValue() + "\t");
  }
}
```

The output from the sample program is below. Looks like all of the predictions were accurate!

```
Expect 'true':     true
Expect '0':        0
Expect 'null':     null
Expect 'false':    false
Expect '5:         5
Expect 'true':     true
Expect 'false':    false
Expect 'dog':      dog
Expect 'null':     null
Expect 'cat':      cat
Expect 'cow':      cow
Expect 5 animals: dog        pig        ant        fox        cow
Expect 'pig':      pig
Expect 'dog':      dog
Expect 3 animals plus a 'null': ant       fox        cow        null
```

8.2   Map Implementations

There are many ways to implement our Map ADT. Any of the internal representations we have used so far for collections can also form the basis for a map implementation. This is not surprising since a map can be viewed as a collection of MapEntry objects with the additional requirement that no two objects have the same key.

Let us briefly consider some possible approaches.

Unsorted Array

The array holds MapEntry objects. The put operation creates a new MapEntry object using the arguments provided by the client code. It then performs a brute force search of all the current keys in the array to prevent key duplication. If a duplicate key is found, then the associated MapEntry object is replaced by the new object and its value attribute is returned. For example,

```
map.put('C', "cow");
```

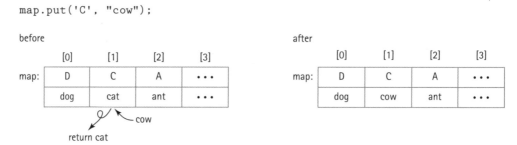

Otherwise, the new object is simply added at the "end" of the array, that is, in the first available array slot. For example:

```
map.put('B', "bat");
```

before

	[0]	[1]	[2]	[3]	
map:	D	C	A	•••	
	dog	cat	ant	•••	

after

	[0]	[1]	[2]	[3]	
map:	D	C	A	B	•••
	dog	cat	ant	bat	•••

Like put, the get, remove, and contains operations would all require brute force searches of the current array contents, so they are all O(N).

Sorted Array

A sorted array is the same as an unsorted array except the entries are maintained in sorted order by key. Depending on the implementation details, clients may be required to use Comparable keys or provide a Comparator object. With this approach the binary search algorithm can be used, greatly improving the efficiency of the important get and contains operations. Although it is not a requirement, in general it is expected that a map will provide fast implementation of these two operations.

Unsorted Linked List

As with the unsorted array, a brute force search of the linked list is required for most operations. Therefore, there is no time efficiency advantage to using an unsorted linked list as compared to an unsorted array. The put operation, for example, looks much the same as the put operation for the unsorted array. The following figure depicts what happens when a key is reused to put a second value into the map.

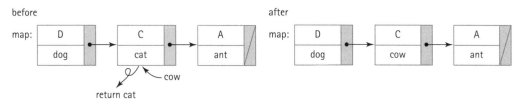

When a new key is put into a map, the map still must be searched to make sure there are no duplicates. Then, the new entry is placed in an "easy" location, probably either the front or the rear of the linked list. There is conceivably some benefit to using the front of the array for insertion of a new key/value pair, as for many applications, an entry recently inserted into a map is highly likely to be searched for soon afterward.

In terms of space, a linked list grows and shrinks as needed so it is possible that some advantage can be found in terms of memory management, as compared to an array. Do not forget, however, that a linked list uses an extra memory reference, to hold the link, for each element.

Sorted Linked List

Even though a linked list is kept sorted, it does not permit use of the binary search algorithm as there is no efficient way to inspect the "middle" element. So there is not much advantage to using a sorted linked list to implement a map, as compared to an unsorted linked list. It is possible to make use of the sorted nature of the list to discontinue a search for a given key once a key with a higher value has been encountered. Although helpful, this approach does not provide a faster order of growth efficiency.

Binary Search Tree

If a map can be implemented as a *balanced* binary search tree, then all of the primary operations (put, get, remove, and contains) can exhibit efficiency $O(\log_2 N)$. The tree may use the key of each entry for comparison purposes and so, as with the sorted array approach, clients would be required to use Comparable keys or provide a Comparator object. The time efficiency benefits depend on the tree remaining balanced:

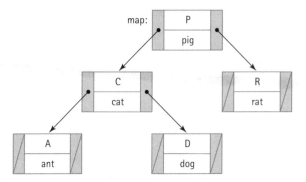

An ArrayList-Based Implementation

We provide an implementation of a map using an ArrayList of MapEntry objects as the internal representation. The ArrayList is unsorted so the analysis above in the subsection "Unsorted Array" applies. This implementation, although not a good example of an efficient approach, does clearly show the relationships among the various operations and the use of the helper class MapEntry.

```
//---------------------------------------------------------------------------
// ArrayListMap.java          by Dale/Joyce/Weems          Chapter 8
//
// Implements a map using an ArrayList.
//
// A map provides (K = key, V = value) pairs, mapping the key onto the value.
// Keys are unique. Keys cannot be null.
//
// Methods throw IllegalArgumentException if passed a null key argument.
//
```

```java
// Values can be null, so a null value returned by put, get, or remove does
// not necessarily mean that an entry did not exist.
//------------------------------------------------------------------------
package ch08.maps;

import java.util.*;   // Iterator, ArrayList

public class ArrayListMap<K, V>  implements MapInterface<K,V>
{
  protected ArrayList<MapEntry<K, V>> map;

  public ArrayListMap()
  {
    map = new ArrayList<MapEntry<K, V>>();
  }

  public ArrayListMap(int initCapacity)
  {
    map = new ArrayList<MapEntry<K, V>>(initCapacity);
  }

  public V put(K k, V v)
  // If an entry in this map with key k already exists then the value
  // associated with that entry is replaced by value v and the original
  // value is returned; otherwise, adds the (k, v) pair to the map and
  // returns null.
  {
    if (k == null)
      throw new IllegalArgumentException("Maps do not allow null keys.");

    MapEntry<K, V> entry = new MapEntry<K, V>(k, v);

    MapEntry<K,V> temp;
    Iterator<MapEntry<K,V>> search = map.iterator(); // Arraylist iterator
    while (search.hasNext())
    {
      temp = search.next();
      if (temp.getKey().equals(k))
      {
        search.remove();
        map.add(entry);
        return temp.getValue(); // k found, exits method
      }
    }
```

```
    // No entry is associated with k.
    map.add(entry);
    return null;
}

public V get(K k)
// If an entry in this map with a key k exists then the value associated
// with that entry is returned; otherwise null is returned.
{
  if (k == null)
    throw new IllegalArgumentException("Maps do not allow null keys.");

  for (MapEntry<K,V> temp: map)     // uses ArrayList iterator
    if (temp.getKey().equals(k))
      return temp.getValue();        // k found, exits method

  // No entry is associated with k.
  return null;
}

public V remove(K k)
// If an entry in this map with key k exists then the entry is removed
// from the map and the value associated with that entry is returned;
// otherwise null is returned.
{
  if (k == null)
    throw new IllegalArgumentException("Maps do not allow null keys.");

  MapEntry<K,V> temp;
  Iterator<MapEntry<K,V>> search = map.iterator(); // Arraylist iterator
  while (search.hasNext())
  {
    temp = search.next();
    if (temp.getKey().equals(k))
    {
      search.remove();
      return temp.getValue();     // k found, exits method
    }
  }

  // No entry is associated with k.
  return null;
}
```

```java
public boolean contains(K k)
// Returns true if an entry in this map with key k exists;
// Returns false otherwise.
{
  if (k == null)
    throw new IllegalArgumentException("Maps do not allow null keys.");

  for (MapEntry<K,V> temp: map)
    if (temp.getKey().equals(k))
      return true;       // k found, exits method

  // No entry is associated with k.
  return false;
}

public boolean isEmpty()
// Returns true if this map is empty; otherwise, returns false.
{
  return (map.size() == 0);   // uses ArrayList size
}

public boolean isFull()
// Returns true if this map is full; otherwise, returns false.
{
  return false;  // An ArrayListMap is never full
}

public int size()
// Returns the number of entries in this map.
{
  return map.size();   // uses ArrayList size
}

public Iterator<MapEntry<K,V>> iterator()
// Returns the Iterator provided by ArrayList.
{
  return map.iterator();  // returns ArrayList iterator
}
}
```

A few notes about the implementation:

- Two constructors are provided, one for which the client indicates the original capacity and one that uses the default capacity of an `ArrayList`, 10, for the original capacity.

- Since an `ArrayList` is unbounded, our `ArrayListMap` is unbounded and the `isFull` method simply returns `false`.

- Within the code, in order to determine if an entry with a particular key exists, we create an iterator on the `ArrayList` and walk through it, checking the keys of the map entries. Alternately, if an `equals` method is defined for our `MapEntry` class which returns `true` if two `MapEntry` objects have the same key attribute, then it is possible to use the `contains` method of the `ArrayList` class (which in turn would use the `MapEntry equals` method). Although this would make the code for our `ArrayListMap` class simpler, it does not improve efficiency since in either case the `ArrayList` entries must be traversed.

- For the `iterator` method we simply return the `Iterator` provided by the `ArrayList` class. This same approach could be used by any other implementation approach that uses a wrapped `Iterable` object as its internal representation of the map.

- Because we also make use of the built-in `ArrayList iterator` method within our `put` method implementation, `put` does not act exactly like the aforementioned *put* operation for an unsorted array approach. Can you see the difference? If we attempt to put an entry that duplicates a previously entered key, rather than replacing its associated value, we remove the entry altogether (which causes the remaining entries to be shifted) and insert a new entry at the end of the list.

8.3 Application: String-to-String Map

Here we develop a short yet versatile application that demonstrates the use of our Map ADT. Suppose there is a text file containing pairs of related strings, one pair per line. Assume that none of the strings contain the character #—we can use # as a delimiter to separate the strings. Assume that there are no empty strings included and that the first string of each pair is unique—the first string will act as a key.

Our application reads the text file line by line, putting the information into a map object, using the first string on a line as the key and the second string as the associated value. The application then prompts the user to enter a string and if the user replies with one of the previously read keys, the application displays the associated value. In order to allow the application to provide appropriate prompts, the first line of the text file contains a pair of strings indicating the meanings of the keys and the values. As an example, suppose the file `numbers.txt` contains

```
Number between 0 and 100#The Number is:
0#Zero
1#One
2#Two

. . .

99#Ninety-Nine
100#One Hundred
```

A run of the application using `numbers.txt` as input reads the text file, builds the maps, and then interacts with the user:

```
Enter Number between 0 and 100 (XX to exit):
12
The Number is:        Twelve

Enter Number between 0 and 100 (XX to exit):
134
        No information available.

Enter Number between 0 and 100 (XX to exit):
56
The Number is:        Fifty-Six

Enter Number between 0 and 100 (XX to exit):
XX
```

Assuming one understands the Map ADT and its interface the application is straightforward and easy to create. A command line argument indicates the location and name of the input file, and a `Scanner` object, set up with appropriate delimiters, is used to scan the file. The application first scans and saves the information from the first line to use when interacting with the user. Next it scans the key/value string pairs until it reaches the end of the file, saving the information in the `pairs` map. Finally, it repeatedly prompts the user for a string and if a matching key exists in the `pairs` map, it displays the corresponding value. Otherwise it reports, "No information available." Here is the code with the map-related commands <u>emphasized</u>.

```
//-------------------------------------------------------------------------
// StringPairApp.java          by Dale/Joyce/Weems          Chapter 8
//
// Reads # separated pairs of strings from specified input file.
// First pair of strings provides descriptive info.
// Remaining pairs of strings stored in a map as key - value pairs.
// Prompts user for a key and if it exists, displays the associated value.
//-------------------------------------------------------------------------
package ch08.apps;

import java.io.*;
import java.util.*;
import ch08.maps.*;

public class StringPairApp
{
  public static void main(String[] args) throws IOException
```

```java
{
    // Create map
    MapInterface<String, String> pairs = new ArrayListMap<String, String>();

    // Set up file reading
    String fname = args[0];            // input file of text
    FileReader fin = new FileReader(fname);
    Scanner info = new Scanner(fin);
    info.useDelimiter("[#\\n\\r]");     // delimiters are # signs, line feeds,
                                        // carriage returns

    // get information about the key and value
    String keyInfo = info.next();
    String valueInfo = info.next();
    info.nextLine();

    // Reads the key/value pairs from the file and puts them into the map
    String key, value;
    while (info.hasNext())
    {
        key = info.next();   value = info.next();
        info.nextLine();
        pairs.put(key, value);
    }

    // Interact with user, getting keys and displaying value
    Scanner scan = new Scanner(System.in);
    final String STOP = "XX";
    key = null;
    while (!STOP.equals(key))
    {
        System.out.println("\nEnter " + keyInfo + " (" + STOP + " to exit):");
        key = scan.next();
        if (!STOP.equals(key))
            if (pairs.contains(key))
                System.out.println(valueInfo + "\t" + pairs.get(key));
            else
                System.out.println("\tNo information available.");
    }
}
}
```

Now we look at a few more examples of how one might use this application. The file `glossary.txt`, found in the `input` folder, contains this text's definitions as key/value pairs. Using it as input to the `StringPairApp` application we get a means to look up definitions:

```
Enter Data Structure's Term (XX to exit):
Leaf
Definition      A tree node that has no children

Enter Data Structure's Term (XX to exit):
Ancestor
Definition      A parent of a node, or a parent of an ancestor

Enter Data Structure's Term (XX to exit):
Garbage
Definition      The set of currently unreachable objects

Enter Data Structure's Term (XX to exit):
XX
```

Nice! OK, one more example. The file `periodic.txt` contains a list of atomic element numbers and names:

```
Atomic Number#Element Name
1# Hydrogen
2# Helium
3# Lithium
. . .
118# Ununoctium
```

Our application lets us look up element names based on number:

```
Enter Atomic Number (XX to exit):
6
Element Name    Carbon

Enter Atomic Number (XX to exit):
36
Element Name    Krypton

Enter Atomic Number (XX to exit):
200
        No information available.

Enter Atomic Number (XX to exit):
118
Element Name    Ununoctium

Enter Atomic Number (XX to exit):
XX
```

8.4 Hashing

As the name implies, the purpose of a Map ADT is to map keys onto their corresponding values. Although an efficient mapping is not required as part of the specification of the ADT, it is implied and expected. In particular, when using an implementation of a Map ADT, a programmer expects efficient implementations of the observer methods `get` and `contains`. If we consider the approaches discussed in Section 8.2, "Map Implementations," we see that the unsorted array (including the `ArrayList`-based implementation we presented later in the section), unsorted linked list, and sorted linked list all support $O(N)$ implementations of the observer methods—this is not efficient. Both the sorted array and balanced binary search tree approaches do better, allowing `get` and `contains` implementations that are $O(\log_2 N)$. That is good.

Let us do better!

Consider the first example of Section 8.3, "Application: String-to-String Map" where, based on the contents of the `numbers.txt` file, the integers between 0 and 100 were mapped onto their description as words. By the time all of the data is loaded into the underlying array it looks something like this:

	[00]	[01]	[02]		[99]	[100]
map:	0	1	2	. . .	99	100
	zero	one	two		ninety-nine	one hundred

Consider, for example, a call to `map.contains("91")`. Our `ArrayList`-based application searches the first 92 slots of the array before finding a match and returning `true`. The `contains` method is $O(N)$. Even if we chose a sorted array-based implementation for our map that can use binary search, the search would require seven comparisons ($O(\log_2 N)$) before locating the target key. However, in this case, we can see that it would be possible to simply read the user's input as an integer and use that integer as the index into the underlying array (the value associated with 91 is in array location 91). That is $O(1)$—a constant time search for the entry.

This is promising. Let us further explore this idea of using the key as an index into an array of entries. Can we somehow get this approach to work in the general case? In theory, that is not an impossible dream. The approach presented next is called **hashing** (you will learn why in the next section) and the underlying data structure—the array that holds the entries—is called a **hash table**.

Hashing involves determining array indices directly from the key of the entry being stored/accessed. Hashing is an important approach involving many inter-related considerations. Here we present the related ideas one at a time, so although you may have concerns about holes in the approach as we first start to describe it, we hope that by the time you reach the end of the discussion you will agree that this is a clever and interesting solution to efficient storage/retrieval.

Let us continue by looking at a more pragmatic example, a list of employees of a fairly small company. First we will consider a company with 100 employees, each of whom has an ID number in the range 0 to 99. We want to access the employee information by the key idNum. If we store the entries in a hash table that is indexed from 0 to 99, we can directly access any employee's information through the array index, just as discussed for the numbers example above. A one-to-one correspondence exists between the entry keys and the array indices; in effect, the array index functions as the key of each entry.

In practice, this perfect relationship between the key value and the location of an entry is not so easy to establish or maintain. Consider a similar small company with 100 employees, but this company uses five-digit ID numbers to identify employees. If we use the five-digit ID number as our key, then the range of key values is from 00000 to 99999. It seems wasteful to set up a hash table of 100,000 locations, of which only 100 are needed, just to make sure that each employee's entry is in a perfectly unique and predictable location.

What if we limit the hash table size to the size that we actually need (an array of 100 entries) and use just the last two digits of the key to identify each employee? For instance, the entry for employee 53374 is stored in employeeList[74], and the entry for employee 81235 is in employeeList[35]. The entries are located in the hash table based on a function of the key value:

```
location = (idNum % 100);
```

The key idNum is divided by 100, and the remainder is used as an index into the hash table of employee entries, as illustrated in **Figure 8.3**. This function assumes that the hash table is indexed from 0 to 99 (MAX_ENTRIES = 100). In the general case, given an integral key, for example idNum, and the size of the storage array, such as MAX_ENTRIES, we can associate a hash table location with the key using the statement:

```
location = (idNum % MAX_ENTRIES);
```

The function f(idNum) = idNum % MAX_ENTRIES used here is called a **compression function** because it "compresses" the wider domain of numbers (0 to idNum), representing the keys, into the smaller range of numbers (0 to MAX_ENTRIES - 1), representing the indices of the hash table. Of course, keys will not always be integral—for now we assume they are and we will address the important issue of nonintegral keys in Section 8.5, "Hash Functions."

The compression function has two uses. First it is used to determine where in the hash table to store an entry. **Figure 8.4** shows a hash table whose entries—information for the employees with the key values (unique ID numbers) 12704, 31300, 49001, 52202, and 65606—were added using the compression function (idNum % 100) to determine the storage index. To simplify our figures in the remainder of this section, we use the key value, in this case the idNum, to represent the entire entry stored along with the key. Note that with this approach the entries are *not* stored contiguously as has been done with all previous array-based approaches in the text. For example, because no entries whose keys produce the hash values 3 or 5 have been added yet in Figure 8.4, the hash table slots [03] and [05] are logically "empty."

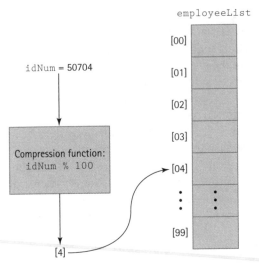

Figure 8.3   Using a compression function to determine the location of the entry in a hash table

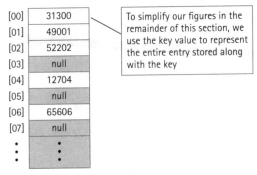

Figure 8.4   Result of adding entries based on a compression function

The second use of the compression function is to determine where to look for an entry. If the information corresponding to idNum 65606 is requested, the retrieval method uses 65606 % 100 = 06 as the index into the hash table to retrieve the information.

It is not quite that simple, which is OK. We cannot expect to obtain constant time storage and retrieval without some complexity, correct?

Collisions

By now you are probably objecting to this scheme on the grounds that it does not guarantee unique array locations for each key. For example, unique ID numbers 01234 and 91234 both "compress" to the same location: 34. This is called a **collision**. The problem of minimizing such collisions is the biggest challenge in designing a good hashing system and we discuss it in Section 8.5, "Hash Functions."

Assuming that some collisions occur, where should the entries be stored that cause them? We briefly describe several popular collision-handling algorithms next. Whatever scheme is used to find the place to store an entry will also need to be used when trying to find the entry. The choice of collision-handling algorithm also impacts entry removal options.

In our discussion of collision resolution policies, we will assume use of an array `info` to hold the information, and the `int` variable `location` to indicate an array/hash-table slot.

Linear Probing

A simple scheme for resolving collisions is to store the colliding entry into the next available space. This technique is known as **linear probing**. In the situation depicted in **Figure 8.5**, we want to add the employee entry with the key ID number 77003. The compression function returns 03. But there already is an entry stored in this hash table slot, the record for employee 50003. The `location` is incremented to 04, and the next hash table slot is examined. Because `info[04]` is also in use, `location` is incremented again. This time a slot that is empty is found, so the new entry is stored into `info[05]`.

What happens if the last index in the hash table is reached and that space is in use? The hash table can be considered to be a circular structure so searching for an empty slot can continue at the beginning of the table. This approach is similar to our circular array-based queue presented in Chapter 4.

How do we know whether a hash table slot is "empty"? Assuming we have an array of objects, this is easy—just check whether the value of the array slot is `null`.

To search for an entry in support of the `get` and `contains` operations using this collision-handling technique, the compression function is evaluated on the target key, and the result is used to obtain an entry from the table. The target key is compared to the key of the entry from the table. If the keys do not match, linear probing is used, beginning at the next slot in the hash table. Searching continues until either a matching entry is found (a successful search) or a `null` entry is found (an unsuccessful search).

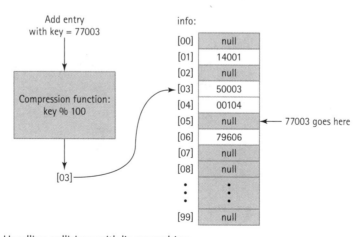

Figure 8.5   Handling collisions with linear probing

There is a boundary-case issue or bug with our search approach. If searching for an entry that is not contained in the hash table and the hash table is full, the code will continuously wrap around, fruitlessly searching forever. We can solve this issue by storing the original location returned by the compression function and then discontinuing the search if it returns to that location. In practice this is not an issue—as we will discuss later, most hashing schemes increase the size of the underlying array if their load factor (the percentage of array slots being used) rises above a preset threshold. In that case, the array will never be full and we need not worry about the infinite loop.

Entry Removal

Although we have discussed the insertion and retrieval of entries in the hash table, we have not yet mentioned how to remove an entry. Look at an example. Consider **Figure 8.6**. Suppose we remove the entry with the key 77003 by setting info[05] to null. A subsequent search for the entry with the key 42504 would begin at info[04]. The entry in this slot is not the one being searched for, so the code next tests info[05]. This slot, which formerly was occupied by the entry that was removed, is now empty (contains null), but the search cannot be terminated—the record being searched for is in the next slot.

Not being able to assume that an empty array slot indicates the end of a linear probe severely undermines the efficiency of this approach. Even when the hash table is sparsely populated, every location must be examined before determining that an entry is not present. Because the primary goal of a hashing approach is to provide fast search, this is not a tenable solution. What else can we do?

One approach is to indicate, with a special reserved value stored in a hash table slot, that the slot once held an entry, but that the entry has been deleted. For example, if we use the value 00000 as the special value, then the hash table in **Figure 8.7** shows what the hash table from Figure 8.6 contains after removal of the entry with key 77003.

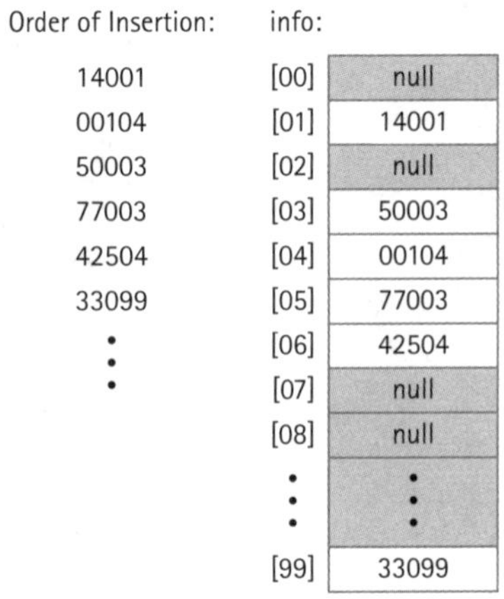

Order of Insertion:	info:	
14001	[00]	null
00104	[01]	14001
50003	[02]	null
77003	[03]	50003
42504	[04]	00104
33099	[05]	77003
⋮	[06]	42504
	[07]	null
	[08]	null
	⋮	⋮
	[99]	33099

Figure 8.6   Linear probing

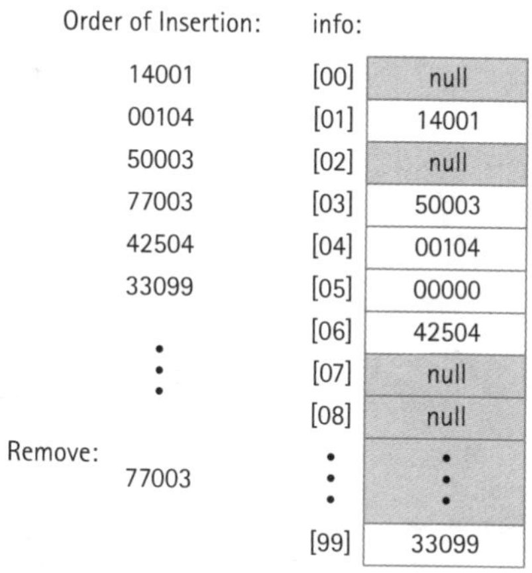

Figure 8.7   Using 00000 to indicate removal

With this approach, when searching the hash table to support `get`, `contains`, or `remove`, any hash table slot containing the special value is skipped over. The `add` operation, on the other hand, upon seeing the special value, acts as if it has seen a `null` and uses the slot for the new entry. After all, the location is available and can be used to hold real information. Note that with this approach, when searching for a key, the code *can* terminate the search (unsuccessfully) when a `null` value is encountered. For example, if checking to see if the hash table pictured in Figure 8.7 contains the key 17203, the code would inspect hash table slots 03 (not a match), 04 (not a match), 05 (special value), 06 (not a match), and 07 (null).

For the special value approach to work we must assume that no entry actually uses the value as its key. A similar approach does not suffer from this restriction. If an additional value, for example, a `boolean` value, is associated with each hash table slot, it can be used to indicate whether or not the slot previously held a value (see **Figure 8.8**). This is essentially the same as the special value approach except the code checks the boolean value instead of looking for the special value.

Another approach to this issue is to disallow removal of entries. Make `remove` an illegal operation. Although this may seem like a drastic approach there are many situations where it is not an issue. Collections are often used to store static information for fast retrieval, in which case, the `remove` operation is not needed.

Quadratic Probing

One problem with linear probing is that it results in a situation called **clustering**. Suppose keys end up being distributed randomly, resulting in a uniform distribution of used indices throughout the hash table's index range. Initially, entries are added throughout the hash table, with

> **Data Structures and Algorithms**
>
> In many cases our data structures and algorithms evolve concurrently. We design a data structure to solve a problem. During its use "in the wild" issues arise and patterns emerge. So we adjust the definition and/or implementation of the structure to address the issues or take advantage of the observed patterns. Quadratic probing is an example of a case where a new operation approach was created due to patterns observed (the observation of clustering) as the original structure was being used in real applications.

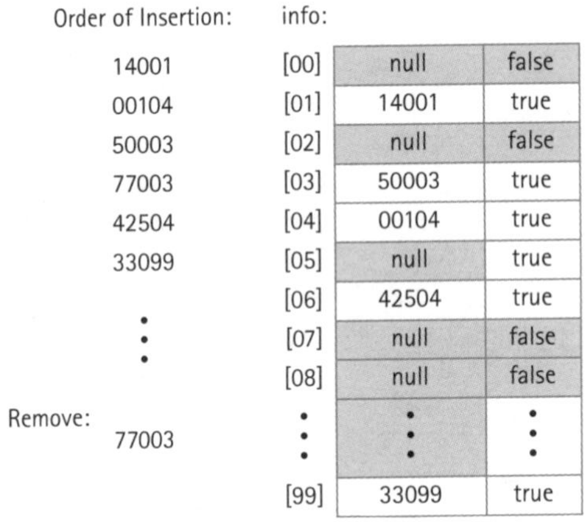

Order of Insertion:	info:		
14001	[00]	null	false
00104	[01]	14001	true
50003	[02]	null	false
77003	[03]	50003	true
42504	[04]	00104	true
33099	[05]	null	true
	[06]	42504	true
⋮	[07]	null	false
	[08]	null	false
Remove:	⋮	⋮	⋮
77003			
	[99]	33099	true

Figure 8.8   Using a `boolean` to indicate removal

each slot being equally likely to be filled. Over time, after a number of collisions have been resolved, the distribution of entries in the hash table becomes less and less uniform. The entries tend to cluster together, as multiple keys begin to compete for a single location. This phenomena happens even with a good random distribution of keys. Why?

Consider the hash table in Figure 8.6. Only an entry whose key produces the compression value 08 would be inserted into hash table slot [08]. However, any entries with keys that produce a compression value of 03, 04, 05, 06, or 07 would be inserted into hash table slot [07]. That is, hash table slot [07] is five times more likely than hash table slot [08] to be filled. As soon as there is a collision or two entries otherwise end up beside each other in the hash table, the probability that the two of them viewed as a unit are "hit" is twice as high as any other slot in the hash table. And this probability-driven effect escalates as more entries are added, resulting in clusters of used locations throughout the hash table. Clustering results in inconsistent efficiency of collection operations and makes the use of a load threshold for the underlying array even more important when linear probing is used.

Clustering is a side effect of linear probing. Another collision resolution approach, called quadratic probing, reduces the cluster effect. In linear probing, the code adds the constant value 1 to the location until it finds an open hash table slot. With **quadratic probing** the value added at each step is dependent on how many locations have already been inspected. The first time it looks for a new location it adds 1 to the original location, the second time it adds 4 to the original location, the third time it adds 9 to the original location, and so on—the ith time it adds i^2.

Because we jump ahead more and more spaces, each time a "probe" fails to find an available slot, the clustering effect is reduced. The example shown in **Figure 8.9** makes the difference clear to see. We must take care with this approach, however, because we could find ourselves in an infinite loop of probes even though there are empty slots in the hash table. We can solve this issue by keeping track of how many probes have been attempted and if the count reaches the size of the hash table, discontinuing our search.

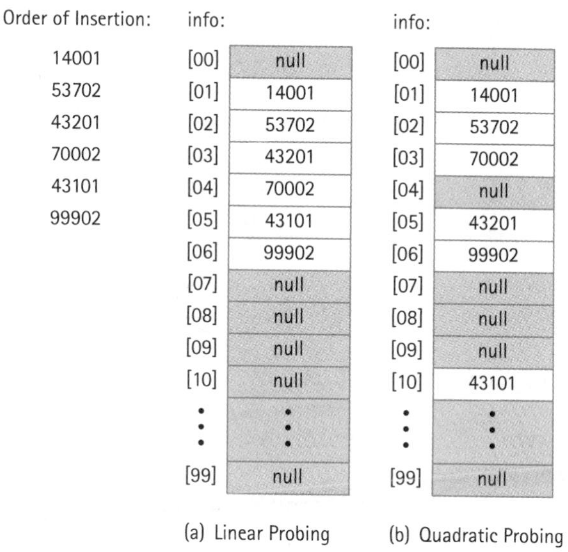

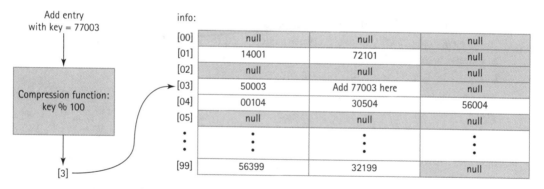

Figure 8.9 Linear versus quadratic probing

Figure 8.10 Handling collisions with buckets

Even better we can maintain a load threshold below 50% and use a hash table size that is a prime number. Theorists have proven that the degenerate, infinite loop situation will not occur as long as we meet those conditions.

Buckets and Chaining

Another, perhaps better, alternative for handling collisions is to allow entries to share the same location. One approach lets each computed location contain slots for multiple entries, rather than just a single entry. Each of these multientry locations is called a **bucket**. **Figure 8.10** shows an example with buckets that can contain three entries each. Using this approach, we can allow collisions to produce duplicate entries at the same location,

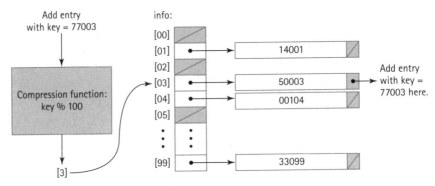

Figure 8.11 Handling collisions with chaining

up to a point. When the bucket becomes full, we must again deal with the problem of determining a new location.

Another solution, which avoids this problem, is to store a linked list of entries at each location. Each hash table slot accesses a **chain** of entries. **Figure 8.11** illustrates this approach. The entry in the hash table at each location contains a reference to a linked list of entries.

To search for a given entry, we first apply the compression function to the key and then search the indicated chain for the entry. Searching is not eliminated, but it is limited to entries that actually share a compression value. By contrast, with linear probing we may have to search through many additional entries if the slots following the location are filled with entries from collisions on other locations.

8.5   Hash Functions

To get the most benefit from the hashing system described in the previous section we need for the eventual locations used in the underlying array to be as spread out as possible. Two factors affect this spread—the size of the underlying array and the set of integral values presented to the compression function. First we will discuss the size factor and then turn our attention to the primary topic of this section—generating a good set of integral values.

Array Size

One way to minimize collisions with a hash system is to use an array that has significantly more space than is actually needed for the number of entries, thereby increasing the range of the compression function. This extra space reduces the negative impact of collisions by providing a wide range of target values.

Selecting the array size involves a space versus time trade-off. The larger the range of array indices, the less likely it is that two keys will end up at the same location. However, allocating an array that contains too large a number of empty slots wastes space. In most cases though, we prefer to err on the side of using too much space, because in most cases, space is not an issue.

Hash systems will often monitor their own load—the percentage of array indices being used. Once the load reaches a certain level, for example 75%, the system is rebuilt using a larger array. This approach is similar to the one we used to create unbounded array-based ADTs in previous chapters, although in those cases we only executed the private `enlarge` method when the underlying structure was full, and in this case we enlarge it preemptively, when it is 75% full, to help ensure efficient operation. This approach is used within the Java Library hash-based classes and is also the approach we use for the map implementation we present in the next section. This approach is often called **rehashing** because after the array is enlarged all of the previous entries have to be "rehashed", that is they have to be reinserted into the new array—they cannot just remain in their previous locations.

The Hash Function

In the discussion of hashing systems so far we have been assuming that our keys are integral and that when these keys are fed to the compression function the result will be a nice spread of target hash table locations. These assumptions allowed us to concentrate on the processes of a hash system, but it is not difficult to see that neither assumption is well founded:

- Key information might not be integral. For example, it is not unusual for a string to be used as a key—perhaps a person's full name, the name of a country, a word in a glossary, an identifier in a computer program, a Web URL, and so on.

- Even if the key information within a certain domain is integral, it might not be well suited for use as input to the compression function. Imagine, for example, an encoding system for cities that assigns a nine-digit code to each city in the world, with the first four digits representing a city's name, the next two digits representing a city's region, and the last three digits representing the city's country:

Yiyang, Hunan, China
3217   32   038

Such a system is capable of assigning unique nine-digit keys to up to 10,000 cities in each of up to 100 regions, in each of up to 1,000 countries. But if you used this key to store information about the cities, in a hash system with an underlying array of size 1,000 that used buckets of linked lists to resolve collisions, you will likely end up with an inefficient system. For example, if your data set consists of 5,000 cities from China your array will consist of 999 empty slots and one slot, slot [038], that holds a 5,000-entry linked list. This is not what we hope for when we decide to use hash-based storage.

The solution to these issues is to add another level of transformation that takes us from key value to the hash table location. This new transformation is provided by a function called the **hash function** and occurs before applying the compression function. The hash function accepts a key as input and produces an integer as output (in our case, using Java, it produces an `int`). It does this whether or not the key is integral. The `int` produced by the hash function is called the **hash code** for the key, and is passed to the compression function so that the final result represents an index in the target hash table as shown below. Synonyms for "hash code" include "hash value," and sometimes we just use the word "hash."

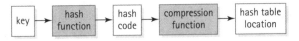

A good hash function minimizes collisions by generating hash codes, which ultimately lead to a uniform spread of entries throughout the hash table. We say "minimizes collisions" because it is extremely difficult to avoid them completely.

So, how do we create a hash function and more importantly, how do we create a good hash function?

Selecting, Digitizing, and Combining

Anything stored on a computer is composed of a sequence of bits, 1s and 0s. Movies, sounds, images, strings, books, songs, student records—everything. Since a sequence of bits can be interpreted as a binary number people sometimes say that "computers only operate on binary numbers." While that is a simplification of computing it is technically true, and it tells us that no matter what form a key takes it is possible to transform it into a binary number. Given a binary number it is possible to generate a related `int`—for example, simply use the most significant (or least significant) 32 bits of the binary number.

We typically do not want to follow this exact procedure in practice, but it does demonstrate, in theory, it is possible to create a hash function that transforms keys of any data type/class into hash codes of type `int`.

Let us consider how we might create a hash function for use with our nine-digit city code example. As we have seen, we do not want to simply use the nine-digit code directly because it will most likely not provide a good spread of

Hash

zkruger/Shutterstock, Inc.

Hash is a yummy dish (ok, that is a matter of personal taste) created by choosing a variety of ingredients (Selecting), transforming them by slicing and dicing (Digitizing), and then mixing them together (Combining). Now we finally see why the approach under study here is called hashing!

hash codes. So what do we do? A common approach is to split the hash function activity into three steps:

- *Selecting*. Identify selected parts of the key to be used in the next step. In our city code example, we make the obvious choice and identify part A = first four digits (the city code), part B = next two digits (the region code), and part C = last three digits (the country code). Although in this case we use the entire key, this is not required. For example, if the key is a string we could use every other character as a "part," or if the key is an image we could use the values of a subset of pixels.

- *Digitizing*. The selected parts are all transformed to integers. For the city codes just use the code as a number, for a string character use its underlying character code, and for a pixel use its gray scale level or some arithmetic combination of its color codes.

- *Combining*. Combine the digitized parts using some arithmetic function. In our city code example, we might try [(A × C) + B] or [A² + (B × C)], for example. The result is our hash code. In other situations we might concatenate or exclusive-OR some parts together. We hope to find a function that minimizes collisions yet at the same time is not too expensive to calculate.

In practice it might be possible to combine or skip steps, depending on the data being hashed.

Once the hash code is computed, it is passed to the compression function (if necessary) and the result is used as an index into the hash table. If a collision occurs, then more processing, some sort of probing, is needed to find the final target location. We sometimes shorten the description of application of a hash function to just the word "hashes," as in "'Yiyang, Hunan, China' hashes to 122,278".

Many different schemes are used for computing hash functions, with variations for all three steps possible. Schemes have impressive-sounding names such as polynomial, midsquare, cyclic-shift, boundary, and/or shift folding, and so forth. No matter how fancy the names, all the methods consist of one or more of the aforementioned steps.

Other Considerations

There are many things to consider when defining and using a hash function:

- A hash code is *not* unique. The input to a hash function is typically a key of some sort, but do not forget that two separate keys might generate the same hash code. For example, if a hash function for a string consists of adding together the ASCII code values of its first six characters, then the following two strings hash to the same value: "listen" and "silent." Do *not* use a hash code as a key.

- If two entries are considered to be equal, then they should hash to the same value. For example, suppose we have Gem objects with attributes `weight`, `color`, and `quality`, and within our domain two gems are considered equal if they have the same `weight` and `quality`. In that case the hash function should not use the `color` attribute when computing the hash code. Although a red gem of weight 16.4

and quality level 2.3 might appear different to us than a green gem of the same weight and quality, since within the domain they are considered equal then their hash values must be equal. Otherwise we cannot use a hashing system for storage and retrieval—storage and retrieval is based on the concept of equality.

- Be aware of the range of the compression function. For example, in Java the % operator can return a negative value: $-23 \% 5$ is -3. If % is used for the compression function in a Java implementation, you must ensure that the output from the hash function is nonnegative. Otherwise, a negative hash table location might be generated by the compression function which would lead to an `ArrayIndexOut OfBoundsException` being thrown. It is easy to prevent this problem by using an *if-else* guard statement or the `Math` class's `abs` (absolute value) method. Alternatively you can just ensure it is not possible to generate a negative number by carefully choosing your hash function. If using this latter approach, be aware that arithmetic overflow may occur during the execution of your hash function, in which case although it appears negative numbers cannot be generated, they might appear as a result of the overflow.

- When defining a hash function, we should consider the work required to calculate the function. Even if a hash function always produces unique values, it is not a good choice if it takes too long to compute. In some cases clever algorithms can be used to reduce computation time. For example, if you have parts A, B, and C selected and wish to apply the mathematical function $5A^3 + BA^2 + CA$ you could implement it as follows:

```
hashcode = (5 * A * A * A) + (B * A * A) + (C * A);
```

A more clever approach, known as Horner's method, gives the following equivalent implementation:

```
hashcode = ((((5 * A) + B) * A) + C) * A;
```

and reduces the number of costly multiplications from 6 to 3. Similarly, a knowledge of bit-level representations and the effects of left and right shifts can be used to decrease computation time in some cases.

- Do not overcompensate in terms of calculation efficiency. The previous example (see the first bulleted item) of a hash function for strings that consisted of adding together the ASCII code values of the string's first eight characters is efficient (additions are "cheap") but not a good choice if you have a large hash table. Suppose your hash table size is 100,000. Inasmuch as ASCII character codes are at most 127 then the maximum hash code you can generate with your mathematical function is $8 \times 127 = 1,016$. The range of potentially generated values uses only about 1% of the table! An alternate hash function, perhaps one that combines multiplication and addition of ASCII code values that results in a larger range of potential hash codes, will likely mean less collisions and a more efficient hashing system.

- It is possible to use knowledge of the domain of a required hash function to help you devise a good function, or conversely, to avoid creating a poor function. In our city code example used previously, we showed how knowledge of the nine-digit code cautions us against using only the last three digits (the country code) as the hash code. We can imagine many other similar situations. Suppose, for example, we devise a hash function aimed at transforming strings into hash codes that uses a well-conceived mathematical combination of the first and last four characters of the string. Such a scheme might work well in many situations. But what happens if we try to use it to store information about Web addresses:

- www.somebusiness.com

- www.someplace.com

- www.somesearchengine.com

- etc.

See the problem? Many, and we do mean many, Web addresses begin and end with the same characters and in the scheme described here they would all hash to the same location. Knowing that your hash function is to be used to hash Web locations should inform you not to use this approach.

Java's Support for Hashing

Java provides good support for hashing. The Java library includes two important hash-based collection classes—the HashMap, which we discuss in Section 8.7, "Map Variations," and the HashSet which uses a hash table approach to implementing a set (see Section 5.7, "Collection Variations," for a definition of the Set ADT). More importantly for the current discussion, the Java Object class exports a hashCode method that returns an int hash code. Because all Java objects ultimately inherit from Object, all Java objects have an associated hash code. Therefore, just as we can assume that all objects in Java support the toString and equals methods, we can assume that all objects support the hashCode method.

Similar to the way the Object class treats equals and toString, the standard Java hashCode for an object is a function of the object's memory location. As a consequence, it cannot be used to relate separate objects with identical contents. For example, even if circleA and circleB have identical attribute values, it is very unlikely that they have the same hash code. Of course, if circleA and circleB are aliases, if they both reference the same object, then their Object-based hash codes are identical because they hold the same memory reference.

For most applications, hash codes based on memory locations are not useful. Therefore, many of the Java classes that define commonly used objects (such as String and Integer) override the Object class's hashCode method with one that is based on the contents of the object. Just as we override the Object class's toString and equals methods when defining a class whose objects may need to support those methods, we should override the hashCode method as necessary. In fact, it is good programming practice to always override the equals and hashCode methods together, if you intend to override either one. It is important that these two methods are consistent with one another.

In Chapter 5 we defined a `FamousPerson` class. An object of this class has `String` attributes `firstName`, `lastName`, and `fact`, and an `int` attribute `yearOfBirth`. The `equals` method for this class is based on names only, that is two `FamousPerson` objects are considered equal if and only if both their first and last names are equal. Any definition of the `hashCode` method for this class should therefore be based strictly on the first and last name attributes. Here is an example:

```
@Override
public int hashCode()
// Returns a hash code value for this FamousPerson object.
{
   return Math.abs((lastName.hashCode() * 3) + firstName.hashCode());
}
```

As you can see, the above method makes use of the predefined `hashCode` method of the `String` class. The call to the absolute value method of the `Math` class ensures that it will return a positive result. Here is an example of what this method returns for a sample of famous people:

```
Edsger Dijkstra:      1960658654
Grace Hopper:         2019100524
Alan Turing:          1038687573
```

Complexity

We began our discussion of hashing by trying to find a collection implementation where the addition, removal, and most importantly, the discovery of entries had a complexity of O(1). If our hash function is efficient and never produces duplicates, and the hash table size is large compared to the expected number of entries in the collection, then we have reached our goal. In general, this is not the case.

Clearly, as the number of entries approaches the array size, the efficiency of the algorithms deteriorates. This is why the load of the hash table is monitored. If the table needs to be resized and the entries all need to be rehashed, a one-time heavy cost is incurred.

A precise analysis of the complexity of hashing depends on the domain and distribution of keys, the hash function, the size of the table, and the collision resolution policy. In practice it is usually not difficult to achieve close to O(1) efficiency using hashing. For any given application area, it is possible to test variations of hashing schemes to see which works best.

8.6 A Hash-Based Map

In Section 8.1, "The Map Interface," we introduced the Map, an ADT that maps keys to values with a goal of supporting fast retrieval. In Sections 8.4, "Hashing," and 8.5, "Hash Functions," we learned about hashing, a system for fast storage and retrieval of information. It is time to put the two together. Here we present an implementation of our Map ADT called the HMap with the following characteristics:

- HMap is implemented with an internal hash table that uses the `hashCode` method of the key class (the argument passed through the generic parameter K) and linear probing to determine storage locations. To guard against a key class that might return negative hash code values, we apply the absolute value operation from the `Math` class to all returned hash codes.

- An HMap is unbounded. A private `enlarge` method increases the size of the internal hash table (i.e., the internal array) by an amount equal to the original capacity on an as-needed basis. The `isFull` method always returns `false`.

- The internal hash table has a default capacity of 1,000 and a default load factor of 75%. Thus, if an HMap object is instantiated using the default constructor (the constructor with no parameters) and the number of `MapEntry` objects held by the table reaches 751, the size of the hash table is increased to 2,000. The next increase, if necessary, is to 3,000, and so on.

- Two constructors are provided, the default constructor described in the previous bullet item and a constructor which allows the client to indicate the original capacity and load factor.

- Recall that in the Map interface, `remove` is listed as an optional operation. Our HMap does not support the `remove` operation. Invoking `remove` will result in the unchecked `Unsupported-OperationException` being thrown. The `remove` operation is similarly prohibited by any returned `Iterator`. A client using HMap can `add` and `put` key/value pairs but cannot `remove` them. Although this approach does somewhat limit how an HMap can be used, there are still many clients that can productively use the class, and it permits us to disregard the complexities normally associated with hash table entry removal.

The Implementation

Here is the HMap code listing. The listing is followed by some discussion and examples of how to use the HMap.

```
//-----------------------------------------------------------------------------
// HMap.java                   by Dale/Joyce/Weems                  Chapter 8
//
// Implements a map using an array-based hash table, linear probing collision
// resolution.
//
// The remove operation is not supported. Invoking it will result in the
// unchecked UnsupportedOperationException being thrown.
//
// A map provides (K = key, V = value) pairs, mapping the key onto the value.
```

```java
// Keys are unique. Keys cannot be null.
//
// Methods throw IllegalArgumentException if passed a null key argument.
//
// Values can be null, so a null value returned by put or get does
// not necessarily mean that an entry did not exist.
//--------------------------------------------------------------------------
package ch08.maps;

import java.util.Iterator;

public class HMap<K, V> implements MapInterface<K,V>
{
  protected MapEntry[] map;

  protected final int DEFCAP = 1000;      // default capacity
  protected final double DEFLOAD = 0.75; // default load

  protected int origCap;  // original capacity
  protected int currCap;  // current capacity
  protected double load;

  protected int numPairs = 0;     // number of pairs in this map

  public HMap()
  {
    map =  new MapEntry[DEFCAP];
    origCap = DEFCAP;
    currCap = DEFCAP;
    load = DEFLOAD;
  }

  public HMap(int initCap, double initLoad)
  {
    map = new MapEntry[initCap];
    origCap = initCap;
    currCap = initCap;
    load = initLoad;
  }

  private void enlarge()
  // Increments the capacity of the map by an amount
  // equal to the original capacity.
```

```
{
  // create a snapshot iterator of the map and save current size
  Iterator<MapEntry<K,V>> i = iterator();
  int count = numPairs;

  // create the larger array and reset variables
  map = new MapEntry[currCap + origCap];
  currCap = currCap + origCap;
  numPairs = 0;

  // put the contents of the current map into the larger array
  MapEntry entry;
  for (int n = 1; n <= count; n++)
  {
    entry = i.next();
    this.put((K)entry.getKey(), (V)entry.getValue());
  }
}


public V put(K k, V v)
// If an entry in this map with key k already exists then the value
// associated with that entry is replaced by value v and the original
// value is returned; otherwise, adds the (k, v) pair to the map and
// returns null.
{
  if (k == null)
    throw new IllegalArgumentException("Maps do not allow null keys.");

  MapEntry<K, V> entry = new MapEntry<K, V>(k, v);

  int location = Math.abs(k.hashCode()) % currCap;
  while ((map[location] != null) && !(map[location].getKey().equals(k)))
    location = (location + 1) % currCap;

  if (map[location] == null)  // k was not in map
  {
    map[location] = entry;
    numPairs++;
    if ((float)numPairs/currCap > load)
      enlarge();
    return null;
  }
  else     // k already in map
```

```
    {
      V temp = (V)map[location].getValue();
      map[location] = entry;
      return temp;
    }
}

public V get(K k)
// If an entry in this map with a key k exists then the value associated
// with that entry is returned; otherwise null is returned.
{
  if (k == null)
    throw new IllegalArgumentException("Maps do not allow null keys.");

  int location = Math.abs(k.hashCode()) % currCap;
  while ((map[location] != null) && !(map[location].getKey().equals(k)))
    location = (location + 1) % currCap;

  if (map[location] == null)  // k was not in map
    return null;
  else                        // k in map
    return (V)map[location].getValue();
}

public V remove(K k)
// Throws UnsupportedOperationException.
{
  throw new UnsupportedOperationException("HMap does not allow remove.");
}

public boolean contains(K k)
// Returns true if an entry in this map with key k exists;
// Returns false otherwise.
{
  if (k == null)
    throw new IllegalArgumentException("Maps do not allow null keys.");

  int location = Math.abs(k.hashCode()) % currCap;
  while (map[location] != null)
    if (map[location].getKey().equals(k))
      return true;
    else
      location = (location + 1) % currCap;
```

```
  // if get this far then no current entry is associated with k
  return false;
}

public boolean isEmpty()
// Returns true if this map is empty; otherwise, returns false.
{
  return (numPairs == 0);
}

public boolean isFull()
// Returns true if this map is full; otherwise, returns false.
{
  return false;   // An HMap is never full
}

public int size()
// Returns the number of entries in this map.
{
  return numPairs;
}

private class MapIterator implements Iterator<MapEntry<K,V>>
// Provides a snapshot Iterator over this map.
// Remove is not supported and throws UnsupportedOperationException.
{
  int listSize = size();
  private MapEntry[] list = new MapEntry[listSize];
  private int previousPos = -1; // previous position returned from list

  public MapIterator()
  {
    int next = -1;
    for (int i = 0; i < listSize; i++)
    {
      next++;
      while (map[next] == null)
        next++;
      list[i] = map[next];
    }
  }

  public boolean hasNext()
```

```
  // Returns true if iteration has more entries; otherwise returns false.
  {
    return (previousPos < (listSize - 1));
  }


  public MapEntry<K,V> next()
  // Returns the next entry in the iteration.
  // Throws NoSuchElementException - if the iteration has no more entries
  {
    if (!hasNext())
      throw new IndexOutOfBoundsException("illegal invocation of next " +
                            " in HMap iterator.\n");
    previousPos++;
    return list[previousPos];
  }


  public void remove()
  // Throws UnsupportedOperationException.
  // Not supported. Removal from snapshot iteration is meaningless.
  {
    throw new UnsupportedOperationException("Unsupported remove attempted "
                              + "on HMap iterator.\n");

  }
}


public Iterator<MapEntry<K,V>> iterator()
// Returns a snapshot Iterator over this map.
// Remove is not supported and throws UnsupportedOperationException.
{
  return new MapIterator();
}
}
```

The three operations (put, get, and contains) that must determine if the map holds a given key k, all follow the same general pattern exemplified by the following code:

```
int location = Math.abs(k.hashCode()) % currCap;
while ((map[location] != null) && !(map[location].getKey().equals(k)))
    location = (location + 1) % currCap;
```

First, location is set using the hashCode method of the key class. Then linear probing is used until either an empty array slot is found (one where map[location] == null) or a MapEntry object with key k is found (note that we make use of the short-circuit property of the Java && operation to protect ourselves from using a null reference). If the object with key k is found then the appropriate action takes place—replacement for the put operation, return for the get operation, and return true for the contains operation. Otherwise, in the case of a location containing null being found, again the appropriate action takes place—insertion for the put opera-

> **Java Note**
>
> Java uses short-circuit evaluation for both && and ||. This means that if the result of a boolean expression using one of these operators is determined completely by the value of its first operand, then the second operand is not evaluated. So when evaluating (A && B), for example, if A evaluates to false no matter what the value of B, the expression will be false, so the evaluation of B is skipped.

tion, return null for the get operation, and return false for the contains operation.

The private enlarge method deserves some discussion. Because put is the only way to add information to the map it is the only place where enlarge is invoked:

```
if (map[location] == null)  // k was not in map
{
  map[location] = entry;
  numPairs++;
  if ((float)numPairs/currCap > load)
    enlarge();
  return null;
}
```

The enlarge method first stores all of the current entries of the map by creating an Iterator. It then instantiates a new array of MapEntry objects of the appropriate size. Finally, it "walks through" the saved Iterator, adding each of the MapEntry objects into the new array using the put operation. The put operation spreads the entries across the newly enlarged array.

Overall, enlarge is a costly operation, especially if an expensive hash function is in use. Although enlarge only executes on a rare basis and we can amortize its cost across the large number of put operations that must precede its invocation, the actual cost does all occur at once. If you are designing a system where consistent rapid response is a requirement you need to be aware of this and consider how you can originally allocate enough space to your hash table to avoid the use of enlarge.

Finally, we should note why we did not use an anonymous inner class to provide the required Iterator object that is returned by the iterator method, as we have done for previous ADT implementations. For the hash table–based map, our approach to iteration is to search through the entire underlying map array, creating a new array, list, that holds references to only the non-null entries. In other words, the list array will hold a "snapshot" of the MapEntry entries that have been stored so far, without all of the intervening null entries.

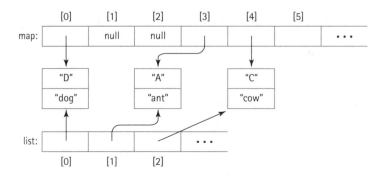

The `list` array is then used to provide the `hasNext` and `next` operations. The `remove` operation is not supported. In any case, in order to set up the `list` array we need to perform some initial processing, when the `Iterator` object is created. This processing must take place in a constructor. But constructors are not supported by anonymous classes— after all, an anonymous class does not have a name, so there is no way to "name" the constructor. Thus, we use a "regular" inner class in this case to support iteration.

Using the HMap class

We can use the `HMap` class in the same way we used our `ArrayListMap` class. For example, to use the `HMap` class to support the `StringPairApp` application presented in Section 8.3, "Application: String-to-String Map," all we need to do is change the line

```
MapInterface<String, String> pairs = new ArrayListMap<String, String>();
```
          to
```
MapInterface<String, String> pairs = new HMap<String, String>();
```

It might be interesting to see how `HMap` performs on the Text Analysis experiment we used in both Chapter 5, "The Collection ADT," and Chapter 7, "The Binary Search Tree ADT." You may recall that our application, `VocabularyDensity`, reads a given text file and computes the ratio of its number of unique words to total number of words. We used the application to analyze a collection of texts including, among others, the *Complete Works of Shakespeare* and an edition of the *Encyclopaeda Brittanica*. Perhaps the most interesting text file analyzed was one we called "Mashup," which consisted of a concatenation of 121 files from the Gutenberg site including novels, "complete works," dictionaries, and technical manuals, plus Spanish, French, and German language texts in addition to the English. What happens if we "hash the mash"?

The `VocDensMeasureHMap` application can be found in package `ch08.apps`. As before, the application reads through the words from the input text, checking each word to see whether or not it already exists in the map. If not, the word is added, and if so, the word is skipped. In either case we increment the number of total words. When finished we simply divide the number of words in the map by the total number of words. Because we are only interested in the words themselves, which are used as the keys, we use `null` values when putting information into the map. We set the initial capacity to 2,404,198, which is exactly twice the number of unique words in the `mashup.txt` file. How do the results compare to previous attempts, in terms of execution time? (Times are approximate):

- *Unsorted Array*: 10 hours
- *Sorted Array* (uses binary search): 7 minutes, 10 seconds
- *Binary Search Tree*: 100 seconds
- *Hash Map*: 66 seconds

Well, that is a little disappointing although requiring 66% of the time needed by the binary search tree is some improvement. But wait—there is quite a bit of overhead associated with just reading the input file word by word. Experimentation shows that the cost of this activity, which is unavoidable for our application yet is not directly related to the storage/ retrieval mechanism, is approximately 51 seconds. We can relist our last two results, subtracting out this overhead cost, and get (approximately):

- *Binary Search Tree*: 50 seconds
- *Hash Map*: 15 seconds

Now we can state that the hash map approach only takes about 30% of the time of the binary search tree result, a more satisfying result.

8.7 Map Variations

The Map ADT is important, versatile, and widely used. Some programming languages, (e.g., Awk, Haskell, JavaScript, Lisp, MUMPS, Perl, PHP, Python, and Ruby), directly support it as part of the base language, although in some cases there are limitations on what can be used as a key and/or value. Many other languages, including Java, C++, Objective-C, and Smalltalk provide map functionality through their standard code libraries.

Maps are known by many names:

- *Symbol table.* As discussed in the chapter introduction, symbol tables were one of the first carefully studied and designed data structures, and were related to compiler design. Classically they associate a program symbol with its attributes—so they are indeed maps.
- *Dictionary.* The idea of looking up a word (the key) in a dictionary to find its definition (the value) makes the concept of a dictionary a good fit for maps. So in some textbooks and some programming libraries you will find maps are called dictionaries.
- *Hashes.* Because a hash system is a very efficient and common way to implement a map, you will sometimes see the two terms used interchangeably. For example, when using the Perl language one might say "hashes are a powerful structure" or "insert the element into a hash."

- *Associative Arrays.* You can view a standard array as a map—it maps indices onto values. With a little bit more imagination you can view a map as an array—one that associates keys with values rather than indices with values. Therefore, the term "associative array" is becoming the commonly used term that represents symbol tables, dictionaries, hashes, and maps.

A Hybrid Structure

We have seen how a hash table, under the right conditions, supports fast storage and retrieval of information. Suppose we have a situation where we need fast storage and retrieval, but we also need to be able to iterate through the stored entries in the order in which they were placed into the collection. The only structures that we have studied so far that support such an iteration are the unsorted array (assuming the *remove* operation is implemented carefully) and the unsorted linked list (assuming we insert entries at the end of the list)—but neither of these provide efficient storage and retrieval. They are both $O(N)$ for these operations.

Is there some way we could use a hash table to solve our problem?

The problem is that a hash table spreads things all across the underlying array in no particular order. Suppose we create a map with the following declaration:

```
HMap<Character, String> animals = new HMap<Character, String>;
```

and then execute:

```
animals.put('A', "ant"); animals.put('B', "bat"); animals.put('C', "cat");
```

The result might look something like this:

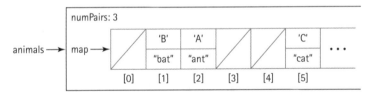

As you can see, the entries are spread around and there is no way to recapture the original order of insertion. If we expand the contents of the internal data to hold a count of how many entries have been entered so far, and associate the value of that count with each entry as it is stored in the array, then at least we have saved the order of insertion for later use. The result might look like this:

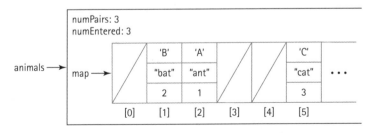

Now at least we have captured the entry order information and can, with a bit of work, create the desired iteration. To do this we need to look through the entire internal array, find the entries, and then sort them in increasing order of entry. Seems like a lot of work to reclaim information that was already available to us. Is there a better way?

What if we maintain a second internal array named `list`, with references into the `map` array, kept in the desired order:

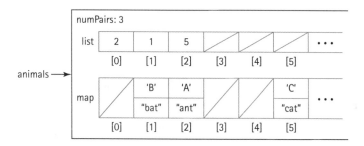

Now we are getting somewhere. The hashing scheme works as before so this approach supports fast storage and retrieval, and when we need to iterate on insertion order we can just use values from the `list` array to access the entries in the `map` array in the desired sequence.

But what happens when an entry is removed? Maintaining the information correctly after a `remove` operation is going to be difficult and costly. When the `remove` operation is invoked it is not difficult to find the entry in the `map` array—we just use the hash function and collision resolution approach. Once the entry is found the contents of the `map` array at that index can be set to `null`. But the `list` array also needs to be updated. Because there is no link back to the `list` array from `map`, we need to search the `list` array to find the correct location to update—and once found in order to remove the information at that location we need to shift all remaining entries to the "left" one slot. So, if we use this approach we have transformed `remove` from an expected efficiency of O(1) to a best case efficiency of O(N). For some systems this might be too high a cost.

Let us try one more time. We need a support structure that supports fast addition. We need to be able to iterate through the entries in the order in which they are inserted into the map. And we need a reasonably quick remove operation. A doubly linked list (see Section 4.7, "Queue Variations") supports fast removal. If we embed the list within the map entries themselves then we have the desired relationship between the map entries and the list elements. The result might look something like this:

> **Hybrid Data Structures**
>
> Our final solution is an example of what is called a hybrid data structure—hybrid because it is a combination of two data structures—a hash table and a doubly linked list. We have seen another example of a hybrid data structure before in this chapter when we discussed using linked lists as the buckets for a hash table. In place of the linked lists we could use binary search trees, giving us a third example of a hybrid data structure. As you may have guessed, many hybrid structures are possible. Studying their properties and uses is a good topic for an advanced data structures course.

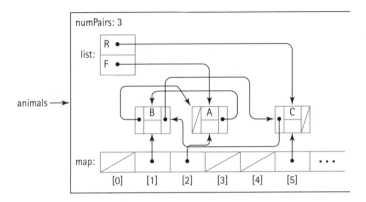

Although the figure looks complex, this approach meets our requirements. It is a hash table–based map with an embedded doubly linked list. This is very similar by the way, to a Java Library class—the LinkedHashMap.

Java Support for Maps

The Java Library includes a Map interface. Like our maps, the maps in the library use two generic parameters—K for the types of keys and V for the types of values. A nested class, Entry, fulfills the role of our MapEntry class. The interface, being a part of a professional API, is more complex than our MapInterface. It defines 25 abstract methods, has eight subinterfaces, and is implemented by 19 classes within the library. Nevertheless, in terms of its core functionality, it is equivalent to our map interface.

Of the 19 implementing classes, of special note to us is the HashMap class. The Hash-Map class permits null keys. Other than that it is very similar to our HMap class (or per-haps we should state that the other way around—our HMap class is similar to the library class!). HashMap provides both a default capacity and load factor, and allows the client to set these through a constructor if they wish, just like our HMap. And like our HMap, assum-ing a reasonably well-behaved hash function and distribution of keys, HashMap provides constant time storage, removal, and retrieval. The library's hash map provides more op-erations than our version does; in fact it implements 24 operations in addition to the 12 it inherits from its ancestors. Professional Java programmers typically make heavy use of the HashMap class to support their work.

Summary

Maps associate unique keys with values. The Map is our only data structure that requires *two* generic parameters, one to indicate the *key* class and the other to indicate the *value* class. Following our typical pattern we first defined an interface for our Map ADT using Java's interface construct. We then discussed many implementation approaches and provided an ArrayList-based implementation. The StringPairApp exemplified a simple yet powerful program using a map, in this case our ArrayListMap.

One map implementation approach in particular is very important. The goal of hashing is to produce a search that approaches O(1) efficiency. Because of collisions of hash locations, searching or rehashing is sometimes necessary. A good hash function minimizes collisions and distributes the entries randomly across the hash table. Our hash table–based implementation of the map, the HMap, produced the fastest processing yet (and we will not do better) for the vocabulary density problem.

In the *Variations* section we surveyed how maps are provided and named in several programming languages. Finally, we discussed a hybrid structure consisting of a hash table with a linked list threaded through the entries, a structure providing the benefits of hashing while still allowing easy insertion order-based iteration.

Exercises

8.1 The Map Interface

1. Give an example of a mathematical function such that
   a. it maps some of its input values to identical output values (a → x, b → x).
   b. none of its input values map to the same output value (this is called a one-to-one mapping).
   c. it has an inverse function.

2. Describe an information processing situation where you might use a mapping that
   a. is one to one (see previous question).
   b. is not one to one.

3. The first paragraph of Section 8.1 states that a rule limiting a mapping so that each key maps to exactly one value is equivalent to a rule requiring a mapping to have unique keys. Explain.

4. Show how you would declare a map of type ArrayListMap
   a. representing student (unique) names mapped onto their birthdays.
   b. representing countries mapped onto their populations.
   c. representing the number of sides of a polygon, mapped to the name of the polygon.

5. Critique the following code which is intended to print out whether or not a key value k1 is used in a map named relationships:

```
if (relationships.get(k1) != null)
    System.out.println("yes it does");
else
    System.out.println("no it does not");
```

Now rewrite the code so that it works correctly.

6. What is the output of the following code—ArrayListMap is an implementation of the MapInterface and is presented in Section 8.2:

```
MapInterface<Character, String> question;
question = new ArrayListMap<Character, String>();
System.out.println(question.isEmpty());
System.out.println(question.size());

System.out.println(question.put('M', "map"));
question.put('D', "dog");    question.put('T', "Top");
question.put('A', "ant");    question.put('t', "Top");
System.out.println(question.isEmpty());
System.out.println(question.size());
System.out.println(question.contains('D'));
System.out.println(question.contains('E'));
System.out.println(question.get('D'));
System.out.println(question.get('E'));

System.out.println(question.put('D', "dig"));
System.out.println(question.get('D'));
for (MapEntry<Character,String> m: question)
    System.out.print(m.getValue() + "\t");

System.out.println(question.remove('D'));
System.out.println(question.remove('D'));
for (MapEntry<Character,String> m: question)
    System.out.print(m.getValue() + "\t");
```

8.2 Map Implementations

7. In this section we discussed several approaches to implementing a map using previously studied data structures, and in some cases we discussed the implementation of the put operation. For each approach (Unsorted Array, Sorted Array, Unsorted Linked List, Sorted Linked List, and Binary Search Tree), describe how you would implement the following operations.

   a. isEmpty()

   b. contains(K k)

   c. remove(K k)

   d. iterator()

8. Bob studies the code for ArrayListMap and announces that he has discovered an "easier approach to the contains method" as shown below. What do you tell Bob?

```
public boolean contains(K k)
// Returns true if an entry in this map with key k exists;
// Returns false otherwise.
{
    return map.contains(k);
}
```

9. Describe the ramifications of each of the following changes to `ArrayListMap`:

   a. In the single statement of the second constructor `initCapacity` is changed to 10.

   b. The *if* statement is removed from the beginning of the `put` method.

   c. Within the `put` method the boolean expression (`temp.getKey().equals(k)`) is changed to (`k.equals(temp.getKey())`).

   d. The `get` method is rewritten as follows:

```
public V get(K k)
// If an entry in this map with a key k exists then the value
// associated with that entry is returned; otherwise null
   is returned.
{
  if (k == null)
    throw new IllegalArgumentException("Maps do not allow
    null keys.");

  V result = null;
  for (MapEntry<K,V> temp: map)
    if (temp.getKey().equals(k))
      result = temp.getValue();

  return result;
}
```

   e. the `contains` method is rewritten as follows:

```
public boolean contains(K k)
// Returns true if an entry in this map with key k exists;
// Returns false otherwise.
{
  if (k == null)
    throw new IllegalArgumentException("Maps do not allow
    null keys.");

  boolean result = false;
  for (MapEntry<K,V> temp: map)
    if (temp.getKey().equals(k))
      result = true;

  return result;
}
```

10. Implement the Map ADT using

    a. an Unsorted Array.

    b. a Sorted Array.

    c. an Unsorted Linked List.

    d. a Binary Search Tree.

8.3 Application: String-to-String Map

11. Create a text file similar to `numbers.txt` and `periodic.txt` of your own devising that captures an interesting "string-to-string map." Use it as input to the `StringPairApp` application.

12. Create an application, similar to `StringPairApp`, which acts as a chemistry quiz. It randomly generates a periodic number between 1 and 118 and asks the user for the corresponding element. It then checks their answer against the correct answer (using a map based on the `periodic.txt` file) and reports the result, displaying the correct answer if they get it wrong. It repeats this for 10 questions and then reports the percentage of correct answers. How can your application be made more generally usable?

13. Java reserved words can be categorized into subsets such as "primitive types," "control," "access control," etc. Research the reserved words and create your own categorization scheme. Then

    a. Create an application called `Categories` that first creates a map based on your categorization of reserved words (e.g., `int` → "primitive type") and then reads a `.java` file and displays the keyword types found in the file. For example, if `MapEntry.java` is the input file then the output, depending on your categorization, might look like this:

        `control, organization, access control, definition, control . . .`

        because of the sequence of reserved words `for` (see opening comment), `package`, `public`, `class`, `protected`,...

    b. Improve your application so that it ignores the contents of literal strings.

    c. Improve your application so that it ignores the contents of comments.

8.4 Hashing

14. For each of the following array sizes indicate whether or not the following sequence of key insertions 21, 75, 240, 413, 1368, 9021, 9513 using a hashing system causes a collision when the appropriate compression function is used:

    a. 10   b. 15   c. 17   d. 21   e. 50   f. 100   g. 1,000   h. 10,000

15. Show the array that results from the following sequence of key insertions using a hashing system under the given conditions: 5, 205, 406, 5205, 8205, 307 (you can simply list the non-null array slots and their contents)

a. array size is 100, linear probing used.

b. array size is 100, quadratic probing used.

c. array size is 101, linear probing used.

d. array size is 1,000, linear probing used.

e. array size is 100, with buckets consisting of linked lists.

16. For each of the situations described in Exercise 15, indicate how many comparisons are required to search for the key 307, after all insertions were made. The key 406? The key 506?

17. Show the array that results from the following sequence of operations using a hashing system under the given conditions: insert 5, insert 205, insert 406, remove 205, insert 407, insert 806, insert 305 (you can simply list the non-null array slots and their contents)

a. array size is 100, linear probing used, the value −1 indicates a removed entry.

b. array size is 10, linear probing used, the value −1 indicates a removed entry.

c. array size is 10, linear probing used, an additional value of type `boolean` is used, with `true` indicating a slot has been used.

d. array size is 10, with buckets consisting of linked lists.

8.5 Hash Functions

18. Describe three domains/application areas where you might expect to be able to define a perfect hash function (no collisions).

19. Discuss rehashing (enlarging a hash table dynamically). Why? When? How?

20. In the nine-digit city code example suppose the hash function used is $[(A \times C) + B]$. What is the hash code for each of the following cities?

a. Hangzhou, Zhejiang, China: 001112038

b. Lancaster, Pennsylvania, USA: 012113103

c. Yiyang, Hunan, China: 321732038

d. Beaver Falls, Pennsylvania, USA: 54213103

e. Seoul, Seoul, South Korea: 010313121

21. Critique the following hash functions for a domain consisting of people with attributes `firstName`, `lastName`, `number` (used to resolve identical first and last names, e.g., "John Smith 0," "John Smith 1," etc.), and `age`. The names are of class `String` and the other two attributes are of type `int`.

a. hash function returns $(age)^2$

b. hash function returns $(age)^2 + $ `lastName.hashCode()`

c. hash function returns `lastName.hashCode() + firstName.hashCode()`

d. hash function returns `lastName.hashCode() + firstName.hashCode() + number`

22. Define a viable hash function for the following domains with a targeted hash code size of five digits:

    a.   randomized citizen identification numbers of length 10 digits.

    b.   randomized citizen identification numbers of length 10 where the last three digits indicate occupation.

    c.   Web URLs.

    d.   file names.

    e.   country names.

    f.   telephone numbers consisting of two-digit country code, three-digit area code, three-digit exchange code, and four-digit number.

23. Add `equals` and `hashCode` methods (unless they are already defined) to the following classes. Create a test driver to show that your code works properly.

    a.   The `FamousPerson` class defined in Chapter 5 and found in the `support` package.

    b.   The `Date` class defined in Chapter 1 and found in the `ch01.dates` package.

    c.   The `WordFreq` class defined in Chapter 7 and found in the `support` package.

    d.   The `Card` class defined in Chapter 6 and found in the `support.cards` package.

    e.   The `CardDeck` class defined in Chapter 6 and found in the `support.cards` package.

24. Add the `hashCode` method defined in Section 8.5 on page 530 to the `FamousPerson` class. Write an application that reads the `input/FamousCS.txt` file, creates a `FamousPerson` object for each line of the file, and generates and saves its associated `hashCode()` value in an array.

    a.   Output the values from the array in sorted order.

    b.   Replace each array value A with the value A % 1,000, and again output the values in the array in sorted order.

    c.   Replace each array value A with the value A % 100, and again output the values in the array in sorted order.

    d.   Replace each array value A with the value A % 10, and again output the values in the array in sorted order.

    e.   Write a report about your observations on the output.

    f.   Repeat this entire exercise, but use a hash function of your own devising.

8.6 A Hash-Based Map

25. If our `HMap` implementation is used (load factor of 75% and an initial capacity of 1,000), how many times is the `enlarge` method called if the number of unique entries put into the map is

    a.   100   b.   750   c.   2,000   d.   10,000   e.   100,000

26. Your friend Diane says "my hash map implementation uses buckets of linked lists, so I don't need to worry about load factors." What do you tell her?

27. Describe the ramifications of each of the following changes to `HMap`:

   a. The signature of the second constructor is changed from

   ```
   public HMap(int initCap, double initLoad)
   ```
   to
   ```
   public HMap(double initLoad, int initCap)
   ```

   b. The call to the `Math.abs` method within `put` is dropped.

   c. The statement `currCap = currCap + origCap;` is dropped from the `enlarge` method.

   d. The opening *if* statement is removed from the `put` method.

   e. The opening *if* statement is removed from the `get` method.

   f. The code for the `remove` method is changed to:

   ```
   if (k == null)
      throw new IllegalArgumentException("null keys not allowed");

   int location = Math.abs(k.hashCode()) % currCap;
   while ((map[location] != null)
            &&
            !(map[location].getKey().equals(k)))
      location = (location + 1) % currCap;

   if (map[location] == null)   // k was not in map
      return null;
   else                         // k in map
   {
      V hold = (V)map[location].getValue();
      map[location] = null;
      return V;
   }
   ```

   g. Within the *for* loop of the `MapIterator` constructor the first `next++` is dropped.

28. Change the `HMap` class (and create a test driver to show that your changes work correctly) so that:

   a. It includes a `toString` method that prints out the entire contents of the internal array, showing the array index along with its contents. This is helpful for testing the rest of this exercise and some of the following exercises also.

   b. It uses quadratic probing.

    c. It provides a working `remove` method, using an additional `boolean` value associated with each hash table slot to track removal.

    d. Instead of probing it uses buckets of linked lists of `MapEntry` objects.

29. Create an application that uses `HMap` and reads a list of words from a provided file and outputs whether or not any word repeats. As soon as the application determines there is at least one repeated word it can display "<such and such word> repeats" and terminate. If no words repeat it displays "No words repeat" and terminates.

30. Add a `toString` method to the `HMap` class (see Exercise 28a). Modify `String-PairMap2`, found in the `ch08.apps` package so that instead of interacting with the user it simply reads the information from the file, stores the information in the `HMap`, and then "prints" the `HMap`. Run the application on each of the following files, using a reasonable starting capacity (150% the number of pairs) and a load threshold of 80%, and discuss what you see.

    a. `input/numbers.txt`

    b. `input/periodic.txt`

    c. `input/glossary.txt`

8.7 Map Variations

31. Research: Write a short report about the support for maps in two different languages—one language for which the support is part of the language itself and another for which the support is provided through a standard library.

32. Our final solution to the problem of creating an efficient storage/retrieval structure that supports iterating through the entries in insertion order was a hash map with an embedded doubly linked list. Create a drawing similar to the one shown at the end of the section for the internal view of this structure under each of the following situations:

    a. The structure has just been instantiated. Nothing has been added yet.

    b. Continuing from part (a) you put("b," "bat") which hashes to location 2, put("p," "pig") which hashes to location 4, and put("g," "goat") which hashes to location 6.

    c. Continuing from part (b), you put("a," "ant") which hashes to location 0, and then remove("p").

    d. Continuing from part (c) you put("b," "bear").

33. Implement the hash map with an embedded doubly linked list described in the "A Hybrid Structure" subsection. Include a test driver to show that your implementation works properly.

34. Create a new version of the `StringPairApp`, found in the `ch08.apps` package, that uses the Java Library `HashMap` class in place of this text's `ArrayListMap` class.

The Priority Queue ADT

Knowledge Goals

You should be able to

- describe a priority queue at the abstract level
- discuss uses for a priority queue
- discuss alternative implementation approaches for a priority queue and their efficiencies
- define full and complete binary trees
- describe the shape and order properties of a heap
- define the heap operations reheap up and reheap down
- describe how a binary tree can be represented as an array, with implicit positional links between elements

Skill Goals

You should be able to

- given a binary tree, identify whether it is full, complete, both, or neither
- given an array-based representation of a binary tree and an index indicating a node of the tree, determine the indices of the node's parent, left child, and right child, if they exist
- implement a priority queue using an array, an `ArrayList`, a linked list, or a `BinarySearchTree`
- given an array-based representation of a heap, trace the reheap up and reheap down operations
- draw trees that show the results of enqueuing or dequeuing from a heap-based representation of a priority queue
- implement a priority queue as a heap
- use the Priority Queue ADT as a component of a solution to a problem

Chapter 4 focused on the queue, a first-in, first-out (FIFO) structure. In this short chapter we look at a related structure, the priority queue. Rather than dequeuing the element that has been in the queue for the longest time, with a priority queue we dequeue the element with the highest priority. Here we define priority queues, how they are used, and how they are implemented. In particular, we look at a clever implementation approach called the "heap," which features fast insertion and removal of elements.

9.1 The Priority Queue Interface

A **priority queue** is an abstract data type with an interesting accessing protocol. Only the highest-priority element can be accessed. "Highest priority" can mean different things, depending on the application. Consider, for example:

- A small company with one IT specialist. When several employees need IT support at the same time, which request gets handled first? The requests are processed in order of the employee's importance in the company; the specialist handles the president's request before starting on the vice president's, and so on. The priority of each request relates to the level of the employee who initiated it.

- An ice cream vendor serves customers in the order that they arrive; that is, the highest-priority customer is the one who has been waiting the longest. The FIFO queue studied in Chapter 4 can be considered a priority queue whose highest-priority element is the one that has been queued the longest time.

- Sometimes a printer shared by a number of computers is configured to always print the smallest job in its queue first. This way, someone who is printing only a few pages does not have to wait for large jobs to finish. For such printers, the priority of the jobs relates to the size of the job: shortest job first.

Using Priority Queues

Priority queues are useful for any application that involves processing elements by priority.

In discussing FIFO queue applications in Chapter 4, we said that an operating system often maintains a queue of processes that are ready to execute. It is common, however, for such processes to have different priority levels, so that rather than using a standard queue, an operating system may use a priority queue to manage process execution.

In Section 4.8, "Application: Average Waiting Time," we used queues to help us model a customer service system. This was a relatively simple model that generated all the information about the customers first, and then simulated servicing them. For more complex models it is possible to generate customer information during processing—consider, for example, that a man arrives at the service counter only to discover he incorrectly filled out a form; he needs to redo the form and get back in the queue. His reentry to the queue is a dynamic event that could not have been predicted ahead of time. Modeling this type of system is termed *discrete event simulation* and is an interesting area of study. A common approach with discrete event models is to maintain a priority queue of events. As events are generated they are enqueued, with a priority level equal to the time at which the event is to take place. Earlier events have higher priority. The event-driven simulation proceeds by dequeuing the highest-priority event (the earliest event available) and then modeling that event, which may generate subsequent events to be enqueued.

Starvation

When priority queues are used in busy real-time systems, designers must be careful that queued items do not "starve"—that is, they do not spend an inordinate amount of time waiting to be processed because higher-priority elements keep arriving. One solution to the starvation problem is to "age" elements—the longer they wait the better their priority becomes, so that eventually they are processed.

Priority queues are also useful for sorting data. Given a set of elements to sort, the elements can be enqueued into a priority queue, and then dequeued in sorted order (from largest to smallest). We look at how priority queues and their implementations can be used in sorting in Chapter 11.

The Interface

The operations defined for the Priority Queue ADT include enqueuing elements and dequeuing elements, as well as testing for an empty or full-priority queue and determining the queue's size. These operations are very similar to those specified for the FIFO queue discussed in Chapter 4. In fact, except for the information in the comments and the name and package of the interface, the queue interface and the priority queue interface are indistinguishable. Functionally, the difference between the two types of queues is due to how the `dequeue` operation is implemented. The Priority Queue ADT does not follow the "FIFO" approach; instead, it always returns the highest-priority element from the current set of enqueued elements, no matter when the element was enqueued. For our purposes we define highest priority as the "largest" element based on the indicated ordering of elements. Here is the interface:

```
//-------------------------------------------------------------------------
// PriQueueInterface.java          by Dale/Joyce/Weems          Chapter 9
//
// Interface for a class that implements a priority queue of T.
// The largest element as determined by the indicated comparison has the
// highest priority.
//
// Null elements are not allowed. Duplicate elements are allowed.
//-------------------------------------------------------------------------
package ch09.priorityQueues;

public interface PriQueueInterface<T>
{
  void enqueue(T element);
  // Throws PriQOverflowException if this priority queue is full;
  // otherwise, adds element to this priority queue.
```

```
T dequeue();
// Throws PriQUnderflowException if this priority queue is empty;
// otherwise, removes element with highest priority from this
// priority queue and returns it.

boolean isEmpty();
// Returns true if this priority queue is empty; otherwise, returns false.

boolean isFull();
// Returns true if this priority queue is full; otherwise, returns false.

int size();
// Returns the number of elements in this priority queue.
}
```

The exception objects mentioned in the comments are defined as part of the `ch09.priorityQueues` package. They are unchecked exceptions.

As with all of the ADTs we have studied, variations of the Priority Queue ADT exist. In particular, it is common to include operations that allow an application to reach into a priority queue to examine, manipulate, or remove elements. For some applications such operations are necessary. Consider the previously discussed use of priority queues for discrete event simulation. With some discrete event models the result of handling an event may affect other scheduled events, delaying or canceling them. The additional priority queue functionality allows them to be used for such models. Here though, we focus solely on the basic Priority Queue operations as listed in `PriQueueInterface`.

9.2 Priority Queue Implementations

There are many ways to implement a priority queue. In any implementation, we want to be able to access the element with the highest priority quickly and easily.

Let us briefly consider some possible approaches.

Unsorted Array

Enqueuing an element would be very easy with an unsorted array—simply insert it in the next available array slot, an $O(1)$ operation. Dequeuing, however, would require searching through the entire array to find the largest element, an $O(N)$ operation.

Sorted Array

Dequeuing is very easy with this array-based approach: Simply return the last array element (which is the largest) and reduce the size of the queue; dequeue is a $O(1)$ operation. Enqueuing, however, would be more expensive, because we have to find the place to insert the element. This is an $O(\log_2 N)$ step if we use a binary search. Shifting the elements of the array to make room for the new element is an $O(N)$ step, so overall the enqueue operation is $O(N)$.

The SortedABPriQ class implements the PriQueueInterface using the approach outlined earlier. It provides two constructors, one of which allows the client to pass a Comparator argument to be used to determine priority, and the other which has no parameters, indicating that the natural order of the elements should be used. This is an unbounded array-based implementation. To enable easy testing it includes a toString method. The reader is invited to study the code found in the ch09.priorityQueues package. Here is a short program that demonstrates use of the SortedABPriQ class, followed by its output.

```
//----------------------------------------------------------------------
// UseSortedABPriQ.java              by Dale/Joyce/Weems          Chapter 9
//
// Example use of the SortedABPriQ
//----------------------------------------------------------------------
package ch09.apps;
import ch09.priorityQueues.*;

public class UseSortedABPriQ
{
  public static void main(String[] args)
  {
    PriQueueInterface<String> pq = new SortedABPriQ<String>();

    pq.enqueue("C");    pq.enqueue("O");    pq.enqueue("M");
    pq.enqueue("P");    pq.enqueue("U");    pq.enqueue("T");
    pq.enqueue("E");    pq.enqueue("R");

    System.out.println(pq);
    System.out.println(pq.dequeue());
    System.out.println(pq.dequeue());
    System.out.println(pq);
  }
}
```

The output is:

```
Priority Queue:    C  E  M  O  P  R  T  U

U
T

Priority Queue:    C  E  M  O  P  R
```

Sorted Linked List

Assume the linked list is kept sorted from largest to smallest. Dequeuing with this reference-based approach simply requires removing and returning the first list element, an operation that takes only a few steps. But enqueuing again is an $O(N)$ operation, because we must search the list one element at a time to find the insertion location.

Binary Search Tree

For this approach, the `enqueue` operation is implemented as a standard binary search tree `insert` operation. We know that operation requires $O(\log_2 N)$ steps on average. Assuming access to the underlying implementation structure of the tree, we can implement the `dequeue` operation by returning the largest element, which is the rightmost tree element. We follow the right subtree references down, maintaining a trailing reference, until reaching a node with an empty right subtree. The trailing reference allows us to "unlink" the node from the tree. We then return the element contained in the node. This is also a $O(\log_2 N)$ operation, on average.

The binary search tree approach is the best so far—it requires, on average, only $O(\log_2 N)$ steps for both `enqueue` and `dequeue`. If the tree is skewed, however, the performance degenerates to $O(N)$ steps for each operation. The time efficiency benefits depend on the tree remaining balanced. Unless a self-balancing tree is used it is likely the tree will become skewed—after all, elements will continually be removed from the far right of the tree only, which will result in a tree that is heavier on its left side. We can do better.

The next section presents a very clever approach, called the heap, that guarantees $O(\log_2 N)$ steps, even in the worst case.

9.3 The Heap

A **heap** is an implementation of a priority queue that uses a binary tree that satisfies two properties, one concerning its shape and the other concerning the order of its elements. Before discussing these properties we need to expand our tree-related terminology.[1]

A **full binary tree** is a binary tree in which all of the leaves are on the same level and every nonleaf node has two children. The basic shape of a full binary tree is triangular:

---

[1] "Heap" is also a synonym for the free store of a computer—the area of memory available for dynamically allocated data. The heap as a data structure is not to be confused with this unrelated computer system concept of the same name.

A **complete binary tree** is a binary tree that is either full or full through the next-to-last level, with the leaves on the last level as far to the left as possible. The shape of a complete binary tree is either triangular (if the tree is full) or something like the following:

Figure 9.1 shows some examples of different types of binary trees.

Now we are ready to define a heap. As previously stated, a heap is an implementation of a priority queue that uses a binary tree that satisfies two properties: one concerning its shape and the other concerning the order of its elements. The **shape property** is simply stated: The underlying tree must be a complete binary tree. The **order property** says that, for every node in the tree, the value stored in that node is greater than or equal to the value in each of its children.

It might be more accurate to call this structure a "maximum heap," because the root node contains the maximum value in the structure. It is also possible to create a "minimum heap," each of whose elements contains a value that is less than or equal to the value of each of its children.

The term *heap* is used for both the abstract concept, that is, a binary tree that maintains the shape and order properties, and the underlying structure, usually an efficient array-based tree implementation. This section concentrates on the properties of heaps and how a heap is used to implement a priority queue. The next section describes the standard implementation of the heap itself, using an array.

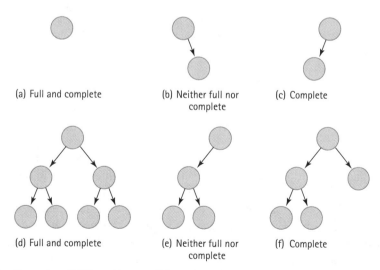

Figure 9.1   Examples of different types of binary trees

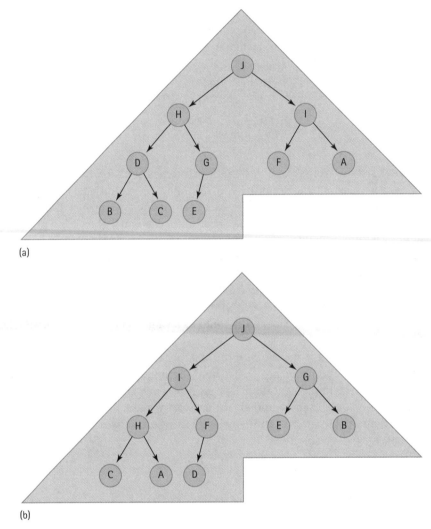

(a)

(b)

Figure 9.2 Two heaps containing the letters *A* through *J*

Figure 9.2 shows two trees containing the letters *A* through *J* that fulfill both the shape and order properties. The placement of the values differs in the two trees, but the shape is the same: a complete binary tree of 10 elements. The two trees have the same root node. A group of values can be stored in a binary tree in many ways and still satisfy the order property of heaps. Because of the shape property, we know that all heap trees with a given number of elements have the same shape. We also know, because of the order property, that the root node always contains the largest value in the tree. This helps us implement an efficient `dequeue` operation, supporting the Priority Queue ADT.

Let us say we want to dequeue an element from the heap in Figure 9.2a—in other words, we want to remove and return the element with the largest value from the tree, the J. The largest element is in the root node, and since we know exactly where to find it we can easily remove it, as illustrated in **Figure 9.3a**. Of course, this leaves a hole in the root position (Figure 9.3b). Because the heap's tree must be complete, we decide to fill the hole with the bottom rightmost element from the tree; now the structure satisfies the shape property (Figure 9.3c). The replacement value, however, came from the bottom of the tree, where the smaller values are; as a consequence, the tree no longer satisfies the order property of heaps.

This situation suggests one of the standard heap-support operations: Given a binary tree that satisfies the heap properties, *except that the root position is empty*, insert an element into the structure so that it again becomes a heap. This operation, called `reheapDown`, involves starting at the root position and moving the new element down,

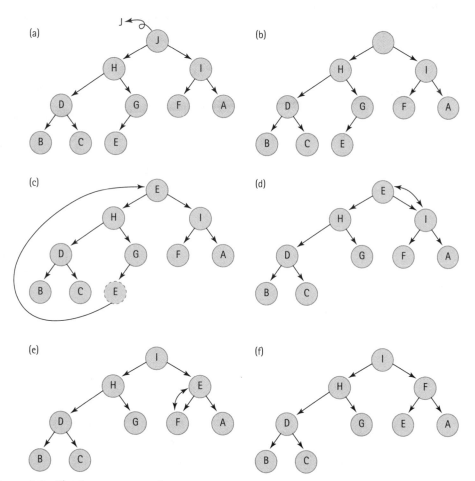

Figure 9.3 The dequeue operation

while moving child elements up, until we find a legal position for the newelement (see Figure 9.3d and e). We *swap* the element with one of its children—its largest child, in fact, so that the order property will be restored.

To dequeue an element from the heap, we remove and return the root element, remove the bottom rightmost element, and then pass the bottom rightmost element to `reheapDown` to restore the heap (Figure 9.3f).

Now suppose we want to enqueue an element to the heap—where do we put it? Let us enqueue the element 'I' into the heap represented in Figure 9.3f. Yes, it is true that 'I' is already in the heap, but heaps (and priority queues) are allowed to contain duplicate elements. The shape property tells us that the tree must be complete, so we put the new element in the next bottom rightmost place in the tree, as illustrated in **Figure 9.4a**. Now the shape property is satisfied, but the order property may be violated. This situation illustrates the need for another heap-support operation: Given a binary tree that satisfies the heap properties, except that the last position is empty, insert a given element into the structure so that it again becomes a heap. After inserting the element in the next bottom rightmost position in the tree, we float the element up the tree, while moving tree elements down, until the element is in a position that satisfies the order property (see Figure 9.4b and c) resulting once again in a legal heap (Figure 9.4d). This operation is called `reheapUp`—it adds an element to the heap, assuming the last index position of the array-based tree implementation is empty.

To review how our heap supports a priority queue we show the results of a sequence of enqueues and dequeues in **Figure 9.5**. Initially the priority queue is empty. The sequence of operations that correspond to the changes depicted in the figure are listed in the text box embedded in the figure. At each stage we show only the final result of the

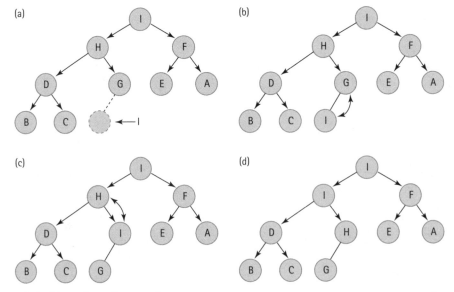

Figure 9.4 The `reheapUp` operation

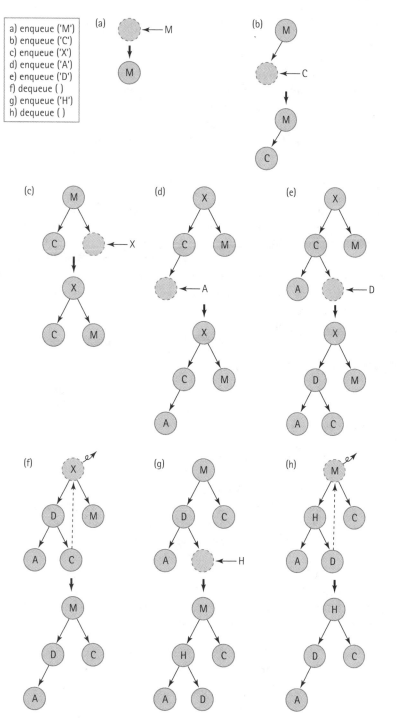

a) enqueue ('M')
b) enqueue ('C')
c) enqueue ('X')
d) enqueue ('A')
e) enqueue ('D')
f) dequeue ( )
g) enqueue ('H')
h) dequeue ( )

Figure 9.5 A sequence of priority queue operations performed by a heap

reheap up or *reheap down* operation, allowing you to fill in the details of how the heap elements are adjusted to maintain the heap properties.

Note that because a heap is always a complete tree, the height of a heap is always at most $\lfloor \log_2 N \rfloor$, where N represents the number of elements in the heap. The *reheap up* and *reheap down* operations involve moving an element up the tree or down the tree through these $\lfloor \log_2 N \rfloor$ levels. Assuming we can implement the primitive statements involved in these operations in constant time, we can support both `enqueue` and `dequeue` priority queue methods with $O(\log_2 N)$ efficiency. In the next section we learn how to do this.

9.4 The Heap Implementation

Although we have graphically depicted heaps as binary trees with nodes and links, it would be very impractical to implement the heap operations using the linked binary tree representation presented in Chapter 7. For example, our binary search tree implementation does not efficiently support "moving" elements up a tree. Due to the shape property of heaps an alternate representation is possible, one that supports constant time implementation of all of the operations we need to manage our heaps. We first explore this tree implementation approach and then see how it can be used to implement a heap (and therefore a priority queue).

A Nonlinked Representation of Binary Trees

The implementation of binary trees we studied in Chapter 7 used a scheme in which the links from parent to children are *explicit* in the implementation structure. In other words, instance variables were declared in each node for the reference to the left child and the reference to the right child.

A binary tree can be stored in an array in such a way that the relationships in the tree are not directly represented by references, but rather are *implicit* in the positions used within the array to hold the elements.

Let us take a binary tree and store it in an array in such a way that the parent–child relationships are not lost. We store the tree elements in the array, level by level, from left to right. We call the array `elements` and store the index of the last tree element in a variable `lastIndex`, as illustrated in **Figure 9.6**. The tree elements are stored with the root in `elements[0]` and the last node in `elements[lastIndex]`.

To implement the algorithms that manipulate the tree, we must be able to find the left and right children of a node in the tree. Comparing the tree and the array in Figure 9.6, we make the following observations:

`elements[0]`'s children are in `elements[1]` and `elements[2]`.

`elements[1]`'s children are in `elements[3]` and `elements[4]`.

`elements[2]`'s children are in `elements[5]` and `elements[6]`.

Do you see the pattern? For any node `elements[index]`, its left child is in `elements[index * 2 + 1]` and its right child is in `elements[(index * 2) + 2]`

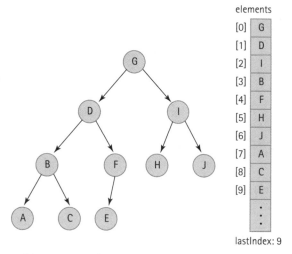

elements

[0]	G
[1]	D
[2]	I
[3]	B
[4]	F
[5]	H
[6]	J
[7]	A
[8]	C
[9]	E

lastIndex: 9

Figure 9.6   An abstract binary tree and its concrete array-based representation

(provided that these child nodes exist). Notice that nodes from `elements[(tree.lastIndex + 1) / 2]` to `elements[tree.lastindex]` are leaf nodes.

Not only can we easily calculate the location of a node's children, but we can also determine the location of its parent node, a required operation for `reheapUp`. This task is not an easy one in a binary tree linked together with references from parent to child nodes, but it is very simple in our implicit link implementation: `elements[index]`'s parent is in `elements[(index - 1) / 2]`.

Because integer division truncates any remainder, `(index - 1) / 2` is the correct parent index for either a left or right child. Thus, this implementation of a binary tree is linked in both directions: from parent to child, and from child to parent.

The array-based representation is simple to implement for trees that are full or complete, because the elements occupy contiguous array slots. If a tree is not full or complete, however, we must account for the gaps where nodes are missing. To use the array representation, we must store a dummy value in those positions in the ar-

> **Authors' Note**
>
> As we have done before, to simplify the figures in this section we use single letters to represent the objects stored in the heap. Keep in mind that what is actually stored in each array location is a reference to an object.

ray to maintain the proper parent–child relationship. The choice of a dummy value depends on the information that is stored in the tree. For instance, if the elements in the tree are nonnegative integers, a negative value can be stored in the dummy nodes; if the elements are objects, we can use a null value.

Figure 9.7 illustrates an incomplete tree and its corresponding array. Some of the array slots do not contain actual tree elements, but rather dummy values. The algorithms to manipulate the tree must reflect this situation. For example, to determine that the node in

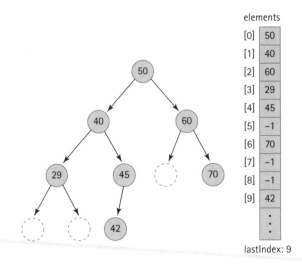

Figure 9.7   An abstract binary tree and its concrete array-based representation using dummy values

`elements[index]` has a left child, we must verify that `(index * 2) + 1 <= last-Index`, and that the value in `elements[(index * 2) + 1]` is not the dummy value.

Implementing a Heap

Although when there are many "holes" in the tree, the array-based binary tree implementation can waste a lot of space, in the case of the heap it is a perfect representation. The shape property of heaps tells us that the binary tree is complete, so we know that it is never unbalanced. Thus, we can easily store the tree in an array with implicit links without wasting any space. **Figure 9.8** shows how the values in a heap would be stored in the array-based representation.

If a heap with *N* elements is implemented this way, the shape property says that the heap elements are stored in *N* consecutive slots in the array, with the root element in the first slot (index 0) and the last leaf node in the slot with index `lastIndex = N - 1`. Therefore, when implementing this approach there is no need for dummy values—there are never gaps in the tree.

Recall that when we use this representation of a binary tree, the following relationships hold for an element at position `index`:

- If the element is not the root, its parent is at position `(index - 1) / 2`.
- If the element has a left child, the child is at position `(index * 2) + 1`.
- If the element has a right child, the child is at position `(index * 2) + 2`.

These relationships allow us to efficiently calculate the parent, left child, or right child of any node. Also, because the tree is complete, no space is wasted using the array representation. Time efficiency and space efficiency! We make use of these features in our heap implementation.

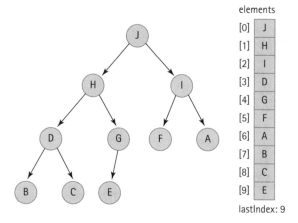

elements
[0] J
[1] H
[2] I
[3] D
[4] G
[5] F
[6] A
[7] B
[8] C
[9] E
lastIndex: 9

Figure 9.8 An abstract heap and its concrete array-based representation

Rather than directly use an array to implement our heaps we use the Java library's `ArrayList` class. This allows us to create a generic heap without needing to deal with the troublesome issues surrounding the use of generics and arrays in Java. An `ArrayList` is essentially just a wrapper around an array—therefore, the use of an `ArrayList` does not cost much, if anything, in terms of efficiency. This is especially true since we design our heap-based priority queue to be of a fixed capacity, and therefore prevent the use of the automatic, time-inefficient copying of the underlying array that occurs when an `Array-List` object needs to be resized. Furthermore, the code only ever adds or removes elements at the "end" of the `ArrayList`—adding or removing anywhere else would require costly element shifting.

Here is the beginning of our `HeapPriQ` class. As you can see, it implements `PriQueueInterface`. Because it implements a priority queue, we placed it in the `ch09.priorityQueues` package. Also, note that both constructors require an integer argument, used to set the size of the underlying `ArrayList`. As with several of our ADTs, one constructor accepts a `Comparator` argument and the other creates a `Comparator` based on the "natural order" of T. The `isEmpty`, `isFull`, and `size` operations are trivial.

```
//-------------------------------------------------------------------------------
// Heap.java                    by Dale/Joyce/Weems                   Chapter 9
// Priority Queue using Heap (implemented with an ArrayList)
//
// Two constructors are provided: one that use the natural order of the
// elements as defined by their compareTo method and one that uses an
// ordering based on a comparator argument.
//-------------------------------------------------------------------------------

package ch09.priorityQueues;
```

```java
import java.util.*;  // ArrayList, Comparator

public class HeapPriQ<T> implements PriQueueInterface<T>
{
  protected ArrayList<T> elements; // priority queue elements
  protected int lastIndex;         // index of last element in priority queue
  protected int maxIndex;          // index of last position in ArrayList

  protected Comparator<T> comp;

  public HeapPriQ(int maxSize)
  // Precondition: T implements Comparable
  {
    elements = new ArrayList<T>(maxSize);
    lastIndex = -1;
    maxIndex = maxSize - 1;

    comp = new Comparator<T>()
    {
      public int compare(T element1, T element2)
      {
        return ((Comparable)element1).compareTo(element2);
      }
    };
  }

  public HeapPriQ(int maxSize, Comparator<T> comp)
  // Precondition: T implements Comparable
  {
    elements = new ArrayList<T>(maxSize);
    lastIndex = -1;
    maxIndex = maxSize - 1;

    this.comp = comp;
  }

  public boolean isEmpty()
  // Returns true if this priority queue is empty; otherwise, returns false.
  {
    return (lastIndex == -1);
  }

  public boolean isFull()
  // Returns true if this priority queue is full; otherwise, returns false.
```

```
{
  return (lastIndex == maxIndex);
}


public int size()
// Returns the number of elements on this priority queue.
{
  return lastIndex + 1;
}
```

The enqueue Method

We next look at the enqueue method, which is the simpler of the two transformer methods. Assuming the existence of a reheapUp helper method, as specified previously, the enqueue method is

```
public void enqueue(T element) throws PriQOverflowException
// Throws PriQOverflowException if this priority queue is full;
// otherwise, adds element to this priority queue.
{
  if (lastIndex == maxIndex)
    throw new PriQOverflowException("Priority queue is full");
  else
  {
    lastIndex++;
    elements.add(lastIndex,element);
    reheapUp(element);
  }
}
```

If the heap is already full, the appropriate exception is thrown. Otherwise, we increase the lastIndex value, add the element to the heap at that location, and call the reheapUp method. Of course, the reheapUp method is doing all of the interesting work. Let us look at it more closely.

The reheapUp algorithm starts with a tree whose last node is empty; we call this empty node the "hole." We swap the hole up the tree until it reaches a spot where the element argument can be placed into the hole without violating the order property of the heap. While the hole moves up the tree, the elements it is

Using ArrayList

In our description of the reheapUp algorithm we speak of "starting with a tree whose last node is empty" and moving a "hole" up the tree until it is in the correct location to receive element. But in our enqueue code, before invoking reheapUp, we add element at that "last node." We must place something in the array location that represents that last node so that the ArrayList set method, invoked in the reheapUp code, will not throw an exception when attempting to use that location. The code eventually overwrites the value placed in that node, but there must be something there first for it to be overwritten. The truth is, any value of type T could have been used—the location really does represent a "hole."

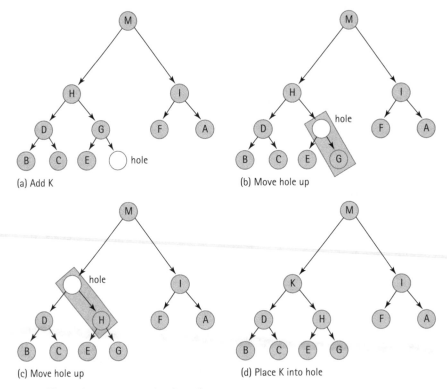

(a) Add K   (b) Move hole up

(c) Move hole up   (d) Place K into hole

Figure 9.9 The reheapUp operation in action

replacing move down the tree, filling in the previous location of the hole. This situation is illustrated in **Figure 9.9**.

The sequence of nodes between a leaf and the root of a heap can be viewed as a sorted linked list. This is guaranteed by the heap's order property. The reheapUp algorithm is essentially inserting an element into this sorted linked list. As we progress from the leaf to the root along this path, we compare the value of element with the value in the hole's parent node. If the parent's value is smaller, we cannot place element into the current hole, because the order property would be violated, so we move the hole up. Moving the hole up really means copying the value of the hole's parent into the hole's location. Now the parent's location is available, and it becomes the new hole. We repeat this process until (1) the hole is the root of the heap or (2) element's value is less than or equal to the value in the hole's parent node. In either case, we can now safely copy element into the hole's position.

This approach requires us to be able to find a given node's parent quickly. This task appears difficult, based on our experiences with references that can be traversed in only one direction. But, as we saw earlier, it is very simple with our implicit link implementation:

- If the element is not the root, its parent is at position (index - 1) / 2.

Here is the code for the `reheapUp` method:

```
private void reheapUp(T element)
// Current lastIndex position is empty.
// Inserts element into the tree and ensures shape and order properties.
{
  int hole = lastIndex;
  while ((hole > 0)      // hole is not root and element > hole's parent
         &&
    (comp.compare(element, elements.get((hole - 1) / 2)) > 0))
    {
    // move hole's parent down and then move hole up
    elements.set(hole,elements.get((hole - 1) / 2));
    hole = (hole - 1) / 2;
  }
  elements.set(hole, element);   // place element into final hole
}
```

This method takes advantage of the short-circuit nature of Java's && operator. If the current `hole` is the root of the heap, then the first half of the *while* loop control expression

```
(hole > 0)
```

is `false`, and the second half

```
(element.compareTo(elements.get((hole - 1) / 2)) > 0))
```

is not evaluated. If it was evaluated in that case, it would cause an `IndexOutOfBounds-Exception` to be thrown.

The dequeue Method

Finally, we look at the `dequeue` method. As for enqueue, assuming the existence of the helper method, in this case the `reheapDown` method, the `dequeue` method is relatively simple:

```
public T dequeue() throws PriQUnderflowException
// Throws PriQUnderflowException if this priority queue is empty;
// otherwise, removes element with highest priority from this
// priority queue and returns it.
{
  T hold;      // element to be dequeued and returned
  T toMove;    // element to move down heap

  if (lastIndex == -1)
    throw new PriQUnderflowException("Priority queue is empty");
  else
```

```
      {
         hold = elements.get(0);                       // remember element to be returned
         toMove = elements.remove(lastIndex);          // element to reheap down
         lastIndex--;                                  // decrease priority queue size
         if (lastIndex != -1)                          // if priority queue is not empty
            reheapDown(toMove);                        //   restore heap properties
         return hold;                                  // return largest element
      }
   }
}
```

If the heap is empty, the appropriate exception is thrown. Otherwise, we first store a reference to the root element (the maximum element in the tree), so that it can be returned to the client program when finished. We also store a reference to the element in the "last" position and remove it from the ArrayList. Recall that this is the element used to move into the hole vacated by the root element, so we call it the toMove element. We decrement the lastIndex variable to reflect the new bounds of the heap and, assuming the heap is not now empty, pass the toMove element to the reheapDown method. The only thing remaining to do is to return the saved value of the previous root element, the hold variable, to the client.

Look at the reheapDown algorithm more closely. In many ways, it is similar to the reheapUp algorithm. In both cases, we have a "hole" in the tree and an element to be placed into the tree so that the tree remains a heap. In both cases, we move the hole through the tree (actually moving tree elements into the hole) until it reaches a location where it can legally hold the element. The reheapDown operation, however, is a more complex operation because it is moving the hole down the tree instead of up the tree. When we are moving down, there are more decisions to make.

When reheapDown is first called, the root of the tree can be considered a hole; that position in the tree is available, because the dequeue method has already saved the contents in its hold variable. The job of reheapDown is to "move" the hole down the tree until it reaches a spot where element can replace it. See **Figure 9.10**.

Before we can move the hole, we need to know where to move it. It should move either to its left child or to its right child, or it should stay where it is. Assume the existence of another helper method, called newHole, that provides us this information. The newHole method accepts arguments representing the index of the hole (hole), and the element to be inserted (element). The specification for newHole is

```
private int newHole(int hole, T element)
// If either child of hole is larger than element, return the index
// of the larger child; otherwise, return the index of hole.
```

Given the index of the hole, newHole returns the index of the next location for the hole. If newHole returns the same index that is passed to it, we know the hole is at its final location. The reheapDown algorithm repeatedly calls newHole to find the next index for the hole, and then moves the hole down to that location. It does this until newHole returns

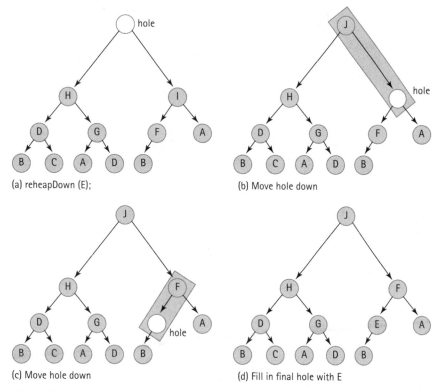

(a) reheapDown (E);

(b) Move hole down

(c) Move hole down

(d) Fill in final hole with E

Figure 9.10 The `reheapDown` operation in action

the same index that is passed to it. The existence of `newHole` simplifies `reheapDown` so that we can now create its code:

```
private void reheapDown(T element)
// Current root position is "empty";
// Inserts element into the tree and ensures shape and order properties.
{
    int hole = 0;        // current index of hole
    int next;            // next index where hole should move to

    next = newHole(hole, element);    // find next hole
    while (next != hole)
    {
        elements.set(hole,elements.get(next));   // move element up
        hole = next;                             // move hole down
        next = newHole(hole, element);           // find next hole
    }
    elements.set(hole, element);                 // fill in the final hole
}
```

Now the only thing left to do is create the `newHole` method. This method does quite a lot of work for us. Consider Figure 9.10 again. Given the initial configuration, `newHole` should return the index of the node containing J, the right child of the hole node; J is larger than either the element (E) or the left child of the hole node (H). Thus, `newHole` must compare three values (the values in `element`, the left child of the hole node, and the right child of the hole node) and return the index of the greatest value. Think about that. It does not seem very hard, but it does require quite a few steps:

Greatest(left, right, element) returns index

```
if (left < right)
      if (right <= element)
            return element
      else
            return right
else
if (left <= element)
      return element;
else
    return left;
```

Other approaches to this algorithm are possible, but they all require about the same number of comparisons. One benefit of the preceding algorithm is that if `element` is tied for being the largest of the three arguments, its index is returned. This choice increases the efficiency of our program because in this situation we want the hole to stop moving (`reheapDown` breaks out of its loop when the value of `hole` is returned). Trace the algorithm with various combinations of arguments to convince yourself that it works.

Our algorithm applies only to the case when the hole node has two children. Of course, the `newHole` method must also handle the cases where the hole node is a leaf and where the hole node has only one child. How can we tell if a node is a leaf or if it has only one child? Easily, based on the fact that our tree is complete. First, we calculate the expected position of the left child; if this position is greater than `lastIndex`, then the tree has no node at this position and the hole node is a leaf. (Remember, if it does not have a left child, it cannot have a right child because the tree is complete.) In this case `newHole` just returns the index of its hole parameter, because the hole cannot move anymore. If the expected position of the left child is equal to `lastIndex`, then the node has only one child, and `newHole` returns the index of that child if the child's value is larger than the value of `element`.

Here is the code for `newHole`. As you can see, it is a sequence of *if-else* statements that capture the approaches described in the preceding paragraphs.

```
private int newHole(int hole, T element)
// If either child of hole is larger than element, return the index
// of the larger child; otherwise, return the index of hole.
{
  int left = (hole * 2) + 1;
  int right = (hole * 2) + 2;

  if (left > lastIndex)
    // hole has no children
    return hole;
  else
  if (left == lastIndex)
    // hole has left child only
    if (comp.compare(element, elements.get(left)) < 0)
      // element < left child
      return left;
    else
      // element >= left child
      return hole;
  else
  // hole has two children
  if (comp.compare(elements.get(left), elements.get(right)) < 0)
    // left child < right child
    if (comp.compare(elements.get(right), element) <= 0)
      // right child <= element
      return hole;
    else
      // element < right child
      return right;
  else
  // left child >= right child
  if (comp.compare(elements.get(left), element) <= 0)
    // left child <= element
    return hole;
  else
    // element < left child
    return left;
}
```

A Sample Use

To allow us to test our heap we include the following `toString` method within its implementation:

```java
@Override
public String toString()
// Returns a string of all the heap elements.
{
    String theHeap = new String("the heap is:\n");
    for (int index = 0; index <= lastIndex; index++)
        theHeap = theHeap + index + ". " + elements.get(index) + "\n";
    return theHeap;
}
```

This `toString` method simply returns a string indicating each index used in the heap, along with the corresponding element contained at that index. It allows us to devise test programs that create and manipulate heaps, and then displays their structure.

Suppose you enqueue the strings "J", "A", "M", "B", "L", and "E" into a new heap. How would you draw our abstract view of the ensuing heap? Which values would be in which `ArrayList` slots? Suppose you dequeue an element and print it? Which element would be printed, and how would the realigned heap appear?

To demonstrate how you might declare and use a heap in an application we provide a short example of a program that performs those operations, and we show the output from the program. Were your predictions correct?

```java
//-------------------------------------------------------------------------
// UseHeap.java               by Dale/Joyce/Weems              Chapter 9
//
// Example of a simple use of the HeapPriQ.
//-------------------------------------------------------------------------
package ch09.apps;

import ch09.priorityQueues.*;

public class UseHeap
{
    public static void main(String[] args)
    {
        PriQueueInterface<String> h = new HeapPriQ<String>(10);
        h.enqueue("J");
        h.enqueue("A");
        h.enqueue("M");
        h.enqueue("B");
        h.enqueue("L");
        h.enqueue("E");
```

```
System.out.println(h);

System.out.println(h.dequeue() + "\n");

System.out.println(h);
    }
}
```

Here is the output from the program, with our abstract view of the heap, both before and after dequeuing the largest element, drawn to the right:

```
the heap is:
0. M
1. L
2. J
3. A
4. B
5. E

M

the heap is:
0. L
1. E
2. J
3. A
4. B
```

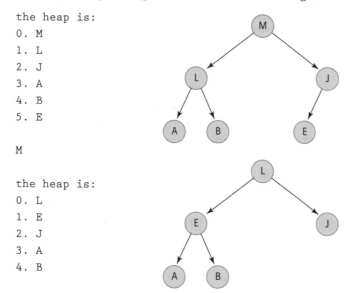

Heaps Versus Other Representations of Priority Queues

How efficient is the heap implementation of a priority queue? The constructors, isEmpty, isFull, and size methods are trivial, so we examine only the operations to add and remove elements. The enqueue and dequeue methods both consist of a few basic operations plus a call to a helper method. The reheapUp method creates a slot for a new element by moving a hole up the tree, level by level; because a complete tree is of minimum height, there are at most $\lfloor \log_2 N \rfloor$ levels above the leaf level (N = number of elements). Thus, enqueue is an $O(\log_2 N)$ operation. The reheapDown method is invoked to fill the hole in the root created by

> **Heaps Are Amazing**
>
> A heap provides a near-perfect implementation of a priority queue— $O(\log_2 N)$ enqueue and dequeue operations plus efficient space usage. The combination of elegant, clever algorithms and an efficient array-based storage structure results in what can only be classified as an amazing data structure.

the dequeue method. This operation moves the hole down in the tree, level by level. Again, there are at most $\lfloor \log_2 N \rfloor$ levels below the root, so dequeue is also an $O(\log_2 N)$ operation.

How does this implementation compare to the others we mentioned in Section 9.2, "Priority Queue Implementations"? As discussed there, the only approach with comparable efficiency is the binary search tree approach; however, in that case the efficiency of the operations depends on the shape of the tree. When the tree is bushy, both `dequeue` and `enqueue` are $O(\log_2 N)$ operations. In the worst case, if the tree degenerates to a linked list, both `enqueue` and `dequeue` have $O(N)$ efficiency.

Overall, the binary search tree looks good if it is balanced. It can, however, become skewed, which reduces the efficiency of the operations. The heap, by contrast, is always a tree of minimum height. It is not a good structure for accessing a randomly selected element, but that is not one of the operations defined for priority queues. The accessing protocol of a priority queue specifies that only the largest (or highest-priority) element can be accessed. For the operations specified for priority queues; therefore, the heap is an excellent choice.

Summary

In this chapter, we discussed the Priority Queue ADT—what it is, how it is used, and how to implement it. In particular, we studied an elegant implementation called a heap. A heap is based on a binary tree with special shape and order properties, constructed from an array rather than with links as is typical for a tree representation. The properties of heaps make them particularly well suited to implementing the priority queue. Although the algorithms for maintaining the heap in the correct shape and order are relatively complex, they allow us to create $O(\log_2 N)$ enqueue and dequeue operations, all while using a space-efficient array-based structure. The heap can also be used to provide a very time- and space-efficient sorting algorithm, the Heap Sort, which is presented in Chapter 11.

Exercises

9.1 The Priority Queue Interface

1. Give an example from everyday life that involves a priority queue.

2. If a priority queue is used to implement a busy queue it is conceivable that some elements may spend a very long time in the queue, waiting to be serviced. We say such elements "starve."

   a. Describe two examples where this type of "starvation" might be an issue.

   b. For each of your examples, describe an approach to prevent the starvation from occurring.

3. What is the output of the following code (remember, the "largest" string lexicographically, i.e., lexicographically last, has the highest priority)—`SortedABPriQ` is an implementation of the `PriQInterface` that is developed in Section 9.2, "Priority Queue Implementations."

```
PriQInterface<String> question;
question = new SortedABPriQ<String>();
System.out.println(question.isEmpty());
System.out.println(question.size());

question.enqueue("map"); question.enqueue("ant");
question.enqueue("sit"); question.enqueue("dog");
```

```
System.out.println(question.isEmpty());
System.out.println(question.size());
System.out.println(question.dequeue());
System.out.println(question.dequeue());
System.out.println(question.size());
```

9.2 Priority Queue Implementations

4. In this section we discussed several approaches to implementing a priority queue using previously studied data structures (Unsorted Array, Sorted Array, Sorted Linked List, and Binary Search Tree). Discuss, in a similar fashion, using

   a. an Unsorted Linked List.

   b. a Hash Table.

5. Bill announces that he has found a clever approach to implementing a Priority Queue with an Unsorted Array that supports an O(1) dequeue operation. He states "It is simple actually, I just create an `int` instance variable `highest` that holds the index of the largest element enqueued so far. That is easy to check and update whenever an element is enqueued, and when it is time to dequeue I return the element at index `highest`— constant time dequeue!" What do you tell Bill, or maybe, what do you ask Bill?

6. Describe the ramifications of each of the following changes to `SortedABPriQ` (code is in the `ch09.priorityQueues` package):

   a. In the first constructor the statement

   ```
   return ((Comparable)element1).compareTo(element2);
   ```

   is changed to

   ```
   return ((Comparable)element2).compareTo(element1);
   ```

   b. In the boolean expression for the *while loop* of the enqueue method the first `>` is changed to `>=`.

   c. In the boolean expression for the *while loop* of the enqueue method the second `>` is changed to `>=`.

7. Suppose a priority queue is implemented as a binary search tree of integers. Draw the tree resulting from

   a. enqueuing, in this order, the following integers: 15, 10, 27, 8, 18, 56, 4, 9.

   b. continuing from part a, three dequeues are invoked.

   Discuss the results.

8. Implement the Priority Queue ADT using

   a. an Unsorted Array.

   b. an Unsorted Linked List.

   c. a Sorted Linked List (sort in decreasing order).

   d. our Binary Search Tree (wrap the tree inside your priority queue implementation).

9. Use the `SortedABPriQ` class to help solve the following problem. Create an application `Random10K` that generates 100 numbers between 1 and 10,000, stores them in a priority queue (you can wrap them in an `Integer` object), and then prints them out in columns 10 integers wide in

   a. decreasing order.

   b. increasing order.

   c. ordered increasingly by the sum of the digits in the number.

9.3 The Heap

10. Consider the following trees.

    a. Classify each as either full, complete, both full and complete, or neither full nor complete.

    b. Which of the trees can be considered a heap? If they are not, why not?

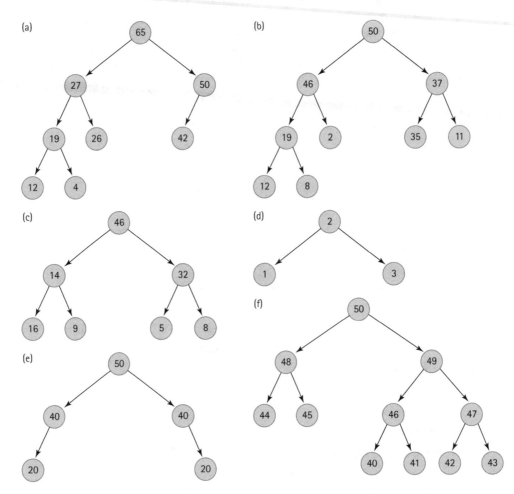

11. Consider a tree with the following number of levels: 1 (contains only the root), 2, 3, 5, 10, *N*.

    a.   If full, how many nodes does it contain?

    b.   If complete, what is the minimum number of nodes it contains?

    c.   If complete, what is the maximum number of nodes it contains?

12. Draw three separate heaps containing the nodes 1, 2, 3, and 4.

13. Starting with the priority queue represented by the heap shown below (start over again with this heap for each part of the question) draw the heap that results from

    a.   one dequeue.

    b.   two dequeues.

    c.   three dequeues.

    d.   enqueue 1.

    e.   enqueue 47.

    f.   enqueue 56.

    g.   the following sequence: dequeue, enqueue 50.

    h.   the following sequence: dequeue, dequeue, enqueue 46, enqueue 50.

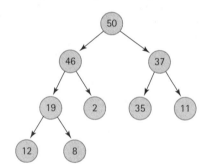

14. Starting with an empty priority queue, represented as a heap, draw the heap that results from:

    a.   enqueue 25, enqueue 13, enqueue 30, enqueue 10, enqueue 39, enqueue 27, dequeue

    b.   enqueue 1, enqueue 2, enqueue 3, enqueue 4, enqueue 5, enqueue 6, enqueue 7, dequeue

    c.   enqueue 7, enqueue 6, enqueue 5, enqueue 4, enqueue 3, enqueue 2, enqueue 1, dequeue

    d.   enqueue 4, enqueue 2, enqueue 6, enqueue 1, enqueue 3, enqueue 5, enqueue 7, dequeue

9.4 The Heap Implementation

15. The elements in a binary tree are to be stored in an array, as described in this section. Each element is a nonnegative `int` value.

    a. Which value can you use as the dummy value, if the binary tree is not complete?

    b. Draw the array that would represent the following tree:

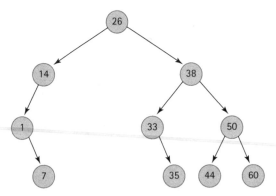

16. The elements in a complete binary tree are to be stored in an array, as described in this section. Each element is a nonnegative `int` value. Show the contents of the array, given the following tree:

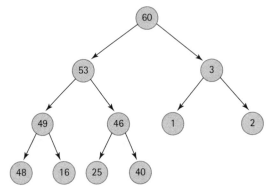

17. Given the array pictured below, draw the binary tree that can be created from its elements. (The elements are arranged in the array to represent a tree as discussed in this section.)

[0]	[1]	[2]	[3]	[4]	[5]	[6]	[7]	[8]	[9]
15	10	12	3	47	8	3	20	17	8

18. A complete binary tree is stored in an array called `treeNodes`, which is indexed from 0 to 99, as described in this section. The tree contains 85 elements. Mark each of the following statements as true or false, and explain your answers.

    a. `treeNodes[42]` is a leaf node.

    b. `treeNodes[41]` has only one child.

    c. The right child of `treeNodes[12]` is `treeNodes[25]`.

    d. The subtree rooted at `treeNodes[7]` is a full binary tree with four levels.

    e. The tree has seven levels that are full, and one additional level that contains some elements.

19. The `enqueue` method listed in this section uses the `ArrayList add` method to add the argument to the internal array list. But the `ArrayList add` method will add the argument in the next available slot, in other words to the "right" of all the other current elements. This might not be the correct location. Explain how this is resolved.

Questions 20, 21, and 22 use the following heap:

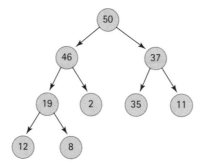

20. Show the array that stores the above heap.

21. Given the array that stores the above heap indicate the sequence of indices of the array which would be occupied by the hole during the `reheapDown` method execution of our `HeapPriQ` class

    a. if `dequeue()` is invoked.

    b. if `dequeue()` is invoked a second time.

22. Given the array that stores the above heap, indicate the sequence of indices of the array which would be occupied by the hole during the `reheapUp` method execution of `HeapPriQ` class

    a. if `enqueue(48)` is invoked.

    b. if `enqueue(60)` is then invoked.

23. Show the expected output of the following program:

```
package ch09.apps;
import ch09.priorityQueues.*;

public class UseHeap
{
  public static void main(String[] args)
  {
    PriQueueInterface<String> h = new HeapPriQ<String>(10);
    h.enqueue("C");   h.enqueue("O");
    h.enqueue("M");   h.enqueue("P");
    h.enqueue("U");   h.enqueue("T");
    h.enqueue("E");   h.enqueue("R");

    System.out.println(h);
    System.out.println(h.dequeue() + "\n");
    System.out.println(h);
  }
}
```

The Graph ADT

Knowledge Goals

You should be able to

- define the following terms related to graphs:
  - graph
  - vertex
  - edge
  - undirected graph
  - directed graph
  - adjacent vertices
  - path
  - cycle
  - connected vertices
  - connected graph
  - disconnected graph
  - connected component
  - complete graph
- describe the purpose of each of the methods defined in the `WeightedGraphInterface`
- explain how to implement a graph using arrays
- explain how to implement a graph using linked lists
- discuss the benefits and drawbacks of the two primary graph implementation approaches
- explain the difference between a depth-first search and a breadth-first search of a graph
- describe the shortest-path algorithm for graphs

Skill Goals

You should be able to

- trace the depth-first "is-path" algorithm, listing the vertices in the order marked and the order visited
- trace the breadth-first "is-path" algorithm, listing the vertices in the order marked and the order visited
- trace the "shortest paths" algorithm, listing the shortest path and distance to all vertices from a given vertex
- implement a graph using an adjacency matrix to represent the edges
- implement a graph using adjacency lists
- implement the depth-first searching strategy for a graph using a stack for auxiliary storage
- implement the breadth-first searching strategy for a graph using a queue for auxiliary storage
- implement a shortest-paths operation for a graph, using a priority queue to access the edge with the minimum weight

In Chapter 7 we looked at how a branching structure—the binary search tree—facilitates searching for data. In this chapter we see how another branching structure, the graph, is defined and implemented to support a variety of applications. Graphs consist of vertices and edges. The information held in a graph often is related to the structure of the graph itself, the relationships among the vertices and edges.

10.1   Introduction to Graphs

In Chapter 7 we studied trees. Trees provide a very useful way of representing relationships in which a hierarchy exists. That is, a node is pointed to by at most one other node (its parent), as pictured below.

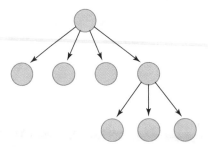

If we remove the restriction that each node may have only one parent node, we have a data structure called a **graph**. A graph is made up of a set of nodes called **vertices** and a set of lines called **edges** (or **arcs**) that connect the vertices. The information held in a graph is related to the structure of the graph itself, the relationships among the vertices and edges. In this section we introduce the vocabulary of these relationships.

Graph Definitions

The many definitions related to graphs presented in this section are collected in Figure 10.4 at the end of the section and can also be found in the glossary.

The set of edges describes relationships among the vertices. For instance, if the vertices are the names of cities, the edges that link the vertices could represent roads between pairs of cities. Because the road that runs between Houston and Austin also runs between Austin and Houston, the edges in this graph have no direction. This is called an **undirected graph**. If the edges that link the vertices represent flights from one city to another, however, the direction of each edge is important. The existence of a flight (edge) from Houston to Austin does not assure the existence of a flight (edge) from Austin to Houston. A graph whose edges are directed from one vertex to another is called a **directed graph**, or **digraph**.

From a programmer's perspective, vertices represent whatever is the subject of our study: people, houses, cities, courses, and so on. Mathematically, however, vertices are the abstract concept upon which graph theory rests. In fact, a great deal of formal mathematics is associated with graphs. In other computing courses, you may analyze graphs and prove theorems about them. This text introduces the graph as an abstract data type, teaches some basic terminology, discusses how a graph might be implemented, and describes how algorithms that manipulate graphs make use of stacks, queues, and priority queues.

Formally, a graph G is defined as follows:

$$G = (V, E)$$

where

V(G) is a finite, nonempty set of vertices and E(G) is a set of edges (written as pairs of vertices).

The set of vertices is specified by listing them in set notation, within { } braces. The following set defines the six vertices of Graph1 pictured in **Figure 10.1a**:

$$V(Graph1) = \{A, B, C, D, E, F\}$$

(a) Graph1 is an undirected graph

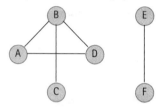

V(Graph1) = {A, B, C, D, E, F}
E(Graph1) = {(A, B), (A, D), (B, C), (B, D), (E, F)}

(b) Graph2 is a directed graph

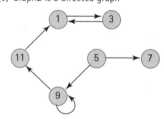

V(Graph2) = {1, 3, 5, 7, 9, 11}
E(Graph2) = {(1, 3), (3, 1), (5, 7), (5, 9), (9, 11), (9, 9), (11, 1)}

(c) Graph3 is a directed graph

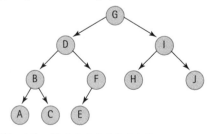

V(Graph3) = {A, B, C, D, E, F, G, H, I, J}
E(Graph3) = {(G, D), (G, I), (D, B), (D, F), (I, H), (I, J), (B, A), (B, C), (F, E)}

Figure 10.1   Examples of graphs

The set of edges is specified by listing a sequence of edges. Each edge is denoted by writing the names of the two vertices it connects in parentheses, with a comma between them. For instance, the vertices in Graph1 are connected by the five edges described below:

$$E(\text{Graph1}) = \{(A, B), (A, D), (B, C), (B, D), (E, F)\}$$

Because Graph 1 is an undirected graph, the order of the vertices in each edge is unimportant. The set of edges in Graph 1 can also be described as follows:

$$E(\text{Graph1}) = \{(B, A), (D, A), (C, B), (D, B), (F, E)\}$$

If the graph is a digraph, the direction of the edge is indicated by which vertex is listed first. For instance, in Graph 2 pictured in Figure 10.1b, the edge (5, 7) represents a link from vertex 5 to vertex 7. There is no corresponding edge (7, 5) in Graph 2. In pictures of digraphs, the arrows indicate the direction of the relationship.

We do not have duplicate vertices or edges in a graph. This point is implied in the definition, because sets do not have repeated elements.

If two vertices in a graph are connected by an edge, they are said to be *adjacent*. In Graph 1 vertices A and B are adjacent, but vertices A and C are not. If the vertices are connected by a directed edge, then the first vertex is said to be **adjacent to** the second, and the second vertex is said to be **adjacent from** the first. For example, in Graph 2 vertex 5 is adjacent to vertices 7 and 9, while vertex 1 is adjacent from vertices 3 and 11.

The picture of Graph 3 in Figure 10.1c may look familiar; it is the tree we looked at in Chapter 9 in connection with the nonlinked representation of a binary tree. A tree is a special case of a directed graph in which each vertex may only be adjacent from one other vertex (its parent) and one vertex (the root) is not adjacent from any other vertex.

A **path** from one vertex to another consists of a sequence of vertices that connect them. For a path to exist, there must be an uninterrupted sequence of edges from the first vertex, through any number of vertices, to the second vertex. For example, in Graph 2, there is a path from vertex 5 to vertex 3, but not from vertex 3 to vertex 5. In a tree, such as Graph 3, there is a unique path from the root to every other vertex in the tree.

A **cycle** is a path that begins and ends at the same vertex. For example, in Graph 1 the path A-B-D-A is a cycle.

In an undirected graph we say that two *vertices are connected* (**connected vertices**) if there is a path between them. Note that in Graph 1, vertex A is connected to vertices B, C, and D but not to E or F. A **connected component** is a maximal set of vertices that are connected to each other, along with the edges associated with those vertices. Graph 1 consists of two connected components {A, B, C, D} and {E, F}. Each vertex of an undirected graph belongs to one connected component. So does each edge.

An undirected graph is a **connected graph** when it consists of a single connected component. Otherwise it is a **disconnected graph**.

A **complete graph** is one in which every vertex is adjacent to every other vertex. **Figure 10.2** shows two complete graphs. If there are N vertices, there are $N * (N - 1)$

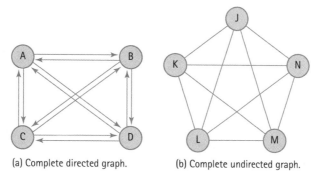

(a) Complete directed graph.　(b) Complete undirected graph.

Figure 10.2 Two complete graphs

edges in a complete directed graph and $N * (N - 1) / 2$ edges in a complete undirected graph.

A **weighted graph** is a graph in which each edge carries a value. Weighted graphs can be used to represent applications in which the *value* of the connection between the vertices is important, not just the *existence* of a connection. For instance, in the weighted graph pictured in **Figure 10.3**, the vertices represent cities and the edges indicate the Air Busters Airlines flights that connect the cities. The weights attached to the edges represent the air distances between pairs of cities.

To see whether we can get from Denver to Washington, we look for a path between them. If the total travel distance is determined by the sum of the distances between each pair of cities along the way, we can calculate the travel distance by adding the weights attached to the edges that constitute the path between them. There may be multiple paths between two vertices. Later in this chapter, we talk about a way to find the shortest path between two vertices (**Figure 10.4**).

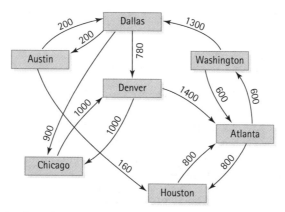

Figure 10.3 A weighted graph

Adjacent vertices   Two vertices in a graph that are connected by an edge

Adjacent from   If vertex A is connected to vertex B in a directed graph by an edge (A, B) then B is adjacent to A

Adjacent to   If vertex A is connected to vertex B in a directed graph by an edge (A, B) then A is adjacent to B

Complete graph   A graph in which every vertex is directly connected to every other vertex

Connected component   A maximal set of vertices of a graph that are connected to each other, along with the edges associated with those vertices

Connected graph   A graph that consists of a single connected component

Connected vertices   In an undirected graph we say that two vertices are connected if there is a path between them

Cycle   A path that begins and ends at the same vertex

Directed graph (digraph)   A graph in which each edge is directed from one vertex to another (or the same) vertex

Disconnected graph   A graph that is not connected

Edge (arc)   A pair of vertices representing a connection between the two vertices in a graph

Graph   A data structure that consists of a set of vertices and a set of edges that relate the vertices to each other

Path   A sequence of vertices that connects two vertices in a graph

Undirected graph   A graph in which the edges have no direction

Vertex   A node in a graph

Weighted graph   A graph in which each edge carries a value

Figure 10.4   Graph terminology

10.2   The Graph Interface

We described a graph at the abstract level as a set of vertices and a set of edges that connect some or all of the vertices to one another. What kind of operations are defined on a graph? In this chapter we specify and implement a small set of useful graph operations for a directed, weighted graph. Many other operations on graphs can be defined as well. We have chosen operations that are useful when building applications to answer typical questions one might ask about graphs. For example:

- Does a path exist between vertex A and vertex D? Can we fly from Atlanta to Detroit?
- What is the total weight along this path from A to D? How much does it cost to fly from Atlanta to Detroit? What is the total distance?

- What is the shortest path from A to D? What is the cheapest way to get from Atlanta to Detroit?

- If I start at vertex A, where can I go? What cities are accessible if I start in Atlanta?

- How many connected components are in the graph? What groups of cities are connected to each other?

> **Graph Operations**
>
> The operations specified for our Graph ADT are the building blocks used by applications that need to answer questions about any given graph. By carefully combining the provided simple operations a programmer can implement the more complex algorithms needed to obtain information from graph data.

Note that we do not implement operations that directly answer any of the above questions within our Graph ADT. Instead we provide more primitive operations that can be used, in combination with each other, to answer these questions and more. In Section 10.4, "Application: Graph Traversals," we show how this is accomplished for a few of the above questions. Others are left as exercises.

Our specification for the Graph ADT, found in the `WeightedGraphInterface` listing below, includes 11 public methods. As expected, it includes methods to check whether the graph is empty or full, and methods to add vertices and edges. Here we describe the remaining, more unusual methods.

The `hasVertex` method can be used to check whether the argument object is used as a vertex in the graph. This issue is important because many of the other methods that accept a vertex as an argument assume, as a precondition, that the given vertex exists within the graph. Equivalence of vertices is determined using the vertices' `equals` method—so if the vertex class has overwritten the `Object` class `equals` method, then equality will be as defined within the vertex class; otherwise, it is defined using the default approach of comparing references.

The `weightIs` method returns the weight of the edge between two given vertices; if there is no such edge, it returns a special value indicating that fact. The special value could vary from one application to another. For example, the value −1 could be used for a graph whose edges represent distances, because there is no such thing as a negative distance. The special value for a specific application could be passed to the Graph constructor, if that capability is provided by the class that implements the interface. The `weightIs` method lets us determine whether a given edge is in the graph, which is useful, for example, to see if two vertices are connected. Of course, if two vertices are connected it is used to determine the weight of the edge between them, useful for answering questions about the total weight of a path between two vertices or the shortest path in terms of weight.

A very interesting method is `getToVertices`, which returns a queue of vertex objects. The idea is that an application may need to know which vertices a given vertex is adjacent *to* in order to determine what paths exist through the graph. This method returns the collection of such vertices as a queue. The application can then dequeue the vertices one at a time, as needed. The return value of the method is of "type" `QueueInterface`. The implementation programmer can choose to use any queue class that implements this interface.

Marking Vertices

During execution of a graph-related algorithm we often need to mark vertices as they are processed or stored for processing. This prevents us from repeatedly examining the same vertices over and over again. At the beginning of any such processing it is important to "clear all the marks," so that marks left over from previous work do not interfere with the new problem solution.

Another approach to solving the "get to vertices" problem is to have the method return a Java `Iterator` object. We have used iterators with many of our previous collection ADTs, but in this case we will use the queue.

To answer many of the questions we listed above, an application must be able to traverse the graph—that is, it must visit the vertices of the graph and perform some operation at each vertex. Because so many paths through a graph are possible, it is not unusual for the traversal algorithm to attempt to visit a vertex more than once. In such cases it is important for the application to "know" that it has previously visited the vertex. To facilitate this, our interface includes several methods related to marking vertices as visited. The `markVertex` and `isMarked` methods are used to mark vertices and check for marks, respectively. The `clearMarks` method clears all of the marks throughout the graph; it is used to prepare for a new traversal. Finally, the `getUnmarked` method returns an unmarked vertex. This ability is useful for beginning a traversal or for continuing a traversal, when the application is not sure it has visited every vertex. The ability to mark vertices is used to answer questions about shortest paths and the number of connected components.

Below is the `WeightedGraphInterface`. It is found in the `ch10.graphs` package.

```
//---------------------------------------------------------------------
// WeightedGraphInterface.java      by Dale/Joyce/Weems      Chapter 10
//
// Interface for classes that implement a directed graph with weighted edges.
// Vertices are objects of class T and can be marked as having been visited.
// Edge weights are integers.
// Equivalence of vertices is determined by the vertices' equals method.
//
// General precondition: Except for the addVertex and hasVertex methods,
// any vertex passed as an argument to a method is in this graph.
//---------------------------------------------------------------------

package ch10.graphs;

import ch04.queues.*;

public interface WeightedGraphInterface<T>
{
  boolean isEmpty();
  // Returns true if this graph is empty; otherwise, returns false.

  boolean isFull();
  // Returns true if this graph is full; otherwise, returns false.
```

```
void addVertex(T vertex);
// Preconditions:    This graph is not full.
//                   vertex is not already in this graph.
//                   vertex is not null.
//
// Adds vertex to this graph.

boolean hasVertex(T vertex);
// Returns true if this graph contains vertex; otherwise, returns false.

void addEdge(T fromVertex, T toVertex, int weight);
// Adds an edge with the specified weight from fromVertex to toVertex.

int weightIs(T fromVertex, T toVertex);
// If edge from fromVertex to toVertex exists, returns the weight of edge;
// otherwise, returns a special "null-edge" value.

QueueInterface<T> getToVertices(T vertex);
// Returns a queue of the vertices that vertex is adjacent to.

void clearMarks();
// Unmarks all vertices.

void markVertex(T vertex);
// Marks vertex.

boolean isMarked(T vertex);
// Returns true if vertex is marked; otherwise, returns false.

T getUnmarked();
// Returns an unmarked vertex if any exist; otherwise, returns null.
}
```

10.3   Implementations of Graphs

Array-Based Implementation

A simple way to represent V(graph), the vertices in the graph, is to use an array where the array elements are the vertices. For example, if the vertices represent city names, the array might hold strings. A simple way to represent E(graph), the edges in a graph, is to use an **adjacency matrix**, a two-dimensional array of edge values (weights), where the indices of a weight correspond to the vertices connected by the edge. Thus, a graph consists of an integer variable numVertices, a one-dimensional array vertices, and

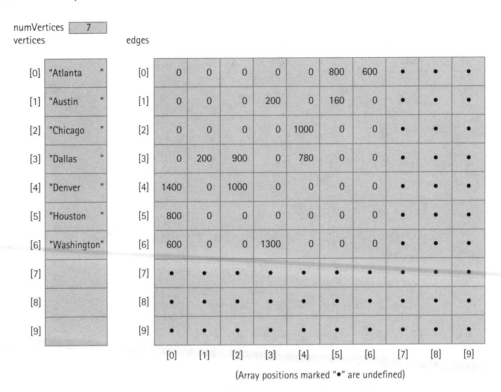

Figure 10.5   Matrix representation of graph of flight connections between cities

a two-dimensional array `edges`. **Figure 10.5** depicts the implementation of the graph of Air Busters' flights among the seven cities shown in Figure 10.3. For simplicity, we omit the additional `boolean` data needed to mark vertices as "visited" during a traversal from the figure. Although the city names in Figure 10.5 are in alphabetical order, there is no requirement that the elements in this array be sorted.

At any time, within this representation of a graph,

- `numVertices` is the number of vertices in the graph.
- V(graph) is contained in `vertices[0]` to `vertices[numVertices - 1]`.
- E(graph) is contained in the square matrix `edges[0][0]` to `edges[numVertices - 1][numVertices 1]`.

The names of the cities are contained in `vertices`. The weight of each edge in `edges` represents the air distance between two cities that are connected by a flight. For example, the value in `edges[1][3]` tells us that there is a direct flight between Austin and Dallas, and that the air distance is 200 miles. A `NULL_EDGE` value (0) in `edges[1][6]` tells us that the airline has no direct flights between Austin and Washington. Because this is a weighted graph in which the weights are air distances, we use `int` for the edge value type. If it were not a weighted graph, the edge value type could be `boolean`, with each position in the adjacency matrix being `true` if an edge exists between the pair of vertices, and `false` if no edge exists.

Here is the beginning of the definition of class `WeightedGraph`. We assume that the edge value type is `int` and that a null edge is indicated by a 0 value.

```
//-----------------------------------------------------------------------
// WeightedGraph.java              by Dale/Joyce/Weems        Chapter 10
//
// Implements a directed graph with weighted edges.
// Vertices are objects of class T and can be marked as having been visited.
// Edge weights are integers.
// Equivalence of vertices is determined by the vertices' equals method.
//
// General precondition: Except for the addVertex and hasVertex methods,
// any vertex passed as an argument to a method is in this graph.
//-----------------------------------------------------------------------

package ch10.graphs;

import ch04.queues.*;

public class WeightedGraph<T> implements WeightedGraphInterface<T>
{
  public static final int NULL_EDGE = 0;
  private static final int DEFCAP = 50;  // default capacity
  private int numVertices;
  private int maxVertices;
  private T[] vertices;
  private int[][] edges;
  private boolean[] marks;  // marks[i] is mark for vertices[i]

  public WeightedGraph()
  // Instantiates a graph with capacity DEFCAP vertices.
  {
    numVertices = 0;
    maxVertices = DEFCAP;
    vertices = (T[]) new Object[DEFCAP];[1]
    marks = new boolean[DEFCAP];
    edges = new int[DEFCAP][DEFCAP];
  }
```

[1] An unchecked cast warning may be generated because the compiler cannot ensure that the array contains objects of class T—the warning can safely be ignored.

```
public WeightedGraph(int maxV)
// Instantiates a graph with capacity maxV.
{
  numVertices = 0;
  maxVertices = maxV;
  vertices = (T[]) new Object[maxV];¹
  marks = new boolean[maxV];
  edges = new int[maxV][maxV];
}
```

The class constructors have to allocate the space for vertices, marks (the boolean array indicating whether a vertex has been marked), and edges. The default constructor sets up space for a graph with DEFCAP (50) vertices. The parameterized constructor lets the user specify the maximum number of vertices.

The addVertex operation puts a vertex into the next free space in the array of vertices and increments the number of vertices. Because the new vertex has no edges defined yet, it also initializes the appropriate row and column of edges to contain NULL_EDGE (0 in this case).

```
public void addVertex(T vertex)
// Preconditions:    This graph is not full.
//                   vertex is not already in this graph.
//                   vertex is not null.
//
// Adds vertex to this graph.
{
  vertices[numVertices] = vertex;
  for (int index = 0; index < numVertices; index++)
  {
    edges[numVertices][index] = NULL_EDGE;
    edges[index][numVertices] = NULL_EDGE;
  }
  numVertices++;
}
```

To add an edge to the graph, we must first locate the fromVertex and toVertex that define the edge being added. These values become the arguments to addEdge and are of the generic T class. Of course, the client really passes references to the vertex objects, because that is how we manipulate objects in Java. We are implementing our graphs "by reference" so this strategy should not pose a problem for the client. To index the correct matrix slot, we need the index in the vertices array that corresponds to each vertex. Once we know the indices, it is a simple matter to set the weight of the edge in the matrix.

---

[1] An unchecked cast warning may be generated because the compiler cannot ensure that the array contains objects of class T—the warning can safely be ignored.

To find the index of each vertex, let us write a `private` search method that receives a vertex and returns its location (index) in `vertices`. Based on the general precondition stated in the opening comment of the `WeightedGraph` class, we assume that the `fromVertex` and `toVertex` arguments passed to `addEdge` are already in V(graph). This assumption simplifies the search method, which we code as helper method `indexIs`. Here is the code for `indexIs` and `addEdge`:

```
private int indexIs(T vertex)
// Returns the index of vertex in vertices.
{
  int index = 0;
  while (!vertex.equals(vertices[index]))
    index++;
  return index;
}


public void addEdge(T fromVertex, T toVertex, int weight)
// Adds an edge with the specified weight from fromVertex to toVertex.
{
  int row;
  int column;

  row = indexIs(fromVertex);
  column = indexIs(toVertex);
  edges[row][column] = weight;
}
```

The `weightIs` operation is the mirror image of `addEdge`.

```
public int weightIs(T fromVertex, T toVertex)
// If edge from fromVertex to toVertex exists, returns the weight of edge;
// otherwise, returns a special "null-edge" value.
{
  int row;
  int column;

  row = indexIs(fromVertex);
  column = indexIs(toVertex);
  return edges[row][column];
}
```

The last graph operation that we address is `getToVertices`. This method receives a vertex as an argument, and it returns a queue of vertices that the vertex is *adjacent to* (or, another way of looking at it, that are *adjacent from* the designated vertex). That is, it returns a queue of all the vertices that we can get to from this vertex in one step. Using an adjacency matrix to represent the edges, it is a simple matter to determine the vertices to which the vertex is adjacent. We merely loop through the appropriate row in edges; whenever a value is found that is not NULL_EDGE, we add the corresponding vertex to the queue.

```
public QueueInterface<T> getToVertices(T vertex)
// Returns a queue of the vertices that are adjacent from vertex.
{
  QueueInterface<T> adjVertices = new LinkedQueue<T>();
  int fromIndex, toIndex;
  fromIndex = indexIs(vertex);
  for (toIndex = 0; toIndex < numVertices; toIndex++)
    if (edges[fromIndex][toIndex] != NULL_EDGE)
      adjVertices.enqueue(vertices[toIndex]);
  return adjVertices;
}
```

We leave writing isFull, isEmpty, hasVertex, and the marking operations (clearMarks, markVertex, isMarked, and getUnmarked) for you as exercises.

Linked Implementation

The advantages of representing the edges in a graph with an adjacency matrix are two-fold: speed and simplicity. Given the indices of two vertices, determining the existence (or the weight) of an edge between them is an O(1) operation. The problem with adjacency matrices is that their use of space to store the edge information is $O(N^2)$, where N is the maximum number of vertices in the graph. If the maximum number of vertices is large but the number of actual vertices is small, or if a graph is sparse (the ratio between the number of edges and number of vertices is small), adjacency matrices waste a lot of space. We can save space by allocating memory as needed at run time, using linked structures. Adjacency lists are linked lists, one list per vertex, that identify the vertices to which each vertex is connected. They can be implemented in several different ways. **Figures 10.6** and **10.7** show two different adjacency list representations of the graph in Figure 10.3.

In Figure 10.6, the vertices are stored in an array. Each component of this array contains a reference to a linked list of edge information. Each item in these linked lists contains an index number, a weight, and a reference to the next item in the adjacency list. Look at the adjacency list for Denver. The first item in the list indicates that there is a 1,400-mile flight from Denver to Atlanta (the vertex whose index is 0) and the second item indicates a 1,000-mile flight from Denver to Chicago (the vertex whose index is 2).

No arrays are used in the implementation illustrated in Figure 10.7. Instead, the list of vertices is also implemented as a linked list. Now each item in the adjacency list contains a reference to the vertex information rather than the index of the vertex. Because Figure 10.7 includes so many of these references, we have used text to describe the vertex that each reference designates rather than draw them as arrows.

We leave the implementation of the Graph class methods using the linked approaches as a programming exercise.

Space Efficiency

When a graph has a large number of vertices but a small number of edges the adjacency list approaches to implementation are much more space efficient than the adjacency matrix approach.

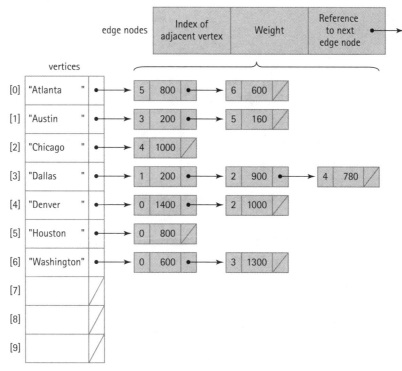

Figure 10.6   Adjacency list representation of graphs

10.4   Application: Graph Traversals

The graph specification given in Section 10.2, "The Graph Interface," includes only the most basic operations; it does not include any traversal operations. As you might imagine, we can traverse a graph in many different orders. Therefore, we treat traversal as a graph application rather than as an innate operation. The basic operations given in our specification allow us to implement different traversals *independent* of how the graph itself is implemented.

In Section 7.1, "Trees," we discussed two ways of traversing a general tree, *depth-first*, that repeatedly goes as deep as it can in the tree and then backs up, and *breadth-first*, that fans out across the tree level by level. With graphs, both depth-first and breadth-first strategies are also *extremely* important. We discuss algorithms for employing both strategies within the context of determining whether two cities are connected in our airline example. Note that these same basic approaches can be used

> **Code Files**
>
> The application `UseGraph` in the `ch10.apps` package contains the code for all the algorithms presented in Sections 10.4 and 10.5, "Application: Graph Traversals" and "Application: The Single-Source Shortest-Paths Problem." Each algorithm is implemented as a separate private method within the application. The main method of `UseGraph` acts as a test driver for this code. Because `UseGraph` uses the `WeightedGraph` class partially developed in Section 10.3, "Implementations of Graphs," in order to use the program you must finish coding that class. See Exercise 17.

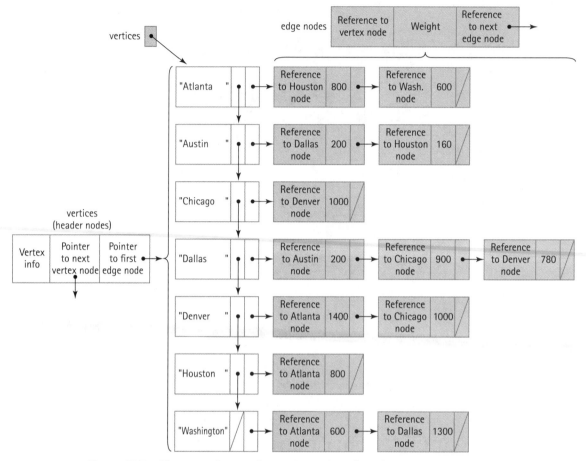

Figure 10.7 Alternate adjacency list representation of graphs

to solve *many* other problems, when traversing the vertices of a graph in an organized fashion is required.

Depth-First Searching

One question we can answer using the graph in Figure 10.3 is "Can I get from city X to city Y on my favorite airline?" This is equivalent to asking, "Does a path exist in the graph from vertex X to vertex Y?" Using a depth-first strategy, we develop an algorithm *IsPathDF* that determines whether a path exists from startVertex to endVertex.

We need a systematic way to keep track of the cities as we investigate them. With a depth-first search, we examine the first vertex that is adjacent from startVertex; if it is endVertex, the search is over. Otherwise, we examine all of the vertices that can be reached in one step (are adjacent) from this first vertex. While we examine these vertices, we need to store the remaining vertices adjacent from `startVertex` that have not yet been examined. If a path does not exist from the first vertex, we come back and try the second vertex, third vertex, and so on. Because we want to travel as far as we can down one path, backtracking if the `endVertex` is not found, a stack is a good structure for storing the vertices.

However, there is a problem with the approach we just described. Graphs can contain cycles. We can fly from Washington to Dallas to Denver and then back to Washington. Do you see why this is an issue in the approach described above? Not only is it likely that we will unnecessarily repeat the processing of a city (a vertex), it is even possible to get caught in an infinite loop (e.g., when processing Washington we push Atlanta onto the stack, and when processing Atlanta we push Washington onto the stack). We did not have this issue when designing our tree traversals in Chapter 7 because trees by definition do *not* have cycles.

How can we fix this? You probably recall that addressing this problem was the reason we included the ability to mark vertices within our Graph ADT. Our solution is to mark vertices to indicate that they have been placed on the stack. And, of course, to use those marks to prevent pushing a vertex onto the stack more than once. This way we eliminate repetitiously processing a vertex and the possibility of an infinite loop. Here is the algorithm:

IsPathDF (startVertex, endVertex): returns boolean

```
Set found to false
Clear all marks
Mark the startVertex
Push the startVertex onto the stack
do
    Set current vertex = stack.top()
    stack.pop()
    if current vertex equals endVertex
        Set found to true
    else
    for each adjacent vertex
        if adjacent vertex is not marked
            Mark the adjacent vertex and
            Push it onto the stack
while !stack.isEmpty() AND !found
return found
```

Let us apply this algorithm to the sample airline-route graph in Figure 10.3. We will trace the algorithm applied to the case where Austin is the starting city and Washington is the desired destination. In **Figure 10.8** we repeat the airport graph, abbreviating the names of the cities using their first two letters and dropping the distances, because they are

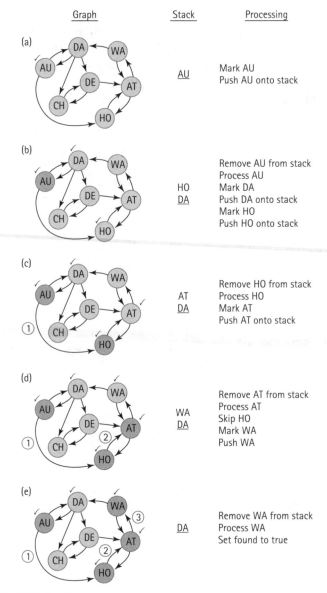

Figure 10.8 IsPathDF algorithm trace

not pertinent to our current question. We use boldface to indicate that a city has been processed—that it has been checked to see if it is the destination and if not then its adjacent cities have been placed on the stack if appropriate. We also sequentially number the entry edge into a city when it is processed, the edge that is followed to lead to the processing of the city. Finally, we indicate that a city has been marked by placing a checkmark beside it.

Okay, so we want to fly from Austin to Washington. We initialize our search by marking our starting city and pushing it onto the stack (Figure 10.8a). At the beginning of the *do-while* loop we retrieve the current city, Austin, from the stack using the top method and then remove it from the stack using the `pop` method. Because Austin is not our final destination we examine the places we can reach directly from it—Dallas and Houston (we will process adjacent vertices in alphabetical order); neither of these is marked so we mark them and push them onto the stack (Figure 10.8b). That completes the processing of Austin.

At the beginning of the second iteration we retrieve and remove the top vertex from the stack—Houston. Houston is not our destination, so we resume our search from there. There is only one flight out of Houston, to Atlanta; Atlanta has not yet been marked so we mark it and push it onto the stack (Figure 10.8c), finishing our processing of Houston. Again we retrieve and remove the top vertex from the stack. Atlanta is not our destination, so we continue searching from there. Atlanta has flights to two cities: Houston and Washington. Houston was already marked so at this stage we mark only Washington and push it onto the stack (Figure 10.8d).

Finally, we retrieve and remove the top vertex from the stack, Washington. This is our destination, so the search is complete (Figure 10.8e).

As indicated by the final part of Figure 10.8e we had a very successful and efficient search, processing only four cities during our search including the source and destination cities. Although the algorithm (since it is correct!) guarantees success in that it will always correctly identify whether a path exists, it might not always be so efficient. Consider a new question: can we fly from Dallas to Austin. A quick check of the graph tells us that yes we can, in fact it is a one hop trip. Yet in this case the algorithm will process every vertex in the graph before determining that the path exists. The reader is encouraged to verify this for themselves by tracing the algorithm on the new problem.

Method `isPathDF` receives a graph object, a starting vertex, and a target vertex. It uses the depth-first algorithm described above to determine whether a path exists from the starting city to the ending city, displaying the names of all cities processed in the search. Nothing in the method depends on the implementation of the graph. The method is implemented as a graph application; it uses the Graph ADT operations without knowing how the graph is represented. We use a graph of strings, since we can represent a city by its name. In the following code, we assume that a stack and a queue implementation have been imported into the client class. (The `isPathDF` method is included in the `UseGraph.java` application, available in the `ch10.apps` package.)

```
private static boolean isPathDF(WeightedGraphInterface<String> graph,
                        String startVertex, String endVertex)
// Returns true if a path exists on graph, from startVertex to endVertex;
// otherwise returns false. Uses depth-first search algorithm.
{
   StackInterface<String> stack = new LinkedStack<String>();
   QueueInterface<String> vertexQueue = new LinkedQueue<String>();
```

```
    boolean found = false;
    String currVertex;        // vertex being processed
    String adjVertex;         // adjacent to currVertex

    graph.clearMarks();
    graph.markVertex(startVertex);
    stack.push(startVertex);

    do
    {
      currVertex = stack.top();
      stack.pop();
      System.out.println(currVertex);
      if (currVertex.equals(endVertex))
          found = true;
      else
      {
        vertexQueue = graph.getToVertices(currVertex);
        while (!vertexQueue.isEmpty())
        {
          adjVertex = vertexQueue.dequeue();
          if (!graph.isMarked(adjVertex))
          {
            graph.markVertex(adjVertex);
            stack.push(adjVertex);
          }
        }
      }
    } while (!stack.isEmpty() && !found);
    return found;
}
```

Depth-First or Breadth-First

The best search approach to use for a particular problem depends upon the structure of the graph and the nature of the problem. In general, if you are likely to find the end vertex close to the start vertex then breadth-first search is probably preferred. On the other hand, if you expect there may be several target vertices that fulfill your needs but believe they might be far away from the start vertex then depth-first is probably best. For any given problem and environment it might be wise to perform some experiments before selecting an approach.

Breadth-First Searching

A breadth-first search looks at all possible paths at the same depth before it goes to a deeper level. In our flight example, a breadth-first search checks all possible one-stop connections before checking any two-stop connections. For most travelers, this strategy is the preferred approach for booking flights.

When we come to a dead end in a depth-first search, we back up as little as possible. We then try another route from a recent vertex—the route on top of our stack. In a breadth-first search, we want to back up as far as possible to find a route originating from the earliest vertices. The stack is not the right structure for finding an early route, because it keeps track of things in the order opposite of their occurrence—the latest route is on top. To keep track of things in the order in which they happened, we use a FIFO queue. The route at the front of this queue is a route from an earlier vertex; the route at the back of the queue is from a later vertex. To modify the search to use a breadth-first strategy, we change all calls to stack operations to the analogous FIFO queue operations in the previous algorithm. Just as we did with the depth-first search, we mark a vertex before placing it in the queue, to avoid repetitive processing. Here is the breadth-first algorithm:

IsPathBF (startVertex, endVertex): returns boolean

```
Set found to false
Clear all marks
Mark the startVertex
Enqueue the startVertex into the queue
do
    Set current vertex = queue.dequeue()
    if current vertex equals endVertex
        Set found to true
    else
    for each adjacent vertex
        if adjacent vertex is not marked
            Mark the adjacent vertex and
            Enqueue it into the queue
while !queue.isEmpty() AND !found
return found
```

Figure 10.9 shows the sequence in which vertices are visited for several depth-first and breadth-first searches using our flights example. The numbers in the figure indicate the order in which entry edges are used to "visit" vertices. Keep in mind our assumption that vertices are placed into the queue (or stack) in alphabetical order.

Let us revisit our previous example, searching for a path from Austin to Washington, but this time with a breadth-first search. We start with Austin in the queue. We dequeue Austin and enqueue all the cities that can be reached directly from it: Dallas and Houston. Then we dequeue the front queue element, Dallas (indicated by the circled 1 in Figure 10.9b). Because Dallas is not the destination we seek, we enqueue all the adjacent cities from Dallas that have not yet been marked: Chicago and Denver. (Austin has been visited already, so it is not enqueued.) Again we dequeue the front element from the queue. This element is the other "one-stop" city: Houston (indicated by the circled 2 in Figure 10.9b). Houston is not the desired destination, so we continue the search. There is

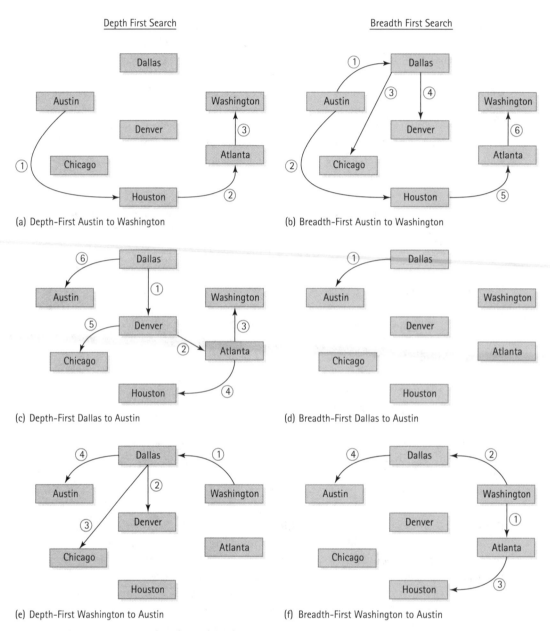

Figure 10.9 Examples of search paths

only one flight out of Houston, and it is to Atlanta. Because we have not marked Atlanta before, it is enqueued. This processing continues until Washington is put into the queue (from Atlanta), and is finally dequeued. We have found the desired city, and the search is complete.

As you can see in Figure 10.9b the breadth-first search of a path from Austin to Washington processed every city in the graph before determining that the path existed. It was not as efficient as the depth-first search for the same path (Figure 10.9a). On the other hand, a comparison of Figures 10.9c and 10.9d shows that in another case, searching for a path from Dallas to Austin, the breadth-first search is more efficient. It is really just a matter of luck—the number of steps depends on the graph configuration and the source and destination vertices. Comparing Figures 10.9e and 10.9f shows an example, searching for a path from Washington to Austin, where the same number of entry edges are used in each approach.

The source code for the breadth-first search approach is identical to the depth-first search code, except for the replacement of the stack with a FIFO queue. It is also included in the `UseGraph.java` application, as the method `isPathBF`, available in the `ch10.apps` package.

10.5   Application: The Single-Source Shortest-Paths Problem

We know from the two search operations discussed in Section 10.4, "Application: Graph Traversals," that there may be multiple paths from one vertex to another. Continuing the example scenario from that section, suppose that we want to find the shortest path from Austin to each of the other cities that Air Busters serves. By "shortest path" we mean the path whose edge values (weights), added together, have the smallest sum. Consider the following two paths from Austin to Washington:

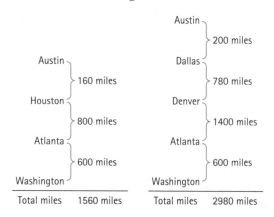

Clearly, the first path is preferable, unless we want to collect extra frequent-flyer miles.

Let us develop an algorithm that displays the shortest path from a designated starting city to *every other city* in the graph. As in the two graph search algorithms described earlier, we need an auxiliary structure for storing cities that we process later. By retrieving the city that was most recently put into the structure, the depth-first search tries to keep going "forward." It tries a one-flight solution, then a two-flight solution, then a three-flight solution, and so on. It backtracks to a fewer-flight solution only when it reaches a dead end. That approach is not suitable for our shortest-paths problem.

By retrieving the city that had been in the structure the longest time, the breadth-first search tries all one-flight solutions, then all two-flight solutions, and so on. The breadth-first search finds a path with a minimum number of flights. But a minimum *number* of flights does not necessarily mean the minimum *total distance*. That approach is also unsuitable for our shortest-paths problem.

Dijkstra's Algorithm

The algorithm presented in this section for finding the shortest past is attributed to computer scientist Edsger W. Dijkstra who conceived of the algorithm in 1956 and published it in 1959. Dijkstra contributed a great deal to many facets of computer science.

Unlike the depth-first and breadth-first searches, this *shortest-path traversal* must use the number of miles (edge weights) between cities. We want to retrieve the vertex that is *closest* to the current vertex—that is, the vertex connected with the minimum edge weight. By always adding the next shortest path we are guaranteed to identify the correct paths. If we consider minimum distance to be the highest priority, then we know the perfect structure—the priority queue. Our algorithm can use a priority queue whose elements are flights (edges) with the distance *from the starting city* as the priority. That is, the elements in the priority queue are objects with three attributes: `fromVertex`, `toVertex`, and `distance`. We use a class named `Flight` to define these objects. The class implements the `Comparable<Flight>` interface, using the `distance` attribute to compare two flights (shorter is better). It provides a constructor that accepts three arguments, one for each attribute, and it provides the standard setter and getter methods for the attributes. The code is found in our `support` package. Here is the shortest-path algorithm:

```
shortestPaths(graph, startVertex)

graph.ClearMarks()
Create flight(startVertex, startVertex, 0)
pq.enqueue(flight)                                      Caution:
do                                                      Contains subtle error

    flight = pq.dequeue()
    if flight.getToVertex() is not marked
        Mark flight.getToVertex()
        Write flight.getFromVertex, flight.getToVertex, flight.getDistance
        flight.setFromVertex(flight.getToVertex())
        Set minDistance to flight.getDistance()
        Get queue vertexQueue of vertices adjacent from flight.getFromVertex()
        while more vertices in vertexQueue
            Get next vertex from vertexQueue
            if vertex not marked
                flight.setToVertex(vertex)
                flight.setDistance(minDistance + graph.weightIs(flight.getFromVertex(), vertex))
                pq.enqueue(flight)
while !pq.isEmpty()
```

The algorithm for the shortest-path traversal is similar to those we used for the depth-first and breadth-first searches, albeit with three major differences:

1. We use a priority queue rather than a FIFO queue or stack. Note that when processing halts there can still be many flights left on the priority queue, but they are longer flights than the ones that have been identified as being part of the solution.

2. We stop only when there are no more cities to process; there is no destination.

3. It is incorrect if we use a store-by-reference priority queue!

When we code this algorithm, we are likely to make a subtle, but crucial error. This error is related to the fact that our queues store information "by reference" and not "by copy." Take a minute to review the algorithm to see if you can spot the error before continuing.

Recall the feature section in Chapter 5 that discussed the dangers of storing information by reference. In particular, it warned us to be careful when inserting an object into a structure and later making changes to that object. If we use the same reference to the object when we make changes to it, the changes are made to the object that is in the structure. Sometimes this outcome is what we want (see the word frequency counter application in Chapter 7); at other times it causes problems, as in the current example. Here is the incorrect part of the algorithm:

```
while more vertices in vertexQueue
   Get next vertex from vertexQueue
   if vertex not marked
      flight.setToVertex(vertex)
      flight.setDistance(minDistance + graph.weightIs(flight.getFromVertex(), vertex))
      pq.enqueue(flight)
```

Now can you see the problem? This part of the algorithm walks through the queue of vertices adjacent to the current vertex and enqueues `Flight` objects onto the priority queue `pq` based on the information discovered there. The `flight` variable is actually a reference to a `Flight` object. Suppose the queue of adjacent vertices holds information related to the cities Atlanta and Houston. The first time through this loop, we insert information related to Atlanta in `flight` and enqueue it in `pq`. The next time through the loop, however, we make changes to the `Flight` object referenced by `flight`. We update it to contain information about Houston using the setter methods; and again we enqueue it in `pq`. So now `pq` contains information about Atlanta and Houston, correct? Nope. When we change the information in `flight` to the Houston information, those changes are reflected in the `flight` that is already on `pq`. The `flight` variable still references that object. In reality, the `pq` structure now contains two references to the same `flight`, and that `flight` contains Houston information.

To solve this problem, we must create a new flight object before storing on pq. Here is the corrected version of that part of the algorithm:

```
while more vertices in vertexQueue
    Get next vertex from vertexQueue
    if vertex not marked
        Set newDistance to minDistance + graph.weightIs(flight.getFromVertex(), vertex)
        Create new Flight(flight.getFromVertex(), vertex, newDistance)
        pq.enqueue(newFlight)
```

Here is the source code for the shortest-path algorithm (also included in the UseGraph.java application). As before, the code assumes that a priority queue and a queue implementation have been imported into the client class. For the priority queue, we use our HeapPriQ class from Chapter 9. We want a smaller distance to indicate a higher priority, but our HeapPriQ class implements a *maximum* heap, returning the *largest* value from the dequeue method. To fix this problem, we could define a new heap class, a minimum heap. But there is an easier way. The current HeapPriQ class bases its decision about what is "larger" on the values returned by the flight's compareTo method. Thus, we just define the compareTo method of the Flight class to indicate that the current flight is "larger" than the argument flight if its distance is smaller. For every flight in the heap's tree, flight.distance is then less than or equal to the distance value of each of its children. We can still use our maximum heap.

```java
private static void shortestPaths(WeightedGraphInterface<String> graph,
                                  String startVertex)
// Writes the shortest distance from startVertex to every
// other reachable vertex in graph.
{
  Flight flight;
  Flight saveFlight;          // for saving on priority queue
  int minDistance;
  int newDistance;

  PriQueueInterface<Flight> pq = new HeapPriQ<Flight>(20);
  String vertex;
  QueueInterface<String> vertexQueue = new LinkedQueue<String>();

  graph.clearMarks();
  saveFlight = new Flight(startVertex, startVertex, 0);
  pq.enqueue(saveFlight);

  System.out.println("Last Vertex    Destination    Distance");
  System.out.println("-----------------------------------");
```

```
do
{
  flight = pq.dequeue();
  if (!graph.isMarked(flight.getToVertex()))
  {
    graph.markVertex(flight.getToVertex());
    System.out.println(flight);
    flight.setFromVertex(flight.getToVertex());
    minDistance = flight.getDistance();
    vertexQueue = graph.getToVertices(flight.getFromVertex());
    while (!vertexQueue.isEmpty())
    {
      vertex = vertexQueue.dequeue();
      if (!graph.isMarked(vertex))
      {
        newDistance = minDistance
                      + graph.weightIs(flight.getFromVertex(), vertex);
        saveFlight = new Flight(flight.getFromVertex(), vertex,
                                newDistance);
        pq.enqueue(saveFlight);
      }
    }
  }
} while (!pq.isEmpty());
System.out.println();
}
```

The output from this method is a table of city pairs (edges) showing the total minimum distance from startVertex to each of the other vertices in the graph, as well as the last vertex visited before the destination. We assume that printing a vertex means printing the name of the corresponding city. If graph contains the information shown in Figure 10.3, the method called

shortestPaths(graph, startVertex);

where startVertex corresponds to Washington, would print the following:

Last Vertex	Destination	Distance
Washington	Washington	0
Washington	Atlanta	600
Washington	Dallas	1,300
Atlanta	Houston	1,400
Dallas	Austin	1,500
Dallas	Denver	2,080
Dallas	Chicago	2,200

The shortest-path distance from Washington to each destination is shown in the two columns to the right. For example, our flights from Washington to Chicago total 2,200 miles. The left-hand column shows which city immediately preceded the destination in the traversal. We want to figure out the shortest path from Washington to Chicago. First we find our destination, Chicago, in the Destination (middle) column, and see from the left-hand column that the next-to-last vertex in the path is Dallas. Now we look up Dallas in the Destination (middle) column—the vertex before Dallas is Washington. The whole path is Washington–Dallas–Chicago. (We might want to consider another airline for a more direct route!)

Unreachable Vertices

You may have noticed that in all of our examples so far we have been able to "reach" all of the other vertices in our graphs from our given starting vertex. What if this is not the case? Consider the weighted graph in **Figure 10.10**, which depicts a new set of airline-flight legs. It is identical to Figure 10.3 except that we removed the Washington–Dallas leg. If we invoke our shortestPaths method, passing it this graph and a starting vertex of Washington, we get the following output:

Last Vertex	Destination	Distance
Washington	Washington	0
Washington	Atlanta	600
Atlanta	Houston	1,400

A careful study of the new graph confirms that one can reach Atlanta and Houston only, when starting in Washington, at least when flying Air Buster Airlines.

Suppose we extend the specification of our shortestPaths method to require that it also prints the unreachable vertices. How can we determine the unreachable vertices

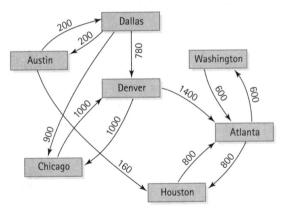

Figure 10.10 A new set of airline-flight legs

after we have generated the information about the reachable ones? Easy! The unreachable vertices are the unmarked vertices. We simply need to check whether any vertices remain unmarked. Our Graph ADT provides the operation `getUnmarked` specifically for this situation. So we simply add the following code to our method:

```
System.out.println("The unreachable vertices are:");
vertex = graph.getUnmarked();
while (vertex != null)
{
   System.out.println(vertex);
   graph.markVertex(vertex);
   vertex = graph.getUnmarked();
}
```

Now the output from the call to `shortestPaths` would be

Last Vertex	Destination	Distance
Washington	Washington	0
Washington	Atlanta	600
Atlanta	Houston	1,400

The unreachable vertices are:

Austin

Chicago

Dallas

Denver

In Exercise 43 we ask you to investigate counting the "connected components" of a graph. This is another interesting application of the `getUnmarked` method.

Summary

In this chapter, we discussed graphs. After reviewing graph terminology we defined a Graph ADT and discussed implementation approaches, providing a partially finished array-based implementation. The set of abstract methods included in `WeightedGraph-Interface` is designed to allow an application to implement graph-related algorithms. Three such algorithms, depth-first path discovery, breadth-first path discovery, and shortest paths, were presented.

The array-based graph implementation provides time-efficient operations. We also discussed a space-efficient reference-based implementation. Time and space efficiency trade-offs are often the key considerations when choosing among alternative implementations of a data structure.

Graphs are the most complex structure we have studied. They are very versatile and are a good way to model many real-world objects and situations. Because many different types of applications could potentially use graphs, numerous variations and generalizations of their definitions and implementations exist. In addition, many advanced algorithms for manipulating and traversing graphs have been discovered. They are generally covered in detail in advanced computer science courses on algorithms.

Exercises

10.1 Introduction to Graphs

1. True/False. Explain your answer—in some cases drawing an example figure suffices for an explanation.
   a. A graph can have more vertices than edges.
   b. A graph can have more edges than vertices.
   c. A graph with just one vertex is connected.
   d. An edgeless graph with two or more vertices is disconnected.
   e. A graph with three vertices and one edge is disconnected.
   f. A connected graph with N vertices must have at least $N-1$ edges.
   g. A graph with five vertices and four edges is connected.
   h. An edge cannot connect a vertex to itself.
   i. All graphs are trees.
   j. All trees are graphs.
   k. A directed graph must be weighted.

2. Each of the following can be modeled as graphs. Describe in each case how you would define the vertices and how you would define the edges.
   a. Friendships
   b. Television show costars
   c. Research literature citations
   d. The Internet
   e. The Web

3. For each example in Exercise 2, describe how the graph could be weighted; that is, what might the weights on the edges of the graph represent?

4. Draw an undirected graph, if possible (if not possible explain why not) that has
   a. five vertices and three edges and is connected.
   b. five vertices, three edges, and two connected components.
   c. five vertices, two edges, and three connected components.
   d. five vertices, two edges, and two connected components.
   e. five vertices, six edges, and two connected components.

Use the following description of an undirected graph in Exercises 5 and 6:

> EmployeeGraph   =   (V, E)
>
> V(EmployeeGraph) =   {Susan, Darlene, Mike, Fred, John, Sander, Lance, Jean, Brent, Fran}
>
> E(EmployeeGraph) =   {(Susan, Darlene), (Fred, Brent), (Sander, Susan), (Lance, Fran), (Sander, Fran), (Fran, John), (Lance, Jean), (Jean, Susan), (Mike, Darlene), (Brent, Lance), (Susan, John)}

5. Draw a picture of `EmployeeGraph`.

6. Which one of the following phrases best describes the relationship represented by the edges between the vertices in `EmployeeGraph`?

    a. "works for"

    b. "is the supervisor of "

    c. "is senior to"

    d. "works with"

Use the following specification of a directed graph in Exercises 7–9:

> ZooGraph   =   (V, E)
>
> V(ZooGraph) =   {dog, cat, animal, vertebrate, oyster, shellfish, invertebrate, crab, poodle, monkey, banana, dalmatian, dachshund}
>
> E(ZooGraph) =   {(vertebrate, animal), (invertebrate, animal), (dog, vertebrate), (cat, vertebrate), (monkey, vertebrate), (shellfish, invertebrate), (crab, shellfish), (oyster, shellfish), (poodle, dog), (dalmatian, dog), (dachshund, dog)}

7. Draw a picture of `ZooGraph`.

8. To tell if one element in `ZooGraph` has relation X to another element, you look for a path between them. Show whether the following statements are true, using your picture or the specification.

    a. dalmatian X dog

    b. dalmatian X vertebrate

    c. dalmatian X poodle

    d. banana X invertebrate

    e. oyster X invertebrate

    f. monkey X invertebrate

9. Which of the following phrases best describes relation X in Exercise 8?

    a.   "has a"

    b. "is an example of "

    c. "is a generalization of "

    d. "eats"

Use the following graph for Exercises 10 and 11:

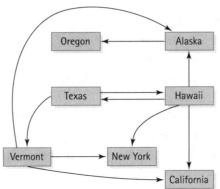

10. Describe the graph pictured above, using the formal graph notation.

V(StateGraph) =

E(StateGraph) =

11. In the states graph:

    a.   Is there a path from Oregon to any other state in the graph?

    b.   Is there a path from Hawaii to every other state in the graph?

    c.   From which state(s) in the graph is there a path to Hawaii?

10.2 The Graph Interface

12. Classify the methods defined in the `WeightedGraphInterface` as observers or transformers or both.

13. It is possible to define more operations for a Graph ADT. Describe two operations that you think would be useful additions to the `WeightedGraphInterface`, and explain why.

14. Suppose g has been declared to be of type `WeightedGraphInterface` and instantiated as an object of a class that implements that interface. Assume that g consists of seven vertices A, B, C, D, E, F, G and seven directed edges A-B, B-C, C-D, D-C, D-F, F-B, and G-E with all weights equal to 1. Show the expected output of the section of code below. Assume that capital letters A through G are of type T (the vertex type), that `getToVertices` returns a queue with the vertices in alphabetical order, that `getUnmarked` returns unmarked vertices in alphabetical order, that the null edge value is 0, and that printing a vertex displays its corresponding letter.

```
System.out.println(g.isEmpty());
System.out.println(g.weightIs(A,B));
System.out.println(g.weightIs(B,A));
System.out.println(g.weightIs(A,C));
g.clearmarks(); g.markVertex(A); g.markVertex(C);
System.out.println(g.ismarked(B));
```

```
g.markVertex(g.getUnmarked())
System.out.println(g.isMarked(B));
System.out.println(g.getUnmarked());
System.out.println(g.getToVertices(D).dequeue());
```

10.3 Implementations of Graphs

15. Draw the adjacency matrix for `EmployeeGraph` (see Exercise 5). Store the vertices in alphabetical order.

16. Draw the adjacency matrix for `ZooGraph` (see Exercise 7). Store the vertices in alphabetical order.

Note: Exercises 18–22, 38, and 42 are dependent on the completion of Exercise 17.

17. Complete the implementation of the Weighted Graph (`WeightedGraph.java`) that we began in this chapter by providing bodies for the methods `isEmpty`, `isFull`, `hasVertex`, `clearMarks`, `markVertex`, `isMarked`, and `getUnmarked` in the `WeightedGraph.java` file. Test the completed implementation using the `UseGraph` class. When implementing `hasVertex`, do not forget to use the `equals` method to compare vertices.

18. For each of the methods in the `WeightedGraph` implementation, identify its order of growth efficiency.

19. Class `WeightedGraph` in this chapter is to be extended to include a `boolean` `edgeExists` operation that determines whether two vertices are connected by an edge.

    a. Write the declaration of this method. Include adequate comments.

    b. Implement the method.

20. Class `WeightedGraph` in this chapter is to be extended to include an `int connects` operation, passed two arguments a and b of type T representing two vertices in the graph (guaranteed as a precondition that both a and b are vertices) that returns a count of the number of vertices v such that v is connected to both a and b.

    a. Write the declaration of this method. Include adequate comments.

    b. Implement the method.

21. Class `WeightedGraph` in this chapter is to be extended to include a `removeEdge` operation that removes a given edge.

    a. Write the declaration of this method. Include adequate comments.

    b. Implement the method.

22. Class `WeightedGraph` in this chapter is to be extended to include a `removeVertex` operation that removes a vertex from the graph.

    a. Deleting a vertex is more complicated than deleting an edge from the graph. Discuss the reasons for this operation's greater complexity. Write the declaration of this method. Include adequate comments.

    b. Implement the method.

23. Graphs can be implemented using arrays or references. For the states graph (see Exercise 10):

   a. Show the adjacency matrix that would describe the edges in this graph. Store the vertices in alphabetical order.

   b. Show the array of adjacency lists that would describe the edges in this graph.

24. What percent of the adjacency matrix representation of a graph consists of null edges if the graph contains

   a. 10 vertices and 10 edges?

   b. 100 vertices and 100 edges?

   c. 1,000 vertices and 1,000 edges?

25. Assuming an adjacency matrix-based directed graph implementation as described in Section 10.3, "Implementations of Graphs," describe an algorithm that solves each of the following problems; include an efficiency analysis of your solutions.

   a. Return the number of vertices in the graph.

   b. Return the number of edges in the graph.

   c. Return the highest number of "out edges" exhibited by a vertex; for example, for the graph in Figure 10.3 this would return 3 because Dallas has three cities adjacent to it

   d. Return the highest number of "in edges" exhibited by a vertex. For example, for the graph in Figure 10.3 this would return 3 because Atlanta has three cities it is adjacent from.

   e. Return the number of "singleton" vertices, that is, vertices that are not connected to any other vertex.

26. Repeat Exercise 25 using the adjacency list–directed graph implementation approach represented in Figure 10.6.

27. Specify, design, and code an undirected, weighted graph class using an adjacency matrix representation.

28. Specify, design, and code an undirected, unweighted graph class using an adjacency matrix representation.

29. Design and code a reference-based weighted graph class with the vertices stored in an array as in Figure 10.6. Your class should implement our `WeightedGraphInterface`.

30. Design and code a reference-based weighted graph class with the vertices stored in a linked list as in Figure 10.7. Your class should implement our `WeightedGraphInterface`.

10.4 Application: Graph Traversals

For exercises 31–36 assume `getToVertices` and `getUnmarked` return information in alphabetical order.

31. Using the `EmployeeGraph` (see Exercise 5) describe both the order in which vertices would be marked and the order they would be visited/processed using the depth-first "is there a path" algorithm, when searching for a path:

    a. from Susan to Lance

    b. from Brent to John

    c. from Sander to Darlene

32. Repeat Exercise 31 using the breadth-first algorithm.

33. Using the `StateGraph` (see Exercise 10) describe both the order in which vertices would be marked and the order they would be visited/processed using the depth-first "is there a path" algorithm, when searching for a path:

    a. from Texas to Alaska

    b. from Hawaii to California

    c. from Hawaii to Texas

34. Repeat Exercise 33 using the breadth-first algorithm.

35. We reconfigure the Air Busters Airlines graph in Figure 10.3 so that the edges from Dallas to Austin and from Denver to Atlanta are dropped and an edge from Denver to Washington with weight 700 is added. Describe both the order in which vertices would be marked and the order they would be visited/processed using the depth-first "is there a path" algorithm, when searching for a path:

    a. from Dallas to Houston

    b. from Denver to Austin

36. Repeat Exercise 35 using the breadth-first algorithm.

37. Consider the following full graph of seven vertices.

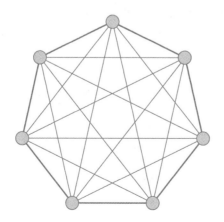

   a. Recreate the drawing of the graph so that it shows only the lead-in edges to vertices that would be visited by a depth-first search starting from the vertex at the top of the image. Note that there are many possible answers.

   b. Recreate the drawing of the graph so that it shows only the lead-in edges to vertices that would be visited by a breadth-first search starting from the vertex at the top of the image. Note that there is only one possible answer.

38. A text file contains information about a directed unweighted graph, where the vertices are strings, by listing the edges line by line. Each line contains the from-vertex, followed by the symbol #, followed by the to-vertex. For example,

```
heap#priority queue
```

represents an edge from the vertex "heap" to the vertex "priority queue" perhaps in this case representing the fact that a heap is used to implement a priority queue.

   Create an application that is given the name of such a text file as a command line argument, generates the corresponding graph using `WeightedGraph` from the `ch10.graphs` package, and then repeatedly prompts the user to enter a from-vertex and a to-vertex, reporting back to the user (a) one or both of the vertices does not exist or (b) whether there exists a path from the given from-vertex to the given to-vertex.

   Create a suitable input file and test your program. Submit a report.

10.5 Application: The Single-Source Shortest-Paths Problem

39. Trace the Shortest Paths algorithm (or code) including the latter section about unreachable vertices and show what it would output for our Air Busters Airlines example (Figure 10.3) if the starting vertex is

   a. Dallas

   b. Atlanta

40. We reconfigure the Air Busters Airlines graph in Figure 10.3 so that the edges from Dallas to Austin, Denver to Atlanta, Washington to Dallas, and Austin to Houston are dropped and an edge from Denver to Washington with weight 700 is added. Trace the Shortest Paths algorithm (or code) including the latter section about unreachable vertices and show what it would output for this new graph if the starting vertex is

   a. Austin

   b. Atlanta

41. For the `StateGraph` (see Exercise 10) list the unreachable vertices for each of the vertices in the graph.

42. Our `shortestPaths` method is concerned with the minimum *distance* between two vertices of a graph. Create a minEdges method that returns the minimum *number of edges* that exist on a path between two given vertices. You can put your new method in our `useGraph` class and use it to test your code.

43. Counting connected components. Informally, a connected component of a graph is a subset of the vertices of the graph such that all of the vertices in the subset are connected to each other by a path. For example, the following graph consists of three connected components.

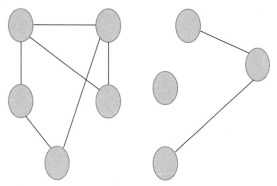

a.   Create an undirected, unweighted graph ADT (similar to Exercise 26 but you can use a linked representation if you wish).

b.   Test it.

c.   Create an application that generates a graph and counts the number of connected components. The graph can be "hard coded," read from a file, or randomly generated.

d.   Create an application that generates graphs with 26 vertices and:

   • 4, 8, 12, 16, 20, 24, 28, 32, 36, and 40 unique random edges.

   • five graphs for each of the number of edges (so you are generating 50 random graphs altogether).

   • outputs the average number of connected components for each edge count.

e.   Submit a report that contains your code, the output, and a discussion.

Sorting and Searching Algorithms

Knowledge Goals

You should be able to

- describe the following sorting algorithms:
  - selection sort
  - bubble sort (two versions)
  - insertion sort
  - quick sort
  - merge sort
  - heap sort
- analyze the efficiency of the six sorting algorithms, in terms of time and space requirements
- discuss other sorting efficiency considerations: overhead, elimination of method calls, programmer time
- describe the concept of stability with respect to sorting algorithms
- describe and discuss the performance of the following search algorithms:
  - sequential search of an unsorted list
  - sequential search of a sorted list
  - binary search
  - searching a high-probability sorted list

Skill Goals

You should be able to

- implement the following sorting algorithms
  - selection sort
  - bubble sort (two versions)
  - insertion sort
  - quick sort
  - merge sort
  - heap sort
- determine the stability of a specific implementation of a sorting algorithm
- identify an appropriate search algorithm, given a description of the way data is organized

A t many points in this text we have gone to great trouble to keep information in sorted order: famous people sorted by name or year of birth, airline routes sorted by distance, integers sorted from smallest to largest, and words sorted alphabetically. One reason to keep lists sorted is to facilitate searching; given an appropriate implementation structure, a particular list element can be found faster if the list is sorted.

In this chapter we directly examine several strategies for both sorting and searching, contrast and compare them, and discuss sorting/searching concerns in general. Even though sorting and searching are already supported by most modern software development platforms, we believe their study is beneficial for computer science students—for the same reasons you study data structures even though language libraries provide powerful structuring APIs, you should study sorting and searching. Their study provides a good way to learn basic algorithmic and analysis techniques that help form a foundation of problem-solving tools. Studying the fundamentals prepares you for further growth so that eventually you will be able to create your own unique solutions to the unique problems that you are sure to encounter one day.

11.1   Sorting

Putting an unsorted list of data elements into order—*sorting*—is a very common and useful operation. Entire books have been written about sorting algorithms as well as algorithms for searching a sorted list to find a particular element.

Sorting Efficiency

We elect to measure sorting efficiency by focusing on the number of comparisons made during a sort. Alternately, we could focus on the number of "swaps"—the exchange of two values, or the number of "moves"— changing the location of an element. In Java when we swap or move elements we are actually manipulating references to elements. In some languages this is not the case and the actual elements themselves have to be moved, a potentially costly operation. In such cases programmers sometime mimic the "by-reference" model used by Java, using an array to store the elements and then manipulating array indices rather than the elements themselves.

Because sorting a large number of elements can be extremely time consuming, an efficient sorting algorithm is very important. How do we describe efficiency? List element comparison—that is, the operation that compares two list elements to see which is smaller—is an operation central to most sorting algorithms. We use the number of required element comparisons as a measure of the efficiency of each algorithm. For each algorithm we calculate the number of comparisons relative to the size of the list being sorted. We then use order of growth notation, based on the result of our calculation, to succinctly describe the efficiency of the algorithm.

In addition to comparing elements, each of our algorithms includes another basic operation: swapping the locations of two elements on the list. The number of element swaps needed to sort a list is another measure of sorting efficiency. In the exercises we ask you to analyze the sorting algorithms developed in this chapter in terms of that alternative measure.

Another efficiency consideration is the amount of extra memory space required by an algorithm. For most applications memory space is not an important factor when choosing a sorting algorithm. We look at only two sorts in which space would be a consideration. The usual time versus space trade-off applies to sorts—more space often means less time, and vice versa.

A Test Harness

To facilitate our study of sorting we develop a standard **test harness**, a driver program that we can use to test each of our sorting algorithms. Because we are using this program just to test our implementations and facilitate our study, we keep it simple. It consists of a single class called `Sorts`. The class defines an array that can hold 50 integers. The array is named `values`. Several static methods are defined:

- `initValues`. Initializes the `values` array with random numbers between 0 and 99; uses the `abs` method (absolute value) from the Java library's `Math` class and the `nextInt` method from the `Random` class.
- `isSorted`. Returns a `boolean` value indicating whether the `values` array is currently sorted.
- `swap`. Swapping data values between two array locations is common in many sorting algorithms—this method swaps the integers between `values[index1]` and `values[index2]`, where `index1` and `index2` are parameters of the method.
- `printValues`. Prints the contents of the `values` array to the `System.out` stream; the output is arranged evenly in 10 columns.

Here is the code for the test harness:

```
//----------------------------------------------------------------------
// Sorts.java              by Dale/Joyce/Weems          Chapter 11
//
// Test harness used to run sorting algorithms.
//----------------------------------------------------------------------
package ch11.sorts;

import java.util.*;
import java.text.DecimalFormat;

public class Sorts
{
  static final int SIZE = 50;           // size of array to be sorted
  static int[] values = new int[SIZE];  // values to be sorted

  static void initValues()
  // Initializes the values array with random integers from 0 to 99.
  {
    Random rand = new Random();
    for (int index = 0; index < SIZE; index++)
      values[index] = Math.abs(rand.nextInt()) % 100;
  }

  static public boolean isSorted()
```

```
// Returns true if the array values are sorted and false otherwise.
{
  for (int index = 0; index < (SIZE - 1); index++)
    if (values[index] > values[index + 1])
      return false;
  return true;
}


static public void swap(int index1, int index2)
// Precondition: index1 and index2 are >= 0 and < SIZE.
//
// Swaps the integers at locations index1 and index2 of the values array.
{
  int temp = values[index1];
  values[index1] = values[index2];
  values[index2] = temp;
}


static public void printValues()
// Prints all the values integers.
{
  int value;
  DecimalFormat fmt = new DecimalFormat("00");
  System.out.println("The values array is:");
  for (int index = 0; index < SIZE; index++)
  {
    value = values[index];
    if (((index + 1) % 10) == 0)
      System.out.println(fmt.format(value));
    else
      System.out.print(fmt.format(value) + " ");
  }
  System.out.println();
}


public static void main(String[] args) throws IOException
{
  initValues();
  printValues();
  System.out.println("values is sorted: " + isSorted());
  System.out.println();
```

```
    swap(0, 1);
    printValues();
    System.out.println("values is sorted: " + isSorted());
    System.out.println();
  }
}
```

In this version of Sorts the main method initializes the values array, prints the array, prints the value of isSorted, swaps the first two values of the array, and again prints information about the array. The output from this class as currently defined would look something like this:

```
the values array is:
20 49 07 50 45 69 20 07 88 02
89 87 35 98 23 98 61 03 75 48
25 81 97 79 40 78 47 56 24 07
63 39 52 80 11 63 51 45 25 78
35 62 72 05 98 83 05 14 30 23

values is sorted: false

the values array is:
49 20 07 50 45 69 20 07 88 02
89 87 35 98 23 98 61 03 75 48
25 81 97 79 40 78 47 56 24 07
63 39 52 80 11 63 51 45 25 78
35 62 72 05 98 83 05 14 30 23

values is sorted: false
```

As we proceed in our study of sorting algorithms, we will add methods that implement the algorithms to the Sorts class and change the main method to invoke those methods. We can use the isSorted and printValues methods to help us check the results.

Because our sorting methods are implemented for use with this test harness, they can directly access the static values array. In the general case, we could modify each sorting method to accept a reference to an array-based list to be sorted as an argument.

11.2   Simple Sorts

In this section we present three "simple" sorts, so called because they use an unsophisticated brute force approach. This means they are not very efficient; but they are easy to understand and to implement. Two of these algorithms were presented earlier in the text—the Selection Sort and the Insertion Sort. Here we revisit those algorithms, plus introduce the Bubble Sort, looking at them more formally than we did in the previous coverage.

Selection Sort

In Section 1.6, "Comparing Algorithms," we introduced the Selection Sort. Here we present this algorithm more formally.

   If we were handed a list of names on a sheet of paper and asked to put them in alphabetical order, we might use this general approach:

1. *Select* the name that comes first in alphabetical order, and write it on a second sheet of paper.

2. *Cross* the name out on the original sheet.

3. *Repeat* steps 1 and 2 for the second name, the third name, and so on until all the names on the original sheet have been crossed out and written onto the second sheet, at which point the list on the second sheet is sorted.

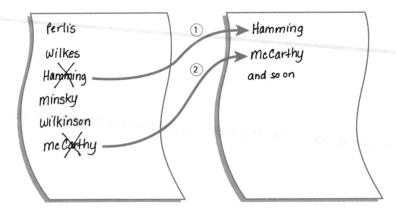

This algorithm is simple to translate into a computer program, but it has one drawback: It requires space in memory to store two complete lists. This duplication is clearly wasteful. A slight adjustment to this manual approach does away with the need to duplicate space. Instead of writing the "first" name onto a separate sheet of paper, exchange it with the name in the first location on the original sheet.

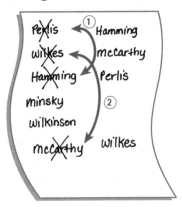

Repeating this until finished results in a sorted list on the original sheet of paper.

Within our program the "by-hand list" is represented as an array. Here is a more formal algorithm.

SelectionSort

for current going from 0 to SIZE – 2
    Find the index in the array of the smallest unsorted element
    Swap the current element with the smallest unsorted one

Figure 11.1 shows the steps taken by the algorithm to sort a five-element array. Each section of the figure represents one iteration of the *for* loop. The first part of a section represents the "find the smallest unsorted array element" step. To do so, we repeatedly examine the unsorted elements, asking if each one is the smallest we have seen so far. The second part of a figure section shows the two array elements to be swapped, and the final part shows the result of the swap.

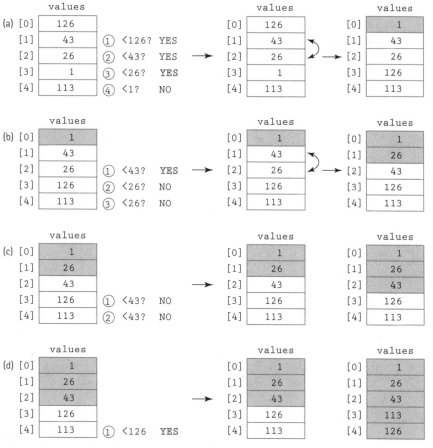

Figure 11.1 Example of a selection sort (sorted elements are shaded)

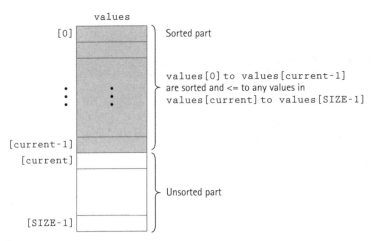

Figure 11.2 A snapshot of the selection sort algorithm

During the progression, we can view the array as being divided into a sorted part and an unsorted part. Each time we perform the body of the *for* loop, the sorted part grows by one element and the unsorted part shrinks by one element. The exception is the very last step, when the sorted part grows by two elements. Do you see why? When all of the array elements except the last one are in their correct locations, the last one is in its correct location by default. This is why our *for* loop can stop at index SIZE - 2 instead of at the end of the array, index SIZE - 1.

We implement the algorithm with a method selectionSort that becomes part of our Sorts class. This method sorts the values array that is declared in that class. It has access to the SIZE constant that indicates the number of elements in the array. Within the selectionSort method we use a variable, current, to mark the beginning of the unsorted part of the array. Thus the unsorted part of the array goes from index current to index SIZE - 1. We start out by setting current to the index of the first position (0). **Figure 11.2** provides a snapshot of the array during the selection sort algorithm.

We use a helper method to find the index of the smallest value in the unsorted part of the array. The minIndex method receives the first and last indices of the unsorted part, and returns the index of the smallest value in this part of the array. We also use the swap method that is part of our test harness.

Here is the code for the minIndex and selectionSort methods. Because they are placed directly in our test harness class, a class with a main method, they are declared as static methods.

```
static int minIndex(int startIndex, int endIndex)
// Returns the index of the smallest value in
// values[startIndex]to values[endIndex].
{
    int indexOfMin = startIndex;
    for (int index = startIndex + 1; index <= endIndex; index++)
```

```
        if (values[index] < values[indexOfMin])
            indexOfMin = index;
    return indexOfMin;
}

static void selectionSort()
// Sorts the values array using the selection sort algorithm.
{
    int endIndex = SIZE - 1;
    for (int current = 0; current < endIndex; current++)
        swap(current, minIndex(current, endIndex));
}
```

Let us change the main body of the test harness:

```
initValues();
printValues();
System.out.println("values is sorted: " + isSorted());
System.out.println();
selectionSort();
System.out.println("Selection Sort called\n");
printValues();
System.out.println("values is sorted: " + isSorted());
System.out.println();
```

Now we get an output from the program that looks like this:

```
The values array is:
92 66 38 17 21 78 10 43 69 19
17 96 29 19 77 24 47 01 97 91
13 33 84 93 49 85 09 54 13 06
21 21 93 49 67 42 25 29 05 74
96 82 26 25 11 74 03 76 29 10

values is sorted: false

Selection Sort called

The values array is:
01 03 05 06 09 10 10 11 13 13
17 17 19 19 21 21 21 24 25 25
26 29 29 29 33 38 42 43 47 49
49 54 66 67 69 74 74 76 77 78
82 84 85 91 92 93 93 96 96 97
values is sorted: true
```

We can test all of our sorting methods using this same approach.

Analyzing the Selection Sort

Now we try measuring the amount of "work" required by this algorithm. We describe the number of comparisons as a function of the number of elements in the array—that is, SIZE. To be concise, in this discussion we refer to SIZE as N.

The comparison operation is in the minIndex method. We know from the loop condition in the selectionSort method that minIndex is called $N - 1$ times. Within minIndex, the number of comparisons varies, depending on the values of startIndex and endIndex:

```
for (int index = startIndex + 1; index <= endIndex; index++)
   if (values[index] < values[indexOfMin])
      indexOfMin = index;
```

In the first call to minIndex, startIndex is 0 and endIndex is SIZE - 1, so there are $N - 1$ comparisons; in the next call, there are $N - 2$ comparisons; and so on; until the last call, when there is only one comparison. The total number of comparisons is

$$(N - 1) + (N - 2) + (N - 3) + ... + 1 = N (N - 1) / 2$$

To accomplish our goal of sorting an array of N elements, the selection sort requires $N(N - 1)/2$ comparisons. The particular arrangement of values in the array does not affect the amount of work required. Even if the array is in sorted order before the call to selectionSort, the method still makes $N(N - 1)/2$ comparisons. **Table 11.1** shows the number of comparisons required for arrays of various sizes.

How do we describe this algorithm in terms of order of growth notation? If we express $N(N - 1)/2$ as $\frac{1}{2}N^2 - \frac{1}{2}N$, the complexity is easy to determine. In O notation we consider only the term $\frac{1}{2}N^2$, because it increases fastest relative to N. Further, we ignore the constant, $\frac{1}{2}$, making this algorithm $O(N^2)$. Thus, for large values of N, the computation time is approximately proportional to N^2. Looking at Table 11.1, we see that multiplying the number of elements by 10 increases the number of comparisons by a factor of about 100; that is, the number of comparisons is multiplied by approximately the square of the increase in the number of elements. Looking at this table makes us appreciate why sorting algorithms are the subject of so much attention: Using selectionSort to sort an array of 1,000 elements requires almost a half million comparisons!

Table 11.1 Number of Comparisons Required to Sort Arrays of Different Sizes Using Selection Sort

Number of Elements	Number of Comparisons
10	45
20	190
100	4,950
1,000	499,500
10,000	49,995,000

In the selection sort, each iteration finds the smallest unsorted element and puts it into its correct place. If we had made the helper method find the largest value instead of the smallest one, the algorithm would have sorted in descending order. We could also have made the loop go down from SIZE - 1 to 1, putting the elements into the end of the array first. All of these approaches are variations on the selection sort. The variations do not change the basic way that the minimum (or maximum) element is found, nor do they improve the algorithm's efficiency.

Bubble Sort

The bubble sort uses a different scheme for finding the minimum (or maximum) value. Each iteration puts the smallest unsorted element into its correct place, but it also makes changes in the locations of the other elements in the array. The first iteration puts the smallest element in the array into the first array position. Starting with the last array element, we compare successive pairs of elements, swapping whenever the bottom element of the pair is smaller than the one above it. In this way the smallest element "bubbles up" to the top of the array.

Figure 11.3a shows the result of the first iteration through a five-element array. The next iteration puts the smallest element in the unsorted part of the array into the second array position, using the same technique, as shown in Figure 11.3b. The rest of the sorting process is represented in Figures 11.3c and d. In addition to putting one element into its proper place, each iteration can cause some intermediate changes in the array. Also note that as with selection sort, the last iteration effectively puts two elements into their correct places.

The basic algorithm for the bubble sort:

BubbleSort

Set current to the index of first element in the array
while more elements in unsorted part of array
   "Bubble up" the smallest element in the unsorted part, causing intermediate swaps as needed
   Shrink the unsorted part of the array by incrementing current

---

The overall approach is similar to that followed in the selectionSort. The unsorted part of the array is the area from values[current] to values[SIZE - 1]. The value of current begins at 0, and we loop until current reaches SIZE - 2, with current incremented in each iteration. On entrance to each iteration of the loop body, the first current values are already sorted, and all the elements in the unsorted part of the array are greater than or equal to the sorted elements.

The inside of the loop body is different, however. Each iteration of the loop "bubbles up" the smallest value in the unsorted part of the array to the current position. The algorithm for the bubbling task is

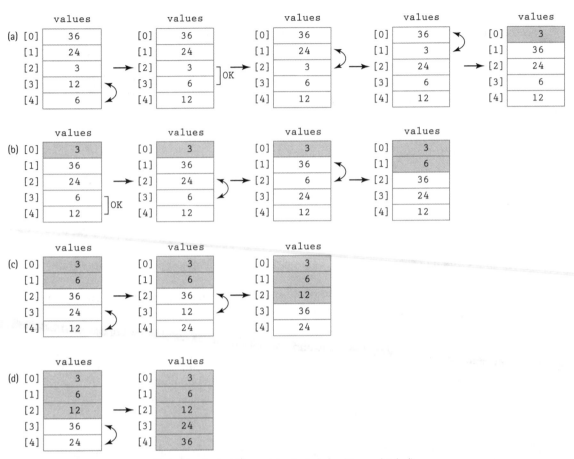

Figure 11.3   Example of a bubble sort (sorted elements are shaded)

bubbleUp(startIndex, endIndex)

for index going from endIndex DOWNTO startIndex +1
  if values[index] < values[index - 1]
      Swap the value at index with the value at index - 1

A snapshot of the array during this algorithm is shown in **Figure 11.4**. We use the swap method as before. The code for methods bubbleUp and bubbleSort follows. The code can be tested using our test harness.

```
static void bubbleUp(int startIndex, int endIndex)
// Switches adjacent pairs that are out of order
// between values[startIndex]to values[endIndex]
// beginning at values[endIndex].
```

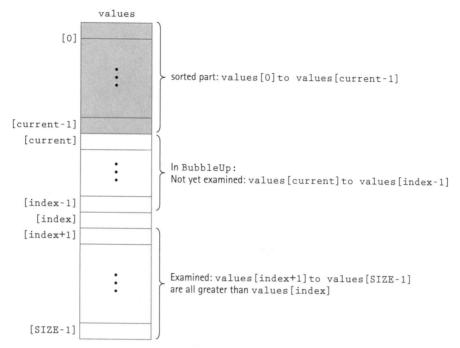

Figure 11.4 A snapshot of the bubble sort algorithm

```
{
  for (int index = endIndex; index > startIndex; index--)
    if (values[index] < values[index - 1])
      swap(index, index - 1);
}

static void bubbleSort()
// Sorts the values array using the bubble sort algorithm.
{
  int current = 0;
  while (current < (SIZE - 1))
  {
    bubbleUp(current, SIZE - 1);
    current++;
  }
}
```

Analyzing the Bubble Sort

Analyzing the work required by `bubbleSort` is easy, because it is the same as for the selection sort algorithm. The comparisons are in `bubbleUp`, which is called $N - 1$ times. There are $N - 1$ comparisons the first time, $N - 2$ comparisons the second time, and so on.

Therefore, both `bubbleSort` and `selectionSort` require the same amount of work in terms of the number of comparisons. The `bubbleSort` code does more than just make comparisons; however, `selectionSort` has only one data swap per iteration, but `bubbleSort` may do many additional data swaps.

What is the result of these intermediate data swaps? By reversing out-of-order pairs of data as they are noticed, bubble sort can move several elements closer to their final destination during each pass. It is possible that the method will get the array in sorted order before $N - 1$ calls to `bubbleUp`. This version of the bubble sort, however, makes no provision for stopping when the array is completely sorted. Even if the array is already in sorted order when `bubbleSort` is called, this method continues to call `bubbleUp` (which changes nothing) $N - 1$ times.

We could quit before the maximum number of iterations if `bubbleUp` returns a `boolean` flag, telling us when the array is sorted. Within `bubbleUp`, we initially set a variable `sorted` to `true`; then in the loop, if any swaps are made, we reset `sorted` to `false`. If no elements have been swapped, we know that the array is already in order. Now the bubble sort needs to make only one extra call to `bubbleUp` when the array is in order. This version of the bubble sort is as follows:

```
static boolean bubbleUp2(int startIndex, int endIndex)
// Switches adjacent pairs that are out of order between
// values[startIndex]to values[endIndex] beginning at values[endIndex].
//
// Returns false if a swap was made; otherwise, returns true.
{
  boolean sorted = true;
  for (int index = endIndex; index > startIndex; index--)
    if (values[index] < values[index - 1])
    {
      swap(index, index - 1);
      sorted = false;
    }
  return sorted;
}


static void shortBubble()
// Sorts the values array using the bubble sort algorithm.
// The process stops as soon as values is sorted.
{
  int current = 0;
  boolean sorted = false;
  while ((current < (SIZE - 1)) && !sorted)
  {
    sorted = bubbleUp2(current, SIZE - 1);
    current++;
  }
}
```

The analysis of `shortBubble` is more difficult. Clearly, if the array is already sorted to begin with, one call to `bubbleUp` tells us so. In this best-case scenario, `shortBubble` is O(*N*); only *N* − 1 comparisons are required for the sort. But what if the original array was actually sorted in descending order before the call to `shortBubble`? This is the worst possible case: `shortBubble` requires as many comparisons as `bubbleSort` and `selectionSort`, not to mention the "overhead"—all the extra swaps and setting and resetting the `sorted` flag. Can we calculate an average case? In the first call to `bubbleUp`, when `current` is 0, there are `SIZE - 1` comparisons; on the second call, when `current` is 1, there are `SIZE - 2` comparisons. The number of comparisons in any call to `bubbleUp` is `SIZE - current - 1`. If we let *N* indicate SIZE and *K* indicate the number of calls to `bubbleUp` executed before `shortBubble` finishes its work, the total number of comparisons required is

$$(N-1) + (N-2) + (N-3) + \ldots + (N-K)$$

    1st call   2nd call   3rd call   *K*th call

A little algebra changes this to

$$(2KN - 2K^2 - K) / 2$$

In O notation, the term that is increasing the fastest relative to *N* is 2*KN*. We know that *K* is between 1 and *N* − 1. On average, over all possible input orders, *K* is proportional to *N*. Therefore, 2*KN* is proportional to N^2; that is, the `shortBubble` algorithm is also O(N^2).

Why do we even bother to discuss the bubble sort algorithm if it is O(N^2) and requires extra data movements? Due to the extra intermediate swaps performed by the bubble sort, it can quickly sort an array that is "almost" sorted. If the `shortBubble` variation is used, a bubble sort can be very efficient in this situation.

Insertion Sort

In Section 6.4, "Sorted Array-Based List Implementation," we described the Insertion Sort algorithm and how it could be used to maintain a list in sorted order. Here we present essentially the same algorithm, although for the present discussion we assume we start with an unsorted array and use Insertion Sort to change it into a sorted array.

The principle of the insertion sort is quite simple: Each successive element in the array to be sorted is inserted into its proper place with respect to the other, already sorted elements. As with the previously mentioned sorting strategies, we divide our array into a sorted part and an unsorted part. (Unlike with the selection and bubble sorts, there may be values in the unsorted part that are less than values in the sorted part.) Initially, the sorted portion contains only one element: the first element in the array. Now we take the second element in the array and insert it into its correct place in the sorted part; that is, `values[0]` and `values[1]` are in order with respect to each other. Now the value in `values[2]` is inserted into its proper place; so `values[0]` to `values[2]` are in order with respect to each other. This process continues until all elements have been sorted.

In Chapter 6, our strategy was to search for the insertion point using a binary search and then to shift the elements from the insertion point down one slot to make room for the new element. We can combine the searching and shifting by beginning at the end of the sorted part of the array. We compare the element at `values [current]` to the one before it. If it is less than its predecessor, we swap the two elements. We then compare the element at `values [current - 1]` to the one before it, and swap if necessary. The process stops when the comparison shows that the values are in order or we have swapped into the first place in the array.

Figure 11.5 illustrates this process, which is described in the following algorithm, and **Figure 11.6** shows a snapshot of the array during the algorithm.

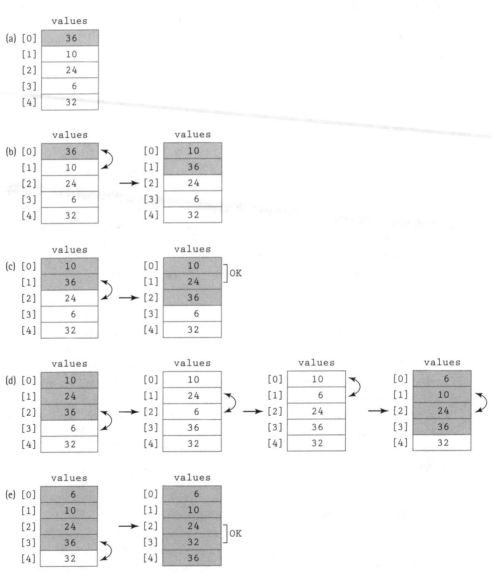

Figure 11.5 Example of an insertion sort

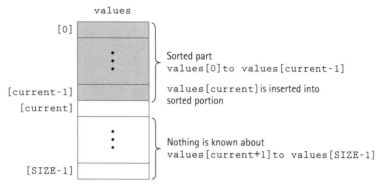

Figure 11.6   A snapshot of the insertion sort algorithm

---

insertionSort

for count going from 1 through SIZE – 1
   insertElement(0, count)

InsertElement(startIndex, endIndex)

Set finished to false
Set current to endIndex
Set moreToSearch to true
while moreToSearch AND NOT finished
   if values[current] < values[current – 1]
      swap(values[current], values[current –1])
      Decrement current
      Set moreToSearch to (current does not equal startIndex)
   else
      Set finished to true

Here are the coded versions of `insertElement` and `insertionSort`:

```
static void insertElement(int startIndex, int endIndex)
// Upon completion, values[0]to values[endIndex] are sorted.
{
  boolean finished = false; int current = endIndex; boolean moreToSearch = true;
  while (moreToSearch && !finished)
  {
    if (values[current] < values[current - 1])
```

```
    {
      swap(current, current - 1);
      current--;
      moreToSearch = (current != startIndex);
    }
    else
      finished = true;
  }
}


static void insertionSort()
// Sorts the values array using the insertion sort algorithm.
{
  for (int count = 1; count < SIZE; count++)
    insertElement(0, count);
}
```

Analyzing the Insertion Sort

The general case for this algorithm mirrors the selectionSort and the bubbleSort; so the general case is $O(N^2)$. But as for shortBubble, insertionSort has a best case: The data are already sorted in ascending order. When the data are in ascending order, insertElement is called N times, but only one comparison is made each time and no swaps are necessary. The maximum number of comparisons is made only when the elements in the array are in reverse order.

The insertion sort takes the "next" element from the unsorted part of the array and *inserts* it into the sorted part, so that the sorted part is kept sorted. Therefore, it is a good choice for sorting when faced with a situation where elements are presented one at a time—perhaps across a network or by an interactive user. During the lull between element arrivals the insertion sort processing moves forward so that by the time the final element is presented it is a simple matter to finish the sorting.

If we know nothing about the original order of the data to be sorted, selectionSort, shortBubble, and insertionSort are all $O(N^2)$ sorts and are very time consuming for sorting large arrays. Several sorting methods that work better when N is large are presented in the next section.

11.3 $O(N \log_2 N)$ Sorts

The sorting algorithms covered in Section 11.2, "Simple Sorts," are all $O(N^2)$. Considering how rapidly N^2 grows as the size of the array increases, can we do better? We note that N^2 is a lot larger than $(\frac{1}{2}N)^2 + (\frac{1}{2}N)^2$. If we could cut the array into two pieces, sort each segment, and then merge the two back together, we should end up sorting the entire array with a lot less work. An example of this approach is shown in **Figure 11.7**.

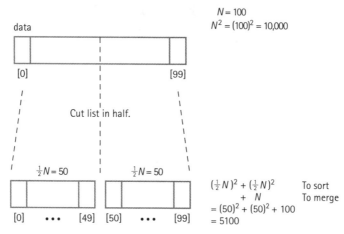

Figure 11.7   Rationale for divide-and-conquer sorts

The idea of "divide and conquer" has been applied to the sorting problem in different ways, resulting in a number of algorithms that can do the job much more efficiently than $O(N^2)$. In fact, there is a category of sorting algorithms that are $O(N \log_2 N)$. We examine three of these algorithms here: `mergeSort`, `quickSort`, and `heapSort`. As you might guess, the efficiency of these algorithms is achieved at the expense of the simplicity seen in the selection, bubble, and insertion sorts.

Merge Sort

The merge sort algorithm is taken directly from the idea presented above.

mergeSort
Cut the array in half
Sort the left half
Sort the right half
Merge the two sorted halves into one sorted array

Merging the two halves together is an $O(N)$ task: We merely go through the sorted halves, comparing successive pairs of values (one in each half) and putting the smaller value into the next slot in the final solution. Even if the sorting algorithm used for each half is $O(N^2)$, we should see some improvement over sorting the whole array at once, as indicated in Figure 11.7.

Actually, because `mergeSort` is itself a sorting algorithm, we might as well use it to sort the two halves. That is right—we can make `mergeSort` a recursive method and let it call itself to sort each of the two subarrays:

---

mergeSort—Recursive

Cut the array in half
mergeSort the left half
mergeSort the right half
Merge the two sorted halves into one sorted array

This is the general case. What is the base case, the case that does not involve any recursive calls to `mergeSort`? If the "half" to be sorted does not hold more than one element, we can consider it already sorted and just return.

Here we summarize `mergeSort` in the format we used for other recursive algorithms. The initial method call would be `mergeSort(0, SIZE - 1)`.

Method `mergeSort(first, last)`

Definition:	Sorts the array elements in ascending order.
Size:	last – first + 1
Base case:	If size less than 2, do nothing.
General case:	Cut the array in half.
	mergeSort the left half.
	mergeSort the right half.
	Merge the sorted halves into one sorted array.

Cutting the array in half is simply a matter of finding the midpoint between the first and last indices:

```
middle = (first + last) / 2;
```

Then, in the smaller-caller tradition, we can make the recursive calls to `mergeSort`:

```
mergeSort(first, middle);
mergeSort(middle + 1, last);
```

So far this is simple enough. Now we just have to merge the two halves and we are done.

Merging the Sorted Halves

For the merge sort all the serious work takes place in the merge step. Look first at the general algorithm for merging two sorted arrays, and then we can look at the specific problem of our subarrays.

To merge two sorted arrays, we compare successive pairs of elements, one from each array, moving the smaller of each pair to the "final" array. We can stop when one array runs out of elements, and then move all of the remaining elements from the other array to the final array. **Figure 11.8** illustrates the general algorithm. In our specific problem, the two "arrays" to be merged are actually subarrays of the original array (**Figure 11.9**). Just as in Figure 11.8, where we merged array1 and array2 into a third array, we need to merge our two subarrays into some auxiliary structure. We need this structure, another array, only temporarily. After the merge step, we can copy the now-sorted elements back into the original array. The entire process is shown in **Figure 11.10**.

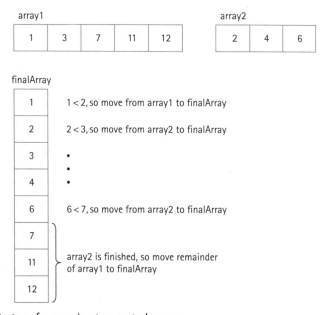

Figure 11.8   Strategy for merging two sorted arrays

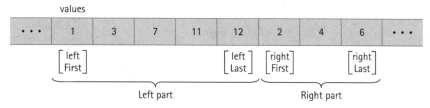

Figure 11.9   Two subarrays

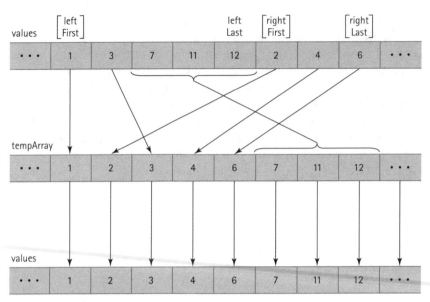

Figure 11.10 Merging sorted halves

Here is the algorithm for merge:

merge (leftFirst, leftLast, rightFirst, rightLast)

(uses a local array, tempArray)
Set index to leftFirst
while more elements in left half AND more elements in right half
    if values[leftFirst] < values[rightFirst]
        Set tempArray[index] to values[leftFirst]
        Increment leftFirst
    else
        Set tempArray[index] to values[rightFirst]
        Increment rightFirst
    Increment index
Copy any remaining elements from left half to tempArray
Copy any remaining elements from right half to tempArray
Copy the sorted elements from tempArray back into values

In the coding of method merge, we use leftFirst and rightFirst to indicate the "current" position in the left and right halves, respectively. Because these variables are values of the primitive type int and not objects, copies of these parameters are passed to method merge, rather than references to the parameters. These copies are changed in the method; changing the copies does not affect the original values. Both of the "copy any remaining elements" loops are included. During the execution of this method, one of these loops never executes. Can you explain why?

```
static void merge (int leftFirst, int leftLast, int rightFirst, int rightLast)
// Preconditions: values[leftFirst]to values[leftLast] are sorted.
//      values[rightFirst]to values[rightLast] are sorted.
//
// Sorts values[leftFirst]to values[rightLast] by merging the two subarrays.
{
  int[] tempArray = new int [SIZE];
  int index = leftFirst;
  int saveFirst = leftFirst;       // to remember where to copy back

  while ((leftFirst <= leftLast) && (rightFirst <= rightLast))
  {
    if (values[leftFirst] < values[rightFirst])
    {
      tempArray[index] = values[leftFirst];
      leftFirst++;
    }
    else
    {
      tempArray[index] = values[rightFirst];
      rightFirst++;
    }
    index++;
  }

  while (leftFirst <= leftLast)
  // Copy remaining elements from left half.
  {
    tempArray[index] = values[leftFirst];
    leftFirst++;
    index++;
  }

  while (rightFirst <= rightLast)
  // Copy remaining elements from right half.
  {
    tempArray[index] = values[rightFirst];
    rightFirst++;
    index++;
  }

  for (index = saveFirst; index <= rightLast; index++)
    values[index] = tempArray[index];
}
```

As we said, most of the work occurs in the merge task. The actual mergeSort method is short and simple:

```
static void mergeSort(int first, int last)
// Sorts the values array using the merge sort algorithm.
{
  if (first < last)
  {
    int middle = (first + last) / 2;
    mergeSort(first, middle);
    mergeSort(middle + 1,    last);
     merge(first, middle, middle + 1, last);
  }
}
```

Analyzing mergeSort

The mergeSort method splits the original array into two halves. It first sorts the first half of the array; it then sorts the second half of the array using the same approach; finally, it merges the two halves. To sort the first half of the array, it follows the same approach of splitting and merging. It does likewise for the second half. During the sorting process, the splitting and merging operations all become intermingled. Analysis is simplified if we imagine that all of the splitting occurs first, followed by all of the merging—we can view the process this way without affecting the correctness of the algorithm.

We view the mergeSort algorithm as continually dividing the original array (of size N) in two, until it has created N one-element subarrays. **Figure 11.11** shows this point of view for an array with an original size of 16. The total work needed to divide the array in half, over and over again until we reach subarrays of size 1, is O(N). After all, we end up with N subarrays of size 1.

Each subarray of size 1 is obviously a sorted subarray. The real work of the algorithm involves merging the smaller sorted subarrays back into the larger sorted subarrays. To merge two sorted subarrays of size X and size Y into a single sorted subarray using the merge operation requires O($X + Y$) steps. We can see this because each time through the *while* loops of the merge method we advance either the leftFirst index or the rightFirst index by 1. Because we stop processing when these indices become greater than their "last" counterparts, we know that we take a total of (leftLast - leftFirst + 1) + (rightLast - rightFirst + 1) steps. This expression represents the sum of the lengths of the two subarrays being processed.

How many times must we perform the merge operation? And what are the sizes of the subarrays involved? Here we work from the bottom up. The original array of size N is eventually split into N subarrays of size 1. Merging two of those subarrays into a subarray of size 2 requires $1 + 1 = 2$ steps, based on the analysis of the preceding paragraph. We must perform this merge operation a total of ½N times (we have N one-element

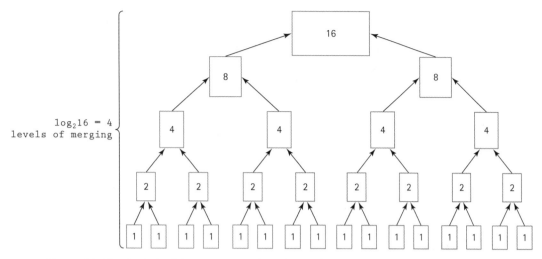

Figure 11.11   Analysis of the merge sort algorithm with $N = 16$

subarrays and we are merging them two at a time). Thus, the total number of steps to create all of the sorted two-element subarrays is $O(N)$ because $(2 * \frac{1}{2}N = N)$.

Now we repeat this process to create four-element subarrays. It takes four steps to merge two two-element subarrays. We must perform this merge operation a total of $-\frac{1}{4}N$ times (we have $\frac{1}{2}N$ two-element subarrays and we are merging them two at a time). Thus, the total number of steps to create all of the sorted four-element subarrays is also $O(N)$ because $(4 * \frac{1}{4}N = N)$. The same reasoning leads us to conclude that each of the other levels of merging requires $O(N)$ steps—at each level the sizes of the subarrays double, but the number of subarrays is cut in half, balancing them out.

We now know that it takes $O(N)$ total steps to perform merging at each "level" of merging. How many levels are there? The number of levels of merging is equal to the number of times we can split the original array in half. If the original array is size N, we have $\log_2 N$ levels. For example, in Figure 11.11 the size of the original array is 16 and the number of levels of merging is 4.

Because we have $\log_2 N$ levels, and we require $O(N)$ steps at each level, the total cost of the merge operation is $O(N \log_2 N)$. Because the splitting phase was only $O(N)$, we conclude that the merge sort algorithm is $O(N \log_2 N)$. **Table 11.2** illustrates that, for large values of N, $O(N \log_2 N)$ is a big improvement over $O(N^2)$.

A disadvantage of `mergeSort` is that it requires an auxiliary array that is as large as the original array to be sorted. If the array is large and space is a critical factor, then this sort may not be an appropriate choice. Variations of merge sort exist that do not use an auxiliary array; however, they are more complex and therefore less time efficient. Next we discuss two $O(N \log_2 N)$ sorts that move elements around in the original array and do not need an auxiliary array.

Table 11.2 Comparing N^2 and $N \log_2 N$

N	$\log_2 N$	N^2	$N \log_2 N$
32	5	1,024	160
64	6	4,096	384
128	7	16,384	896
256	8	65,536	2,048
512	9	262,144	4,608
1,024	10	1,048,576	10,240
2,048	11	4,194,304	22,528
4,096	12	16,777,216	49,152

Quick Sort

Similar to the merge sort, the quick sort is a divide-and-conquer algorithm, which is inherently recursive. Given a large stack of final exams to sort by name, we might use the following approach (see **Figure 11.12**): Pick a splitting value—say, L—and divide the stack of tests into two piles, A–L and M–Z. (The two piles do not necessarily contain the same number of tests.) Then take the first pile and subdivide it into two piles, A–F and G–L. The A–F pile can be further broken down into A–C and D–F. This division process goes on until the piles are small enough to be easily sorted. The same process is applied to the M–Z pile. Eventually, all the small sorted piles can be collected one on top of the other to produce a sorted set of tests.

This strategy is recursive: On each attempt to sort the pile of tests, the pile is divided, and then the same approach is used to sort each of the smaller piles (a smaller case). This process continues until the small piles do not need to be further divided (the base case). The parameter list of the quickSort method reflects the part of the list that is currently

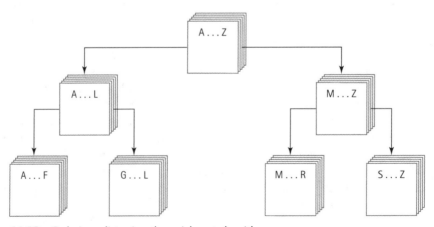

Figure 11.12 Ordering a list using the quick sort algorithm

being processed; we pass the first and last indices that define the part of the array to be processed on this call. The initial call to quickSort is

```
quickSort(0, SIZE - 1);
```

Method quickSort(first, last)

Definition:	Sorts the elements in subarray values[first] to values[last].
Size:	last – first + 1
Base case:	If size less than 2, do nothing.
General case:	Split the array according to splitting value.
	quickSort the elements <= splitting value.
	quickSort the elements > splitting value.

quickSort

```
if there is more than one element in values[first] to values[last]
   Select splitVal
   Split the array so that
      values[first] to values[splitPoint - 1] <= splitVal
      values[splitPoint] = splitVal
      values[splitPoint + 1] to values[last] > splitVal
   quickSort the left subarray
   quickSort the right subarray
```

As you can see, the algorithm depends on the selection of a "split value," called splitVal, that is used to divide the array into two subarrays. How do we select splitVal? One simple solution is to use the value in values[first] as the splitting value. (We discuss other approaches later.)

splitVal = 9

9	20	6	10	14	8	60	11

[first]   [last]

We create a helper method split, to rearrange the array elements as planned. After the call to split, all of the elements that are less than or equal to splitVal appear on the left side of the array and all of the elements that are greater than splitVal appear on the right side of the array.

smaller or equal values   larger values

9	8	6	10	14	20	60	11

[first]   [splitPoint]   [last]

The two subarrays meet at splitPoint, the index of the last element that is less than or equal to splitVal. We do not know the value of splitPoint until the splitting process is complete. Its value is returned by split. We can then swap splitVal with the value at splitPoint.

smaller or equal values				larger values			
6	8	9	10	14	20	60	11
[first]		[splitPoint]					[last]

Our recursive calls to quickSort use this index (splitPoint) to reduce the size of the problem in the general case.

quickSort(first, splitPoint - 1) sorts the left subarray. quickSort (splitPoint + 1, last) sorts the right subarray. splitVal is already in its correct position in the array.

What is the base case? When the segment being examined holds fewer than two elements, we do not need to go on. In other words, we continue processing as long as first < last. We can now code our quickSort method.

```
static void quickSort(int first, int last)
{
  if (first < last)
  {
    int splitPoint;

    splitPoint = split(first, last);
    // values[first]to values[splitPoint - 1] <= splitVal
    // values[splitPoint] = splitVal
    // values[splitPoint+1]to values[last] > splitVal

    quickSort(first, splitPoint - 1);
    quickSort(splitPoint + 1, last);
  }
}
```

Now we must develop our splitting algorithm. We must find a way to get all of the elements equal to or less than splitVal on one side of splitVal and the elements greater than splitVal on the other side.

We do so by moving the indices, first and last, toward the middle of the array, looking for elements that are on the wrong side of the split point and swapping them (**Figure 11.13**). While this operation is proceeding, the splitVal remains in the first position of the subarray being processed. As a final step, we swap it with the value at the splitPoint; therefore, we save the original value of first in a local variable, saveF (Figure 11.13a).

We start out by moving first to the right, toward the middle, comparing values[first] to splitVal. If values[first] is less than or equal to splitVal, we

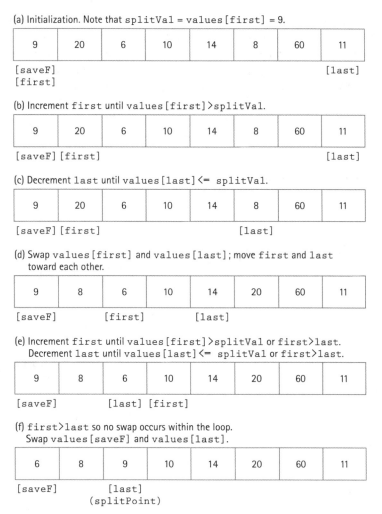

(a) Initialization. Note that `splitVal = values[first] = 9`.

9	20	6	10	14	8	60	11

[saveF]   [last]
[first]

(b) Increment `first` until `values[first] > splitVal`.

9	20	6	10	14	8	60	11

[saveF] [first]   [last]

(c) Decrement `last` until `values[last] <= splitVal`.

9	20	6	10	14	8	60	11

[saveF] [first]   [last]

(d) Swap `values[first]` and `values[last]`; move first and last
    toward each other.

9	8	6	10	14	20	60	11

[saveF]   [first]   [last]

(e) Increment `first` until `values[first] > splitVal` or `first > last`.
    Decrement `last` until `values[last] <= splitVal` or `first > last`.

9	8	6	10	14	20	60	11

[saveF]   [last] [first]

(f) `first > last` so no swap occurs within the loop.
    Swap `values[saveF]` and `values[last]`.

6	8	9	10	14	20	60	11

[saveF]   [last]
       (splitPoint)

Figure 11.13   The split operation

keep incrementing `first`; otherwise, we leave `first` where it is and begin moving `last` toward the middle (Figure 11.13b).

Now `values[last]` is compared to `splitVal`. If it is greater than `splitVal`, we continue decrementing `last`; otherwise, we leave `last` in place (Figure 11.13c). At this point, it is clear that both `values[last]` and `values[first]` are on the wrong sides of the array. The elements to the left of `values[first]` and to the right of `values[last]` are not necessarily sorted; they are just on the correct side of the array with respect to `splitVal`. To put `values[first]` and `values[last]` into their correct sides, we merely swap them; we then increment `first` and decrement `last` (Figure 11.13d).

Now we repeat the whole cycle, incrementing `first` until we encounter a value that is greater than `splitVal`, then decrementing `last` until we encounter a value that is less than or equal to `splitVal` (Figure 11.13e).

When does the process stop? When `first` and `last` meet each other, no further swaps are necessary. Where they meet determines the `splitPoint`. This is the location where `splitVal` belongs; so we swap `values[saveF]`, which contains `splitVal`, with the element at `values[last]` (Figure 11.13f). The index `last` is returned from the method, to be used by `quickSort` as the `splitPoint` for the next pair of recursive calls.

```
static int split(int first, int last)
{
  int splitVal = values[first];
  int saveF = first;
  boolean onCorrectSide;

  first++;
  do
  {
    onCorrectSide = true;
    while (onCorrectSide)      // move first toward last
      if (values[first] > splitVal)
        onCorrectSide = false;
      else
      {
        first++;
        onCorrectSide = (first <= last);
      }

    onCorrectSide = (first <= last);
    while (onCorrectSide)      // move last toward first
      if (values[last] <= splitVal)
        onCorrectSide = false;
      else
      {
      last--;
      onCorrectSide = (first <= last);
      }

    if (first < last)
    {
      swap(first, last);
      first++;
      last--;
    }
  } while (first <= last);

  swap(saveF, last);
  return last;
}
```

What happens if our splitting value is the largest value or the smallest value in the segment? The algorithm still works correctly, but because the split is lopsided, it is not so quick.

Is this situation likely to occur? That depends on how we choose our splitting value and on the original order of the data in the array. If we use `values[first]` as the splitting value and the array is already sorted, then *every* split is lopsided. One side contains one element, whereas the other side contains all but one of the elements. Thus our `quickSort` method is not a "quick" sort. Our splitting algorithm works best for an array in random order.

It is not unusual, however, to want to sort an array that is already in nearly sorted order. If this is the case, a better splitting value would be the middle value:

```
values[(first + last) / 2]
```

This value could be swapped with `values[first]` at the beginning of the method. It is also possible to sample three or more values in the subarray being sorted and to use their median. In some cases this will help prevent lopsided splits.

Analyzing `quickSort`

The analysis of `quickSort` is very similar to that of `mergeSort`. On the first call, every element in the array is compared to the dividing value (the "split value"), so the work done is O(N). The array is divided into two subarrays (not necessarily halves), which are then examined.

Each of these pieces is then divided in two, and so on. If each piece is split approximately in half, there are O($\log_2 N$) levels of splits. At each level, we make O(N) comparisons. Thus, the quick sort is also an O($N \log_2 N$) algorithm, which is quicker than the O(N^2) sorts we discussed at the beginning of this chapter.

But the quick sort is not always quicker. We have $\log_2 N$ levels of splits if each split divides the segment of the array approximately in half. As we have seen, the array division of the quick sort is sensitive to the order of the data—that is, to the choice of the splitting value.

What happens if the array is already sorted when our version of `quickSort` is called? The splits are very lopsided, and the subsequent recursive calls to `quickSort` break our data into a segment containing one element and a segment containing all the rest of the array. This situation produces a sort that is not at all quick. In fact, there are $N - 1$ levels; in this case, the complexity of the quick sort is O(N^2).

Such a situation is very unlikely to occur by chance. By way of analogy, consider the odds of shuffling a deck of cards and coming up with a sorted deck. Of course, in some applications we may know that the original array is likely to be sorted or nearly sorted. In such cases we would want to use either a different splitting algorithm or a different sort—maybe even `shortBubble`!

What about space requirements? A quick sort does not require an extra array, as a merge sort does. Are there any extra space requirements, besides the few local variables? Yes—recall that the quick sort uses a recursive approach. Many levels of recursion may be "saved" on the system stack at any time. On average, the algorithm requires O($\log_2 N$) extra space to hold this information and in the worst case requires O(N) extra space, the same as a merge sort.

Heap Sort

In each iteration of the selection sort, we searched the array for the next-smallest element and put it into its correct place in the array. Another way to write a selection sort is to find the maximum value in the array and swap it with the last array element, then find the next-to-largest element and put it into its place, and so on. Most of the work involved in this sorting algorithm comes from searching the remaining part of the array in each iteration, looking for the maximum value.

In Chapter 9, we discussed the *heap*, a data structure with a very special feature: We always know where to find its largest element. Because of the order property of heaps, the maximum value of a heap is in the root node. We can take advantage of this situation by using a heap to help us sort data. The general approach of the heap sort is as follows:

1. Take the root (maximum) element off the heap, and put it into its place.
2. Reheap the remaining elements. (This puts the next-largest element into the root position.)
3. Repeat until there are no more elements.

The first part of this algorithm sounds a lot like the selection sort. What makes the heap sort rapid is the second step: finding the next-largest element. Because the shape property of heaps guarantees a binary tree of minimum height, we make only $O(\log_2 N)$ comparisons in each iteration, as compared with $O(N)$ comparisons in each iteration of the selection sort.

Building a Heap

By now you are probably protesting that we are dealing with an unsorted array of elements, not a heap. Where does the original heap come from? Before we go on, we have to convert the unsorted array, `values`, into a heap.

Look at how the heap relates to our array of unsorted elements. In Chapter 9, we saw how heaps can be represented in an array with implicit links. Because of the shape property, we know that the heap elements take up consecutive positions in the array. In fact, the unsorted array of data elements already satisfies the shape property of heaps. **Figure 11.14** shows an unsorted array and its equivalent tree.

We also need to make the unsorted array elements satisfy the order property of heaps. First, we need to discover whether any part of the tree already satisfies the order property. All of the leaf nodes (subtrees with only a single node) are heaps. In **Figure 11.15a**, the subtrees whose roots contain the values 19, 7, 3, 100, and 1 are heaps because they consist solely of root nodes.

Now let us look at the first *nonleaf* node, the one containing the value 2 (Figure 11.15b). The subtree rooted at this node is not a heap, but it is *almost* a heap—all of the nodes *except the root node* of this subtree satisfy the order property. We know how to fix this problem. In Chapter 9, we developed a heap utility method, `reheapDown`, that we can use to handle this same situation. Given a tree whose elements satisfy the order property of heaps, except that the tree has an empty root, and a value to insert into the heap,

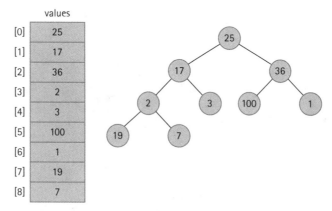

Figure 11.14 An unsorted array and its tree

reheapDown rearranges the nodes, leaving the (sub)tree containing the new element as a heap. We can just invoke reheapDown on the subtree, passing it the current root value of the subtree as the element to be inserted.

We apply this method to all the subtrees on this level, and then we move up a level in the tree and continue reheaping until we reach the root node. After reheapDown has been called for the root node, the entire tree should satisfy the order property of heaps. Figure 11.15 illustrates this heap-building process; **Figure 11.16** shows the changing contents of the array.

In Chapter 9, we defined reheapDown as a private method of the Heap class. There, the method had only one parameter: the element being inserted into the heap. It always worked on the entire tree; that is, it always started with an empty node at index 0 and assumed that the last tree index of the heap was lastIndex. Here, we use a slight variation: reheapDown is a static method of our Sorts class that takes a second parameter—the index of the node that is the root of the subtree that is to be made into a heap. This is an easy change; if we call the parameter root, we simply add the following statement to the beginning of the reheapDown method:

```
int hole = root;        // Current index of hole
```

The algorithm for building a heap is summarized here:

---

buildHeap

for index going from first nonleaf node up to the root node
    reheapDown(values[index], index)

We know where the root node is stored in our array representation of heaps: values[0]. Where is the first nonleaf node? From our knowledge of the array-based representation of a complete binary tree we know the first nonleaf node is found at position SIZE/2 - 1.

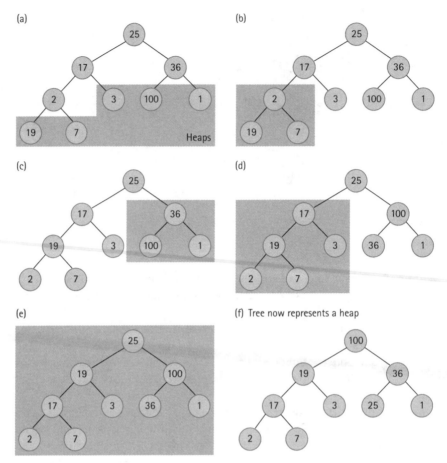

Figure 11.15 The heap-building process

	[0]	[1]	[2]	[3]	[4]	[5]	[6]	[7]	[8]
Original values	25	17	36	2	3	100	1	19	7
After reheapDown index = 3	25	17	36	19	3	100	1	2	7
After index = 2	25	17	100	19	3	36	1	2	7
After index = 1	25	19	100	17	3	36	1	2	7
After index = 0	100	19	36	17	3	25	1	2	7

Tree is a heap.

Figure 11.16 Changing contents of the array

During this heap construction the furthest any node moves is equal to its distance from a leaf. The sum of these distances in a complete tree is O(N), so building a heap in this manner is an O(N) operation.

Sorting Using the Heap

Now that we are satisfied that we can turn the unsorted array of elements into a heap, let us take another look at the sorting algorithm.

We can easily access the largest element from the original heap—it is in the root node. In our array representation of heaps, the location of the largest element is `values[0]`. This value belongs in the last-used array position `values[SIZE - 1]`, so we can just swap the values in these two positions. Because `values[SIZE - 1]` now contains the largest value in the array (its correct sorted value), we want to leave this position alone. Now we are dealing with a set of elements, from `values[0]` through `values[SIZE - 2]`, that is almost a heap. We know that all of these elements satisfy the order property of heaps, except (perhaps) the root node. To correct this condition, we call our heap utility, `reheapDown`. (But our original `reheapDown` method assumed that the heap's tree ends at position `lastIndex`. We must again redefine `reheapDown`, so that it now accepts three parameters, with the third being the ending index of the heap. Once again the change is easy; the new code for `reheapDown` is included in the `Sorts` class.)

After `reheapDown` returns we know that the next-largest element in the array is in the root node of the heap. To put this element in its correct position, we swap it with the element in `values[SIZE - 2]`. Now the two largest elements are in their final correct positions, and the elements in `values[0]` through `values[SIZE - 3]` are almost a heap. We call `reheapDown` again, and now the third-largest element is in the root of the heap.

We repeat this process until all of the elements are in their correct positions—that is, until the heap contains only a single element, which must be the smallest element in the array, in `values[0]`. This is its correct position, so the array is now completely sorted from the smallest to the largest element. At each iteration, the size of the unsorted portion (represented as a heap) gets smaller and the size of the sorted portion gets larger. When the algorithm ends, the size of the sorted portion is the size of the original array.

The heap sort algorithm, as we have described it here, sounds like a recursive process: each time, we swap and reheap a smaller portion of the total array. Because it uses tail recursion, we can code the repetition just as clearly using a simple *for* loop. The node-sorting algorithm is as follows:

Sort Nodes

for index going from last node up to next-to-root node
  Swap data in root node with values[index]
  reheapDown(values[0], 0, index − 1)

Method `heapSort` first builds the heap and then sorts the nodes, using the algorithms just discussed.

```
static void heapSort()
// Post: The elements in the array values are sorted by key
{
  int index;
  // Convert the array of values into a heap
  for (index = SIZE/2 - 1; index >= 0; index--)
    reheapDown(values[index], index, SIZE - 1);

  // Sort the array
  for (index = SIZE - 1; index >=1; index--)
  {
    swap(0, index);
    reheapDown(values[0], 0, index - 1);
  }
}
```

Figure 11.17 shows how each iteration of the sorting loop (the second *for* loop) would change the heap created in Figure 11.16. Each line represents the array after one operation. The sorted elements are shaded.

	[0]	[1]	[2]	[3]	[4]	[5]	[6]	[7]	[8]
values	100	19	36	17	3	25	1	2	7
swap	7	19	36	17	3	25	1	2	100
reheapDown	36	19	25	17	3	7	1	2	100
swap	2	19	25	17	3	7	1	36	100
reheapDown	25	19	7	17	3	2	1	36	100
swap	1	19	7	17	3	2	25	36	100
reheapDown	19	17	7	1	3	2	25	36	100
swap	2	17	7	1	3	19	25	36	100
reheapDown	17	3	7	1	2	19	25	36	100
swap	2	3	7	1	17	19	25	36	100
reheapDown	7	3	2	1	17	19	25	36	100
swap	1	3	2	7	17	19	25	36	100
reheapDown	3	1	2	7	17	19	25	36	100
swap	2	1	3	7	17	19	25	36	100
reheapDown	2	1	3	7	17	19	25	36	100
swap	1	2	3	7	17	19	25	36	100
reheapDown	1	2	3	7	17	19	25	36	100
Exit from sorting loop	1	2	3	7	17	19	25	36	100

Figure 11.17 Effect of `heapSort` on the array

We entered the `heapSort` method with a simple array of unsorted values and returned with an array of the same values sorted in ascending order. Where did the heap go? The heap in `heapSort` is just a temporary structure, internal to the sorting algorithm. It is created at the beginning of the method to aid in the sorting process, but then is methodically diminished element by element as the sorted part of the array grows. When the method ends, the sorted part fills the array and the heap has completely disappeared. When we used heaps to implement priority queues in Chapter 9, the heap structure stayed around for the duration of the use of the priority queue. The heap in `heapSort`, by contrast, is not a retained data structure. It exists only temporarily, during the execution of the `heapSort` method.

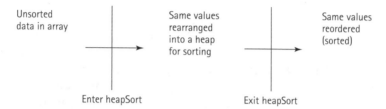

Analyzing `heapSort`

The code for method `heapSort` is very short—only a few lines of new code plus the helper method `reheapDown`, which we developed in Chapter 9 (albeit slightly revised). These few lines of code, however, do quite a bit of work. All of the elements in the original array are rearranged to satisfy the order property of heaps, moving the largest element up to the top of the array, only to put it immediately into its place at the bottom. It is hard to believe from a small example such as the one in Figures 11.16 and 11.17 that `heapSort` is very efficient.

In fact, for small arrays, `heapSort` is not very efficient because of its "overhead." For large arrays, however, `heapSort` is very efficient. Consider the sorting loop. We loop through $N - 1$ times, swapping elements and `reheaping`. The comparisons occur in `reheapDown` (actually in its helper method `newHole`). A complete binary tree with N nodes has $\lfloor \log_2 N \rfloor$ levels. In the worst case, if the root element had to be bumped down to a leaf position, the `reheapDown` method would make O($\log_2 N$) comparisons. Thus method `reheapDown` is O($\log_2 N$). Multiplying this activity by the $N - 1$ iterations shows that the sorting loop is O($N \log_2 N$).

Combining the original heap build that is O(N), and the sorting loop, we can see that the heap sort requires O($N \log_2 N$) comparisons. Unlike the quick sort, the heap sort's efficiency is not affected by the initial order of the elements. Even in the worst case it is O($N \log_2 N$). A heap sort is just as efficient in terms of space; only one array is used to store the data. The heap sort requires only constant extra space.

The heap sort is an elegant, fast, robust, space-efficient algorithm!

11.4 More Sorting Considerations

This section wraps up our coverage of sorting by revisiting testing and efficiency, considering the "stability" of sorting algorithms, and discussing special concerns involved with sorting objects rather than primitive types.

Testing

All of our sorts are implemented within the test harness presented in Section 11.1, "Sorting." That test harness program, `Sorts`, allows us to generate a random array of size 50, sort it with one of our algorithms, and view the sorted array. It is easy to determine whether the sort was successful. If we do not want to verify success by eyeballing the output, we can always use a call to the `isSorted` method of the `Sorts` class.

The `Sorts` program is a useful tool for helping evaluate the correctness of our sorting methods. To thoroughly test them, however, we should vary the size of the array they are sorting. A small revision to `Sorts`, allowing the user to pass the array size as a command line parameter, would facilitate this process. We should also vary the original order of the array—for example, test an array that is in reverse order, one that is almost sorted, and one that has all identical elements (to make sure we do not generate an "array index out of bounds" error).

Besides validating that our sort methods create a sorted array, we can check their performance. At the start of the sorting phase we can initialize two variables, `numSwaps` and `numCompares`, to 0. By carefully placing statements incrementing these variables throughout our code, we can use them to track how many times the code performs swaps and comparisons. Once we output these values, we can compare them to the predicted theoretical values. Inconsistencies would require further review of the code (or maybe the theory!).

Efficiency

When *N* Is Small

As emphasized throughout this chapter, our analysis of efficiency relies on the number of comparisons made by a sorting algorithm. This number gives us a rough estimate of the computation time involved. The other activities that accompany the comparison (swapping, keeping track of `boolean` flags, and so forth) contribute to the "constant of proportionality" of the algorithm.

In comparing order of growth evaluations, we ignored constants and smaller-order terms because we want to know how the algorithm performs for large values of N. In general, an $O(N^2)$ sort requires few extra activities in addition to the comparisons, so its constant of proportionality is fairly small. Conversely, an $O(N \log_2 N)$ sort may be more complex, with more overhead and thus a larger constant of proportionality. This situation may cause anomalies in the relative performances of the algorithms when the value of N

is small. In this case, N^2 is not much greater than $N \log_2 N$, and the constants may dominate instead, causing an $O(N^2)$ sort to run faster than an $O(N \log_2 N)$ sort. A programmer can leverage this fact to improve the running time of sort code, by having the code switch between an $O(N \log_2 N)$ sort for large portions of the array and an $O(N^2)$ sort for small portions.

We have discussed sorting algorithms that have complexity of either $O(N^2)$ or $(N \log_2 N)$. Now we ask an obvious question: Do algorithms that are better than $(N \log_2 N)$ exist? No, it has been proven theoretically that we cannot do better than $(N \log_2 N)$ for sorting algorithms that are based on comparing keys—that is, on pairwise comparison of elements.

Eliminating Calls to Methods

Sometimes it may be desirable, for efficiency reasons, to streamline the code as much as possible, even at the expense of readability. For instance, we have consistently used

```
swap(index1, index2);
```

when we wanted to swap two elements in the `values` array. We would achieve slightly better execution efficiency by dropping the method call and directly coding

```
tempValue = values[index1];
values[index1] = values[index2];
values[index2] = tempValue;
```

Coding the swap operation as a method made the code simpler to write and to understand, avoiding a cluttered sort method. However, method calls require extra overhead that we may prefer to avoid during a real sort, where the method is called over and over again within a loop.

The recursive sorting methods, `mergeSort` and `quickSort`, bring up a similar situation: They require the extra overhead involved in executing the recursive calls. We may want to avoid this overhead by coding nonrecursive versions of these methods.

In some cases, an optimizing compiler replaces method calls with the inline expansion of the code of the method. In that case, we get the benefits of both readability and efficiency.

Programmer Time

If the recursive calls are less efficient, why would anyone ever decide to use a recursive version of a sort? This decision involves a choice between types of efficiency. Until now, we have been concerned only with minimizing computer time. While computers are becoming faster and cheaper, however, it is not at all clear that computer programmers are following that trend. In fact, programmers are becoming more expensive. Therefore, in some situations, programmer time may be an important consideration in choosing an algorithm and its implementation. In this respect, the recursive version of the quick sort is more desirable than its nonrecursive counterpart, which requires the programmer to simulate recursion.

If a programmer is familiar with a language's support library, the programmer can use the sort routines provided there. The `Arrays` class in the Java library's `util` package defines a number of sorts for sorting arrays. Likewise, the Java Collections Framework, which was introduced in Section 2.10, "Stack Variations," provides methods for sorting many of its collection objects.

Space Considerations

Another efficiency consideration is the amount of memory space required. In small applications, memory space is not a very important factor in choosing a sorting algorithm. In large applications, such as a database with many gigabytes of data, space may pose a serious concern. We looked at only two sorts, `mergeSort` and `quickSort`, that required more than constant extra space. The usual time versus space trade-off applies to sorts: More space often means less time, and vice versa.

Because processing time is the factor that applies most often to sorting algorithms, we have considered it in detail here. Of course, as in any application, the programmer must determine the program's goals and requirements before selecting an algorithm and starting to code.

Objects and References

So that we could concentrate on the algorithms, we limited our implementations to sorting arrays of integers. Do the same approaches work for sorting objects? Of course, although a few special considerations apply.

Keep in mind that when we sort an array of objects, we are manipulating references to the objects, not the objects themselves (**Figure 11.18**). This point does not affect any of our algorithms, but it is still important to understand. For example, if we decide to swap the objects at index 0 and index 1 of an array, it is actually the references to the objects that we swap, not the objects themselves. In one sense, we view objects, and the references to the objects, as identical, because using a reference is the only way we can access an object.

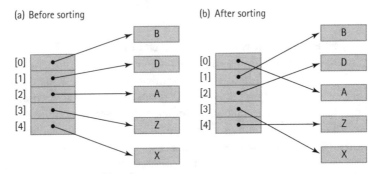

Figure 11.18   Sorting arrays with references

Comparing Objects

When sorting objects, we must have a way to compare two objects and decide which is "larger." Two basic approaches are used when dealing with Java objects, both of which you are familiar with from previous chapters. If the object class exports a `compareTo` operation, or something similar, it can be used to provide the needed comparison.

As we have seen, the Java library provides another interface related to comparing objects, a generic interface called `Comparator`. A programmer can define more than one `Comparator` for a class, allowing more flexibility.

Any sort implementation must compare elements. Our sorting methods so far have used built-in integer comparison operations such as `<` or `<=`. If we sort `Comparable` objects instead of integers, we could use the `compareTo` method that is guaranteed to exist by that interface. Alternatively, we could use the versatile approach supported by the `Comparator` interface. If we pass a `Comparator` object `comp` to a sorting method as a parameter, the method can use `comp.compare` to determine the relative order of two objects and base its sort on that relative order. Passing a different `Comparator` object results in a different sorting order. Perhaps one `Comparator` object defines an increasing order, and another defines a decreasing order. Or perhaps the different `Comparator` objects could define order based on different attributes of the objects. Now, with a single sorting method, we can produce many different sort orders.

Stability

The stability of a sorting algorithm is based on what it does with duplicate values. Of course, the duplicate values all appear consecutively in the final order. For example, if we sort the list A B B A, we get A A B B. But is the relative order of the duplicates the same in the final order as it was in the original order? If that property is guaranteed, we have a **stable sort**.

In our descriptions of the various sorts, we showed examples of sorting arrays of integers. Stability is not important when sorting primitive types. If we sort objects, however, the stability of a sorting algorithm can become more important. We may want to preserve the original order of unique objects considered identical by the comparison operation.

Suppose the elements in our array are student objects with instance values representing their names, postal codes, and identification numbers. The list may normally be sorted by the unique identification numbers. For some purposes we might want to see a listing in order by name. In this case the comparison would be based on the name variable. To sort by postal code, we would sort on that instance variable.

If the sort is stable, we can get a listing by postal code, with the names in alphabetical order within each postal code, by sorting twice: the first time by name and the second time by postal code. A stable sort preserves the order of the elements when it finds a match. The second sort, by postal code, produces many such matches, but the alphabetical order imposed by the first sort is preserved.

Of the various types of sorts that we have discussed in this text, only `heapSort` and `quickSort` are inherently unstable. The stability of the other sorts depends on how the code handles duplicate values. In some cases, stability depends on whether a $<$ or a $<=$ comparison is used in some crucial comparison statement. In the exercises at the end of this chapter, you are asked to examine the code for the various sorts and determine whether they are stable.

If we can directly control the comparison operation used by our sort method, we can allow more than one variable to be used in determining a sort order. Thus another, more efficient approach to sorting our students by ZIP code and name is to define an appropriate `compareTo` method for determining sort order as follows (for simplicity, this code assumes we can directly compare the name values):

```
if (postalcode < other.postalcode)
   return -1;
else
if (postalcode > other.postalcode)
   return +1;
else
// Postal codes are equal
if (name < other.name)
   return -1;
else
if (name > other.name)
   return +1;
else
   return 0;
```

With this approach we need to sort the array only once.

11.5 Searching

This section reviews material scattered throughout the text related to searching. Here we bring these topics together to be considered in relationship to each other to gain an overall perspective. Searching is a crucially important information processing activity. Options are closely related to the way data is structured and organized.

Sometimes access to a needed element stored in a collection can be achieved directly. For example, with both our array-based and link-based stack ADT implementations, we can directly access the top element on the stack; the top method is $O(1)$. Access to our array-based indexed lists, given a position on the list, is also direct; $O(1)$ time is needed. Often, however, direct access is not possible, especially when we want to access an element based on its value. For instance, if a list contains student records, we may want to find the record of the student named Suzy Brown or the record of the student whose ID number is 203557. In such cases, some kind of *searching technique* is needed to allow retrieval of the desired record.

In this section we look at some of the basic "search by value" techniques for collections. Most of these techniques were encountered previously in the text—sequential search in Section 1.6, binary search in Sections 1.6 and 3.3, and hashing in Section 8.4.

Sequential Searching

We cannot discuss efficient ways to find an element in a collection without considering how the elements were added into the collection. Therefore, our discussion of search algorithms is related to the issue of a collection's add operation. Suppose that we want to add elements as quickly as possible, and are not overly concerned about how long it takes to find them. We would put the element into the last slot in an array-based collection or the first slot in a linked collection. Both are O(1) insertion algorithms. The resulting collection is sorted according to the time of insertion, not according to key value.

To search this collection for the element with a given key, we must use a simple *sequential* (or *linear*) *search*. For example, we used a sequential search for the find method of our ArrayCollection class in Chapter 5. Beginning with the first element in the collection, we search for the desired element by examining each subsequent element's key until either the search is successful or the collection is exhausted.

Based on the number of comparisons, this search is O(N), where N represents the number of elements. In the worst case, in which we are looking for the last element in the collection or for a nonexistent element, we will make N key comparisons. On average, assuming that there is an equal probability of searching for any element in the collection, we will make N/2 comparisons for a successful search; that is, on average we must search half of the collection.

High-Probability Ordering

The assumption of equal probability for every element in the collection is not always valid. Sometimes certain collection elements are in much greater demand than others. This observation suggests a way to improve the search: Put the most-often-desired elements at the beginning of the collection.[1] Using this scheme, we are more likely to make a hit in the first few tries, and rarely do we have to search the whole collection.

If the elements in the collection are not static or if we cannot predict their relative demand, we need some scheme to keep the most frequently used elements at the front of the collection. One way to accomplish this goal is to move each element accessed to the front of the collection. Of course, there is no guarantee that this element is later frequently used. If the element is not retrieved again, however, it drifts toward the end of the collection as other elements move to the front. This scheme is easy to implement for linked collections,

---

[1] This approach cannot be used with sorted or indexed lists, because with those lists the positions of elements is predetermined.

requiring only a few pointer changes. It is less desirable for collections kept sequentially in arrays, because we need to move all the other elements down to make room at the front.

An alternative approach, which causes elements to move toward the front of the collection gradually, is appropriate for either linked or array-based collection representations. As an element is found, it is swapped with the element that precedes it. Over many collection retrievals, the most frequently desired elements tend to be grouped at the front of the collection. To implement this approach, we need to modify only the end of the algorithm to exchange the found element with the one before it in the collection (unless it is the first element). This change should be documented; it is an unexpected side effect of searching the collection.

Keeping the most active elements at the front of the collection does not affect the worst case; if the search value is the last element or is not in the collection, the search still takes N comparisons. It is still an O(N) search. However, the *average* performance on successful searches should improve. Both of these high-probability ordering algorithms depend on the assumption that some elements in the collection are used much more often than others. If this assumption is erroneous, a different ordering strategy is needed to improve the efficiency of the search technique.

Collections in which the relative positions of the elements are changed in an attempt to improve search efficiency are called **self-organizing** or **self-adjusting collections**.

Sorted Collections

As discussed in Section 1.6, "Comparing Algorithms," if a collection is sorted, we can write more efficient search routines.

First of all, if the collection is sorted, a sequential search no longer needs to search the whole collection to discover that an element does *not* exist. It just needs to search until it has passed the element's logical place in the collection—that is, until it encounters an element with a larger key value.

Therefore, one advantage of sequential searching a sorted collection is the ability to stop searching before the collection is exhausted if the element does not exist. Again, the search is O(N)—the worst case, searching for the largest element, still requires N comparisons. The average number of comparisons for an unsuccessful search is now $N/2$, however, instead of a guaranteed N.

Another advantage of sequential searching is its simplicity. The disadvantage is its performance: In the worst case we have to make N comparisons. If the collection is sorted and stored in an array, we can improve the search time to a worst case of O($\log_2 N$) by using a binary search (see Section 1.6, "Comparing Algorithms"). This improvement in efficiency, however, comes at the expense of simplicity.

The binary search is not guaranteed to be faster for searching very small collections. Even though such a search generally requires fewer comparisons, each comparison involves more computation. When N is very small, this extra work (the constants and smaller terms that we ignore in determining the order of growth approximation) may dominate. For instance, in one assembly-language program, the sequential search required 5 time units per comparison, whereas the binary search took 35. For a collection size of 16 elements, therefore, the worst-case sequential search would require 5 * 16 = 80 time units. The worst-case binary search requires only 4 comparisons, but at 35 time units each, the comparisons take 140 time units. In cases where the number of elements in the collection is small, a sequential search is certainly adequate and sometimes faster than a binary search.

As the number of elements increases, the magnitude of the difference between the sequential search and the binary search grows very quickly. Look back at the Vocabulary Density experiment results in Table 5.1 on page 324 for an example of this effect.

The binary search discussed here is appropriate only for collection elements stored in a sequential array-based representation. After all, how can we efficiently find the mid-point of a linked collection? We already know one structure that allows us to perform a binary search on a linked data representation: the binary search tree. The operations used to search a binary tree were discussed in Chapter 7.

Hashing

So far, we have succeeded in paring down our $O(N)$ search to a complexity of $O(\log_2 N)$ by keeping the collection sorted sequentially with respect to the key value. That is, the key in the first element is less than (or equal to) the key in the second element, which is less than (or equal to) the key in the third, and so on. Can we do better than that? Is it possible to design a search of $O(1)$—that is, one with a constant search time, no matter where the element is in the collection? Yes, the hash table approach to storage presented in Sections 4 through 6 of Chapter 8 allows constant search time in many situations.

If our hash function is efficient, never produces duplicates and the hash table size is large compared to the expected number of entries in the collection, then we have reached our goal—constant search time. In general, this is not the case, although in many practical situations it is possible.

Clearly, as the number of entries in a collection approaches the size of the hash table's internal array, the efficiency of the hash table deteriorates. This is why the load of the hash table is monitored. If the table needs to be resized and the entries all rehashed there is a one-time heavy cost incurred.

As discussed in Chapter 8, a precise analysis of the complexity of hashing is difficult. It depends on the domain and distribution of keys, the hash function, the size of the table, and the collision resolution policy. In practice it is usually not difficult to achieve close to $O(1)$ efficiency using hashing. For any given application area it is possible to test variations of hashing schemes to see which works best.

Summary

We have not attempted in this chapter to describe every known sorting algorithm. Instead, we presented a few of the popular sorts, of which many variations exist. It should be clear from this discussion that no single sort is best for all applications. The simpler, generally $O(N^2)$ sorts work as well as, and sometimes better than, the more complicated sorts for fairly small values of N. Because they are simple, these sorts require relatively little programmer time to write and maintain. As we add features to improve sorts, we also increase the complexity of the algorithms, expanding both the work required by the routines and the programmer time needed to maintain them.

Another consideration in choosing a sort algorithm is the order of the original data. If the data are already sorted (or almost sorted), shortBubble is $O(N)$, whereas some versions of quickSort are $O(N^2)$.

As always, the first step in choosing an algorithm is to determine the goals of the particular application. This effort usually narrows the choice of options considerably. After that, knowledge of the strong and weak points of the various algorithms assists us in selecting a sorting method.

Table 11.3 compares the sorts discussed in this chapter in terms of O notation.

Searching, similar to sorting, is a topic that is closely tied to the goal of efficiency. We speak of a sequential search of a collection as an $O(N)$ search, because it may require as many as N comparisons to locate an element. (N refers to the number of elements in the collection.) Binary searches are considered to be $O(\log_2 N)$ and are appropriate for array-based collections if they are sorted. A binary search tree may be used to allow binary searches on a linked structure. The goal of hashing is to produce a search that approaches $O(1)$ time efficiency. Because of collisions of hash locations, some searching is usually necessary. A good hash function minimizes collisions and distributes the elements randomly throughout the table.

Table 11.3 Comparison of Sorting Algorithms

Sort	Order of Growth		
	Best Case	Average Case	Worst Case
selectionSort	$O(N^2)$	$O(N^2)$	$O(N^2)$
bubbleSort	$O(N^2)$	$O(N^2)$	$O(N^2)$
shortBubble	$O(N)^*$	$O(N^2)$	$O(N^2)$
insertionSort	$O(N)^*$	$O(N^2)$	$O(N^2)$
mergeSort	$O(N \log_2 N)$	$O(N \log_2 N)$	$O(N \log_2 N)$
quickSort	$O(N \log_2 N)$	$O(N \log_2 N)$	$O(N^2)$ (depends on split)
heapSort	$O(N \log_2 N)$	$O(N \log_2 N)$	$O(N \log_2 N)$

*Data almost sorted.

In the chapter introduction we addressed the fact that modern programming environments usually provide predefined sort and search facilities. Professional programmers usually use these packaged sort and search tools when they need to sort/search data. Nevertheless, as a student of computing, it is good for you to become familiar with basic sorting and searching techniques.

Exercises

11.1 Sorting

1. A test harness program for testing sorting methods is provided with the program files. It is in the file `Sorts.java` in the `ch11.sorts` package. The program includes a swap method that is used by all of the sorting methods to swap array elements.

   a. Describe an approach to modifying the program so that after calling a sorting method the program prints out the number of swaps needed by the sorting method.

   b. Implement your approach.

   c. Test your new program by running the `selectionSort` method. Your program should report 49 swaps.

11.2 Simple Sorts

2. Determine the order of growth complexity for the selection sort based on the number of elements moved rather than on the number of comparisons

   a. For the best case.

   b. For the worst case.

3. In what case(s), if any, is the complexity of the selection sort $O(\log_2 N)$?

4. Write a version of the bubble sort algorithm that sorts a list of integers in descending order.

5. In what case(s), if any, is the complexity of the bubble sort $O(N)$?

6. How many comparisons would be needed to sort an array containing 100 elements using `shortBubble`

   a. in the worst case?

   b. in the best case?

7. Show the contents of the array

43	7	10	23	18	4	19	5	66	14
[0]	[1]	[2]	[3]	[4]	[5]	[6]	[7]	[8]	[9]

after the fourth iteration of

a. `selectionSort`.

b. `bubbleSort`.

c. `insertionSort`.

8. For each of the sorting algorithms presented in Section 11.2 (selection sort, bubble sort, short bubble, and insertion sort) how many comparisons would be needed to sort an array containing 100 elements if the original array values

a. were already sorted?

b. were sorted in reverse order?

c. were all identical?

9. Repeat Exercise 8 but report the number of "swaps."

10. In Exercise 1 you were asked to modify the `Sorts` program so that it would output the number of swaps used by a sorting method. It is a little more difficult to have the program also output the number of comparisons (compares) needed. You must include one or more statements to increment your counter within the sorting methods themselves. For each of the listed methods, make and test the changes needed, and list both the number of swaps and the number of compares needed by the `Sorts` program to sort an array of 50 random integers.

a. `selectionSort`   swaps: ____   compares: ____

b. `bubbleSort`   swaps: ____   compares: ____

c. `shortBubble`   swaps: ____   compares: ____

d. `insertionSort`   swaps: ____   compares: ____

11.3 O($N \log_2 N$) Sorts

11. A merge sort is used to sort an array of 1,000 test scores in descending order. Which one of the following statements is true?

a. The sort is fastest if the original test scores are sorted from smallest to largest.

b. The sort is fastest if the original test scores are in completely random order.

c. The sort is fastest if the original test scores are sorted from largest to smallest.

d. The sort is the same, no matter what the order of the original elements.

12. Show how the values in the array in Exercise 7 would be arranged immediately before the execution of method `merge` in the original (nonrecursive) call to `mergeSort`.

13. Determine the order of growth complexity for `mergeSort` based on the number of elements moved rather than on the number of comparisons

a. for the best case.

b. for the worst case.

14. Use the Three-Question Method to verify `mergeSort`.

15. In what case(s), if any, is the complexity of the quick sort $O(N^2)$?

16. Which is true about the quick sort?

    a. A recursive version executes faster than a nonrecursive version.

    b. A recursive version has fewer lines of code than a nonrecursive version.

    c. A nonrecursive version takes more space on the run-time stack than a recursive version.

    d. It can be programmed only as a recursive function.

17. Determine the order of growth complexity for `quickSort` based on the number of elements moved rather than on the number of comparisons

    a. for the best case.

    b. for the worst case.

18. Use the Three-Question Method to verify `quickSort`.

19. Using the algorithms for creating a heap and sorting an array using a heap-based approach:

    a. Show how the values in the array in Exercise 7 would have to be rearranged to satisfy the heap property.

    b. Show how the array would look with four values in the sorted portion after reheaping.

20. A sorting function is called to sort a list of 100 integers that have been read from a file. If all 100 values are zero, what would the execution costs (in terms of O notation) be if the sort used was

    a. `mergeSort`?

    b. `quickSort`, with the first element used as the split value?

    c. `heapSort`?

21. Suppose a list is already sorted from smallest to largest when a sort is called. Which of the following sorts would take the longest time to execute and which would take the shortest time?

    a. `quickSort`, with the first element used as the split value

    b. `shortBubble`

    c. `selectionSort`

    d. `heapSort`

    e. `insertionSort`

    f. `mergeSort`

22. A very large array of elements is to be sorted. The program will be run on a personal computer with limited memory. Which sort would be a better choice: a heap sort or a merge sort? Why?

23. True or False? Explain your answers.

    a. `mergeSort` requires more space to execute than `heapSort`.

    b. `quickSort` (using the first element as the split value) is better for nearly sorted data than `heapSort`.

    c. The efficiency of `heapSort` is not affected by the original order of the elements.

24. In Exercise 1 you were asked to modify the `Sorts` program so that it would output the number of swaps used by a sorting method. It is a little more difficult to have the program also output the number of comparisons needed. You must include one or more statements to increment your counter within the sorting methods themselves. For each of the listed methods, make and test the changes needed, and list the number of comparisons needed by `Sorts` to sort an array of 50 random integers.

    a. `mergeSort`   compares: ____

    b. `quicksort`   compares: ____

    c. `heapSort`   compares: ____

11.4 More Sorting Considerations

25. For small values of N, the number of steps required for an $O(N^2)$ sort might be less than the number of steps required for a sort of a lower degree. For each of the following pairs of mathematical functions f and g below, determine a value N such that if $n > N$, $g(n) > f(n)$. This value represents the cutoff point, above which the $O(n^2)$ function is always larger than the other function.

    a. $f(n) = 4n$ $g(n) = n^2 + 1$

    b. $f(n) = 3n + 20$ $g(n) = \frac{1}{2}n^2 + 2$

    c. $f(n) = 4\log_2 n + 10$ $g(n) = n^2$

    d. $f(n) = 100\log_2 n$ $g(n) = n^2$

    e. $f(n) = 1000\log_2 n$ $g(n) = n^2$

26. Give arguments for and against using methods (such as `swap`) to encapsulate frequently used code in a sorting routine.

27. What is meant by this statement: "Programmer time is an efficiency consideration." Give an example of a situation in which programmer time is used to justify the choice of an algorithm, possibly at the expense of other efficiency considerations.

28. Go through the sorting algorithms coded in this chapter and determine which ones are stable as coded. Identify the key statement in the corresponding method that determines the stability.

29. We said that the heap sort algorithm is inherently unstable. Explain why.

30. Which sorting algorithm would you *not* use under each of the following conditions?

    a. The sort must be stable.

    b. Space is very limited.

11.5 Searching

31. Fill in the following table, showing the number of comparisons needed either to find the value or to determine that the value is not in the indicated structure based on the given approach and given the following values:

26, 15, 27, 12, 33, 95, 9, 5, 99, 14

Value	Unsorted Array in the order shown, Sequential Search	Sorted Array, Sequential Search	Sorted Array, BinarySearch	Binary Search Tree with elements added in the order shown
15				
17				
14				
5				
99				
100				
0				

32. If you know the index of an element stored in an array of N unsorted elements, which of the following best describes the order of the algorithm to find the element?

a. $O(1)$

b. $O(N)$

c. $O(\log_2 N)$

d. $O(N^2)$

e. $O(0.5N)$

33. The element being searched for *is not* in an array of 100 elements. What is the *average* number of comparisons needed in a sequential search to determine that the element is not there

a. if the elements are completely unsorted?

b. if the elements are sorted from smallest to largest?

c. if the elements are sorted from largest to smallest?

34. The element being searched for *is not* in an array of 100 elements. What is the *maximum* number of comparisons needed in a sequential search to determine that the element is not there

    a. if the elements are completely unsorted?

    b. if the elements are sorted from smallest to largest?

    c. if the elements are sorted from largest to smallest?

35. The element being searched for *is* in an array of 100 elements. What is the *average* number of comparisons needed in a sequential search to determine the position of the element

    a. if the elements are completely unsorted?

    b. if the elements are sorted from smallest to largest?

    c. if the elements are sorted from largest to smallest?

36. Choose the answer that correctly completes the following sentence: The elements in an array may be sorted by highest probability of being requested to reduce

    a. the average number of comparisons needed to find an element in the list.

    b. the maximum number of comparisons needed to detect that an element is not in the list.

    c. the average number of comparisons needed to detect that an element is not in the list.

    d. the maximum number of comparisons needed to find an element that is in the list.

37. True or False? Explain your answers.

    a. A binary search of a sorted set of elements in an array is always faster than a sequential search of the elements.

    b. A binary search is an $O(N \log_2 N)$ algorithm.

    c. A binary search of elements in an array requires that the elements be sorted from smallest to largest.

    d. A high-probability ordering scheme would be a poor choice for arranging an array of elements that are equally likely to be requested.

38. How might you order the elements in a list of Java's reserved words to use the idea of high-probability ordering?

© Ake Bild/Shutterstock

Appendices

Appendix A

Java Reserved Words

abstract	continue	for	new	switch
assert	default	goto	package	synchronized
boolean	do	if	private	this
break	double	implements	protected	throw
byte	else	import	public	throws
case	enum	instanceof	return	transient
catch	extends	int	short	try
char	final	interface	static	void
class	finally	long	strictfp	volatile
const	float	native	super	while

Appendix B

Operator Precedence

In the following table, the operators are grouped by precedence level (highest to lowest), and a horizontal line separates each precedence level from the next-lower level.

Precedence (highest to lowest)

Operator	Assoc.*	Operand Type(s)	Operation Performed
.	LR	object, member	object member access
[]	LR	array, int	array element access
(args)	LR	method, arglist	method invocation
++, --	LR	variable	post-increment, decrement
++, --	RL	variable	pre-increment, decrement
+, -	RL	number	unary plus, unary minus
~	RL	integer	bitwise complement
!	RL	boolean	boolean NOT
new	RL	class, arglist	object creation
(type)	RL	type, any	cast (type conversion)
*, /, %	LR	number, number	multiplication, division, remainder
+, -	LR	number, number	addition, subtraction
+	LR	string, any	string concatenation
<<	LR	integer, integer	left shift
>>	LR	integer, integer	right shift with sign extension
>>>	LR	integer, integer	right shift with zero extension
<, <=	LR	number, number	less than, less than or equal
>, >=	LR	number, number	greater than, greater than or equal
instanceof	LR	reference, type	type comparison
==	LR	primitive, primitive	equal (have identical values)
!=	LR	primitive, primitive	not equal (have different values)
==	LR	reference, reference	equal (refer to the same object)
!=	LR	reference, reference	not equal (refer to different objects)
&	LR	integer, integer	bitwise AND
&	LR	boolean, boolean	boolean AND
^	LR	integer, integer	bitwise XOR
^	LR	boolean, boolean	boolean XOR

*LR means left-to-right associativity; RL means right-to-left associativity.

Precedence (highest to lowest)

Operator	Assoc.*	Operand Types(s)	Operation Performed
|	LR	integer, integer	bitwise OR
|	LR	boolean, boolean	boolean OR
&&	LR	boolean, boolean	conditional AND (short circuit evaluation)
||	LR	boolean, boolean	conditional OR (short circuit evaluation)
? :	RL	boolean, any, any	conditional (ternary) operator
=	RL	variable, any	assignment
*=, /=, %=, +=, -=, <<=, >>=, >>>=, &=, ^=, |=	RL	variable, any	assignment with operation

*LR means left-to-right associativity; RL means right-to-left associativity.

Appendix C

Primitive Data Types

Type	Value Stored	Default Value	Size	Range of Values
char	Unicode character	Character code 0	16 bits	0 to 65535
byte	Integer value	0	8 bits	−128 to 127
short	Integer value	0	16 bits	−32768 to 32767
int	Integer value	0	32 bits	−2147483648 to −147483647
long	Integer value	0	64 bits	−9223372036854775808 to 9223372036854775807
float	Real value	0.0	32 bits	±1.4E-45 to ±3.4028235E+38
double	Real value	0.0	64 bits	±4.9E-324 to ±1.7976931348623157E+308
boolean	true or false	false	1 bit	NA

Appendix D

ASCII Subset of Unicode

The following chart shows the ordering of characters in the ASCII (American Standard Code for Information Interchange) subset of Unicode. The internal representation for each character is shown in decimal. For example, the letter *A* is represented internally as the integer 65. The space (blank) character is denoted by a "□".

Left Digit(s)	Right Digit	ASCII									
		0	**1**	**2**	**3**	**4**	**5**	**6**	**7**	**8**	**9**
0		NUL	SOH	STX	ETX	EOT	ENQ	ACK	BEL	BS	HT
1		LF	VT	FF	CR	SO	SI	DLE	DC1	DC2	DC3
2		DC4	NAK	SYN	ETB	CAN	EM	SUB	ESC	FS	GS
3		RS	US	□	!	"	#	$	%	&	'
4		(	)	*	+	,	−	.	/	0	1
5		2	3	4	5	6	7	8	9	:	;
6		<	=	>	?	@	A	B	C	D	E
7		F	G	H	I	J	K	L	M	N	O
8		P	Q	R	S	T	U	V	W	X	Y
9		Z	[	\	]	^	_	`	a	b	c
10		d	e	f	g	h	i	j	k	l	m
11		n	o	p	q	r	s	t	u	v	w
12		x	y	z	{			}	~	DEL		

Codes 00–31 and 127 are the following nonprintable control characters:

NUL	Null character	VT	Vertical tab	SYN	Synchronous idle
SOH	Start of header	FF	Form feed	ETB	End of transmitted block
STX	Start of text	CR	Carriage return	CAN	Cancel
ETX	End of text	SO	Shift out	EM	End of medium
EOT	End of transmission	SI	Shift in	SUB	Substitute
ENQ	Enquiry	DLE	Data link escape	ESC	Escape
ACK	Acknowledge	DC1	Device control one	FS	File separator
BEL	Bell character (beep)	DC2	Device control two	GS	Group separator
BS	Back space	DC3	Device control three	RS	Record separator
HT	Horizontal tab	DC4	Device control four	US	Unit separator
LF	Line feed	NAK	Negative acknowledge	DEL	Delete

Glossary

Abstract data type (ADT)   A data type whose properties (domain and operations) are specified independently of any particular implementation

Abstract method   A method declared in a class or an interface without a method body

Abstraction   A model of a system that includes only the details essential to the perspective of the viewer of the system

Access modifier   Indicates the availability of a Java construct: public, protected, package, or private

Activation record (stack frame)   Space used at run time to store information about a method call, including the parameters, local variables, and return address

Adjacency list   A list that identifies all the vertices to which a particular vertex is connected; each vertex has its own adjacency list

Adjacency matrix   For a graph with *N* nodes, an *N* by *N* table that shows the existence (and weights) of all edges in the graph

Adjacent from   If vertex A is connected to vertex B in a directed graph by an edge (A, B) then B is adjacent from A

Adjacent to   If vertex A is connected to vertex B in a directed graph by an edge (A, B) then A is adjacent to B

Adjacent vertices   Two vertices in a graph that are connected by an edge

Algorithm   A sequence of unambiguous instructions that solve a problem, within a finite amount of time, given a set of valid input

Alias   When two variables reference the same object, they are aliases of each other

Amortized analysis   Using average case analysis in place of worst case analysis to spread the cost of unusual extra processing that is only incurred occasionally

Ancestor   A parent of a node, or a parent of an ancestor, in a tree

Anonymous inner class   An anonymous class is a class without a name; instead of defining a class in one place and then instantiating it somewhere else, as is the usual approach, we can define a class exactly at the place in the code where it is being instantiated; because it is created at the same place it is defined, there is no need for a class name

Application (Java application)   The part of a Java program where processing begins; the class of a Java program that contains the main method

Average case complexity   Related to the average number of steps required by an algorithm, calculated across all possible sets of input values

Bag   A Collection-like ADT that also provides operations *grab*, *count*, *removeAll*, and *clear*

Base case   The case for which the solution can be stated nonrecursively

Best case complexity   Related to the minimum number of steps required by an algorithm, given an ideal set of input values, in terms of efficiency

Binary search   A search approach that eliminates half the remaining possibilities at each step

Binary search tree   A binary tree in which the value in any node is greater than or equal to the value in its left child and any of its descendants (the nodes in the left subtree) and less than the value in its right child and any of its descendants (the nodes in the right subtree)

Binary tree   A tree in which each node is capable of having two child nodes: a left child node and a right child node

Breadth-first traversal (level order traversal)   A tree traversal that first visits the root of the tree, then next visits, in turn, the children of the root (typically from leftmost to rightmost), followed by visiting the children of the children of the root and so on until all of the nodes have been visited

Bucket   A collection of elements associated with a particular hash location

Bushy   A well-balanced tree

Chain   A linked list of elements that share the same hash location

Checked exception   Java exception that when thrown, must be either caught by the surrounding code or rethrown by the surrounding method

Children   The successor nodes of a node in a tree

Circular linked list   A list in which every node has a successor; the "last" element is succeeded by the "first" element

Client   A client of a class/ADT is any code that uses the class/ADT, be it an application or another class/ADT

Clustering   The tendency of elements to become unevenly distributed in the hash table, with many adjacent locations containing elements

Collection   An object that holds other objects; typically we are interested in inserting, removing, searching, and iterating through the contents of a collection

Collections Framework (Java Collections Framework)   The set of classes and interfaces that implement Collection ADTs

Collision   The condition resulting when two or more keys produce the same hash location

Complete binary tree   A binary tree that is either full or full through the next-to-last level, with the leaves on the last level as far to the left as possible

Complete graph   A graph in which every vertex is directly connected to every other vertex

Compression function   A function that "compresses" the wider domain of numbers, representing the hash codes of the elements being inserted into a hash table, into the smaller range of numbers, representing the indices of the hash table

Concurrent programs   Several interacting code sequences are executing simultaneously, possibly through an interleaving of their statements by a single processor, possibly through execution on distinct processors

Connected component   A maximal set of vertices of a graph that are connected to each other, along with the edges associated with those vertices

Connected graph   A graph that consists of a single connected component

Connected vertices   In an undirected graph we say that two vertices are connected if there is a path between them

Constructor   An operation that creates a new instance of a class

Cycle   A path in a graph that begins and ends at the same vertex

Data abstraction   The separation of a data type's logical properties from its implementation

Data encapsulation   A programming language feature that enforces information hiding

Deallocate   To return the storage space for an object to the pool of free memory so that it can be reallocated to new objects

Depth-first traversal   A tree traversal that first visits the root of the tree, then next traverses as far as possible along the leftmost path, until reaching a leaf, and then "backing up" as little as needed before traversing again down to a leaf and so on until all of the nodes have been visited

Depth of the recursion   The number of activation records on the system stack associated with a given recursive method

Deque (double-ended queue)   A linear structure that only allows access (insertion/removal of elements) at its ends, that is, at its front and at its rear

Descendant   A child of a node, or a child of a descendant, in a tree

Direct recursion   Recursion in which a method directly calls itself

Directed graph (digraph)   A graph in which each edge is directed from one vertex to another (or the same) vertex

Disconnected graph   A graph that is not connected

Double-ended queue (deque)   A linear structure that only allows access (insertion/removal of elements) at its ends, that is, at its front and at its rear

Doubly linked list   A linked list in which each node is linked to both its successor and its predecessor

Dynamic (run-time) binding   When the association between a variable or method and the actual memory location containing the variable or method is made during the execution of a program

Dynamic memory management   The allocation and deallocation of storage space as needed while an application is executing

Edge (arc)   A pair of vertices representing a connection between the two vertices in a graph

Exception   Associated with an unusual, sometimes unpredictable event, detectable by software or hardware, which requires special processing; the event may or may not be erroneous

Factory method   A method that creates and returns objects

Full binary tree   A binary tree in which all of the leaves are on the same level and every nonleaf node has two children

Garbage   The set of currently unreachable objects

Garbage collection   The process of finding all unreachable objects and deallocating their storage space

General (recursive) case   The case for which the solution is expressed in terms of a smaller version of itself

Generics   Parameterized types; allow us to define a set of operations that manipulate objects of a particular class, without specifying the class of the objects being manipulated until a later time

Graph   A data structure that consists of a set of vertices and a set of edges that relate the vertices to each other

Hash code   The output of the hash function that is associated with the input object

Hash function   A function that takes as input the key of an element and produces an integer as output

Hash table   The data structure used to store elements using hashing

Hashing   The technique used for ordering and accessing elements in a collection in a relatively constant amount of time by manipulating the element's key to identify the element's location in the collection

Header node   A placeholder node at the beginning of a list; used to simplify list processing

Heap   An implementation of a priority queue based on a complete binary tree, each of whose elements contains a value that is greater than or equal to the value of each of its children

Height   The maximum level of a tree

Hybrid data structure   A synergetic combination of two data structures

Immutable object   An object that once instantiated cannot be changed

Indirect recursion   *See* Recursion (indirect)

Information hiding   The practice of hiding details within a module with the goal of controlling access to the details from the rest of the system

Inheritance of classes   A Java class can extend one other Java class, inheriting its attributes and methods

Inheritance of interfaces   A Java interface can extend another Java interface, inheriting its requirements; if interface B extends interface A, then classes that implement interface B must also implement interface A; usually, interface B adds abstract methods to those required by interface A

Inheritance tree   A tree, rooted in the Object class, representing all of the inherited class relationships between Java classes

Inorder traversal   A systematic way of visiting all the nodes in a binary tree by visiting the nodes in the left subtree of a node, then visiting the node, and then visiting the nodes in the right subtree of the node

Instantiation   Using the *new* command to create a new instance/object of a Java class

Interior node   A tree node that is not a leaf

Key   The attributes that are used to determine the identity and logical order of the elements in a collection

Leaf   A tree node that has no children

Level   The level of a tree node is its distance from the root (the number of connections between itself and the root)

Level order traversal (breadth-first traversal)   A tree traversal that first visits the root of the tree, then next visits, in turn, the children of the root (typically from leftmost to rightmost), followed by visiting the children of the children of the root and so on until all of the nodes have been visited

Linear probing   Resolving a hash collision by sequentially searching a hash table beginning at the location returned by the hash/compression function

Linear relationship   Each element except the first has a unique predecessor, and each element except the last has a unique successor

List   A collection that exhibits a linear relationship among its elements

Load threshold   When the ratio of entries to total space in a hash table rises above the load threshold the size of the hash table is increased

Map   An ADT that associates keys with unique values

Methodology   A collection of specific procedures for creating a software system to meet a user's needs

Multiple inheritance of interfaces   A Java interface may extend more than one interface; if interface C extends both interface A and interface B, then classes that implement interface C must also implement both interface A and interface B; sometimes multiple inheritance of interfaces is used simply to combine the requirements of two interfaces, without adding any more methods

Multitasking   Perform more than one task at a time

Natural order   The order established by a class's *compareTo* method

Observer   An operation that allows us to observe the state of an object without changing it

Optional operation/method   Some operations fit well with one implementation of an ADT but do not make sense for another implementation; in these cases we indicate in our interface that an operation is optional; implementations can elect not to support such operations

Order of growth complexity   A notation that expresses computing time (complexity) as the term in a function that increases most rapidly relative to the size of a problem

Order property of heaps   For every node in the underlying tree, the value stored in that node is greater than or equal to the value in each of its children

Override   Redefining a method of a superclass in a subclass

Parent   A tree node's unique predecessor is its parent

Path   A sequence of vertices that connects two vertices in a graph

Polymorphism   The ability of an object variable to reference objects of different classes at different times during the execution of a program

Postconditions (effects)   The results expected at the exit of a method, assuming that the preconditions are true

Postorder traversal   A systematic way of visiting all the nodes in a binary tree by visiting the nodes in the left subtree of a node, then visiting the nodes in the right subtree of the node, and then visiting the node

Preconditions   Assumptions that must be true on entry into a method for it to work correctly

Preorder traversal   A systematic way of visiting all the nodes in a binary tree by visiting a node, then visiting the nodes in the left subtree of the node, and then visiting the nodes in the right subtree of the node

Primitive variable   A Java variable of one of the eight directly supported types (*byte, char, short, int, long, float, double, and boolean*) that stores its contents by-value, that is, the actual value of the variable is held in the memory location associated with the variable

Priority queue   An abstract data type where only the highest-priority element can be accessed/removed

Quadratic probing   Resolving a hash collision by using the formula (hash value $+ I^2$) % array-size

Queue   A structure in which elements are added to the rear and removed from the front; a "first in, first out" (FIFO) structure

Recursion (indirect)   *See* Indirect recursion

Recursive algorithm   A solution that is expressed in terms of (1) smaller instances of itself, and (2) a base case

Recursive call   A method call in which the method being called is the same as the one making the call

Recursive (general) case   The case for which the solution is expressed in terms of a smaller version of itself

Recursive definition   A definition in which something is defined in terms of smaller versions of itself

Reference variable   A Java variable associated with an object defined by a Java class—it stores its contents by-reference, that is, the variable holds the address where the object resides in memory

Rehash Recomputing the locations for all of the elements in a hash table, for example, when the underlying hash table is resized

Root The top node of a tree structure; a node with no parent

Run-time (dynamic) binding When the association between a variable or method and the actual memory location associated with the variable or method is made during the execution of a program

Run-time (system) stack A system data structure that keeps track of activation records during the execution of a program

Self-organizing (adjusting/balancing) tree A tree that adjusts its pattern of nodes to keep itself "balanced" after nodes are added or removed

Self-referential class A class that includes an instance variable or variables that can hold a reference to an object of the same class

Sequential search A search approach that examines each element in a collection one by one sequentially

Set A *Collection* class that does not allow duplicate elements

Shape property of heaps The underlying tree must be a complete binary tree

Siblings Tree nodes with the same parent

Signature The distinguishing features of a method heading; the combination of a method name with the number and type(s) of its parameters in their given order

Skewed tree A tree that is long and narrow; the opposite of a bushy/balanced tree

Snapshot A copy of a data structure at some point in time

Stable sort A sorting algorithm that preserves the order of duplicates

Stack A structure in which elements are added and removed from only one end; a "last in, first out" (LIFO) structure

Subclass If class A inherits from class B, then we say that "A is a subclass of B"

Subtree A node and all of its descendants form a subtree rooted at the node

Superclass If class A inherits from class B, then we say that "B is a superclass of A"

System (run-time) stack A system data structure that keeps track of activation records during the execution of a program

Tail recursion The case in which a method contains only a single recursive invocation and it is the last statement to be executed in the method

Test driver A program that calls operations exported from a class, allowing us to test the results of the operations

Test harness A stand-alone program designed to facilitate testing of the implementations of algorithms

Trailer node A placeholder node at the end of a list; used to simplify list processing

Transformer An operation that changes the internal state of an object

Tree A structure with a unique starting node (the root), in which each node is capable of having multiple child nodes, and in which a unique path exists from the root to every other node

Unchecked exception An exception of the *RunTimeException* class; it does not have to be explicitly handled by the method within which it might be raised

Undirected graph A graph in which the edges have no direction

Unified Modeling Language (UML) A collection of diagramming techniques used to describe software

Vertex A node in a graph

Weighted graph A graph in which each edge carries a value

Worst case complexity Related to the maximum number of steps required by an algorithm, given the worst possible set of input values in terms of efficiency

Index

Note: Italicized page locators indicate a figure; tables are noted with a *t*.